# CULTS IN CONTEXT

## Readings in the Study of New Religious Movements

*edited by*

## Lorne L. Dawson

Transaction Publishers
New Brunswick (U.S.A.) and London (U.K.)

Published in the United States of America by Transaction Publishers, New Brunswick, New Jersey.

Original material copyright © 1998 Canadian Scholars' Press, the editor and the contributing authors.

This book printed on acid-free paper that meets the American National standard for Permanence of Paper for Printed Library Materials.

Library of Congress Catalog Number: 98-22986
ISBN: 0-7658-0478-6
Printed in Canada

**Library of Congress Cataloging-in-Publication Data**

Cults in context : readings in the study of new religious movements /
    edited by Lorne L. Dawson.
        p.    cm.
    Originally published: Toronto : Canadian Scholars' Press, 1996.
    Includes bibliographical references.
    ISBN 0-7658-0478-6 (pbk. : alk. paper)
        1. Cults—United States. 2. Cults—Canada. 3. United States—Religion.
4. Canada—Religion. I Dawson, Lorne L., 1954-
[BL2525.C86  1998]
200'.973—dc21
                                                                                98-22986
                                                                                CIP

# TABLE OF CONTENTS

# ABOUT THE EDITOR

Lorne Dawson is an interdisciplinary scholar working in the fields of religious studies and sociology. He has a Ph.D. in religious studies from McMaster University (1986) and teaches in the departments of sociology and religious studies at the University of Waterloo (Waterloo, Ontario, Canada). He is the author of *Reason, Freedom and Religion* (1988) and numerous articles on questions of method and theory in the study of religion published in such journals as *Studies in Religion, Religion, Journal of the American Academy of Religion, Journal for the Social Scientific Study of Religion*, and *Method and Theory in the Study of Religion*. He also writes on the use of rational action theory in sociology and the influence of postmodernist thought on the practice of sociological ethnography. *Cults in Context* grows out of years of teaching classes on new religious movements at two universities. It is designed to provide students and others with a convenient and comprehensive introduction to the issues and findings of the social scientific study of new religious movements. The primary readings collected offer a reliable and flexible resource for faculty and students curious about the public controversy over cults and the changing face of religion in our times.

# THE BOOK
# AND THE SUBJECT

The most immediate, important, and prevailing context of the study of cults is controversy. Controversy over the very existence of so many religions. Controversy over the seemingly sudden conversion of young people to religions so strange to their families. Religion, in the guise of what sociologists prefer to call "new religious movements," has become a "social problem" in our supposedly secular age.

In the contemporary Western world, religious beliefs and practices are commonly deemed to be a matter of private choice. In sharp contrast to our heritage, it is now often considered unusual, even perverse, for someone to seek to seriously carry their religious commitments beyond the bounds of their family life or their personal quest for meaning. Religious principles are no longer suppose to be invoked to determine how we are governed, manage our finances, educate ourselves, or care for our physical well-being. Rather religion is often treated today as if it were a leisure activity, segmented off from the rest of life. But when the ruling concensus of Catholic, Protestant, and Jewish worldviews (Herberg, 1955; Wuthnow, 1988) began to wane in the 1960s, a plethora of new religions of unusual cast and intensity emerged in North America and Europe. Defying the functional marginalization of religion to the private sphere of life and aiming to transform society itself through the avid pursuit of religious ideals, many of the new religious movements challenged the integrity of modern American culture. Their continued existence, relative success, and proliferation cast doubt on the adequacy and legitimacy of the accommodations struck by most North Americans between the demands of the head and the heart, the pocket book and the soul, the needs of the individual and the community.

By some estimates as many as three thousand new religions have appeared in the last few decades. These religions, often stigmatized as "cults," are part of an interest in things "other-worldly" or "supernatural" that has persisted in strength, particularly in the United States. Whether Christian and evangelical, or new age, Eastern and mystical in inspiration, these new religions demand a level of religious knowledge, personal sacrifice and commitment no longer consonant with the norms of our individualistic and materialistic culture. Attracting the young, relatively well-healed, and well-educated, in many cases these new religions threaten the middle class dreams of happiness and prosperity envisioned by parents for their children. But for many an awareness of the new religious forces in our midst really only struck home when the "private troubles" of families struggling to understand the conversions of their sons and daughters escalated into such "public problems" (Mills, 1959) as the Jonestown massacre in 1978, the Waco debacle in 1993, the Solar Temple mass murder/suicide in 1994, and the Aum Shinrikyo subway poisonings in Tokyo in 1995. To comprehend these tragedies we need a better grasp of the nature and dynamics of the new religious life in our culture as a whole. Violence and deviance of this kind is as aberrant for most new religious movements as it is for other religions. But there is a continuity between the tensions and misunderstandings characteristic of these violent episodes and the plights experienced by many other people as a result of their unorthodox religious activities. Abuses occur, at the hands of both the leaders of cults and those who oppose them. There is little evidence, however, that new religious movements are intrinsically dangerous for their members or the public.

No more than 10% of the American population may ever have participated in any new religious movement, and the real numbers may be as low as 1-3%. Those who do join a group rarely stay members for more than two years. But it is not the numbers who have converted that count. The attention drawn by such conspicuous new religions as the Hare Krishna (The International Society for Krishna Consciousness), the Moonies (The Holy Spirit Association for the Unification of World Christianity), and the Church of Scientology, to name only a few prominent organizations, reflects and hastens the rise of a new religious and cultural pluralism that may be profoundly effecting the religious sensibilities of everyone. As Robert Wuthnow evocatively comments in *The Restructuring of American Religion* (1988: 152), with the birth of the new religions it is "... as if the bits of mosaic that had given shape to the religious topography had been thrown into the air, never to land exactly in the same positions as before."

In the face of the increasingly variegated ideological landscape of contemporary America, cults have become the target of a religious and cultural backlash. The growth of new religions has been matched by the development of an organized and vocal opposition, the anti-cult movement (e.g., The Cult Awareness Network, The American Family Foundation, The Council on Mind Abuse). Led by disgruntled parents and professional deprogrammers, the anti-cult movement has persuaded the public, if not always the legal authorities, to attribute the success of new religions to the systematic practice of deception and sophisticated methods of "brainwashing" or "mind control." In fact, the "cults," it is stressed, are not truly religions at all. They are just elaborate schemes for the personal aggrandizement, wealth, and sexual titillation of their charismatic leaders. Consequently such groups should not be accorded the freedoms and rights conventionally and constitutionally guaranteed to other religions.

These charges and demands, and the need to forestall future tragedies, has prompted an extensive investigation of new religious movements (NRMs) by sociologists and psychologists of religion, as well as some historians and religious studies scholars. After more than twenty years of effort a sizable body of detailed information is now available, information that tends to contradict the claims of the anti-cult movement. With the unique opportunity provided by the rise of NRMs to study the very birth, life, and sometimes death of religions, sociologists and others have significantly improved our grasp of how and why people become religious, especially radically so, how religious organizations arise and develop, and why they succeed or fail. These issues are extremely complex, but after years of heated debate empirical evidence has begun to displace conjecture and animosity as the basis of public discussion, particularly in the courts where numerous suits have been filed in attempts to suppress and destroy new religious movements (see e.g., Richardson, 1991; Anthony and Robbins, 1995).

The readings collected here seek to foster this shift in the context of debate about cults by sampling some of the best and most accessible publications from the academic study of NRMs. These readings do many things, ranging from historically and conceptually framing the issues under dispute to broadening the explanatory framework under consideration and summarizing the results of years of social scientific research. The literature available is now vast, but the readings chosen are representative of the scope and the quality of the analyses done to date, within the limits posed by fashioning an "introduction" to the study of NRMs. An explanation of the selection and usefulness of each reading is provided in the brief introduction to each section of the book. The readings stand on their own, but it is advisable that they be read in conjunction with a textbook. I will be using them in conjunction with my new book *Comprehending Cults: The Sociology of New Religious Movements* (Oxford University Press, 1998), which discusses the issues at stake in greater breadth and detail. It is best to see the findings of the social scientific study of NRMs in the light of a knowledge of the actual beliefs and practices of some new religions and vice versa.

● ● ● ● ● ● ● ● ● ● ● ● ● ● ● ● ● ● ● ● ● ● ● ●

# References

Anthony, Dick and Thomas Robbins
    1995      "Negligence, Coercion, and the Protection of Religious Belief." *Journal of Church and State* 37: 509-536.

Dawson, Lorne L.
    n.d.        *Understanding New Religious Movements: The Cult Controversy in Context.* Toronto and
                New York: Oxford University Press (forthcoming).

Herberg, Will
    1955        *Protestant, Catholic, Jew.* New York: Doubleday.

Mills, C. Wright
    1959        *The Sociological Imagination.* New York: Oxford University Press.

Richardson, James T.
    1991        "Cult/Brainwashing Cases and Freedom of Religion." *Journal of Church and State* 33: 56-
                74

Wuthnow, Robert
    1988        *The Restructuring of American Religion.* Princeton, NJ: Princeton University Press.

# THE NATURE AND STUDY OF CULTS

## Introduction to the Readings

In studying cults a number of basic points need to be established from the beginning. First, as Eileen Barker's "The Scientific Study of Religion? You Must be Joking?" displays with considerable finesse, there are many competing voices to be heard in the debate about cults: the new religions themselves, the anti-cult movement, the media, the law, therapists, and sociologists of religion (and other academics). Each group has its agenda and while some of these agendas coincide some of the time (e.g., the media tend to rely on the anti-cult movement and vice versa), most of the time they are at odds with one another (e.g., sociologists of religion and the anti-cult movement). Being aware of the differences and conflicts is essential if members of the public wish to secure reliable information about the new religions. This selection from Barker, a leading sociologist of new religious movements from England, uniquely describes and compares these competing voices and their consequences for the study of cults. Chief amongst these consequences is the precarious position of the sociologist of religion dedicated (in principle at least) to achieving an "objective" account. Unlike other sociologists, scholars in this field must chart a course with care between the Scylla and Charybdis of an active, organized, and often belligerent opposition from the anti-cult movement and the attempts of the new religious movements (NRMs) to either resist their investigations or somewhat manipulatively appropriate them for propagandistic purposes. They run the risk of being either sued or duped and can more or less always count on someone denouncing what they say. As Barker candidly reveals, this methodological dilemma has both its galvanizing and debilitating effects on the work done by sociologists of NRMs.

Second, as should be apparent by now, the very language used to talk about this subject is itself in dispute. The term "cult" was used in a relatively clear descriptive manner in the sociology of religion prior to the rise of the anti-cult movement. But the success of this movement in bringing about the "symbolic degradation" of the cults in the popular consciousness (see e.g., Van Driel and Richardson, 1988; Bromley and Shupe, 1993) has turned the term "cult" into a pejorative label. In the search for a more neutral terminology, free of the prejudice now clearly associated with the word cult, the phrase "new religious movements" has gained currency. The reading from James Richardson, a prominent American sociologist of new religions, traces the path of this development, discussing the advantages and disadvantages of this choice and some of the other options proposed along the way. Calling on a highly instructive experiment by psychologist Jeffry Pfeiffer, he documents the overwhelming nature of the bias now directed towards any group identified as a "cult." In addressing the legal ramifications of this dispute he also highlights the fact that language use in this field is not just a matter of semantics.

The third reading in this section, Roy Wallis' "Three Types of New Religious Movements," serves many purposes. First and foremost, it establishes the need to recognize that the common tendency to lump all cults together, to generalize from one group to others, is unsound and unhelpful. Contrary to the rhetoric of the anti-cult movement, there are true and telling differences between NRMs. In fact, as Wallis delineates, some new religions are starkly opposed to others in their most basic orientations. Following in the footsteps of Max Weber (1963), Wallis distinguishes cults by their orientations to the social world in which they emerge. He argues that a "new movement may embrace the world, *affirming* its normatively approved goals and values; it may *reject* that world, denigrating those things held dear within it; or it may remain as far as possible indifferent to the world in terms of its religious practice, *accommodating* to it otherwise, and exhibiting only mild acquiescence to, or disapprobation of, the ways of the world" (Wallis, 1984: 4; emphasis added). Each orientation gives rise to a distinctive social structure. This social structure shapes the daily life experience of members in ways that render the groups in question as different from one another as they are similar.

In the process of demonstrating these differences Wallis' discussion serves at least two other ends. It provides a first and quite effective exposure to the beliefs, practices, and prospects of some specific groups. It gets us thinking, in other words, about what NRMs are about and not just how we should study them. On this latter count, however, Wallis' work also illustrates the ways in which sociologists manage to find order in the great diversity and complexity of data available, facilitating systematic comparisons, analysis, and the generation of theoretical insights pertinent to the study of all religions, new and old.

● ● ● ● ● ● ● ● ● ● ● ● ● ● ● ● ● ● ● ● ● ● ● ● ●

## References

Bromley, David G. and Anson D. Shupe, Jr.
    1993     "Organized Opposition to New Religious Movements," in D.G. Bromley and J.K. Hadden, eds., *Religion and the Social Order, Vol. 3, The Handbook on Cults and Sects in America, Part A*. Greenwich, CT: JAI Press, pp. 177-198.

Van Driel, Barend and James T. Richardson
    1988     "Print Media Coverage of New Religious Movements: A Longitudinal Study." *Journal of Communication* 38 (3): 37-61.

Weber, Max
    1963     *The Sociology of Religion*. Translated by Ephraim Fischoff. Boston: Beacon Press.

# THE SCIENTIFIC STUDY OF RELIGION? YOU MUST BE JOKING!*

EILEEN BARKER**

*Those who aspire to engage in the scientific study of religion may, in the course of their research, affect the data that they are studying. The paper examines some ways the study of new religions can result in the researcher's "making a difference" for both methodological and ethical or political reasons. A comparison is drawn between the interests of the social scientist and those of the new religions, the anti-cult movement, the media, the law, and therapists. Finally, it discusses some potential effects on the meta-values of science that may arise out of involvement in the market of competing accounts of new religions.*

● ● ● ● ● ● ● ● ● ● ● ● ● ● ● ● ● ● ● ● ● ● ● ● ●

...The very name "Society for the Scientific Study of Religion" makes some people shudder with horror. For others it stands for something that is itself almost a religion: dispassionate, objective, systematic, and accurate research. *Is* the concept a somewhat ridiculous joke? Or are we claiming something important when we define ourselves as a community of scholars dedicated to the scientific study of religion?

My underlying question is: How might the "methods and the politics of involvement" affect the meta-values that lie at the basis of a scientific study of religion? I shall be discussing where members of the SSSR might stand — and where some of us *are* standing — in the marketplace of reality construction, and in what

Eileen Barker. "The Scientific Study of Religion? You Must be Joking!" *Journal for the Scientific Study of Religion* 34, 1995: 287-310.

ways the fact that we are operating in a highly competitive market might threaten our claims to a special "scientific" status.

Although I hope that what I say will have a wider relevance, this is very much a personal story which poses questions that I and other members of the SSSR have found ourselves facing as a result of our research into new religious movements (NRMs). Many of the illustrations are drawn from my own experience, but most of them could have been replicated with stories that others have told. My aim is, however, to go beyond the merely anecdotal by attempting to raise for public debate a number of issues, some of which have been touched upon elsewhere but are not as yet routinely addressed in methodological handbooks.

Most of us who have been involved in the study of NRMs during the past quarter of a century or so have enjoyed learning much of interest for the study of religion in general. But several of us have also been bruised and confused, a few of us quite sorely, because of the threat that we have presented to others by our claims to have a more "scientific" — or at least a more balanced, objective, and accurate — or, at very least, a less biased, subjective, and wrong — understanding of the movements than they have.

This has led to a certain amount of navel contemplation about how we might justify our research. *Are* we "doing" a scientific study of religion? What *is* a scientific study of religion? To what extent and why might we claim that we "know better" than some others, including even those who provide the raw data of our research? And, just as importantly, on what matters must we be wary to acknowledge "that whereof we may not speak" — not, that is, as persons claiming to speak as social scientists?...

## Primary and Secondary Constructions of Social Reality

For the sake of the argument, an analytical distinction needs to be made between primary and secondary constructions of reality. The former comprise the basic data of social science; the latter are accounts of the former. The primary construction of an NRM is the product of direct and indirect interactions between the members of the movement and, to some extent, between members and the rest of society.

Secondary constructions are depictions of the movement that are offered in the public arena by sociologists and others, including the movement itself, *about* the movement. Secondary constructions are, thus, more conscious than primary constructions, although part of the process of the latter may be quite conscious, and the former are by no means always consciously thought through. It should, however, be recognized that the distinction between primary and secondary constructions becomes blurred when one is taking a wider reality into account. Thus, if (as in this paper) we are concerned with "the cult scene," secondary constructions, including those of the sociologist, make a difference and must be considered as part of the primary construction of *that* social reality.

The concept of social reality is fraught with tensions and paradox. It appeals to both realism and idealism insofar as it is an objective reality, the existence of which no individual members of a social group can wish away any more than they can wish away the existence of a brick wall. At the same time, social reality exists only as ideas in people's heads; if *no one* took it into account (positively or negatively, consciously or unconsciously), it would not exist (Berger and Luckmann 1966). Put another way, although social reality exists independently of the volition of any particular individual, it can exist only insofar as individual human minds are continually recognizing it and acting as the media through which are processed the cultural ideas and meanings, and the roles and expectations that arise from and result in its existence.

This means that, *pace* Wuthnow (1987), if as social scientists we want to understand what is going on, we have no option but to use ourselves as "a medium." A robot cannot do social science; it is not capable of *Verstehen*. It cannot further our understanding beyond the very important ways that logic can further our understanding of what we already know. We need to have some knowledge about the meanings that situations have for individuals. We need to be able to understand how a situation can be perceived.

*Of course*, others will not perceive it in the same way as we do — *no* two people will perceive a situation in exactly the same way — none of us *ever* has the exact same understanding or perception as anyone else. But — and this is just as important — our perceptions are more or less shared. If they were not shared at all, we would have no society (and no possibility of a social science); and if they were totally shared, again we would have no society, for there would be no dynamic — no force for change, negotiation, or adjustment to external circumstances.

But these differences between individual perceptions of social reality are not random. The variations will depend upon such factors as people's innate characteristics, their past experiences, hopes, fears, interests, assumptions, values, and expectations and the social position from which they view the reality that confronts them. A new convert will view the NRM from one perspective, seasoned leaders from a different perspective; members' perceptions will differ from nonmembers'; and different groups of nonmembers will perceive the NRM in the light of their own particular interests.

Not only will people *perceive* the movement from different perspectives, they will also *describe* and, perhaps, explain the movement in different ways. Consciously or unconsciously, they will *select* from among the features presented to them. Again, what is included and what is excluded in the process of creating their secondary constructions will not be random, but significantly influenced according to their interests.

The interests of some personally or professionally motivated secondary constructors may lead them to take matters further than a passive reception of their perception.

Some, wanting to reinforce an image that has already been delineated, will place themselves in a position that will protect it from disconfirmation and/or supply confirming evidences. Others, wanting to test their secondary construction...will systematically try to refute their hypotheses. To do this they may actively engage in research which involves as close a scrutiny as possible of the primary construction.

## Making a Difference

When I was a student, it was part of the conventional wisdom of the methodology which we were taught that social scientists should be clinically detached observers who noted what was going on but did not allow their observations to affect the data. Such as position is to some extent possible when the scientist is observing through a one-way glass, watching a covertly shot film or reading diaries or other written materials. But for a number of reasons discussed elsewhere (Barker 1987), I and others have come to believe that such an approach is not only difficult but methodologically inappropriate for the kind of research that is needed for an acceptable secondary construction of NRMs. There is some information that one can acquire only by becoming part of the data and, thus, playing a role in the ongoing social construction of reality. I would even go so far as to say that to remain physically distanced from the data can be methodologically reprehensible — an abrogation of one's responsibility as a social scientist.

But as we step outside the Ivory Tower of academia and become part of the process that we are researching, we are, of course, placing our pristine purity in jeopardy. Most social scientists who have worked "in the field" are aware of the impact that they might have and take this into account when they come to analyze their data. To what extent does the involvement enhance or diminish our "scientific" study of religion? Before addressing this question, let me give some examples to illustrate the variety of ways in which I personally have become conscious that my research was "making a difference."

First of all, just being there can make a difference. When I began studying the Unification Church in the early 1970s, it was a relatively closed community with strong boundaries distinguishing "them" from "us." To have someone living in the community who was not part of "us" threatened and weakened the boundary and, thus, the beliefs and actions associated with a strong-group situation (Douglas 1970).[1] The very fact that a normally impermeable boundary *can* be permeated by an outsider affects the group and its members in a number of concrete ways. For example, one girl left, not because I advised her to do so but, she said, because my anomalous existence as someone who could live both within and without led her to realize that she did not have to make the stark choice between *either* a godly *or* a satanic life-style; that there could be a middle way which would allow her to pursue an alternative way of serving God without having to deny all that was good about her Unification experience.

At the same time, it is possible that others stayed in the movement, at least for slightly longer than they might otherwise have done, because of the existence of a "professional stranger" (Barker 1987). My presence meant there was someone who would neither report back to the leadership, nor go to the media but on whom they could off-load their anxieties and frustrations.

Asking questions (in formal interviews, general discussions, or through questionnaire) that no one else has previously asked can lead to an unexpected "raising of consciousness." In the words of one respondent, "It made me take out and look at some of the things I'd been keeping in the pending tray." Sometimes, I was told, the result was a deeper understanding of the theology, but on other occasions the consequence was a growing irritation or suspicion of the leadership. Occasionally a change would be brought about as the result of a group interview offering members the opportunity to discuss openly matters about which they normally kept silent. I gather that a number of fairly radical changes were introduced to an American ISKCON Temple following a day I had spent with a group of female devotees who had not previously shared their feelings of how they were treated by the male hierarchy.

As my research into NRMs progressed, I found myself affecting the situation more consciously. First, I was being asked to mediate between members of movements and their parents, who also formed part of my data. The fact that I could explain the perspective of the movement to nonmembers (and that of nonmembers to members) meant that there was frequently an increased communication and, sometimes, accommodation to the others' points of view as they each reached an increased understanding of how "the other side" saw things.

Then "making a difference" became not merely a result of face-to-face interaction with those individuals who formed part of my data. Publishing books and papers, appearing as a witness in court cases and making statements in various media about my conception of the NRMs meant that my findings were being presented to a wider audience. Like other scholars, I was offering an alternative perspective that questioned many of the existing secondary constructions and their taken-for-granted assumptions. I was affecting the data not only as part of a methodological procedure, but also as part of a political action.

Once the results of my research became public it became increasingly obvious that they were not to go unchallenged. I had initially contacted the anticult movement (ACM) with the somewhat naive belief that, as we were both interested in finding out about NRMs, we might exchange information that could be helpful to us both. My overtures were not merely rejected, the anticultists started to launch a full-scale *ad hominem* attack on anything I said or wrote in public; having gone to NRMs for a significant, though by no means complete part of my research, I was clearly "on the other side." To the astonishment and/or amusement of anyone who knew me, I found myself being labeled a Moonie, a Scientologist, a fundamentalist Christian or a cult lover — or, by the more benign, an innocent who was being deceived by the movements. *What* I said was rarely questioned — except, curiously enough, for statements for which I had incontrovertible evidence. The first major bone of contention was the membership figures that I publicized, both to the annoyance of the Unification Church (who did not want either their members or the general public to be aware of the very high turnover rates) and to the fury of those members of the ACM who were (and in some cases still are) insistent that the movements use irresistible and irreversible mind control techniques — which would, of course, imply that Unification membership was in the hundreds of thousands if not in the millions, rather than the rather paltry hundreds that I was reporting.

The shift from a methodological to a more politico-ethical involvement in the "cult scene" became even more marked when I reached the conclusion that a considerable amount of unnecessary suffering and unhappiness might be avoided were social scientific constructions of NRMs to compete more robustly in the market place. My "Road to Damascus" was an ACM Family Support Group meeting at which an ex-member, whom I happened to know as a thoughtful and honest woman, had been invited to tell her story. It soon became evident that things were not going according to plan. She was resisting the pressure that was being put on her to say how she had suffered, how she had been deceived, and how she had been under the influence of mind control. It was suggested that she had not *really* left the movement and that she was determined to deceive the assembled company. Trying to pour oil on troubled waters, someone asked if she had anything to say that would help the assembled parents. A woman then stood up and shouted "We don't want to hear this; it's just deceit and lies. It's not helpful at all. We don't want to hear any more." At that point I stopped taking notes. Something more, it seemed, needed to be done.

With the support of the British government and mainstream churches, I set up a charity called INFORM (Information Network Focus on Religious Movements) with the aim of providing information that was as objective, balanced, and up-to-date as possible. In the seven years that have ensued, thousands of relatives and friends of NRM members, ex-members, the media, local and national government, police, social welfare workers, prison chaplains, schools, universities and colleges, traditional religions, and NRMs themselves have contacted the office (located at the London School of Economics) for information and help (Barker 1989a).

I did not consider the founding of INFORM to be part of my research, although it has certainly resulted in my learning a great deal more about the "cult scene." Rather, the aim was to *use* professional knowledge to challenge alternative secondary constructions. It was not to fight for The Truth in any ideological sense but, minimally, to contest *untrue* statements about NRMs (whether they originate from an NRM or anyone else). Apart from providing information directly, enquirers are referred to an international network of experts which includes scholars, lawyers, doctors, and therapists. Day-long seminars on a particular subject (such as *Authority and Dependence in NRMs*; *The Law and NRMs*; *Children in NRMs*; *Leaving an NRM*; or *Changes in the New Religions*) are organized twice yearly, with videos and speakers among whom are academics and other experts, parents of members, ex-members, and members of the movements themselves; and in 1993, a four-day Conference on *NRMs and the New Europe* attracted over 200 participants from 23 different countries. Professionally trained counselors and therapists have met on a regular basis to learn about the NRMs and problems associated with them. A range of literature, from pamphlets about individual movements to a book giving information and practical suggestions which was published for the Home Office by Her Majesty's Stationery Office (Barker 1989a) is available. Talks by INFORM's staff, governors, and members of its network are given to schools, universities, local churches, and a variety of other groups.

Although INFORM does not see itself as an advice center, it points out the likely consequences of a variety of actions, ranging from joining a new religion to trying to abduct someone from one; it has also been instrumental in mediating between members and their families, and while it certainly does not have a magic wand with which it can solve all problems, the reliability of INFORM's information and its knowledge of the social processes involved in their relationships with the outside world has meant that it has been able to relate to the NRMs in such a way that many of them are willing to cooperate in such matters as putting parents back in touch with their children, or refunding money obtained under duress. In short, INFORM's policy is to use secondary constructs according to the logic of the social sciences in order to try to bring about a resolution of problems through amelioration and accommodation and avoid "deviance amplification" and the exacerbation of problems.

It would have been ingenuous to assume that there would not be opposition to an organization such as INFORM. What was unexpected, however, was the virulence with which it has been attacked by a few NRMs, the ACM, some sections of the media, and a small number of individuals with opposing interests. By the late 1980s, it appeared that British anticultists were directing more of their resources to trying to discredit us rather than the new religions. The director of my university received letters suggesting that it would be better for his students if I were removed from the faculty; a member of Parliament, who knew nothing of our work but had been carefully briefed by the ACM, accused us of all kinds of rubbish in the House of Commons[2]; a petition was delivered to 10 Downing Street, and radio and television programs as well as a variety of newspaper articles offered the general public a series of features exposing me in particular and INFORM in general as posing a dangerous threat to the nation.

Strangely enough, in a number of ways the negative publicity was helpful — although it is not something that I would recommend to a friend. It prompted a thorough investigation of INFORM's work by the Home Office, which then extended its original three years' funding for a further three years and continues to this day to use INFORM's services rather than those of any other group. Moreover, the mainstream churches, large sections of the more responsible media, and countless individuals seem to be of the opinion that INFORM's balanced information, which both alerts them to potential problems and allays unnecessary fears, is considerably more helpful than the more sensational and one-sided information produced by its competitors.

The battles continue of course, and while we are making a difference, other people's secondary constructions are also making a difference to "the cult scene" *and* to us. But before giving further consideration to the methodological, ethical, and political implications of such involvement, let us turn to the marketplace and compare the secondary constructs of social science with the competition.

## The Competitors

Table 1 summarizes some basic differences between six ideal types of secondary constructors: sociologists and others involved in the scientific study of religion, members of the new religions themselves, the anticult movement, the media, the legal profession, and therapists (the first four constructors are analyzed in greater detail in Barker 1993a). The types were chosen on the grounds that it is they who feature most prominently in the competition with social scientists, but the table could be extended to include the police, the social services, clergy, theologians, educationalists, and any number of other categories of constructors.

It is important to stress that it is not merely personal commitments to particular outcomes that are at issue here, nor is it a question of whether individual constructors are efficient, stupid, honest, or deceitful in their depictions of new religions. What we are concerned with is an exercise in the sociology of knowledge, examining how the socio-logic of group aims and interests can give rise to systematic differences between the various secondary constructions.

### THE SOCIOLOGY OF RELIGION

Obviously the particular aims of those concerned with the scientific study of religion will differ from person to person, but most would agree that they wish to present as accurate, objective, and unbiased an account as possible. They will want to describe, understand, and explain social groupings and such phenomena as the power structures, communication networks, and belief systems that enable members to do (or prevent them from doing) things that they could not (or could) do in other social situations. Social scientists will also want to explore and account for the range of different perceptions held by individual actors and to assess the consequences of such differences. The nature of social reality means that the regularities of social science are relative to social space and time in a way that the laws of nature seldom are. Nonetheless, sociological constructions do contain empirically refutable statements, and it is part of the logic of science that the methods and results of its research should be available for public scrutiny: "Our great instrument for progress is criticism" (Popper 1972:34).

**Table 1 Competing Logics in Secondary Constructions of Reality**

| 2ry constructors | Interest and/or aim | Method | Data selected for inclusion | Data systematically excluded | Mode of communication | Relationship with SoR |
|---|---|---|---|---|---|---|
| Sociology of Religion | Unbiased & objective sociological description, understanding & explanation | Comparison Methodological agnosticism; Interview; Questionnaire; Observation | Individual & social levels; Control groups; Wider context | Non-empirical evaluation; Transcendent variables; Definitional essentialism | Scholarly publications; Through other secondary constructs | Effect of methods of research; Effect of use made of research |
| NRMs | Primary construction; Good PR, Promote beliefs | Selective reflection on primary construction | Good Behaviour; Supernatural claims | Bad skeletons; Esoteric gnoses | Literature; Witnessing | Control of access; Use positive evidence |
| ACM | Warn; Expose; Control; Destroy | Ex-members; Parent; Media (may be circular) | Atrocity tales | Good behaviour; Changes for the better | Lobbying; Newsletters; Media | Use negative data; Attack when positive data |
| Media | Good story; get/keep readers, viewers, and/or listeners | Interview where easy access &/or subject willing to talk; Investigative journalism; Press releases | Topical; Relevant; Sensational | Every-day; 'Normal'; Unexceptional | Newspapers Magazines, TV, Radio; Large public; Short shelf-life; Difficult to check or question | Preferred use of ACM where complementary interests SoR used more if new, pithy, sexy &/or sensational |
| Law | 'Justice' according to the law of the land; Winning case for individual | Adversarial; Confrontational; Positive vs negative | Evidence presented by the two opposing sides; Expert witnesses Legal precedent | Middle ground, not making +ve or -ve point; What deemed irrelevant to the case; Inadmissible evidence | Legal judgements; Common law; Media reports | Impartial Expert or Whore Witness? |
| Therapy | Help client to get better and to cope with 'reality' | Listen, accept, and/or Construct client's version of reality | Individual's perception; Pragmatic constructs | Other versions of reality | Direct to client; Courts; Media; Professional carers | Competition over importance of 'whole' & professional expertise |

There are those who believe that the task of science is to find out the truth, the whole truth, and nothing but the truth. I disagree. *No one* ever tells the whole truth; no one ever *could*. All secondary constructions consist of both more and less than the primary construction. Although looking for nothing but the truth in the sense that we are committed to accuracy and eliminating falsehoods from both our own and others' constructions, social scientists *select* what will go into our constructions, excluding some aspects that others include, and including further aspects that others exclude.

Not only do social scientists include and exclude for methodological reasons, but also, perhaps paradoxically, because it is only by doing this that an understanding of the primary construction may be transmitted to others. An example I sometimes use to illustrate the importance of *not* replicating the original too precisely is that of an actor playing a bore. The actor is successful in communicating something of the essence of being a bore only insofar as he is not boring. Similarly, in order to communicate something of the essence of an NRM, social scientists have to "interpret" or "translate" the primary construction so that their audience can understand what may have been incomprehensible when they were looking at the movement itself. Raëlians can tell their parents what it means to them to be a Raëlian, but the parents may be incapable of hearing what is being said. There would be absolutely no point in the sociologist's merely reproducing what the Raëlian says and does — this has to be put in a wider context; both more and less has to be offered to the parent — less, in that we do not tell the parent things that seem irrelevant (that they clean their teeth every morning) — more, in that we add information that relates what they believe and do to the understanding of the parent. For this we need to know not only what Raëlians believe and do, but also what the parent can understand. We are not being selective in the sense that we are being untruthful or keeping back truths; we are representing rather than presenting.

Thus, the constructs of social science *exclude details that do not seem to be of particular interest*. Part of what we decide is of interest will depend upon what we and our potential audience consider useful knowledge — either because we believe it will further our general understanding of social behaviour, or because we believe that it could be of practical use in implementing our own or society's interests.

Next, the constructs of social science *exclude theological judgments*. The sociology of religion is concerned with who believes what under what circumstances, how beliefs become part of the cultural milieu and are used to interpret people's experiences, and what the consequences of holding particular beliefs may be; but it can neither deny nor confirm ideological beliefs. Social scientists *qua* social scientists have to remain *methodologically agnostic*. The epistemology of an empirical science has no way of knowing whether God, gods, the Devil, angels, evil spirits, or the Holy Spirit have been acting as independent variables; and miracles, by definition, are beyond the purview of science.

Then, social scientists *stipulate* what they mean by particular concepts or use ideal types (Weber 1947:92) for the purposes of a particular study, but they cannot claim that these definitions are either true or false, merely that they are more or less useful. Of course, concepts are "given" (data) in the sense that they are part of primary constructions and our accounts will *report* what people mean by concepts such as "religion." We also note that different groups use, negotiate, or manipulate definitions to further their own interests (Barker 1994; Douglas 1966)... .

Most social scientists would agree that they ought to try to *exclude their own subjective evaluations* from the actual collection and analysis of data... .Of course, as any methodology book will testify, there are many ways in which our values *do* enter the research and skew the outcome: We cannot interpret the reality that we are studying except by using our own subjective perception; concepts can be value laden; We may be working with unexamined assumptions which have implications for our perception; and so on. But we do try to be aware of and counter such obstacles by various techniques so as to produce descriptions that are as objective as possible in the sense that they are concerned with the object of our study rather than our own or others' subjective beliefs.

Social scientists are, however, quite likely to choose a subject that is of interest to them and which they may well believe *ought* to be researched... .In theory at least, this need not interfere with the outcome of the research. Similarly, social scientists may be concerned about the use to which the results of their research are put — that, perhaps, they *ought* to be used to improve understanding and tolerance of others...and, again in theory at least, this can be separated from the research itself.

That the people whom the sociologist is studying hold strong values is, once more in theory at least, irrelevant to the researcher's values insofar as he or she is concerned with finding out to what extent this, as a question of fact, *is* the case... .We may, of course, point to the difficulties involved in achieving a valued goal or suggest that it is realizable only by using means or with consequences that would violate either the value or other valued goals (Barker 1993b; Runciman 1969)... .

But social science not only excludes ideological, definitional, and evaluative concerns, it *includes* interests that extend beyond any NRM under study. Study of the primary construction through interview, questionnaire, participant observation, and the examination of written material needs to be supplemented with data from further sources, all of which may be necessary, but none sufficient for the kind of picture that the sociologist needs to construct (Barker 1984: 124-33). We may want to check where individual members are "coming from" by speaking to people who have known them both before and after their conversion. Ex-members comprise an invaluable source of further information and for checking the veracity of what members are reporting. It does, however, have to be remembered that no single member (past or present) is likely to know everything that is going on in the movement. The sociological construction of an NRM requires, moreover, information about yet others who have no relationship whatsoever with the movement. This is because a fundamental component of science is the comparative method, which, by putting the NRM in a wider frame of reference, brings *balance* into the equation. In order to be able to understand and test "what variable varies with what," the primary construction has to be compared with other primary constructions, using control groups (although this has become distressingly rare in monographs) and techniques such as the statistical manipulation of data about the population as a whole to test for correlations. Such tools of the trade serve, minimally, to eliminate some mistakes that we might otherwise make.

## THE NEW RELIGIONS

NRMs have an interest in gaining new members and, perhaps, political and financial or legal advantage by presenting a secondary construction of their own primary reality in the public domain. As with most organizations, one would expect the movement to select those aspects that show it in a favorable light and be less forthcoming about skeletons in the cupboard. Unlike the social scientist, the NRM will draw on nonempirical revelations to describe and explain at least part of its construction of reality (that, for example, God is responsible for revelations and conversions, and/or that evil forces are responsible for things that go wrong); and it will, of course, be anxious to proclaim the truth of its theological teachings — unless there are esoteric gnoses, in which case these will be kept secret.

Clearly, there is a sense in which an NRM has privileged access to its own reality — but it is also possible to argue that the very fact of their involvement means that members are unable or unwilling to see what is going on with the same detachment as some outsiders (Wilson 1970:ix-xiii). There are, however, members of NRMs such as Mickler (1980, 1992) and Jules-Rosette (1975) who, as *social scientists*, have done excellent work on their own NRMs.

## THE ANTICULT MOVEMENT (ACM)

The ACM includes a wide variety of organizations with members as diverse as anxious parents, ex-members, professional deprogrammers, and "exit counselors." In some ways, the ACM can be seen as a mirror image of the NRM. Both tend to want a clear, unambiguous division between "us" and "them"; but while the NRM will select only good aspects, the ACM selects only bad aspects. Most ACM pronouncements tend to be about "destructive cults," lumping all NRMs together as though they were a single entity, the sins of one being visited on all. Any evidence or argument that could complicate or disprove their negative construction (or reform that may be introduced) is more likely to be ignored or dismissed than denied.[3]

As lobbyists, anticultists have to be proactive not only in promoting their constructions but also in denying or dismissing other constructions and denigrating the constructors.[4] Sociological secondary constructions may appear more threatening to the ACM than those of the NRMs, the latter being more likely to agree with the ACM where there are clear boundaries; they can, furthermore, be goaded into reinforcing the anticult position by responding to it in an unambiguously negative fashion, exacerbating the process of "deviance amplification" and, thereby, justifying further accusations by the ACM.

Social scientists, members of the media, the legal profession, and therapists have a professional interest in their secondary constructions' achieving their relevant aims, but they do not usually expect to gain much more from their work in the area of NRMs than they would by doing their work well in any other area. When we turn to the ACM and NRMs, however, we find that most of the rank and file membership do their work either on a purely voluntary basis or with little more that living expenses because they believe, sometimes quite passionately, that what they are doing is right — they have a mission to fight evil.

There are, however, also "charismatic leaders" in the NRMs and "leading experts" in the ACM, both of whom may reap enormous financial benefits from having their constructions of reality accepted. Stories about the wealth controlled by Sun Myung Moon, L. Ron Hubbard, or Bhagwan Rajneesh (with his 97 Rolls Royces and collection of Rolex watches) are common enough. What is less well known is the vast amount of money at stake in the fostering of the brainwashing or mind control thesis in ACM secondary constructions. On the one hand, "deprogrammers" and, to a somewhat lesser extent, "exit counselors" can charge tens of thousands of dollars for their services; on the other hand, "expert witnesses" have charged enormous fees for giving evidence about brainwashing in court cases. The sums involved are illustrated by the fact that both Richard Ofshe and Margaret Singer recently attempted to sue certain members of the SSSR and both the American Sociological Association and the American Psychological Association for several tens of millions of dollars in loss of earnings after it had been argued in court that their theories of mind control and brainwashing lacked any scientific support. (The eventual outcome was that Singer and Ofshe were ordered to pay considerable legal costs for both sides.) Not surprisingly, given the money involved, the mind control issue has proved to be one of the fiercest battlegrounds.

The sharp "them/us" perspective of the ACM is reflected in the fact that it frequently operates under a cloak of secrecy. Not only the NRMs, but also social scientists may be denied access to allegedly open meetings and refused requests for information or evidence that could corroborate assertions made in ACM constructions of reality. One anticultist who repeatedly claims that NRMs use hypnosis to recruit members refuses to tell me which movements he is talking about on the grounds that he does not trust me because I am "on the other side." Other information that is presumably nonconfidential and which one might have thought the ACM would want widely disseminated is jealously guarded. The secrecy is, of course, perfectly understandable when it concerns the planning of an illegal kidnapping and deprogramming.

Given its aims, the ACM does not lay stress on either objectivity or balance in its secondary constructions of reality — in fact, members will frequently admit quite openly that they consider a balanced presentation of the facts counterproductive. Once, the editor of a journal in which I had written an article received a telephone call from the then-chairman of FAIR (Family Action Information and Rescue) to protest that "Eileen Barker's article had been so balanced and objective, he demanded the right to redress the balance."

As a matter of principle, anticultists are likely to refuse to have direct contact with the primary construction itself as a source of information. This is justified by the premise that cults are, almost by definition, bound to practice deception and are probably dangerous. Data for ACM stories tend, therefore, to be collected from anxious parents, disillusioned ex-members, and negative media reports. Often there is a circularity involved in that the anxious parents have been alerted to the negative aspects of their child's movement by anticult "atrocity tales" (Shupe and Bromley 1980); the ex-members have been taught by deprogrammers or exit counselors to believe that they were brainwashed and that their whole experience is to be interpreted in negative terms (Lewis 1986; Solomon 1981; Wright 1987); and the media frequently get their stories from the ACM which then uses the fact that the story appeared in print as proof that it has been independently verified. There have been cases where the media have included rebuttals to a story supplied to them by the ACM, which has then innocently asked why the question was raised in the first place, suggesting that there is no smoke without a fire — even when they themselves had kindled the fire... .

Some of the differences between the interests of the ACM and social scientists were fairly stated at the 1990 Annual Meeting of FAIR by another chairman, the late Lord Rodney:

> The majority of us here this afternoon have come because of our concern about cults. This concern in most cases stems from our personal experience....I believe by and large this concern is unselfish and motivated by a desire that others may be spared the trauma we have experienced. Some accuse us of being oversentimental and overreacting; maybe some of us are, but with good reason: It is hard to stay calm and collected when you see your family being split asunder.
>
> There are those — mostly academics — who set out to examine these cults in a cool and logical way: What motivates people to join them? Are they free agents? How long does the average member remain in a cult? and so forth. I have nothing against this approach, but I do not think those adopting it can quantify the human suffering involved. I do not wish ill to anyone, but let them have a loved one duped into joining a cult, and I wonder how detached they would remain. The other objection I have is that their association with these cults helps the groups in their search for credibility. Otherwise why are

they welcomed at their meetings and featured in their newsletters! Ladies and gentlemen, I believe in the end you either consider the activities of cults antisocial, deceptive, and destructive of family life — or you don't. I do not think we can sit on the fence (*FAIR News* Autumn 1990:1).

Unlike some anticultists who refuse to have anything to do with me in case they become contaminated, Lord Rodney accepted an invitation to lunch at LSE and was generous enough to invite me to tea at the House of Lords a couple of times.... .On each occasion he made it quite clear that he did not disagree with the facts that I produced, but he did object strongly to my "muddying the waters" by including qualifications and information about the movements that could be taken to mean that they had some benign aspects. "People cannot hear you unless you have a clear message — you just confuse them," he insisted. And, to some extent, he was right.

## THE MEDIA

The overriding interest of the mass media is to get a good story that will keep the loyalty of readers, viewers, and/or listeners and, if possible, to gain new audiences. They are unlikely to be interested in presenting an everyday story of how "ordinary" life in an NRM can be, or even of the rewards that it offers contented members — unless it can expose these as fraudulent, fantastic, or sensational. The media are nearly always working to a tight deadline — very tight compared to the months or years that scholars may spend on their research. They are also limited in the amount of time or space that they have to present their story. Only rarely will the electronic media concentrate on a single topic for more than thirty minutes and only rarely do the printed media allocated more than a few hundred words. [5]

Pressure of space and time means that members of the media collect their data from sources selected for accessibility and the provision of good quotes. "The grieving mother" or "The man who risked prison to save a helpless victim from the clutches of a bizarre cult" are far more valuable informants than "The mother whose devotee son visits her on a regular basis," "The Moonie who passed his exams with good marks" — or, indeed, the academic who is full of long-winded qualifications. Many (though by no means all) of the media tend, moreover, to be remarkably reluctant to ask members of NRMs for their own versions of reality, and to dismiss press releases from the movements far more readily than they dismiss the information handed out by the ACM. This may seem somewhat surprising to anyone who has researched NRMs and learned what extraordinary statements they themselves are capable of producing; yet on numerous occasions when I have offered to give journalists a contact number for one of the movements, they have dismissed the offer, saying either that they would not get the truth or that their editors would expect them to use a more reliable source.

Unlike social scientists, the media are under no obligation to introduce comparisons to assess the relative rates of negative incidents. Thus, when reporting a tragedy or some kind of malpractice, they note in the headline that the victim or the perpetrator was a cultist, but are unlikely to mention it anywhere in the report if he or she were a Methodist. The result is that even if such tragedies and malpractices are relatively *infrequent* they would still be more visible and, thereby, become disproportionately associated with the NRMs in the public mind.

Not only does the logic of the aims and interests of the media result in their seldom being able to go into the kind of depth or ensure the kind of balance that social science would demand, their social position means that the secondary constructions that they create are both powerful (due to their widespread circulation and interest-appeal) and extremely difficult to check or correct. Complaints and apologies can be made, but they rarely attract as much attention as the original story. Usually it is difficult to track down the story for a second look; a transient television report or a story in the newspaper or magazine long since thrown away leaves an impression but not something that can be scrutinized, and there are seldom references than can be followed up. Even with more balanced programs and articles, it is the more sensationalist images that are likely to stick in the mind. It is only those programs and stories selected by the ACM for quotation that are likely to be preserved for recycling.

## The Law

The primary interest of the law as represented by a judge and, sometimes, jury, is to ensure that justice is carried out according to the law of the land. No attempt is made to present a complete or balanced picture of a primary construction, but only to point to those aspects that could be of relevance to the case. Indeed, some information (such as previous convictions) that might be pertinent for a more general understanding are ruled out of court as inadmissible evidence. As far as the defense and the prosecution are concerned, their specific interest is to win the case for their clients. Each side will attempt to construct a picture of reality that is advantageous to its own position and disadvantageous to the other side. Although it might be argued that, adjudicating between two opposing sides, the judge (or jury) would be able to reach a middle position, there is no guarantee that a middle position is a true position. To being with, we may ask, middle of what? It is the court that has set the goal posts and the true position might or might not be somewhere (anywhere) between them.

The law does make use of "expert witnesses" who usually present their credentials as representatives of the scientific community, so one might, *prima facie*, expect the expert witness to produce a secondary construction of reality that corresponds to that of the social scientist, but in fact this is not necessarily the case. One reason is that lawyers will invite those witnesses who are known to hold views that support their client's case, but a more fundamental reason is that it is the court that decides what questions will and will not be asked and, thus, answered.

In short, the adversarial procedure is to argue for and against opposing versions of reality, either or both of which may be grossly distorted versions of a primary construction. This might not matter if the procedure were used only for the purposes of the court. But there is plenty of evidence that decisions on one matter are frequently used by others to "prove" a version of reality that may have little relevance, even to what came up in the case (Barker 1989b: 197-201).

## THERAPISTS

Like defense lawyers, therapists and counselors have an interest in helping their client. But instead of needing to establish their client's version of reality to score a public victory over an opposing version, they may need to help the client to construct privately a new reality that he or she can live with and feel good about. Practices do, of course, vary enormously — many therapists will try to help the client to reach a clearer understanding of the primary construction in which the client is or was a participant — but it will be a practical construction that has the client at its center, rather than a balanced appraisal of the group as a whole. In fact, therapists who have been interested enough in NRMs to attend the INFORM counseling seminars will, when a particular client is referred to them, ask not to be given background information such as a detailed account of the movement in question. This is because they feel it might interfere with their relationship with the client — it would be a kind of betrayal to hear a point of view other than that of the client.

Let me be quite clear, this is not a criticism of these therapists who play an effective role in their clients' recovery from difficult experiences. It is merely to point out that they have a different aim from social scientists and will, therefore, use different methods and employ different kinds of knowledge; the secondary construction of the therapist can be different from but complementary to that of the social scientist. Conflicts between the two constructors emerge, however, when counselors and therapists claim to know what a particular movement — or NRMs in general — are like through their client-focused work. This is likely to arise when therapists give evidence as expert witnesses in court or present their stories to the media and/or at public meetings. Again, there would be no conflict if the stories were confined to descriptions of ways in which people might be helped rather than claims being made that these are proven accurate, balanced portrayals of the primary construction as they come from a "professional" source. They are, of course, from a professional source, but, as with the court, the profession is not one that aims primarily to construct an accurate and balanced account.

Two of the main situations in which counselors and therapists have crossed swords with sociologists are (a) over the so-called brainwashing or mind-control thesis (see above) and (b) over allegations of ritual satanic abuse. Studies in the latter area have revealed a considerable body of evidence showing that therapists may not only help clients to construct a secondary version of reality, but some construct a version of reality themselves, and then put considerable pressure on the client to accept it (Mulhern 1994; Richardson et al. 1991; but see also Houston 1993:9).

## Beyond the Ivory Tower

Although social science cannot claim to be as "scientific" as the natural sciences, it is unquestionably more scientific than its competitors. The *logic* of its approach is infinitely superior for producing balanced and accurate accounts of NRMs than is that of any of its competitors. Undifferentiated relativism, as espoused by some of the exponents of deconstructionism and postmodernism, seems to me to be just plain silly. The rules of science (even loosely characterized as in this paper) are not merely a language game; they are an assurance of a minimal, albeit limited, epistemological status. We would be crazy to argue that *anything* goes— some things are patently false, and empirical observation can demonstrate this to anyone with their faculties in good working order. Assuredly, some statements (moral evaluations and claims about the supernatural) are not empirically testable and it would be equally crazy to believe that we could prove or disprove them to someone holding a different opinion. But such statements are not within the purview of social science. I am not suggesting that social science holds a monopoly on The Truth. Far from it. But I am suggesting that the methods of social science (its openness to criticism and empirical testing and, above all, its use of the comparative method) ought to ensure that it produces a more balanced and *more useful* account than that of its competitors for seeing the way things are and the way things might be — *not* for deciding how they ought to be, but for *implementing* decisions about how they ought to be.

Should social scientists get involved with the use to which their secondary constructions are put and, thereby, become part of the primary construction of the wider "cult scene" not merely for methodological reasons (as discussed earlier), but for ethical or political purposes? Is such involvement compatible with, inimical to, or a question of indifference for the scientific study of religion? What if, in the course of our research, we frequently come across misunderstandings, misinformation, and/or gross distortions that appear to cause unnecessary suffering and are related to a subject that we have been investigating by methods that we believe to be superior to those that have given rise to the errors? What if we find that there are people who, claiming a professional expertise, maintain that they have arrived at certain conclusions using the scientific method, yet they provide no testable evidence, and we suspect that the scientific method not only does not, but could not, produce such conclusions? Should we not, both as individuals and as members of a professional society, fight ignorance, exploitation, and prejudice or at least correct inaccurate statements in our own field? Or do we just publish our misgivings in the *JSSR* on the chance that someone else might read what we have written and use it to challenge the alternative versions?

I know of nothing in the scientific enterprise that suggests social scientists *ought* to champion their versions of reality in the marketplace. At the same time, I know of nothing intrinsic to science that would proscribe such involvement. Indeed, those of us who *have* felt drawn to use the secondary constructs of the social scientific study of religion are, rightly or wrongly, of the opinion that we have as much right as anyone (and more relevant knowledge than many) not only to promote the social scientific perspective, but also to question others' secondary constructions when we consider them to be either inaccurate or biased.

But life is not that simple. As we step outside the relative protection of the Ivory Tower, we can find ourselves being affected by our competitors. I have already intimated that, while our presence is welcomed by some, it poses a threat to others. But it poses a threat to us too — not just the unpleasantness of the ways we are sometimes attacked, but a more insidious threat to the very meta-values and methods that can give us the edge over our competitors... .

The means by which the different secondary constructors sell their wares is of crucial significance for their success or failure, and the first hurdle social scientists face is how to set up our stall in a good position in the marketplace. When social scientists have completed their research they are quite likely to publish the results in scholarly books or journals which may sit on dusty shelves with few save other social scientists being aware of their existence. Placing monographs in the SSSR annual meeting's book exhibition, even getting published or reviewed in the *JSSR*, is not enough — it might give rise to internal debates, but if we are not heard by outsiders not only may we be missing some valuable feedback, we are also likely to be excluding ourselves from making any difference to "the cult scene."

We may need to be more conscious than is our wont that what we present should come across as being of relevance for the audience we want to reach. I am not suggesting that we fudge our results so that they are acceptable. On the contrary, I am suggesting that, like the actor playing the bore, we need to present our results so that they are understandable and *heard*, whether or not they are welcomed — especially, perhaps, if we suspect that they are not going to be welcomed. There may be lessons to be learned (and warnings to be heeded) by looking a bit more closely at both the media and the ACM. The former clearly have the largest audience and can make and enormous impact, despite (perhaps because of) the limitations of a short shelf-life and the difficulties of checking or recapturing their content. The ACM offers a dozen or so unambiguous points that can be applied to any situation; and, like the seasoned politician, they can be adept at avoiding probing questions. The ACM message is, furthermore, a popular one — not only are the cults fascinatingly evil compared to the rest of us, but also, because of their mind control techniques, they provide a simple explanation of why people reject "normal" society to follow "incredible" beliefs and lead "impossible" lives; and, moreover, they (the cults) can be held responsible for any problems that exist between members and their families.

If we want to preserve our sanity, we have to recognize that some battles will never be won. There are those who will continue to advance their version of reality whatever disconfirming evidence is presented to them, and there are others (sometimes the same people) who will persist in portraying our secondary constructions in a distorted manner. It is not that all individuals from the other categories are bound to reject our versions of reality — two erstwhile members of the FAIR Committee became valuable members of INFORM's Board of Governors; several members of the media who used to rely on the ACM now make copious use of INFORM's resources and international contacts — but the more realistic challenge is to communicate to those who, with no particular axe to grind, are interested in accurate and balanced accounts of NRMs. But how can we make our construction available without jeopardizing the integrity of our account?...

## Conclusion

Social reality is not an unchanging structure; it is an ongoing process that exists only insofar as individuals recognize its existence and act as the media through which it is processed. Whilst some perceptions always overlap, no two people ever share exactly the same vision of reality. All constructions of social reality are more or less affected not only by subjective understandings (previous experiences, values, assumptions, hopes, fears, and expectations), but also by the social position from which the social reality is perceived. Secondary constructions exhibit differences that can be observed to vary systematically and significantly according to the professional or group interests of the constructors.

As social scientists, we are interested in producing accurate and balanced constructions. To achieve this objective, we may believe that, rather than remaining clinically removed, part of our research necessitates an involvement with the people we are studying. This gives rise to the complication that we are likely to affect, and may ourselves be affected by, our data — a complication that become even more acute if, as individuals holding certain values, we actively engage in competing in the open market with others who are trying to sell their secondary constructions of the same primary reality.

...I do not believe that the idea of a scientific study of religion is utterly ridiculous. I would like to affirm that the exercise of social science is, despite its problems, an important and valuable discipline. We have a method-o-logic that can produce a more accurate and balanced account of social reality than those adopted by other secondary constructors. So far as "the cult scene" is concerned, I have argued that methodologically we ought to "get in there" to find out what's going on, and that politically we may, perhaps even should, "make a difference." We ought to communicate so that we can be *heard*; there is no reason why we should not fight ignorance and misinformation when we see it. Nor is there any reason why, *as citizens*, we should not use the findings of social science to fight bigotry, injustice, and what we conceive to be unnecessary misery.

But if we are to take on this mission, we also need to be careful that we do not throw the baby out with the bathwater or, to mix my metaphors still further, let the political tail wag the empirical dog. We need to be more aware, careful and true to our meta-values as professional social scientists than has sometimes been the case. We need to recognize that others may start defining our agenda — that we could be starting to select and evaluate according to criteria that violate the interests of social sciences. And when promoting and defending our versions of reality, we must remember that we can claim professional proficiency only within a limited area — that there are many legitimate questions which we cannot and should not address — *qua* social scientists... .

●●●●●●●●●●●●●●●●●●●●●●●●●●

# Notes

\*   This is a slightly revised version of a Presidential Address given at the Annual Meeting of the Society for the Scientific Study of Religion in Raleigh, NC, November 1993.

\*\*  Eileen Barker is a professor of sociology with special reference to the study of religion at the London School of Economics, Houghton St, London WC2A 2AE, England.

1   While doing participant observation at the London headquarters of the Unification Church, I would occasionally bump into the national leader. We had come to an implicit agreement that we could best cope with each other by developing a joking relationship (Radcliffe-Brown 1950), and he would almost inevitably greet me with the reminder: "Don't forget, you're either with us or against us!" to which I would invariably reply "But I'm a value-free objective social scientist!" whereupon we would exchange slightly uneasy laughter and some banter about who was brainwashing whom these days before going our separate ways.

2   Unfortunately, MPs are protected by "Parliamentary Privilege" from being sued for slander for anything they say in the House. Were it not so, INFORM might have been able to solve all its financial problems in one fell swoop!

3   Theologically motivated "countercultists" whose interests are primarily in what they consider to be the heretical and/or blasphemous beliefs of the movements are more likely to use their own hermeneutic of Holy Scripture to disprove the NRM's beliefs (Introvigne 1995). Just as the anticultist will ignore any positive aspects of an NRM, the countercultist will usually ignore any points of overlap between their beliefs and those of the NRM.

[4]    One of my colleagues met an active anticultist who told him I did nothing but praise the cults. Rather surprised, my colleague asked what she had read. "Oh, I wouldn't dream of reading anything she wrote!" she replied.

[5]    Exceptions would be full-length books, such as the paperbacks by Kilduff (1978) and Krause (1978) that appeared a few *days* after the Jonestown tragedy. Also, some books, such as Hounam and Hogg (1984) and Fitzgerald (1986), which started as articles in newspapers or popular journals involved impressive in-depth research.

# References

Asch, Solomon E.
    1959      Effects of group pressure upon the modification and distortion of judgments. In *Readings in social psychology* (3rd edition), edited by Eleanor E. Maccoby et al., 174-183. London: Methuen.

Barker, Eileen
    1984      *The making of a Moonie: Brainwashing or choice?* Reprinted by Gregg Revivals, Aldershot, 1993.
    1987      Brahmins don't eat mushrooms: Participant observation and the new religions. *LSE Quarterly* 1:127-152.
    1989a     *New religious movements: A practical introduction.* London: HMSO.
    1989b     Tolerant discrimination: Church, state and the new religions. In *Religion, state and society in modern Britain*, edited by Paul Badham, 185-208. Lewiston, NY: Edwin Mellen Press.
    1992      Authority and dependence in new religious movements. In *Religion: Contemporary issues. The All Souls Seminars in the sociology of religion*, edited by Bryan Wilson, 237-255. London: Bellew.
    1993a     Will the real cult please stand up? In *Religion and the social order: The handbook of cults and sects in America*, edited by David G. Bromley and Jeffrey Hadden, 193-211. Greenwich, CT, and London: JAI Press.
    1993b     Behold the New Jerusalems! *Sociology of Religion* 54:337-352.
    1994      But is it a genuine religion? In *Between sacred and secular: Research and theory on quasi-religion*, edited by Arthur L. Greil and Thomas Robbins, 69-88. Greenwich, CT, and London: JAI Press.
    1995      Plus ça change. In *20 years on: Changes in new religious movements.* Special edition of *Social Compass* 42, edited by Eileen Barker and Jean-François Mayer, 165-180.

Berger, Peter and Thomas Luckmann
    1966      *The Social Construction of Reality.* London: Penguin.

Bromley, David G. and Anson Shupe
    1995      Anti-cultism in the United States. *Social Compass* 42:221-236.

Douglas, Mary
    1966      *Purity and danger.* London: Routledge and Kegan Paul.
    1970      *Natural symbols: Explorations in cosmology.* London: Barrie and Rockliff

Fitzgerald, Frances
    1986      *Cities on a hill.* New York and London: Simon and Schuster.

Hounam, Peter and Andrew Hogg
    1984      *Secret cult.* Tring: Lion.

Houston, Gaie
1993 The meanings of power. *Self and Society* 21:4-9.

Introvigne, Massimo
1995 L'évolution du 'movement contre les sectes' chrétien 1978-1993. *Social Compass* 42:237-247.

Jules-Rosette, Bennetta
1975 *African apostles.* Ithaca: Cornell University Press.

Kilduff, Marshall and Ron Javers
1978 *The suicide cult.* New York: Bantam.

Krause, Charles A.
1978 *Guyana massacre: The eyewitness account.* New York: Berkley Books.

Lewis, James R.
1986 Restructuring the 'cult' experience. *Sociological Analysis* 47:151-9.

Mickler, Michael L.
1980 *A history of the Unification Church in the Bay Area: 1960-74.* MA thesis. Graduate Theological Union, University of California, Berkeley.
1992 The politics and political influence of the Unification Church. Paper given at SSSR, Washington, DC.

Mulhern, Sherrill
1994 Satanism, ritual abuse, and multiple personality disorder: A sociohistorical perspective. *The International Journal of Clinical and Experimental Hypnosis* 42:265-88.

Popper, Karl
1972 *Objective knowledge: An evolutionary approach.* Oxford: Clarendon Press.

Radcliffe-Brown, A.R.
1950 On joking relationships. *Africa* 13: 195-210.

Richardson, James T., Joel Best, and David G. Bromley (eds)
1991 *The satanism scare.* New York: de Gruyter.

Runciman, W.G.
1969 Sociological evidence and political theory. In *Philosophy, politics and society,* 2nd series, edited by Peter Laslett and W.G. Runciman, 34-47. Oxford: Blackwell.

Shupe, Anson D. and David G. Bromley
1980 *The new vigilantes.* Beverly Hills: Sage.

Solomon, Trudy
1981 Integrating the 'Moonie' experience. In *In Gods we trust,* edited by Thomas Robbins and Dick Anthony, 275-294. New Brunswick, NJ, and London: Transaction.

Weber, Max
1947 *The theory of social and economic organization.* New York: Free Press.

Wilson, Bryan (ed.)
1970 *Rationality.* Oxford: Blackwell.

Wright, Stuart
1987 *Leaving cults: The dynamics of defection.* Washington, DC: SSSR.

Wuthnow, Robert
1987 *Meaning and moral order: Explorations in cultural analysis.* Berkeley: University of California Press.

# DEFINITIONS OF CULT: FROM SOCIOLOGICAL-TECHNICAL TO POPULAR-NEGATIVE

## JAMES T. RICHARDSON

*This paper examines the theoretical and historical development of the term "cult," from its inception in the work of Troeltsch to more modern delineations of the term in the work of researchers studying new religious groups. The usurpation of the term by popular usage associated with strong negative connotations is discussed, along with efforts by a few contemporary scholars to salvage the term by redefining it in ways which attempt to combine traditional and popular meanings. The futility of this approach is discussed, and the paper concludes with suggestions that scholars should avoid the term and that it should not be allowed to be used in legal proceedings because of its confused and negatively connoted meaning in contemporary society.*

● ● ● ● ● ● ● ● ● ● ● ● ● ● ● ● ● ● ● ● ● ● ● ● ●

## Introduction

The term cult has a long and revered history in the sociology of religion, deriving from the work of Troeltsch (1931) and being developed since by a number of theorists (see Richardson, 1978, and van Driel and Richardson, 1988, for fuller discussions). The concept, as Campbell (1972) has noted, is a "Cinderella term" within the sociology of religion, consistently overlooked in favor of other concepts such as sect, church and denomination. Troeltsch developed the term as something of a residual category in his

James T. Richardson. "Definitions of Cult: From Sociological-Technical to Popular-Negative." *Review of Religious Research* 34, 1993: 348-356.

theoretical scheme of religious forms in Western culture. Since then the term has served "as a 'rug' under which were swept the troublesome and idiosyncratic religious experiences of mystics and other religious deviants..."(Richardson, 1978:29).

In recent years the term cult has become widely used popular term, usually connoting some group that is at least unfamiliar and perhaps even disliked or feared (Dillon and Richardson, 1991). This popular use of the term has gained such credence and momentum that it has virtually swallowed up the more neutral historical meaning of the term from the sociology of religion. Indeed, some would claim that the term cult is useless, and should be avoided because of the confusion between the historic meaning of the term and current pejorative use.

This paper will compare these two usages of the term cult, and make some recommendations about resolving the dilemma, especially since the new, negatively connoted usage of the term cult has invaded so many areas of life. First we will look at the traditional use of the term within the sociology of religion.

## Cult in the Sociological Tradition

In an earlier paper (Richardson, 1978:31) I defined the term as follows:

> ...a cult is usually defined as a small informal group lacking a definite
> authority structure, somewhat spontaneous in its development (although
> often possessing a somewhat charismatic leader or group of leaders),
> transitory, somewhat mystical and individualistically oriented, and
> deriving its inspiration and ideology from outside the predominant
> religious culture.

This definition relied heavily on the work of Nelson (1969), whose work on Spiritualism had revealed serious problems with usual scholarly application of the church-sect typology. Nelson was attempting to develop and generalize the term cult so that it might be useful in describing entities not fitting usual notions of church, sect, or denomination well. He also wanted a concept useful beyond the Judeo-Christian orbit. Nelson stressed the "break with tradition" idea, and also incorporated a focus on individualism and on mystical, psychic, or ecstatic experiences.

The just-cited typical definition from Richardson (1978) is not without controversy. Wallis (1974:300) argues that to include the idea of "deriving its inspiration from outside the dominant culture" makes the term cult too culturebound. He suggests that a more sociological approach would focus on "...changes in organizational form, modes of social control, and relations with the surrounding society." Wallis, however, goes on to develop a conceptualization of cult emphasizing Martin's (1965) notion of individualism, which is itself quite content-oriented.

In the 1978 paper I developed an "oppositional" conceptualization of cult more generalizable than usual delineations within sociology of religion. Two major dimensions were used — "individualistic-collectivistic" and "mystical-rational" to demonstrate how an oppositional approach to cult might operate (see Table 1). If a society has as dominant values individualism and rationality, then cultic responses would be indvidualistic-mystical, collectivistic-rational or collectivistic-mystical. More specifically (1979:38):

> If dominant cultural values are individualistic-rational (as some would say about modern American society), then cultic responses could be the hippie subculture (individualistic-mystical, a communist cell (collectivistic-rational), and a religious commune, either eastern or Christian mystical (collectivistic-mystical). If one were willing to categorize the culture of a communist country as "collectivistic-rational" a mystically oriented artist group (individualistic-mystical) would illustrate a cultic response. If we consider the Catholic-dominated period prior to the Reformation as "collectivistic-mystical," then certainly the initial stages of the Protestant Reformation would be an individualistic-rational" response...

Most earlier treatments simply state that a cult develops in opposition to the dominant culture, or they only talk of cults in religious terms (Yinger, 1957; Glock and

**Table 1** **Relationship of dominant and counter-cultural values, using 'individualistic-collectivistic' and 'rational-mystical' as major characterizing variables.**

| Dominant values | Values of 'counter-cultural' response | | | |
|---|---|---|---|---|
| | Individualistic | | Collectivistic | |
| | Rational | Mystical | Rational | Mystical |
| Individualistic rational | | | | |
| Individualistic mystical | | | | |
| Collectivistic rational | | | | |
| Collectivistic mystical | | | | |

Stark, 1965). The oppositional conceptualization is derivative of traditional approaches within the sociology of religion, but adds an element of specificity that most treatments omit. The conceptionalization is also suggestive of some interesting ideas for possible research in other areas of study (Richardson, 1978:34).

> (T)here could be cultic responses to sects, denominations, churches, and even other cults (or the "cultic milieu"). And regarding other areas of life and of sociology it seems just as obvious that there could be cultic responses in art, music, politics, medicine, education, and many other areas (even sociology itself).

The oppositional conceptualization seemed a fruit way to proceed with research in sociology of religion and other areas as well. The so-called Jesus Movement of the later 1960s and 1970s had been used in the earlier paper as an example of a cult-like movement in which the oppositional conceptualization was developed. Such a characterization of the Jesus Movement was counter to usual application of the notion of cult in the sociology of religion (which emphasize that cults are counter to the dominant values of the society). The cult characterization of Jesus Movement beginnings was explained as follows (1978:43):

> ...much of the initial impetus for the movement did come from outside the primary religion of the culture. Interviews with the members of several different movement groups indicated that the movement developed in reaction to excesses in the counter-cultural cultic milieu, and used a form of traditional Christianity as a vehicle of rebellion against the counterculture, while at the same time retaining some elements of counter-cultural beliefs and behavior with which to...contrast...its own position and that of the dominant culture.

In another paper I used the oppositional approach to develop a theory of how cult groups evolve into what sociologists would call sects. Again the Jesus Movement was used as an example of how the process might work. I had expanded the theorizing of Wallis (1974), developed in his research on Dianetics (better known as Scientology). The expansion was incorporated in a theoretical model that included several sets of analytically distinct factors: (1) group factors, (2) individual factors, (3) external factors, and (4) "bridges" or links between the cultic milieu and the Jesus Movement and other new religions (Richardson, 1979: 143).

Details of this theory of cult to sect change will not be discussed here. The point of this discussion is that in the late 1970s I and other sociologist of religion were making use of the term cult in a technical sense and were developing theories incorporating that term. But these promising theoretical and empirical efforts to use the term were obliterated by growing use of the term cult as a catch-all to refer to any new and unusual groups which had engendered animosity among some interest groups in the society. This usage will now be discussed.

# The "New" Cult Definition

Robbins and Anthony (1982:283) delineate the new, more popular definition of cult as follows:

> ...certain manipulative and authoritarian groups which allegedly employ mind control and pose a threat to mental health are universally labeled cults. These groups are usually: (1) authoritarian in their leadership; (2) communal and totalistic in their organization; (3) aggressive in their proselytizing; (4) systematic in their programs of indoctrination; (5) relatively new and unfamiliar in the United States; and (6) middle class in their clientele.

This definition clearly shows the problems associated with the new, popularized definition of cult. The emotionally charged terms used in the definition evidence the meaning of the term for those who employ it. To call a group manipulative and authoritarian, and to allege that it poses a threat to the mental health of participants shows strong feelings. Calling such groups "totalistic" and "aggressive" and saying that they systematically indoctrinate members adds to the baggage carried by popular use of the term.

Aside from the obvious negative stereotype offered by the use of such language, there are other problems with the delineation. There is little in the definition except for the "new and unfamiliar in the U.S." which resembles the traditional sociological definition of the term. Indeed, there are elements in the definition which are counter to the sociological delineation. This popular use of the term does not refer to a "small informal group lacking in a definite authority structure...spontaneous in development." The notion of communal is not part of the traditional definition, and aggressive recruitment seems at the odds with the notion of a small informal group with relatively amorphous boundaries of belief and behavior.

Thus the new definition of cult is a hodgepodge of elements which do not hang together in any logical sense, as did elements of the traditional definition. The new definition's elements are a list of things which some interest groups in our society do not like, or which they attribute to disfavored groups. If those opposing certain groups can successfully attach the label "cult" to a group, then they virtually automatically get to heap the negative baggage of the popular definition on that group. In short, the term has become a "social weapon" to use against groups which are not viewed with favor.

The new use of the term cult has become widespread. Media use it indiscriminantly (see van Driel and Richardson, 1988), which evidences the success of the Anti-Cult Movement (Shupe and Bromley, 1980) in promoting its view of the world. Professionals and lay persons who oppose the new religions use the term as frequently as possible, and in an every-expanding way, as evidenced by the recent focus on activities of alleged "satanic cults" (Richardson, Best, and Bromley, 1991). Even more interesting is growing use of the popular term in scholarly writings about new religions and related phenomena. Some scholars attempt to avoid the term because of negative stereotyping which accompanies its use (Dillon and Richardson, 1991). The term "new religions" or "new religious movements" has been developed as a somewhat amorphous term of art by some scholars. Others, however, have, in a sense, given up to the inevitable and employ the term cult so that people who read their writings will know they are talking about phenomena popularly referred to as cults. Thus the popular usage of the term has virtually swept the more technical and historical use of the term from writings both popular and scholarly.

Ellwood (1986) attempts to develop a definition of cult that combines some traditional concerns from the sociology of religion with the newer meaning of the term. He admits (1986:217) to "approaching the job phenomenologically...seek(ing) only to give a name to that which has already appeared and...defined itself by exhibiting special features or constellations of features." Ellwood adds:

> ...the word *cult* is so intimately intertwined with the popular connotations the word has acquired as to make it, in my view, ultimately undesirable. The label has too often been used to isolate groups in *a priori* theological or social grounds and then endow them with a wide range of characteristics associated in the user's mind with cults.

Ellwood's efforts to salvage the term are laudatory. In reasonably neutral language he offers (1986:218-222) a delineation which includes the following elements:

1. A group that "presents a distinct alternative to dominant patterns within the society in fundamental areas of religious life." This includes a small size with "distinctly different" forms of belief and practice, carried on by a uniquely organized group (see p. 219 for details).
2. Possessing "strong authoritarian and charismatic leadership."
3. Oriented toward "inducing powerful subjective experiences and meeting personal needs."
4  Is "separatist in that it strives to maintain distinct boundaries between it and the 'outside,'" and "requiring a high degree of conformity and commitment."

5. A tendency "to see itself as legitimated by a long tradition of
wisdom or practice of which it is the current manifestation."

This integrative effort is defended by Ellwood, who says the definition will not
apply to some groups being referred to popularly (and by some professionals) as cults.
He states (1986:221) that it will apply more to newer religious movements "in their
first generation and subsequently become less applicable as they, through routinization
of charisma and institutionalization, become something else sociologically, even if
still small and alternative."

Ellwood also attempted to distinguish his delineation from the term sect (1986:22):

> [o]ur definition allows the customary sociological distinction between
> cult and sect, unless the sect is quite heterodox, for though many
> characteristics would obtain in both instances — separatism or relation
> to a legitimating tradition for example — the sect, as a particularly
> intense version of the dominant religion with withdrawal features, is
> usually said to possess more legalistic that charismatic authority and to
> represent a spiritual alternative only in a much narrower sense than the
> cult.

Ellwood has made a valiant effort to define the term cult in a useful, non-
stereotypical way. He apparently is not satisfied with his efforts, however, as he
proceeds (1986:23) to recommend use of the alternative term "emergent religion" in
place of the term cult. I share his concerns, based on personal experiences with trying
to use the term in a technical sense with new religious phenomena. Indeed, I would
take the regrettable position that the term should be abandoned by scholars as currently
being misleading and not very useful. For scholars to attempt to make use of a term
with such strong and negative popular meanings seems to be folly, and it plays into the
hands of those who would oppose the development of new religious forms in our
society.

## Use of the Term Cult in Other Settings

As problematic as the term cult is for scholars, its use in other settings may be
worse. For instance, the term has such negative connotations that for it to be allowed in
court proceedings is a major victory for those opposing groups being referred to as
cults. If a group being sued is referred to with impunity as a cult, many of those
hearing the term can be expected to assume the "baggage" which often accompanies
the term in its popular usage. There is suggestive evidence that this attribution process
may occur with regularity. For example, Tyner (1991) notes that custody disputes

involving minority or deviant religious groups nearly always result in custody awards to the parent involved in a traditional religious group. Richardson (1991) discusses tort actions involving groups often referred to as cults, and notes the difficulty such groups have in defending themselves. Bromley and Breschel (1992) find strong support among the general public and institutional elites for social control of groups referred to as cults.

Jeffrey Pfeiffer, a psychologist, has done research relevant to the question (Pfeiffer, 1992). His research, grounded in psychological framing theory as developed by Tversky and Kahneman (1981), offers some empirical test of the claim that the term "cult" carries significant "baggage." Pfeiffer states (1992:533) that "when an individual is asked to evaluate an object, person, or event, his or her judgment may be based upon a previously developed cognitive representation such as a schema." He adds, "there is a negativity bias...[That] has been illustrated by a number of studies which suggest that negative information often carries more weight than positive information in terms of biasing judgments."

Pfeiffer then points out the general negative coverage of cults in the media and suggests that inundating people with the negative images from the media may result in the formation of "negative schemata regarding the indoctrination processes employed by cults" (1992:533-534). He refers to Tversky and Kahneman's (1981) point that when a person is asked to make a judgment about something unfamiliar they may "anchor the response to any piece of relevant information the person has...and subsequently frame their decision around this anchor" (1992:534). Pfeiffer thinks the term cult is a significant anchor which frames interpretations given to anything referred to by that term.

Pfeiffer's research is supportive of our point. He developed a scenario of someone joining a group and going through its indoctrination process. He had 100 subjects read a scenario, similar in all respects except changed so that subjects thought the person was being recruited by a cult, identified as the Unification Church or "Moonies", by a Catholic seminary, or by the Marines.

The results of this research show an overwhelming bias against groups such as the Unification Church, and those who join them. For instance, subjects defined the person who joined the Unification Church as significantly less happy, less intelligent, and less responsible than those who joined the Marines or the seminary. They also thought the person may have been coerced and treated less fairly by the Unification Church.

In a survey administered to subjects afterward, they were asked to describe their feelings about cults. Seventy-four percent offered a negative interpretation, and 82% described the average cult member in negative terms. Of note, 92% said their perceptions were based on news media accounts, and 78% said they have had no personal contact with cult members. Pfeiffer's conclusion included the following statement (1992:541): "(S)ubjects tend to rate both the group, and the individual joining the group, in more negative terms if they are led to believe the group is a cult."

## Conclusion and Recommendations

Given the obvious negative connotations of the term cult, as shown by a number of surveys and by Pfeiffer's research, it seems reasonable to suggest that the term "cult" should be severely limited in scholarly and other writings about religious groups. To do otherwise promotes the agenda of those deliberately using the term as a social weapon against new and exotic religious groups and experiences, even if those using the term do so more or less innocent of such intentions (Dillon and Richardson, 1991). Scholars should abandon the term cult, in favor of terms which have not been so taken over with popular negative usage. Perhaps Ellwood's term "emergent religion" will be found to be useful. But if it does not, then some other should be tried, so that dispassionate discussion and research can proceed.

The term cult should also be disallowed in legal proceedings where involvement in an exotic religious group is an issue. Those defending in actions against new religions popularly referred to as cults should consider making pre-trial motions to suppress the use of that term in the court room. The term simply carries too much baggage to allow its casual use in proceedings designed to have rational judgments made about important issues.

Some years ago I co-authored a somewhat tongue-in-cheek piece entitled "Cultphobia" (Kilbourne and Richardson, 1986), in which we described a new mental disorder involving phobia about cults. I would now close with the suggestion, somewhat more seriously, that those concerned with the misuse of the term cult should themselves become literally "cultphobic" and develop a strong aversion to using the misleading term. To make any use of the term "cult" offers solace to those promoting the new, negatively-loaded definition of the term, and such use should be stopped.

● ● ● ● ● ● ● ● ● ● ● ● ● ● ● ● ● ● ● ● ● ● ● ● ● ●

## References

Bromley, D. and E. Breschel
    1989      "General population and institutional elite perceptions of cults: Evidence from national surveys." *Behavioral Sciences and the Law* 10:39-52.

Campbell, C.
    1972      "The cult, the cultic milieu and secularization." Pp. 119-136 in M. Hill (ed.). *A Sociological Yearbook of Religion in Britain*. London: SCM Press.

Dillon, J. and J. Richardson
    1991      "A politics of representation analysis of social construction of the term 'cult'." Paper presented at annual meeting of the Society for the Scientific Study of Religion, Pittsburgh, PA.

Ellwood, R.
1986        "The several meanings of cult." *Thought* LXI (241):212-224.

Glock, C. and Stark, R.
1965        *Religion and Society in Tension*. Chicago: Rand McNally.

Kilbourne, B. and J. Richardson
1986        "Cultphobia." *Thought* LXI(241):258-266.

Martin, D.
1965        *Pacificism*. London: Routledge and Kegan-Paul.

Nelson, G.
1969        "The Spiritualist movement and the need for a redefinition of cult." *Journal for the Scientific Study of Religion* 8:152-160.

Pfeiffer, J.
1989        "The psychological framing of cults: Schematic presentations and cult evaluations." *Journal of Applied Social Psychology* 22:531-544.

Richardson, J.
1978        "An oppositional and general conceptualization of cult." *Annual Review of the Social Sciences of Religion* 2:29-52.
1979        "From cult to sect: Creative eclecticism in new religious movements." *Pacific Sociological Review* 22:139-166.
1991        "Cult/brainwashing cases and freedom of religion." *Journal of Church and State* 33:55-74.

Robbins, T. and D. Anthony
1982        "Deprogramming, brainwashing and the medicalization of deviant religious groups." *Social Problems* 29:283-297.

Shupe, A. and D. Bromley
1980        *The New Vigilantes*. Beverly Hills: Sage.

Troeltsch, E.
1931        *The Social Teachings of the Christian Churches*. New York: MacMillan.

Tversky, A. and D. Kahneman
1981        "The framing of decisions and the psychology of choice." *Science* 211:453-458.

Tyner, M.A.
1991        "Who gets the kid?" *Liberty* May/June:8-11.

van Driel, Barend and J. Richardson
1988        "Cult versus sect: Categorization of new religions in American print media." *Sociological Analysis* 49:171-183.

Wallis, R.
1974        "Ideology, authority, and the development of cultic movements." *Social Research* 41:299-327.

Yinger, M.
1957        *Religion, Society, and the Individual*. New York: McGraw-Hill.

# THREE TYPES OF NEW RELIGIOUS MOVEMENTS

## ROY WALLIS

*... I propose to provide a characterisation of the three types of new religion, illustrating the characteristics of each type from actual movements which appear to approximate them particularly closely, or to embody features of the type in a sharply visible form.*

• • • • • • • • • • • • • • • • • • • • • • • • •

## The World-Rejecting New Religion

The world-rejecting movement, no matter what religious tradition it draws upon, is much more *recognisably* religious than the world-affirming type. It possesses a clear conception of God as at the same time a *personal* entity but yet radically distinct from man and prescribing a clear and uncompromising set of moral demands upon him. For example, in the International Society for Krishna Consciousness (ISKCON) — the saffron-robed devotees of Swami Bhaktivedanta (also knows as Prabuphada), an Indian guru who travelled to America in 1965 to spread devotion to Krishna and the ecstatic practices of his worship, such as chanting the Hare Krishna mantra — Krishna 'is not an idea or abstract principle but a person not unlike every human, however unfathomably greater, more magnificent, opulent and omnipotent he may be' (Reis, 1975: 54).

---

Roy Wallis. "Three Types of New Religious Movements," in Roy Wallis, *The Elementary Forms of the New Religious Life*. London: Routledge and Kegan Paul, 1984, pp. 9-39.

The Children of God derive from a quite different tradition, that of American fundamentalism, adapted to the counter-cultural youth revolt of the 1960s. Founded in 1968 by David Brandt Berg (later known as Moses David, or Mo) in California among the youthful rebels and drop-outs of the West Coast, it subsequently spread nomadically throughout the world. The deity of the Children of God is a variation upon the traditional Judeo-Christian God, highly personalistic even when referred to more impersonally as 'Love' and possessed of the same whims, emotions, arbitrariness, and tendencies to favouritism as any human being.

The Unification Church, whose followers are popularly known as the 'Moonies', also emerged from within the Judeo-Christian tradition. But in this case fundamentalism was syncretised with Asian religious conceptions in Korea where the Reverend Sun Myung Moon, its founder, was born. Although missionaries of the church arrived in America late in 1959, it was not until the late 1960s and early 1970s that it began to expand significantly and to attain an almost unrivalled public notoriety. For all its novel features, however, the deity of the Unification Church is a Heavenly Father, to whom conventional attitudes of prayer and supplication are taken.

The world-rejecting movement views the prevailing social order as having departed substantially from God's prescriptions and plan. Mankind has lost touch with God and spiritual things, and, in the pursuit of purely material interests, has succeeded in creating a polluted environment; a vice-ridden society in which individuals treat each other purely as means rather than as ends; a world filled with conflict, greed, insincerity and despair. The world-rejecting movement condemns urban industrial society and its values, particularly that of individual success as measured by wealth or consumption patterns. It rejects the materialism of the advanced industrial world, calling for a return to a more rural way of life, and a reorientation of secular life to God.

Moses David, leader of the Children of God, observed in disappointment after a visit to Israel, that it:

> reminds us more of America than any country we visited with all its busy materialism, its riches, power, and armaments, its noisy traffic and air pollution, and its increasingly materialistically-minded younger generation. (Moses David, 'The promised land?', 4 February 1971)[1]

> God's government is going to be based on the small village plan. ... Each village will be virtually completely self-contained, self-controlled and self-sufficient unto itself, like one big happy family or local tribe, just the way God started man out in the beginning. His ideal economy, society and government based on His own created productive land for man's simple necessities.
> We're going to go back to those days with only the beautiful creation of God around us and the wonderful creatures of God to help

> us plow and power and transport what little we have to do to supply
> our meagre needs (Moses David, 'Heavenly homes', 21 October 1974)

These sentiments are echoed by the Krishna Consciousness movement in its references to New Vrndavana, its model agricultural community established in West Virginia, to

> show that one need not depend upon factories, movies, department
> stores, or nightclubs for happiness; one may live peacefully and happily
> with little more than some land, cows, and the association of devotees
> in a transcendental atmosphere of Krishna Consciousness. (*Back to*
> *Godhead*, 60, 1973: 14)

Jonestown in the Guyana jungle was viewed as a potential rural paradise by Jim Jones's followers in the People's Temple. The prospèct of a communist agrarian idyll where food would be plentiful, prejudice and discrimination non-existent, and all would share as they had need, was attractive indeed for under-privileged black ghetto-dwellers in northern California, and for white middle-class radicals alike.

Rather than a life pursuing *self-interest*, the world-rejecting sect requires a life of *service* to the guru or prophet and to others who likewise follow him. Through long hours of proselytising on the street or distributing the movement's literature, through an arduous round of devotional ritual before the deities or unpaid domestic duties for leaders or other members, the devotee will suppress his own desires and goals in expression of his commitment to the greater good of the movement, or love of God and His agent. Reis observes of the Krishna Consciousness devotee that:

> Although one has a duty to provide financial support for the maintenance
> and expansion of the organisation, this is not done for the self, the
> fragile illusionary ego, but out of love for Krishna and his personal
> representative, Prabhupada (Reis, 1975: 159-60).

Such a movement may anticipate an imminent and major transformation of the world. The Children of God, for example, expect a progressive movement toward the prophesied End Time with the rise of the Anti-Christ shortly to occur or even now under way, the confirmation of the Covenant in 1985 and the inauguration thereby of the final seven years of world history. In 1989 the Tribulation will begin as the Anti-Christ demands to be worshipped as God, turning against the saints; and in 1993 Jesus is to return. Many members of the Unification Church, too, regard themselves as living in the Last Days (Edwards, 1979: 80-9) in which the Lord of the Second Advent is destined to take up the task which Jesus failed to complete because of his crucifixion. Jesus was able only to establish God's spiritual kingdom on earth when his mission had been to establish both a spiritual *and* a physical kingdom. The Christian tradition has held — in some of its varieties — to a conception of the physical return of Christ at the Second Coming to establish his millennial reign after defeating the forces of evil. Members of the Unification Church see the Reverend Sun Myung Moon as occupying the role of Christ (rather than being Jesus returned), and engaged in a God-directed mission to establish the basis for the physical kingdom of God, and the restoration of the world to His dominion after wresting it from Satan.

The world-rejecting movement expects that the millennium will shortly commence or that the movement will sweep the world, and, when, all have become members or when they are in a majority, or when they have become guides and counsellors to kings and presidents, then a new world-order will begin, a simpler, more loving, more humane and more spiritual order in which the old evils and mistakes will be eradicated, and utopia will have begun. These examples illustrate the close link between religious and political aspirations among world-rejecting sects. Their rejection of the world clearly embraces secular institutions. Since their aim to recover the world for God, they deny the conventional distinction between a secular and a religious realm, the secular must be restored to its 'original' religious character. Their tendency to reject a distinction between the religious and the political also follows from a conception of mundane events as implicated in a cosmic plan, one based on a struggle between God and evil, truth and illusion, now near culmination. Political differences thus mirror cosmic positions in this struggle, with communism typically seen as the Satanic representative on earth. It also follows from this that, with the final struggle so close, the faithful cannot hope to change the world sufficiently one soul at a time. Thus, although they seek to convert among the world's masses, they also address themselves to the influential, who are in a position to affect a much wider range of people and events and thus to meet the pressing cosmic timetable more effectively. Hence, a number of such movements have cultivated the company of the powerful. Judah quotes a Krishna devotee on the benefits of such a policy:

> So the idea is that the politicians ... take advice from Krishna Consciousness.... Just try to conceive for a moment the potency of a political candidate running for office having spiritual advisers who are telling him that his only goal should be to serve Krishna. (Judah, 1974: 119)

The Unification Church, too, has sought to gain a role for some of its members as advisers to, and confidantes of, prominent American politicians. The Children of God have also seen themselves as aides and counsellors to rulers and, more especially, to the world-ruler they believe to be about to rise. After Armageddon and the return of Christ, they believe that 'we, the Children of God, shall rule and reign with Him ...' (Moses David, 'Daniel 7', May 1975).

So active have some groups been in this direction that their claim to a *religious* mission comes to be regarded as little more than a front for political aspirations. Such accusations have been levelled against Sun Myung Moon and the Unification Church, who have been vigorous in their opposition to communism, and their support for anti-communist figures and regimes such as Richard Nixon, and successive South Korean military dictatorships. Jim Jones, founder of the People's Temple, was courted by many Californian politicians. Manson's gory group are not perhaps readily conceived as 'religious', but it appears that Charles Manson did view himself as a composite of Christ and Satan, returned to earth in preparation for the imminent cataclysm of Armageddon (Bugliosi, 1977: 581), which would largely consist of a terrible violent revolution of the blacks against the whites in America. Thereafter his political role would emerge. He is said to have believed that the American blacks, having vanquished the whites, would eventually have to turn to him to guide them.

Meanwhile, in such movements, characteristically the faithful have come out of the world until Armageddon or the millennium transpires, setting themselves apart from it, anticipating utopia in the communal life wherein they can keep themselves separated, uncontaminated by the worldly order, able to cultivate their collective spiritual state unmolested. The religious involvement of members is thus a full-time activity. The committed adherent will need to break completely with the worldly life in order to fulfill the movement's expectations, and separation may result in a rift with family and former friends, with conventional education and career. The movement is a 'total institution', regulating all its adherents' activities, programming all of their day but for the briefest periods of recreation or private time. Not only will the member live in the community, normally he will also work for it. Although this may sometimes mean taking a job 'in the world', the risks of this are quite high for a movement that so heartily condemns the prevailing social order. Usually an economic base for the movement will be devised which limits involvement in the world. Often this can be combined with proselytising, as in the case of Krishna Consciousness devotees who offer copies of their magazine, books, or flowers, or the Children of God who offer copies of their leader's letters printed in pamphlet form, in return for a donation. Contact with non-members can then be highly routinised and ritualised. It is, anyway, transient; it can be interpreted in terms confirmatory of the movement's beliefs as, for example, when a hostile response is received from someone approached on the street, which serves only to confirm the evil nature of the world; but such forms of fund-raising do provide the opportunity for contact with people who may show some interest in, or sympathy with, what they are being offered, and thus provide occasions for conversion.

An alternative approach is to separate economic activity and proselytism, or to establish an independent source of income, for example, farming, as in the case of some Jesus People groups, or various manufacturing activities such as those conducted by the Unification Church. Most movements tend to have multiple economic bases often also deriving income from the possessions of new members handed over to the collective fund on joining; donations from sympathetic or unwary businessmen; and remittances from parents of members; as well as the street sales and manufacturing enterprises. Despite their rejection of the world and its materialism, members are often encouraged to collect state welfare payments, rent subsidies, child allowances, etc.

Two hundred of the Jonestown, Guyana residents were receiving social security benefits.

Street solicitation became a major initial economic resource for many of the youthful world-rejecting new religions (Children of God, Unification Church, ISKCON, The Process) for a variety of pressing reasons. Unlike the world-affirming movements they had no commodity or service to purvey. Unlike earlier generations of world-rejecting movements, this cohort emerged into a world where readily available, cultivatable land for producing their own subsistence had virtually disappeared. What remained was, at best, marginal land impossible to farm satisfactorily without agricultural expertise lacking among the primarily urban-raised membership (Whitworth, 1975). While they could support themselves for a time through handing over their resources to a communal fund, most of those recruited were economically marginal and thus had few resources and little capital to offer. Working at conventional jobs for support entailed a consequent loss of time for spreading the word, for proselytising others. They lacked funds initially for investment in other income-producing enterprises such as forms of manufacture. Hence, what they required was an economic base which needed little capital investment; made use of their only resources — people and enthusiasm; and which, if possible, brought them into contact with potential members. Street solicitation — seeking donations in return for some low cost item such as leaflets, magazines, candles, or flowers — met this need. Later, when investment capital had been secured by this means, some of these movements invested in viable agricultural land and book publishing (ISKCON), fishing and manufacture (Unification Church), etc., which supplied some of their resources. The Children of God continued to combine witnessing and fund-raising through the practice of 'flirty fishing': demonstrating 'God's love' through sex, and encouraging the beneficiaries of their favours to provide financial and other assistance in return (Wallis, 1979a: ch. 5).

The People's Temple illustrates the pattern of severe economic self-renunciation characteristic of such movements , particularly in their early years:

> Finances for People's Temple members were fairly simple: everything went to Jim Jones. Families signed over homes, property, and pay-checks to the temple. To raise additional money for the cult, some members occasionally begged on street corners.
>
> Members who did not live in the church had to tithe a minimum of 25 percent of their earnings. Those living on church property gave everything to Jones, who returned to them a two dollar weekly allowance. (Kerns, 1979: 159)

The life-style to be found in world-rejecting movements — despite its deviant appearance — is characteristically highly organised and controlled. The need to generate adequate financial support often imposes severe rigours on members, particularly when combined with an ascetic ethic. Thomas Robbins *et al.* (1976: 115) argue of the Unification Church, for example, that, 'Life in a communal center is disciplined and most of the day is devoted to activities such as "witnessing" on the street, giving and listening to lectures, and attending other functions.'

The rigours of fund-raising in the Unification Church have been described by Christopher Edwards, a former member:

> I had been flower selling for a week now. At the end of each afternoon, we would return to the van, exhausted. For dinner — if lucky, we would receive a generous donation of unusable burgers someone had begged from the McDonald's franchise down the road by telling the manager we were poor missionaries. If we weren't so lucky, we might dine on donated stale doughnuts and cold pizza.
>
> Our group was collecting over a thousand tax-free dollars daily.
>
> Each morning we picked up our order of roses from the San Francisco flower district. We slept in vans at night, eight in a row, brothers at one end, sisters at another. When Family members were on the road for several days, we couldn't change clothes or shower. To even change a shirt in this crowded, smelly vehicle could tempt the sisters to fall again, might stir and excite the sexual drives now buried deep within our unconscious.
>
> Night after night we worked until two in the morning, doing bar runs — blitzing, as we called it, coaxing drunks to buy wilted roses for the angry wives awaiting them at home. At 2.30, we would drive to a local park, praying in unison in the darkness. ... After the gruelling ritual ended, we settled down for a night's sleep, a full hour and a half, for we must soon be up for pledge service Sunday morning. (Edwards, 1979: 161-2)

Success in fund-raising becomes an indicator of the member's own spiritual condition rather than of his worldly skills. Fund-raising is interpreted by members less as an economic necessity than as a method of spiritual growth (Bromley and Shupe, 1979: 123). A Unification Church member reports that:

> Fund-raising was a powerful experience for me. I was out on my own and had to make a decision: do I believe in the *Divine Principle* and am I willing to go through this? To me, fund-raising was a very spiritual experience in that it reaffirmed my faith. Every day I had to question what I believed. (Bryant and Hodges, 1978: 62)

Daner (1976: 77) asserts that in Krishna Consciousness too, 'A devotee must be prepared to give his entire self to lead a life of day to day obedience and service.' Indeed, in the face of the increasing competition from groups and movements offering forms of 'easy' enlightenment, ISKCON'S magazine, *Back to Godhead* has laid *increasing* stress on the necessity of spiritual discipline (Reis, 1975: 133).

The disciplined character of the communal life may extend to the use of physical sanctions to encourage the achievement of movement requirements. When 'litnessing', i.e. the distribution of literature in return for donations, was a major aim of the Children of God, members who failed to reach the quota set for them were, at times, sent out again after a day on the streets and forbidden to return to the colony (i.e. the commune) until the quota target in literature distributed, or daily financial quota, was met. Synanon is a movement that began life as a communal drug-rehabilitation programme in California, which developed a religious self-conception and philosophy only subsequently. It has thus undergone considerable changes during the course of its development which I shall discuss later, but, during its most explicitly world-rejecting phase, physical violence was occasionally inflicted on deviant members. As the People's Temple, too, became more world-rejecting over the course of its development, so physical violence became more normal as a means of social control (Kerns, 1979: 157, 185). This was also, of course, the case in Manson's Family. None the less, the demand for discipline only rather infrequently issues in the routine use of violence in new religious movements. The reason is not far to seek. These movements are voluntary communities living usually in densely populated societies with strong central state authorities. They cannot effectively coerce those who can make their wish to dissent or abandon membership known; they cannot normally hope to isolate effectively members who rebel or resist authority; nor can they compete with the means of violence available to the state if they infringe upon the liberties of members to the degree where they call upon its aid. They must retain their following by persuasion — albeit some may see such persuasion as entailing forms of blackmail — or by the instilling of fear at the prospect of departure. Followers must be given reasons to remain when they cannot in general be coerced. And since *enthusiasm* is normally a prerequisite for the survival and growth of the movement, love, rather than fear, is much the more frequent means of persuasion.

The communal life-style of the world-rejecting movement exhibits a high level of diffuse affectivity. Members of such movements kiss each other and hug in greeting, hold hands with other members, or call endearments and offer constant encouragement. Typically, this highly visible affectivity is coupled with a strongly puritan moral code which permits it to go no further than public display. Or, when sexual relationships are permitted, it is normally primarily for the purpose of reproduction. Married members of the Krishna Consciousness movement, for example, are allowed to engage in sexual intercourse only at the wife's most fertile point in the monthly cycle, and even then only after extensive ritual preparations. Sexual relationships are subordinated to *collective* rather than private, *personal* ends, so that, in the Unification Church and the early Children of God, members were willing to have marriage partners chosen for them even from among complete strangers. In the Unification Church, moreover, members will normally lead lives of rigorous chastity, often for a number of years before marriage.

Married members of Synanon and the People's Temple, on the other hand, were prepared to divorce their mates and take new spouses at their leader's direction. But even when, as in the later Children of God, the movement has become sexually antinomian, such apparent self-indulgence may in fact itself be largely a matter of service. The liberal sexuality of the Children of God is employed at least in part to win converts and to increase the solidarity and commitment of members, and personal pleasure therefore remains a *secondary* consideration to helping others and serving God.

In this quotation, Moses David stresses the use of sex as a means of 'saving souls' and serving God:

> Who knows? — When all other avenues of influence and witnessing are closed to us this may be our only remaining means of spreading the Word and supporting the work, as well as gaining new disciples and workers for the Kingdom of God.
> 
> What better way to show them the love of God than to do your best to supply their desperately hungry needs for love, fellowship, companionship ... affection, a tender loving kiss, a soft warm embrace, the healing touch of your loving hands, the comforting feeling of your body next to theirs — and yes, even *sex* if need be! (Moses David, 'King Arthur's nights: chapter one', 29 April 1976).

Even earlier he had indicated that monogamous marriage was by no means sacrosanct in the Children of God, and could not be permitted to endanger the solidarity of the movement:

> We do not minimise the marriage ties as such. We just consider our ties to the Lord and the larger Family greater and more important. And when the private marriage ties interfere with Our Family and God ties, they can be readily abandoned for the glory of God and the good of the Family! ... partiality toward your own wife or husband or children strikes at the very foundation of communal living — against the unity and supremacy of God's Family and its oneness and wholeness. (Moses David, 'One wife', 28 October 1972)

Moses David is quite explicit about the role sexual relationships can play in generating solidarity in the Children of God, as in his letter reflecting on 'The real meaning of The Lord's Supper!' (Moses David, 1 October 1978):

> Boy, there's a hot one for our Family!: One in the flesh, one body, and one in spirit! ... in our Family we are one body, all the way! Sexually as

well, really one Bride of Christ, One Wife, One Body! How much
more could you be one body than *we* are, amen? PTL! *We're one all
the way!* ...

Thank God, in our Family ... we are not only one in spirit but one in
body, both in sex and sacrificial service to others.

The Manson Family — to take a yet more extreme case — also employed sexual
promiscuity as a means of eliminating the individual ego and subordinating all individual
personality and goals to those of the collectivity, as formulated by Charles Manson:

The lack of sexual discrimination among hard-core Family members
was not so much gross animalism as it was simply a physical parallel
to the lack of emotional favoritism and attachment that Charlie taught
and insisted on. As long as we loved one person more than the others,
we weren't truly dead [to self] and the Family wasn't one. (Watson
1978: 70)

Manson's Family also employed sexuality instrumentally as a means of attracting
converts (Zamora, 1976: 79). Through sexuality the Children of God believed they
showed God's love, and the Manson Family the love of Charlie (Watson, 1978: 68-9).

The life of the world-rejecting movement tends to require considerable
subordination of individual interest, will, and autonomy in order to maximise collective
solidarity and to eliminate disruptive dissent. Naranjo (1979: 27) reports from her
observations that 'members are expected to learn that Synanon places the explicit
needs and demands of the community over and above the needs of any individual.' A
common theme in world-rejecting movements is that of having been *reborn* on joining
the group. A complete break with past desires, interests, statuses, with any past
identity, is made by dating one's birth from the moment of joining (as, for example, in
the Love Israel movement, a small Seattle based, counter-cultural, communal, religious
group). A new identity will be acquired incorporating as its central features the beliefs,
norms and values of the collectivity joined. Typically this nascent identity is signified
by the convert taking a new name as in the Children of God, Love Israel, Krishna
Consciousness, The Process, and the Manson Family.

The ego or former self must be completely repudiated. The Children of God
employ the term 'forsake all' to mean not only the process of handing over all worldly
possessions to the movement on joining, but also the renunciation of the past and of all
self-interest. Enroth reports from some reflections of a COG 'lit shiner' (i.e. a distributor
of the largest number of MO Letters in her area at a time when members were
encouraged to maximise their output), her aspiration to do even better: 'I'm sure it's
possible to hit 12,000 a week. I know it. *I have to die more to myself* and put more
hours in' (Enroth, 1977: 51, my emphasis). Even the exclusiveness of the marital bond
must be abandoned for the collective good. As Moses David, leader of the Children of

God put it in one of his letters to his disciples: 'it's the last vestige of forsaking all to forsake even your husband and wife to share with others' (Moses David, 'One wife', 28 October 1972; on sex and marriage in the Children of God, see Wallis, 1979a: ch. 5). Giving up any exclusive claim upon particular others was an important part of abandoning the self. In similar vein, Watson recounts the beliefs of the Manson Family:

> True freedom means giving up ourselves, letting that [sic] old ego die so we can be free of the self that keeps us from one another. ... 'Cease to exist', Charlie sang in one of the songs he'd written. 'Cease to exist, come say you love me'. The girls repeated it over and over — *cease to exist, kill your ego, die* — so that once you cease to be, you can be free to totally love, totally come together. (Watson, 1978: 54)

Abnegation of personal identity, or self-renunciation to this degree renders more comprehensible the awesome mass suicide of People's Temple members in Jonestown, Guyana. When the cause and the movement are everything, and the self is nothing, giving one's own life may be a small price for what one has had, or for what may be achieved by the gesture.

When individual identity is so thoroughly tied to a collective identity and subordinated to the will and authority of a leader personifying that collective identity, any threat to the leader or the community is a threat to the self. Life is far less important than protection of the leader, defence of the movement's ideal, or indictment of its enemies. The logical extreme of 'forsaking all' for the common good is not — as Moses David supposes — the abandoning of an exclusive sexual claim upon a spouse, but rather it is the *suicidal act*. Members of the Unification Church and the Children of God are warned that they may have to die for their movement or their faith:

> We know that some will suffer and some will have to die for Thee and Thy Gospel. You promised it, Lord, but you said 'Great is your reward in Heaven, for so persecuted they the prophets which were before you! (MT 5: 12).' (Moses David, 'The happy ending', February 1979)

The deindividuation, subordination of self, and the correlated sense of rebirth, of complete break with the past are highlighted, in the case of the Manson Family, by a recollection of Tex Watson. A prolonged intimate relationship normally results in the partners acquiring substantial background knowledge of each other, yet Watson observes of the girl specially assigned to him by Manson that, 'During the months that Mary and I were more or less together, I learned practically nothing about her past. The past was non-existent for the Family, something to discard along with all the materialistic middle-class programming and the ego that it had built' (Watson, 1978: 61).

A collective identity may be fostered by various means as Rosabeth Kanter (1972) has shown, including a common mode of dress and appearance. This is seen at its clearest in Krishna Consciousness, wherein temple residents wear Indian dress and men shave their heads but for a topknot. Observers often commented on the similarity in dress and appearance of members of the Unification Church in its early years of notoriety. To a considerable extent this was also true of the Children of God who might not all look precisely alike, but for whom there was a considerable commonality in style. Another expression of this deindividuation is to be seen in the practice in the Manson Family of keeping all the clothes not in immediate use in one large pile on the floor (see e.g. Watson, 1978: 29). This is echoed in Edwards's (1979: 97) account of induction to the Unification Church:

> I left the shower room house, wearing the crumpled old clothes I had
> pulled out of the collective laundry hamper. ... All our clothes were
> thrown together and we dressed on a first-come, first-serve system,
> those newest in the Family choosing the shabbiest clothes to show
> humility and Family leaders picking out the finest as a sign of their
> status.

Another typical means of fostering and marking collective identity, so usual as almost to be a defining characteristic of the world-rejecting movement, is that of new members handing over on joining all belongings (Unification Church, Children of God, Krishna Consciousness, Manson Family, etc.), or major assets and income (People's Temple). Equally general is the conceptualisation of the movement as a family in which other members are closer than any physical brothers and sisters, and in which the leader occupies the status of father with an appropriate authority over his 'children'. By this means movements as diverse as the Love Family (in Seattle), the Unified Family — a designation employed by the Unification Church; the Manson Family, and the Family of Love — a later name taken by the Children of God, have sought to describe the close, emotional bonding and corporate loyalty felt by members of the group.

Movements such as these, mandated by God through the medium of a messiah, prophet or guru to fulfill His demands, tend to be highly authoritarian. The resulting constraints of the communal life and an authoritarian leadership provide a basis for the claim by hostile outsiders that the youthful members have lost their identity, personality, and even their 'free will' in joining. Such claims have formed a major part of the rhetoric of the 'anti-cult' movement (Shupe, Spielmann and Stigall, 1977; Wallis, 1977. This issue is discussed further below).

# The World-Affirming New Religion

The other end of the continuum presents a sharp contrast. The style of the world-affirming movement lacks most of the features traditionally associated with religion. It may have no 'church', no collective ritual of worship, it may lack any developed theology or ethics (in the sense of general, prescriptive principles of human behaviour and intention — although see Tipton, 1982b [1] on *est*). In comparison to the world-rejecting movement, it views the prevailing social order less contemptuously, seeing it as possessing many highly desirable characteristics. Mankind, too, is not so much reprobate as needlessly restricted, containing within itself enormous potential power which, until now, only a very few individuals have learned to utilise effectively, and even then normally only by withdrawing from the world, and subjecting themselves to the most rigorous disciplines. Silva Mind Control is a training involving techniques of self-hypnosis and visualisation, which is transmitted in 40-48 hours and which:

> can train anyone to remember what appears to be forgotten, to control
> pain, to speed healing, to abandon unwanted habits, to spark intuition
> so that the sixth sense becomes a creative, problem-solving part of
> daily life. With all this comes a cheerful inner peace, a quite optimism
> based on first-hand evidence that we are more in control of our lives
> than we ever imagined. (Silva and Miele, 1977: 12-13)

The method — which brings one 'into direct, working contact with an all-pervading higher intelligence' (ibid.: 17) — was invented by a Mexican American Jose Silva in the 1950s. An advertising leaflet for Silva Mind Control avers that:

> In 48 hours you can learn to use your mind to do *anything* you wish. ...
> There is no limit to how far you can go, ... to what you can do, because
> there is no limit to the power of your mind.

Transcendental Meditation (TM) involves — as its name makes clear — a meditational technique taught to those who are initiated in a relatively brief ceremony in which the initiator conveys to the new meditator a 'personal' mantra, in fact selected according to the new meditator's age, on which the individual meditates for twenty minutes each morning and evening. The technique was brought to the West by the Maharishi Mahesh Yogi in the late 1950s, but achieved celebrity mainly as a result of the Beatles becoming initiated and visiting the Maharishi in India in 1968. Although their interest shortly waned, numbers undertaking initiation into TM increased dramatically in the late 1960s and 1970s. (For data on the expansion of TM in the USA, see Bainbridge and Jackson, 1981.) A pamphlet published by one of the organisations of Transcendental Meditation announces the super-normal powers to which it provides access:

> The TM-Siddhis programme ... creates the ability to function from the level of ... unbounded awareness. Any thought consciously projected from that unbounded awareness will be so powerful, will be so supported by all the laws of nature, that it will be fulfilled without problems, without loss of time. (Mahesh Yogi, 1977)

Movements approximating the world-affirming type claim to possess the means to enable people to unlock their physical, mental and spiritual potential without the need to withdraw from the world, means which are readily available to virtually everyone who learns the technique or principle provided. No arduous prior period of preparation is necessary, no ascetic system of taboos enjoined. No extensive mortification of the flesh nor forceful control of the mind. At most, a brief period abstention from drugs or alcohol may be requested, without any requirement even of continued abstention after the completion of a training or therapy period.

*est* (the italicised initial lower case form is used even at the beginning of a sentence) is the commonly used designation for Erhard Seminar's Training, an organisation which provides a 60-hour training, the purpose of which is 'to transform your ability to experience living so that the situations you have been trying to change or have been putting up with, clear up just in the process of life itself'. While it is one of the less transcendental of the new world-affirming salvational movements, *est* is clearly part of the same domain as its more overtly religious counterparts among movements of this type. As will be argued subsequently, movements of this type tend to possess a more secularised and individualised conception of the divine. Moreover, they offer access to supernatural, magical and spiritual powers and abilities which legitimise the attribution to them of the label 'religious'. Participants in the *est* training are not expected to submit to any severe preparatory trials or rigours. They are required merely to observe a series of rules during the 60 hours the training involves (normally spread over two weekends in four approximately 15-hour days). They may not smoke in the training room, eat except at the specified meal break, drink alcohol or take any drug (except as medically prescribed) during the training period and the intervening week. The 'asceticism' involved in securing enlightenment through *est* goes no further than being permitted breaks for smoking or the lavatory only three or four times during each 15-16 hour day; being required to sit in straight-backed chairs during much of the training with the consequent mild physical discomfort; and being obliged to raise one's hand, be acknowledged, and stand to use a microphone before speaking. Persons wishing to be initiated into Transcendental Meditation are asked to cease drug use for fifteen days beforehand.

Just as no rigorous discipline is normally involved, so, too, no extensive doctrinal commitment is entailed, at least not at the outset. There may even be no initial insistence that the adherent *believe* the theory or doctrine at all, as long as he is willing to try the technique and see if it works. Examples are readily available in Transcendental Meditation and in *est*:

> No one is required to declare a belief in TM, in the Maharishi, or even in the possible effects of the technique in order for it to work. *It works in spite of an individual's disbelief or skepticism.* (Robbins and Fisher, 1972: 7)

> Q. Do I have to believe the training will work in order for the training to work?
> A. No. *est* is not a system of beliefs or techniques to be learned and practised. Some people approach the training with enthusiasm, and some with skepticism — and some with both. Your willingness to be there is all you need.
> (*Questions People Ask About The est Training*, 1977, no pagination)

Nichiren Shoshu, also knows as Soka Gakkai, is a movement of Japanese origin which — although formed prior to the second world war — only flourished with the return of religious liberty to Japan under the post-war American administration. From 1951, it began an aggressive programme of proselytisation which led to rapid expansion in Japan and the conversion of some American service men, often married to members of Soka Gakkai. It was largely as a result of their return to America, bearing their new faith, that it spread to the West (Dator, 1969). From interviews, I understand that it was by a similar process that the movement was brought to Britain. Soka Gakkai members believe that by chanting the Lotus Sutra, believed to be the highest and most powerful scripture, and the mantra *Namu Myoho Renge Kyo* ('Adoration be to the Sutra of the Lotus of the Wondrous Law'), before the *Gohonzon* (a copy of a scroll representing the Buddha, the original of which was inscribed by Nichiren, the thirteenth century monk, founder of this branch of Buddhism) (White, 1970: 30), kept in a household shrine, they can attain personal happiness, economic improvement, and other this-worldly goals as well as spiritual rewards. Individuals drawn into an initial discussion meeting by Nichiren Shoshu proselytisers are customarily told:

> These meetings are to get you to experiment with the practice, not to believe in it. The reason for having you come to this meeting is to get you to try and test the practice. We don't expect you to believe in it right away, but we do want you to give it a try. (Snow, 1976: 236)

While followers of such movements may object to some limited aspects of the present social order, the values and goals which prevail within it are normally accepted. They have joined such a movement not to escape or withdraw from the world and its values, but to acquire the means to achieve them more easily and to experience the world's benefits more fully. Snow (1976: 67) argues that, for most rank and file members, the philosophy of Nichiren Shoshu of America is:

> usually interpreted and defined in terms of the various things which collectively yield a sense of personal satisfaction and well-being in one's everyday life in the immediate here and now. For most, happiness or value creation is thus constituted by the attainment of a semblance of material well-being, family harmony, friends, good health, inner security, and a sense of meaning, purpose and direction.

In world-affirming movements, the social order is not viewed as entirely and irredeemably unjust, nor society as having departed from God as in the world-rejecting case. The beliefs of these movements are essentially individualistic. The source of suffering, of disability, of unhappiness, lies within oneself rather than in the social structure. This view is stated for TM by Forem (1973: 235), but could be duplicated for many movements of this type:

> When individuals within a society are tense, strained and dissatisfied with life, the foundation is laid for conflict in its various forms: riots, demonstrations, strikes, individual and collective crimes, wars. But a society composed of happy, creative individuals could not give rise to such outbreaks of discord.

Hence, it follows that producing social change is dependent upon producing individual change. The individual must 'take responsibility' for the circumstances around him and for transforming them:

> While it does not as yet provide them with political power, NSA [Nichiren Shoshu of America, the corporate name in America for Soka Gakkai] philosophy does teach that responsibility lies with the individual ... rather than despairing or complaining, individuals are encouraged to think about and discuss solutions to the problems they see, chant for them and work in any capacity they can, where they are, to bring about better societal conditions. (Holtzapple, 1977: 138)

Transcendental Meditation articulates its version of this theory through the notion of the 'Maharishi Effect', which refers to the social consequences of the practice of TM by a significant proportion of the population (once 10 per cent was aspired to, but, more recently, as the following quotation shows, the movement has lowered its recruitment expectations):

The phenomenon known as the Maharishi Effect is the basis of Maharishi's prediction that every nation will soon become invincible in the growing sunshine of the Age of Enlightenment. This phenomenon has been verified in about 1,100 cities around the world, where it was found that crime, accidents, sickness, and other negative trends fell sharply, as soon as just one per cent of the population began the Transcendental Meditation technique. The Maharishi Effect on a global scale results in ideal societies everywhere and invincibility for every nation. (*World Government News* No 8, August 1978: 4)

Leading Transcendental Meditators, called 'Governors of the Age of Enlightenment', have been despatched in large numbers to areas of civil crisis. There they in no way participate in relief programmes or in providing physical assistance, but rather engage in meditation and the 'Siddhi programme' (a more advanced set of practices which produce magical abilities, such as levitation), and thus:

Without going out of their comfortable hotel rooms, the Governors of the Age of Enlightenment enliven the ground state of natural law deep within themselves and produce the gentle impulses of coherence which neutralize turbulence and disorder in collective consciousness. ... Violence naturally calms down. (*World Government News*, issue No 2, Nov/Dec 1978, Jan 1979: 6)

The 'Governors' then educate local leaders in the virtues of TM and the 'Siddhi programme', and secure their assistance in teaching these in that locale. By such means world peace is ensured.

Similarly the Hunger Project sponsored by *est* engages in promotional activities connected with ending starvation in the world, and raises money for that purpose. However, the Hunger Project does not send money to feed the starving, nor otherwise directly provide aid to the underdeveloped world, nor even advocate any particular social or economic remedy:

It is not the purpose of The Hunger Project to feed hungry people ... but rather to speak to the world on behalf of hungry people. ... Your contribution to the Hunger Project goes directly to generate the most important process on our planet — creating the end of hunger and starvation as an idea whose time has come. (*A shift in the wind* [The Hunger Project Newspaper], 4, February 1979: 15)

The Hunger Project exists to convey to the world that hunger can be ended within twenty years. Its purpose, that is, is to change our *consciousness* about the possibility of ending starvation. World hunger is inevitable only because we believe it to be inevitable. The Hunger Project therefore exists 'to create a context of commitment among a critical mass of people, to create the elimination of death due to starvation as "an idea whose time has come"' (Babbie, 1978: 16).

This should not be taken to mean that world-affirming movements never have genuinely reformist aims. A number of groups within the Human Potential tradition have aspirations which combine the personal and the political. Human Potential enthusiasts often see a need for action to effect liberation at the level of social structure as well as that of personal psychology. Such issues as feminism, the ecology, peace, siting of nuclear power stations or nuclear weapons facilities, race, and community action are often part of the agenda of such groups as Re-evaluation Counselling which devotes resources to publicising precisely these issues and educating its members and others in their implications. Even a movement such as Scientology has undertaken campaigns for the protection of the civil rights of mental patients, although, as in so much of the activity of this group, it is sometimes difficult to disentangle a disinterested desire for social reform from the pursuit of enhanced power and security for Scientology.

However characteristically in world-affirming movements, the individual is responsible not only for the environment around him but for everything he is and does. The individual's nature and behaviour is not viewed as a composite of predispositions, situations, and a psychological biography, but simply in terms of free choice at the point of performance. *est*, for example, even views stories about predispositions, situations and psychological biographies as part of the individual's 'act', by means of which he avoids experiencing what is happening to him. The individual is the only one who experiences (for him) what is happening to him, and hence he is responsible for (his experience of) life's vicissitudes for him; even his disasters and his illnesses. The individual therefore chooses his (experience of his) circumstances, his illnesses, etc. And as one chooses to be and to behave, so one can choose to change. Linda Dannenberg (1975: 20) observes from a Silva Mind Control lecture: 'You are free to change ... and can make anything of yourself that you wish. You will be as happy, sad, beautiful, ugly, rich or poor, relaxed or nervous as you make up your mind to be.'

The spiritual dimension in particular is a matter of individual experience and individual *subjective* reality rather than social reality or even social concern. Moreover, God is not perceived as a personal deity imposing a set of ethical prescriptions upon human society. If God is referred to at all it is primarily as a diffuse, amorphous and immanent force in the universe, but present most particularly within oneself. Mind Dynamics, for example, encourages its followers to bring their minds into states where they produce alpha waves. Its founder argues that 'when you are working dynamically in Alpha you are in touch with Higher Intelligence. ...' (Silva and Miele, 1977: 37), although Higher Intelligence may be less than God Himself. For many of these groups and movements, the self is the only God there is, or at least the only one that matters. One observer of the Human Potential Movement notes that, rather than 'God', adherents are likely to refer to 'my ground of being, my true nature, the ultimate energy'; and that, 'The most common image of God is the notion of cosmic energy as a life force in which all partake' (Stone, 1976: 102). He also relates the experience of one follower: 'A psychiatric social worker said she formerly used terms like *God* to explain suffering and the source of happiness and love. Subsequent to the *est* (Erhard Seminars Training) training, she did not use these terms so often, sensing that she is god in her universe and thus creator of what she experiences' (Stone, 1976: 103). Maharishi Mahesh Yogi, founder and leader of Transcendental Meditation and the Spiritual Regeneration Movement, makes the same point, that 'the inner man is Divine, is fully Divine, ...' (Mahesh Yogi, 1962: 7), although he may not always know it consciously (Mahesh Yogi, 1962: 14). John-Roger, the American founder of the Movement of Spiritual Inner Awareness, associated with the Insight training, announces to his followers that 'we are the Holy Spirit, we are Gods in manifestation' (John-Roger, 1976: 18). According to Ellwood (1974: 107), in Nichiren Shoshu (Soka Gakkai), 'All the promises of religion are made to apply to this world. All divine potential is within man, it is said, and can be unleashed.'

These movements, then, share a view of man as inherently *perfectible*. People possess a potential far beyond their current level of functioning. The key to attaining the level of their potential lies not in modification of the social order or the structure of social opportunity, but in facilitating the transformation of *individuals*. Moreover, such a transformation is believed to be possible on the basis of techniques and theories which can be rather quickly transmitted and learned.

The world-affirming movements emphasise the *present*, what Kurt Back (1972) refers to as the 'mythology of the here and now'. They are often hostile to intellectualisation and rational evaluation, seeing these as a defence against, or barrier to, feeling and experience. Understanding, Werner Erhard observes of the *est* training and of life in general, 'is the booby prize'. The world-affirming movement offers immediate and automatic benefits of a concrete kind through the practice of some formula or recipe: chanting "Namu Myoho, Renge Kyo' (Soka Gakkai); fifteen minutes' mediation on a mantra morning and evening (TM); or merely by 'keeping your soles in the room and taking what you get' (*est*). Holtzapple summarizes these characteristics in the case of Nichiren Shoshu of America (Soka Gakkai):

> The emphasis within NSA is on practice, i.e. 'doing', 'acting', not theorizing. The 'benefits' which can be achieved are not just in the future. They are here and now, because any goal can be accomplished through the universal mystic law of cause and effect. The right attitude and right effort automatically lead to the right effect. (Holtzapple, 1977: 139)

It follows from this ethos of individual self-realisation that collective activities have little or no sacred quality and indeed are likely to have only a small place in the enterprise unless it is particularly centred upon some group-based or interpersonal technique, such as encounter groups; and even here the group is of importance only as a means to self-liberation. *est*, for example, is presented to 250 trainees at a time yet requires minimal interpersonal contact, and indeed develops a thoroughly subjective idealist theory of knowledge and of the world. So subjective is its epistemology that it appears at times to verge on solipsism. Its ontology, as noted above, rests on the claim that 'You're god in your universe. You caused it.' (Erhard, 1973: n.p.) Scientology, one of the most notorious of the world-affirming new religious movements, was developed by L. Ron Hubbard in America from his lay psychotherapy Dianetics — presented to the public in 1950 — which briefly attained the proportions of a craze in the USA. Scientology, although it describes itself as a church, has only the most rudimentary of religious practices in any conventional sense. So, too, its activities are principally of an individualistic character, with little value placed upon collective or communal enterprise. Its central activity, 'auditing', is undertaken between an 'auditor' and 'pre-clear' on a one-to-one basis, or even by the pre-clear auditing himself; and even training in the theory and practice of Scientology is organised in such a fashion as to enable the student to pursue his course quite alone. Moreover, involvement in Scientology, too, is oriented primarily to the pursuit of individual goals of success, greater power and ability and personal spiritual attainment (Wallis, 1976b). Such developments in therapy and spiritual search have been characterised as a 'new narcissism' (Marin, 1975; see also Tom Wolfe's amusing essay deflating many of the pretensions of such movements as *est* in Wolfe, 1977).

It follows that the world-affirming movement rejects the dualism of the world-rejecting movement, with its concrete conception of the transcendental realm and of the coming transformation of the earth in a physically tangible millennium. Indeed, it rejects the materialist assumptions upon which such a view is predicated. Its philosophy is idealist to the degree that perfection is merely the result of realising that everything is *already* perfect. John Weldon quotes Werner Erhard from an *est* seminar, expressing a sentiment which, with minor modification, could be found in many other cases:

> Life is always perfect just the way it is. When you realize that, then no matter how strongly it may appear to be otherwise, you know that whatever is happening right now will turn out all right. Knowing this, you are in a position to begin mastering life. (John Weldon, n.d.: 5)

Three themes can be identified which seem, albeit in varying degrees, to be central to the beliefs and ethos of the world-affirming movement. Although these can be distinguished analytically, they none the less sometimes co-occur empirically, perhaps as major and minor themes within the same movement. There is first the theme of coping with the demands made upon us to succeed in modern capitalist societies, of coping with the dilemmas of *individual achievement*. Underlying much of the rhetoric of 'awareness' and 'realising potential' is the theme of personal success in securing the valued goals of this world: improved income and personal relationships, greater confidence and self-esteem, enhanced ability to cope with life's vicissitudes (Wallis, 1979b). Intelligence will be increased, social capabilities immeasurably improved, psychosomatic illnesses and psychological disabilities eliminated. The Inner Peace Movement, founded in 1964 by Francisco Coll, provides methods for spiritual and psychological growth through the medium of a pyramid sales corporation which encourages recruits to move into leadership roles marketing the movement's product of spiritual growth and inner peace (Scott, 1980: 24). Scott argues that 'Success and its achievement ... are emphasised repeatedly in IPM programs and songs' (1980: 73).

> To achieve success, the IPMer is encouraged to develop certain personality attributes, such as being positive, enthusiastic, hard working, assertive, dynamic, motivated, committed, confident and organised. ... Given these success concerns, many IPM classes center around success, such as an ALC [American Leadership College] class entitled 'Success, Goals, and Motivation'. Many techniques are designed to show participants what they need to do to obtain success. ... (Scott, 1980: 74-5)

A small sample of Scientologists completed a questionnaire in Wallis's (1976b) study, which included a question asking them what kinds of problems they hoped Scientology would solve for them. Twenty-five of the twenty-nine who answered this question indicated a wide range of problems to which they had been seeking solutions (they could indicate more than one):

| Problem | No. |
|---|---|
| (a) Loneliness | 8 |
| (b) Financial | 4 |
| (c) Marital | 5 |
| (d) Other interpersonal relationships | 14 |
| (e) Psychological | 15 |
| (f) Physical illness | 11 |

(Adapted from Wallis, 1976b: 170)

Re-evaluation Counseling was founded in the early 1950s by Harvey Jackins, a one-time associate of L. Ron Hubbard. Re-evaluation Counseling appears to lean heavily upon Dianetic theory and to develop central features of its practice, notably co-auditing — or, as it is called in Re-evaluation Counseling, 'co-counseling' — by lay peers. A member of Re-evaluation Counseling, interviewed by the author, presents this achievement theme in somewhat lower key:

> People who come into Counseling are functioning quite well, but they know they could be functioning better. They know they're just not

achieving their potential; they're not doing things as well as they could do; they're not behaving to other people as well as they could. Things aren't just quite right. But to all external intents and purposes, they're doing very well.

In some movements this theme of coping with the expectations of individual happiness and achievement prevailing in the western world appears in the form of its converse, i.e. the dominant theme is one of the *reduction of expectations* from life to a realistic level. This has its clearest embodiment in *est* which encourages participants to make the most of their present experience, to live for the present rather than future aims or past aspirations. *est* assures its adherents that 'This is all there is,' and they might as well enjoy it rather than constantly compare their present condition unfavourably with some other, non-existent state of affairs. Even if they did achieve the new job, wife, home, image they want — *est* informs them with considerable, if mortifying, realism — they would only be happy with it for a couple of days before they began to feel as dissatisfied with that as they are with what they have now. Werner Erhard assures his followers that 'Happiness is a function of accepting what is.' Moreover, 'Life is a rip off when you expect to get what you want. Life works when you choose what you get.' (Erhard, 1973: n.p.)

A second theme, clearly closely related to the desire to achieve one's full potential, is that of coping with our sense of constraint, of facilitating the desire for liberation from social inhibitions, of breaking free from the bonds of social roles to reach the 'real' person beneath. The individual will be released from conventional ritual; from habitual modes of speech or interaction; from inhibitions acquired in childhood; from repressions of instinctual life; or from a learned reserve. He will thereby be enabled to 'get in touch with' his feelings, his emotions; and encouraged to express the 'authentic' self beneath the social facade; to celebrate spontaneity, sensual pleasure and the indulgence of natural impulse.

The shifting congeries of groups, organisations and activities which form the Human Potential Movement take this to be a fundamental assumption. Human beings possess vast potential by way of ability, awareness, creativity, empathy, emotional expressiveness, capacity for experience and enjoyment, and the like. The pristine human being possesses these characteristics and qualities, but is believed to lose or to repress them as a result of the impact of society and the constraining structures it imposes upon the individual. Oscar Ichazo, founder of Arica, a gnostic school drawing much upon Gurdjieff, but eclectic in its synthesis of concepts and practices, has said that:

> A person retains the purity of essence for a short time. It is lost between four and six years of age when the child begins to imitate his parents, tell lies and pretend. A contradiction develops between the inner feelings of the child and the social reality to which he must

conform. Ego consciousness is the limited mode of awareness that develops as a result of the fall into society. (Interview with Sam Keen, see Keen, 1973.)

Arica provides practices, exercises, ritual and a conceptual system which will enable the individual to transcend mere 'ego consciousness', and thus to recover some of his capabilities from before the fall. Bernard Gunther, author of two best-selling books on the topic of sensitivity training and a major teacher in the Human Potential Movement, has commented on his own approach as follows:

> I guess largely I feel that most people in our culture tend to carry around a lot of chronic tension, and that they tend to respond largely on the basis of *habit* behavior ... what I call sensory awakening is a method to get people to ... let go their tension and focus their awareness on various parts of the body. And of experiencing the *moment*, experiencing what it is they are actually doing, as opposed to any kind of concept or conditioned kind of habit behavior. (Back, 1972: 81)

In his book, *The Human Side of Human Beings,* Harvey Jackins provides an illustration of the inter-related themes of a desire to achieve one's full capacity, held to be vastly greater than is manifested at present, and a belief that this achievement is to be gained through liberation from those constraints upon our powers which society has imposed upon us. Reminiscent of early Dianetics, Jackins (1978: 19-20) argues that,

> if any of us could preserve in operating condition a very large part of the flexible intelligence that each of us possesses inherently, the one who did so would be accurately described as an 'all round genius' by the current standards of our culture. This is not, of course, the impression that most of us have been conditioned to accept. We have heard, from our earliest age, that 'Some have it and some don't, 'Where were you when the brains were passed out?', 'Don't feel bad, the world needs good dishwashers, too', and similar gems. These impressions and this conditioning, however, seem to be profoundly wrong. Each of us who escaped physical damage to our forebrain began with far more capacity to function intelligently than the best operating adult in our culture is presently able to exhibit.

Successful adults, Jackins calculates, are operating on only about 10 per cent of their 'original resources of intelligence, ability to enjoy life and ability to enjoy other people' (Jackins, 1978: 59). Re-evaluation Counseling offers a method which will enable its practitioners to recover this enormous inherent capacity.

Arianna Stassinopoulos, a recruit to Insight, an American self-realisation movement which she subsequently introduced to Britain, represented particularly sharply the theme of liberation at a public presentation in London in 1979, when she announced that the purpose of Insight could be summarised as 'getting free'. It offered, she said, freedom from the melodrama which goes on in many of our heads most of the time, the fear, anxiety, guilt and recrimination; the burden of the past which continues to dominate our present responses, and produces exaggerated or inappropriate reactions to current circumstances. Freedom from 'self-limiting images and beliefs' which make us feel we are not terribly worthwhile; which sabotage us at points of crisis, by making us feel we simply cannot do whatever the situation requires. But also, from contrary images of ourselves as perfect, leading to self-judgment, guilt and a burden of blame. It offered freedom from the sense of oneself as victim, as the passive recipient of life's circumstances. Thus, like *est* on which it is substantially based, the Insight training purveys the view that we are 'totally responsible for our lives'. Finally, the training offers, it was claimed, freedom from the limitations imposed by a rationalistic and cerebral culture; realisation that the heart is equally in 'energy centre', and thus the opportunity to celebrate one's emotional nature.

A third theme is that of coping with the pervasive loneliness of life in modern society. The desire for liberation, therefore, readily shades over into that of attaining a sense of *intimacy*, of instant if highly attenuated community. In a safe, secure environment — or at least one sufficiently separated from the normal world and normal routine so that rebuff or failure can be effectively isolated from everyday reality — individuals seek not only to discover *themselves*, but to make contact with others, to open themselves to relationships which have hitherto seemed threatening. The activities of these movements may provide opportunities wherein with barriers lowered, participants may find it possible to make contact with others without elaborate and socially sophisticated preliminaries, and indeed without any necessary long-term commitment or enduring responsibilities. Kurt Back (1972: 33) has argued, for example, that 'Encounter groups have become a respectable "lonely hearts club" for newcomers or those without roots in a community.'

Many 'graduates' of the *est* training undertake voluntary work for the movement and Adelaide Bry (1976: 76), a sympathetic commentator, describes how intimacy forms at least one reward of such continued participation:

> Working at est means instant friends, confidants, and people who
> sincerely are interested in one another. ... Someone would burst into
> tears and immediately find both a sympathetic ear and assistance in
> getting whatever the tears related to. The problems shared were intimate
> ones — a bad trip with parents, a lover, a boss. Nothing seemed too
> private, too embarrassing, too crazy to [have to] hide.

As the world-affirming movement does not reject the world and its organisation, it will quite happily model itself upon those aspects of the world which are useful to the movement's purpose. The salvational commodity includes a set of ideas, skills and techniques which can be marketed like any other commodity since no sense of the sacred renders such marketing practice inappropriate (as it might, for example in, say, the idea of marketing the Mass, or Holy Communion). The logic of the market is wholly compatible with the ethos of such movements. Thus the salvational product will be tailored for mass-production, standardising content, instructional method, and price, distributing it through a bureaucratic apparatus which establishes or leases agencies, just as in the distribution of Kentucky Fried Chicken or Ford motor cars. Scientology, for example, possesses a substantial bureaucratic structure which invests a great deal in the collection of statistics, maintenance of records and the implementation of a considerable body of rules. Professional practitioners may operate as employees of the central organisations of the movement, as 'Field Auditors', i.e. relatively independent practitioners teaching and auditing the lower levels of Scientology, or they might establish 'franchises', expected to send a proportion of their receipts to the central organisation in return for assistance, preferential discounts and other concessions (Wallis, 1976b: 127-56).

The Inner Peace Movement is organised on the model of the modern multinational corporation. Like Scientology, it possesses an elaborate fee structure, offering introductory courses as 'loss-leaders' at rates as low as $1.00 per hour, but moving up to as much as $600 for advanced courses. Like Scientology too, it employs modern methods of marketing:

> Besides soliciting business from those already committed, the group
> makes a major effort to recruit newcomers through newspaper, TV and
> radio promotions. ... This kind of hard-driving promotional push draws
> heavily from the corporate business model and systematises the selling
> of spiritual growth. (Scott, 1980: 38)

The methods of mass instruction employed in universities or mail-order colleges are drawn upon for pedagogic technique by world-affirming movements. The outlets are situated in large cities where the market exists, rather than reflecting an aspiration for a return to the rural idyll. And, as with the sale of any commercial service or commodity, the normal round of life of the customer is interfered with as little as possible. Courses of instruction or practice are offered at weekends or in the evenings, or during periods of vacation. *est* offers its basic training over two consecutive weekends, albeit at the rate of 15-16 hours for each of the four days. TM is transmitted on the basis of an initial lecture, a talk with the initiator explaining it in more detail, an initiation and practice session lasting perhaps a couple of hours, and brief checking sessions thereafter, a total of probably no more than 12-15 hours. Encounter and other forms of human potential training are usually programmed to take place over a maximum of a fortnight at a time, in the evenings. Although clients may sometimes subtly be encouraged to engage in further participation, full-time involvement and complete commitment are not normally required. Membership is a leisure activity, one of the multiple role-differentiated pursuits of the urban dweller. His involvement will be partial and segmentary rather than total.

Such movements tend to employ quite normal, commercial means for generating income. Their followers are mostly in orthodox employment, and the movement simply sells them a service or commodity for an established price plus local taxes, sometimes even with facilities for time-payment or discounts for cash! Only for the staff of full-time professionals employed by the organisation will life normally approximate to any degree the 'total institution' setting of the contemporary world-rejecting religions.

It is evident, then, that in the context of a Christian culture, the world-rejecting movement appears much more conventionally religious than the world-affirming movement. Christianity has tended to exhibit a tension between the church and the world, based in part on the institutional differentiation of Christianity from society, which leads us to expect religious institutions to be distinct in form. This differentiation is much less evident in Hindu and Buddhist culture, where, too, the more immanent conception of God, the idea of each individual as a 'divine spark', and that of the existence of hidden wisdom which will lead to salvation, are also familiar. Many of the world-affirming movements have been to some extent influenced by Hindu and Buddhist idealist philosophies. But they have also drawn substantially upon developments in modern science and psychology for their beliefs and practices — or at least for the rhetoric of their presentation — and, marketing a soteriological commodity in quite highly secularised surroundings, the tendency has been to emphasise the *scientific* character of their ideas and techniques, and to suppress the more overtly religious aspects, although an attitude of pragmatism has informed their practice in this regard. Transcendental Meditation, for example, was first presented in the west in much more explicitly religious terms than it is today (see e.g. Mahesh Yogi, 1962), the religious rhetoric being dropped largely on marketing grounds. Robert McCutchan (1977: 146) makes the observation that:

> Publications dating from the late fifties are overtly religious and spiritual. ... Other early publications such as *Love and God, Commentary on the Bhagavad-Gita, The Science of being* and *Art of Living*, are overtly Hindu and religious. After about 1970, however, the movement focused entirely (at least in terms of its public face) on the scientific verification of psychological, physical, and social benefits of TM. None of the more recent publications even mentioned God, much less Hindu cosmology. Simply, one could say that the Hindu cosmology remained, but expressed in more 'sanitized' language. God became cosmic creative intelligence; *atman* became the pure field of creative intelligence within; *karma* became the law of action and reaction; *brahman* became the ground state of physics.

Scott (1978: 217) presents evidence of the rationale behind this shift. He reports a conversion between Professor Robert Bellah and an official of the Maharishi International University in which the latter replied to Dr Bellah's inquiry concerning why TM denied its religious nature, by stating that this was for 'public relations reasons'. He also reports a public lecture by Charles Lutes, a leading figure in TM, in which Lutes declared: 'The popularisation of the movement in non-spiritual terms was strictly for the purpose of gaining the attention of people who wouldn't have paid the movement much mind if it had been put in spiritual terms.' (See also Spiritual Counterfeits Project, 1976, for a report of the affidavit from which this evidence derives. See also Woodrum, 1977 for an analysis of the phases through which the TM movement has passed.) TM has even unsuccessfully fought a legal action to defend itself from being declared a religion in New Jersey, since this would inhibit its presentation in public schools. Scientology, on the other hand, was made more explicitly religious when it seemed this would be a useful public-relations device in the face of government hostility and intervention (Wallis, 1976b; see also the case of Synanon discussed later).

The world-affirming movements could perhaps be conveniently called 'quasi-religious' in recognition of the fact that, although they pursue transcendental goals by largely metaphysical means, they lay little or no stress on the idea of God or transcendent spiritual entities, nor do they normally engage in worship (Soka Gakkai is an exception here, since for this movement worship at the sacred shrine of the *Gohonzon* is a very significant element of its practice). As Donald Stone notes, these movements tend to prefer the term 'spiritual' to 'religious' as a self-description. They straddle a vague boundary between religion and psychology, and which side they are held to fall upon will depend entirely on the nature of the definition of religion employed.

# The World-Accommodating New Religion

The world-accommodating new religion draws a distinction between the spiritual and the worldly in a way quite uncharacteristic of the other two types. Religion is not construed as a primarily social matter; rather it provides solace or stimulation to personal, interior life. Although it may reinvigorate the individual for life in the world, it has relatively few implications for how that life should be lived, except that it should be lived in a more religiously inspired fashion. Any consequences for society will be largely unintended rather than designed. While it may strengthen the individual for secular affairs and heighten his enjoyment of life, these are not the justifications for its practice. The benefits it offers are not of the thorough-going instrumental variety to be found in world-affirming movements. Michael Harper, a leader in Charismatic Renewal, has said that:

> Its main strength, and for many its attractiveness, lies in its spontaneity,
> and in that the fact that it is so far comparatively unstructured. It is not
> basically a protest movement, but a positive affirmation of faith in God
> and His power to change people and institutions. It is a new style of
> Christian life. (Quoted in Quebedeaux, 1976: 71)

Neo-Pentecostalism, or the Charismatic Renewal Movement, comprises a wide range of bodies, organisations and groups both within and beyond the major denominations (including the Catholic Church), which have flourished since the early 1960s. They typically consist of individuals who, although committed Christians before joining the Renewal Movement, felt something to be lacking in their spiritual lives, particularly an active *experience* of God's power working within them and within the church. Involvement in the Renewal Movement was often motivated by the desire for experience of the power of the Holy Spirit, the most obvious and characteristic sign of which was normally glossolalia, the 'gift of tongues'. It would also be accompanied by enthusiastic participation in worship — other religious activities of a less formally structured and more fully participatory kind than the normal religious services — which they would often also continue to attend, perhaps even more zealously than before. Fichter, speaking of the Catholic Pentecostal movement on the issue of its social consequences, argues that:

> The goal of the renewal movement is personal spiritual reform not
> organized social reform, but this does not imply the absence of social
> concern. The movement's basic conviction is that a better society can
> emerge only when people have become better, yet it would be
> completely erroneous to interpret this as an individualistic and self-
> centred attitude. (Fichter, 1975: 144)

Nevertheless, while its beliefs and the benefits of practice are personalistically oriented, the form of practice in worship or ritual will characteristically be collective.

At a conscious level at least, the innovatory religious movement with a world-accommodating orientation will be seen not so much as a protest against the world or society, but as a protest against prevailing religious institutions, or their loss of vitality. These are seen to have abandoned a living spirituality, to have eschewed experience for an empty formalism. The new movement restores an experiential element to the spiritual life and thereby replaces lost certainties in a world where religious institutions have become increasingly relativised. The membership of such movements is drawn from the 'religiously musical' middle and 'respectable' working classes, firmly integrated into the prevailing social order, who are not entirely unhappy with it, but who seek none the less some experiential reassurance of their general spiritual values. Movements approximating this type are likely to draw their associational forms from traditional social models of churches or other religious voluntary associations. Religious activities will tend to be regular and frequent but none the less leisure-time commitments.

As I indicated earlier, all actual cases are likely to be mixed in some degree, but the Charismatic Renewal or Neo-Pentecostal Movement embodies this orientation to a significant extent. Meredith McGuire (1975), for example, argues of the former that:

> pentecostal Catholics can be considered a cognitive minority relative to the rest of American society in general because of their insistence on a religion which over-arches all spheres of every-day life. With the rest of society, however, the pentecostal Catholics tend to accept most of the prevailing social and political system, but interpret it within their religious framework. Nevertheless, the pentecostal belief system, with its emphasis upon interior spiritual concerns, has an inherent bias toward accepting the status-quo in 'worldly' affairs.

Fichter's survey of American Catholic Pentecostals showed them to be predominantly strongly attached to the church before becoming charismatics and for the most part *even more so* afterwards. Eight out of ten affirmed the Pope to be the infallible Vicar of Christ (Fichter, 1975: 25); 76 per cent reported that they attended mass, and 77 per cent that they received Holy Communion *more* than before joining the Charismatic Renewal (ibid.: 30). Fichter argues that the movement originated in the middle classes and that there has been a gradual spread down into the working classes. His sample showed the following distribution (ibid.: 49)

|                          | %    |
|--------------------------|------|
| Professional-Managerial  | 40.5 |
| White collar             | 29.4 |
| Blue collar              | 30.1 |

Bradfield (1975: 98) found 65 per cent of his sample of members of the Protestant Neo-Pentecostal Full Gospel Businessmen's Fellowship to be in professional-managerial occupations (on Catholic charismatics, see also Hammond, 1975).

Such movements need not be of Christian origin, Subud, for example — a Muslim mystic movement introduced to the West by an Indonesian, Pak Subuh — seems to fit this category. A slightly greater admixture of world-rejection produces a group like the Aetherius Society (Wallis, 1974). The Aetherius Society is a movement founded by a Londoner, George King, in the mid-1950s, on the basis of an eclectic synthesis of ideas drawing heavily upon the Theosophical tradition but modified to the degree that the Masters were now to be found not in the Himalayas, but in space craft. Members engage in rituals designed to transmit energies for the good of humanity, and undertake — at set times of the week and in special pilgrimages and ceremonials — a cosmic battle against the forces of evil. The rest of their time, they, by and large, conduct themselves conventionally as accountants, shop-keepers, housewives, and the like (Wallis, 1974). This movement is world-rejecting to the extent that it advances a critique of contemporary greed and materialism which have led to violence and ecological despoliation, and mobilises its efforts to produce social, political and environmental changes, albeit by magical means. But the world is ameliorable. Its ills can be remedied if treated in time, and thus the followers of the Aetherius Society do not cut themselves off from the world around them. Their response to the world is one of accommodation, while they pursue their mission of striving to save it from its self-inflicted fate.

An interesting contrast is formed by the western supporters of the Japanese movement, Soka Gakkai, called in America Nichiren Shoshu of America (NSA), and in Britain Nichiren Shoshu of the United Kingdom (NSUK). In this movement, transition to western, particularly American, culture has led to substantial changes in style which render it an apparently stable combination of world-accommodating and world-affirming types. While its main message is one of individual self-improvement through the chanting of the movement's *mantra*, it began during the late 1960s to recruit larger numbers of American followers and to undergo considerable adaptation as a result. The early membership of the movement in the USA was among Japanese-Americans, many of whom were GI brides, and in some cases their converted husbands. Proselytisation was predominantly among the Japanese community. During the late 1960s, the movement attracted a large number of Caucasian Americans, mostly single, under thirty, and often students or lower white-collar workers (Snow, 1976: 133-4).

In the course of this revolution in its social composition, the movement sought self-consciously to accommodate to American society and to ingratiate itself with Americans. The Japanese-born president of the movement in America became a United States citizen, and changed his name to George Williams. Members are encouraged to dress in a respectable middle-class fashion. English is now used, rather than Japanese as formerly at meetings. The American flag is prominently displayed in movement buildings. NSA participated actively in the American bicentennial celebrations. Thus, by every possible means, it seeks to foster 'the impression that its values, aims, and conduct are in conformity with, or at least not incongruent with certain values, traditions, and normative standards within its community or society of operation' (Snow, 1976: 190).

While much of the discussion will be devoted to the analytical types and cases which best exemplify them, a later section will focus further on some of the more clearly mixed cases variously located within the conceptual space I have delimited, to show the theoretically predictable properties resulting from conflicting orientations. I shall argue that incompatibilities of this kind are significant causal factors in producing characteristic changes which many new religions have undergone.

• • • • • • • • • • • • • • • • • • • • • • • • • •

# References

Babbie, Earl
 1978      "Unseating the Horseman: World Hunger." *Downtown Magazine* (November), Honolulu.

Back, Kurt W.
 1972      *Beyond Words: The Story of Sensitivity Training and the Encounter Movement.* New York: Russell Sage Foundation.

Bainbridge, William Sims and Daniel H. Jackson
 1981      "The Rise and Decline of Transcendental Mediation." Pp. 135-158 in Bryan Wilson, ed., *The Social Impact of New Religious Movements.* New York: The Rose of Sharon Press.

Bradfield, Cecil D.
 1975      "An Investigation of Neo-Pentecostalism." Ph.D. dissertation, American University.

Bry, Adelaide
 1976      *est: 60 Hours that Transform Your Life.* New York: Harper and Row.

Bryant, M. Darroll and Susan Hodges
 1978      *Exploring Unification Theology.* New York: The Rose of Sharon Press.

Bugliosi, Vincent (with Curt Gentry)
 1977      *Helter Skelter: The Manson Murders.* Harmondsworth: Penguin.

Daner, Francine Jeanne
 1976      *The American Children of Krsna: A Study of the Hare Krsna Movement.* New York: Holt, Rhinehart and Winston.

Dannenberg, Linda
 1975      "Tuning in to Mind Control." *Family Circle* (August).

Dator, James Allen
 1969      *Soka Gakkai: Builders of the Third Civilization.* Seattle, WA: University of Washington Press.

Edwards, Christopher
 1979      *Crazy for God: The Nightmare of Cult Life.* Englewood Cliffs, NJ: Prentice-Hall.

Ellwood, Robert S.
 1973      *One Way: The Jesus Movement and Its Meaning.* Englewood Cliffs, NJ: Prentice-Hall.

Enroth, Ronald
 1977      *Youth, Brainwashing and the Extremist Cults.* Grand Rapids, MI: Zondervan.

Erhard, Werner
 1973      "If God had meant man to fly He would have given him wings." (no publisher given).

Fichter, Joseph H.
 1975      *The Catholic Cult of the Paraclete.* New York: Sheed and Ward.

Forem, Jack
 1973      *Transcendental Meditation: Maharishi Mahesh Yogi and the Science of Creative Intelligence.* New York: Dutton.

Hammond, Judith Anne
 1975      "A Sociological Study of the Characteristics and Attitudes of Southern Charismatic Catholics." Ph.D. dissertation, Florida State University.

Holtzapple, Vicki Rea
   1977      "Soka Gakkai in Midwestern America: A Case Study of a Transpositional Movement."
             Ph.D. dissertation, Washington University (St. Louis).

Jackins, Harvey
   1978      *The Human Side of Human Beings: The Theory of Re-evaluation Counselling.* Seattle,
             WA: Rational Island Publishers.

John-Roger
   1976      *The Christ Within.* New York: The Baraka Press.

Judah, J. Stillson
   1974      *Hare Krishna and the Counterculture.* New York: Wiley.

Kanter, Rosabeth Moss
   1972      *Commitment and Community: Communes and Utopias in Sociological Perspective.*
             Cambridge, MA: Harvard University Press.

Keen, Sam
   1973      "Arica." *Psychology Today* (July).

Kerns, Phil (with Doug Wead)
   1979      *People's Temple, People's Tomb.* Plainfield, NJ: Logos International.

Mahesh Yogi, Maharishi
   1962      *The Divine Plan: Enjoy Your Own Inner Divine Nature.* Los Angeles: SRM Foundation.
   1977      *Celebrating Invincibility to Every Nation.* (pamphlet, Oct. 21) Geneva: MERU Press.

Marin, Peter
   1975      "The New Narcissism: The Trouble with the Human Potential Movement." *Harpers* 25,
             1505: 45-56.

MuCutchan, Robert
   1977      "The Social and the Celestial: Mary Douglas and Transcendental Meditation." *The Princeton
             Journal of Arts and Sciences* 1: 130-163.

McGuire, Meredith
   1975      "Toward a Sociological Interpretation of the Catholic Pentecostal Movement." *Review of
             Religious Research* 16: 94-104.

Naranjo, Betty Ann
   1979      "Biobehavioral Belonging: The Reorganization of Behavior and the Reconstruction of
             Social Reality During Rites of Passage at Synanon." Ph.D. dissertation, University of
             California, Irvine.

Quebedeaux, Richard
   1976      *The New Charismatics.* Garden City, NY: Doubleday.

Reis, John P.
   1975      "'God is not dead, he has simply changed his clothes ...': A Study of the International
             Society for Krsna Consciousness." Ph.D. dissertation, University of Wisconsin, Madison.

Robbins, Jhan and David Fisher
   1972      *Tranquillity without Pills.* New York: Peter H. Wyden.

Robbins, Thomas, Dick Anthony, Thomas Curtis and Madalyn Doucas
   1976      "The Last Civil Religion: The Unification Church of Reverend Sun Myung Moon."
             *Sociological Analysis* 37: 111-125.

Scott, Gain Graham
   1980      *Cult and Countercult: A Study of a Spiritual Growth Group and a Witchcraft Order.*
             Westport, CT: Greenwood Press.

Scott, R.D.
   1978      *Transcendental Misconceptions.* San Diego: Beta Books.

Shupe, Anson D., Roger Spielmann and Sam Stigall
   1977      "Deprogramming: the New Exorcism." *American Behavioral Scientist 20: 941-956.*

Silva, Jose and Philip Miele
   1977      *The Silva Mind Control Method.* New York: Pocket Books.

Snow, David Alan
   1976      "The Nichiren Shoshu Buddhist Movement in America: A Sociological Examination of its
             Value Orientation, Recruitment Efforts and Spread." Ph.D. dissertation, University of
             California, Los Angeles.

Stone, Donald
   1976      "The Human Potential Movement." Pp. 93-115 in Charles Glock and Robert Bellah, eds.,
             *The New Religious Consciousness.* Berkeley, CA: University of California Press.

Wallis, Roy
   1974      "The Aetherius Society: A Case Study in the Formation of a Mystagogic Congregation."
             *Sociological Review* 22: 27-44.
   1976      *The Road to Total Freedom: A Sociological Analysis of Scientology.* London: Heinemann.
   1977      "Salvation from Salvation." *The Zetetic* 1: 67-71.
   1979a     *Salvation and Protest: Studies of Social and Religious Movements.* New York: St. Martins
             Press.
   1979b     "Varieties of Psychosalvation." *New Society* 50: 649-651.

Watson, Tex
   1978      *Will You Die For Me?* Old Tappan, NJ: Revell.

Weldon, John
   n.d.      *The Frightening World of est.* (pamphlet) Berkeley, CA: The Spiritual Counterfeits Project.

White, James W.
   n.d.      *The Sokagakkai and Mass Society.* Stanford, CA: Stanford University Press.

Whitworth, John McKeivie
   1975      "Communitarian Groups and the World." Pp. 117-137 in Roy Wallis, ed., *Sectarianism:
             Analyses of Religious and Non-religious Sects.* London: Peter Owen.

Wolfe, Tom
   1977      "The Me Decade and the Third Great Awakening." Pp. 111-147 in Tom Wolfe, *Mauve
             Gloves and Madmen, Clutter and Vine.* London: Bantam.

Woodrum, Eric
   1977      "The Development of the Transcendental Meditation Movement." *The Zetetic* 1: 38-48.

Zamora, William
   1976      *Bloody Family.* New York: Kensington Pub.

# THE HISTORICAL AND SOCIOLOGICAL CONTEXT OF CULTS

## Introduction to the Readings

Why did new religious movements (NRMs) arise? Many theoretical speculations have been proffered, targeting an array of cultural, social, and religious changes (see Robbins, 1988, Chapter Two). The most immediate and frequently cited context of explanation is the counter-culture of the 1960s. As Robert Bellah (1976), Steve Tipton (1982), and many others (see Robbins, 1988) have argued, NRMs are best conceived as "successor movements" to the movements of cultural experimentation and political protest that swept through Western society as the "baby-boomer" generation came of age. Along with the acid rock, drugs, Hippie clothes, free-love, demonstrations against the war in Vietnam, and the race riots of the sixties, came a strong new interest in alternative, and particularly Eastern, religious beliefs and practices (e.g., doing yoga, meditating, being the disciple of a mystical guru and "realizing one's true self").

More than just generational fads, the "youth culture" of the time introduced some fundamental changes to the religious economy of North America. It ushered in a new religious and cultural pluralism. As the bloom of the youth culture faded with bad drug trips, broken hearts, the end of the war in Vietnam, the assassinations of John Kennedy, Robert Kennedy, and Martin Luther King Jr., the Watergate scandal and other disillusioning events, great and small, many young people opted, wholly or in part, to seek to change the world, or just make it a more meaningful place, by reverting from politics to religion (Kent, 1988). In general, as the baby boomers graduated from school to face the daunting responsibilities of adulthood in a world gripped by recessions, environmental crises, and continued racial and sexual discrimination, some of the innovative spiritual choices of the sixties became permanent religious options, substitutes in the 1970s and 1980s for the failed idealism of the sixties.

The first reading in this section, "A Time When Mountains Were Moving" by Wade Clark Roof, tries to convey to a later generation of students a sense of the heady feeling of cultural "revolution" that marked the era of the sixties. He recapitulates some of the traumatic events and shifting sensibilities that helped to initiate an unprecedented surge of new forms of spiritual exploration. In the process he instructively highlights, with empirical data, some of the larger social forces at work in the post-WW II period relevant to understanding the religious changes that occurred (e.g., the new levels of affluence and educational attainment, and the unprecedented exposure to mass media). He also importantly reveals the roots of the contemporary tendency of Americans to divide into liberals and conservatives on questions of religion, sexuality, gender roles, and most other major economic, social, and political issues. Only about half of the baby boomers, he notes, ever did participate in the counter culture of the sixties. The other half largely reacted against the challenges posed to the status quo at that time and ever since, retrenching themselves in more traditional religious and social mores. The opposition to NRMs finds its natural audience and sources of support in this other segment of the population — characterized at various times as the "silent majority" and the "moral majority."

More complexly, the second reading "The New Religions: Demodernization and the Protest Against Modernity" by James Hunter, relates the rise of both NRMs and the New Christian Right to a larger problem: the anomic and alienating conditions of "modern" life. Building on the influential theories of religion and of modernity developed by Peter Berger (Berger, 1967; Berger et al., 1974), Hunter suggests that we can trace the resurgent appeal of all new forms of religious involvement (whether liberal or conservative) to the response of some people to the root dilemma of "de-institutionalization" faced by everyone today.

This assertion may appear rather paradoxical at first. The onset of modernity and the demise of traditional social systems, from tribalism through to feudalism, is commonly associated with a marked increase in the institutionalization of society. At one level, Berger, and hence Hunter, agree. In the "public" sphere of activity, primarily the world of work for most of us, massive bureaucracies are the order of the day. They organize and operate government, the law, business, labour, health care, communications, education, the military, and even religion (e.g., the Catholic church and the other large Protestant denominations). But in the "private" sphere, they argue, more and more aspects of life, aspects of great emotional significance to individuals, are being de-institutionalized: patterns of courtship, marriage, child-rearing, sexuality, gender roles and relations, consumption, vocation, and spirituality. In these matters, that is, what was once taken-for-granted has now become a matter of choice and for many, if not all of us at one point or another, the choices are becoming bewildering. Anomie, a sense of normlessness and consequent fear about what to do, often ensues, especially as meaningful individual choices are simultaneously becoming more restricted in the highly institutionalized public sphere. Increasingly we become who we are by our choices in the private sphere, but the very abundance of choice in these matters renders the choices that we make unstable and unreliable. New religions, by "resacralizing" the activities of daily life provide a greater measure of order, stability, and hence clear meaning to life. Once getting married is again a religious as well as a personal act, for example, it is less likely to be followed by divorce — or so many people believe. For those disturbed by the moral ambiguity of our age of choice, the stronger guidelines for living provided by either the NRMs or the evangelical revival are reassuring. By anchoring our activities and identities in institutions conceived, once again, as reflections of the natural, cosmic, or divine order, people are able to reimpose reliable meanings upon existence. Of course, the contemporary situation delineated so well by Hunter is more complex than these brief words of introduction can convey.

Implicit to both of the first two readings in this section is the theory of secularization. Roof and Hunter, like most sociologists from Karl Marx, Emile Durkheim, and Max Weber on, believe that religion is becoming a less and less important aspect of our society as other kinds of institutions (largely governments and private corporations) and systems of meaning (e.g., the sciences, psychotherapies, and political ideologies) are increasingly taking over the functions traditionally performed by religious organizations (e.g., explaining the nature of the world, helping the poor, healing the sick, teaching the young, guiding sexual behaviour). Roof notes, for instance, the marked increase in the number of baby boomers falling away from religion altogether. Hunter's discussion identifies the attraction of NRMs with an attempt to turn-back-the-clock, to "de-modernize" or in other words "de-secularize" the world, or at least their small part of it. Seen in this light, NRMs often are cast as a transitional phenomenon; they somehow represent a last gasp of religious vitality prior to the complete "withering away" (Marx) of religion in advanced capitalist societies (e.g., Wilson, 1979).

In the third reading of this section, Rodney Stark and William Sims Bainbridge, two of the most prominent sociologists of NRMs, propose an alternative and more optimistic interpretation. Many scholars, they argue, may be mistaking the secularization of certain traditional forms of religious life for "the doom of religion in general" (1985: 3). Positing a more or less inherent human need for meanings grounded in some sense of the supernatural, and arguing that secularization is a recurrent feature of all "religious economies" and not a unique attribute of modernity, Stark and Bainbridge suggest that the rise of NRMs indicates a change in the nature of religion in our society and not its sheer demise. By accommodating themselves too much to the scientific and rationalistic worldview of secular institutions, the large denominations of America have retreated from their anchorage in the supernatural and become dead and hollow formalities disconnected from any moving personal experiences. In doing so they have, in essence, lost their market edge and various sects and cults have emerged to satisfy the continuing spiritual needs of a growing segment of the American populace. Most of these new religious groups will be short lived and, in the larger scheme of things, inconsequential. But as Stark and Bainbridge are fond of observing, all the great salvation religions of the world began as cults (e.g., Buddhism, Christianity, Islam), and the Mormons provide a fine example of just how successful some modern religious innovations can be. In the process of empirically supporting the inverse relationship postulated between the decline of churches and the rise of cults, Stark and Bainbridge also usefully reveal that the constituencies of sects and cults may be distinct. Such being the case, care must be taken to differentiate the two forms of renewed religious growth, for the data suggest that contemporary cults do not represent so much a simple revival of religious life (as Hunter's analysis implies) as a turn to truly new forms of religious life. The careful study of cults or NRMS may pay special dividends, then, in terms of discerning the future nature and functions of religion.

Other reasons have been given for the emergence of NRMs in the West since the 1960s, and in fact Roger Finke and Rodney Stark (1992) have even called into question whether a significant upsurge in new religious activity occurred. But the three readings provided reflect some of the most basic and influential lines of argument entertained by scholars of NRMs in pondering this question.

• • • • • • • • • • • • • • • • • • • • • • • • •

# References

Bellah, Robert
    1976        "New Religious Consciousness and the Crisis of Modernity." Pp. 333-352 in C. Glock and
                R. Bellah, eds., *The New Religious Consciousness*. Berkeley, CA: University of California
                Press.

Berger, Peter L.
    1967        *The Scared Canopy*. New York: Doubleday.

Berger, Peter, Brigitte Berger, Hansfried Kellner
    1974        *The Homeless Mind: Modernization and Consciousness*. New York: Vintage.

Finke, Roger and Rodney Stark
    1992        *The Churching of America, 1776-1990*. New Brunswick, NJ: Rutgers University Press.

Kent, Stephen
    1988    "Slogan Chanters to Mantra Chanters: A Mertonian Deviance Analysis of Conversion to Religiously Ideological Organizations in the Early 1970s." *Sociological Analysis* 49 (2): 104-118.

Robbins, Thomas
    1988    *Cults, Converts, and Charisma.* Newbury Park, CA: Sage.

Stark, Rodney and William Sims Bainbridge
    1985    *The Future of Religion - Secularization, Revival and Cult Formation.* Berkeley, CA: University of California Press.

Tipton, Steven M.
    1982    *Getting Saved from the Sixties.* Berkeley, CA: University of California Press.

Wilson, Bryan
    1979    *Contemporary Transformations of Religion.* Oxford: Clarendon Press.

# A TIME WHEN MOUNTAINS WERE MOVING

## WADE CLARK ROOF

During the late 1980s, the popular television program "thirtysomething" featured a generation of upscale young Americans struggling with careers, marriages, children, and incipient middle age. The struggles were hardly peculiar to this generation, yet the characters seemed to face them in their own way. "There's something nostalgic about the attitudes of 'thirtysomething' people," writes one commentator, "they're like World War I veterans, like they've been through a war together." Television programs depict the lives of boomers, the commentator goes on to say, by "refract[ing] elements of optimism and world-weariness through plots that aren't always neatly tied up at the end of each episode and through realistic, complex characters who don't always behave well."[1]

Nostalgia, optimism, world-weariness, complexity — all are elements bound up in the lives of the people we interviewed. The stories they tell of growing up all reveal these nuanced and refracted interpretations of American life. But what was it about those years that produced such experiences and interpretations? What were the shaping influences of the period that so jolted their religious and spiritual lives? The answers lie in the sweeping social and cultural changes that engulfed the boomers and jarred the cultural narratives that had been passed down to them from their parents. History and demography came together at a crucial moment, at just the time when so many were moving out of childhood into adolescence and adulthood. Other generations were affected, too, but none with the lasting impact and shared *zeitgest* of the boomers. For them, the sixties was more than simply a decade: It had something of a mythic reality with a power and momentum all its own.

---

Wade Clark Roof. "A Time When Mountains Were Moving," in Wade Clark Roof, *A Generation of Seekers*. San Francisco: HarperCollins, 1993, pp. 32–60. Copyright © 1993 Wade Roof Clark. Reprinted by permission of HaprerCollins Publishers Inc.

# The Sixties

As with all myth, "the sixties" has many possible meanings and interpretations. Often the people we talked to described their years growing up and its impact on their lives in metaphorical and semimythical language. Carol McLennon, for example, speaks of her adolescent years as a "really rich era," and Barry Johnson talks about growing up when "things were happening." Perhaps Mollie Stone captured the era best when she spoke of "a time when mountains were moving." Those less articulate stumbled for words to express themselves, but were no less caught up in its mythical realities. Most of our informants looked back on the era as a special time of hope and anticipation, of new horizons. Even those who frowned on some of what happened during those years spoke fondly about many of their memories.

It was a time when many things did change — social and sexual mores especially. Some of the most visible things associated with the sixties' counterculture — drugs, rock-and-roll, casual sex — have taken on legendary character. The 1986 *Rolling Stone* survey reported that 65% of those growing up during the 1960s had engaged in premarital sex; 30% had lived with someone of the opposite sex before marriage; 5% of the females acknowledged having had an abortion. More than one in ten had tried psychedelic drugs like LSD. Fifty-four per cent felt that rock-and-roll music was a positive influence on young people in the 1960s. Commenting on these statistics, the magazine's David Sheff says:

> This generation endorsed sexual freedom and altered consciousness. And rock & roll was the pulse, the heartbeat of a new age. Elvis Presley's music said, "Free your body." The Beatles said, "Free your mind." Their lyric "I'd love to turn you on" had a symbolic as well as a literal meaning. Turning on was a metaphor for becoming enlightened, but it also had a straightforward meaning: having sex and taking drugs.[2]

Yet it is easy to exaggerate. Our survey shows a generation more divided by the social mores than does the *Rolling Stone* survey. One-half of our respondents had smoked marijuana in their earlier years; almost two-thirds said they had attended a rock concert; 20% had taken part in a demonstration, march, or rally. We did not ask about sexual practices. Certainly, the involvement in drugs, rock-and-roll music, and political activism point to major changes in keeping with the reputation of the sixties as a period of profound cultural changes. But we should not overlook the one-half of our population who did not try drugs, the one-third who never attended a rock concert, and the overwhelming 80% who were not politically active. Many were far less caught up in the counterculture, its controversies and protests, than we tend to think. Once we get beyond the stereotypes that still linger on from that era, we discover a generation growing up in the 1960s and 1970s that was incredibly diverse.

**Figure 2.1      Exposure to the Sixties**

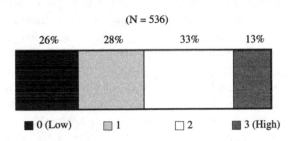

(N = 536)

26%       28%       33%       13%

■ 0 (Low)          □ 1          □ 2          ▨ 3 (High)

This is better shown in Figure 2.1, which combines the several items above into
an index showing the extent of exposure to the sixties' counterculture.[3] Statistics here
are telling: 13% scored "high," indicating a positive response to all three items; but
26% scored "low," with negative responses to all three items. The majority — as we
would expect in a normal distribution of responses — scored in the middle two
categories. Comparing the upper two categories with the lower two categories, we find
a generation deeply divided between traditionalists and counterculturalists, the former
outnumbering the latter 54% to 46%.

Age-cohort differences in countercultural experience are important: The first
wave of boomers, born between the years 1946 and 1954, experienced more directly
the upheavals of the decade that did those of the second wave, born between 1955 and
1962. Caught up in a climate of social and political protest, the former were more
involved in demonstrations, marches, and rallies. But more of the younger ones report
having smoked marijuana and having attended rock concerts. Militant political activism
declined during the 1970s, but the drugs, music, and "new morality" lived on. No
longer were drugs and unmarried sex all that surprising for younger boomers growing
up in a counterculture that had by then become structured by its traditions and rituals.
"The sixties" as a mythic reality lived on even for those who grew up in the 1970s.

The two age groups experienced a different social and political history and so
have differing collective memories. Older boomers remember elementary school
bomb drills in the 1950s; and later, in the 1960s, John F. Kennedy, freedom-rides, city
riots, and Vietnam. They confronted the upheavals of the decade head-on in their late
teens and early twenties. Caught at the epicenter of a cultural earthquake, many were
traumatized and transformed by what was happening around them. A great many of
them became passionate visionaries and dreamed of "building the New Jerusalem." In
contrast, younger boomers remember at an early age the deaths of Martin Luther King,
Jr., and Bobby Kennedy; and later, in the 1970s, long gas lines, Three Mile Island, and
Watergate. They came of age in a quieter time marked less by protest than by scarcity
and environmental scares. Economic recession was a reality of the 1970s, setting
limits and constraints on life possibilities. If the older boomers were "challengers,"

ready to take on "the establishment," the younger ones were "calculators," intent upon setting priorities for what to go after in a world where you cannot have it all.[4] Unlike their older siblings, who saw chaotic change as revolution or as revelation, the younger ones saw it more as the world in which they had been born into, and to which they must adapt.

What they all share is "the sixties," even if they didn't live it the same way. The two waves are much more alike than they are different, more unified than separated. They are bound by a shared sense of time, and an optimism tempered by the disillusionment that came with assassinations, Vietnam, and Watergate. What unites the two waves more than anything else was the changing climate of moral values and sensitivities, a shift in cultural values that would have a lasting impact on them. Especially in the realms of sexuality and family life, of personal lifestyles and preferences, the "New Morality" would distinguish the young from their parents and would become a source of division among themselves of lasting consequence. Those most influenced by the counterculture adopted new outlooks that have, by and large, remained with them and that continue to distinguish them from those who were less involved. Figure 2.2 shows, for example, that those who were highly involved in countercultural activities back when they were growing up — for some, as many as twenty-five years ago — are *still* far more liberal in their view on unmarried couples living together, on whether or not a married woman should be able to obtain a legal abortion, and on homosexual relations. Patterns for the three moral attitude items are remarkably consistent when tabulated with our index of countercultural exposure, suggesting that the sixties had an enormous and apparently lasting impact on members of this generation.

As a cultural or mythic entity, more so than a chronological one, the period had its own *zeitgeist*, or spirit of the times, demarcating it from other times. Annie Gottlieb says the sixties began in 1963 with the death of President Kennedy, and ended in 1973 with the energy crisis and economic recession. That would define the sixties, as she says, "as a decade of *upheaval plus affluence* — the two ingredients that together account for the special character of the time."[5] We would add two other features as well, the *gender revolution* and role of *higher education and television*, that helped define the period and shape the lives of those growing up at the time.

"I can still remember," says Barry Johnson. "I remember sitting in chemistry class in the tenth grade when it came over the loudspeaker. I'll never forget that as long as I live."

November 22, 1963, lives on in the memories of millions of schoolchildren who heard the announcement over the school public address system, went home stunned, and for three long days watched events unfold on television as a nation grieved its loss. President John F. Kennedy's death was a gripping experience, especially for young children, many of whom deeply admired the young president and his family. Schoolchildren at the time knew Kennedy not only as a political leader, but as a father who had young children of his own, and in death he loomed larger than life. Television's

Figure 2.2     Moral Values

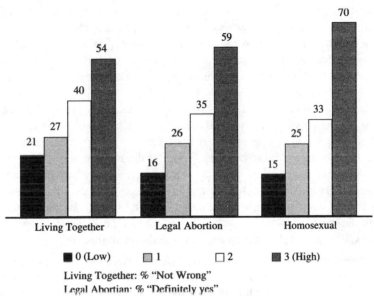

0 (Low)     1     2     3 (High)
Living Together: % "Not Wrong"
Legal Abortion: % "Definitely yes"
Homosexual: % "Only Sometimes," or "Never" Wrong

role in galvanizing an emotional experience was incalculable: the countless replays of the assassination, Jackie Kennedy's bloodstained suit, the flag-draped coffin, little John, Jr.'s, salute, the murder of Lee Harvey Oswald, the long weekend culminating in a state funeral.

For schoolchildren across the country, the event provoked intense reactions and led to serious questions. As a young boy, Barry wondered: "If there's an active God in this world, what is he doing?...The world is out of control. It's just exploding." Many children wondered how the nation would get along without its leader. The feeling of loss seemed to persist longer for children than it did for adults, far longer than in a normal process of grieving. Kennedy had been a symbol of youthful leadership, someone who had a vision of an American future, and who had a caring and personal touch. His death wiped away all of that for children and teenagers who had been hopeful and optimistic about their country. His assassination left a deep emotional scar: Three-quarters of the schoolchildren in a Detroit study at the time said they felt the loss of someone very close and dear, eight in ten felt ashamed that such a tragedy could happen in America.[6] Among our respondents it was the event most frequently cited in shaping their childhood and adolescent years. According to many of them, it marked the time when the mood of the country began to change.

Youth growing up during the 1960s had been born into a world shaped largely by the politics of the cold war and the postwar family life that fit so comfortably with it. The late 1940s and 1950s had a quality all their own: a time of almost uncontested conservatism, as reflected in the emphasis put on family "togetherness" rather than individual needs, conventional gender roles, churchgoing, anticommunism, and free-enterprise capitalism. An expanding economy combined with the GI Bill and VHA loans gave unprecedented numbers of Americans the opportunity to obtain an education, to get a better job, and to buy a home in the newly emerging suburbs. Working-class men and women enjoyed as never before hopes for sharing in the American Dream. With security as the common threat, cold war ideology and domesticity reinforced each other. Young people were expected to follow in their parent's footsteps, embracing the containment ethos that undergirded both foreign policy and family life in the 1950s. Except for a handful of beatniks, youth at the beginning of the decade of the 1960s showed every sign of growing up pretty much as they had the decade before. They reflected their parents' optimism and satisfaction with their lives. In a salute to the new decade, *Look* magazine in January 1960 published a poll saying that all was right with the world: Americans "naturally expect to go on enjoying their peaceable, plentiful existence — right through the 1960s and maybe forever."[7]

But the dream of a peacable, plentiful existence was short-lived. After Kennedy's death optimism faded, as more and more people became disillusioned with the prospects for both peace and a plentiful life for all Americans. The middle years of the decade were unsettling enough, with civil rights demonstrations, urban riots, and the Vietnam War, but 1968 was staggering. For the first time, a majority of Americans actively turned against a war in progress. Sentiment was slow to crystallize, but once it did it was firm. In that unforgettable year, Americans witnessed the Tet offensive, President Lyndon Johnson decided against a bid for reelection, Martin Luther King, Jr., and Robert Kennedy were murdered, and the Democratic Convention in Chicago was the scene of violent confrontations. These events are all seared in the memories of boomers except for the very youngest — the first generation ever to witness history through the unifying image of television.

By 1968 radical students had galvanized into "the Movement" spearheading cultural and political change. A generation that was to be cool turned out to be explosive: They broke out of old social mores and explored sexual freedom, drug use, and the so-called "new morality"; they expressed their frustration over a stalled civil rights movement; they opposed an escalating war in Vietnam. The rebellion amounted to a repudiation of conventional middle-class life — "Culture War," in Loren Baritz's words[8] — aimed at a reordering of human relations and of the values by which people live. The world had to be remade, for that which their parents had created was no longer viable. Containment at home and abroad no longer made sense. Conditions had changed radically in a generation's time. Rather than a continuation of the easy-going, comfortable times of their childhood, the late 1960s emerged as a reversed mirror image of the late 1940s: The fathers of the baby boomers had come home from a glorious war; their sons refused to go to a not-so-glorious war. The mothers had poured into the homes, proud to be wives and mothers; their daughters poured out of them.

The "war of values" was often fought at home — against parents, against brothers and sisters. Debate centered on America itself, what it stood for. The civil rights movement sharpened for many what Gunnar Myrdal had called the "American Dilemma" — the discrepancy between the egalitarian values as professed and racially discriminatory practices. Militant students sought resolution in protests and demonstrations aimed at exposing these ethical inconsistencies. Less politically active young Americans felt their consciences pricked, especially by the violence, intense expressions of racial hatred, and tragic deaths. For many whites the death of Dr. Martin Luther King, Jr., was the event that shocked them into seeing the severity of this discrepancy. Equality, not just as principle but as practice, would thus emerge as a strong commitment on the part of white boomers. Out of the struggle came greater racial justice, and also greater awareness and appreciation of cultural diversity and a concern for people as people, and not because of their social appearances.

The antiwar protests further exposed discrepancies in American-style democracy: If Americans truly believed in the principle of self-determination, why were we in Southeast Asia trying to shape a people's destiny? Nothing divided the nation more during these years than the Vietnam issue. Time has brought about considerable healing, but if you scratch the surface of a boomer, deep emotions still pour out. All seven of our boomers spoke of the impact of the war on their lives. All of them found themselves, as did the great majority of Americans, pulled into support of the war or its opposition; even Pam Fletcher, probably the most apolitical among them, discovered that as much as she wanted to get away from the news on television night after night, she couldn't shut the war out of her life.

Vietnam split the older boomers right down the middle. They are still split: 51% of this age group now say they opposed the war; 43% supported it; and the remaining 6% are still unsure. Women often experienced it as "struggle" and "heartache," both personally and in their relationships with men. It was all these things and more for men, for those who went to Vietnam and for those who didn't. Of the three men — Sonny D'Antonio, Oscar Gantt, and Barry Johnson — one enlisted in the military rather than wait to be drafted and got as close as the Philippines; the other two escaped the draft through the lottery. Neither of the men who owed his life to the luck of the draw (one spoke of being "saved" by it) felt he could discuss the war with his father. All seemed to have learned something about fragile and wounded relationships, and also, perhaps, that in a highly rational, technological world, there is still an element of chance and maybe even a little of the miraculous.

The country was torn between hawks who wanted to win, and win decisively, and doves who wanted simply to get out, the sooner the better. Levels of frustration and alienation ran high. "The country just sort of got involved," as Barry Johnson put it, "with something that totally polarized it." The division ran deep, forcing strains at the most profound levels of national life. Religious talk undergirding national goals and purposes became deeply polarized: Religious conservatives spoke of God as favoring freedom and competition, of America as having a unique, divine role in world affairs, and above all, the importance of personal moral values and salvation; religious liberals spoke in a different voice, emphasizing the common concerns of humanity for peace, justice, and human rights, and of the responsibility of America to take action to help bring about a better world. The two types of discourse are themselves differing versions of America's "civil religion" — that amorphous set of Judeo-Christian beliefs and symbols by which the nation's traditional principles and goals are given sanction. While never a fully coherent set of beliefs and symbols in its functioning in American life, the languages of civil religion became more pulled apart, and themselves a source of tension and discord during these years. For boomers, talk about God, country, and patriotism could never be quite the same as it had been for their parents' generation.

Whether religious or not, many in the boomer generation grew weary of the war. Over time, growing numbers came, as did Barry, to a "fundamental feeling that it was wrong." Having grown up in the South in a politically conservative home, he did not easily find fault with his country; only gradually did he come to the awareness that the war was symbolic of the country's misdirected goals and values. The war taught him two immensely powerful lessons: that America was not always right, and that political leaders weren't always to be trusted. Many young Americans lost faith in their country's moral superiority and in a technology that tried to make the nation's military might increasingly invisible and remote. Seeing the napalm-scarred faces of children on television and hearing day after day about "body counts" and "loss-ratios" eroded what confidence was left in the nation's war machine. Older boomers were the most affected: They had grown up with more confidence in the country than had the younger boomers. They had farther to fall in their disillusionment. Many have yet to regain confidence in the country and its leadership. Twenty-nine percent of the older boomers said they had little or no confidence in the country today, compared with 24% of younger boomers. Among the half within the older cohort opposing the country's involvement in the war, the lack of confidence in the country runs considerably higher today — upwards of 40%.

The impact was even more subtle: Boomers still feel some "distance" from almost every institution, whether the military, banks, public schools, Congress, or organized religion. A 1985 Gallup Poll found that boomers were the least trusting of all age groups toward social and political institutions, even less so than for those younger than themselves.[9] Alienation and estrangement born out of the period continue to express themselves as generalized distrust of government, of major institutions, and of leaders. As Seymour Martin Lipset and William Schneider point out, baby boomers are less polarized in their distrust of both big labor and big business than older generations.[10] Whereas older Americans have tended to distrust one or the other, boomers generally distrust both. Compared with other generations, their distrust of institutions simply runs deeper.

Boomers continue in their separation from traditional social and political roles. The separation is expressed in many ways: in lower levels of political party loyalty, in preferences for talking about who they *are* rather than what they *do*, in an even greater reluctance to use titles like "Mr." or "Mrs." Less inclined to be conformists, they favor instead their own deeply personal and individualistic preferences, which shows up in consumer choices: less loyal to particular brands, more suspicious of advertising, more likely than older consumers to prefer a product made by a new company than by a well-established business, more likely to vote out political incumbents and take chances on new political faces and ideas. Thus they tend to reject social labels that lack individual meaning, labels that remain, as social psychologists Joseph Veroff, Elizabeth Douvan, and Richard Kulka say, "objects of suspicion, as though they were different from — even contradictory to — the core self, the essential person."[11]

Boomers today often lack connections in their local communities. They are less likely than their parents to belong to social organizations concerned with community welfare. They tend to be less locally involved in social activities — except in family and neighborhood affairs. According to the *Rolling Stone* survey, members of this generation are less active in their communities now than they expected to be. Asked whether the phrase "being a concerned citizen, involved in helping others in the community" better describes their generation or their parents', 21% chose their generation, while more than twice that number chose their parents'.[12] The boomers themselves readily admit a difference in generational styles. This appears to be something of a sore spot: Most of the respondents in the survey were not pleased with their record of community participation, and three-quarters of them felt that their reduced involvement was a change for the worse.

## Affluence

Boomers were born in a time of considerable affluence and almost limitless expectations. The 1950s and much of the 1960s were times of economic growth and widespread optimism: The Gross National Product was up, unemployment was down, inflation was low; people were moving out of the cities into the suburbs; more Americans owned their homes than ever before; the country would put a man on the moon within a decade. The American Dream was alive and doing well — at least in the beginning of their lives. Their future was unmatched by that of either their parents' or grandparents' generation. Landon Y. Jones, writing in 1980, summed it all up with the title of his landmark book on the boomers: *Great Expectations*.[13]

Advertising played a big part in shaping their expectations from an early age. Good economic times, a more consumption-oriented society, and the use of television for mass marketing all came together at just the time when the largest cohort of children ever in America was being born. Not surprisingly, the children grew up acutely aware of themselves as consumers. Advertising serves not only to sell products, but to promote consumption as a way of life, and boomers were catered to like no generation before them. Jones writes: "They were the first generation of children to be isolated by Madison Avenue as an identifiable market. That is the appropriate word: isolated. Marketing, and especially television, isolated their needs and wants from those of their parents. From the cradle, the baby boomers had been surrounded by products created especially for them, from Silly Putty to Slinkys to skateboards. New products, new toys, new commercials, new fads — the dictatorship of the new — was integral to the baby boom experience."[14]

Surrounded by so much that was new, middle-class boomers had more than just expectations. They had a sense of entitlement: a right to interesting jobs, livable incomes, goot times, rewarding lives. Children were raised to express themselves and to feel good about themselves, believing that somehow sheer abundance would nurture them. In the early years of school, children were taught to enjoy the process of creative learning and not worry so much about the goal: paint and draw what you feel. Liberal child-rearing philosophies on the part of educated, upper middle-class parents encouraged freedom and personal development, the fulfillment of wants and needs. Not all boomers were brought up on the permissive teachings of Dr. Benjamin Spock, however. Many lower middle-class and working-class children, indeed probably a majority of school-age children in the 1960s and 1970s, were brought up in more traditional ways. Thirty percent of our respondents, mostly from upper middle-class backgrounds, described their upbringing as "permissive" or "very permissive," as compared to 52% who described theirs as "somewhat rigid" and 17% as "very rigid."

But the cultural winds were definitely blowing in the direction of heightened expectations. The upheavals of the period had so profound an impact on their lives growing up, in great part because of these hopes and dreams. Rising expectations widened the gap between aspiration and realities, but also, as political scientist Ronald Inglehart argues, contributed to a "silent revolution" in values.[15] Unlike the revolution that took place in the streets, with civil right marches and antiwar protests, this one was quieter and more subtle, but no less important. Inglehart argues that in times of prosperity — as opposed to economic insecurity — values tend to shift in the direction of greater concern for individual well-being, interesting experiences, quality of life, tolerance of diversity, intellectual and spiritual development. Whereas economic insecurity encourages acquisitive values, economic security fosters greater inwardness and quest for meaning. Building on Abraham Maslow's notion of a "hierarchy of needs," he emphasizes that once economic survival needs are met, then higher-order needs of the self come into play to shape people's values. This latter he describes as "post-materialist," emphasizing the break with more bourgeois, material-oriented values.

These sweeping value changes touched Americans in their inner lives. According to a major study on American culture, a new sense of self was in the making — away from social roles toward a more inner-developed, more psychological view of self. In *The Inner American*, Veroff, Douvan, and Kulka found young Americans more willing in 1976 than in 1957 to mention personality factors in describing how they differed from others. When asked to describe themselves, Americans increasingly focused less on their ascribed characteristics, and more on personal qualities. They observed a sharp decline in social connections and a shift in the "locus of control" — that is, a sense of self more of their own making than created by a conformist culture.[16] An older culture of self-denial that had long guided Americans was giving way to a psychological culture concerned with feelings, with self-expressiveness, with personal adaptation, and therapeutic solutions.

Pollster Daniel Yankelovich saw the changes as a major shift, replacing the old ethic of self-denial with a new ethic of self-fulfillment. He spoke of the "giant plates" of culture moving, of abrupt transformations in orientations to self and to society. Those living closest to society's fault lines — the young — were the first to feel the shifts and the resulting dislocations. He looked to the college educated as the cutting edge, and how the fundamental questions these young Americans were asking had changed:

> Instead of asking, "Will I be able to make a good living?" "Will I be successful?," "Will I raise happy, health, successful children?" — the typical questions asked by average Americans in the 1950s and 1960s — Americans in the 1970s came to ponder more introspective matters. We asked "How can I find self-fulfillment?" "What does personal success really mean?" "What kinds of commitments should I be making?" "What is worth sacrificing for?" "How can I grow?"[17]

Others felt the tremors as well. The new values spread into much of middle-class America, and gradually into those sectors of the population ready to express their discontent — housewives, blue-collar workers, high school students. By the mid-1970s, Yankelovich continues:

> Americans from every walk of life were suddenly eager to give more meaning to their lives, to find fuller self-expression and to add a touch of adventure and grace to their lives and those of others. Where strict norms had prevailed in the fifties and sixties, now all was pluralism and freedom of choice: to marry or live together; to have children early or postpone them, perhaps forever; to come out of the closet or stay in; to keep the old job or return to school; to make commitments or hang loose; to change careers, spouses, houses, states of residence, states of mind.[18]

By the early 1980s, the pendulum appeared to be swinging back. Yankelovich observed an easing away from a more radical quest for self, and an emerging "ethic of commitment" with a growing emphasis on concerns for others and relations with the world. Disillusioned with the excesses of personal freedom and self-fulfillment, the winds of change were blowing in the direction of a better balance between obligations to self and to others. He envisioned a new ethic that would shift the axis away from preoccupation with self (either self-denial or self-fulfillment) toward connectedness with the world — to people, institutions, places, nature. Boomers were still skeptical about institutions, political leaders, and social labels, but they were turning toward some types of commitments. The new ethic was gathering force, as Yankelovich saw it, around two kinds of commitments: closer and deeper personal relationships, and the switch from instrumental values to sacred/expressive ones.

This trend toward commitment is apparent in the boomers we interviewed. Mollie Stone, the single mother in Massachusetts who told us about her days as a "flower child" in Central Park, is the most obvious case of someone deeply immersed in her own self, but who is now trying to revise the giving-receiving compact. Today she would like to be married and to have a more stable family life. Partly a reflection of demographics, many boomers — like Mollie — are now in their mid- to late thirties and early forties and are concerned with marriages, families, and parenting. But there appears to be something more — a profound search for ways to reach out and connect with others, and to find a more satisfying balance of concerns for self and for others. Commitment amounts to what Yankelovich describes as a "giving/receiving social compact," and many today are recognizing that such a compact is open to revision as people's lives and circumstances change.

Though much energy is now directed at working out a meaningful and balanced sense of commitment, this does not mean that boomers, by and large, have abandoned their expectations for fulfilling lives. To the contrary, whatever revisions of the giving/ receiving compact are occurring, it is in the context of some deeply held values that crystallized during their years growing up and continue to be of great importance to them. One is tolerance. Eighty-seven percent in our survey said there should be more acceptance of different lifestyles. Social background, level of education, and region of country do not matter: Boomers generally hold to the view that lifestyles should be a matter of personal choice. Tolerance was extended in their generation to those not just different racially or socioeconomically, but with differing sexual orientations and lifestyles. Options in virtually all realms of life are taken for granted.

Another value they hold dear is belief in themselves. Eighty-six percent of our respondents say that if you believe in yourself, there is almost no limit to what you can do. Seventy-one percent say a person who is strong and determined can pretty much control what happens in life. Even failure is seen as something to be blamed on the individual, not society. Sixty-six percent agree that if someone does not succeed in life, usually it's his or her own fault. The better educated and those most deeply influenced by the counterculture are somewhat less inclined to agree, and more likely to see society as playing a part affecting people's life chances, but self-reliance is a tenet of faith among boomers. "Brought up in an enviornment of change," writes Michael Maccoby, "they have learned to adapt to new people and situations, and to trust their own abilities rather than parents or institutions. They value independence, and they accept responsibility for themselves."[19]

Victims of their own great expectations, many in this generation have experienced a disheartening gap between their perceived potential and realized achievements. Economic opportunities failed to keep pace with their aspirations. Many with college degrees were forced to settle for jobs and incomes lower than what they had assumed was befitting of college status. The optimism of the 1960s faded in the 1970s — a decade remembered for gas lines, inflation, and a rising cost of living. The tightening of the economy came at just the time when many of the older boomers were forming families, trying to buy their first homes, and discovering the difficulties of maintaining marriages, raising children, and having satisfying careers, and optimism gave way to the "big chill." One-third of our respondents report having to "scale down their expectations" — true for both the older and younger waves. Expecting so much in life, they have discovered that nothing — homes, family, love, friendship, wealth — comes easily.

A third value is the belief that strength comes from within. When boomers are asked to describe themselves, they focus on personal, individual qualities. Both their successes and failures may contribute to a greater introspectiveness. A focus on self helps to explain, for example, the high priority given to family, friends, and interpersonal relationships. Having been estranged from more organized formal institutions, many still prefer a more personal means of relating to the social world. Much energy is spent in personal relationships, obviously a source of immense satisfaction. It likely accounts for why so many boomers turn to therapy and counseling as a solution to problems and why they like a high degree of personal service in the marketplace. Introspection also bears on openness and sharing of feelings. Asked to evaluate a list of changes from the time of their parents' generation, respondents in the *Rolling Stone* survey chose one change above all others: 83% felt that greater openness and willingness to share personal feelings was a change for the better.[20]

These are hardly new values. The quest for psychological well-being itself has roots reaching deep into the American past. As early as the mid-1800s, Ralph Waldo Emerson, in his essay on "Self-Reliance," had written of his opposition to tradition and conformity and looked to individuals relying on their own inner resources as a means to truth and wisdom. He called upon people to recognize the power within them and to use that power for their own fulfillment. In his writing on "Nature" and "Wealth," he further elaborated on the expansive qualities of the human spirit: "Who can set bounds to the possibilities of man?" he asks, and then implicitly answers his question by reminding his readers that "the world exists for you."[21] Optimism, personal transformation, and the union of mind and matter were all Emersonian themes that later generations of "positive thinkers" — from Mary Baker Eddy to Norman Vincent

Peale — would draw on. Members of the boomer generation have felt a special affinity with such thinkers and have been inspired by their teachings.

The rise of psychotherapy further liberated the self from its bondages to external authorities. Freud established a new, idealized image of selfhood: a person who has an analytic attitude and strives for well-being as a way of overcoming the neuroses generated out of social life, a sane self in an insane world. After Freud came the "humanistic psychologists" who popularized notions of human potential and self-actualization, again on the assumption that society was detrimental or restrictive to the emergence of a more vibrant, healthy self. Humanistic psychology spread widely among the college educated in the 1960s and 1970s. Influenced by a faith in the flexibility of human nature, and inspired by the traditional American values of self-improvement and individualism, the boomers were to become the carriers of an ethic of self-realization that had been in the making for a long time and was now a dominant cultural theme in American life. It could hardly be otherwise. In a society that had so many inducements to material advancement and self-interest, it is not surprising that "self-fulfillment" and "self-help" would be seen as healthy correlates. Two hundred years have passed from the time Benjamin Franklin published his autobiography, a self-help book of sorts of a man in quest of virtue, to today's flourishing market of books, videos, and audiocassettes catering to psychological needs — the popular expression, as Philip Rieff says, of "the triumph of the therapeutic."[22]

## Gender Revolution

Of all the sixties' revolutions, none had a greater long-term impact than the gender revolution. The changing sexual rules and relationships of the period mushroomed into a major social movement that has radically altered marriage, family, parenting, and career patterns. By the 1980s there were significant increases in the number of couples cohabiting, single-parent families, blended families, lesbian and gay families, couples without children, couples with children no longer at home, and families consisting of an adult and an aging parent. Family types, lifestyles, and new gender roles proliferated. Freedom of choice had invaded the more private, intimate realms of sexuality and family, producing an immense variety of acceptable alternatives.

The boomer generation came into adulthood just at the time the gender revolution was in the making. Events coalesced early in the 1960s to give shape to a broadly based women's movement. In 1963 Betty Friedan published *The Feminine Mystique*, which spoke directly to women who had lived by old standards.[23] Women had far fewer opportunities to break into the labor force; but even more of an impediment was the mystique surrounding women themselves — as wives and mothers. Speaking of the "problem that has no name," Friedan urged them to break away from their domestic confines, go back to school, and pursue careers. The book became an immediate bestseller, giving voice to discontented women across the country. Much of the discontent came from wives and mothers older than the first wave of boomers who were just beginning to reach adulthood, women who had struggled to conform to the prevailing family norms of their time, but who were increasingly disenchanted. Women who had married and raised families in the late 1940s and the 1950s — the period after World War II leading up to the 1960s — especially felt pressures for change. Their discontent over lack of career opportunities and gender roles defining their meaningful activities largely to the kitchens and bedrooms was a powerful outpouring of support for change, bonding them with their younger "sisters" in the movement.

Simultaneously, the birth control pill, approved for sale in 1960, gained widespread usage the first few years it was on the market. Technology converged with the mounting women's movement, giving it an immediate and far-reaching impact. For the first time, a women could truly feel she was in charge of her body, that sex was possible without excessive worry about becoming pregnant. By de-coupling sex and procreation, the pill gave women a degree of choice and control hitherto unknown. Critics feared it would lead to freer sex and changing moral values, which it did, but its greater impact lay in the power it gave women over their own lives. It freed women to accept and assert their sexuality, to demand recognition as human beings with sexual appetites no less pronounced than men's. It freed women for opportunities of their own choosing, emancipated them from old bondages, and therby altered significantly the power relationships between men and women. Women of all social classes were affected, but none more so than middle-class women: "Now, for the first time, millions of middle-class women could rationally and safely plan careers, conceive of marriage as a true partnership, calculate the rational economic future of the family, and think differently about what it meant to be a woman of the middle class."[24]

Catholic women also sought prescriptions. By the mid-1960s about two-thirds as many Catholic women as Protestants and Jews were using the pill. Today, between 80% and 85% of Catholic women approve its use.[25] Its reliability encourages them to ignore the church's centuries-old prohibition against artificial birth control, though not always without personal struggle and guilt. Carol McLennon, the post-Vatican II Catholic from Southern California, tells of her own struggle leading up to her decision about birth control:

> So after the third [baby], I decided, Brad and I will work on this real hard and we'll just not get pregnant. No more shlepping around. It really caused a lot of tension. Because it seems like you get into bed at night and you'd hug, and then you'd start thinking what day of the month is this and, y'know, God, we can't do it now. What are we gonna do? Let's go find this, y'know...and that's not what God meant either. I mean our relationship as husband and wife was meant to be loving and caring and, y'know, I just couldn't imagine living all the rest of those years with that kind of tension. But, as it ended up, we

didn't have to. I ended up pregnant again by the end of the year. And
then came the guilt. Tremendous guilt. Why did I have this horrible
thick guilt? And it was because I really didn't do what I knew was the
right thing to do. So after Carla I had the tubal ligation.

Carol's decision to practice some kind of birth control was a significant step to take.
For her, as for many Catholic women, the pill or its equivalent was their first
significant rebellion against the church, and it meant that their attitude toward the
authority of the church on other issues would never by quite the same again.

The pill provoked profound social changes. It helped lower the birth rate and
brought an end to the postwar baby boom. It helped raise the age at marriage after
decades of decline, as more and more women chose to postpone a committed
relationship. That in itself was a major change — creating a "Postponed Generation,"
or the delaying of the responsibilities of adulthood. It spelled doom to the old
containment ethic of the earlier period. Women could now enter the labor force with
less fear of losing jobs as a result of unexpected births. Marriage need not stand in the
way of pursuing a career. With good "family planning," young working couples could
enjoy the early years of their marriage with double incomes. Even to have children at
all was now an option. It contributed to a changing, more liberal stance toward
divorce: 18% of the boomers we surveyed were themselves currently divorced or
separated, and another 13%, now married, reported previous marriages. It also helped
indirectly to redefine men's roles in the direction of greater gender equality, both in
the workplace and at home.

Thus boomers as a generation would have to deal with an enormous array of
gender and lifestyle changes, affecting the lives of both men and women. The technology
of birth control combined with the burgeoning sixties' youth culture encouraged the
young, as historian Elaine Tyler May points out, to be risk-takers in ways that their
security-oriented parents found unthinkable.[26] They embraced new gender role
definitions and sexual norms; and while many may be concerned today about
promiscuous sex and AIDS, the majority has not turned its back on the gains from the
gender revolution. Indeed, 77% agree that *more* needs to be done to advance equal
opportunities for women. Eighty-one percent agree that it is good for women to have
jobs outside the home, and 71% say it is all right for women to work even if they have
preschool children at home. This generation strongly endorses "egalitarian marriages,"
in which husbands and wives share decision making in family matters: 74% disagree
with the statement that "by and large the husband ought to have the main say-so in
family matters." Three-quarters of boomers say they would like husbands and wives to
share responsibility for work, homemaking, and child-raising; while just one in ten
prefers a "traditional marriage," in which the husband works and the wife stays at
home. Views on shared work, homemaking, and child-raising is one thing, however,
and what actually happens at home is quite another. Indeed, the evidence suggests that
although men have started to "help out" more with domestic chores, working women

still do double duty and are responsible for the lion's share of child care and housework. In the new world of two-career families, women still bear a greater responsibility for, to cite Arlie Hochschild's phrase, the "second shift."[27]

# Education and the Media

Finally, we consider education and the media. The boomer generation is the most educated generation in American history — twice as many baby boomers went to college as their parents, three times as many as their grandparents. Educational institutions expanded at every phase during their childhood and growing-up years — first when they were in kindergarten and elementary school, then in the junior high and high school years, and later still when they went off to colleges and universities. Eighty-five percent of baby boomers in our survey finished high school. Over 60% have attended college, 38% earned college degrees, and 17% have a postgraduate education.

Schools during the 1960s and 1970s exposed students to a wide variety of ideas and influences. The sheer increase in numbers of people living and interacting in one place had an impact: It opened their eyes to diverse ways of living and believing. An expanding curriculum in the humanities and social sciences had an effect as well. New courses in religion and philosophy introduced students to the world religions, to critical thinking about the Bible, and to metaphysical questions never before raised. Oscar Gantt remembers taking such a course in college and his encounter with a Jewish professor with whom he could explore questions and doubts about his own faith. Some of his beliefs arising out of an African-American heritage were challenged, and it helped him, as he says, "to better understand my spiritual self or what I was seeking spiritually." For many like him, college was a time of encountering religious pluralism, of discovering and meeting people who differed in their beliefs about God and the sacred, and of finding out that religious truth is itself something that is deeply personal and deemed by many as more relative than absolute.

On college and university campuses across the country, of course, the counterculture was flourishing. Young people who were in college at the time were almost twice as likely as noncollege student to have attended a rock concert, smoked marijuana, and protested the Vietnam War. The counterculture sensitized the better educated to new values and experiences, encouraging them to be more open and experimental in matters ranging from family and sexual styles to religious views. The so-called "new religions" — Zen Buddhism, Meher Baba, Transcendental Meditation, and many others — also flourished, introducing students to Eastern spirituality. College students were twice as likely as noncollege students to say they practice meditation techniques. Others, however, were not so greatly influenced by the changing cultural and religious climate, especially those attending small colleges or business and technical schools.

Linda Kramer, in a business school at the time, knew about the drugs and different lifestyles that university students were into, but she was effectively sheltered from all of that even while living in the same Ohio city.

During these years a new basis of cultural cleavage emerged that fell along educational lines. With the growth of science and technology, the boomers — more so than any other generation — came to be deeply divided by level of education. Education is probably the best single predictor for a range of attitudes and values, such as racial tolerance, anti-Semitism, egalitarian gender roles, alternative lifestyles, and tolerance of nonconformity of various kinds. And the same holds for traditional religious beliefs and practices. During the 1960s and 1970s, levels of religious belief, of worship attendance, and of participation in organized religion declined considerably among the better educated, and more so than in previous decades. On matters as varied as belief in God, interpretations of the Bible, Sabbath observance, prayer, and church and Sunday school attendance, there were precipitous declines.[28] More than anything else, education contributed to the deepening division between liberals and conservatives within religious communities, and to a growing split between the more conventionally religious and the more secular sector of the population.

So great and widespread were the differences in attitudes, values, and beliefs that some have argued that a "new class" emerged during this time. In an "information-oriented" society, a class that valued knowledge and its uses and interpretations, and was more liberal in its outlook and more supportive of government spending in the areas of education, welfare, and environmental protection especially, seemed increasingly set off from the more traditional classes.[29] Whatever the changing ideological configurations, one thing was certain: The relation of religion and education was undergoing a major shift in society. Whereas for a long time the better educated held to about the same levels of conventional religious belief as the less educated and were more involved in religious activities, in the 1960s these patterns began to reverse with the declines among the better educated.

Higher education generated new and more secular meaning systems competing with theistic interpretations of the nature of reality. Social scientific modes of explanation, for example, have gained ascendancy, emphasizing the role of social forces in shaping people's lives. This is more true for the better educated than the general population. Forty-six percent of postgraduates in our survey, compared with 29% of high school graduates, agree with the statement: "If someone does not succeed in life, often it is because society has not given the person a chance." Postgraduates are less likely to regard God, or supernatural forces, as having a strong influence on them, and more likely to attribute influence to how they were brought up or to those in power in society. Social scientific thinking has become widely diffused in contemporary society, and among boomers especially, who as a generation have been the most exposed to this mode of constructing reality.

American-style individualism, shorn of its religious underpinnings, is a type of meaning system as well. This particular type of thinking elevates the person — rather than God or social forces — as responsible for his or her own destiny. Willpower and determination are the critical factors shaping a person's life and success. Individuals have within them the power to make life as they want it. Pam Fletcher, the Massachusetts housewife, is an example of one who thinks largely in these terms. She holds to a utilitarian philosophy emphasizing her own choices and actions as what are important in life. Decisions influence outcomes: You put your effort into being a good person, or working hard, and hope you succeed. She is hardly alone in her view — well over half of our respondents agree that "hard work always pays off." Even more agree that "a person who is strong and determined can pretty much control what happens in life," and that "if one believes in oneself, there is almost no limit to what one can do." These latter constructions of reality are particularly pronounced among the less well educated.

If education helped to created a variety of meaning systems, the media had an impact as well. The boomers were, as already noted, the first generation to grow up with television: They watched the assassination of a president and other national leaders, civil rights demonstrations, the Vietnam War, nuclear test explosions. Television brought the violence and destructiveness of our national life right into the living room for all to see. More than any other medium, television shaped consumer tastes and raised their levels of expectations for the future. It was also a consuming medium. By the time the average boomer had reached sixteen years of age, television had captured an estimated 12,000 to 15,000 hours of his or her time.[30] Although they watched children's programs, much of that time was spent watching adult programs. In effect, television introduced the generation to a very adult world at a very early age.

Unquestionably, television limited the amount of time boomers had with their peers and parents. It became the major source of information shaping their definitions of reality, exceeding that of books, newspapers, teachers, religious leaders, perhaps supplanting the family itself. Researchers at the University of Michigan, interviewing the high school class of 1965 along with their parents, found considerable evidence that the family socialization process had weakened: There were few agreements between the two generations on racial equality, drug use, gender view, political attitudes, and religion.[31] Although the investigators did not examine the role of television, there can be little doubt that it contributed to the diminished importance of the family in the transmission of cultural values and beliefs.

Perhaps the most important impact of television was that it replaced the *word* with the *image*: Henceforth the dominant medium would be the fleeting, discontinous flow of electromagnetic pictures. Instancy and intimacy would be the distinguishing features of this new medium; seeing, not reading, would become the basis for believing. The implications were staggering, far beyond anything we have yet grasped. And once again boomers could claim a first: the first generation to experience what amounts to a major transformation in mode of communication. Music sensitized them to the auditory dimensions of experience, and television opened up realms of visual experience, both of which have had a powerful effect on how Americans ever since have defined truth and knowledge, and even reality itself.

# Religious Protests and Spiritual Explorations

Upheaval, affluence, gender revolution, education, and the media all shaped boomer experiences. Disruptive events and rapid social changes jolted their lives, distancing them from the major institutions and challenging core values and the cultural narratives by which generations of Americans have understood themselves. They shared the great economic expectations of the 1950s and early 1960s, but they also shared the disillusionments of the 1970s, forcing many to scale down their material dreams. Not surprisingly, as the commentator quoted at the beginning of this chapter suggests, boomers look like veterans, having been through a war together.

Nowhere were the jolts felt more than within institutional religion, in the churches and synagogues across the country. Most dropped out in their late teenage years or early twenties. Those who were involved in the civil rights movement and antiwar protests left in disillusionment with a church that seemed so feeble, so impotent to bring about changes in a world where so much had gone wrong. Many Catholics left in frustration and anger over the church's positions on issues like abortion and divorce. In all the religious traditions, many simply dropped out. Some felt that the mainline churches were spiritually and theologically impoverished; but most, it seems, just stopped going, not out of any strong doctrinal or moral objection, but because church or synagogue seemed irrelevant to them.

The youthful protest against organized religion appears to have been far more broadly based than is often thought. Over 60% of the young adults in our survey dropped out of active involvement for a period of two years or more — somewhat higher for Jews and mainline Protestants, but not less than one-half for Catholics and conservative Protestants. Levels of dropping out were about the same for boomers born before 1955 as for those born afterwards and are only slightly higher for men than for women. Perhaps most surprising of all, education appears to have had little influence on this — those without a college education dropped out about equally with those who had a college degree. In fact, those with a high school education or less dropped out more so than did college graduates, but postgraduates abandoned the churches and synagogues more so than any of the others.

Clearly, something happened to alter fundamentally the generation's ties with religious institutions. The fact is that the religious involvement of boomers changed drastically, and in a relatively short period of time — from when they were children until their early adult years. Nine out of ten people in our survey reported attending religious services weekly or more when they were children eight to ten years old. Many of them were baptized. As children they were as religious as any generation before them in this century — at least in terms of their exposure to and early involvement within religious institutions.[32] But by their early twenties, slightly more than one-fourth were involved to the same extent; the great majority had dropped out altogether or, if still attending, they did so irregularly. Those who had been baptized as children did not join churches through profession of faith, or confirmation, at levels that might have been expected on the basis of their numbers — becoming instead the church's "missing generation."[33] They dropped out of the mainline churches and synagogues in unprecedented numbers, resulting in a substantial loss of members.[34]

Dropping out of organized religion during the young adult years, at least for a transitory period in a person's life, is a deeply embedded cultural pattern in America. Previous generations have drifted away from religious institutions in which they were brought up during their young adult years, when they must decide for themselves what they believe or whether to get involved in a congregation. What is really significant religiously is not that they drift away, but whether or not they return to these institutions later on in their lives — which many are now doing, as we shall see in later chapters. Still, it would appear that for the post-World War II generation, the extent of dropping out was greater than for their parents' generation, and that educated, middle-class young Americans abandoned the religious institutions in proportionally greater numbers in the 1960s and 1970s than in earlier times.[35]

More important than anything else in shaping a religious response were the experiences growing up in the 1960s and 1970s. As Figure 2.3 shows, there is a relationship between exposure to the cultural upheavals and religious involvement. Among those who were the least touched by the music, the drug culture, and the social and political unrest that ripped the country at the seams, well over one-half dropped out. But for those who were more exposed, levels of dropping out rose considerably higher — from 56% up to 84%. The cultural reverberations of this tumultuous period clearly had an enormous impact on the youth's estrangement from organized religion. The patterns hold for men and women, for the younger and the older groups, for those who went to college and those who did not, and in all parts of the country.

The extent of the estrangement and value shift is evident by looking at the changes in generational attitudes. Figure 2.4 shows a discernible break on some key attitudes between pre-boomers and boomers. On measures of strength of religious identity, the importance of arriving at one's own beliefs, whether religious attendance is necessary to being a "good" Christian or Jew, and in views about the rules of morality within churches and synagogues, there is a 5- to 15-point spread between the cohorts born before 1946 and those born after that time. The end of World War II is like a cultural fault line — the differences greater on either side than between those born in cohort 1 (1926-1935) and cohort 2 (1936-1945), or between those born in cohort 3 (1946-1954) and cohort 4 (1955-1962). "In an epoch of change, each person is dominated by his birth date," wrote sociologist Norman Ryder in an essay on generations and social change published in 1965, words that aptly described the boomers.[36]

What happened religiously is much the same as what happened politically. Boomers in the late 1950s and early 1960s were a generation well on their way to a normal respect for the political process: They had high levels of trust in government and felt that political leaders cared about what people thought. But within a span of ten years — from 1963 to 1973 — they abandoned their once hopeful outlook for a new course

**Figure 2.3**        **Religious Dropouts**

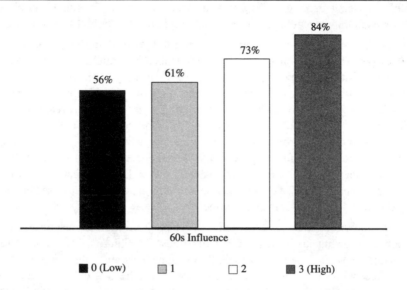

60s Influence

■ 0 (Low)          ▨ 1                □ 2          ■ 3 (High)

of political independence and institutional separation. By their late teens and early twenties, trust in government plummeted, party loyalty declined, and the number of political party "independents" shot up.[37] The analogy to organized religion seems indisputable: greater separation from institutions and a corresponding increase in emphasis on individual choice.

While religious responses were shaped by the cultural ferment of the 1960s, the roots of the protest reach further back into the childhood years of the boomers. The years in which many of the older boomers grew up — the 1950s — were an aberration in many ways. In some respects it was a very religious era, still looked back on with nostalgia; yet in other ways it was very secular and riddled with paradoxes. The close intertwining of domestic ideology and cold war militance may have produced a powerful countercultural response. A stable family life seemed necessary for national security and for maintaining supremacy over the Soviet Union. Cold war tensions may have encouraged a retreat into the home in search of security but may also have sown the seeds for a strong institutional backlash, beginning with the "soft" institutions of the family and religion. The 1950s, as one commentator observes, was "an era of suppressed individuality, of national paranoia, and of largely unrecognized discrimination against minorities, women, the poor, foreigners, homosexuals, and indeed most of those who dared to be different — the era that came to an end with the onset of the '60s was a time bomb waiting to explode."[38] Heightened expectations, too, especially as translated into new, more permissive child-rearing philosophies, had an

Figure 2.4    Birth Cohorts and Attitudes toward Organized Religion

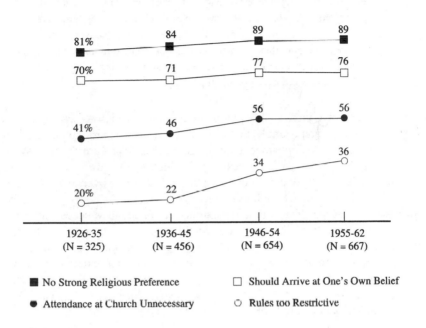

| 81% | 84 | 89 | 89 |
| 70% | 71 | 77 | 76 |
| 41% | 46 | 56 | 56 |
|  |  | 34 | 36 |
| 20% | 22 |  |  |

1926-35          1936-45          1946-54          1955-62
(N = 325)        (N = 456)        (N = 654)        (N = 667)

■ No Strong Religious Preference            □ Should Arrive at One's Own Belief
● Attendance at Church Unnecessary          ○ Rules too Restrictive

impact: Dropouts in our survey were twice as likely as those who did not drop out to describe their upbringing as "permissive" or "very permissive."

But there were other, more positive repercussions from the turbulent 1960s. Jolted out of the established faiths, many turned inward in search of basic answers to life. The so-called "new religions" flourished in the latter years of the decade. Fueled partly by the drug culture, insights from the Eastern mystical religions, and the music of protest, the religious consciousness of college-educated, middle-class youth especially was transformed, paralleling changing notions in the realms of family and sex, in politics and economics, in lifestyles. There was a blossoming of the spirit in a thousand forms — everything from astrology to Zen — known simply as "alternative religions." Later, in the 1970s, there was an evangelical and fundamentalist Christian resurgence. Youth turned to "born again" faiths in surprisingly large numbers. No longer defining themselves through the conventional religious labels they had inherited, they turned inward to their own spiritual explorations.

This turning inward would have a lasting spiritual impact. The impact would last because theirs was a generation whose foundations had been shaken and for whom there was no returning to the old ways of believing. Commenting on the existential depths of the generational experiences, Craig Dykstra recently wrote:

The suspiciousness of the '60s has not gone away, and no escape from it is sought by the new religious seekers. Rather the search is for a truer, healther suspiciousness, one that really can smoke out deceit, oppression, violence, and evil —even in its loveliest and most attractive forms — and tell it for what it is. To support the suspiciousness there must be something that is not suspiciousness itself, something that is not so ultimately suspicious it must finally suspect everything. What we have here, I think, is a search for God.[39]

This search, in an increasingly pluralistic moral and religious setting, produced a new salvational dilemma, namely, that of finding one's own spiritual path in the midst of so many alternatives. Fundamental questions, such as "Who am I?" and "What am I doing with my life?" took on fresh meaning. Religion — like life — was something to be explored. Old cultural and religious scripts had lost power over them, forcing them to think through anew their religious and spiritual options. As a generation they were predisposed to post-material values, to pursuing greater equality, peace, environmental protection, and quality-of-life, far more so than the generation before them. They reasserted values of self-fulfillment and human potential, far more so than did their parents. They led the way in exploring lifestyle choices and extending tolerance to people of all preferences and persuasions, far more so than did their parents. A generation with high expectations for themselves and for others, they came to know what it is like, in poet Emily Dickinson's words, "to dwell in possibility."

Ironically, despite a great deal of alienation from traditional religion, the circumstances of their lives led to a great deal of potential interest in spiritual matters. The period left not just a lasting mark on their lives, it left many marks. Members of the boomer generation were touched in ways that have led to many differing, and even alternative, spiritual and religious trajectories. It is to this array of possibilities that we turn as we take a closer look at our representative boomers.

● ● ● ● ● ● ● ● ● ● ● ● ● ● ● ● ● ● ● ● ● ● ● ● ● ●

# Notes

[1]    See "TV Mirrors a New Generation," by Jeremy Gerard, *The New York Times* (October 30, 1988): Section 2.

[2]    David Sheff, "Portrait of a Generation," *Rolling Stone* (May 5, 1988): 55.

[3]    The three items were worded as follows: "In your late teens and early twenties, did you ever (a) attend a rock concert? (b) smoke marijuana? (c) take part in any demonstrations, marches, or rallies? The three are moderately intercorrelated, ranging from 0.20 to 0.41 (Pearson correlations).

[4]    The terms "challengers" and "calculators" are taken from Douglas A. Walrath. See his *Frameworks: Patterns for Living and Believing Today* (New York: Pilgrim Press, 1987), chapter 3.

5    Annie Gottlieb, *Do You Believe in Magic? The Second Coming of the 60s Generation* (New York: Times Books, 1987), 18.

6    These data are reported in Paul C. Light, *Baby Boomers* (New York: W.W. Norton, 1988), 168.

7    William Atwood, "How America Feels," *Look* 24, 1 (January 5, 1960): 11-15.

8    Loren Baritz, *The Good Life* (New York: Alfred A. Knopf, 1989), chapter 5.

9    Light, *Baby Boomers*, 160-61.

10   Seymour Martin Lipset and William Schneider, *The Confidence Gap* (New York: The Free Press, 1983), 296-98.

11   Joseph Veroff, Elizabeth Douvan, and Richard Kulka, *The Inner American: A Self-Portrait from 1957-1976* (New York: Basic Books, 1981), 141.

12   Sheff, "Portrait of a Generation," 52.

13   Landon Y. Jones, *Great Expectations: America and the Baby Boom Generation* (New York: Ballantine Books, 1980).

14   Jones, *Great Expectations*, 51-52.

15   Ronald Inglehart, "The Silent Revolution in Europe: Intergenerational Change in Post-Industrial Societies," *American Political Science Review* 65 (December 1971): 991-1017. Also see his expanded argument in *Culture Shift in Advanced Industrial Society* (Princeton: Princeton University Press, 1990).

16   Veroff, Douvan, and Kulka, *The Inner American*, 528-29. Many others have written about the cultural shift toward the subjective and the personal. See especially Christopher Lasch, *The Culture of Narcissism* (New York: Norton, 1979); Peter Clecak, *America's Quest for the Ideal Self* (New York: Oxford University Press, 1983); and Robert N. Bellah, Richard Madsen, William M. Sullivan, Ann Swidler, and Steven M. Tipton, *Habits of the Heart* (Berkeley: University of California Press, 1985).

17   Daniel Yankelovich, *New Rules: Searching for Self-Fulfillment in a World Turned Upside Down* (New York: Random House, 1981), 4-5.

18   Yankelovich, *New Rules*, 5.

19   Michael Maccoby, *Why Work?* (New York: Simon and Schuster, 1988), 103.

20   Sheff, "Portrait of a Generation," 54.

21   Ralph Waldo Emerson, "Nature," in *Selected Writings of Emerson*, edited by Brooks Atkinson (New York: Modern Library, 1940), 36.

22   Philip Rieff, *The Triumph of the Therapeutic: Uses of Faith after Freud* (New York: Harper & Row, 1966).

23   Betty Friedan, *The Feminine Mystique* (New York: W.W. Norton, 1963).

24   Loren Baritz, *The Good Life* (New York: Alfred A. Knopf, 1989), 238-39.

25   These statistics are reported in *U.S. News and World Report* (July 11, 1966): 65 and in *Ladies' Home Journal* (June 1990): 186.

26   Elaine Tyler May, *Homeward Bound* (New York: Basic Books, 1988).

27   Arlie Hochschild (with Anne Machung), *The Second Shift: Working Parents and the Revolution at Home* (New York: Viking, 1989).

28   Considerable research has documented these declines. For a review and interpretation of the declines, see Robert Wuthnow, *The Restructuring of American Religion* (Princeton: Princeton University Press, 1988), 153-72. Wuthnow describes a much broader "education gap" emerging in the sixties than had existed before.

29   Wuthnow, *The Restructuring of American Religion*, 157-58.

[30]   Light, *Baby Boomers*, 123.

[31]   M. Kent Jennings and Richard Niemi, "The Transmission of Political Values from Parent to Child," *American Political Science Review* 62 (March 1968): 169-84.

[32]   Dividing the survey into four cohorts, those born between 1926 and 1935, between 1936 and 1945, between 1946 and 1954, and between 1955 and 1962, the differences in childhood religious involvement vary not more than 2 points.

[33]   For a case study of the losses within the United Methodist Church, see Warren J. Hartman, "Our Missing Generation," *Discipleship Trends* 5, no. 4 (August 1987).

[34]   For the four cohorts described in endnote 32, the percentages attending once a week or more when the respondents were in their early twenties are as follows: born between 1926 and 1935, 54%; born between 1936 and 1945, 46%; born between 1946 and 1954, 29%; and born between 1955 and 1962, 27%.

[35]   On the basis of a review of religious periodicals that we conducted, we found that every generation expresses great concern about what is happening to the young and their religious faith. Our review suggests there was an outpouring of concern in the late 1920s, but more so in the 1960s. See Jonathan A. Dorn, "Sodom and Tomorrow: Will the Young be Morally Good," unpublished paper, 1989.

[36]   Norman B. Ryder, "The Cohort as a Concept in the Study of Social Change," *American Sociological Review* 30 (December 1965): 843-61.

[37]   See Light, *Baby Boomers*, chapter 5.

[38]   J. Conger, "Freedom and Commitment: Families, Youth, and Social Change," *American Psychologist* 36, no. 12 (1981): 1477-1478. Also see May, *Homeward Bound*, and Arlene Skolnick, *Embattled Paradise* (New York: Basic Books, 1991), chapter 2.

[39]   Craig Dykstra, Editorial, *Theology Today* 46 (July 1989): 127.

# THE NEW RELIGIONS: DEMODERNIZATION AND THE PROTEST AGAINST MODERNITY

## JAMES DAVISON HUNTER

The development of the pervasive cultural innovations (particularly religious innovations) of the past decade and a half induced a considerable incredulity in the social sciences. Many social scientists had accepted the idea that modern society was increasingly secular in character, and had come to suppose that the secularity of the social system implied not only the decline of religious or supernaturalist assumptions in the operation of the social order, but also the diminution of supernaturalist dispositions on the part of individuals. Even theological currents had reinforced these modern liberal and positivistic assumptions — as evident in the successive fashionability of increasingly anti-traditional theologies, from demythologization, and secularization theology, to eventually the "death of God" theology. In this context, the resurgence of religion, as manifested in the new religious movements, came first as an unpredictable irritation, and eventually as a significant challenge to the long-established and even hallowed assumptions of the majority of social scientists. Only when some of these movements had become routinized did social scientists seriously begin to explore the organizational structure and the substantive features of the plurality of new religions and, perhaps more important, the reasons for their emergence in the first place.

A variety of plausible explanations and interpretations from diverse theoretical perspectives have been offered to account for the appearance of the new movements. Surprisingly, little if any of the research undertaken in Anglo-Saxon countries into these new religions has either utilized or even invoked the insights of the German humanistic tradition of the social sciences — a tradition distinguished by such classical figures as Max Weber, Ernst Troeltsch, and George Simmel— nor made use of the

James D. Hunter. "The New Religions: Demodernization and the Protest Against Modernity," in Bryan Wilson, ed., *The Social Impact of the New Religious Movements*. New York: The Rose of Sharon Press, 1981, pp. 1-19.

extensive and pertinent contributions of such writers as Arnold Gehlen, Peter Berger, Brigitte Berger, Anton Zijderveld, Thomas Luckmann, Hansfried Kellner, René König or Helmut Schelsky. In what follows, I seek to provide the groundwork for a perspective on the rise of the new religions which exploits the insights afforded by the German humanistic tradition, and which uses them to increase our understanding of the constitutive character of the new religious movements. I shall try, in addition, to locate this perspective among a few of the more recent interpretations offered, briefly exploring their commonalities and differences.

## Modernity and the Crises of Meaning

The perspective which is derived from the German humanistic tradition of sociology maintains a deliberate and unflinching affinity with the concerns and aspirations of classical sociological thought. Most generally, these concerns focus on the problem of individual existence in society, and more specifically, on the problem of individual existence in *modern societies*. At issue are the essence and character of modernity and its impact on the nature and course of individual life. These fundamental questions provided the *daemon* of inspiration behind most of the writings of the patristics of sociological thinking; and in this regard, it can be noted that the "early fathers" interpreted this problem as a religious problem, and adduced solutions which relied upon their development of an understanding of the differing aspects of the religious dimensions of social life. This preamble aside, it is within this stream of the classical tradition that one may find the first clue to understanding the riddle posed by the rise of the new religious consciousness.

Modernity is typified by a number of salient features. Among the most important are institutional differentiation[1] and bureaucratic augmentation.[2] This process results in a structural bifurcation — a split between public and private spheres of life;[3] intense cultural pluralism which follows from urbanization and the proliferation of the media of mass communications;[4] and social mobility and geographic mobility, among other things. The resulting effect of the intense convergence of these uniquely modern processes is what the German social theorist, Arnold Gehlen, has aptly described as *de-institutionalization*. Requisite to the full appreciation of the meaning of this concept is its placement within the larger context of Gehlen's general theory of institutions.[5]

The basis of Gehlen's theory of institutions is in an understanding of the biological constitution of the human animal. The biological research of such scientists as Adolf Portmann, J. von Uexkull and F. Butendijk has indicated that in relation to the rest of the animal world, the human organism is incomplete at birth, in the sense of what Gehlen calls *instinctual deprivation*. There is no biologically grounded structure through which humans may channel their externalizing energies; moreover there is no single ecological environment to which the human organism must become accustomed.

Unlike the rest of the animal world, the human experience at birth is open and unchanneled. Yet this is a situation which is to man biologically, and therefore psychologically, intolerable. Institutions, according to Gehlen, are *human artificial constructions* that provide for men what our biology does not. They function like instincts in that they pattern individual conduct and social relationship in an habitual and socially predictable manner. Not only do they establish behavior with a pattern, but institutions also provide human experience at the cognitive level with an intelligibility and a sense of continuity. By living within the well-defined parameters of a matrix of such institutions, humans need not reflect on their actions — they can take their social world for granted. While institutions exist as a stable background to human experience, there is also a foreground — the zone of life in which the individual makes deliberate and purposive choices. The former provides the structural context for the latter. Institutionalization occurs when an aspect of the foreground of human experience becomes habitualized and routinized so as to become a part of the background. Thus, for example, child-rearing is institutionalized when random behavior of the parent towards the child becomes habituated in a society, and then embedded in a normative (often moral) structure of rules, codes, and procedures. Institutionalization is complete when the rules and procedures guiding child-rearing practices become a feature of the society's taken-for-granted experience. De-institutionalization occurs when an item of culture is transferred from the background to the foreground. Thus, for instance, marriage is de-institutionalized when the normative codes regulating a specific type of social arrangement lose their plausibility, and thus the structure and functioning of the nuptial relationship become open-ended — a matter of choice. According to Gehlen, one of the most important aspects of modernity is that the foreground of choice is growing, and the background of stable institutional patterns is receding. Modernity is characterized by an unprecedented degree of de-institutionalization.

Yet the processes of de-institutionalization are not uniformly distributed in the social world. The public sphere — the sphere of massive bureaucracies organizing such areas of human activity as government and law, business and commerce, labor, health care, communications, the military and oftentimes, religion — remains highly institutionalized. All these institutions remain quite capable of patterning the thought and the social relationships of individuals within that public sphere, and, when occasion arises, of imposing the force of social control. Because these institutions in the public sphere are extensive and complex, and because, within the public sphere, what is demanded of men is thought, behavior, and relationships that are functionally rational, so these institutions become remote from the individual, and alien from the private sphere of life in general. As Zijderveld has argued, they are very often experienced as infinitely abstract, incomprehensible, and, in the extreme situation, as possessing the quality of unreality.[6] Experience in the public sphere typically disconfirms and contradicts experience in the private sphere.[7] Thus, while the processes of de-institutionalization have not infiltrated the public sphere, its institutions have, nonetheless, "lost their grip" on the individual. They are intrinsically unable to provide the individual with an overall sense of concrete, personal attachment which reinforces personal meanings and purpose. To find these things, the individual must turn elsewhere. That elsewhere is the private sphere — the sphere of personal and family life and other primary relationships. Yet, it is in the private sphere that the processes of de-institutionalization have gone furthest. The areas of child-rearing; courtship; marriage; sexuality; vocation; religious belief and practice; consuming patterns; leisure; and the basic norms which guide social behavior and social exchange — are, in advanced industrial countries, all radically de-institutionalized.

Thus, the dilemma of modernity, in which all individuals are variously caught, is an oppressively formidable public sphere, which is structurally incapable of providing individuals with concrete and meaningful social confirmation of their sense of reality (including their understanding of social processes, subjective meaning and personal identity), and an enfeebled private sphere, which is distressingly under-institutionalized, and which is structurally unable to provide reliable social parameters for the more mundane activity of everyday life and a plausible, well-integrated system of meaning which gives location and purpose to the individual's total life experience.

The condition of modernity, then, necessarily posits a crisis of meaning for individuals. The situation translates into human consciousness as a psychological anomie, with the individual experiencing a *spiritual hopelessness* (Camus) or *weightlessness*,[8] metaphorically floating without dependable, faithworthy (taken-for-granted) institutional anchors. Simultaneously, these factors converge to fashion an historically unique personality structure — the *other-directed individual*,[9] concerned with *impression management*,[10] or *Protean Man*,[11] performing chameleon-type identity shifts through the course of his biography according to the different social groups of which he is a part — in a situation defined appropriately as a *permanent identity crisis.*[12]

Naturally, the crisis of meaning (the experience of homelessness) varies in degree according to the relative proximity to the forces of modernity of both the individual himself and of the social structure to which he belongs. Those furthest away from the processes of modernization (empirically this means those of low level educational achievement; non-urban domicile; non-industrial and non-bureaucratic occupation; lower income levels; ethnic or minority racial origin; female gender, etc.) are less likely to experience these strains in their fullest and most sustained intensity. Those closest to these processes (those characterized by higher educational achievement; urban-suburban domicile; industrial or bureaucratic type of occupation; higher income level; dominant racial origin; male gender, etc.) are more likely to experience this type of cognitive uneasiness. Yet, despite these apparent social advantages, it is from among those in closest proximity to these forces, and therefore from those who experience these social-psychological strains most acutely, that protest is most likely to come.

# The Anthropological Protest Against Modernity

The protest is, in essence, not cultural, social or political, but rather anthropological. This is to say that the protest against modernity is rooted in the nature of the species, *homo sapiens*.

It is a commonplace that human beings have a remarkable capacity for adjustment in the face of difficult social and natural environments. Nonetheless, there are definite limitations to this human malleablity. The death of the human organism marks the human limit of adjustment to the harshest of natural ecological conditions; insanity marks the limit of adjustment to intemperate socio-cultural conditions. Prior to reaching these limits however, humans almost invariably struggle to resist the environment when the strains endemic to that environment threaten to become too great to bear. Man will in most circumstances pronounce the "No" of protest *when it is perceived* that the "Yes" of accommodation means the end of one's humanity — biological or psychological. Humans have a limited capacity to adjust to the conditions of anomie — a situation which is experienced as lacking any enduring, subjectively meaningful and relevant design. To do so is, as Turnbull's Mountain People exemplify, to risk extinction. Human beings almost inevitably react against these conditions.[13]

Holding these broadest theoretical generalities in reserve, one may say that what we have characterized as modernity structurally engenders precisely those conditions that are anthropologically intolerable. Thus, modernity itself spawns discontents among those who experience and induce protest — a protest that has been called the *demodernizing impulse*.[14]

Although this protest against modernity is fundamentally anthropological, it may and often does take social, cultural, and political expression. Historically, the expression of the demodernizing impulse in all these three forms is not new. The past two centuries of Western history are replete with examples. The mysticism of the Transcendentalist movement which was popularized by Emerson and Thoreau; Eastern mysticism advocated by upper class intellectuals in the Theosophical Society and, later, in the Vedanta Society; the Shaker movement; late nineteenth and early twentieth century Fundamentalism; and even aspects of the larger Romanticist movement in art and literature in the nineteenth century — may all be understood as various cultural expressions of the anthropological protest against modernity. The most recent significant expression of the protest is the counter-cultural movement of the 1960s and early 1970s, which extends, in its successor movements, to the present. Perhaps the most important cultural aspect of this latter phenomenon are the burgeoning myriad of new religions.

Thus, I am now in a position to state propositionally that the source of the new religious consciousness is in the anthropological protest against modernity. More precisely stated, the new religious consciousness is a cultural expression of the anthropological protest against the anomic structures intrinsic to modernity. As a demodernizing movement, the new religions are a sign that in some sectors of modern society, the strains of modernity have reached the limits of human tolerance, and are thus symbolic, at both the collective and the social-psychological levels, of the desire for relief and assuagement.

One point of clarification should be made here. Although new religions are here all classified as demodernizing movements, these movements do differ considerably one from another in the thrust of their challenge to modernity. Some of them embrace ideologies and adopt strategies of organization and activity, and promote life-styles which have the appearance of being not merely consonant with modernity, but even of being an espousal and a celebration of it. Let me exemplify: Scientology and the Unification Church are movements that are both decidedly pro-science and pro-technology, and so, ostensibly pro-modern. Scientology appears to claim, in its very name, as well as in its quasi-scientific therapeutic procedures, the imprimatur of science and technology. Nonetheless, much as it claims to offer its votaries better techniques based on fundamental "scientific" research, for the improvement of their intelligence and their lives, Scientology is itself rejected by modern science. Its claims are unsubstantiated by those outside the movement. In its salesmanship (its attempt to induce those who do become involved to continue in ever more advanced courses); in its development of increasingly metaphysical theories; and also in the segregated and intense total organization of the lives of its inner cadres, Scientology also manifests characteristics that can readily be seen to be at variance with the normal practice and assumptions of modern everyday life. Structurally, if not ideologically, the movement stands counter to much of modern life and social organization. In particular, of course, it claims to neutralize the anomic effects that life in modern society produces, and it offers the prospect of a life without this type of strain and tension, first for individuals and, ultimately, for mankind at large. That utopian ideal is radically anti-modern. The Unification Church also endorses modern science, but the structure of the movement, particularly in its communal organization and in its emphasis on individual care, stands in sharp contrast to the structural arrangements and the value-orientations of modern life.

What is unique about the counter-culture in general and the new religions in particular, in relation to demodernizing movements of the past, is a quantitative shift. Demodernizing movements of the past remained sequestered in fairly small and isolated socio-cultural enclaves. The new religions are representative of a large-scale cultural phenomenon. Never before has a demodernizing movement been so pervasive and so rapidly and so widely disseminated, attesting to the extent to which the discontents of modernity have become diffused. The new religions are unique because of a qualitative shift as well. The protest represented by the rise of the new religions is, as a whole, more extreme than that of most other demodernizing movements of the past, leading to much more radical departures from the assumptions of everyday life. This is brought into relief by the radical disjunction which many of these religions manifest between their own life-style and values and those of the dominant patterns of the modern societies in which they arise.

## Principal Features of the New Religions

More than a symbol of the need for relief, the new religions are concrete attempts to resolve the perplexities experienced by modern man. In attempting to provide such a solution the new religions are distinctively characterized in that they in greater or lesser degree reflect the opposition to the strains imposed by the double-bind of modernity, an overly rational, abstract public sphere and a radically de-institutionalized private sphere. To take the latter dimension first: if the dominant social psychological effect of modernity is the experience of "homelessness," then, the most likely solution will be an attempt to restore a sense of "being at home" by reconstructing or reimposing institutionally reliable meanings upon existence. As it is true for demodernizing movements on the whole, so it is with the new religions, namely, that the principal feature of the spirit of protest is an *absolutism* or *totalism*.[15] This manifests itself at the cognitive level as well as the socio-organizational level of human experience.

At the cognitive level, this is expressed in a variety of ways. Within the new religions absolutism is present, almost by definition — the "pure consciousness" advocated by Transcendental Meditation; "eternal bliss" offered by the Hare Krishna movement; "receiving Knowledge" from the Divine Light Mission; achieving "God Consciousness" through the Healthy Happy Holy Organization; and undergoing "Transpersonal Experience" (*e.g.*, being, essence, self-actualization, "oneness," "Cosmic awareness," "transcendence") in the Human Potential Movement, to name a few. All, in one form or another, profess to offer a superlative, providing its possessor with an ultimate system of relevance which transcends the bland ordinariness and meaninglessness of everyday life in the modern world.

At the social-behavioral level, absolutism is expressed variously as a communitarianism, which may vary from the part-time quasi-communities[16] such as the encounter group and sensitivity training groups of the human potential movement to the communities of the neo-Christian movement and the communal *ashrams* of the neo-Eastern religious movement. As Zablocki points out, communitarianism (specifically the communal structure) is basically a modern phenomenon which, however, may be understood as a demodernizing form of social organization.[17] Indeed the protest and reaction to the experience of homelessness produced by modernity is such that the social structure of the new religions in many cases approximates, when it does not replicate, a *total institutionalization* — a microcosmic totalitarianism as a means of tangibly re-establishing a home-world for its members.[18] Synanon, the Unification Church, and the Children of God are especially notable in this regard.

Parenthetically, it may be noted that it is not happenstance that communitarianism, in its various forms, is a predominant mode of social organization in the new religions. It provides perhaps the only type of social structure by which a socially deviant meaning system can be plausibly maintained among its members. It provides a thorough insulation and protection from the cognitize contamination that a sustained encounter with "the world" necessarily brings about. It therefore performs a cognitive survival function. The quasi-communitarianism of the human potential movement functions similarly to ensure that the individual maintains a cognitive allegiance to his/ her world-view.

Thus the cognitive and organizational absolutism implicitly offered by the new religions is counter-poised against the institutional ambiguity of the modern social world. It offers to bridge the hiatus between public and private spheres, renewing symbolic and actual symmetry in individual life experience. In this way, the new religions offer cognitive easement from the tensions that such institutional ambiguity begets. Although it is certainly the principal characteristic of the spirit of protest, absolutism is not the only one. It must be understood in association with another important feature, one born specifically in protest against the abstract character of the public sphere.

As was previously advanced, social experience in the public sphere is typically unsatisfying. Its structures confront man as an abstract and incomprehensible labyrinth; its rationality is detached from subjectively meaningful values and aspirations. These things are, therefore, perceived as "not real," or as unnatural perversions of social existence. All demodernizing movements exhibit, to a greater or lesser degree, a rejection of the "cold, lifeless and artificial forms" of thought, behavior, and relationship, and manifest an affinity for the expressive and particularistic at all three levels. The emotionally spontaneous is understood to be "more natural" than the rationally engineered; the subjective experience of reality is understood to be "more real" than the objective, institutionally defined reality, and therefore, the former is assigned greater positive value than the latter. This is particularly true for the new religions. The ideological elements of expressivism and particularism can be seen in the mysticism of the neo-oriental and neo-Christian groups (from Zen to Charismatic Renewal) as well as in the orgiastic rituals of the human potential groups (*e.g.*, Silva Mind Control, Arica, est, and others.)

Yet, I should note, in this regard, that the orientation toward expressivism does not simply result from a disaffection with the functional rationalism and utilitarianism of the public sphere. There is an important structural process which encourages this response. That process is what Gehlen refers to as *subjectivization*.

According to Gehlen, subjectivization is a corollary process to de-institutionalization. When, over the course of time, stable institutional routines and habits are rendered implausible or inconceivable — no longer taken for granted — behavior, morality, and the like are transplanted to the realm of choice. Individuals then must necessarily turn inward to the subjective, and must seriously and continuously reflect, ponder and probe their newfound choices. This is not to suggest that each individual constructs *ex nihilo* his own life patterns. Options already exist because of the pluralization of cultures. Although innovation is inevitable, it is essentially this plurality of cultural options upon which the individual must reflect and from among which he must choose. Personal independence (*e.g.*, doing one's own thing in life), then, is not simply a social fashion, but rather a structural necessity. Yet, this process presupposes that the individual may engage in a process of turning to his own subjective apprehensions in determining his choices. Helmut Schelsky called this phenomenon the "permanent-reflectiveness" intrinsic to modernity.

One consequence of subjectivization is a shift in self-perception. In more archaic societies, identities were assigned at birth and were socially reinforced throughout the course of the individual's biography. With the de-institutionalization of identity, the question of personal identity shifted to the foreground of choice. Choosing "who one is" again presupposes the process of subjectivization. Hence the "self" becomes a territory without boundaries, ready to be explored, probed, excavated, and charted. The lack of institutional supports for identity make the territory liable to change. Thus, there are always new depths of the self beckoning to be explored.[19]

Subjectivization, the structural process necessitating a "turn within" to reflect on life patterns and identity (and not so much a failure of the moral character of the individual), fosters a *subjectivism* within the culture — an orientation marked not so much by vanity and egoism as it is by an incessant preoccupation with the complexities of one's individual subjectivity, pleasing or displeasing as that may be. Subjectivism may vary in degree from society to society. In the extreme, subjectivism may translate into a narcissism.[20] The latter is particularly encouraged by the dynamics of modern monopoly capitalism. Regardless of this variability, it is an orientation built into modernity and therefore a salient feature within the culture of all modern societies.

This structurally-rooted subjectivism provides a buttress, if not an added dimension, to the highly subjective expressiveness which ensues from the protest against the abstract rationalism of the public sphere. Most demodernizing movements, then, are accented by strong traces of subjectivism.[21] This is particularly true of the new religions. Within the human potential movement "transpersonal techniques are used to achieve the sense realization of Self beyond the everyday self. Put another way, they facilitate an encounter with one's being."[22] Thus, personal-growth programs overtly foster a subjectivism among those who follow them. By fostering it, they also legitimate such subjectivism. Although usually less overtly, the neo-Eastern and neo-Christian religions perform the same function. In this latter case, the exploration of one's subjectivity is usually couched in terms of aligning one's being with one or a number of cosmic forces or deities — an exercise which may take a considerable time, effort and, often, expense. In all of this, there are, as Joseph Fichter has noted, strong narcissistic qualities about the movements.[23] They are narcissistic in the sense that the "self" is deliberately assigned an inflated significance, indeed, an historically unprecedented preeminence as against the collective weal.

What is suggested, then, is that there is an underlying infrastructure to all cultural manifestations of the anthropological protest against modernity. It takes shape in opposition to the dilemma of modernity. Its most rudimentary feature is a cognitive and socio-organizational absolutism. This is accented, however, by an orientation toward expressivism and subjectivism which may reach narcissine proportions.

## Other Theory on the Topic

It is, of course, clear that the interpretation offered here is not in fundamental conflict with that put forward from other theoretical perspectives. It is not presumed that this perspective offers an entirely unique approach to the phenomenon. Yet, it can be argued that it does have its own distinctiveness and, at least, that it throws new light on the subject, providing a basis on which an integration of previous theory on the subject may be accomplished.

A number of attempts to account for the rise of the new religions have been advanced and have been catalogued under several broadly defined rubrics.[24] One perspective contends that the cause of the re-charismatization within the culture is found in the response to *normative breakdown* and *value dissensus*. One important proponent of this view is Charles Glock, who argues that it is the proliferation of scientific rationalism in the culture which "undermines the underlying assumptions of the old imageries, the cultural values and social arrangements informed by them and the inherent ability of these world-views to give meaning and purpose" while offering "no clear alternative formula either for organizing society or for living one's life."[25] Along similar lines, Robert Bellah contends that "the deepest cause...was...the inability of utilitarian individualism" and technical reason, dominant within the culture, "to provide a meaningful pattern of personal and social existence, especially when its alliance with biblical religion began to sag because biblical religion itself had been gutted in the process."[26]

From a related perspective it is argued that the effect of structural differentiation on individual existence (*e.g.*, the fragmentation of identity into functionally specific roles) encourages the formation of groups which offer a holistic conception of both reality and the self.[27] Very closely connected with this perspective is the view which emphasizes the quest for a sense of community among individuals who are dissatisfied with their life experience in an atomized and structurally disjointed "mass society."[28] The result of such a quest is the development of functional alternatives to extended families and traditional communities — communes and quasi-communes — which are capable of solving the problems of disjuncture by reintegrating the individual's life experience into a coherent totality, thus protecting their members from the world, or providing them with adjustment for a renewed participation in the world.[29]

Without belaboring a body of literature familiar to all students of modern religion, it is clear that there is a great deal of overlap between these explanations and the perspective put forth here. Yet, most of the interpretations that are offered focus upon one or another isolated aspect of a larger problem. The problems of scientific rationalism, the instrumentalism of utilitarianism and technical reason, structural differentiation, and the atomization of mass society are all different though related features of modernity. The *composite effect* of these is captured in what has here been labeled the dilemma of modernity, in a word, an abstract and overly-rational public sphere, and a de-institutionalized private sphere. The elaboration of the perspective offered here, especially of the concepts of de-institutionalization and subjectivization, brings into relief structural dimensions hitherto unaccounted for in the literature which seeks to account for the rise and character of the new religions.

Perhaps the most important contribution of the perspective offered here is the deliberate connection of the perplexities intrinsic to modernity with a philosophical anthropology. The varying perspectives gain added coherence when viewed in relation to a philosophical conception of man. The answer to the question "why have the new religions emerged?" may, then, be more adequately understood.

Normative breakdown, value dissensus, and the resulting moral ambiguity are causal factors in the upsurge of the new religions because there is an anthropological requirement of stable and reliable parameters for individual existence. This latter is something which modernity fails adequately to provide, but something which the new religions promise to supply. There is a quest for community, not simply for unnamed "needs," but because of the anthropologically grounded fact of human sociality — something obstructed by modernity: something promised by the new religions. Finally, a fragmented personal identity and a fragmented general conception of reality is a causal factor because of the anthropologically-rooted demand for a world that has a more or less total and integrated intelligibility, a world that makes sense — which is again something intrinsically denied by modernity, but something which is offered by the new religions. All of the perspectives of causality that we have reviewed declare, or imply, that the new religions offer to meet a human need not presently met. But rarely, if ever, do they state what that need is and why it exists. I suggest that these differing perspectives might be interpreted in light of these philosophical considerations, specifically as rooted in the anthropological protest against modernity.

As such, this perspective offers a broader interpretive framework for understanding the new religions. The new religions are to be understood as a demodernizing movement, unique in its own right, to be sure, yet still one among others in the historical legacy of modernity in the West.

## Conclusions

The foregoing are broad brush strokes. They lack shade and nuance, detail, and qualification. Clearly a major theoretical synthesis is necessary to refine, and improve upon, the propositions here outlined. Notwithstanding theoretical imprecision, the foregoing has offered a purview of a theoretical tradition, the contributions of which have been largely ignored in research on the new religions, but the insights of which invite serious consideration. Its proposition are not abstract and/or merely the results of "grand theory," but are capable of being subjected to the rigor of empirical analysis. The assimilation of the special insights of this tradition within empirical research on the new religions might prove to be a very fruitful alliance in a further understanding of the rise of the new religions in the modern world.

• • • • • • • • • • • • • • • • • • • • • • • • • • • •

# Notes

1   See Talcott Parsons, *The System of Modern Societies*, Englewood Cliffs, N.J.: Prentice Hall, 1971, Anton Zijderveld, *The Abstract Society*, Garden City, N.Y.: Doubleday, 1970, and Thomas Luckmann, *The Invisible Religion*, New York: Macmillan, 1967.

2   See Peter Blau, *Bureaucracy in Modern Society*, New York: Random House, 1956, Jacques Ellul, *The Technological Society*, New York: Vintage, 1960.

3   See Peter Berger, Brigitte Berger, and Hansfried Kellner, *The Homeless Mind*, New York: Vintage, 1974, T. Luckmann, *op. cit.*, Richard Sennett, *The Fall of Public Man*, New York: Vintage, 1978, Jürgen Habermas, "The Public Sphere," *The New German Critique*, 3, 1974.

4   Peter Berger, *The Heretical Imperative*, Garden City, N.Y.: Doubleday, 1979; P. Berger *et al.*, *op. cit.*; Robert Nisbet, *The Quest for Community*, New York: Oxford University Press, 1953.

5   See Arnold Gehlen, *Urmensch und Spätkultur*, Bonn: Athanauem, 1956; see also P. Berger and H. Kellner, "Arnold Gehlen and the Theory of Institutions," *Social Research*, 32, 1, 1965.

6   See A. Zijderveld, *op. cit.*

7   P. Berger *et al.*, *op. cit.*

8   Lionel Trilling, *Sincerity and Authenticity*, Cambridge, Mass.: Harvard University Press, 1972.

9   See David Riesman, *The Lonely Crowd*, New Haven: Yale University Press, 1966.

10  See Erving Goffman, *The Presentation of the Self in Everyday Life*, Garden City, N.Y.: Doubleday, 1959.

11  Robert Jay Lifton, "Protean Man," *Partisan Review*, 25, 1, 1968.

12  P. Berger, "Modern Identity: Crisis and Continuity" in Wilton Dillon (ed.), *The Cultural Drama*, Washington: Smithsonian, 1974; Orrin Klapp, *Collective Search for Identity*, New York: Holt, Rinehart and Winston, 1969.

13  Let me be direct about what is implied in this point. Namely, that at the core of these propositions is a certain philosophical anthropology — one that underlies the entire German humanistic tradition in sociology. The central presupposition of this philosophical anthropology is that man has a craving for meaning that has the force of an innate drive. Berger's elaboration of this in *The Sacred Canopy* is helpful. Men are congenitally compelled to impose a meaningful order upon reality. This order, however, presupposes the social enterprise of ordering world-construction. To be separated from society exposes the individual to a multiplicity of dangers with which he is unable to cope by himself, in the extreme case to the danger of imminent extinction. Separation from society also inflicts unbearable psychological tensions upon the individual, tensions that are grounded in the root anthropological fact of sociality. The ultimate danger of such separation, however, is the danger of meaninglessness. This danger is the nightmare *par excellence*, in which the individual is submerged in a world of disorder, senselessness and madness (Berger, 1969:22). While all philosophical anthropologies

reside in the domain of unverifiable conjecture, the validity and utility of this particular philosophical anthropology is supported by the aforementioned research on the biological constitution of man. Without the instinct to order human activity and thought, the human organism is rendered helpless. Instinctual deprivation *requires* humans to make up for this inadequacy through the construction of institutions which function like instincts. The biological, and therefore psychological, survival of the human organism depends upon this.

14    P. Berger, B. Berger and H. Kellner, *op. cit.*

15    See A. Zijderveld, *op. cit.*, p. 120.

16    See J. Marx and D. Ellison, "Sensitivity Training and Communes: Contemporary Quests for Community," *Pacific Sociological Review*, 18, 4, 1975.

17    See Benjamin Zablocki, *Alienation and Charisma*, Riverside N.J.: The Free Press, 1980.

18    The total institution is an ideal-type, not to be found in social reality. Even in the most totalitarian societies or micro-societies there can be found non-institutional or anti-institutional behavior and thought. Social organizations are *more* or *less* institutionalized or *more* or *less* totalitarian than others. The new religions, in most cases, tend to be among the *more* institutionalized examples. Thus, for example, in the Unification Church, although members do have the choice whether to marry a particular individual (after three years of membership), the selection has already been made for them. They have only to answer 'yes or no' not 'which one?' Yet should they agree with the Rev. Moon's selection, they do not have a choice as to when they get married, how they get married, or whether to live in proximity to one another before or after marriage. These aspects of the church's organization are totalitarian. The list of examples to be found in the Unification Church or in many of the other new religions of totalitarian control could easily be extended.

19    See Ralph Turner, "The Real Self: From Institution to Impulse," *American Journal of Sociology*, 85, 6, 1976.

20    See Christopher Lasch, The Culture of Narcissism, New York. W.W. Norton & Co., 1979, Tom Wolfe, "The Me Generation," *New York Magazine*, August, 1976, and R. Sennett, *op. cit.*

21    There is one qualification to this. Subjectivization occurs in situations where there is a high degree of institutional ambiguity. Thus the strong institutional control which some new religions impose upon their membership militates against this subjectivism.

22    D. Stone, "The Human Potential Movement" in Charles Y. Glock and Robert N. Bellah (eds.), T*he New Religious Consciousness*, Berkeley: University of California Press, 1976.

23    Joseph Fichter, "The Trend to Spiritual Narcissism," *Commonweal*, 105, 6, 1978.

24    T. Robbins, D. Anthony, and J. Richardson, "Theory and Research on Today's 'New Religions,'" *Sociological Analysis*, 39, 2, 1978.

25    C.Y. Glock, "Consciousness among Contemporary Youth: An Interpretation" in C.Y. Glock and R.N. Bellah (eds.), *op. cit.*; see also Allan Eister, "Culture Crises and New Religious Movements: A Paradigmatic Statement of a Theory of Cults" in Irving Zaretsky and Mark Leone (eds.), *Religious Movements in Contemporary America*, Princeton: Princeton University Press, 1974.

26    See R.N. Bellah, "The New Religious Consciousness and the Crisis of Modernity" in C.Y. Glock and R.N. Bellah (eds.), *op. cit.*, p. 339; see also, Steven Tipton, "Getting Saved from the Sixties," unpubd. doctoral dissertation, Harvard University, 1978; Christopher Evans, *Cults of Unreason*, New York: Spectrum, 1973; A. Mauss and D. Petersen, "Les 'Jesus Freaks' et Retour à la Respectabilité, ou la Prédiction des Fils Prodiques," *Social Compass*, 21, 3, 1974.

27    Cecil Bradfield, "Neo-Pentecostalism: A Preliminary Inquiry," paper presented to the Eastern Sociological Society, 1975; see also, John Marx and Buckart Holzner, "Ideological Primary Groups in Contemporary Cultural Movements," *Sociological Focus*, 8, 4, 1975.

[28]   See J. Richardson, M. Stewart, and R.B. Simmonds, *Organized Miracles: A Sociological Study of the Jesus Movement Organization*, New Brunswick, N.J.: Transaction Books, 1978; see also, Cecil Bradfield, "Our Kind of People: The Consequences of Neo-Pentecostalism for Social Participation," paper presented at the Association for the Sociology of Religion, 1976.

[29]   See J. Marx and D. Ellison, *op. cit.*

# SECULARIZATION, REVIVAL, AND CULT FORMATION

## RODNEY STARK and WILLIAM SIMS BAINBRIDGE

Secularization is the dominant theme in modern assessments of the future of religion. According to Webster, the term *secular* means "of or belonging to the world and worldly things as distinguished from the church and religious affairs." Secularization, then, means to become worldly. More specifically, modern writers use the term *secularization* to mean the erosion of belief in the supernatural — a loss of faith in the existence of otherworldly forces.

...[W]e argue that secularization is nothing new, that it is occurring constantly in all religious economies. Through secularization, sects are tamed and transformed into churches. Their initial otherworldliness is reduced and worldliness is accommodated. Secularization also eventually leads to the collapse of religious organizations as their extreme worldliness — their weak and vague conceptions of the supernatural — leaves them without the means to satisfy even the universal dimension of religious commitment. Thus, we regard secularization as the primary dynamic of religious economies, a self-limiting process that engenders revival (sect formation) and innovation (cult formation).

Most modern scholars, however, do not regard current trends of secularization as the harbinger of religious change, but as the final twilight of the gods. Many recognize that, in the past, secularization resulted only in the rise of new faiths, but they are convinced that a new factor has entered into and canceled the old equation: the rise of science. Science is expected to make religion implausible, and hence modern secularization will not produce new major religions, but an era of rationality in which

---

Rodney Stark and William Sims Bainbridge. "Secularization, Revival, and Cult Formation," in Rodney Stark and William Sims Bainbridge, *The Future of Religion*. Berkeley: University of California Press, 1985, pp. 429-456. Reproduced by permission.

mysticism can no longer find a significant place. Anthony F.C. Wallace (1966:264-265), among the most distinguished anthropologists of religion, spoke for the vast majority of modern social scientists when he wrote:

> ...the evolutionary future of religion is extinction. Belief in supernatural beings and in supernatural forces that affect nature without obeying nature's laws will erode and become only an interesting historical memory. To be sure, this event is not likely to occur in the next generation; the process will very likely take several hundred years, and there will always remain individuals, or even occasional small cult groups, who respond to hallucination, trance, and obsession with a supernaturalist interpretation. But as a cultural trait, belief in supernatural powers is doomed to die out, all over the world, as a result of the increasing adequacy and diffusion of scientific knowledge...the process is inevitable.

Clearly, science is a new and potent cultural force, and it has had dramatic impact on many religious organizations. Indeed, a major element in modern secularization involves the retreat by religious bodies from supernatural explanations of various phenomena as science has revealed the natural causes of these phenomena. Moreover, the impact of science has undoubtedly created a period of unusually rapid and extreme secularization. Today, many of the leading religious organizations of Western civilization are so secularized that, to the extent they refer to God at all, it is to the most distant, indistinct, impersonal, and inactive entity.

Thus, the issue is posed. Is this the end of the era of faith? Is science the basis for the "final secularization" of societies? Or is this simply a very dramatic swing of the age-old pendulum? Will this wave of secularization also be self-limiting?

Our theory of religion forces the conclusion that religion is not in its last days. We think that most modern scholars have misread the future because they have mistakenly identified the dominant religious traditions in modern society with the phenomenon of religion in general. Most observers have noted correctly that major Christian-Judaic organizations are failing, but they have not seen or appreciated the vigor of religion in less "respectable" quarters.

Our confidence that religion will persist follows directly from our analysis of what religion is and does, which we outline in Chapter 1. We conclude that supernatural assumptions are the only plausible source for many rewards that humans seem to desire intensely. Only the gods can assure us that suffering in this life will be compensated in the next. Indeed, only the gods can offer a next life — an escape from individual extinction. Only the gods can formulate a coherent plan for life, that is, make meaningful in a fully human way the existence of the natural world of our senses. It can be easily demonstrated that, as long as humans persist in such desires, systems of thought that posit the supernatural will always have a competitive edge over purely naturalistic meaning systems....

We see no reason to suppose that the diffusion of science will make humans in the future less motivated to escape death, less affected by tragedy, less inclined to ask, "What does it all mean?" True, science can challenge *some* of the claims made by historic religions, but it cannot provide the primary satisfactions that have long been the raison d'être of religions.

Our theory permits us to understand the rise and persistence of intellectual elites who can live without feeling intense religious needs. But it cannot be made compatible with the eventual mass triumph of scientific rationalism over supernaturalism. This means either that our theory is deeply flawed or that projections of secularization toward a religionless future are simply wrong.

Of course, we believe the latter is the case. Moreover, throughout previous chapters, we have examined many signs that religion per se remains robust in the modern era. One such sign is that those who have abandoned a specific religious affiliation and who report their religion as "none" are hardly the scientific, secular humanists they often are thought to be. ...[W]e find that "nones" often accept such deviant supernaturalism as astrology and are exceptionally attracted to yoga, Zen, and Transcendental Meditation. A second sign ... is that the majority of Americans who grew up in irreligious homes ("none") today belong to a Christian denomination (more often a very traditional one). Secularity in one generation typically is followed by reaffiliation in the next. Third, we ... note the relative vigor of the more evangelical Christian denominations. Although the most secularized churches are crumbling, those least secularized still thrive. Finally, it is myopic to note only the weakening of once-potent religious organizations while dismissing the significance of the rise of hundreds of new religions.

## The Secularization Process

[Elsewhere] we demonstrate ... that some very general explanations, about how humans can obtain valued rewards and avoid feared costs, can take the form only of compensators and also must postulate the existence of the supernatural. We define *religion* as a system of very general compensators based on supernatural assumptions. This permits a crucial distinction between magic and religion. Following Durkheim (1915), we characterize magic as offering only compensators for specific rewards. The most general compensators are beyond empirical test, but the same does not apply to very specific compensators. Thus, although religion may offer eternal life beyond the grave, a claim beyond evaluation, magic may offer to cure a specific ailment here and now. Indeed, magic competes with science in attempting to produce tangible results. Hence, magic often is very vulnerable to empirical disconfirmation. That magic is often disconfirmed empirically, although religion *need never* face such tests, provides the key to our arguments about science and secularization.

Religions that arise prior to the development of organized science will tend to include magic in their offerings. That is, they will deal not only in very general compensators (which are not subject to empirical evaluation), but will also offer some specific compensators that are subject to empirical evaluation. This will especially be the case for religions that attempt to monopolize a religious economy. ...[M]onopoly faiths must offer a considerable amount of magic.

*Science* is simply the name for the development of systematic procedures for evaluating explanations. The process of evaluation will always tend to drive out empirically testable explanations that are false or at least less efficient than some other explanation. In consequence, as science is more widely practiced, it will tend to drive out magic. This is no more than an application of Malinowski's famous middle-range proposition about magic, which, as deduced in our theory, takes the form: People will not exchange with the gods when a cheaper or more efficient alternative is known and available. This simply means that magical explanations about how to gain a desired reward (or avoid a damaging cost) will tend to be discredited by scientific test and to be discarded in favor of scientifically verified explanations.

This tendency has serious consequences for religions that include a significant magical component. Consider the case of the lightning rod (White, 1896). For centuries, the Christian church held that lightning was the palpable manifestation of divine wrath and that safety against lightning could be gained only by conforming to divine will. Because the bell towers of churches and cathedrals tended to be the only tall structures, they were the most common targets of lightning. Following damage or destruction of a bell tower by lightning, campaigns were launched to stamp out local wickedness and to raise funds to repair the tower.

Ben Franklin's invention of the lightning rod caused a crisis for the church. The rod demonstrably worked. The laity began to demand its installation on church towers — backing their demands with a threat to withhold funds to restore the tower should lightning strike it. The church had to admit either that Ben Franklin had the power to thwart divine retribution or that lightning was merely a natural phenomenon. Of course, they chose the latter. But, in so doing, they surrendered a well-known and dramatic magical claim about the nature of the supernatural. Such admissions call into question other claims made by a religion, including even those that are eternally immune from empirical disconfirmation.

Thus, the rise of science meant a retreat by religions that, originating in prescientific ages, contained significant elements of magic. In this way, these religions became increasingly secularized — they made progressively fewer claims about the powers of the supernatural and the extent to which the supernatural was active in the empirical world. Each of these retreats was noted and recorded for posterity.

Meanwhile, because science resulted in more efficacious explanations than did magic (indeed, science is the selection of efficacious explanations), scientists increasingly possessed highly valuable exchange resources. Hence, scientists have tended to become an elite and thus able to withstand opposition from religious elites. Because it can never be clear a priori just where the boundary between magic and religion lies — what seems beyond verification in one time often is easily verified in another — science engenders skepticism toward religion. And, as an elite, scientists are rewarded for such skepticism, and their skepticism tends to permeate all intellectual elites.

As this occurred, a somewhat novel instance of the church-sect process took place. Secularization usually transforms religious groups to bring them into lower tension with their environments. With the rise of science, some low tension bodies found their environment moving away from them. That is, as the general culture was made less hospitable to traditional supernaturalism, major Christian and Jewish groups found themselves in greater tension with their environment. To hold tightly to Genesis, for example was to move from lower to higher tension. To regain (or retain) low tension with society, and thus to best serve the needs of their most dominant and privileged members, these denominations had to water down their doctrines concerning the supernatural — especially those, such as faith healing, that involved demonstrable magic. And, of course, these groups have jettisoned one traditional tenet after another in order to stay in low tension.

Granted that, in the beginning, religious elites fought against the challenge of science. But, being committed to empirically vulnerable positions and opposing a new culture with obvious and profound practical payoffs, they lost. In this century, it has been religious intellectuals, not scientists, who have done the recanting. In recent decades, religious intellectuals have outdone themselves in disparaging traditional supernaturalism in an apparent effort to seek respectability in the eyes of secular intellectuals (cf. Robinson, 1963; Cox, 1965; Kueng, 1976).

Obviously, this is a much oversimplified sketch of modern secularization. We think it does identify key processes, but clearly it omits the rich complexities of concrete historical events (cf. Martin, 1978). These details are beyond the scope of our present needs. We also have not explained the rise of science beyond noting that more efficacious explanations will tend to drive out the less efficacious. Some scholars have even suggested that religion of certain kinds may itself stimulate growth of science, thus unintentionally accelerating its own decline (Westfall, 1958; Merton, 1970). This is not the place to assess social and historical processes of such magnitude. It is sufficient for present purposes to note the vulnerability of magical elements in religions to scientific disconfirmation. Therefore, let us turn our attention to modern times, when science is highly developed and the dominant religious organizations are severely eroded by repeated retreats from scientific disconfirmation.

When we examine these religious organizations, we find that today they offer only very weak general compensators. The conception of the supernatural they sustain has receded to a remote, inactive, almost nonexistent divinity. We see bishops and theologians denouncing as mere superstition the notion of a god "up there." Does a god who is not "up there" plausibly presside over heaven and offer triumph over death? Many of the most prestigious denominations offer mixed signals at best in answer to this question. Such religions have reached the point where they can no longer offer the quality of general compensators that has been the historic raison d'être of religions. They offer little solace to the bereaved, to the dying, to the poor, or to those who seek to understand the enigmas of existence (Stark and Glock, 1968; Kelley, 1972).

Simply because human societies have the blessings of advanced science does not mean that they are free from existential anxieties or from a desire for rewards that remain unobtainable. These desires persist because science cannot satisfy them. In similar fashion, radical politics ultimately fails to eradicate them. People may commit themselves to radicalism in hopes of satisfying desires for scarce rewards. But, should the revolution occur, relative scarcity (stratification) continues and unmet desires persist (in combination with those desires for unobtainable rewards that the revolutionary movement could not effectively address in the first place).

Given churches (and revolutionary regimes) that fail to meet the desires for efficacious compensators, faiths that effectively offer such compensators will have a most favorable market position. And, to the extent that religious innovation or dissent is possible, such faiths ought to thrive as a result of the secularization of the dominant religious organizations. This reaction against secularization is likely to take two primary forms: *revival* and *innovation*.

## REVIVAL

In response to an unmet demand for more efficacious compensators, movements will arise to restore the potency of the conventional religious traditions. This pattern is typified by the vigor of evangelical Protestantism and the growth of the Catholic charismatic movement in contemporary America. The tactic involved is simply to reassert the validity of the general compensators of traditional faith because these have not been (and cannot be) invalidated by scientific discovery.

However, such a reassertion raises the problems that led to the extreme secularization of the major denominations in the first place. Many elements of the Christian-Judaic tradition have, in fact, been disconfirmed by science. Not merely lightning, but the literal interpretation of creation and of the flood, indeed, the underlying astronomical and geological assumptions of the Bible clearly are discrepant with secular knowledge: The sun does not go around the earth and it seems incredible that it ever was stationary in the sky, no matter what God wanted to signal to His people. Thus, the trouble with revival is that it is heir to a whole cultural history, and this history is replete with defeats of doctrine by science. Moreover, as soon as this problem is dealt with by picking and choosing those parts of the tradition that remain invulnerable to disproof, secularization has been reintroduced as legitimate — science will dictate what doctrines can be accepted. Thus, revival seems to be chronically vulnerable to secularization and to lack long-term staying power, especially if there is an alternative. Such alternatives are created by the rise of new religious traditions.

## INNOVATION

The dominant faiths of today arose a very long time ago and offered desired explanations unavailable from science. That is, they were well suited to the culture in which they arose — they did not make claims that were obviously false at that time. In consequence, the dominant faiths suffer from an ineradicable history of defeat because they were not designed for our present culture. But this is not necessarily so for new faiths — faiths that arise to meet the circumstances of *this* culture. A new faith can offer a set of general compensators invulnerable to secularization. Such a faith will have no history of futile holding actions and past defeats by science. It will not have to admit to picking and choosing among its tenets, for it has none at risk. Put another way, new faiths can be fully in harmony with the culture without having to be in any way subservient to it.

A case in point is Mormonism. Although it claims to be merely the next unfolding of the Christian-Judaic tradition, it appeared in the 19th century and was fully compatible with scientific knowledge of that time. Indeed, a major denunciation of the Book of Mormon made by 19th-century Christian theologians was its modernity. Unlike the Bible, which posits a tiny earth and seems to regard the Mediterranean as the whole of the oceans, the Book of Mormon, although claiming to be of ancient origins, bases its accounts on the existence of a large world and on knowledge of all the continents and oceans. Indeed, its primary setting is in the New World; thus, it is aware of the existence of the western hemisphere and of details of the cultures and peoples to be found there. "Unfair," charged the Christian clergy. "How easy to prophesy of the past or of the present time!" wrote Alexander Campbell (1832:12).

As a new faith, Mormonism is much less vulnerable to empirical disconfirmation (although too great reliance on empirical arguments rooted in 19th-century anthropology may be a source of trouble). More recent faiths may entirely eschew empirically vulnerable claims and thus be wholly accommodated to science. This does not mean that a new faith must accommodate itself to prevailing *moral* norms. To the contrary, it would probably be strengthened if it fostered a stricter morality — faiths can lose credibility by being too inexpensive.

Thus, new faiths would appear to have much better long-run chances than do old faiths for maintaining highly efficacious compensators in the midst of a culture that is corrosive to magic. Of course, our predictions depend upon the continuing social influence of organized science. Although a new dark age might restore traditional Christianity to its former throne (Miller, 1960), a collapse of civilization could as easily establish contemporary cults as the dominant churches (Sorokin, 1941).

The argument we have developed thus far is incompatible with the dominant view of the relationship between secularization and religious innovation. The prevailing wisdom, best expressed by Bryan Wilson (1975b) and Richard Fenn (1978), is that the prevalence of cults or "new religions" in the modern world is part and parcel of the process of secularization *as such*. Thus, Wilson (1975b:80) argues that the modern world produces "a supermarket of faiths; received, jazzed-up, homespun, restored, imported and exotic. But all of them co-exist only because the wider society is so secular, because they are relatively unimportant consumer items." Wilson's evaluation of new religions as superficial and inauthentic is echoed by many others (Truzzi, 1970; Fenn, 1978).

This evaluation of cults is rooted in Christian-Judaic parochialism. That cults fall outside the dominant, respectable, religious traditions of Western civilization is taken a prima facie evidence of their fundamental inferiority. That, in the first century, Christianity was both deviant and unimpressive is ignored. New faiths are dismissed as inauthentic because they are new.

We suggest that anyone with a serious interest in empirically testing the worth of this judgment spend some time in one of the highly respectable denominations (Episcopalian, for example) and then spend some time with Mormons or Moonies. Then make a comparative judgment about the depth of commitment and the authenticity of these religious groups. It will be patent that Mormonism and the Unification Church are not "relatively unimportant consumer items." Furthermore, if we can demonstrate that cult movements are serving as alternatives to conventional faiths, what grounds remain for calling the one authentic and the other superficial? However, many modern cults do seem in many ways to be ill conceived and implausible. We expect that many of these will be short-lived and insignificant. But it takes only a *few* effective cults to serve as the vehicle for a massive religious renewal. Indeed, it might take only one.

Simply to equate cults with religious trivia and to make them a *symptom* of secularization is to miss the opportunity to investigate the link between secularization and religious innovation. Surely it is to deprive the concept of secularization of coherent meaning if we describe persons deeply engrossed in supernatural belief and worship as secularized. We therefore propose to examine cult formation as a religious reaction to secularization and to suggest that simply because some faiths retain little religious content is no reason to suppose that all faiths have been emptied of the power to satisfy fundamental human needs.

Another problem with the view that cults reflect secularization per se has been the failure to distinguish among cultic phenomena. ...[Elsewhere we argue that] not all cults are full-fledged religions. ...[O]nly cult movements are religions. Client cults deal primarily in magic, not religion, and consequently cannot bind their clients into stable organizations. Audience cults deal primarily in myth and entertainment. Because they function primarily through the mass media, audience cults attract considerable attention and may well be the basis for judgment of all cults as unimportant consumer items. Surely such a blanket judgment is absurd in light of the deaths of 917 members of the Jim Jones cult. People do not commit mass suicide on behalf of unimportant consumer items.

Given our line of analysis, it follows that the weaker the established religions become, the more religious innovation ought to occur and the more such innovation will be sustained by a growing population in search of new religious alternatives. Daniel Bell (1971:474) expressed the idea succinctly:

> Where religions fail, cults appear. This situation is the reverse of early Christian history where the new, coherent religion competed with multiple cults and drove them out because it had the superior strength of a theology and an organization. But when theology erodes and organization crumbles, when the institutional framework of religion begins to break up, the search for a direct experience which people can feel to be religious facilitates the rise of cults.

Although the low tension denominations are threatened everywhere and the challenge of science is a worldwide antagonist, the organizational and social weakness of conventional religion is more pronounced in some places than in others. For example, wherever rates of geographical migration are especially high, a greater proportion of the population will be free to experiment in search of more efficacious systems of compensators because their social bonds to the old organizations are loosened. Thus, we can expect great geographic variations and can test our theory through a geographic hypothesis: *Cults will abound where conventional churches are weakest.*

To follow the logic of the dominant view of secularization leads to a contrary prediction. Secularization is seen as an unstoppable trend. If we mean by secularization a decline in the credibility of all systems of thought that postulate the existence of the supernatural, then it follows that secularization produces people who resist supernatural explanations. To the extent that occurs, there will not exist a clientele for religion, whether new or old, or for magic. People who have turned their backs on the rich variety available within the Christian-Judaic tradition are unlikely to take up with exotic cults. This leads to a hypothesis wholly opposite to the one we have advanced: *Cults will be weakest where conventional churches are weakest.*

We have argued that the conventional religious organizations have been eroded by centuries of conflict and science. We have *not* argued that this has caused masses of people to lose their belief in some form of supernatural or their interest in very general compensators based on supernatural assumptions. Rather, we have argued that the mainline churches in the United States are failing to offer such compensators in effective form because these organizations have adopted very vague conceptions of the supernatural. Thus, our primary concern is with *organizational weakness* of the religious bodies within the Christian-Judaic tradition. Indeed, the hypotheses to be investigated make contradictory predictions about the relationship between the strength of traditional religious organizations and the vigor of religious innovation — the formation of cults. Hence, the most appropriate of available measures of organizational weakness is the rate of membership in conventional churches....

## Church Membership and Cult Movements in the 1970s

If our conclusions about the self-limiting character of secularization are correct, we ought to find that there is a significant *negative* correlation between the church membership rate and the cult movement rate... . That is, the higher the church membership rate of a state, the lower its cult movement rate ought to be.

If others are correct that secularization is a process that leads to the demise of religion — that people drop out of the traditional churches comfortably to accept a nonreligious outlook — then the sign of the correlation ought to be *positive*. Cults ought to flourish where traditional religion is strongest — where large numbers of "religious" people are still to be found. Two so diametrically opposed hypotheses provide a rare opportunity to conduct a crucial test of two lines of argument.

Our first computation revealed an $r$ of -.37 between the church membership rate and the cult rate using all 50 states as our units of analysis (see Table 19.1). This correlation is highly significant: .004. This is strong confirmation of our hypothesis that cult formation thrives in response to crumbling commitment to traditional religion. Cults do not flourish where traditional religion is strong, but in areas that, judging by membership in conventional religious groups, are the most secularized.

However, we were not satisfied that our initial analysis did justice to the real strength of the relationship. A major problem is a defect in our measure of the cult movement rate, which puts an artificial limit on the observed correlation. Nine states score zero on the index. This does not mean that they have no cult activity. Nor does it mean that they have the same amount of cult activity. It merely means that whatever level they have is unmeasured. Because these states differ considerably in terms of their church membership rates, they add a great deal of noise to the data and severely restrict the size of the potential correlation.

We therefore removed these nine states from the data. Recomputing $r$ based on the remaining 41 cases, the correlation increased to -.49 and significance improved beyond .001. Considering that a number of additional states with extremely similar and low cult rates (probably also poorly measured) still remain in the data, this seems to us a very high correlation lending considerable plausibility to our analysis of secularization.

---

**Table 19.1    Correlations (r) Between the Church Membership Rate and Various Cult Rates for States**

---

| Measure of Cult Activity | Correlation with Church Membership Rate | Significance |
|---|---|---|
| 1a. Cult Movement Rate | -.37 | .004 |
| 1b. Cult Movement Rate (with nine zero-rate states and New Mexico omitted) | -.61 | .001 |
| 2. Cult Centers Rate | -.52 | .001 |
| 3. New Age Stores and Restaurants Rate | -.33 | .009 |
| 4. *Fate* Letter Writers Rate | -.58 | .001 |
| 5. *Fate* Subscription Rate | -.68 | .001 |
| 6. Psychic Practitioners Rate | -.45 | .001 |
| 7. TM Initiation Rate 1970 | -.42 | .001 |
| 8. TM Initiation Rate 1975 | -.51 | .001 |
| 9. Astrologers Rate * | -.35 | .007 |

---

* N = 47; all others, N = 50.

However, we felt justified in making one additional change in the data. New Mexico is an extremely deviant case, lying far out from the slope of the observed correlation and greatly influencing it. This is easy to see, given that New Mexico is second highest in terms of cults (with a rate of 9.1 per million residents) while standing twelfth from the top in terms of church membership: 640 per 1,000. Deviant cases can occur by chance, by measurement error, or for quite specific reasons. This led us to make a laborious county-by-county analysis of how New Mexico produced its high rates. States are not the ideal unit of analysis for our study because they are not always very homogeneous in terms of social and cultural patterns. Thus, for example, the very low church membership rate of California tends to mask somewhat higher rates in less populous counties well inland from the coast. We have utilized states as our unit of analysis simply because it was not possible to create cult rates for smaller ecological units.

In the case of New Mexico, use of state as the unit of analysis turned out to be extremely misleading. New Mexico contains many counties with extraordinarily high church membership rates and others with very low rates. Summed, these produce a quite high overall membership rate for the state. However, the cults that give New Mexico its high rate on that measure are located in those counties with extremely low church membership rates. That is, within New Mexico, the expected relationship between secularization and cult formation holds very clearly. But, when New Mexico is taken as a whole, these extreme internal variations produce a highly deviant case that reduces the correlation between church membership and cult formation. For these reasons, we omitted New Mexico from the data set and recomputed the correlation on the basis of 40 cases. This resulted in an $r$ of -.61, significant beyond the .001 level.

We believe that we observed good methodological practices in dropping cases, as we have reported, and that the correlation of -.61 is the best of the three estimates of the extent to which the vigor of traditional religious bodies is negatively correlated with cult activity. Some readers, of course, may disagree. If so, we direct them to the highly significant correlation ($r = -1.37$) observed when all 50 cases were used. If we take that as the most credible estimate, we are still in the position of having clearly eliminated one hypothesis and supported the other. Cults flourish where membership in traditional religious bodies is low. They are rare where membership in traditional religious bodies is high.

...Belief in the supernatural does not vary nearly so much across regions of the United States as do church membership rates. Although a smaller proportion of persons along the West Coast hold such beliefs than elsewhere (and this is also the region where church membership is lowest), levels of belief remain quite high — for example, the great majority of persons living in California, Washington, and Oregon believe in a personal God and may pray frequently. Thus, although some persons in this region are not members of established churches because they have embraced a secular outlook, the modal person in this region retains belief in the supernatural while being unchurched. Secularization has reduced the traditional churches to a minority status, but it has not created an irreligious culture, only an unchurched one. This is precisely the condition under which we theorize that cults are bound to arise (if they are not ruthlessly suppressed).

What we have argued is that centuries of secularization have made ruins of many of the traditional religious bodies. But the process of secularization has not caused people to reject the possible existence of supernatural forces or caused them no longer to desire things that are difficult or impossible to obtain in this world. A simple application of the laws of supply and demand would lead one to expect that such a vacuum would tend to be filled. Indeed, many cults are founded in a purely entrepreneurial fashion. ...The data show that new religious movements are making many efforts to fill the vacuum being left by declining adherence to the traditional faiths.

# Other Cult Activity Measures

We have noted several limitations to the data on cult movements, particularly the inability to measure variations across states that lack a cult headquarters. In consequence, we sought other means to measure cult activity within states....

Our second measure is based on the *Spiritual Community Guide* (Singh, 1974). This guide does not list all the groups on which our cult movement rates are based, but it has the advantage of listing each of the centers or outposts of groups it covers, rather than just their headquarters. One section lists 1,345 centers and communities "devoted to the spiritual path, raising one's consciousness, transmitting higher knowledge or promoting universal love and unity," (Singh, 1974:110). Only three states failed to achieve at least one entry. Thus, in transforming these data into a rate of cult centers and communities per million residents for each state, we were able to distinguish among many states that were not differentiated by the cult movement rate. And the large number of cases probably helps distinguish among states with only one or two cult movements as well. The church membership rate is strongly negatively correlated with the cult centers rate: -.52 (significant at the .001 level). Again our hypothesis is sustained.

For a third measure of cult activity, we returned to the *Spiritual Community Guide*, which also provides a national list of "New Age" bookstores, foodstores, and restaurants offering magical nourishment for body and soul. The 1,023 stores and restaurants listed in the guide provided a new set of state rates for this very different indicator of cult activity. Again our hypothesis is confirmed by a correlation of -.33 with the church membership rate (significant at the .009 level). This measure is flawed because Vermont has a highly deviant rate, 60 per million, 3 times the second place state and 12 times the national average. When Vermont is removed, the correlation rises to -.56, significant well beyond the .001 level.

Our fourth measure of cult activity is based on coding 2,086 letters from readers published in *Fate* magazine from January 1960 through September 1979. Although the *Spiritual Community Guide* is the result of great diligence on the part of its editors, the fact that it comes from California suggests a possible geographic bias; so it is worth remembering that *Fate* magazine is edited and published in Illinois. Again we transformed the data into state rates per million residents. As can be seen in Table 19.1, once again our hypothesis is confirmed. Church membership is correlated -.58 with the *Fate* letter writers rate (significant at the .001 level).

Our fifth measure also comes from *Fate*, the tabulation of subscribers to the magazine kindly provided by the publisher, Curtis G. Fuller. A total of 82,812 persons received the November 1979 issue through the mail, 79,907 of them residents of the 50 states. These data on the magazine's circulation do not merely duplicate our earlier count of stories submitted by readers because most subscribers may enjoy *Fate* privately without risking censure from friends and family, but published stories broadcast their authors' involvement with the occult. This measure also shows a strong negative correlation with the church member rate, -.68.

A sixth measure of cult activity is based on *The International Psychic Register* (McQuaid, 1979), published in Erie, Pennsylvania. This comprehensive guide lists 705 "psychic and metaphysical practitioners" in the United States, including aura readers, dowsers, psychic investigators, parapsychologists, past lives readers, and tarot readers. Converting these listings into state rates per million residents, we found the psychic practitioners rate was highly correlated with each of our other measures. As shown in Table 19.1, this rate also replicates our previous results: It is correlated - .45 with the church membership rate.

Our seventh and eighth measures are complete figures for urban initiates to Transcendental Meditation for the years 1970 and 1975... . TM accepted the status of deviant cult movement in 1977, although it had previously presented itself as a relatively low tension client cult. The particular data set analyzed here lists the number of persons initiated each year whose homes were in 5,629 urban areas, a total of 16,066 in 1970 and 232,306 in 1975. In calculating rates, we divided each state's total initiates for a given year by the estimated urban population. We chose 1970 because it was the earliest single year for which we could calculate state rates and 1975 because it was the peak year for TM. Thus, we measured two different stages in the life cycle of one of the most popular recent cults. Again the correlations are significant and in the predicted direction, -.42 for 1970 and -.51 for 1975.

Our ninth and last measure is a tabulation of all 571 professional astrologers listed in all classified telephone directories for the nation's 277 standard metropolitan statistical areas. We found that this measure has a rather strong bias toward large cities compared with other measures, but, in a sense, this merely adds variety to what is, in toto, a very comprehensive set of indicators of cult activity. Unfortunately, two states lack metropolitan areas, and an anti-fortune-telling law in Pennsylvania prevents astrologers from advertising; so here we are reduced from 50 to 47 cases. But again we see an association that supports our hypothesis, -.35.

To sum up: Nine independent measures of cult activity yield identical results. Cult activity seems to be a *response* to secularization. Cults flourish where the conventional churches are weakest. Indeed, as already noted, the failure of the conventional churches to attract the majority of residents of West Coast states is not a symptom of the emergence of a population of atheists and agnostics; in that sense, secularization has made very little headway in American society. What organizational secularization has produced is a large population of unchurched people who retain their acceptance of the existence of the supernatural. They seem only to have lost their faith in the ability of the conventional churches to interpret and serve their belief in the supernatural. Hence, it should be no surprise that many of these unchurched believers are willing, perhaps eager, to examine new religions, to find a faith that can offer an active and vigorous conception of the supernatural that is compatible with modern culture.

# Secularization and Revival

Because revival represents an effort to protect and maintain deep attachments to the traditional religions, rather than the efforts to create new religions, we do not expect it to flourish where the traditional churches are weakest. To the contrary, we expect efforts at revival to be centered where the traditional churches are still reasonably vigorous. Put another way, if cult formation reflects the efforts of the unchurched to become churched, revival reflects the efforts of the churched to remain churched.

We conceive of religious revival primarily in terms of the emergence and growth of sect movements. As the traditional faiths move toward greater accommodation with secular society, they give birth to many groups that desire to retain or to reinstate more otherworldly versions of that faith. Sects are high tension, schismatic movements within a conventional (nondeviant) religious tradition.

Our analysis leads to the conclusion that cult and sect formation are not direct functional alternatives. Rather, we think they are quite different responses to secularization that predominate at different stages in the secularization process. Sect formation is, in part, a response to early stages of weakness in the general compensators provided by the conventional churches. Cult formation tends to erupt in later stages of church weakness, when large sectors of the population have drifted away from all organizational ties to the prevailing faiths.

Applied to cross-sectional data, this line of reasoning leads to the prediction that sect formation will be concentrated in areas with higher, rather than lower, church membership rates. But the situation is not as simple as with cults, and we might not expect as strong a relationship. For example, it might be that the relationship between the church membership rate and sect formation is slightly curvilinear, high in areas of moderate institutional decay of the low tension denominations and low where they are either well entrenched or very weak. Our data set, limited to a mere 50 cases (the states), does not permit sensitive statistical analysis to resolve all these complexities, but it is adequate for testing the main propositions.

[We have examined] American-born sects and identify a list slightly shorter than that of cult movements. We tabulate them similarly and code each existing sect group in the nation according to the state in which its headquarters is located. As with cults, many sects are small and have all their members in one state. But although few cults have an extensive membership, many sects are quite large and have members in many states. Having been forced to code a sect in one state only leaves much to be desired in terms of measurement. However, lacking state-by-state membership data on most sects, we had no other choice. And, as with the data on cult movements, a number of states were essentially unmeasured in terms of their sect activity, having no sect headquarters located within their borders.

When we compared the data on cult and sect movements, we found that the average sect is much older than the average cult. Sixty-one percent of the cult movements we identified had been founded since 1959, but only 20 percent of sects were this new. If we are right about sects tending to occur at an earlier stage of the secularization process, this is the kind of difference we ought to find between cults and sects. These findings also indicate that, at present, many more cults than sects are being formed. However, it appears that sects have been better able to survive in the United States, especially in earlier eras; hence, some of the difference in the average age of cults and sects is caused by the greater longevity of sects. Because only existing sects and cults can be counted with any accuracy, we are not able to show that many more sects than cults were forming in the United States 50 or 100 years ago. Our data conform to such a conclusion but cannot fully sustain it.

However, when we examine the correlation between the church membership rate and the sect rate, we find additional support for our hypothesis. Although the cult movement rate was strongly negatively correlated with the church membership rate, the sect movement rate is positively correlated with church membership. The correlation is +.25, significant at the .02 level. Sects tend to thrive where the conventional churches are stronger. This is not merely a case of autocorrelation, because few of our sects were willing, able, or asked to provide state and county data to the survey by the National Council of Churches; hence, they are not included in the church membership rates. Thus, it seems reasonable to conclude that sects and cults are not simply interchangeable responses to secularization, but are relatively different.

An additional way to demonstrate that cult and sect movements are not basically the same is to examine the relationships between them. We expect to find the absence of a positive correlation, which would indicate they are indeed phenomena with distinctive social significance and causes, and perhaps a slight negative correlation. Table 19.2 shows the correlations between the sect rate and our nine measures of cult activity.

The findings are very persuasive. All nine measures of cult activity are negatively correlated with the sect rate, five of them significantly. None shows a significant positive correlation. Two factors account for the lack of a significant negative correlation between cult and sect movement rates. First, both rates suffer from a lack of differentiation among a number of states having no cult and/or no sect headquarters. Many other states are virtually not differentiated on one or both measures because their rates are extremely low and hence about the same. (To remove all these cases would eliminate so many states that there are too few left for adequate analysis.) Because a lack of cult or sect headquarters tends to be associated with having a small population, some pressure toward a positive correlation is produced by many small states with artificially similar low scores on both cult and sect headquarters rates. A second problem is that there is a modest tendency for cult and sect headquarters to be located in regional urban centers as a matter of convenience. This tendency will also cause some positive correlation between the two rates. The net result is no correlation at all because negative and positive tendencies cancel out.

**Table 19.2 Correlations ($r$) Between the Sect Movement Rate and Various Cult Rates for States**

| Measure of Cult Activity | | Correlation with Sect Movement Rate | Significance |
|---|---|---|---|
| 1. | Cult Movement Rate | -.03 | .42 |
| 2. | Cult Centers Rate | -.40 | .002 |
| 3. | "New Age" Stores and Restaurants Rate | -.37 | .004 |
| 4. | *Fate* Letter Writers Rate | -.17 | .12 |
| 5. | *Fate* Subscription Rate | -.30 | .02 |
| 6. | Psychic Practitioners Rate | -.17 | .12 |
| 7. | TM Initiation Rate 1970 | -.43 | .001 |
| 8. | TM Initiation Rate 1975 | -.52 | .001 |
| 9. | Astrologers Rate* | -.17 | .13 |

*N – 47; all others, N = 50

The other eight measures of cult activity do not suffer from these problems — each gives a somewhat more sensitive measurement of interstate differences in cult activity. Although three of the eight correlations fall short of the .10 level of significance, the remaining five are individually significant, and the entire set adds up to a very convincing rejection of the null hypothesis. If Vermont is removed from the New Age stores and restaurants rate, its correlation with the sect movement rate strengthens to -.39, significant at the .003 level. Of course, our theory would have been confirmed merely by the lack of a positive correlation. These negative correlations give powerful confirmation that cults and sects are responses to very different stages in secularization.

We have worked with the best data available, but none of these measures is as good as might be desired. The best data can be produced only by a census or an extremely large survey study that would permit us to examine actual membership rates in all the various cult and sect movements in existence. Such data do not exist and probably never will.

Despite the limits of our various measures, the findings offer reasonably substantial support for our fundamental thesis. The weakening of the traditional churches does not seem to portend the sudden demise of religion. Secularization seems instead to be prompting its own religious solutions. While the mainline denominations discard their traditional confessions, clash over the ordination of women and homosexuals, and often seem to regard the governance of South Africa as the central religious matter of the day (and, in so doing, alienate thousands more of their current members), other movements, both sects and cults, are dealing in a far richer expression of the supernatural.

Given that our rates are based on 501 current cult movements and 417 active sects, the nation does not lack for religious alternatives. These data lead to the conclusion that the current wonderment over the present wave of deviant religion and mysticism is misplaced. The current vitality of deviant religion is amazing only on the assumption that religion in general is being overwhelmed by secularization. If we see that only particular religious organizations, albeit those with the longest history and the highest social standing, are crumbling, not religion in general, then it should be no surprise that new organizations are moving in on the market no longer effectively served by the old ones....

## Conclusion

Secularization, even in the scientific age, is a self-limiting process. This theoretical proposition is supported by consistent correlations linking cult activity with low rates of church membership. Whether we look at cult formation, represented by the cult movements rate, or at client cult offices and occult magazine readers, we see the same thing. The statistical associations hold steady over a span of five decades and are based on thousands of cases. Cults do abound where the conventional churches are weakest.

We are *not* suggesting that cult movements are currently filling the gap left by the weakness of conventional religion. It is clear in our American data that, even with all the cult members added in, the Pacific region still has a very low religious membership rate. ...

We do not posit a steady-state religious economy in which cults immediately make up deficits in conventional religious affiliation. We argue only that, to the degree a population is unchurched, there will be *efforts* to fill the void. Most such efforts will be abortive, for most cults are ill conceived and badly led or lose heart as even a high rate of annual growth produces only a small absolute number of members over the first several decades of recruitment efforts. Thus, most cults will have no impact on the void left by secularization. Only once in a while will an effective, rapidly growing cult movement appear. We cannot predict accurately *when* that will happen. But we think we can say *where* this is apt to happen and *why*.

Until effective cult movements appear, an area may remain indefinitely low in church membership — indeed, the Unchurched Belt along the West Coast of the

United States has persisted for a century. Hundreds of cult movements have arisen there, as our theory predicts. When one of them will achieve real success, we cannot say. We notice, however, that the Mormons have greatly increased their membership each decade during this century. Should their growth continue for only a few more decades, the Pacific region may no longer be low in religious affiliation. Or perhaps the new religion for the Pacific region has but 50 members today.

However, we do not expect any single new religious movement to rise to the dominant position so long enjoyed by Christianity. ...[P]luralism is the natural state of religious economies, and even the limited success of Christianity in achieving a religious monopoly depended on enlisting the coercive powers of the state. Hence, unless a massive cultural shift enables a new religion to gain an exclusive franchise, no one religion will ever again even appear to be universal. Rather, we anticipate that the future will more closely resemble the Roman Empire than the Holy Roman Empire. A number of vigorous religious traditions will coexist.

Most cults in America do not conform to our expectations of what a really successful faith of the future would be like. Many current cults, such as the various witchcraft and pagan groups, have reacted to secularization by a headlong plunge back into magic. They reject the whole scientific culture as well as Christian-Judaic religious traditions. They succeed in gathering a few members because they claim to offer extremely efficacious compensators. They unblushingly promise to give the individual the power to harness supernatural powers to manipulate the natural world. In our judgment, these cults are reactionary and have little future. They are utterly vulnerable to the same forces of secularization that have corroded much better organized and accommodated faiths. They will not thrive unless the modern world itself collapses.

Other current cult movements have reacted to secularization by adopting a scientific facade. TM used this tactic for a considerable time, and Scientology remains an outstanding example. The problem with these groups is that their "science" is very vulnerable to empirical evaluation and most likely will be revealed as magic if and when such evaluations are made. But that may not do them real harm so long as true science is unable to offer the specific rewards for which these cults offer mere compensators. There is an immense literature exposing the scientific inadequacy of Psychoanalysis, but it remains a very lucrative profession....

In our judgment, faiths suited to the future will contain no magic, only religion This will not, of course, allow them to escape the long run forces of secularization — all successful faiths are fated to be tamed by the world. But faiths containing only religion will be immune to scientific attack and thus will avoid the accelerated secularization in effect during recent centuries.

Perhaps all contemporary cult movements contain too much magic to become really successful mass movements. But simply because we cannot point to an apt example does not mean that none exists or that one will not be born tomorrow.

Contemporary observers also failed to notice earlier great world religions during their formative periods. As the poet William Butler Yeats asked,

And what rough beast, its hour come round at last,
Slouches towards Bethlehem to be born?

• • • • • • • • • • • • • • • • • • • • • • • • •

# References

Bell, Daniel
    1971      "Religion in the Sixties." *Social research* 38: 447-497.

Campbell, Alexander
    1832      *An Analysis of the Book of Mormon.* Boston: Benjamin H. Greene.

Cox, Harvey
    1965      *The Secular City.* New York: Macmillan

Fenn, Richard K.
    1978      *Toward a Theory of Secularization.* Ellingon, CT: Society for the Scientific Study of Religion.

Kelly, Dean
    1972      *Why Conservative Churches Are Growing.* New York: Harper and Row.

Kung, Hans
    1976      *On Being a Christian.* Garden City, NY: Doubleday.

Martin, David
    1978      *A General Theory of Secularization.* New York: Harper and Row.

McQuaid, Donald A.
    1979      *The International Psychic Register.* Erie, PA: Orion Press.

Merton, Robert K.
    1970      *Science, Technology and Society in Seventeenth-Century England.* New York: Harper and Row.

Miller, Walter M., Jr.
    1960      *A Canticle for Leibowitz.* Philadelphia: Lippincott.

Robinson, John A.T.
    1963      *Honest to God.* Philadelphia: Westminster Press.

Singh, Parmatma (Howard Weiss)
    1974      *Spiritual Community Guide, 1975-76.* San Rafael, CA: Spiritual Community Pub.

Sorokin, Pitirim A.
    1941      *The Crisis of Our Age.* New York: Dutton.

Stark, Rodney and Charles Y. Glock
    1968      *American Piety.* Berkeley, CA: University of California Press.

Truzzi, Marcello
    1970     "The Occult Revival as Popular Culture: Some Random Observations on Old and Nouveau Witch." *Sociological Quarterly* 13: 16-36.

Wallace, Anthony F.C.
    1966     *Religion: An Anthropological View*. New York: Random House.

Westfall, Richard S.
    1958     *Science and Religion in Seventeenth-Century England*. New Haven, CT: Yale University Press.

White, A.D.
    1896     *A History of the Warfare of Science and Theology in Christendom*. Gloucester, MA: Peter Smith (1978).

Wilson, Bryan R.
    1975     "The Secularization Debate." *Encounter* 45: 77-83.

# WHO JOINS NEW RELIGIOUS MOVEMENTS AND WHY?

## Introduction to the Readings

The most common question asked by the public about NRMs is "Why would anyone join a cult?" Some obvious initial answers are proposed by the readings in the previous section of this book. NRMs seem to satisfy the strong need of some people for a life with more moral certainty and purpose, and some kind of distinct "spiritual" or "transcendental" focus. But such broad generalizations do not sufficiently delimit the appeal of NRMs. Many people identify with the dis-ease of de-institutionalization discussed by Hunter, or with the idealism and disillusionment of the baby boomers as discussed by Robert Bellah (1976) and others like Roof. But only a small percentage of these ever entertain joining an NRM. Without pretending to be able to accurately discern the motivations of others, in this section I have tried to provide a more detailed insight into why someone might join an NRM by bringing together three important essays striving to give more specific social-psychological form to the anomie and alienation that Hunter, Bellah and others have hypothesized are afflicting the young people in our society.

Discussion of this point leads us into the heart of the controversy surrounding NRMs: the persistently reiterated charge of the anti-cult movement that NRMs use deceptive and injurious techniques of "brainwashing" to recruit members. This is the specific subject matter of the next section of readings. Attention is directed here at setting the stage further by first reading two of the best known and most influential social scientific analyses of why people join marginal or deviant religions: Charles Glock's "The Role of Deprivation in the Origin and Evolution of Religious Groups" (1964) and John Lofland and Rodney Stark's "On Becoming a World-Saver: A Theory of Conversion to a Deviant Perspective" (1965). These two essays have framed three decades of research on religious conversions.

Sociologists, historians, and others have traditionally explained why people join sects and cults in terms of some complementary set of "pushes" and "pulls." People are predisposed, it is argued, by certain social and psychological forces or characteristics to have certain interests or to take certain actions which push them towards joining unusual groups. Likewise, the beliefs or ideology of these groups are thought to exert an attraction, pulling people with the appropriate predispositions into group membership. Studies of why people joined various Christian sects in the nineteenth century and early twentieth century (e.g., Seventh Day Adventists, Christian Scientists, Jehovah's Witnesses, Pentecostalism) proposed that the primary push was economic deprivation. The pull was threefold: (1) the promise of reward in the next life for accepting one's lowly lot in this life with proper Christian humility, (2) spiritual compensation in this life from the consequent belief that "while we may be poor, we are virtuous," (3) and more immediate psychic compensations from being involved in ecstatic and highly emotional religious experiences. Genuinely poor people, it is argued, were seeking an escape from the hardships and humiliations of life.

The basic elements of this scheme are displayed in the essays of Glock and of Lofland and Stark. But by the time they were writing it was already apparent that the socio-economic status of sectarians was on the rise (e.g., Wilson, 1961; Calley, 1965). Not only the poor join sects. It was also increasingly apparent that the processes by which conversions occurred are more complicated than previously acknowledged. In response to the changing sensibilities of scholarship, Glock (along with others like Aberle, 1962) argued that whether people really are deprived or not may not be very important in determining who joins NRMs. If people perceive a discrepancy between the social rewards they feel entitled to and the rewards they think they are getting, or they believe others are getting, and if they fail to perceive or accept some rational conception of the causes of their deprivation, then there will be an incentive to launch or join a movement that promises change or compensation. The deprivation in question is "relative" and "subjective" (though it may also be real), and as Glock suggests there may be at least five different forms of this subjective sense of deprivation (1964: 27-28): economic, social, organismic, psychic, and ethical deprivation.

Glock proposes that relative deprivation in one of these form, or some combination, is a "necessary" condition for the rise of NRMs. It explains why even relatively privileged individuals are willing to incur sacrifices to join NRMs and change their lives. It is not, however, a "sufficient" condition — it is not enough, by itself, to explain the emergence of an NRM. To bring an NRM into being it is also necessary "that the deprivation be shared, that no alternative institutional arrangements for [the] resolution [of the relative deprivation] are perceived, and that a leadership emerge with an innovating idea for building a movement out of the existing deprivation" (Glock, 1964: 29). Nevertheless, study of the beliefs, practices, and organization of particular groups, Glock implies, should tell us quite a bit about what kinds of deprivations probably motivated people to join the groups in question, since the former can be interpreted as responses to the latter (Glock, 1964: 33).

Lofland and Stark responded to the changing sensibilities of scholarship by doing one of the earliest and certainly most rewarding participant observation field studies of a contemporary NRM. From the accounts of converts to a small and obscure group, soon to become, however, one of the largest and most controversial NRMs, namely the "Moonies" (The Unification Church of Reverend Sun Myung Moon), they formulated a sequential seven step model of the process of conversion. Their model, which laid the foundation for a plethora of later conversion studies (see, e.g., Greil and Rudy, 1984), proposes that conversions can be traced to the combined effects of three "predisposing conditions" and four "situational contingencies." People are predisposed to become converts to NRMs by their (1) experience of enduring, acutely felt **tensions** in their lives, (2) within a **religious problem-solving perspective** (as opposed to a psychiatric or political problem-solving perspective), (3) which leads them to think of themselves as **religious seekers**. But conversion depends on such predisposed people (4) encountering the NRM to which they convert at a **turning point** in their lives, (5) forming **affective bonds** with one or more members of the group, (6) reducing or eliminating their **extracult attachments**, and (7) being exposed to **intensive interaction** with previous converts. It is the cumulative effect of all of these experiences, Lofland and Stark assert, that produces a true conversion. Each step is necessary, but only the whole process is sufficient.

Each of these theories has been subjected to vigorous criticism (e.g., Gurney and Tierney, 1982; Snow and Phillips, 1980), but their essential features continue to inform most discussions, popular and scholarly, of why people join NRMs. Much of the reliable empirical evidence we now possess about "who" joins NRMs comes directly or indirectly from tests of the adequacy and applicability of the theories of Glock, Lofland and Stark. The picture that emerges from these studies and analyses of specific new religions tends to contradict the popular prejudices about converts, prejudices bolstered in part by the work of Glock, Lofland and Stark and unquestioningly promoted by the anti-cult movement. As the reading by Roof in the previous section indicates, the cults active in the 1960s through to the 90s have drawn most of their converts from university and college campuses, and not from the poor, abused, marginal, or mentally deficient elements of society. In the words of Stark and Bainbridge

(1985: 395), the successful cults of today "skim more of the cream of society than the dregs."

In the third reading by the Canadian psychiatrist Saul Levine, "The Joiners," the theme of relative deprivation recurs, but so does the recognition of the relatively young, healthy, well-off, and well-educated nature of converts to NRMs. From interviews with hundreds of young people who joined NRMs, Levine develops a much more nuanced understanding of who converts and why. As with Lofland and Stark's study, we gain a more humane grasp of these converts through Levine's presentation of nine typical conversion stories. The picture he draws from the experiences of these nine people, however, reflects his dealings (in the 1970s and 80s) with converts to more mature manifestations of new religious life than those scrutinized by Glock, Lofland and Stark (in the early 1960s). These are no longer the obviously marginal or troubled people drawn to the nascent Moonie organization that Lofland and Stark stumbled upon in the streets of San Francisco.

Without endorsing the reductionistic thrust of Levine's psychological reading of the dynamics of conversion, his detailed account is instructive. Levine emphatically asserts that he found "no more sign of pathology among [the members and ex-members of NRMs that he studied] than ... in any youthful population." Yet these seemingly normal kids engaged in the kind of "radical departures," as he calls them, that were highly disturbing to their families and friends. While extraordinary, these radical departures, he argues, also make sense, if seen in the right light. "They are desperate attempts to grow up in a society that places obstacles in the way of the normal yearnings of youth" (1984: 11). The young people who join NRMs, he believes, are distinguished by their curious inability to effect the kind of separation from their families consonant with passage into young adulthood (see 1984: 31-38, 46-47, 61). They are psychological "children" trapped in a dilemma that our fragmented and indulgent society may have induced. They wish to sever the parental bond and achieve independence, but they lack a sufficient sense of self to do so. On the one hand, the prospect of relinquishing the overly close ties they do have, in "reality or fantasy," with their mothers and fathers is terrifying; it instills a great fear of personal "depletion." On the other hand, the self they display, whether seemingly normal or rebellious, feels "fraudulent." Such young people feel trapped: they can live neither with nor without their parents, within or without their truncated adolescent lives. Enduring this kind of acutely felt tension (Lofland and Stark, 1965), these young people yearn for a quick fix to their sense of isolation and confusion. They seek a sense of full belonging and purpose in life, independent of their families, but without engaging in the struggle to achieve true "mutual understanding" between individuals or the serious "analysis" of their situation required to find and shape their own identity. With so little real self esteem in place, they are seeking to avoid, for a time at least, the responsibility of making choices. Then at a moment of crisis, a turning point in Lofland and Stark's terminology (1965), they encounter the missionaries of one or another NRM offering just such an alternative path to (or temporary detour from) maturity.                •

Similar lines of analysis have been independently developed by Steven Tipton (1982), Eileen Barker (1984), Janet Jacobs (1987), Susan Palmer (1994) and others. But these accounts bring other broader and less reductive social influences and processes to bear on our understanding of the motivations of converts to NRMs. But I would guess that Levine's account will resonate with readers of this text and help establish the empathy with converts to NRMs that lays the foundation for understanding amidst the salvos of rhetoric generated by the cult controversy. Certainly, Levine's perspective fits with the finding that most converts to NRMs leave voluntarily within about two years (e.g., Barker, 1984; Stark and Bainbridge, 1985; Jacobs, 1987; Wright, 1987; Galanter, 1989). In doing so, it also runs flatly counter to the assertion of the anti-cult movement that converts are the naive victims of "brainwashing."

● ● ● ● ● ● ● ● ● ● ● ● ● ● ● ● ● ● ● ● ● ● ● ● ●

# References

Aberle, David
    1962    "Millennial Dreams in Action." Pp. 209-214 in S.L. Thrupp, ed., *Comparative Studies in Society and History*, Supplement II. The Hague, The Netherlands: Mouton.

Barker, Eileen
    1984    *The Making of A Moonie: Choice or Brainwashing?* Oxford: Basil Blackwell.

Bellah, Robert
    1976    "New Religious Consciousness and the Crisis of Modernity." Pp. 333-352 in C. Glock and R. Bellah, eds., *The New Religious Consciousness*. Berkeley, CA: University of California Press.

Calley, Malcolm
    1965    *God's People: West Indian Pentecostal Sects in England*. London: Oxford University Press.

Galanter, Marc
    1989    *Cults - Faith, Healing and Coercion*. New York: Oxford University Press.

Glock, Charles Y.
    1964    "The Role of Deprivation in the Origin and Evolution of Religious Groups." Pp. 24-36 in R. Lee and M. Marty, eds., *Religion and Social Conflict*. New York: Oxford University Press.

Gurney, Joan Neff and Kathleen J. Tierney
    1982    "Relative Deprivation and Social Movements: A Critical Look at Twenty Years of Theory and Research." *The Sociological Quarterly* 23 (4): 33-47.

Jacobs, Janet Liebman
    1989    *Divine Disenchantment: Deconverting from New Religions*. Bloomington, IN: Indiana University Press.

Levine, Saul
    1984    *Radical Departures: Desparate Detours to Growing Up*. New York: Harcourt Brace Jovanovich.

Lofland, John and Rodney Stark
    1965      "On Becoming a World-Saver: A Theory of Conversion to a Deviant Perspective." *American Sociological Review* 30 (5): 863-874.

Palmer, Susan Jean
    1994      *Moon Sisters, Krishna Mothers, Rajneesh Lovers: Women's Roles in New Religions.* Syracuse, NY: Syracuse University Press.

Snow, David A. and Cynthia L. Phillips
    1980      "The Lofland-Stark Conversion Model: A Critical Reassessment." *Social Problems* 27 (4): 430-447.

Stark, Rodney and William Sims Bainbridge
    1985      *The Future of Religion - Secularization, Revival and Cult Formation.* Berkeley, CA: University of California Press.

Tipton, Steven M.
    1982      *Getting Saved from the Sixties.* Berkeley, CA: University of California Press.

Wilson, Bryan R.
    1961      *Sects and Society.* Berkeley, CA: University of California Press

Wright, Stuart A.
    1987      *Leaving Cults: The Dynamics of Defection.* Washington, D.C.: Society for the Scientific Study of Religion Monograph Series, Number 7.

# THE ROLE OF DEPRIVATION IN THE ORIGIN AND EVOLUTION OF RELIGIOUS GROUPS

## CHARLES Y. GLOCK

*This essay[1] discusses an old problem in the sociology of religion: what accounts for the rise and evolution of religious groups in society? Three aims may be listed:*

*1. To review briefly what sociologists have previously said concerning the conditions which give rise to new religious groups, with particular attention to that part of existing theory which attributes such formations to class differences in society.*

*2. To propose a more general theory, based on the concept of deprivation, to help explain the origin of religious groups.*

*3. To suggest how this broader theory can help to account for the directions in which religious groups evolve.*

● ● ● ● ● ● ● ● ● ● ● ● ● ● ● ● ● ● ● ● ● ● ● ● ●

## I. The Formation of Religious Groups: The "Sect-Church" Theory

Current thinking about the origin and development of religious groups in Western society has been largely informed by so-called "sect-church" theory. The distinction between church and sect, as formulated in the work of Max Weber[2] and his contemporary, Ernst Troeltsch,[3] was initially an attempt to distinguish types of religious

Charles Y. Glock. "The Role of Deprivation in the Origin and Evolution of Religious Groups," in Robert Lee and Martin Marty, eds., *Religion and Social Conflict*. New York: Oxford University Press, 1964, pp. 24-36. Copyright © 1964 by Oxford University Press. Reprinted by permission of Oxford University Press.

groups and not an effort to discover the condition under which religious groups originate. Sects were characterized, for example, as being in tension with the world, as having a converted rather than an inherited membership, and as being highly emotional in character. Churches, in contrast, were seen as compromising with the world, as having a predominantly inherited membership, and as restrained and ritualistic in their services.

The sect-church distinction was later refined by H. Richard Niebuhr, who postulated a *dynamic inter-relationship* between the two types. In this inter-relationship he saw a way to understand the development of new religious groups.[4] Briefly, the compromising tendencies of the church lead some of its members to feel that the church is no longer faithful to its religious traditions. These dissenting members then break away to form new religious groups. At the outset, these new groups take on a highly sect-like character, eschewing the dominant characteristics of the church they have rejected. They assume an uncompromising posture toward the world, they gainsay a professional clergy, they insist on a conversion experience as a condition for membership, and they adopt a strict and literalistic theology.

Over a period of time, however, the conditions which gave rise to the sect change, and the sect slowly takes on the church-like qualities which it had originally repudiated. Once it has made the transition from sect to church, the religious group then becomes the breeding ground for new sects which proceed anew through the same process.

New sects, according to sect-church theory, recruit their membership primarily from the economically deprived, or as Niebuhr calls them, "the disinherited" classes of society. Their emergence is therefore to be understood as a result not only of religious dissent but of social unrest as well. The theological dissent masks an underlying social protest. The new sect functions, however, to contain the incipient social protest, and then to help eliminate the conditions which produced it.

The containment is accomplished through a process of *derailment*. Sects provide a channel through which their members come to transcend their feelings of deprivation by replacing them with feelings of religious privilege. Sect members no longer compare themselves to others in terms of their relatively lower economic position but in terms of their superior religious status.

Built into the sect ideology is a puritanical ethic which stresses self-discipline. Thrift, frugality, and industry are highly valued. Over time, the ideology helps to elevate sect members to middle-class status which in turn socializes them to middle-class values. Because the economic deprivation itself has been eliminated, feelings of economic deprivation no longer need to be assuaged. As the sect members become accommodated to the larger society, their religious movement proceeds to accommodate itself too. In so doing, it makes the transition from sect to church.

This is an admittedly brief and simplified account of sect-church theory and omits the many refinements that have been made in it over the last decades.[5] However, for our purposes, it conveys the essential points of traditional theory: (1) new religious movements begin by being sect-like in character, (2) they arise by breaking off from church-type bodies, (3) they are rooted in economic deprivation, (4) they gradually transform themselves into churches.

While valid in many cases, this theory falls short of being a general theory of the origin and evolution of religious groups. It overlooks the fact that not all religious groups emerge as sects. Some are churches in their original form. This was true of Reform Judaism in Europe and of Conservative Judaism in America. Most Protestant groups were from their beginnings more like churches than like sects.

Not only may new religious groups emerge in other than sect form, they need not, contrary to the theory, draw their membership primarily from the lower class. The American Ethical Union was clearly a middle-class movement from its inception, as was Unity and probably Christian Science.

The theory also does not take into account religious movements which draw their inspiration from other than the primary religion of the culture, and which are consequently not schismatic movements in the same sense as sects — concerned to preserve the traditional faith in purer form. Thus, while the theory may be adequate to explain the Pentecostal movement or the evolution of such religious groups as the Disciples of Christ (The Christian Church) and the Church of God in Jesus Christ, it does not provide a way to account for Theosophy, or the I Am movement, or the Black Muslims. Nor does the theory account for religious movements which show no signs of evolving toward the church form. Finally, the theory ignores the question of the conditions which produce a religious rather than a secular response to economic deprivation.

## II The Deprivation Theory and Religious Organization

The theory of religious organization that will now be outlined is not so much an alternative to existing theory as a generalization of it. In this revised formulation, deprivation is still seen as a necessary condition for the rise of new religious movements. However, the concept of deprivation is broadened and generalized beyond its customary usage in sect-church theory.[6]

Sect-church theory conceives of deprivation almost entirely in economic terms. To be sure, in every society there are individuals and groups which are economically underprivileged relative to others; there are some whose deprivation places them at the very bottom of the economic scale. However, there are forms of deprivation other than economic ones, and these too have implications for the development of religious and secular movements as well.

Deprivation, as we conceive it, refers to any and all of the ways that an individual or group may be, or feel, disadvantaged in comparison either to other individuals or groups or to an internalized set of standards. The experience of deprivation may be conscious, in which case the individual or group may be aware of its causes. Or it may be experienced as something other than deprivation, in which case its causes will be unknown to the individual or the group. But whether directly or indirectly experienced, whether its causes are known or unknown, deprivation tends to be accompanied by a desire to overcome it.[7] Efforts to deal with deprivation will differ, however, according to the degree to which its nature is correctly perceived and individuals and groups are in a position to eliminate its cause. It is primarily the attempt, then, to overcome some of the deprivation, that leads to social conflict and may ultimately lead to the formation of a new social or religious group. We must now examine the major types of deprivation in order to understand the relationship of the deprivation to the reaction of the person who perceives the deprivation.

There are five kinds of deprivation to which individuals or groups may be subject relative to others in society. We shall call these five, economic, social, organismic, ethical, and psychic. The types are not pure; any one individual or group may experience more than one kind of deprivation. However, we can distinguish among them not only analytically but empirically since one type of deprivation is likely to be dominant for particular individuals and groups in particular situations.

*Economic deprivation* has its source in the differential distribution of income in societies and in the limited access of some individuals to the necessities and luxuries of life. Economic deprivation may be judged on objective or on subjective criteria. The person who appears economically privileged on objective criteria might nevertheless perceive himself as economically deprived. For our purposes the subjective assessment is likely to be the more important.

*Social deprivation* is a derivative of the social propensity to value some attributes of individuals and groups more highly than others and to distribute societal rewards such as prestige, power, status, and opportunity for social participation. Social deprivation, then, arises out of the differential distribution of highly regarded attributes. The grounds for such differentiation are virtually endless. In our society, for example, we regard youth more highly than old age. The greater rewards tend to go to men rather than to women. The "gifted" person is given privileges denied to the mediocre.

Social deprivation is additive in the sense that the fewer the number of desirable attributes the individual possesses, the lower his relative status, and vice versa. In our society, it is in general "better" to be educated than uneducated. But one's status is further enhanced if one is white rather than Negro, Protestant rather than Catholic, and youthful rather than old.

The distinction between economic and social deprivation is akin to the distinction sociologists make between social class and social status. Designations of social class tend to be made on economic criteria. Social status distinctions, on the other hand, give greater attention to considerations of prestige and acceptance. While the two tend to go together, the correlation is not perfect. For our present purposes, we will consider social deprivation to be limited to situations in which it exists independently of economic deprivation.

*Organismic deprivation* refers to the fact that some individuals are deprived, relative to others, of good mental or physical health. It would include persons suffering from neuroses and psychoses, the blind, the deaf, the crippled, and the chronically ill.

Economic, social, and organismic deprivation share the characteristic that the individual does not measure up to society's standards. In ethical and psychological deprivation, on the other hand, the individual feels that he is not living up to his own standards. *Ethical deprivation* exists when the individual comes to feel that the dominant values of the society no longer provide him with a meaningful way of organizing his life, and that it is necessary for him to find an alternative. The deprivation is, in part, a philosophical one, but the philosophy sought is one which will provide ethical prescriptions as to how the individual should organize his everyday life.

Ethical deprivation is relatively independent of other forms of deprivation; in fact, it is more likely to arise when other forms of deprivation are not present. It would be exemplified by the person who becomes satiated with the economic and social rewards of life and with the efforts necessary to obtain them, and who seeks some alternative system of values which will inform him as to how he should act.

*Psychic deprivation* is somewhat akin to ethical deprivation. Here, too, there is a concern with philosophical meaning, but in this case philosophy is sought for its own sake rather than as a source of ethical prescriptions as to how one is to behave in relation to others. Psychic deprivation is primarily a consequence of severe and unresolved social deprivation. The individual is not missing the material advantages of life but has been denied its psychic rewards.

We suggest that a necessary pre-condition for the rise of any organized social movement, whether it be religious or secular, is a situation of felt deprivation. However, while a necessary condition, deprivation is not in itself a sufficient condition. Also required are the additional conditions that the deprivation be shared, that no alternative institutional arrangements for its resolution are perceived, and that a leadership emerge with an innovating idea for building a movement out of the existing deprivation.

Where these conditions exist, the organizational effort to overcome deprivation may be religious or it may be secular. In the case of economic, social, and organismic deprivation — the three characterized by deprivation relative to others — *religious* resolutions are more likely to occur where the nature of the deprivation is inaccurately perceived or where those experiencing the deprivation are not in a position to work directly at eliminating the causes. The resolution is likely to be *secular* under the opposite conditions — where the nature of the deprivation is correctly assessed by those experiencing it and they have the power, or feel they have the power, to deal with it directly.

Religious resolutions, then, are likely to compensate for feelings of deprivation rather than to eliminate its causes. Secular resolutions, where they are successful, are more likely to eliminate the causes, and therefore also the feelings.

These tendencies do not hold for ethical and psychic deprivation. In the case of ethical and psychic deprivation, as we shall see, a religious resolution may be as efficacious as a secular one in overcoming the deprivation directly. Resolutions to psychic deprivation tend in practice to be always religious, defined in the broad sense of invoking some transcendental authority. However, secular solutions are conceivable.

Both religious and secular resolutions may follow from each kind of deprivation. However, whether religious or secular, the resolution will be different in character according to which type stimulates it.

Economic deprivation, once it becomes intense, has in it the seed of revolution. When the movements which it stimulates are secular, they are likely to be revolutionary. However, to be successful, revolutions require a degree of power which the deprived group is unlikely to be able to muster. Consequently, even when it is intense, economic deprivation seldom leads to revolution.

Religious resolutions to economic deprivation, while not literally revolutionary, are symbolically so. The latent resentment against society tends to be expressed in an ideology which rejects and radically devalues the society. Thus, for those in the movement, the society is symbolically transformed; actually it is left relatively untouched.

This is characteristically what sects do, and it is this form of religious organization which is likely to arise out of economic deprivation. This is in accord with what we have said earlier in our discussion of sect-church theory, and we need not further elaborate on the way that sect members compensate for economic disadvantage by substituting religious privilege in its place. We would add, however, that the religious movement which grows out of economic deprivation need not have its theological base in the traditional religion of the society. The Black Muslim movement, for example, borrows heavily from an "alien" religious doctrine. Yet in its strong tone of social protest and its doctrine of Negro superiority it exemplifies the kind of religious movement which grows out of economic deprivation (with its accompanying social deprivation).

Social deprivation, where it exists without a strong economic component, ordinarily does not require a complete transformation of society, either literally or symbolically, to produce relief. What is at fault is not the basic organization of society but one or several of its parts. Consequently, efforts at resolution are likely to be directed at the parts without questioning the whole. As with economic deprivation, however, resolutions are not always possible. Once again, responses to the deprivation are most likely to be secular where its cause can be attacked more or less directly.

Many secular movements with roots in one or another kind of social deprivation have arisen in America over the last century. The women's suffrage movement, the Townsend movement, the many hyphenated American societies, the NAACP, all represent movements whose purpose was to eliminate the social deprivation of a particular group.

Social deprivation may be experienced as religious deprivation and, where this is the case, efforts at resolution will take a religious form. Such religious groups as the African Methodist Episcopal Church, the ethnic sub-denominations of Lutheranism, and Conservative Judaism were organized because the existing religious structure was incapable of meeting the religious needs of the groups involved. While overtly a means to overcome religious disadvantage, these organizations also served to overcome social deprivation. For example, the organization of the Augustana Lutheran Church did not immediately produce an increase in the status of the Swedish immigrants who founded it, but it did help to ease their accommodation to American society and hence to relieve incipient feelings of social deprivation. This is generally characteristic, as we have said before, of religious resolutions to deprivation.

The organizational form of religious groups that emerge out of social deprivation tends to be church-like rather than sect-like. This is because the basic interest of the socially deprived is to accommodate themselves to the larger society rather than to escape from it or alternatively to completely transform it. Consequently, they tend to adopt those institutional arrangements with which the larger society is most comfortable.

The psychoanalytic movement, group dynamics, and Alcoholics Anonymous are examples of a secular response to organismic deprivation where the mental component of this form of deprivation is dominant. In turn, the Society for the Blind, the Society for Crippled Children, and the American Cancer Society would exemplify secular efforts toward resolution where the physiological element is primary. However successful or unsuccessful these movements, they all represent attempts to deal with a problem directly. They are revolutionary in that they seek to transform the individual either mentally or physiologically. However, they do not question the value system of the society *per se.*

There have been religious movements — healing cults, for example — which are organized primarily as resolutions to organismic deprivation. More often, however, we find that religious responses to this form of deprivation are not the entire *raison d'être* of a religious movement, but are included as one aspect of it. We note that a faith healing movement has been organized within the Episcopal Church. Many sects — such as that of Father Divine, for example — include a healing element, as do cults such as Christian Science and Unity. Thus, religious responses seem not to be identified with any particular organizational form. We suspect, however, that where healing is the exclusive concern of the religious movement, as with the snake charming movement, it is more likely to be cult-like in character than to be a sect or a church.

As we have already suggested, religious resolutions to ethical deprivation may be as efficacious as secular ones in overcoming the deprivation. However, while alike in providing a direct means of overcoming ethical deprivation, secular responses do differ from religious ones in their source. Secular responses — for example, the existentialist movement and the beatniks — reflect a rejection of the general value system around which the society is organized. Religious responses, on the other hand, represent an alienation from the dominant religious system.

The religious movements which grow out of ethical deprivation cannot be as easily classified as those which emerge out of economic, social, and psychic deprivation. They tend to be more church-like than sect-like; at the same time, they might be more appropriately classified as societies than churches. Thus, the Ethical Culture Union might be loosely considered a church. Or, it may be thought of as having an organizational form which is distinct from the familiar ways in which religious groups tend to be organized. Unitarianism, too, has the quality of being an association, particularly in the way that the Unitarian Fellowships are now organized.

These organizational deviations are to be explained, we would suggest, by the fact that religious responses to intellectual deprivation tend to be deistic rather than theistic. Consequently, some of the accoutrements of more traditional religious groups are no longer relevant.

Responses to psychic deprivation often have religious overtones in that they invoke some form of transcendental authority. However, this authority may or may not derive from the predominant religion of the culture and indeed, as in the case of the flying saucer movement, may not even borrow from an existing religion. However, whether they are offshoots of the dominant religion — Christian Science or Unity, for example — or borrow from alien religions — Theosophy, Vedanta, or the I Am movement — or are essentially new inventions, these movements almost invariably assume a cult-like rather than a sect-like or church-like form. They tend to draw their membership from the severely socially deprived middle class, they require a certain amount of intellectual facility on the part of their adherents and function to relieve the deprivation by stimulating an attitude of mind over matter. At the same time, they avoid the ritualistic trappings of the church and gainsay a professional clergy.

Deprivation need not be immediately present to stimulate an organizational response. The prospect of deprivation may produce a similar effect. The White Citizens' Councils in the South, for example, can be conceived of as organizations growing out of anticipated economic and social deprivation. The John Birch Society is a response to anticipated social deprivation. Protestants and Other Americans United is an example of a religious movement organized around anticipated ethical and social deprivation.

In sum, present or anticipated deprivation would appear to be a central factor in the rise of new movements. The organizational response to deprivation may be either religious or secular. In the case of economic, social, and organismic deprivation, religious responses tend to function as compensations for the deprivation, secular ones as means to overcome it. The type of deprivation around which a movement arises is influential in shaping its character in all cases except organismic deprivation. Generally speaking, religious movements emerge as sects where they are stimulated by economic deprivation, as churches where the deprivation is social, and as cults where it is psychic. Religious movements arising out of ethical deprivation tend to develop an organizational form which is distinct from that of traditional religions.

## III Deprivation and the Development of Religious Groups

Deprivation is important not only to the rise of new movements but to the path of their development and their potentiality for survival. Movements may evolve in a myriad of ways, and we have no intention of trying to cope with all of their variety. We would suggest, however, that movements tend to follow one of three basic patterns. (1) They may flower briefly and then die. (2) They may survive indefinitely in substantially their original form. (3) They may survive but in a form radically different from their original one.

How movements develop, and whether or not they survive, is influenced by the type of deprivation which stimulated them, how they deal with this deprivation, and the degree to which the deprivation persists in the society and, therefore, provides a continuing source of new recruits.

Movements arising out of economic deprivation tend to follow a pattern of either disappearing relatively quickly or of having to change their organizational form to survive. They seldom survive indefinitely in their original form. This is because the deprivation they respond to may itself be short-lived or because they themselves help to overcome the deprivation of their adherents.

Few sects survive as sects. They either disappear or evolve from a sect to a church. Where they follow the former course, it is likely that their source of recruitment suddenly withers because of conditions over which they have no control. Thus, depression-born sects tend to have a low survival rate, lasting only as long as the depression itself. Sects also have the tendency, noted earlier, to socialize their members to higher economic status. In the process, their organizational form is transformed to conform to the changing status of their membership.

Secular responses to economic deprivation follow a similar pattern. Depression-born movements — technocracy, for example — tend to flower briefly and then die. More fundamental movements, such as revolutions, tend, where they are successful, to lose their revolutionary character and to survive as movements functioning to maintain the advantages which have been gained.

Organizational responses to social deprivation may also follow a pattern of disappearing quickly, but where they survive, they are likely to do so without radical alteration of their original form. Which of these paths is followed is largely dependent on the persistence of the deprivation which gave rise to the movement. Successful elimination of the experienced deprivation — for example, the successful attempt of women to gain the right to vote — is likely to produce an early end to the movement.

It is characteristic of many kinds of social deprivation to persist over extended periods of time and to continue from generation to generation. This is because the value systems of societies tend to change slowly, and the differential social rewards and punishments of one era are not likely, in the natural course of events, to be radically altered in the next.

The ability of churches to survive in basically unchanged form is, in substantial part, a consequence of the persistence of social deprivation. Participation in a church, we would suggest, functions to provide individuals with a source of gratification which they cannot find in the society-at-large. Since there are always individuals who are socially deprived in this sense, there exists a continuing source of new recruits to the church. Furthermore, church participation only compensates for the deprivation; it does not eliminate it. Thus, the condition does not arise, as with the sect, that a primary reason for the existence of the church is dissipated over time.

The contention that a major function of church participation is to relieve members' feelings of social deprivation is made here primarily on theoretical grounds. What little empirical evidence there is, however, suggests that churches tend to gain their greatest commitment from individuals who are most deprived of the rewards of the larger society. Thus, it is the less gifted intellectually, the aged, women, and those without normal family lives who are most often actively involved in the church.[8]

Organismic deprivation produces movements whose evolution is likely to be influenced by the development of new knowledge about the causes and treatment of mental and physical disorders. Existing movements can expect to thrive only so long as the therapies they provide are subjectively perceived as efficacious and superior to prevailing alternatives. However, the survival of these movements is constantly threatened by innovations in therapy or treatment which eliminate their *raison d'être*. Under such conditions, they may simply disband — like the Sister Kenny Foundation, for example — or they may elect to chart their course along a different path, like the National Foundation.

Religious movements or sub-movements which are sustained by organismic deprivation may survive for a very long time and recruit new members from those who cannot find relief through secular sources. In the long run they too may become victims of innovations coming from increments in secular knowledge.

Movements which originate in ethical deprivation have a great propensity, we would suggest, to be short-lived. This is not because ethical deprivation is not a persistent element in society; there are always likely to be some individuals who feel that the dominant value system provides an inadequate answer to this concern. However, resolutions which seem appropriate at one time are not likely to be so at another. In effect, ethical deprivation tends to be subject to fads. Consequently, organizational responses to ethical deprivation tend to capture attention for the moment and to be quickly replaced by alternative and new solutions. The beatnik movement exemplifies this propensity.

The exceptions — the movements of this kind which survive — do so because they provide solutions which have relevance to long-term trends in society. These trends function to provide these movements with a continuing source of new recruits. For example, the long-term trend toward secularization in American life is, we suspect, a major factor in the survival and recent acceleration in growth of the

Unitarian movement. In general, ethical deprivation characterizes only a small minority of a population at a given time and movements which respond to such deprivation are likely — whether they survive or not — always to be minority movements.

For much the same reasons movements which arise out of psychic deprivation share this tendency to be short-lived. Theosophy and the I Am society were short-lived movements, and we suspect that this will be true of the flying saucer movement also. Christian Science seems clearly to be more than a fad and so would be an exception to our generalization. The success of this movement to relieve not only psychic deprivation but also the social deprivation which almost invariably accompanies it may account for its survival. Other movements, like Theosophy and I Am may be less capable of relieving psychic and social deprivation because of their reliance on alien religious ideas.

Our aim in this essay has been to assess theoretically the general role of deprivation in the origin and evolution of social movements and to specify its special significance for religious organization. The essay has been informed by the view that religion functions to compensate for deprivations for which direct means of resolution either do not exist or are not possible of employment. By reducing the propensities toward self-destructive behavior which are loosed whenever feelings of deprivation are not resolved, religion, we are asserting, plays an important role in the maintenance of personal and social integration.

It may seem to some readers that we have reduced religion to a sociological variable. This is definitely not our intention. To say that religion relieves deprivation in no sense comprehends all that religion is or does. It merely confirms one claim which religions make: that those who accept the faith will be relieved of the cares of the world. However, religion cannot be understood only in terms of what its adherents receive from it; the question of what they give to it — of what consequences follow from being religious — needs also to be considered. Our essay has been concerned exclusively with the first of these questions. The task of studying the consequences of religion for the individual and the society has, in our judgment, still to be done effectively.

● ● ● ● ● ● ● ● ● ● ● ● ● ● ● ● ● ● ● ● ● ● ● ● ● ●

## Notes

1. The author is indebted to his colleagues, Gertrude Jaeger Selznick and Robert E Mitchell, for constructive criticism and editorial advice.

2. Max Weber, "The Social Psychology of the World's Religions" in Gerth and Mills, eds., *From Max Weber: Essays in Sociology* (New York: Oxford University Press, 1940).

3. Ernst Troeltsch, *Social Teachings of the Christian Churches* (New York: Macmillan, 1949), esp. Vol. 1, pp. 331-43.

[4]   H. Richard Niebuhr, *The Social Sources of Denominationalism* (New York: Henry Holt and Co., 1929).

[5]   See, for example J.M. Yinger, *Religion in the Struggle for Power* (Durham, N.C.: Duke University Press, 1946); Bryan Wilson, "An Analysis of Sect Development," *American Sociological Review*, 22 (Feb. 1957); and Leopold Von Wiese and Howard Becker, *Systematic Sociology* (New York: John Wiley and Sons, 1932).

[6]   This paper has also been informed by Robert K. Merson, "Social Structure and Anomie" in *Social Theory and Social Structure* (Glencoe, Ill.: The Free Press, 1957).

[7]   This is not the case, however, where the value system of the society warrants deprivation, for example, the Hindu caste system.

[8]   See Charles Y. Glock, "A Sociologist Looks at the Parish Church," Afterword in Walter Kloetzli, *The City Church: Death or Renewal* (Philadelphia: The Muhlenberg Press, 1961).

# ON BECOMING A WORLD-SAVER: A THEORY OF CONVERSION TO A DEVIANT PERSPECTIVE

## JOHN LOFLAND and RODNEY STARK

*Materials derived from observation of a West Coast millenarian cult are employed to develop a "value-added" model of the conditions under which conversion occurs. For conversion a person must experience, within a religious problem-solving perspective, enduring, acutely-felt tensions that lead him to define himself as a religious seeker; he must encounter the cult at a turning point in his life; within the cult an affective bond must be formed (or pre-exist) and any extra-cult attachments, neutralized; and there he must be exposed to intensive interaction if he is to become a "deployable agent."*

● ● ● ● ● ● ● ● ● ● ● ● ● ● ● ● ● ● ● ● ● ● ● ● ● ●

All men and all human groups have ultimate values, a world view, or a perspective furnishing them a more or less orderly and comprehensible picture of the world. Clyde Kluckhohn remarked that no matter how primitive and crude it may be, there is a "philosophy behind the way of life of every individual and of every relatively homogenous group at any given point in their histories."[1] When a person gives up one such perspective or ordered view of the world for another we refer to this process as *conversion.*[2]

Frequently such conversions are between popular and widely held perspectives — from Catholicism to Communism, or from the world view of an underdeveloped or primitive culture to that of a technically more advanced society, as from the Peyote Cult of the Southwest Indians to Christianity. The continual emergence of tiny cults

John Lofland and Rodney Stark. "On Becoming a World-Saver: A Theory of Conversion to a Deviant Perspective." *American Sociological Review* 30, 1965: 862-875.

and sects in western industrial nations makes it clear, however, that sometimes persons relinquish a more widely held perspective for an unknown, obscure and often, socially devalued one.

In this paper we shall outline a model of the conversion process through which a group of people came to see the world in terms set by the doctrines of one such obscure and devalued perspective — a small millenarian religious cult. Although it is based on only a single group, we think the model suggests some rudiments of a general account of conversion to deviant perspectives. But the degree to which this scheme applies to shifts between widely held perspectives must, for now, remain problematic.

## Background

Our discussion is based on observation of a small, millenarian cult headquartered in Bay City,[3] a major urban center on the West Coast. This "movement" constitutes the American following of a self-proclaimed "Lord of the Second Advent," a Mr. Chang, who has attracted more than 5,000 converts in Korea since 1954. The "Divine Precepts," the doctrine Chang claims was revealed to him by God, concerns a complete "Restoration of the World" to the conditions of the Garden of Eden by 1967. The message was brought to this country by Miss Yoon-Sook Lee, a graduate of Methodist seminaries, and a former professor of social welfare at a large, church-supported, women's college in Seoul.

In 1959 Miss Lee arrived in a university town (here called Northwest Town) in the Pacific Northwest, and, in two years gained five totally committed converts to the Divine Precepts (hereafter referred to as the D.P.). In December, 1960, after difficulties with local clergymen and public opinion, largely touched off when two female converts deserted their husbands and children, the group moved to Bay City.

By mid-1963, 15 more converts had been gained and by the end of 1964 the cult numbered more than 150 adherents. Converts were expected to devote their lives to spreading "God's New Revelation" and preparing for the New Age theocracy which God and a host of active spirits were expected to create on earth shortly. Typically the converts lived communally in a series of houses and flats, contributed their salaries from menial jobs to the common treasury, thus supporting Miss Lee as a full-time leader, and gave all their spare time to witnessing and otherwise proselytizing.

In this brief report, analysis will be limited to the single problem of conversion.[4] Under what conditions and through what mechanisms did persons come to share the D.P. view of the world, and, conversely, who rejected this perspective?

The logical and methodological structure of the analysis is based on a "value-added"[5] conception. That is, we shall offer a series of seven (more or less) successively accumulating factors, which in their total combination seem to account for conversion to the D.P. All seven factors seem necessary for conversion, and together they appear to be sufficient conditions.

The sequential arrangement of the seven conditions may be conceived in the imagery of a funnel; that is, as a structure that systematically reduces the number of persons who can be considered available for recruitment, and also increasingly specifies who is available. At least theoretically, since the mission of the cult was to "convert America," all Americans are potential recruits. Each condition narrows the range of clientele: ultimately, only a handful of persons responded to the D.P. call.

Typically, and perhaps ideally, the conditions develop as presented here, but the temporal order may vary. The ordering principle is *activation*, rather than temporal occurrence alone: the time of activation is the same whether a condition exists for a considerable time prior to its becoming relevant to D.P. conversion or only develops in time to accomplish conversion.

Data were gathered through participant observation in the cult from early 1962 to mid-1963. Further information was obtained from interviews with converts, their acquaintances, families, and work-mates; with persons who took some interest in the D.P. but were not converts; and with a variety of clergymen, officials, neighbors, employers and others in contact with the adherents. Less intensive observation was conducted through mid-1964.

Although complete data pertinent to all seven steps of the conversion model were not obtainable for all 21 persons who were classified as converts by mid-1963, full information on all seven factors was available for 15 converts. All the available data conform to the model. In presenting biographical information to explicate and document the model, we shall focus on the most central of the early converts, drawing on material from less central and later converts for illustrations. The converts were primarily white, Protestant, and young (typically below 35); some had college training, and most were Americans of lower middle-class and small-town origins.

## Conversion Operationally Defined

How does one determine when a person has "really" taken up a different perspective? The most obvious evidence, of course, is his own declaration that he has done so. This frequently takes the form of a tale of regeneration, about how terrible life was before and how wonderful it is now.[6] But verbal claims are easily made and simple to falsify. Indeed, several persons who professed belief in the D.P. were regarded as insincere by all core members. A display of loyalty and commitment, such as giving time, energy, and money to the D.P. enterprise, invariably brought ratification of the conversion from all core members, but to require such a display as evidence of "actual" conversion overlooks four persons who made only verbal professions but were universally regarded as converts by core members. To avoid this difficulty two classes or degrees of conversion may be distinguished: *verbal converts*, or fellow-travelers and followers who professed belief and were accepted by core members as sincere, but took no active role in the D.P. enterprise; and *total converts*, who exhibited their commitment through deeds as well as words.

Up to a point, the same factors that account for total conversion also account for verbal conversion and initially we shall discuss the two groups together. Later we shall attempt to show that verbal conversion is transformed into total conversion only when the last stage in the conversion sequence develops.

## A Model of Conversion

To account for the process by which persons came to be world-savers for the D.P., we shall investigate two genres of conditions or factors. The first, which might be called *predisposing conditions,* comprises attributes of persons *prior* to their contact with the cult. These are background factors, the conjunction of which forms a pool of potential D.P. converts. Unfortunately, it has become conventional in sociology to treat demographic characteristics, structural or personal frustrations, and the like, as completely responsible for "pushing" persons into collectivities dedicated to protest against the prevailing social order. These factors are not unimportant, but a model composed entirely of them is woefully incomplete. The character of their incompleteness is expressed by a Meadian paraphrase of T.S. Eliot: "Between the impulse and the act falls the shadow." The second genre of conditions is this shadowed area, the situational contingencies.

*Situational contingencies* are conditions that lead to the successful recruitment of persons predisposed to the D.P. enterprise. These conditions arise from confrontation and interaction between the potential convert and D.P. members. Many persons who qualified for conversion on the basis of predisposing factors entered interpersonal relations with D.P. members, but because the proper situational conditions were not met, they did not become converts.

With these two classes of factors in mind, we may turn to a discussion of the first and most general of predisposing conditions.

1. *Tension.* No model of human conduct entirely lacks a conception of tension, strain, frustration, deprivation, or other version of the hedonic calculus. And, not surprisingly, even the most cursory examination of the life situations of converts before they embraced the D.P. reveals what they at least *perceived* as considerable tension.[7]

This tension is best characterized as a felt discrepancy between some imaginary, ideal state of affairs and the circumstances in which these people saw themselves caught up. We suggest that acutely felt tension is a necessary, but far from sufficient condition for conversion. That is, it creates some disposition to act. But tension may be resolved in a number of ways (or remain unresolved); hence, that these people are in a tension situation does not indicate *what* action they may take.

Just as tension can have myriad consequences, its sources can also be exceedingly disparate. Some concrete varieties we discovered were: longing for unrealized wealth, knowledge, fame, and prestige; hallucinatory activity for which the person lacked any successful definition: frustrated sexual and marital relations; homosexual guilt; acute fear of face-to-face interaction; disabling and disfiguring physical conditions; and — perhaps of a slightly different order — a frustrated desire for a significant, even heroic, religious status, to "know the mind of God intimately," and to be a famous agent for his divine purposes.[8]

Brief life histories of a few central believers will indicate concretely what bothered them as pre-converts. The case of Miss Lee, the "Messiah's" emissary in America, illustrates the aspiration to be an important religious figure.

> *Miss Lee* was born and raised in Korea and converted to Chang's cult in 1954 when she was 39. During her early teens she was subject to fits of depression and used to sit on a secluded hilltop and seek spirit contacts. Shortly she began receiving visions and hearing voices — a hallucinatory pattern she was to maintain thereafter. Her adolescent mystical experience convinced her she had a special mission to perform for God and at the age of 19 she entered a Methodist seminary in Japan. She was immediately disenchanted by the "worldly concern" of the seminarians and the training she received, although she stuck out the five-year course. Prior to entering the seminary she had become engrossed in the Spiritualistic writings of Emmanuel Swedenborg, who soon began to appear to her in visions. Her estrangement from conventional religious roles was so great that upon graduating from seminary she, alone among her classmates, refused ordination. She returned to Korea at the start of World War II, and by 1945 was professor of social welfare at a denominational university in Seoul. In 1949 the Methodist Board of Missions sent her to a Canadian university for further theological training. There she wrote her thesis on Swedenborg, who continued to visit her in spirit form. In Canada, as in Japan, she was bitterly disappointed by the "neglect of things of the spirit," caused concern among the faculty by constantly hiding to pray and seek visions, and occasionally stole away to Swedenborgian services. Her spirits continued to tell her that she was a religious figure of great importance. Returning to her academic life in Korea she feel ill with chronic diarrhea and eventually nephritis, both of which resisted all medical treatment. After two years of this, her health was broken and she was completely bedridden. At this time her servant took her to see Chang.

Thus is summarized a portrait of a desperately estranged maiden lady, with secret convictions of grandeur, frequent "heterodox" hallucinations, and failing health, who felt herself badly entangled in the mundane affairs of modern religious bureaucracy.

Although the cultural context is rather different, the cases of *Bertha* and *Lester* follow lines rather similar to Miss Lee's, but include an important sexual theme.

> *Bertha*, 29 at conversion, was the daughter of German immigrants and was raised in a suburban town. After high school she attended a modeling school, the kind operated in large cities for naive, fame-hungry girls, regardless of suitability. She returned to marry a local boy who was employed as a stereotyper in a printing plant. On her wedding night she spent two hours locked in their hotel bathroom, and subsequently did not improve her evaluation of sexual intercourse. Later the couple separated briefly, reunited, and after five years of marriage had their first child (1955). The second came in 1957, and they moved to the West Coast. There Bertha began having private religious hallucinations, including "sanctification" — being made holy and free of all sin. She went to various ministers to tell of her marvelous experiences, but was not warmly received; indeed, most advised psychiatric help. She began, then, to tell her husband that one day she would be very important in the service of the Lord. Following a homosexual episode with a neighbor woman, Bertha demanded to be taken elsewhere and the family went to Northwest Town in April 1959. There they settled in rural Elm Knoll, a collection of half a dozen houses about seven miles from town. This was soon to be the scene of the initial formation of the cult group, and here she came to know two neighbors, Minnie Mae and Alice. These young housewives drew the attention of other neighbors by spending many hours hanging around the nearby general stores, sometimes drinking beer and often complaining a good deal about their husbands. During this period, Bertha attended churches of various denominations and continued to have frequent ecstatic religious experiences, mostly while sitting alone in a clump of bushes near her house, where she was also reported to have spent a good deal of time crying and moaning.

> Like *Miss Lee, Lester* (25 at conversion) went to a seminary (Lutheran) after a series of hallucinatory, spiritualistic experiences and aroused a good deal of curiosity and opposition among his fellows and the faculty. He left after an abortive part-time year to take up full-time graduate work in linguistics at a large state university in the same Bay City as the seminary. He remained convinced he was destined to be a one-man revitalization movement in the church. He took an extremely

active role in campus student religious programs, meanwhile increasing his preoccupation with spiritualism and his own psychic experiences. For his first full-time year of graduate school he was awarded a Woodrow Wilson fellowship. But he was much more concerned about his religious life, and a new interest: he went to live with a young Hungarian ex-aristocrat, well-known in the area as a practicing homosexual. The young Hungarian led Lester to organized Spiritualism, where his religious preoccupations and hallucinations were greatly reinforced and increased, but Lester found these groups wanting. They contented themselves with very mundane affairs and seemed uninterested in speculations on larger theological matters. In addition, Lester was very ambivalent about his homosexuality, unable to explain it, unable to accept it, and unable to quit it. Then he met Miss Lee.

Bertha's friend, *Minnie Mae*, did not aspire to significant status, religious or otherwise. She pined, rather, for the more modest goal of marital satisfaction.

*Minnie Mae* (27 at conversion) was born in Possum Trot, Arkansas, of hillbilly farmers. She was one of 11 children, began dating at 12, and married at 15, having completed only rural elementary school. She and her young husband left Arkansas for lack of jobs and settled in Northwest Town. Her husband took a job as a laborer in a plywood factory. Although the young couple did not join a church, they came from a religious background (Minnie Mae's mother was a Pentecostal lay preacher), and they began attending tent meetings near Northwest Town. During one of these Minnie Mae began speaking in "tongues" and fell into a several-hour trance. After this her husband discouraged church activities. The couple had three children at roughly two year intervals, and until 1960 Minnie Mae seems to have spent most of her time caring for these children and watching television. She reported tuning in a local channel when she got up in the morning and keeping it on until sign-off at night. In 1958 the couple built a small house in Elm Knoll. Here, in her behavior and conversations with neighbors, she began to reveal severe dissatisfactions in her marriage. She repeatedly complained that her husband only had intercourse with her about once a month, but she also reported being very afraid of getting pregnant again. Furthermore, she wanted to get out and have some fun, go dancing, etc., but her husband only wanted to watch TV and to fish. She wondered if she had let life pass her by because she had been married too young. And, often, she complained about her husband's opposition to fundamentalist religious activities.

*Merwin and Alice* followed quite a different pattern. Theirs was not an intensely religious concern, indeed their grandiose ambitions were for fortune.

*Merwin* (29 at conversion) was raised in a Kansas hamlet where his father was the railroad depot agent. After high school he tried a small Kansas junior college for a year, did poorly, and joined the Marines. Discharged in 1952, he spent one year at the University of Kansas majoring in architecture, and did well, so he transferred to what he felt was a better school in Northwest Town. Here he didn't do well and adopted a pattern of frequently dropping out, then going back. Estranged and alone, he bought a few acres in Elm Knoll with a small ramshackle cottage and took up a recluse's existence — he rarely shaved or washed, brewed his own beer, and dabbled in health foods, left-wing political writings, and occult publications, while supporting himself by working in a plywood plant. Next door, about 20 yards away, lived Alice, her two children and her husband, also a plywood plant worker. Alice's husband, however, worked a swing shift, while Merwin worked days. The result was that Alice filed for divorce and moved over to Merwin's. The husband departed without undue resistance. After their marriage, Merwin began to put his plans for financial empires into action. He considered a housing development, a junkyard, and finally bought a large frame house in Northwest Town to convert into a boarding house for students. After he had bought furniture and made other investments in the property, the city condemned it. Merwin filed bankruptcy and returned to Elm Knoll to lick his wounds and contemplate his next business venture. Merwin had long been disaffected with the established religions, had considered himself an agnostic, but was also interested in the occult. These interests were developed by his work partner, Elmer, whom we shall meet in a moment.

*Alice*, also a small town girl, had traded for what she felt was a better man, one who was "going places," but these hopes seemed to be fading after the bankruptcy. She still bragged to Minnie Mae and Bertha that Merwin would be a big man someday, but there was little evidence to support her.

Elmer's case illustrates yet another kind of frustrated ambition, that of attaining status as a man of knowledge and invention.

*Elmer* was born on a farm in North Dakota but his parents fled the drought and depression for the West Coast during the late thirties and settled on a farm near Northwest Town. Elmer, 26 at the time of his conversion, was slightly built with something of a vacant stare. After high school, he flunked out of the university after one semester and spent the next two years in the army where he flunked medical technician school. After the army he enrolled in a nearby state college and again lasted only one semester. He then returned to his parents' farm and took a job in the plywood factory. Elmer conceived of himself as an intellectual and aspired to be a learned man. He undertook to educate himself, and collected a large library toward this end. Unfortunately, he was virtually illiterate. In addition to more conventional books (including much of the Random House Modern Library), he subscribed to occult periodicals such as *Fate, Flying Saucers, Search,* etc. He also viewed himself as a practical man of invention, a young Thomas Edison, and dreamed of constructing revolutionary gadgets. He actually began assembling materials for a tiny helicopter (to use for herding cattle) and a huge television antenna to bring in stations hundreds of miles away. On top of all this, Elmer was unable to speak to other above a whisper and looked constantly at his feet while talking. Furthermore, he had great difficulty sustaining a conversation, often appearing to forget what he was talking about. But despite his "objective" failures at intellectual accomplishment, Elmer clung to a belief in his own potential. The consequences of failure were largely to make him withdraw, to protect this self image from his inability to demonstrate it.

These case histories provide a concrete notion of the kinds of things that bothered pre-converts. These problems apparently are not qualitatively different from the problems presumably experienced by a significant, albeit unknown, proportion of the general population. Their peculiarity, if any, appears to be that pre-converts felt their problems were quite acute, and they experienced high levels of tension concerning them over rather long periods.

From the point of view of an outside observer, however, their circumstances were not extraordinarily oppressive; in the general population, many persons undoubtedly labor under tensions considerably more acute and prolonged. Perhaps the strongest qualitative generalization supported by the data is that pre-converts felt themselves frustrated in their rather diverse aspirations. Most people probably have some type of frustrated aspiration, but pre-converts *experienced* the tension rather more acutely and over longer periods than most people do.

Explanation cannot rest here, for such tensions could have resulted in any number of other resolutions, and in fact they usually do. Thus, these unresolved problems in living are part of the necessary scenery for the stage, but the rest of the props, the stage itself, and the drama of conversion remain to be constructed.

2. *Type of Problem-Solving Perspective.* Since conversion to the D.P. is hardly the only thing people can do about their problems, it becomes important to ask what else

these particular people could have done, and why they didn't. Because people have a number of conventional and readily available alternative definitions for, and means of coping with, their problems, there were, in the end, very few converts to the D.P. An alternative solution is a perspective or rhetoric defining the nature and sources of problems in living and offering some program for their resolution. Many such alternative solutions exist in modern society. Briefly, three particular genres of solution are relevant here: *the psychiatric, the political* and *the religious*. In the first, the origin of problems is typically traced to the psyche, and manipulation of the self is advocated as a solution. Political solutions, mainly radical, locate the sources of problems in the social structure and advocate reorganization of the system as a solution. The religious perspective tends to see both sources and solutions as emanating from an unseen and, in principle, unseeable realm.

The first two secular rhetorics bear the major weight of usage in contemporary society. No longer is it considered appropriate to regard recalcitrant and aberrant actors as possessed of devils. Indeed, modern religious institutions tend to offer a secular, frequently psychiatric, rhetoric concerning problems in living. The prevalence of secular definitions of tension is a major reason for the scarcity of D.P. converts. Several persons, whose circumstances met other conditions of the model, had adopted a psychiatric definition of their tensions and failed to become converts. In one exaggerated instance, an ex-GI literally alternated residence between the D.P. headquarters and the psychiatric ward of the veterans' hospital, never able to make a final decision as to which rhetoric he should adopt.

All pre-converts were surprisingly uninformed about conventional psychiatric and political perspectives for defining their problems. Perhaps those from small towns and rural communities in particular had long been accustomed to define the world in religious terms. Although all pre-converts had discarded conventional religious outlooks as inadequate, "spiritless," "dead," etc., prior to contact with the D.P., they retained a *general propensity to impose religious meaning on events*.

Even with these restrictions on the solutions available for acutely felt problems, a number of alternative responses still remain. First, people can persist in stressful situations with little or no relief. Second, persons often take specifically problem-directed action to change troublesome portions of their lives, without adopting a different world view to interpret them. Bertha and Minnie Mae might have simply divorced their husbands, for instance, and presumably, Lester could have embraced homosexuality. Clearly many pre-converts attempted such action (Merwin *did* start a boarding house, Elmer *did* attend college, etc.) but none found a successful direct solution to his difficulties.

Third, a number of maneuvers exist to "put the problem out of mind." In general these are compensations for or distractions from problems in living: e.g., addictive consumption of the mass media, pre-occupation with child-rearing, or immersion in work. More spectacular examples include alcoholism, suicide, promiscuity, and so on. Recall, for example, that Minnie Mae, Alice and Bertha, "hung around" the general store during the day getting high on beer during the summer of 1959. Had they done this in a more urban setting, in bars with strange men available, their subsequent lives might have been different.

In any event, we may assume that many persons with tensions not only explore these possible strategies, but succeed in some cases in "making it," and hence, are no longer potential D.P. recruits.[9]

3. *Seekership*. Whatever the reasons, pre-converts failed to find a way out of their difficulties through any of the strategies outlined above. Their need for solutions persisted, and their problem-solving perspective was restricted to a religious outlook, but all pre-converts found conventional religious institutions inadequate as a source of solution. Subsequently, each came to define himself as a religious seeker, a person searching for some satisfactory system of religious meaning to interpret and resolve his discontent, and each had taken some action to achieve this end.

Some hopped from church to church and prayer group to prayer group, pursuing their religious search through relatively conventional institutions. A male convert in his early twenties recounted:

> My religious training consisted of various denominations such as Baptist, Methodist, Congregationalist, Jehovah's Witnesses and Catholicism. Through all my experiences, I refused to accept ... religious dogma ... because it was the Truth I was seeking, and not a limited belief or concept.

Others began to explore the occult milieu, reading the voluminous literature of the strange, the mystical and the spiritual and tentatively trying a series of such occult groups as Rosicrucians, Spiritualists and the various divine sciences.

> In April, 1960, my wife and I ... [began] to seek a church connection. [We] began an association with Yokefellow, a spiritual growth organization in our local church. My whole religious outlook took on a new meaning and a broader vision. I grew emotionally and spiritually during the next two and one half years.

> However, as I grew, many spiritual things remained unanswered and new questions came up demanding answers which Yokefellow and the Church seemed not to even begin to touch upon. ... My wife and I became interested in the revelation of Edgar Cayce and the idea of reincarnation which seemed to answer so much, we read searchingly about the Dead Sea Scrolls, we decided to pursue Rosicrucianism, we read books on the secret disclosures to be gained from Yogi-type meditation. The more we searched the more questions seemed to come

up. Through Emmet Fox's writings I thought I had discovered a path through Metaphysics which through study would give me the breakthrough I longed for.

Or, the seeker might display some amalgam of conventional and unusual religious conceptions, as illustrated by a male convert's sad tale:

I was reared in a Pentecostal church and as a child was a very ardent follower of Christianity. Because of family situations, I began to fall away and search for other meanings in life. This began ... when I was about 12 years old. From that time one, my life was most of the time an odious existence, with a great deal of mental anguish. These last two years have brought me from church to church trying to find some fusion among them. I ended up going to Religious Science in the morning and fundamentalist in the evening.

Floundering about among religions was accompanied by two fundamental postulates that define more specifically the ideological components of the religious-seeker pattern. Although concrete per-convert beliefs varied a good deal, all of them espoused these postulates about the nature of ultimate reality.

First, they believed that spirits of some variety came from an active supernatural realm to intervene in the "material world." Such entities could, at least sometimes, "break through" from the beyond and impart information, cause "experiences" or take a hand in the course of events.

Second, their conception of the universe was teleological, in the sense that beyond all appearances in the "sensate world" exists a purpose for which every object or event is created and exists. The earth is as it is to meet the needs of man, for example, and man manifests the physical structure he does to do the things he does. More important, man himself as a phenomenon must "be on earth" because, somewhere, sometime, somehow, it was decided that *homo sapiens* should "fulfill" a purpose or purposes. Accordingly, each person must have been "put on earth" for some reason, with some sort of "job" to perform.

Beliefs were typically no more specific than this. The religious seeking itself was in terms of finding some more detailed formulation of these problematically vague existential axes.

A few words on the general question of the importance of prior beliefs in effecting conversion are necessary at this point. A number of discussions of conversion have emphasized congruence between previous ideology and a given group's "appeal,"[10] while others treat the degree of congruence as unimportant so long as the ideology is seen as embodied in what appears to be a successful movement.[11] Both views seem extreme.[12]

Our data suggest that only the two gross kinds of congruence that make up the ideology of religious seekership are necessary for conversion to the D.P. Presumptively important items, such as fundamentalist Christianity, millenarian expectations, and hallucinatory experience were far from universal among pre-converts. Most pre-converts believed in a vaguely defined "New Age" that would appear gradually, but they *became* apocalyptic pre-millenarian only upon conversion.

The role of these gross points of congruence is suggested in the substantive D.P. appeals to pre-converts. Active spirits were rampant in their view of reality. Converts lived with an immediate sense of unseen forces operating on the physical order (e.g., the weather) and intervening in human affairs — in relations among nations, in the latest national disaster, and in their own moment-to-moment lives. Nothing occurred that was not related to the intentions of God's or Satan's spirits. For persons holding a teleological conception of reality, the D.P. doctrine had the virtue of offering a minute and lawful explanation of the whole of human history. It systematically defined and revealed the hidden meaning of individual lives that had lacked coherence and purpose, and of course, it explained all hallucinatory behavior in terms of spirit manifestations. These spirits had been preparing the pre-convert to see the truth of the D.P.

Although acute and enduring tensions in the form of frustrated aspirations is not an ideological component, in the sense of being a more abstract postulate about the nature of reality, it should be noted here, in relation to the matter of congruence, that the D.P. also offered a proximate and major solution. Converts were assured of being virtual demi-gods for all eternity, beginning with a rule over the restored and reformed earth in the immediate future. By 1967 God was to impose the millennium upon earth, and those who converted early, before the truth of this message became self-evident, would occupy the most favored positions in the divine hegemony. Converts particularly stressed this advantage of conversion in their proselytization: "those who get in early," as one member often put it, "will be in on the ground floor of something big."

Religious seekership emerges, then, as another part of the path through the maze of life contingencies leading to D.P. conversion. It is a floundering among religious alternatives, an openness to a variety of religious views, frequently esoteric, combined with failure to embrace the specific ideology and fellowship of some set of believers.[13] Seekership provided the minimal points of ideological congruence to make these people available for D.P. conversion.

4. *The Turning Point.* The necessary attributes of pre-converts stated thus far had all persisted for some time before the pre-converts encountered the D.P.; they can be considered "background" factors, or predispositions. Although they apparently arose and were active in the order specified, they are important here as accumulated and simultaneously active factors during the development of succeeding conditions.

We now turn to situational factors in which timing becomes much more significant. The first of these is the rather striking circumstance that *shortly* before, and *concurrently* with their encounter with the D.P., all pre-converts had reached or were about to reach what they perceived as a "turning point" in their lives. That is, each had come to a moment when old lines of action were complete, had failed or been disrupted, or were about to be so, and when they faced the opportunity (or necessity), and possibly the burden, of doing something different with their lives.[14] Thus, Miss Lee's academic career had been disrupted by long illness from which she recovered upon meeting Chang; Bertha was newly arrived in a strange town; Lester was disaffected from graduate studies after having quit the seminary; Minnie Mae no longer had a pre-school child at home to care for; Merwin had just failed in business after dropping out of school; and Elmer had returned to his parents' farm after failing in college for the second time.

Turning points in general derived from recent migration; loss of employment (a business failure in Merwin's case); and completion, failure, or withdrawal from school. Perhaps because most converts were young adults, turning points involving educational institutions were relatively frequent. Illustrations in addition to the cases described above are a graduate student who had just failed his Ph.D. qualifying examinations, two second-semester college seniors who had vague and unsatisfying plans for the future, and a seventeen year-old who had just graduated from high school. Recovery from or the onset of an illness, marital dissolution and other changes, extant or imminent, such as Minnie Mae's new freedom, were relatively infrequent. The significance of these various turning points is that they increased the pre-convert's awareness of and desire to take some action about his problems, *at the same time giving him a new opportunity to do so.* Turning points were situations in which old obligations and lines of action were diminished, and new involvements became desirable and possible.

5. *Cult Affective Bonds.* We come now to the contact between a potential recruit and the D.P. If persons who go through all four of the previous steps are to be further drawn down the road to full conversion, an affective bond must develop, if it does not already exist, between the potential recruit and one or more of the D.P. members. The development or presence of some positive, emotional, interpersonal response seems necessary to bridge the gap between the first exposure to the D.P. message and accepting its truth. That is, persons developed affective ties with the group or some of its members while they still regarded the D.P. perspective as problematic, or even "way out." In a manner of speaking, final conversion was coming to accept the opinions of one's friends.[15]

Miss Lee's recollections of her conversion provide a graphic illustration:

> In addition to this change [her recovery from illness] I felt very good spiritually. I felt as if I had come to life from a numb state and there was spiritual *liveliness and vitality within me by being among this group.* As one feels when he comes from a closed stuffy room in the fresh air, or the goodness and warmth after freezing coldness was how my spirit witnessed its happiness. *Although I could not agree with the*

> *message intellectually I found myself one with it spiritually.* I reserved
> my conclusions and waited for guidance from God. [Italics added.]

Miss Lee further revealed she was particularly attracted to Mr. Chang and resided in his dwelling to enjoy the pleasure of his company, until, finally, she decided his message was true. Her statement that she "could not agree with the message intellectually" is particularly significant. Other converts reported and were observed to experience similar reservations as they nevertheless developed strong bonds with members of the group. Thus, for example, Lester, the most highly intellectual of the converts, displayed an extremely strong attachment to the middle-aged Miss Lee and manifested the "intellect problem" for some weeks after he had turned his life over to her. At one point late in this period he could still reflectively comment an observer:

> I have not entirely reconciled [the D.P. world view] with my intellect,
> but [Miss Lee] keeps answering more and more questions that are in
> my mind so I am beginning to close the holes I have found in it.

It is particularly important to note that conversions frequently moved through *pre-existing* friendship pairs or nets. In the formation of the original core group, an affective bond first developed between Miss Lee and Bertha (the first to meet Miss Lee and begin to espouse her views). Once that had happened, the rest of the original conversions were supported by prior friendships. Bertha was part of the housewife trio of Minnie Mae and Alice; Merwin was Alice's husband, and Elmer was Merwin's friend and workmate. Subsequent conversions also followed friendship paths, or friendships developed between the pre-convert and the converts, prior to conversion.

Bonds that were unsupported by previous friendships with a new convert often took the form of a sense of instant and powerful rapport with a believer. Consider , for example a young housewife's account of her first view of Lester while attending an Edgar Cayce Foundation retreat:[16]

> I went to [one of the] Bible class[es] and saw [Lester] in our class — I
> had seen him for the first time the night before and had felt such love
> for him — he was my brother, yet I had not met him. He looked as if he
> were luminous! After the class I wanted to talk to him — but our
> project groups had a discipline that day — complete silence — I did
> not want to break it, yet I felt such a need to talk to him. I prayed and
> asked God what He would have me do — I received such a positive
> feeling — I took this as an answer and sought out [Lester]. When I
> found him, I did not have anything to say — I just mumbled something
> — But he seemed to understand and took me to the beach where he
> told me "He is on earth!" Oh, what a joy I felt! My whole body was
> filled with electricity.

The less-than-latent sexual overtones of this encounter appeared in a number of other heterosexual attachments that led to conversion (and quite a few that did not). Even after four years of cult membership Elmer could hardly hide his feelings in this testimonial:

> Early in 1960, after a desperate prayer, which was nothing more than the words, "Father if there is any truth in this world, please reveal it to me," I met [Miss Lee]. This day I desire to never forget. Although I didn't fully understand yet, I desired to unite with her. ...

Although a potential convert might have some initial difficulty in taking up the D.P. perspective, given the four previous conditions *and* an affective tie, he began seriously to consider the D.P. and to accept it as his personal construction of reality.

6. *Extra-Cult Affective Bonds*. One might suppose that non-D.P. associates of a convert-in-process would not be entirely neutral to the now immediate possibility that he would join the D.P. group. We must inquire, then, into the conditions under which extra-cult controls are activated through emotional attachments, and how they restrain or fail to restrain persons from D.P. conversion.

Recent migration, disaffection with geographically distant families and spouses and very few nearby acquaintances made a few converts "social atoms;" for them extra-cult attachments were irrelevant. More typically, converts were acquainted with nearby persons, but none was intimate enough to be aware that a conversion was in progress or to feel that the mutual attachment was sufficient to justify intervention. Thus, for example, Lester's social round was built primarily around participation in religious groups. Although he was well-known and appreciated for his contributions, he was not included in any local circles of intimacy. Many people knew him, but no one was a *personal* friend. Further, Lester's relations with both parents and step-parents manifested considerable strain and ambivalence, and his homosexual liaison was shot through with strain.

In many cases, positive attachments outside the cult were to other religious seekers, who, even though not yet budding converts themselves, encouraged continued "investigation" or entertainment of the D.P. rather than exercising a countervailing force. Indeed, such an extra-cult person might be only slightly behind his friend in his own conversion process.

In the relatively few cases where positive attachments existed between conventional extra-cult persons and a convert-in-process, control was minimal or absent, because of geographical distance or intentional avoidance of communication about the topic while the convert was solidifying his faith. Thus, for example, a German immigrant in his early thirties failed to inform his mother in Germany, to whom he was strongly attached, during his period of entertainment and only wrote her about the D.P. months after his firm acceptance. (She disowned him.)

During the period of tentative acceptance, and afterwards, converts, of course, possessed a rhetoric that helped to neutralize affective conflicts. An account by a newly converted solider in Oklahoma conveys the powerful (and classic) content of this facilitating and justifying rhetoric:

> I wrote my family a very long but yet very plain letter about our movement and exactly what I received in spiritual ways plus the fact that Jesus had come to me himself. The weeks passed and I heard nothing but I waited with deep trust in God.

> This morning I received a letter from my mother. She ... surmised that I was working with a group other than those with the "stamp of approval by man." She ... called me a fanatic, and went on to say: "My fervent constant prayer is that time will show you the fruitlessness of the way you have chosen before it consumes you entirely. A real true religion is deep in the heart and shines through your countenance for all to see. One need not shout it to the house tops either."

> At first it was the deepest hurt I had ever experienced. But, I remember what others in [the D.P.] family have given up and how they too experienced a similar rejection. But so truly, I can now know a little of the rejection that our beloved Master experienced. I can now begin to understand his deep grief for the Father as he sat peering out of a window singing love songs to Him because he knew that the Father would feel such grief. I can now begin to feel the pain that our Father in heaven felt for 6,000 years. I can now begin to see that to come into the Kingdom of heaven is not as easy as formerly thought. I can now see why many are called but few are chosen. I began to understand why men will be separated, yes even from their families. I begin to see the shallowness of human concern for God as a Father and their true blindness. Oh my heart cries out to Our Father in greatful [*sic*] praise and love for what He has given.

> \* \* \*

> [In the words of Miss Lee:] "As we get close to the Father the road shall become more difficult;" "Only by truly suffering, can we know the Leader and the heart of the Father;" "You shall be tested." "He will come with a double-edged blade." Only now am I beginning to know the heart of the Father and the great suffering of our Lord.

When there were emotional attachments to outsiders who were physically present and cognizant of the incipient transformation, conversion became a "nip-and-tuck" affair. Pulled about by competing emotional loyalties and discordant versions of reality, such persons were subjected to intense emotional strain. A particularly poignant instance of this involved a newly-wed senior at the local state university. He began tentatively to espouse the D.P. as he developed strong ties with Lester and Miss Lee. His young wife struggled to accept, but she did not meet a number of the conditions leading to conversion, and in the end, seemed nervous, embarrassed, and even ashamed to be at D.P. gatherings. One night, just before the group began a prayer meeting, he rushed in and tearfully announced that he would have nothing further to do with the D.P., though he still thought the message was probably true. Torn between affective bonds, he opted for his young bride, but it was only months later that he finally lost all belief in the D.P.

When extra-cult bonds withstood the strain of affective and ideological flirtation with the D.P., conversion was not consummated. Most converts, however, lacked external affiliations close enough to permit informal control over belief. Affectively, they were so "unintegrated" that they could, for the most part, simply fall out of relatively conventional society unnoticed, taking their co-seeker friends, if any, with them.

7. *Intensive Interaction.* In combination, the six previous factors suffice to bring a person to *verbal conversion* to the D.P. but one more contingency must be met if he is to become a "deployable agent,"[17] or what we have termed a *total convert.* Most, but not all, verbal converts ultimately put their lives at the disposal of the cult. Such transformations in commitment took place, we suggest, as a result of intensive interaction with D.P. members, and failed to result when such interaction was absent.

Intensive interaction means concrete, daily, and even hourly accessibility to D.P. members, which implies physical proximity to total converts. Intensive exposure offers an opportunity to reinforce and elaborate an initial, tentative assent to the D.P. world view, and in prolonged association the perspective "comes alive" as a device for interpreting the moment-to-moment events in the convert's life.

The D.P. doctrine has a variety of resources for explicating the most minor everyday events in terms of a cosmic battle between good and evil spirits, in a way that placed the convert at the center of this war. Since all D.P. interpretations pointed to the imminence of the end, to participate in these explications of daily life was to come more and more to see the necessity of one's personal participation as a totally committed agent in this cosmic struggle.[18]

Reminders and discussion of the need to make other converts, and the necessity of supporting the cause in every way, were the main themes of verbal exchanges among the tentatively accepting and the total converts, and, indeed, among the total converts themselves. Away from this close association with those already totally committed, one failed to "appreciate" the need for one's transformation into a total convert.

In recognition of this fact, the D.P. members gave highest priority to attempts to persuade verbal converts (even the merely interested) to move into the cult's communal dwellings. During her early efforts in Northwest Town, Miss Lee gained verbal conversions from Bertha, Minnie Mae, Alice, Merwin, and Elmer, many months before she was able to turn them into total converts. This transformation did not occur, in fact, until Miss Lee moved into Alice and Merwin's home (along with Elmer), placing her within a few dozen yards of the homes of Minnie Mae and Bertha. The resulting daily exposure of the verbal converts to Miss Lee's total conversion increasingly engrossed them in D.P. activities, until they came to give it all their personal and material resources.[19] Recalling this period, Minnie Mae reported a process that occurred during other verbal converts' periods of intensive interaction. When one of them began to waver in his faith, unwavering believers were fortunately present to carry him through this "attack of Satan."

Most verbally assenting converts were induced out of this tenuous state, through contrived or spontaneous intensive interaction, within a few weeks, or more typically, a few months. In a few instances the interval between assent and total commitment spanned a year or more. When the unmarried older sister of the German immigrant mentioned above came to entertain the D.P. perspective, some 11 months of subtle and not-so-subtle pressures were required to get her to leave her private apartment and move into the communal dwelling. Within two months she went from rather lukewarm belief to total dedication and subsequent return to Germany as a D.P. missionary. The following ecstatic testimonial given during her second month of cult residence contrasts sharply with her previously reserved and inhibited statements:

> In the beginning of May I moved into our center in [Bay City]. A complete new life started for me. Why had I not cut off my self-centered life earlier! Here under [Miss Lee's] care and guidance I felt God's power and love tremendously and very soon it became my only desire to wholeheartedly serve our Father. How fortunate I am being a child and student of our beloved mother and teacher, [Miss Lee]. She reflects in all her gestures, words and works the love and wisdom of our Lord and Master.

Thus, verbal conversion and even a resolution to reorganize one's life for the D.P. is not automatically translated into total conversion. One must be intensively exposed to the group supporting these new standards of conduct. D.P. members did not find proselytizing, the primary task of total converts, very easy, but in the presence of persons who reciprocally supported each other, such a transformation of one's life became possible. Persons who accepted the truth of the doctrine, but lacked intensive interaction with the core group, remained partisan spectators, who played no active part in the battle to usher in God's kingdom.

# Summary

We have presented a model of the accumulating conditions that appear to describe and account for conversion to an obscure millenarian perspective. These necessary and constellationally-sufficient conditions may be summarized as follows:

For conversion a person must:

1. Experience enduring, acutely felt tensions
2. Within a religious problem-solving perspective,
3. Which leads him to define himself as a religious seeker;
4. Encountering the D.P. at a turning point in his life,
5. Wherein an affective bond is formed (or pre-exists) with one or more converts;
6. Where extra-cult attachments are absent or neutralized;
7. And, where, if he is to become a deployable agent, he is exposed to intensive interaction.

Because this model was developed from the study of a small set of converts to a minor millenarian doctrine, it may possess few generalizable features. We suggest, however, that its terms are general enough, and its elements articulated in such a way as to provide a reasonable starting point for the study of conversion to other types of groups and perspectives.

A closing *caveat*. The D.P. had few competitive advantages, if any, over other unusual religious groups, in terms of the potential converts' predispositions. In terms of situational conditions the D.P. advantage was simply that they were on the scene and able to make their "pitch," develop affective bonds and induce intensive interaction. We hope our effort will help dispel the tendency to assume some "deep," almost mystical, connection between world views and their carriers. Like conceptions holding that criminals and delinquents must be "really different," our thinking about other deviants has too often assumed some extensive characterological conjunction between participant and pattern of participation.

• • • • • • • • • • • • • • • • • • • • • • • • • •

# Notes

[1]  Clyde Kluckhohn, "Values and Value-Orientations in the Theory of Action: An Exploration in Definition and Classification," in Talcott Parsons and Edward Shils (eds.), *Toward a General Theory of Action*, New York: Harper Torchbooks, 1962, p.409.

[2]  The meaning of this term has been muddied by the inconsistent usage of Christian religious writers. Often they have used "conversion" to refer to an aroused concern among persons who already accept the essential truth of the ideological system. Yet, in keeping with the earliest Christian examples of

conversion, such as that of St. Paul, they have also used the word to describe changes from one such system to another. These are very different events and ought to be indicated by different words.

3    All names that might compromise converts' anonymity have been changed.

4    Other aspects of the cult's formation, development, maintenance and proselytization procedures are analyzed in John Lofland, *The World-Savers*, Englewood Cliffs, N.J.: Prentice-Hall, forthcoming.

5    Neil J. Smelser, *Theory of Collective Behavior*, New York: The Free Press of Glencoe, 1963, pp. 12-21. See also Ralph Turner, "The Quest for Universals in Sociological Research," *American Sociological Review*, 18 (1953), pp. 604-611.

6    Peter Berger has given us a delightful characterization of the reconstructive functions of such tales. See his *Invitation to Sociology*, New York: Doubleday Anchor, 1933, Ch. 3.

7    We conceive this tension as subjective to avoid judgments about how tension-producing the "objective" circumstances actually were, attending instead to the way these circumstances were experienced.

8    It is currently fashionable to reduce this last to more mundane "real" causes, but it is not necessary here to pre-judge the phenomenology.

9    Our analysis is confined to isolating the elements of the conversion sequence. Extended analysis would refer to the factors that *in turn* bring each conversion condition into existence. That is, it would be necessary to develop a theory for each of the seven elements, specifying the conditions under which each appears. On the form such theory would probably take, see Ralph Turner's discussion of "the intrusive factor," *op. cit.*, pp. 609-611.

10    E.g., H.G. Brown, "The Appeal of Communist Ideology," *American Journal of Economics and Sociology*, 2 (1943), pp. 161-174; Gabriel Almond, *The Appeals of Communism*, Princeton: Princeton University Press, 1954.

11    E.g., Eric Hoffer, *The True Believer*, New York: Mentor 1958 (copyright 1951), p. 10.

12    Cf. Herbert Blumer, Collective Behavior" in Joseph B. Gittler (ed.), *Review of Sociology*, New York: Wiley, 1957, pp. 147-148.

13    For further suggestive materials on seekers and seeking see H.T. Dohrman, *California Cult*, Boston: Beacon, 1958; Leon Festinger, Henry Riecken and Stanley Schacter, *When Prophecy Fails*, Minneapolis: University of Minnesota Press, 1956; Sanctus De Santis, *Religious Conversion*, London: Routledge and Kegan Paul, 1927, esp. pp. 260-261; H. Taylor Buckner, "Deviant-Group Organizations," Unpublished M.A. thesis, University of California, Berkeley, 1964, Ch. 2. For discussion of a generically similar phenomenon in a different context, see Edgar H. Schein, *Coercive Persuasion*, New York: Norton, 1961, pp. 120-136, 270-277.

14    Everett C. Hughes, *Men and Their Work*, Glencoe: Free Press, 1958, Ch. 1; Anselm Strauss, "Transformations of Identity," in Arnold Rose (ed.), *Human Behavior and Social Processes*, Boston: Houghton Mifflin, 1962, pp. 67-71. Cf. the often-noted, "cultural dislocation" and migration pattern found in the background of converts to many groups, especially cults.

15    Cf. Tamatsu Shibutani, *Society and Personality*, Englewood Cliffs, N.J.: Prentice-Hall, 1961, pp. 523-532, 588-592. Schein (*op. cit.*, p. 277) reports that "the most potent source of influence in coercive persuasion was the identification which arose between a prisoner and his more reformed cellmate." See also Alan Kerckhoff, Kurt Back and Norman Miller, "Sociometric Patterns in Hysterical Contagion," *Sociometry*, 28, (1965), pp. 2-15.

16    Lester was at this retreat precisely for the purpose of meeting potential converts. Attendance at religious gatherings in the masquerade of a religious seeker was the primary D.P. mode of recruiting.

17    On the concept of the "deployable agent" or "deployable personnel" in social movements see Philip Selznick, *The Organizational Weapon*, New York: The Free Press, 1960 (copyright 1952), pp. 18-29.

18    Cf. Schein, *op. cit.*, pp. 136-139, 280-282.

[19]    Although a number of our illustrative cases are drawn from the period of the group's formation, the process of cult formation itself should not be confused with the analytically distinct process of conversion. The two are merely empirically compounded. Cult formation occurs when a network of friends who meet the first four conditions develop affective bonds with a world-view carrier and collectively develop the last two conditions, except that condition seven, intensive interaction, requires exposure *to each other* in addition to the world-view carrier. (For a different conception of "sub-culture" formation see Albert K. Cohen, *Delinquent Boys*, Glencoe, Ill.: The Free Press, 1955, Ch. 3.)

# CHAPTER NINE

# THE JOINERS

SAUL LEVINE

Dennis Ericson's radical departure was among the first I came to know about. In 1969, when I was working among draft dodgers and deserters in Toronto and other cities in Canada, Dennis was a 20-year-old sophomore studying engineering at the University of Cincinnati. He had no trouble with technical courses, but had to work hard to maintain his grades in the required dose of literature and history. Dennis's stock figure and sandy hair, cropped short even in those long-haired days, resembled those of his father, Jack. Mr. Ericson had worked as a design engineer since his retirement, as a colonel, from the U.S. Army. Ivy Ericson worked as a loan adviser in a bank. An older brother had already graduated with a degree in engineering, and it was a family joke that one day the three men would hoist a sign: Ericson & Sons, Engineers.

The family lived in a pleasant suburb of San Diego. In keeping with their traditionally conservative professions and with their middle-class, Protestant backgrounds, they supported President Nixon and the Vietnam War effort wholeheartedly. Like other students of his day, Dennis anticipated being drafted to serve in Vietnam, and he and his family seemed to be in fundamental agreement that serving one's country was not only an obligation, but also a correct and honorable one.

Dennis had no tolerance for antiwar groups such as Students for a Democratic Society and the Student Nonviolent Coordinating Committee; he had considered joining the Young Republicans.

This seamless agreement in principle showed a slightly frayed edge in practice. Dennis on several occasions confided to his parents a certain eagerness to be drafted, and was surprised to find his urge met with nervous amusement. The Ericsons supported the war but didn't want their son to serve in Vietnam.

Dennis had not, however, confided the full extent of his concerns or the underlying reasons for his urge to join the army. Raised in a career-oriented home and enrolled in a career-oriented course of study, he was nevertheless becoming increasingly unsure of the direction in which he was headed. He was bored with his friends, his activities, his studies, himself. Talking about the months just prior to receiving his draft notice, he said, "All I knew then was that I needed some excitement or adventure in my life. I could get into terrific arguments on campus about the war, but for me it was all a mental game. I wished that I believed what I said." Joining up, he felt, might relieve his overwhelming sense of tedium.

When the draft notice did arrive, Dennis abruptly, to his own and his family's confusion, changed his mind. He joined the other draft dodgers in a commune in Vancouver. Within weeks he had left this group to become a member of Healthy Happy Holy Organization, usually called "3HO." This spiritual-rehabilitation group followed Yogi Bhajan, an Indian teacher of Tantrum and Kundalini Yoga in the United States and Canada.

Philip Holtzman at 21 was the success story all parents wish for their children. He was an excellent student, a star athlete, and popular with both boys and girls; he had a steady girl, Marcie, with whom he was quite taken. During the summer of 1978 this tall boy with tightly curling red hair was living at home in Denver after completing his sophomore year at the University of Colorado. He had taken a variety of arts and science courses, had made the dean's list in both years, but felt unready to declare a major. Hoping to come upon some one thing that interested him particularly, he planned to take a year's leave of absence from school to travel and work abroad, and his parents, Sam and Ellen, encouraged the idea. They had no doubt that their older son could take on this new adventure with the same responsibility he had always shown; to them, this challenging year was to be an extension of his education.

Education was a central value to the Holtzmans. Sam was a prominent physician. Ellen was a high-school librarian studying for her doctorate in library science. Phil's two younger brothers and a sister were all doing well in school, though not quite at the level of their older brother. Like Phil, his parent were what one would call "well-rounded" people. They regularly attended the local symphony and the theater, and found time for tennis and jogging.

Dr. Holtzman had been brought up in an Orthodox Jewish home in New York City; Yiddish was his parents' native tongue. Mrs. Holtzman came from a Conservative, quite devout Jewish background. Although neither grew up to be deeply religious, they felt strongly about their commitment to Judaism and to Israel. They attended Sabbath services at the Reform temple sporadically, never misses the High Holy Day services, and had seen to it that all of their children received religious training and read some Hebrew.

The "ideal" family was further flavored with idealism. In their own words, they had always encouraged their children to "make a contribution," to "leave the world better than they found it." Their only tension with Phil stemmed from the fact that he had been unable to translate this idealism within the context of their religion. As Phil put it, "I never felt much identification with Judaism or Israel. Mom and Dad got annoyed whenever I spoke this way, but I couldn't help it. Actually, I felt that this was the only area in which I disappointed them. I knew I was Jewish, but I didn't feel much else about it."

That summer, abroad, this model youth made his radical departure into the mysticism and narrow intellectualism of an Orthodox Jewish seminary, a yeshiva in Jerusalem.

Jennifer Green was a 19-year-old beauty. She wore her glistening black hair tied back simply from her perfectly oval, creamy-complexioned face. Her gray eyes sparkled with laughter — "bubbly" laughter, as her mother described it. Jennifer showed the sort of native talent that is peculiarly gratifying to parents. She was a gifted pianist, and the Greens took justifiable pride in their expectation that she would go on to a career as a concert pianist.

The whole family had participated in her talent, even to the extent of moving from their home in the Midwest to Houston, where a sought-after teacher had consented to supervise her training. By the winter after her graduation from high school in 1972, their efforts seemed about to pay off: Jennifer had auditioned for and been accepted by two conservatories, Curtis and Julliard.

The Greens, however, showed signs of family strain. Allen Green an accountant and tax consultant employed by a well-heeled clientele, was a busy man whose recipe for getting along with his wife and daughter was to lie low. Linda Green was preoccupied with a campaign to achieve "self-realization" — an endeavor that had led her to espouse at various times Gestalt, Rolfing, Esalen, Bioenergetics, and other therapeutic schemes. Jennifer's older brother, Jason, was completing his doctoral thesis in behavioral modification. Indeed, this faith, for that was what their fervor for therapy seemed to amount to, was practiced by everyone in the family except Mr. Green. From the time Jennifer was 15, Mrs. Green had been convinced that her beautiful, talented daughter needed professional help; and that it was true that Jennifer, for all her appeal to her schoolmates, had tended to isolate herself from other children her age. At her mother's behest, she was in group, family, or individual therapy for the next four years, while Mrs. Green harped on the refrain "Develop yourself."

But Jennifer seemed to lose the strands of whatever self she was supposed to be developing. By the time she was accepted by a conservatory, she was only going through the motions in her music; she could work at it, but took no pleasure in practice. Her mother was too adamant to notice. As Jennifer explained, about this period prior to her departure, "My mother was on a tear all the time about my career and the latest guru who would cure my woes."

Jennifer found her "guru" on her own through an ad in a psychology magazine; Kurt, the charismatic leader of the Healing Workshop, a therapeutic commune and another variety of radical departure.


Suzanne Marquette, 18 in 1975, lived with her family in Minneapolis, where she had completed a year of junior college, though with little interest and declining grades. This, and the fact that this pretty, diminutive blond had never had a boyfriend and didn't participate in the active social life her friends enjoyed, might have concerned her parents were it not for the special circumstances of their daughter's life. Suzanne had one overriding passion: figure skating. She was extremely talented and had since the age of five devoted thousands of hours to what she considered one of the higher art forms.

Her mother, Barbara, was deeply involved in that pursuit, chaperoning her daughter to practice, shows, and competitions and always being extremely supportive of her continuing progress. Peter Marquette, Suzanne's father, was perhaps too distracted by his own pursuits to contribute to those of his daughter. He owned a small but thriving printing business, and evidently had to be there morning, noon, and night — the sort of driven man one would call a "workaholic."

Suzanne had the air of constant busyness. She did everything with a competence and thoroughness unusual in a girl that age. Besides the demands of skating, she did volunteer work at a nursing home and was very helpful around the house. She was particularly tender with her tow-headed twin brothers, whom, though they were only four, she coaxed along on the ice until they were really quite good skaters. "Maybe I was too busy in those days," Suzanne was to tell me later. "I don't know — when I wasn't helping out around the house or at the nursing home, I knew that I had to be skating. And it didn't fell like a burden; I mean I had done that most of my life, and that was just the way things were."

Ice-skating had, indeed, become a career choice as well as a recreation. Suzanne planned to turn professional during the coming fall, when she was scheduled to try out for a well-known ice show in Santa Monica, California. Acceptance into the troupe would mean going on tour. "I was busy but I wasn't involved in things," she explained. "For some reason I knew I couldn't wait to get away on tour, even though I was getting tired of skating."

Lying on the beach in Santa Monica the day of the audition, Suzanne was approached by members of the Unification Church. Sometime in the next three days, and after a most successful audition, she had thrown the years of practice to the wind. She had become a Moonie.

Other young men and women who shocked family and friends with their radical departures were more troublesome to their parents than Dennis, Phil, Jennifer, and Suzanne were.

Nancy Lewis was in constant conflict with her parents over her choice of career and her behavior in general. Her parents had wanted her to go to a small business college not far from their home in northern New Jersey to learn a marketable skill. Nancy, with some contempt for her father's job as a rug salesman, was convinced he saw everything as marketable, even her. She had complied with their wish for one term, then dropped out in favor of informal drama classes run by a New York City actor her father labeled "a loser." Her mother seemed no less crass to Nancy. Mrs. Lewis often remarked on how hard they had worked, how much they had earned, to make her life a happy one.

Nancy's perceptions were not entirely wrong; her parents were not sophisticated and were too often preoccupied with maintaining their middle-class standard of life. The Lewises were nominally Methodist and had sent their three daughters — Nancy was the middle one — to Sunday school, but they themselves rarely attended church. They had few cultural interests. Although their split-level development house was scrupulously cared for, it did not reflect Nancy's idea of creative expression. Mrs. Lewis shopped for supermarket specials on Saturdays; Mr. Lewis watched the ball game and worked around the house on Sundays. All through the week both parents worked hard but unimaginatively to maintain the financial and household standards that, to both of them, stood between them and the much poorer backgrounds both had come from. They were rightly proud of their achievement, but Nancy found their ordinariness dreary. Lillian and George Lewis resented Nancy' apparent ungratefulness.

Nancy responded with what she later called her "grande artiste" front — the belief that she, unlike her parents, was creative, sensitive, cultured. She escaped her house as often as possible to hang out with the guys at "the Elm," smoke a few joints, spend the night with a boyfriend her parents called "a no-good bum," or pick up someone new. She thought these people at least appreciated her creativity, but in fact she was locally known as an "easy lay," which she perhaps inadvertently advertised with overdramatic costuming that accentuated her full breasts and hips.

This desultory sort of life continued for three years without Nancy getting a job, moving away form home, or, as far as the Lewises could see, getting any closer to any acting career. In the winter of 1976, now 22 years old, Nancy looked forward to some relief from the stresses of home life in the form of a two-week vacation in Fort Lauderdale with her close friend, Flo. There she met and joined the Children of God, her radical departure.

Equally bitter but less comprehensible and certainly less likable was Fred Vitelli, a smug young man who by the age of 20 had long since decided that school was "bullshit" and those that remained there "browners." He spoke of others, all others, with contempt weighted with obscenity. If one could ignore his manner, Fred was otherwise attractive: over six feet tall, well built, and with sensual features.

He spent much of his time high or stoned on drugs. He had been suspended from public high school in a wealthy Chicago suburb on two occasions. He had completed secondary education at a private school that specialized in "problem" children, but had refused to apply for college. He had also been in chronic, if minor, trouble with the law — possession of marijuana, reckless driving. Mr. Vitelli, at his wife's pleading for the "baby" in this large family, always bailed Fred out of trouble.

Anthony and Maria Vitelli were one of those couples who by working together in what was originally a small family business — making trophies and commemorative plaques — built their enterprise into a major national concern. They were able to give Fred a Porsche when he was only 17, with the conditional message that the gift was proof of their love but would be taken from him unless he stopped abusing drugs and improved his schoolwork. Fred didn't keep his end of the bargain, but before the Vitelli's could reclaim the costly sports car Fred had totaled it. His driver's license was revoked.

By the fall of 1979, parents and son had made another deal. Fred was to go to Europe for a few months, using his own money (which was in fact an accumulation of cash gifts from relatives, not earnings), on condition that he begin college when he returned. Brazen and cocksure on the surface, he intended to spend the forthcoming months stoned, then return to "make a killing" in his family's or some other business. His parents were worn out by this son, unwilling to take him into their business, uncertain of what else to do, yet hopeful that three months on his own would give him the maturity he lacked.

Fred didn't return. In Rome one autumn day he found his radical departure: a militant leftist group of anarchists who called themselves the Armed Guard.


Jamie Gould, 26 years old, was the oldest of the radical departers in this representative sample. His father, John, had made millions as a stockbroker and then moved with his wife to the Bahamas, a location they saw as combining tax haven, retirement home, and center for wheeling and dealing. After a long marriage, they had separated just before Jamie's birthday that year of 1977, and Joanne Gould had begun to divide her time between her own house on Barbados and a villa on the Riviera both provided by her husband. Jamie accepted a trust fund worth $4 million when he turned 30. While awaiting this largesse he was free to use the substantial income from the trust as he wished, and he also received a monthly allowance from his father that was expressly to support a lavish brownstone house in New York City.

After graduating from Northwestern University with an arts degree and being accepted into law school, Jamie had turned his back on education. This brief flirtation with becoming a lawyer was one example of his lifelong pattern of transient enthusiasms followed by inertia. The pattern was not unlike that of Mrs. Gould, who suffered from endless fits and starts — collecting Chinese porcelain, sponsoring a local historical society, organizing through her church a drive to aid famine victims, participating in political demonstrations, raising Persian cats. People had often remarked that Jamie and his mother looked alike, with their almost mahogany hair and precisely chiseled features.

Between bouts of optimism, Jamie's aimlessness was crushing. He had no job and no longstanding interests; a girl who lived with him in the luxury of his brownstone was seen as a sexual convenience.

Jamie's parents called him regularly, using a three-way connection, a "conference call," but conversation was largely perfunctory. The Gould's main concern, or so it appeared to Jamie, was that he wore and earring in one ear. Their hesitancy about criticizing him any more deeply than that was in contrast to the outspokenness of their older son John Jr., who had become a lawyer. John Jr. was furious at Jamie's total apathy, but his anger didn't really bother Jamie. "I just felt that my brother was a pain. If he wanted to work so hard that was his business, but I felt that I had the bread, why not enjoy it?"

Neither Jamie nor his parents seemed able to overcome the physical and emotional distance from which their cash currency of love was disbursed. "In a strange way," Jamie told me, "I think that money paralyzed me" — until he joined the Church of Scientology, a quasi-religion, quasi-psychology which follows the bizarre teachings of L. Ron Hubbard.

Kathy O'Connor, unlike Jamie, had been very close to her family, until the age of 23. Although she lived in Montreal and they lived in a rural area some miles north of the city, she had visited them often. She was a senior nurse at a university medical center, and was described by those who knew this five-foot-five freckle-faced young woman as "warm," "cheerful," "energetic," and "humane." Fellow nurses especially used the word "wholesome" to sum up Kathy's personality.

The O'Connor family itself might have been described that way. Katherine O'Connor was a bustling, brisk woman who not only had cared for her four daughters with unflappable good cheer, but also had seemed to feed the whole neighborhood's kids while they were growing up. She was always involved in this or that minor crisis among her numerous relatives. Her personal dedication to Catholicism was equally cheerful; she believed that it held all the instruction for managing whatever life might deliver.

Charles O'Connor was a public-works administrator for the Montreal city government, and donated time and effort as scoutmaster. Charles and Katherine were well satisfied that they had devoted their lives to charity, one in the public sphere, the other in service to the family.

But Kathy's relationship with her parents had taken a nose dive the year, 1970, she fell in love with Michael, a young Protestant intern at her hospital. Kathy and

Michael both called what had happened between them "love at first sight"; their love was exuberantly sexual. The O'Connors were unable to accept the blatant way in which the two lovers made clear they were living together. Their three other daughters, one younger and two older than Kathy, were already married, within their faith, to men of whom the family wholeheartedly approved. They could foresee nothing but problems in a mixed marriage, and blamed what was to them their daughter's sinful behavior on her straying from her faith.

Kathy said to me in retrospect, "They wanted what was best for me. It's true they didn't like Michael's religion, but they also resented his liberal politics. I was happy to leave Montreal after our wedding."

The newly married couple moved to New Orleans, where Michael entered an arduous residency in surgery. Kathy saw little of her husband during those months; she couldn't find a senior nursing position; the other residents' wives struck her as shallow people.

After less than a year of marriage, Kathy left her husband and career to join the Maharaj Ji and his Divine Light Mission.

I was struck by Ethan Browning's intensity when I first met him. He wasn't particularly handsome, though his slight, tanned body emitted energy and his wide hazel eyes were appealing. He was shy, or perhaps reserved is a better way to describe him, for he had learned his manners so well that little spontaneity came through. He used a vocabulary astonishing in one so young.

Ethan, at 16, was the youngest of the joiners in this sample. He was the only child of Stuart Browning, a vice president of a major oil company, and his wife, Patricia, who devoted herself to Ethan's upbringing and to Episcopal church activities. Ethan was in the tenth grade at a special high school for gifted students. Rather a loner, he had only one close friend, also a restrained, bookish boy.

Quiet as he was, Ethan did engage in activities that others saw as social. He was the top chess player in his school and regularly participated in competitions. He was an avid and skilled sailor, both solo and as crew in races. A flutist as well, he was given most of the solo parts in the school ensemble to which he belonged. While he did extremely well in school, he learned so easily that he didn't need to devote a great deal of time to his studies. In his ample spare time, he read voraciously, several books at a time, in subjects as diverse as history, science, and philosophy.

The Browning household was comfortable, if somewhat austere. The year before Ethan's departure in 1976 the family had sold their large home in the suburbs and purchased a well-appointed town house in Boston from which they could walk to work, school, and church. They felt that with Ethan so uninvolved with the suburban life style, they could easily live in the city. Mealtime at the Brownings was polite, a time of well-regulated conversation on a variety of intellectual topics. It held a special place within the family's ordered routine, especially for Ethan, perhaps the most orderly of all, who particularly enjoyed formal debate with his father over dinner.

Ethan never participated, however, in his parents' Episcopal church activities, not even accompanying them to Sunday services. He had said for years that he was an atheist. This bothered the Brownings. Ethan could be obstinately opinionated, and though his parents recognized obstinacy as almost a family trademark, this particular expression of it made them uncomfortable. Their church was central to their lives.

"I knew that at the age of 16, I wasn't a happy person," Ethan confided to me later. "I wasn't suicidal or even depressed, but I felt that something was missing from my life. I learned so much and did so well, yet nothing contented me. I felt there had to be more to my life."

Ethan found what was missing in his radical departure into the Hare Krishna.

Different as these joiners were in personality, talent, and interests, there are similarities among them. Whereas a person who succumbs to a radical departure is as likely to be a girl as a boy, she or he is not likely to be younger than Ethan Browning, 16, or older than Jamie Gould, 26. Those few years from adolescence to early adulthood are about the only time in our society when people *can* depart. Younger than 16 they are too dependent on their families, both emotionally and economically. Older than 26 they are likely to have responsibilities of their own — jobs, families — that they cannot easily abandon.

For a similar reason, radical departures are made almost exclusively by as yet unmarried youngsters from the middle or upper middle class, or from among the decidedly rich. Less affluent young people have neither the luxury nor the leisure to depart from obligations; they must pay their own way and often help their families too. Those who make radical departures do not have to pay their own way, nor do their families rely on support from their children. Jennifer Green's family even paid for her membership in the Healing Workshop, as Phil Holtzman's family paid for his year abroad and Suzanne Marquette's family supported her skating.

Thus, although I have seen one boy as young as 14 and occasional joiners in their 30s, radical departures are, with few exceptions, a phenomenon of late adolescence and early adulthood — the only time when there is the luxury and the leisure suddenly to drop out of usual pursuits.

Because of their age and economic situation, the vast majority of these young people are well educated; most are in their college years when they make their decision to leave their traditional paths. Almost all are white. The connection between race and radical departure is indirect, partly because of the underrepresentation of other groups in the middle class, and partly a result of the fact that joiners look especially for groups made up of members almost exactly like themselves.

Cults such as the People's Temple, which was made up of adults and entire families, most of them black, rarely attract those youths who make radical departures.

Indeed, such groups are themselves a rarity; adults who look for impassioned causes or religions seldom depart from other responsibilities in order to satisfy their need, nor do they ordinarily leave home to live communally. That these young people do leave home is all the more extraordinary in that almost all of them come from intact families. Reviews of all the statistics that have been gathered about radical departures indicate that the divorce rate in joiners' families is considerably below the national rate.

But these are constraints on who *can* become a radical departer, and not an explanation of who chooses to depart. Obviously, few of all those affluent youths who might give up education, career, family, and friendships to immerse themselves in the Hare Krishna, the Children of God, the Armed Guard, or the Healing Workshop do so. To understand what it is about them that is different from their contemporaries who struggle on in the larger society, it is necessary to take a look at what is happening internally during the decade from 16 years old to 26.

The school years up to about the age of 12 are ordinarily a time of quite smooth progress. By his birthday each year, a child had grown an inch or so taller, reads at a grade level higher than the year before, and conducts himself with measurably greater sophistication. In the following six years, adolescents may grow five inches between one birthday and the next. Their bodies change shape so radically and rapidly that they have to look at themselves in the mirror constantly to see who they are and how they like it. They may leap in a single bound from reading Judy Blume to enjoying Dostoevsky. And as far as behavior is concerned, parents, and they themselves, hardly know what to expect from hour to hour, much less from month to month.

These physical, emotional, and intellectual changes are biological in nature, a result of built-in programs of maturation over which children have no control. Nature dumps on them, so to speak, the makings of adulthood but doesn't necessarily tell them what to make of it. That's the job of society, the nexus where nature and nurture meet to produce what each culture considers to be the best way to realize the potential of the next generation.

Middle-class culture strongly believes that to be a successful adult, a child must during these years separate from his family and establish his individualism from both a practical and a psychological standpoint.

Teen-agers have long since come partway along this road to autonomy. Infants, as far as can be told, have no clear sense that their internal world is distinct from the external world, so that their wishing for milk and their mother providing milk arise from a union that encompasses both of them. As babies become able to get some distance from their mother — literal physical distance as they learn to crawl and emotional distance as they discover that their wish and her fulfillment aren't always in accord — they begin to construct a self-awareness separate from that of their parents.

By toddlerhood what they are up to can clearly be seen. Toddlers test out all sorts of distinctions between themselves and others — who wants to wear what, eat what, touch what, and go to bed when — that will serve as markers of their separate estate.

Realistically though, pre-schoolers know themselves to be dependent on parents and wisely don't push their differences too far. Indeed, they look out for their own safety by establishing bonds with their parents in the form of identifications ("Don't I look like Mommy?") and behaviors that their parents will love them for ("I'm a good boy!"). When by the age of 5 or 6 the bonds are safely tied, and yet the child has sufficient distance to enjoy a modicum of self-reliance, a time of peace descends. There is perhaps no nicer time within a family than when the children are all of school age but not yet into the upheavals of adolescence.

When the latter stage is reached, the maneuvers to see who's who resume. By then, the child is working from a position of much greater strength. He has self-care skills: selecting clothes, earning money, pursuing interests independently, and regulating his own life through the whole panoply of negotiations that have, over the years, replaced mere infantile demands. The bonds that assure him he is loved extend beyond mother and father to relatives, neighbors, teachers, and, above all, his peers. His identifications are derived from these actual relationships and also from fantasy — folk heroes, fictional characters, and public leaders.

From these practical and psychological achievements most children derive sufficient self-esteem to begin the process of detachment from their childhood relationship with their parents. How detachment is conducted depends on the quality of the attachment. Those who feel most dependent on parents may the more fiercely launch themselves away. Those who derive pleasure already from a degree of independence may separate from their parents and construct new kinds of bonds with barely a ripple.

Of middle-class adolescents, for example, only about half go through the emotional storms and nasty rebellions many associate with these years. Of the fifty percent who show evidence of turmoil, again only half have worse than moderate problems with their families, their peers, and, above all, with themselves. On the other hand, lack of any apparent rebelliousness can indicate a failure to face the dilemmas of growing up. Radical departures are made by children who, outwardly at least, show this whole range from no rebellion at all to quite troublesome behavior.

The word "rebellion" summons forth images of unleashed criticism, challenges to parents standards, angry confrontation, and anti-social or dangerous behavior. There is no word that easily substitutes, so I will have to speak of rebellion when I really mean something that can be, and often is, entirely acceptable and even likable. A child who announces his weekend plans instead of asking permission is rebelling. So is a boy who wants his family to switch to nonphosphate detergents, and a girl who says she can do a better job of fixing the lawn mower than her father can. A child is rebelling when he or she discovers Thoreau, true love, or meditation and thinks the older generation knows nothing of such things. Most teen-agers enact much of their rebellion en masse: they dress to irritate, but they all dress the same. Rebellion is a process of distinguishing and distancing oneself from one's parents by probing for difference and disagreement; there need be nothing awful about it.

As teen-agers grow into young adults their separation is a mutual endeavor. Over time, children's demands for autonomy are matched by parents' willing relinquishment of control. Children come to see themselves more independently, but parents also have to readjust their view of themselves. Mothers and fathers have deeply participated in their child's self for many years. His or her looks, accomplishments, and personality are not just items to take pride in, but partially define who they are too. Women in particular have often lived for and through children. As parents let a son or daughter loosen childhood bonds, they lose something of themselves, and must work to restore it.

Given a long and gradual development toward maturity, parents don't find their task so hard. To be sure, it is difficult at times to have those nice kids who have eaten our cookies and "borrowed" our tools for so many years disagree with our politics ("You're going to vote for *who*?") and, in general, skirt our influence in many everyday matters ("Oh, mom, you wouldn't understand"). But on the whole most families have the humor to survive a certain amount of criticism in return for the freedom to develop new interests of their own and the gratification of having raised children who can now conduct their own lives. That's as it should be, but it isn't always that way.

No radical departer — not the nine I am using to illustrate the general predicament of any of the hundreds of others I have known — has thus gradually been able to separate from his or her family to everyone's mutual satisfaction. Few have been able to engage their peers in their own form of rebellion, or have sought safety in numbers by rebelling among peers. Some, like Dennis Ericson, enter their 20s without ever having disagreed with their families. They haven't rebelled at all. Others, like Nancy Lewis, don't find ways to control their own lives. They rebel to no effect. And all of them, without exception, are still so closely tied to their parents either in reality or fantasy that I will often use the word "children" to refer to joiners in spite of their chronological age. Each has been felled by some obstacle that others manage to scramble over, even if it bruises both them and their families for a while.

The process of formulating one's identity is, of course, never over. One is forever having to reformulate oneself to catch up, so to speak, with the changing context as one pursues a career, gets married, becomes a parent, suffers tragedies, grows older. Change is so rapid during adolescence, however, that the task of identity formulation then is more demanding than it is likely ever to be again. Also, society demands it of teen-agers whether they like it or not.

Parents withdraw support. They no longer wish to supervise children's homework or to chaperone them everywhere. Even if they wish to, they can no longer control children's aggressive and sexual impulses. So adolescents are forced to a degree of independence. They must arrange their own social lives, care for their own bodies, make many of their own decisions, and begin to earn their own money. They are now too muscularly strong for others to subdue easily; they must take over the control of their physical aggression. Both sexes were able to manage the rather mild sexuality of childhood; now sexual impulses are insistent, unpredictable, and sometimes quite unmanageable.

Parents also make it clear to high-school students that adult responsibilities loom ahead. By 16, students know that their present academic industry will determine which college they can hope to attend. By 18, they are asked to make tentative choices of college curriculum and to articulate their reasons for that choice. Most of them are expected to leave home. By 21, they are required to narrow their career choice either by declaring a major or, if they have gone to junior college, by entering the work force. These challenges are unlike those of childhood: they smack of permanence.

There is some suggestion that families of radical departers are hesitant to withdraw support or relinquish control. Fred Vitelli's father protected his son from the consequences of his delinquencies. Mr. Gould paid Jamie's way even into his mid-20s. Jennifer Green's mother masterminded both her daughter's psyche and her piano career.

At the same time that parents are withdrawing support and control, their sons and daughters are withdrawing the unconditional love for and faith in parents that typifies earlier childhood. But children can't continue into adulthood loveless and faithless. They seek intimacy with others — friends and lovers. Instead of relying on the belief system that was on loan to them during childhood, they now formulate ideologies that will serve the unique person each has come to be.

Of those radical departers toward the upper end of the age group, who might have been expected to enjoy intimacy with a lover, only Kathy O'Connor had a relationship that was more than exploitive or tentative, and her marriage didn't last out the year. Some joiners have no friends at all. They are convinced that peers couldn't possibly understand them — a conviction that certainly precludes intimacy. Those who go through the motions of a social life often use the word "plastic" to describe their relationships. They have no sense of deep connection or even of genuineness with their friends, and can't use their affection and admiration as sources of self-esteem.

No radical departers I have studies felt committed to a value system at the time of their joining. Indeed, to all of them, nothing they were doing made any sense, nor did the activities of others. One could sum up their desolation by saying that radical departers feel they belong with no one, believe in nothing.

This is a risk that is incurred by all adolescents as they sever themselves from childhood. By denigrating the family from whose love and values that have derived the very core of their self-esteem, they may also devalue whatever "good" portion of their self relied on family approval. In other words, they may reject a part of themselves as they reject their parents, and thus find themselves unlovable and of no significance. The trick of withdrawing from the curriculum of a family self is to have built an extracurricular self that is equally laudable.

Most teen-agers do have moments of grave doubt: no one likes them, they're ugly, everything's stupid, what's the sense of even trying? But these are moments only, and give way more and more to positive feelings of accomplishment, significance, and worth. Those who will join radical groups behave as though so great a portion of whatever they have found good about themselves has been built on parental ties that were they to sever them they would be terribly depleted, if not entirely empty. Every joiner I have spoken with was, at the time of his or her departure, at a low self-esteem so devastating that there seemed to be no self at all.

Teen-agers want — and it is required of them — a self of their very own, unique, authentic, and separate from the selves of parents. By coincidence, the tasks that children must tackle to differentiate, rearrange, and fortify their sense of self all begin with *I*: Independence, Individuation, Impulse control, Industry, Intimacy, Ideological commitment, and, of course, Identity itself. One might call these the years of the I.

This preoccupation with internal and private psychological issues has led adults to accuse youth of an excess of narcissism. Self-involvement is, however, a trademark of the times. "Develop yourself," Mrs. Green admonished Jennifer, and that theme of self-realization, self-actualization, liberation, and autonomy is echoed throughout the middle class. The message can make individuals ruthlessly oblivious of the needs of others, and blind to the fact of all people's mutual dependency. No wonder youth is selfish, since society demands that it be so.

Worse, by stressing the early achievement of an independent self parents may be out of step with the psychological realities of adolescent development. There seems plenty of evidence from the young people I have worked with, especially those who have made radical departures but also those who have not, that the self is for years tentative and in constant flux. They themselves don't think it can bear much scrutiny.

By demanding that the self be "actualized" prior to reaching the 20s, society is handing children a double-edged sword. With so much attention focused on the self, they tend to protect their fragility with selfishness, egotism, and the kind of acting out Nancy Lewis attempted with her theatrics and precocious "liberation." At the same time, the assumption that they should have no fragility to hide convinces these children that no one else experiences doubt and pain. All nine of these representative radical departers kept their distress secret because they felt "no one would understand."

Again, a modicum of such loneliness is to be expected in adolescence. All through one's life one harbors some core that one knows to be unreachable by others. But adolescents learn that with the effort of reaching out and inviting others to do the same, sufficient intimacy can be found to ease loneliness. Joiners seem to long for a belonging with others that requires no such effort at mutual understanding. Unlike those who, among less judgmental peers at least, become able endlessly to probe, analyze, confess, explore, and lay bare their very souls to one another over these years, radical departers hold aloof while hoping for some unconditional mutual capitulation in which others would not ask a single question. This is their version of belonging.

Joiner's version of belief is equally conditional. To them an ideology should, without the effort of their own analysis, offer ever answer absolutely.

To some extent, longing for the Answer is an inevitable consequence of intellectual maturation. Younger children are poor debaters: something is either true or false, right or wrong, and if there is an argument it is won by the person with the loudest voice. Adolescents can step outside themselves to see issues from various vantage points, and each view, they realize, contains some truth. In Ethan Browning's school for gifted children, this talent was formalized in a debating club to which Ethan belonged, and was a point of pride at home, where right opinions were considered the offspring of free inquiry.

This intellectual experience can be heady, and it can be unsettling. How, if different things have different meanings to different people, can there be any meaning at all? What, deep down, do *I* really believe? *Who am I? Where am I going?* And *why?*

One can catch Ethan Browning at just that moment of unsettling awareness. His extensive reading had given him histories of the Crusades and the Inquisition, Oriental philosophies, Kafka, Emerson, and *Death of a Salesman.* This array of distraught and dissenting humanity was discussed around his family's civilized dinner table as though it were so many specimens to be dissected. Certainly there was something "missing": some heart of the matter that was ultimately undissectible.

This was not the Browning's particular fault. What is merely intellectual discussion among adult members of the middle class may be a desperate search for practical and personal applications among their sons and daughters.

Perhaps too much has been made of the "generation gap"; most parents are far more able to appreciate their children's concerns than their children give them credit for. But a rapidly changing world really does alter perceptions abruptly, particularly for the young, who will have to track the future among shifting sands. For Kathy O'Connor's parents, Catholicism had answers for pain and suffering, but as a nurse Kathy came face to face with the appalling reality of moral dilemmas — the "right to die" and the "right to life" — for which there seemed no answers. Jack Ericson had as a soldier defended the Western world from totalitarianism; in what way was that parallel to the ideological issues (if they were that) in Southeast Asia? To the Holtzman's, a liberal arts education was the key to every sort of success, but by 1978, when Phil had completed two years of college, liberal arts students faced unemployment after graduation.

The sureties that guided parents no longer seem reliable to children who came of age during recent decades. Half of all marriages now end in divorce. These are the days of dioxin, the population explosion, downward mobility, and the threat of nuclear war. Moreover, these are children of the electronic age.

It must often look to them as if adults' daily concerns — which brand of toaster to choose, whether to buy more life insurance, how to get into the best college — are sheer insanity. How can parents, who once seemed so strong and wise, not be *doing* something to make the world safe for their children?

They are, of course, doing the best they know how. They understand the many reasons why they can't cut through the Gordian knot of ethical and practical dilemmas with one neat slice of an answer. To a 16-year-old, however, parents begin to look like fallen idols. This is especially so among the families from whom radical departers come, and it is owing to the mixed messages they give.

While organizing rescue for starving Africans, Jamie Gould's mother enjoyed her porcelains and Persian cats. While espousing honesty, churchgoing Mr. Browning was observed by Ethan to be fudging his income tax. Mrs. Green flirted with radical dreams while pushing the orthodox virtues of daily four-hour piano practice for Jennifer. Middle-class children are often raised with a gloss of idealism that their parents hope they will have the sense not to take too literally as they reach adulthood.

Most do have that good sense. As they separate, adolescents put their parents through their paces: they challenge, provoke, argue, and criticize. They adopt moral stances of their own, which are both extreme, to make a point, and tentative, to test the waters. But the common result is that they gradually define the boundaries of their own and their parents' capabilities and limitations, keep whatever portions of the family's value system seem workable to them, add snippets of personal ideals that seem to be proved out through their own experimentation, and come through the trial without any prolonged crisis of belief. They become willing, in other words, to face the personal and public moral dilemmas that no ideology can guarantee against.

In contrast, joiners look to belief as a way to avoid any personal dilemma at all. Feeling so little self-esteem, they can't shoulder the responsibility of perhaps making a wrong moral choice and thereby feeling more worthless still. They hope for an ideology that will bolster the "good me," that part of them which is admirable to themselves. They long to be purged of all badness, to be pure — and this their parents cannot do for them.

Parents have, in fact, few outward clues that might warn them of an impending departure. Joiners closely guard the secret of their inner desolation. Even as their unhappiness mounts to critical proportions they may continue to, as so many put it, "go through the motions" of whatever has been their accustomed life. Only in the few months — sometimes mere weeks — before their departure do families notice a visible decline in buoyancy that marks their inner sinking. Before then, they have seemed to be in a steady state. And that's what should be the giveaway.

While other children, tumultuously or uneventfully, are piecing together their separate selves, those who will join radical groups are peculiarly stalled. Whatever they are like, they have been that way for years. Others are learning to say, "I know who I am"; these children gain no notion of what a self might feel like. Most young adults begin to need others and to feel needed, love others and feel loved; potential joiners remain bereft. While their peers are becoming increasingly captivated by all sorts of interests, they become weighted with tedium or aimlessly drift. By the time the overwhelming proportion of adolescents enters the 20s, these young men and women have a sense of optimism and enthusiasm for their future. Radical departers have been unable to conceive of a future for themselves.

And then the future presents itself. Out of the blue, the Hare Krishna, Divine Light Mission, Healing Workshop, Children of God, or Armed Guard offer on a silver platter every ingredient that has been missing from their unhappy youth.

● ● ● ● ● ● ● ● ● ● ● ● ● ● ● ● ● ● ● ● ● ● ● ● ●

# THE COERCIVE CONVERSION CONTROVERSY

## Introduction to the Readings

In the early 1970s, after the first significant numbers of young people in America began to convert to various NRMs like The Unification Church, Krishna Consciousness, The Children of God, Divine Light Mission, and many other less prominent groups, some worried and confused parents turned to the legal system to compel their children to leave these "cults" and resume their previous lives. Legally, however, the "children" we are speaking of were adults with the right to determine their own behaviour, particularly in matters of religion. Freedom of religious expression is a core value of the "American way." It is a right guaranteed by the first amendment to the constitution of the United States. To circumvent this guarantee the parents in some states asked the courts to grant them powers of "conservatorship" over their children. The laws of conservatorship were designed to allow family members or others to intercede in the affairs of a person judged to be "incompetent" (temporarily or permanently) — unable to properly take care of themselves or manage their property. To make their case the parents and their supporters turned to certain psychological and medical experts willing to testify that the young people in question were incapable of handling their own affairs because they were the victims of "brainwashing." Their conversions to NRMs were not the result of a free choice, the kind of choice protected by the constitution. Rather they had been systematically deceived and psychologically manipulated by cult recruiters applying subtle and illicit techniques of persuasion like those developed by the Communist Chinese and others to "correct" the thought and behaviour of political prisoners (for an overview of the legal disputes and their consequences see Richardson, 1991 or Anthony and Robbins, 1995).

Just how this particular justification for invoking conservatorships was struck upon is unclear. At first glance the existing accounts of brainwashing did appear to provide one possible explanation for the seemingly sudden, strange, and "unacceptable" actions of many converts to NRMs. Thus for some time, through recourse to this legal argument, some parents were allowed to forcibly remove their children (i.e., kidnap them) and subject them to "deprogramming" (i.e., coercive counter-brainwashing). Soon the legal authorities realized the insufficiency of this justification for such grievous interference in the constitutional rights of individuals. But in the battle for public opinion the anti-cult movement scored a substantial propaganda victory by establishing a strong link in the public mind between NRMs and some kind of fearful process of conversion. In the absence of sound evidence about *who* converts, *why*, and *how*, it was easy to make and maintain this identification for most people are distrustful of new and often foreign beliefs and practices.

The exaggerated and indiscriminate charges levelled against the NRMs, however, prompted sustained research into the topic by many sociologists and psychologists of religion. In the end, twenty years of research has provided little support for the accusation of brainwashing. In fact the evidence of historical and contemporary analyses contradicts the very reality or possibility of "brainwashing" anyone (Anthony and Robbins, 1994). Only recently, though, have the strong academic arguments against brainwashing or "mind-control" had any impact on the biased perceptions of the public. The majority of people continue to doubt that "normal" individuals would join NRMs under "normal" circumstances (e.g., Pfiefer, 1992).

The first reading in this section, "The Seduction Syndrome," drawn from Ronald Enroth's popular book *Youth, Brainwashing and the Extremist Cults* (1977), is illustrative of the voluminous literature from the late 1970s and early 1980s that fuelled the "cult scare." Note the patterns of the argument Enroth weaves and his skewed use of suggestive language, in lieu of systematically attained and statistically significant evidence or the detailed analysis of conversion accounts. The style of argument differs little from that still employed by prominent representatives of the anti-cult movement (e.g., Singer and Lalich, 1995), despite a rising tide of contrary evidence.

In the second and third readings, "A Critique of 'Brainwashing' Claims About New Religious Movements," and "Clinical and Personality Assessment of Participants in New Religions," James Richardson provides an effective summary of the rising tide of contrary evidence, marshalled as a specific critique of the theoretical and empirical claims of the brainwashing scenario. Richardson succinctly reviews the data and ideas developed in numerous sociological and psychological studies of NRMs scattered over the last twenty or more years. Highlighting the numerous errors of logic, evidence, and omissions committed by exponents of the brainwashing scenario, Richardson effectively illustrates just how misleading the anti-cult movement is willing to be in service of its cause. The record of systematic study tends overwhelmingly to contradict the impressions cultivated by the anecdotal reports circulated so widely by this movement to the mass media. Far from being the passive victims of brainwashing, recruits to NRMs are actively engaged in converting themselves (see Richardson, 1985; Dawson, 1990).

What does the psychological testing of hundreds of participants in different NRMs reveal? On the whole the picture that emerges is one of mental health normality. There is little to choose between the members of mainstream religions and the followers of NRMs. In fact, there is no one convert type for NRMs. Rather the evidence suggests discernible differences between the types of people (as measured in various ways) drawn to discernibly different kinds of NRMs (an assessment reinforced by the participant observation studies of Susan Palmer, 1994). Moreover, there is substantial reason to believe that most of those who do join most NRMs find the experience therapeutically beneficial (e.g., in terms of providing relief from drug and alcohol abuse, reduced levels of anxiety, and increased levels of personal well-being and satisfaction with life). Study after study have failed to find the signs of psychological impairment expected of victims of brainwashing. Therefore, the only sound course of action left for all involved, the members of NRMs, the families of members of NRMs, and the public in general, is trusting and open dialogue about the real differences that do exist in our perceptions of the world and our place in it.

• • • • • • • • • • • • • • • • • • • • • • • • •

# References

Anthony, Dick and Thomas Robbins
   1994      "Brainwashing and Totalitarian Influence." Pp. 457-471 in V.S. Ramachandran, ed., *Encyclopedia of Human Behavior*, Vol. 1. San Diego, CA: Academic Press.
   1995      "Negligence, Coercion and the Protection of Religious Belief." *Journal of Church and State* 37 (3): 509-536.

Dawson, Lorne
    1990    "Self-Affirmation, Freedom, and Rationality: Theoretically Elaborating 'Active' Conversions." *Journal for the Scientific Study of Religion* 29 (2): 141-163.

Enroth, Ronald
    1977    *Youth, Brainwashing, and the Extremist Cults.* Grand Rapids, MI: Zondervan.

Palmer, Susan Jean
    1994    *Moon Sisters, Krishna Mothers, Rajneesh Lovers: Women's Roles in New Religions.* Syracuse, NY: Syracuse University Press.

Pfeifer, Jeffrey E.
    1992    "The Psychological Framing of Cults: Schematic Representations and Cult Evaluations." *Journal of Applied Social Psychology* 22 (7): 531-544.

Richardson, James T.
    1985    "The Active vs. Passive Convert: Paradigm Conflict in Conversion/Recruitment Research." *Journal for the Scientific Study of Religion* 24 (2): 163-179.

    1991    "Cult/Brainwashing Cases and Freedom of Religion." *Journal of Church and State* 33 (1): 55-74.

Singer, Margaret Thaler and Janja Lalich
    1995    *Cults in Our Midst: The Hidden Menace in Our Everyday Lives.* San Francisco: Jossey-Bass Pub.

# CHAPTER TEN

# THE SEDUCTION SYNDROME

## RONALD ENROTH

To understand the dynamics of the transformation process by which a young person becomes totally enveloped in an extremist cult, it is important to note the context from which he comes. What kind of background factors characterize the young people who are entering the new-age cults in such alarming numbers? Where are they "at" when they first decide to explore the kinds of groups discussed in Part 1 of this book? Why do they find these groups so appealing? How do cults manage to control their converts once they have recruited them?

The majority of people who join new-age cults are between eighteen and twenty-two years old at the time of first contact. In other words, the immediate post-high school period is when a potential joiner is most vulnerable, though persons as young as fourteen have become victims. A profile of the typical cult member reveals that he or she is white, middle or upper-middle class, with at least some college education and a nominally religious upbringing. In short, the typical cult prospect fits the image of the all-American suburban boy or girl next door.

To be sure, some young people in the cults come from the margins of society or have experienced very unstable of nonexistent family relationships. But they do not constitute the norm. Most have grown up in average American homes, and many have experienced varying degrees of communication problems with their parents. A number have known the pain and deprivation of a single-parent home, and perhaps for this reason some have strongly identified with older cult leaders who provide a parental image. Speaking of Victor Paul Wierwille of The Way, one ex-member describes her feelings: "He was very much the father figure, a strong man, and I just really fell in love with him. I sort of had a crush on him."

Shelley Liebert, the young woman who became an instructor in the Unification Church, feels that two types of people pass through the Moonie indoctrination camps. There is the successful, idealistic, very secure kind of person, who represents the most promising prospect as far as the leadership is concerned. On the other hand, there are clearly those recruits who have problem backgrounds and have experienced varying degrees of "failure" according to the standards of middle-class America. These young people have dropped out of school, have been involved in the drug scene, come from broken homes, or have a history of emotional problems and unresolved personal conflicts.

Some seekers who had troubled backgrounds did not survive in the Moonie environment, as Shelley points out. "I always favored the little stray ones. But they weren't usually the ones that made it. I knew I was fighting for a lost cause, like when you bring in a bird with a broken wing — you know it's going to die, but you take care of it anyway. They were drifters, and they didn't have the stamina."

Perhaps more than anything else, the young people pursuing cults today are involved in a search for identity and a quest for spiritual reality that provides clear-cut answers to their questions. Coming to grips with one's identity has always been a part of adolescence in America, but today's youth face difficulties compounded by massive cultural and social upheavals that characterize the contemporary world, especially during the last decade. Much has been written and said about generational gaps, the alienation of youth from the larger society, the disillusionment and disenchantment with the Establishment which led to immersion in drugs by some and involvement in radical politics by others. Eastern mysticism, existential do-your-own-thing philosophies, and a rejection of many traditional virtues and values have resulted in a confusing array of alternative life styles and value systems which were not options for young people only fifteen years ago.

Despite the boom in entertainment and the pervasive impact of the mass media, youth often remain bored, unfulfilled, and lonely. This is reflected in the unprecedented geographic mobility of a growing segment of the youth subculture. An army of hitchhikers and street people signify that American youth are running away from something. The old anchorages are increasingly absent, for whatever reasons. The separation from the familiar; the tendency to drift in and out of jobs, college, and sexual relationships; uncertainty and anxiety regarding the future; discontent with economic and political structures — all contribute to isolation and loneliness.

Nevertheless, young people who have not fled suburbia and their families are also experiencing a crisis of identity. The characteristic ambiguity of adolescence has been compounded in recent years by the liberation ethos that has pervaded our culture and profoundly affected our sex-role relationships. Women's lib, gay liberation, and sexual permissiveness in general stand in contradistinction to the more traditional patterns of the recent past. Appropriate models for adulthood are often unclear or undergoing considerable change. "Even such seemingly universal adult roles as mother and father are amorphous and changing . . . .For youth, therefore, the development of a coherent adult identity and the resolution of generational discontinuities is becoming more difficult," reports Francine Daner in *The American Children of Krishna* (p. 11).

This identity confusion is commonplace among the children of affluence — the chief target of the cults. As an ex-member of the Children of God describes it, "This is such a searching generation, because everything's been so easy for us. Everything's been handed to us. We've never been hungry. It's almost like we're drowned in a sea of possibilities." Or, as Theodore Roszak observes, "Never before has such freedom of choice been available in regard to work, styles of life, and beliefs. Youth may well be victims of the dilemma of overchoice" (quoted by Daner, p. 11).

If young people who are potential candidates for the cults are concerned with developing a sense of identity, they are just as earnestly engaged in a spiritual search. Some who were interviewed as part of this study had been pursuing spiritual rainbows for many months and had moved from church to church or even cult to cult in search of firm answers.

A case in point is one young man who, before joining the Hare Krishna cult, had been deeply involved in astrology and occult practices. "At this time in my life I wanted to devote myself to the pursuit of truth. I was seeking God with all my heart. Quite by accident, I met a young man who was a devout member of the Hare Krishna sect. This man's manner of living was the most detached and unearthly that I had ever encountered. He cared for nothing, obviously, but his relationship to God. His detachment and devotion was what really got ahold of me. Here I was, honestly and earnestly seeking God, and this man had found the way."

In *Today's Health* magazine, Max Gunther describes one young woman's spiritual quest — not unlike thousands of her peers. She had been raised a Catholic, but had dropped her religious faith in her early teens. This lack of commitment troubled her as she entered a university in an "uncertain, groping state of mind."

> I thought I wanted to become a nurse but wasn't sure. I thought
> Christianity meant a lot to me but I wasn't sure of that either. I guess I
> was kind of desperately looking for somebody who had firm yes-and-
> no answers, somebody who was sure about things and could make me
> sure (*Today's Health*, February 1976, p. 16).

During her sophomore year, this same girl encountered a nomadic cult that was combing her campus for converts. She was attracted by the apparent strength of their religious faith and the sureness and calmness of their approach. "I kept going back and asking them questions, and they always knew the answers — I mean really knew them." She joined them and discovered "a world where you had direct, clear, simple rules to tell you how to find salvation. There were no questions, no confusion — and I guess that's what I'd been looking for" (*Today's Health*, p. 16).

The desire for sure, black-and-white answers to life's questions is illustrated in the case histories of Part 1 and is confirmed in the experience of other young people who participated in this research effort. Cultic groups like The Way are very much aware of this perceived need on the part of today's youth. Victor Wierwille's Way observes, "There is plenty of religion about us today, but very little logical, accurate, and effectual principles that answer people's questions. Questions you have about life can be answered with 'a mathematical accuracy and scientific precision,' answers that work today, not in some distant future."

Cults not only provide firm answers to every question, but also make promises that appeal to those needing assurance, confidence, and affirmation. A prime example of this is seen in a flyer advertising The Way's "Power for Abundant Living" course and posted on college campuses across the nation. It announces in bold headlines: BE A WINNER. The passer-by who is living "below par" is invited to read these lines:

> YOU CAN HAVE POWER FOR ABUNDANT LIVING
> Abundant living means you can be SET FREE from all fear, doubt and bondage; DELIVERED from poverty, sickness and poor health; OVERFLOWING with life, vitality and zest; RESCUED from condemnation and self-contempt; CURED of drug and sex abuse. You can RESTORE your broken marriage; ENJOY a happy united family, where there is no generation gap.
> If you have power for abundant living you can GAIN self-respect; enjoy SATISFYING work with more than ADEQUATE income. You can OVERCOME depression, discouragement and disappointment and have LOVE, JOY AND REAL PEACE. There can always be a POSITIVE outlook on life, day after day, with no let down. There can be a new PURPOSE in your life. If you have the more abundant life,
> YOU CAN HAVE WHATEVER YOU WANT
> Every problem you ever had can be overcome when you are fully and accurately instructed.

Although some young people who enter cults have little or no religious background, many have had nominal religious exposure. A few have had extensive experience in traditional churches or synagogues. Invariably cult seekers have found these conventional religious institutions to be lacking in spiritual depth and meaning, incapable of inspiring commitment and providing clear-cut answers, and often (hypocritical) in everyday life. They view the religious life of their parents as shallow and perfunctory.

A former cultist remarks, "Looking at Christianity, I didn't see the devotion there that I did in the Hare Krishna movement."

Any person experiencing an identity crisis or involved in a serious spiritual quest is theoretically vulnerable to the seductive outreach of the cults, but some are more vulnerable than others. On the basis of evidence drawn from the life histories of former members, it is clear that persons who have recently gone through some kind of painful life experience or who find themselves in a state of unusual anxiety, stress, or uncertainty are far more susceptible to cultic involvement.

For example, students just entering that strange and sometimes scary university world are particularly vulnerable to the appeal of a cult masquerading as a warm, friendly group offering fellowship and small-group intimacy to lonely freshmen. An ex-Moonie who was in her first year at the University of California at Berkeley was ripe for such an appeal: "I was really unhappy for a lot of reasons. My roommate and I didn't get along so well. I had a lot of trouble making friends because people at that school are really academic and all they wanted to do was read books. I was feeling basically alone, and then I began to falter in school. I felt like I blew it and couldn't catch up and didn't know what I was going to do. I was frantic."

Other precipitating life experiences that increase vulnerability include such things as a recent divorce of one's parents or similar serious problem in the home; the extended, critical illness of a family member; a break-up with a girlfriend or boyfriend; poor academic performance or failure; and unpleasant experiences with drugs or sex. When someone is feeling exceedingly anxious, uncertain, hurt, lonely, unloved, confused, or guilty, that person is a prime prospect for those who come in the guise of religion offering a way out or "peace of mind."

Some youth have had a single, traumatic life experience that triggers entrance into a cult, but a significant number might be characterized as having chronic emotional or personality problems of a pathological nature. Dr. John G. Clark, a psychiatrist associated with the Harvard Medical School and Massachusetts General Hospital, has spent several years researching the effects of cult membership on the mental and physical health of young people. He concludes that approximately 58 percent of the cult members he has examined fall into this category. In testimony delivered August 18, 1976, before a select Vermont Senate committee in Montpelier, Dr. Clark declared, "These inductees involve themselves in order to feel better, because they are excessively uncomfortable with the outside world and themselves. Such motivated conversions are 'restitutive' in that the 'seekers' are trying to restore themselves to some semblance of comfort in a fresh, though false, reality."

The remaining 42 percent of the individuals examined by Dr. Clark were found to be normal, developing young people struggling with the usual growth crisis of adolescence when, for reasons we have noted, they fall into the trap laid by cults. For the most part, they were strong students facing the expected pains of separation from their families. Dr. Clark reports: "These people tend to be from intact, idealistic, believing families with some religious background. Often they had not truly made any of the major shifts toward independence, and so, left home at the appropriate time believing they were ready for freedom. When this belief was seriously challenged in this brave new world by their first real setbacks or by any real crisis, they became covertly depressed, thus enhancing their susceptibility to the processes of conversion."

Mental health authorities feel that individuals who constitute what Dr. Clark calls the "restitutive group" — those who already have major emotional problems before joining — run the risk of additional damage through prolonged exposure to extremist cults that practice mind control and prevent or inhibit autonomous behavior. The deterioration that may result is analogous to the fate of chronic schizophrenics institutionalized for many years: they eventually lose the ability to think and function with any degree of effectiveness, especially in the outside world.

Even more disturbing is the fact that young people who have no history of mental pathology, and who have relatively normal, healthy personalities upon entering cultic groups, suffer the destructive impact of a very real, very frightening form of thought control or brainwashing that subjugates the will and stifles independent thinking. There is increasing clinical evidence of a syndrome of seduction and mental subversion involving cult converts. This is a matter of both great human concern and professional interest.

In many respects, this phenomenon represents relatively unfamiliar scientific ground, as reported by Dr. Marvin F. Galper, a San Diego clinical psychologist. In a paper presented in June 1976 to a group of mental health professionals in Florida, Dr. Galper reported, "We are confronted with a new clinical syndrome . . . . As time passes, anecdotal evidence accumulates in which the established assessment methods of the psychiatrist and clinical psychologist have failed to identify the brainwashed cult indoctrinee."

Although journalists and other observers have questioned the validity of brainwashing claims, a small but growing segment of the scientific community has had sufficient firsthand contact with the phenomenon to conclude that mind control does take place in new-age cults and that the results are tragically evident. As to the potential effects of membership in these cults, Harvard's Dr. Clark warns: "The health hazards are extreme!" On the basis of his own clinical data, he told the select Vermont Senate committee "that coercive persuasion and thought reform techniques are effectively practiced on naive, uninformed subjects with disastrous health consequences . . . .I must also as a physician draw attention to equally, often life threatening, dangers to physical health."

From the Christian perspective, there clearly are spiritual dimensions to the seduction syndrome, and these will be discussed in a later chapter. First we must consider the psychological and sociological components of mind control, or — as some prefer to call it — "coercive persuasion."

The word *brainwashing* is somewhat imprecise, as it has been variously defined and applied. Nevertheless, it regularly appears in scholarly literature along with more academic-sounding equivalent terms like "thought control," "mind control," "psychological kidnapping," and "coercive persuasion." Brainwashing became a part of the popular vocabulary during the Korean conflict, when American prisoners of war were subjected to psychologically and physically coercive methods of mind manipulation. A number of psychiatric research studies were later published, based on the experiences of POWs. One of the best-known books on brainwashing, *Thought Reform and the Psychology of Totalism*, written by Dr. Robert J. Lifton, is an analysis of techniques used against Chinese intellectuals and Western prisoners in mainland China.

Social scientists have emphasized the very important role that group influences play in thought reform. They have pointed to some striking similarities between what is occurring in the contemporary cults and the brainwashing that took place in China and Korea during the early 1950s. Some also see parallels in the Nazi movement of World War II. Appearing before a group of parents, senators, and other government officials in Washington, D.C., Rabbi Maurice Davis, an outspoken critic of Moon, stated this concerning the Unification Church:

> The last time I ever witnessed a movement that had these qualifications:
> (1) a totally monolithic movement with a single point of view and a
> single authoritarian head; (2) replete with fanatical followers who are
> prepared and programmed to do anything their master says; (3) supplied
> by absolutely unlimited funds; (4) with a hatred of everyone on the
> outside; (5) with suspicion of parents, against their parents — the last
> movement that had those qualifications was the Nazi youth movement,
> and I tell you, I'm scared.

Lifton and others have noted that "religious totalism" is really just one form of a more general ideological totalism characteristic of the techniques of brainwashing developed by the Chinese Communists. And as Dr. Lifton observes, "Despite the vicissitudes of brainwashing, the process which gave rise to the name is very much a reality . . . . thought reform has in fact emerged as one of the most powerful efforts at human manipulation ever undertaken" (pp. 4-5).

The comparison between classical Chinese communist thought reform and cultic brainwashing may not hold up in every respect (some have argued, for example, that direct physical coercion is not employed by cultists), but the evidence now at hand indicates that the parallel demands serious consideration. It is our contention that psychologically persuasive techniques and the dynamics of spiritual seduction combine with group force and processes to cause youth caught up in the cults to accept ideas, attitudes, and behaviors quite foreign to them prior to their involvement in the groups.

We are speaking of a highly emotional, extremely complex phenomenon. Note that in our delineating the process of radical conversion and thought reform, there will always be exceptions in detail or degree. There is some variation with regard to particular cult groups, and of course there will always be some diversity in the response patterns of individuals. Nevertheless, it is our opinion, based on the existing data, that there is a remarkable pattern to the experiences related by ex-members regardless of the cult. There is ample confirmation from other sources as well — parents, siblings not involved in the cults, journalists, ministers, other professionals — of kinds of behavior, thinking, and attitudes which will be discussed.

The transformation of personality and thinking that occurs in the cults includes, as already suggested, a highly seductive process involving individuals who are already quite susceptible. The first crucial element in the syndrome is gaining access to potential converts — recruitment tactics. The cults prey on the kinds of people we have discussed — the lonely, the confused, the idealistic, the searchers. Cultists have an uncanny ability to single out such individuals in a crowd; they seem to sense those who are ripe for the plucking. Frequently, deceitful means are used to entice a young person to make initial inquiry. For example, Moonies will promise a free dinner and lecture without ever identifying the sponsor as the Unification Church. Moon's witnesses have been known to deny flatly any association with the Korean evangelist in their preliminary contacts with potential recruits.

The Children of God, when witnessing on a University of California campus, were known to circulate in the waiting room of the counseling center, ready to prey on those already identified as experiencing problems. A former member of the Moon movement claims he was instructed to be on the lookout for people wearing backpacks, people on the move. He was also told to avoid Mormons and evangelical Christians — anyone holding firm religious beliefs and possessing substantial knowledge of the Bible was not considered worth the effort. Persons with some religious background and slight acquaintance with Scripture were more promising targets. Moreover, college freshmen and seniors are both viewed are good candidates: freshmen because they are making the transition to an unfamiliar and often unsettling life away from home, seniors because of their insecurity and uncertainty as to future plans.

Once tentative interest has been expressed by the potential convert, intense group pressure and group activity are initiated. Lectures, sermons, Bible studies, and indoctrination sessions — sometimes tape-recorded — are part of a constant round of activity designed to surround the new recruit with an all-encompassing rhetoric. Isolated from prior familiar associations and separated from any input or feedback from the "outside" — while at the same time placed in a position where questioning is discouraged and dissent is not tolerated — the individual is deprived of any opportunity to exercise self-expression and independent thought. He is surrounded by a group of singing, chanting, or meditating peers whose verbal interaction is sprinkled with what Lifton calls "thought-terminating clichés."

Of this constant barrage of indoctrination Dr. Clark observes:

> So intense is this that individuals who are under such pressure and are susceptible tend to enter a state of narrowed attention, especially as they are more and more deprived of their ordinary frames of reference and of sleep. . . .From that time there is a relative or complete loss of control of one's own mind and actions which is then placed into the hands of the group of individuals who have the direct contact with the individual inductee.

In her study of the Hare Krishna movement Professor Daner describes a former member who came to the conclusion that devotees were rejecting the mind's ability to think.

> While she was in the movement and attending *Gita* classes, she would look around at the devotees sitting in the temple chatting japa silently and listening to the lecture, and all she could think of was Orwell's novel *1984*. When she was in the Philadelphia temple where Prabhupada's lectures are played over the loud-speaker system for twenty-four hours a day, she was unable to sleep (*The American Children of Krsna*, p. 76).

All ex-members of extremist cults report having experienced some kind of sensory deprivation — usually food and sleep. Starchy, low-protein diets combined with only four or five hours of sleep each night wear down one's physical and psychological defenses and make a person even more vulnerable to indoctrination. According to Dr. Galper, "Suppression of the individual's rational judgment processes is fostered by sleep deprivation and sensory bombardment. Mobilization of guilt and anxiety in the indoctrinee intensifies this inhibition of judgmental processes and at the same time leads to heightened suggestibility" ("The Cult Indoctrinee: A New Clinical Syndrome," unpublished paper).

This imposition of guilt and fear is basic to the brainwashing process. That a person's eternal destiny will be jeopardized if he abandons the group is a common belief: "If you leave us, you will endanger the salvation of your soul." An ex-Moonie notes, "I was made to feel guilty if ever I wanted to be alone and think."

The co-authors of an article entitled, "Thought Reform and the Jesus Movement," discuss the various dimensions of religious totalism, including the demand for purity or the necessity to place all experience in categories of black and white ("He who is not for me is against me"). They note "that a major emphasis of the demand for purity is to bring out feelings of guilt on the part of the participants. The rigorous standards can seldom be met; the individual nearly always falls short and is left remorseful and repentant (and thus more easily manipulable)" (*Youth and Society*, December 1972, p. 197). The reader will recall Shelley Liebert's statement regarding the Moon movement: "You were always given more than you could do, and you always felt that you never accomplished enough."

Alamo Christian Foundation is a prime example of a cult that effects mind control through fear. The Foundation fosters and intense fear of the wrathful God: "A lot of 'God is Love' heresy is around, and people are blinded to the Truth." The group also preaches an apocalyptic fear that borders on paranoia. A young member of the group once wrote to her parents to warn them about the ZIP codes developed by the U.S. Postal Service — they held sinister implications for a possible future takeover by "commies." She wrote, "they are conditioning us to numbers. They have 'camps' for Christians set up already. When these things begin to happen, they will happen *fast*."

Members of extremist cults undergo a dramatic change in world view. Efforts have been made to alter their former attitude toward and conception of the world, the nature of reality, and the ends and purposes of human life. In *The Joyful Community*, a study of the Bruderhof commune, Benjamin Zablocki underscores how difficult it is to effect a change in a person's world view.

> Change in world-view is possible, although rare and difficult. It can occur in a religious conversion and in psychoanalysis. Both of these processes are undergone voluntarily. Classic thought reform, on the other hand, is an involuntary method of changing a person's world-view (p. 247).

In terms of Lifton's analysis of thought reform, this shift in world view is accomplished through a process of resocialization that includes a "stripping process" by which the identity of the individual is greatly weakened, sometimes destroyed. The person is stripped of his personal possessions. In some groups even clothing is communally owned. Frequently the individual's style of dress and appearance is altered to conform to the requirements of the group. The member's sense of self undergoes change as symbols of his former identity are discarded. This is dramatically illustrated in the Hare Krishna movement, where new identities totally supplant both their personal and social identities.

> In order to bring these changes about, a devotee voluntarily subjects himself to a series of abasements, degradations, and profanations of his self. The alienation from his society, from his family and friends begins before an individual becomes a devotee, but entrance into the

> temple is a formal recognition of this alienation and tends to reinforce
> it. The devotee's former life is relegated to the status of a dream . . .
> (Daner, pp. 73-74).

The cultist is stripped of his past. Renunciation and rejection of his prior associations and relationships is mandatory. All connections with family, friends, and the home community are severed. The past must be submerged; reality becomes the present. With regard to Hare Krishna cult, Professor Daner writes, "So deep are the changes that most devotees do not wish to discuss their former lives at all, and the average devotee has to be pressed to reveal any facts of his former life" (p. 74).

A former member of the Children of God relates an incident illustrating the degree to which even mention of the past is reproved: "One time I was traveling with a brother in California and I noticed that there was snow on the mountains. I remarked about their being so beautiful — 'It reminds me of the first time I skied.' I was rebuked for that, for even mentioning anything at all about what I did when I was not in the Children of God."

Parents are naturally among the first to notice the drastic changes in behavior and attitude after their children join a cult. Their testimony to the characteristic change in identity and rejection of the past is tinged with a sad and anguished realization that they, too, have been relegated to a former category of existence. One parent relates,

> The radical change in our son's behavior and personality since he
> joined this group is hard to believe; he is a totally different person —
> dehumanized and zombie-like. He has abandoned his entire past life;
> has no interest in former friends, or in any of his family. His calls and
> letters are very few and far between, despite our numerous attempts to
> communicate with him. When we do speak with him, it can never be
> on a personal level; it's strictly a sermonizing type of conversation.
> There have been serious illnesses within our immediate family, but his
> responses have been negative, completely devoid of emotion.

Cultists not only claim to have discovered a new "spiritual family," but in many cases acquire a new name. Some observers suggest that using Bible names or "spiritual" names helps to avoid detection by searching parents and law enforcement personnel. More pertinent to our analysis is the fact that acquiring a new name reinforces the act of severing all ties, familial and cultural. Daner notes the significance of the ceremony at which the Hare Krishna member receives his spiritual name.

> At this time he makes a lifetime commitment, and receives a new
> spiritual name and insignia. The devotees are aware of and discuss the
> effects of this ceremony upon the person who undergoes it. "A person
> really changes when he is initiated and gets his new name. I almost

didn't recognize my own husband, he had changed so much," said a young woman. The process of stripping, leveling, and purifying the person to be initiated so that he can take his place in a community of ISKCON is believed to alter his identity in readiness to take on his new identity as a servant of the Lord (p. 77).

Without exception, the parents who contributed to this research effort commented on the drastic, sometimes sudden personality changes they observed in their children. Statements like "He is not the same person" and "She's not the same daughter I once knew" are common. One parent notes, "She changed from a person extremely meticulous in her appearance, thoughtful and considerate of family and friends, to a person completely opposite. Soliciting and peddling up to eighteen hours a day left her no time for personal grooming, proper rest or nutrition."

Many parents and friends of cult members have also observed changes in voice, posture, mannerisms, and even handwriting. Not only can parents notice a shift in personality and world view in the unfolding progression of letters received from a cultic son or daughter, but some report that the handwriting changes, usually becoming smaller and childish. Misspellings increase and the vocabulary becomes stylized, reflecting the rhetoric of the group and the transformation of the person's thinking. In his testimony before the Vermont Senate committee, Dr. Clark described the abrupt linguistic changes that sometimes occur.

> This richness of language is that which parents suddenly miss when they first see their thought-reformed children. Their reaction is appropriately panic! They recognize and correctly identify terrifying, sudden, unacceptable changes in the style of language and the style of relating as well as a narrowing and thinning down of the thought processes. Formerly bright, fluent and creative individuals are rendered incapable in the use of irony or a metaphor and they speak with a smaller, carefully constricted vocabulary with clichés and stereotyped ideas. They also appear to have great difficulty using abstractions in their speech or arguments. They do not love except in clichés and established forms. Almost all of the charged, emotion-laden language symbols are shifted to new meanings.

There is ample evidence that brainwashing as practiced by the cults impairs logical reasoning processes and alters interpersonal relationship patterns. In some extreme cases, individuals have experienced a loss of such basic skills as reading and simple arithmetic. This is most evident in the groups that officially disparage the mind.

Finally, the assault on the convert's prior identity and his subsequently assuming a totally new identity sometimes involve a pattern of personality regression. This is especially the case in the Moon movement, where parents and other observers frequently report that converts have regressed to the level of early teen dependence. A childlike ego state is fostered in the person, and the wholesome innocence of early adolescence appears to be upheld as an ideal. Yet it is unclear whether this childlike state is deliberately encouraged and engineered by the leadership to ensure continued dependence on the group. The scriptural injunction to become like a small child in order to enter the kingdom of heaven is sometimes cited, although cultic use of Scripture can be used to justify a multitude of sins.

Although participation in the cults discussed here nearly always involves substantial personal transformation, it would be an inaccurate generalization to state that *all* cult members display zombie-like behavior or are "spaced-out" robots. Such exotic descriptions do seem to apply to some persons, yet journalists and others have tended to overuse the terms. The public relations girls of the Moonie movement, for example, would hardly be able to function in their particular roles in Washington or elsewhere is they walked around in a perpetual trance.

The word *brainwashing* itself may seem harsh and sensational. But to those who have witnessed and experienced the phenomena discussed in this book, the concepts of thought reform and mind control are not abstract, academic speculations. Respected members of the scientific and medical community such as Dr. Robert J. Lifton of Yale, Dr. John G. Clark of Harvard and Dr. Julius Segal of the National Institute of Mental Health have attested to the clinical reality of the destructive syndrome we have described. All agree that additional research is needed.

Based on his study of young people at various stages of involvement in six different cults, Dr. Clark comes to this conclusion: "The fact of a personality shift in my opinion is established. The fact that this is a phenomenon basically unfamiliar to the mental health profession I am certain of. The fact that our ordinary methods of treatment don't work is also clear, as are the frightening hazards to the process of personal growth and mental health.'

● ● ● ● ● ● ● ● ● ● ● ● ● ● ● ● ● ● ● ● ● ● ● ●

# A CRITIQUE OF "BRAINWASHING" CLAIMS ABOUT NEW RELIGIOUS MOVEMENTS

JAMES T. RICHARDSON

## Introduction

Many young people have been involved with new religious movements (NRMs) — sometimes pejoratively called "cults" — over the past several decades in American and other Western societies. These young people have often been among the most affluent and better educated of youth in their societies, which has contributed to controversies erupting about the meaning of such participation. Parents, friends and political and opinion leaders have attempted to understand the phenomenon, and develop methods to control activities of such groups (Beckford 1985; Barker 1984).

Joining NRMs, which may appear quite strange in their beliefs and organizational patterns, is interpreted by some as an act of ultimate rejection of Western cultural values and institutions — including religious, economic and familial ones. This "culture-rejecting" explanation has been difficult for many to accept, prompting a search for other explanations for involvement, a search raising serious ethical issues.

An appealing alternative explanation has been so-called "brainwashing" theories (Bromley and Richardson 1983; Fort 1983). According to those espousing these ideas, youth have not joined NRMs volitionally, but have been manipulated or forced into participating by groups using powerful psychotechnology practiced first by communist, anti-Western societies. This psychotechnology allegedly traps or encapsulates young people in NRMs, allowing subsequent control of their behavior by leaders of the groups, through "mind control."

Originally published as "The Ethics of 'Brainwashing' Claims About New Religious Movements," *Australian Religious Studies Review* 7, 1994: 48-56.

These techniques were originally developed, according to these claims, in Russian purge trials of the 1930s, and later refined by the Chinese communists after their assumption of power in China in 1949, and then used by them with POWs during the Korean War of the early 1950s (Solomon 1983). Now these techniques are allegedly being used by NRM leaders against young people in Western countries, who are supposedly virtually helpless before such sophisticated methods (Richardson and Kilbourne 1983).

When questioned about obvious logical and ethical problems of applying these theories to situations without physical coercion (such as participation in NRMs), proponents have a ready answer. They claim that physical coercion has been replaced by "psychological coercion," which is supposedly more effective than simple physical coercion (Singer 1979). These ideas are referred to as "second generation" brainwashing theories, which take into account new insights about manipulation of individuals. Supposedly physical coercion is unnecessary if recruits can be manipulated by affection, guilt or other psychological influences.

These theories can be considered ideas developed for functional reasons by those who have a vested interest in their being accepted, such as parents of members, therapists, and leaders of competing religious groups. The ideas plainly are a special type of "account" which "explains" why people join the groups and why they stay in them (Beckford 1978). Whatever the origin, and no matter that the veracity of such accounts is questionable, these ideas about NRM participation have become commonly accepted.

For instance, De Witt (1991) reports that 78 percent of a random sample of 383 individuals from Nevada said they believed in brainwashing, and 30 percent agreed that "brainwashing is required to make someone join a religious cult." A similar question asked of a random sample of 1,000 residents in New York prior to the tax evasion trial of Reverend Moon (Richardson 1992) revealed that 43 percent agreed "brainwashing is required to make someone change from organized religion to a cult." Latkin (1991) reported that 69% of a random sample of Oregon residents who were asked about the controversial Rajneesh group centered in Eastern Oregon agreed that members of the group were brainwashed.

These notions about "brainwashing" and "mind control" have pervaded institutional structures in our society as well, even if they are problematic. Such views have influenced actions by governmental entities and the media (van Driel and Richardson 1988; Bromley and Robbins 1992). The legal system has seen a number of efforts to apply brainwashing theories as explanations of why people might participate in new religions. Several civil actions have resulted in multimillion dollar judgments against NRMs allegedly using brainwashing techniques on recruits (Anthony 1990; Richardson 1991; 1994).

Thus it appears that ideas about brainwashing of recruits to new religions have developed a momentum of their own in several Western societies. These notions are impacting society in many ways, including limitations on religious freedom (Richardson

1991). Thus, we need to examine the brainwashing thesis more closely, in order to see if it is an adequate explanation of the process whereby people join and participate in NRMs, and to examine the underlying ethics of offering such explanations of religious participation.

## Critique of "Brainwashing" Theories

Brainwashing theories serve the interests of those espousing them, which is a major reason they are so readily accepted. Parents can blame the groups and their leaders for what were probably volitional decisions to participate by their sons and daughters. Former members can blame the techniques for a decision to participate which the participant later regrets. Deprogrammers can use brainwashing theories as a justification for their new "profession" and as a quasi-legal defense if they are apprehended by legal authorities during attempted deprogrammings, which often have involved physical force and kidnapping. Societal leaders can blame the techniques for seducing society's "brightest and best" away from traditional cultural values and institutions. Competitive religious leaders as well as some psychological and psychiatric clinicians attack the groups with brainwashing theories, to bolster what are basically unfair competition arguments (Kilbourne and Richardson 1984).

Thus it is in the interest of many different entities to *negotiate an account* of "what happened" that makes use of brainwashing notions. Only the NRM of membership, which is usually politically weak, is left culpable after these negotiated explanations about how and why a person joined an NRM. All other parties are, to varying degrees, absolved of responsibility (Richardson, van der Lans and Derks 1986).

The claim that NRMs engage in brainwashing thus becomes a powerful "social weapon" for many partisans in the "cult controversy." Such ideas are used to "label" the exotic religious groups as deviant or even evil (Robbins and Anthony 1982). However, the new "second generation" brainwashing theories have a number of logical and evidentiary problems, and their continued use raises profound ethical issues.

## 1. MISREPRESENTATION OF CLASSICAL TRADITION

Modern brainwashing theories sometimes misrepresent earlier scholarly work on the processes developed in Russia, China, and the Korean POW situation (Anthony 1990). These misrepresentations are as follows: First, the early classical research by Schein (1963) and Lifton (1961) revealed that, contrary to some recent claims, the techniques were generally ineffective at doing more than modifying behavior (obtaining compliance) even for the short term. Such theories would seem less useful to explain long term changes of behavior and belief allegedly occurring with NRM participation.

Second, the degree of determinism associated with contemporary brainwashing applications usually far exceeds that found in the foundational work of Lifton and of Schein. Anthony and Robbins (1992) contrast the "soft determinism" of the work of Lifton and of Schein with the "hard determinism" of contemporary proponents of brainwashing theories such as Singer and Ofshe (1990). The "hard determinism" approach assumes that humans can be turned into robots through application of sophisticated brainwashing techniques, easily becoming deployable "Manchurian Candidates." Classical scholars Lifton and Schein seemed more willing to recognize human beings as more complex entities than do some contemporary brainwashing theorists.

Third, another problem is that classical scholars Lifton and Schein may not be comfortable with their work being applied to noncoercive situations. Lifton (1985: 69) explicitly disclaims use of ideas concerning brainwashing in legal attacks against so-called cults, and earlier (1961: 4) had stated: "...the term (brainwashing) has a far from precise and questionable usefulness; one may even be tempted to forget about the whole subject and return to more constructive pursuits." The work of Schein and of Lifton both evidence difficulty in "drawing the line" between acceptable and unacceptable behaviors on the part of those involved in influencing potential subjects for change (Anthony and Robbins 1992). Group influence processes operate in all areas of life, which makes singling out one area like NRMs for special negative attention quite problematic. Such a focus cannot be adopted on strictly logical, scientific, or ethical grounds.

## 2. IDEOLOGICAL BIASES OF BRAINWASHING THEORISTS

Contemporary applications of brainwashing theories share an ideological bias in opposition to collectivistic solutions to problems of group organization (Richardson and Kilbourne 1983). In the 1950s many Westerners opposed collectivistic communism; in the 1970s and 1980s many share a concern about communally oriented new religions. Another ideological element of contemporary applications concerns the ethnocentrism and even racism which may be related to their use. The fact that a number of new religions are from outside Western culture and were founded and led by foreigners should not be ignored in understanding the propensity to apply simplistic brainwashing theories to explain participation and justify efforts at social control.

## 3. LIMITED RESEARCH BASE OF CLASSICAL WORK

Research on which the classical models are based is quite limited (Richardson and Kilbourne 1983; Anthony 1990). Small nonrepresentative samples were used by both Lifton and Schein, and those in the samples were presented using an anecdotal reporting style, derived from clinical settings, especially with Lifton's work. As Biderman (1962) pointed out, Lifton only studied 40 subjects in all, and gave detailed information on only 11 of those. Schein's original work was based on a sample of only 15 American civilians who returned after imprisonment in China. This work may be insightful, but it does not meet normal scientific standards in terms of sample size and representativeness.

## 4. PREDISPOSING CHARACTERISTICS AND VOLITION IGNORED

Contemporary applications of brainwashing theories to NRM recruitment tactics typically ignores important work on predisposing characteristics of NRM participants (Anthony and Robbins 1992). The techniques of brainwashing supposedly are so successful that they can transform a person's basic beliefs into sharply contrasting beliefs, even against their will. This aspect of brainwashing theory is appealing to proponents who have difficulty recognizing that an individual might have been attracted to a new and exotic religion perceived by the recruit as offering something positive for themselves.

Sizable numbers of participants are from higher social class origins in terms of education level and relative affluence, a finding raising questions about application of brainwashing theories as adequate explanations of participation. Both Barker (1984) and Kilbourne (1986) have found that there are predisposing characteristics for participation in the Unification Church — such as youthful idealism. Thus, the brainwashing argument would seem to be refuted, even if such data are often ignored.

Brainwashing proponents also conveniently ignore volitional aspects of recruitment to new religions. Brainwashing theorists such as Delgado (1982) turn predispositions and interest in exotic religions into susceptibilities and vulnerabilities, adopting an orientation toward recruitment which defines the potential convert in completely passive terms, a philosophical posture that itself raises serious ethical problems. Most participants are "seekers," taking an active interest in changing themselves, and they are often using the NRMs to accomplish planned personal change (Straus 1976, 1989). There is a growing use of an "active" paradigm in conversion/recruitment research which stresses the predispositional and volitional character of participation. This view is derived from research findings that *many participants actually seek out NRMs to accomplish personal goals* (Richardson 1985a). This nonvolitional view ignores an important aspect of classical work in the brainwashing tradition. For instance, Lifton's

(1961) work clearly shows the voluntaristic character of much of the thought reform which went on in China (his last chapter discusses voluntaristic personal change).

## 5. THERAPEUTIC EFFECTS OF PARTICIPATION IGNORED

Brainwashing theorists usually claim that participation in NRMs is a negative experience, claims countered by many lines of research. Participation seems to have a generally positive impact on most participants, an often-replicated finding which undercuts brainwashing arguments, but is usually ignored by proponents of such theories. Robbins and Anthony (1982) summarized positive effects which have been found, listing ten different therapeutic effects, including reduced neurotic distress, termination of illicit drug use, and increased social compassion. One review of a large literature concerning personality assessment of participants concluded (Richardson 1985b: 221): "Personality assessments of these group members reveal that life in the new religions is often therapeutic instead of harmful." Kilbourne (1986) drew similar conclusions in his assessment of outcomes from participation, after finding, for instance, that members of the Unification Church felt they were getting more from their participation than did matched samples of young Presbyterians and Catholics.

Psychiatrist Marc Galanter, who has done considerable assessment research on participants in some of the more prominent NRMs, has even posited a general "relief effect" brought about by participation (Galanter 1978). He wanted to find out what about participation leads to such consistent positive effects, in order that therapists can use the techniques themselves. McGuire (1988) found that many ordinary people participate in exotic religious groups in a search of alternatives to modern medicine, and many think themselves the better for the experience. To ignore such scholarly conclusions seems ethically quite questionable.

## 6. LARGE RESEARCH TRADITION AND "NORMAL" EXPLANATIONS IGNORED

There has been a huge amount of research done on recruitment to and participation in the new religious groups and movements, research almost totally ignored by brainwashing theorists. This work, which is summarized in such reviews as Greil and Rudy (1984), Richardson (1985a), and Robbins (1985), applies standard theories from sociology, social psychology, and psychology to explain why youth join such groups. These explanations seem quite adequate to explain participation, without any "black box" of mystical psychotechnology such as offered by brainwashing theorists.

Examples of such "normalizing" research include Heirich's (1977) study of the Charismatic Renewal Movement, Pilarzyk's (1978) comparison of conversion in the Divine Light Mission and the Hare Krishna, Straus' (1981) "naturalistic social psychological" explanation of seeking religious experiences, Solomon's work (1983) on the social psychology of participation in the Unification Church; and the examination of process models of conversion to the Jesus Movement (Richardson, et al. 1979). The ethics of ignoring such work, while propounding empirically weak notions such as brainwashing and mind control seem questionable.

## 7. LACK OF "SUCCESS" OF NEW RELIGIONS DISREGARDED

Another obvious problem with brainwashing explanations concerns assuming (and misinforming the public about) the efficacy of the powerful recruitment techniques allegedly used by the new religious groups. Most NRMs are actually quite small: the Unification Church probably never had over 10,000 American members, and can now boast only 2,000 to 3,000 members in the U. S.; the American Hare Krishna may not have achieved even the size of the Unification Church. There are no more than a few hundred membrers of the UC or the HK in Australia. Most other NRMs have had similar problems recruiting large numbers of participants.

A related problem concerns attrition rates for the new religions. As a number of scholars have noted, most participants in the new groups remain for only a short time, and most of those proselytized simply ignore or rebuff recruiters and go on with their normal lives (Bird and Reimer 1982; Barker 1984; Galanter 1980). Many people leave the groups after being in them relatively short periods (Wright 1987; Skonovd 1983; Richardson, et al. 1986).

An example of one well publicized group in Australia is The Family (formerly the Children of God) which has had over 57,000 young people world-wide join it over the group's 25 year history. However, the group has only about 3,000 adult members world-wide at this time, which could be construed to mean they have a serious attrition problem!

These histories of meager growth and/or rapid decline raise serious questions about the efficacy of brainwashing explanations of participation. Such powerful techniques should have resulted in much larger groups, a fact conveniently ignored by brainwashing proponents, who seem intent on raising the level of hysteria about NRMs, through misleading the public as to their size and efficiency in keeping members.

## 8. "BRAINWASHING" AS ITS OWN EXPLANATION

A last critique of brainwashing theories is that they are self-perpetuating, through "therapy" offered those who leave, especially those forcibly deprogrammed. As Solomon (1981) has concluded, those who are deprogrammed often accept the views which deprogrammers use to justify their actions, and which are promoted to the deprogrammee as reasons for cooperating with the deprogramming. These views usually include a belief in brainwashing theories. One could say that a successful deprogramming is one in which the deprogrammee comes to accept the view that they were brainwashed, and are now being rescued. Solomon's finding has been collaborated by other research on those who leave, including by Lewis (1986), Lewis and Bromley (1987), and Wright (1987). The social psychological truth that such ideas are *learned interpretations or accounts* undercuts truth claims by brainwashing theorists.

## Conclusions

The preceding critique indicates that brainwashing theories of participation in new religions fail to take into account considerable data about participation in such groups. However, many people still accept such theories, and high levels of concern about the "cult menace" exist, in part because of the promotion of ideologically based brainwashing theories of participation. Serious attention should be paid to alternative explanations which demystify the process of recruitment to and participation in the new religions.

Motivations for accepting such empirically weak theories as "brainwashing" should be examined. Also, those who propound brainwashing theories of participation need to examine the ethics of promoting such powerful "social weapons" against minority religions. When such theories are used to limit people's religious freedom and personal growth, then the society itself may suffer.

• • • • • • • • • • • • • • • • • • • • • • • • •

## Note

This paper was written while on sabbatical leave associated with the Criminology Department at the University of Melbourne and the Anthropology and Sociology Department at Monash University. Appreciation is expressed for this support. The paper derives in part from one presented at the annual meeting of the Australian Association for the Study of Religion, Adelaide, 1994, and from part of a chapter by the author in *Sects and Cults in America*, edited by Jeffrey Hadden and David Bromley (Greenwich, CT: JAI Press, 1994).

# References

Anthony, D.
    1990    "Religious Movements and Brainwashing Litigation: Evaluating Key Testimony." Pp. 295-344 in T. Robbins and D. Anthony (eds.), *In GodsWe Trust*. New Brunswick, NJ: Transaction Books.

Anthony, D. and T. Robbins
    1992    "Law, Social Science and the 'Brainwashing' Exception in the First Amendment." *Behavioral Sciences and the Law*. 10:5-30.

Barker, E.
    1984    *The Making of a Moonie: Choice or Brainwashing?* Oxford: Blackwell.

Beckford, J.
    1978a    "Accounting for Conversion." *British Journal of Sociology*. 29(2): 249-62.
    1985    *Cult Controversies: The Societal Response to the New Religious Movements*. London: Tavistock.

Biderman, A.
    1962    "The Image of 'Brainwashing'." *Public Opinion Quarterly*. 26: 547-563.

Bird, F. and Reimer
    1982    "A Sociological Analysis of New Religious and Para-religious Movements." *Journal for the Scientific Study of Religion* 21(1): 1-14.

Bromley, D. and J. Richardson (eds.)
    1983    *The Brainwashing / Deprogramming Controversy: Sociological, Psychology, Legal, and Historical Perspectives*. New York: Edwin Mellen.

Bromley, D. and T. Robbins
    1992    "The Role of Government in Regulating New and Non-conventional Religions.": In J. Wood and D. Davis (eds.), *The Role of Government in Monitoring and Regulating Religion in Public Life*. Waco, TX: Baylor University.

Delgado, R.
    1982    "Cults and Conversion: The Case for Informed Consent." *Georgia Law Review* 16: 533-74.

DeWitt, J.
    1991    "Novel Scientific Evidence and the Juror: A Social Psychological Approach to the *Frye / Relevancy* Controversy." Doctoral Dissertation in Social Psychology, University of Nevada, Reno.

Fort, J.
    1983    "What is Brainwashing and Who Says So?" In B. Kilbourne (ed.), *Scientific Research and New Religions: Divergent Perspectives*. San Francisco: American Assoc. for the Advancement of Science, Pacific Division.

Galanter, M.
    1978    "The 'Relief Effect': A Sociobiological Model of Neurotic Distress and Large Group Therapy." *American Journal of Psychiatry* 135: 588-91.
    1980    "Psychological Induction in the Large-Group: Findings from a Modern Religious Sect." *American Journal of Psychiatry* 137: 1574-79.

Greil, A. and D. Rudy
    1984    "What Have We Learned About Process Models of Conversion? An Examination of Ten Studies." *Sociological Analysis* 54(3): 115-25.

Heirich, M.
    1977        "Change of Heart: A Test of Some Widely Held Theories About Religious Conversion."
                American Journal of Sociology 85(3): 653-680.

Kilbourne, B.
    1986        "Equity or Exploitation? The Case of the Unification Church." Review of Religious
                Research 28: 143-150.

Kilbourne, B. and J. Richardson
    1984        "Psychotherapy and New Religions in a Pluralistic Society." American Psychologist 39(3):
                237-251.

Latkin, C.
    1991        "Vice and Device: Social Control of Intergroup Conflict." Sociological Analysis 52: 363-
                378.

Lewis, J.
    1986        "Reconstructing the Cult Experience: Post-Involvement Attitudes as a Function of Mode
                of Exit and Post-Involvement Socialization." Sociological Analysis 46: 151-59.

Lewis, J. and D. Bromley
    1987        "The Cult Withdrawal Syndrome: A Case of Misattribution of Cause?" Journal for the
                Scientific Study of Religion 26(4): 508-522.

Lifton, R.
    1963        Thought Reform and the Psychology of Totalism. New York: Norton.
    1985        "Cult Processes, Religious Liberty and Religious Totalism." Pp. 59-70 in T. Robbins, W.
                Shepherd, and J. McBride (eds.). Cults, Culture and the Law. Chico, CA: Scholars Press.

Lofland, J.
    1978        "'Becoming a World-saver' Revisited." In J. Richardson (ed.) Conversion Careers. Beverly
                Hills, CA: Sage.

McGuire, M.
    1988        Ritual Healing in Suburban America. New Brunswick, NJ: Rutgers University Press.

Pilarzyk, T.
    1978        "Conversion and Alienation Processes in the Youth Culture." Pacific Sociological Review
                21(4): 379-405.

Richardson, J. T.
    1985a       "Active verses Passive Converts: Paradigm Conflict in Conversion/Recruitment Research."
                Journal for the Scientific Study of Religion 24: 163-79.
    1985b       "Psychological and Psychiatric Studies of New Religions." In L. Brown, (ed.) Advances in
                the Psychology of Religion. New York: Pergamon Press.
    1991        "Cult/Brainwashing Cases and Freedom of Religion." Journal of Church and State. 33: 55-
                74.
    1992        "Public Opinion and the Tax Evasion Trial of Reverend Moon." Behavioral Sciences and
                the Law 10: 53-64.
    1993        "The Concept of 'Cult': From Sociological-Technical to Popular-Negative." Review of
                Religious Research 34: 348-356.
    1994        "Legal Status of New Religions in America." Forthcoming, Social Compass.

Richardson, and B. Kilbourne
    1983        "Classical and Contemporary Brainwashing Models: A Comparison and Critique." Pp. 29-
                45 in D. Bromley and J. Richardson, op cit.

Richardson, J., J. van der Lans, and F. Derks
  1986       "Leaving and Labeling: Voluntary and Coerced Disaffiliation from Religious Social
             Movements." In K. Lang and G. Lang (eds.) *Research in Social Movements, Conflict and
             Change* no. # 9. Greenwich, CT: JAI Press.

Richardson, J. T., M. Stewart, and R. Simmonds
  1979       *Organized Miracles.* New Brunswick, NJ: Transaction.

Robbins, T.
  1988       *Cults, Converts and Charisma:* The Sociology of New Religious Movements. Newbury
             Park, CA: Sage.

Robbins, T. and D. Anthony
  1982       "Deprogramming, Brainwashing, and the Medicalization of Deviant Religious Groups."
             *Social Problems* 29: 283-297.

Robbins, T., D. Anthony, and J. McCarthy
  1983       "Legitimating Repression." Pp. 319-328 in D. Bromley and J. Richardson, op cit.

Schein, E., I. Schneier, and C. Becker
  1961       *Coercive Persuasion.* New York: Norton.

Singer, M.
  1979       "Coming out of the Cults." *Psychology Today* 12: 72-82.

Singer, M. and R. Ofshe
  1990       "Thought Reform Programs and the Production of Psychiatric Casualties." *Psychiatric
             Annals.* 20: 188-193.

Skonovd, N.
  1983       "Leaving the Cultic Religious Milieu." Pp. 91-105 in D. Bromley and J. Richardson, op cit.

Solomon, T.
  1981       "Integrating the 'Moonie' Experience: A Survey of Ex-members of the Unification Church."
             In T. Robbins and D. Anthony (eds.), *In Gods We Trust.* New Brunswick, NJ: Transaction.

Solomon, T.
  1983       "Programming and Deprogramming the 'Moonies': Social Psychology Applied." Pp. 163-
             181 in D. Bromley and J. Richardson, op cit.

Straus, R.
  1976       "Changing Oneself: Seekers and the Creative Transformation of Life Experience." In J.
             Lofland (ed.), *Doing Social Life.* New York: Wiley.
  1979       "Religious Conversion as a Personal and Collective Accomplishment." *Sociological Analysis.*
             40: 158-165.

van Driel, B. and J. Richardson
  1988       "Print Media Coverage of New Religious Movements: A Longitudinal Study." *Journal of
             Communication* 36(3): 37-61.

Wright, S.
  1987       *Leaving the Cults: The Dynamics of Defection.* Washington, D.C.: Society for the Scientific
             Study of Religion.

# CHAPTER TWELVE

# CLINICAL AND PERSONALITY ASSESSMENT OF PARTICIPANTS IN NEW RELIGIONS

JAMES T. RICHARDSON

Continuing controversy about the new religions, popularly known as "cults," makes the study of mental health of participants in such groups a topic of major importance for the psychology of religion.[1] Over a decade ago I reviewed the literature on psychiatric and personality assessment of members of new religions at an Oxford conference on new developments in psychology of religion (Richardson, 1985b). In 1990 this review was updated for a conference held at the Institute for the Study of Religion at Jagiellonian University in Cracow, Poland. This article presents that material, with additional coverage of more recent scholarship.

The earlier review (Richardson, 1985b) included psychological assessment studies of (a) a nationwide, communal, Jesus Movement organization (Richardson, Stewart, and Simmonds, 1979; Simmonds, 1978; Simmonds, Richardson, and Harder, 1976); (b) an Eastern-oriented, California, "new age" group, Ananda Cooperative Village (Nordquist, 1978; Rosen and Nordquist, 1980); (c) the Unification Church in the United States and Europe (Galanter, 1980; Galanter, Rabkin, Rabkin, and Deutsch, 1979; Kuner, 1983); (d) the Children of God and Ananda Marga groups in Europe (Kuner, 1983); (e) a fundamentalist campus group at an elite American college (Nicholi, 1974); (f) the Divine Light Mission (Galanter, 1978; Galanter and Buckley, 1978); and (g) other assessment research including several groups (Ungerleider and Wellisch, 1979). The review also critiqued one report of a major "anticult" clinical psychologist who has served as a legitimator for groups opposed to new religions (Singer, 1979), as well as discussing other relevant work by social scientists.

---

James T. Richardson. "Clinical and Personality Assessment of Participants in New Religions." *The International Journal for the Psychology of Religion* 5(3), 1995: 145-170.

This earlier body of scholarship was impressive in coverage and consistency of findings. Noteworthy was the finding from studies of communally oriented groups that an unusual personality type was being fostered in or attracted to such groups. For instance, Nordquist and Rosen's (Nordquist, 1978; Rosen and Nordquist, 1980) work on Ananda Cooperative Village showed a typical member to be comparatively high in social compassion and concerned about the environment and living a more simple, noncompetitive life. Their findings were summarized by saying, "Taken as a whole, these results do not suggest personality disorders or major psychopathologies. They reflect a different setting and lifestyle centered around values of self-realization and even altruism" (Richardson, 1985b, pp. 213-214).

Research on the Jesus Movement group revealed a "dependency-prone" personality for many members, but one that participant observation demonstrated to be functional within the communal context of the group. Dramatic behavioral changes associated with participation (stopping use of drugs, alcohol, tobacco, and premarital sex) and the loving atmosphere within the group made us aware that the seemingly maladaptive pattern we found "fit" that particular context well and had positive value for participants (Richardson et al., 1979).

Kuner's (1983) application of the Minnesota Multiphasic Personality Inventory (MMPI) to European members of the Unification Church, Ananda Marga, the Children of God, and a control group revealed overall group profiles within normal ranges, with few members' scores indicating poor mental health. He added that members had better scores than control group members and seemed to live with less worry and psychic stress, concluding that the new religions often serve as therapeutic groups for socially alienated youths.

Psychiatrist Marc Galanter's study of Unification Church members using a number of personality inventories revealed that "affiliation with the Unification Church apparently provided considerable and sustained relief from neurotic distress. Although the improvement was ubiquitous, a greater religious commitment was reported by those who indicated the most improvement" (Galanter et al., 1979, p. 168). His research on the Divine Light Mission led to similar conclusions: "The diversity of specific psychological symptoms alleviated here is notable. A decline was reported in symptoms affected by behavioral norms, such as drug taking and job trouble; it was also found in subjectively experienced symptoms, such as anxiety, not readily regulated" (Galanter and Buckley, 1978, p. 690). Galanter's provocative 1978 article propounded a biologically based relief effect, based on interaction of the human organism with features of the communal setting of the new religious groups. The article derived directly from the consistent finding across groups in Galanter's research of an ameliorative effect of participation for most members.[2]

This earlier review of personality and psychiatric assessment of members of several new religions led me to conclude (Richardson, 1985b) that:

The personality assessments of these groups members reveal that life in the new religions is often therapeutic instead of harmful. Other information suggests that these young people are affirming their idealism by virtue of their involvement in such groups. Certainly there is some "submerging of personality" in groups which are communal or collective, simply because they do not foster the individualistic and competitive lifestyle to which we are accustomed, particularly in American society. However, there is little data to support the almost completely negative picture painted by a few (mental health professionals and others). (p. 221)

# New Research

A number of new research reports by psychologists have appeared since the 1985 review. Included in this article are the follow-up done on the Jesus Movement group studied in the 1970s research (Taslimi, Hood, and Watson, 1991), as well as research done on the Rajneesh group while located in Oregon (Latkin, 1987, 1989, 1990, 1991, 1992, 1993; Latkin, Hagan, Littman, and Sundberg, 1987; Latkin, Littman, Sundberg, and Hagan, 1993; Latkin, Sundberg, Littman, Katsikis, and Hagan, in press; Palmer and Bird, 1992; Sundberg, Goldman, Rotter, and Smyth, 1992; Sundberg, Latkin, Littman, and Hagan, 1990), and the much-publicized Hare Krishna (Poling and Kenny, 1986; Ross, 1983a, 1983b, 1985a, 1985b; Weiss, 1985, 1987; Weiss and Comprey, 1987a, 1987b, 1987c; Weiss and Mendoza, 1990). The Rajneesh and Hare Krishna groups have been involved in considerable controversy (Richardson, 1990, 1991), making that research especially relevant.

# Jesus Movement Group

The Jesus Movement organization studied extensively in the 1970s, "Shiloh," (called "Christ Communal Organization" in earlier publications) has since disbanded. A number of members moved into conservative, nondenominational churches, including particularly Calvary Chapel, the group out of whence it first evolved (Richardson, 1993b). Cheryl Taslimi, a former Shiloh member, completed follow-up research on a sample of former members, administering Gough's Adjective Check List (ACL; which had been used in the early 1970s research) to former members of Shiloh who had been a member for at least 1 year between 1968 and 1978 (Taslimi et al., 1991). As indicated, our earlier conclusion was that the pattern found, although quite functional within the communal context, appeared somewhat maladaptive for more normal living situations (see particularly Simmonds, 1978). We wondered then if Shiloh members could "recover" from this personality pattern and be able to function in more normal, noncommunal settings.

Taslimi gathered data relevant to this question by mailing to 468 former members (some of whom were not eligible for inclusion, based on the minimum 1 year participation criterion). She obtained 101 usable responses (56 men 45 women), including three who had been assessed back in the earlier research in the 1970s. Results were compared with (a) the Simmonds et al. (1976) results in 1972, (b) a normative sample of college students, and (c) a normative sample of adults.

Taslimi et al. (1991) concluded, "There is an overwhelming tendency for the subjects ... to demonstrate group scores like those of normative samples, in sharp contrast to the results of the 1972 studies" (p. 309). They added, "Clearly if any general trend towards relative 'maladaptivity' existed in the past, and if earlier findings were representative of members of Shiloh, this phenomenon has not persisted, at least as demonstrated in these common personality characteristics" (p. 309). In short, the results indicated that these former members of Shiloh have apparently adapted quite adequately to life in noncommunal settings, as shown by their ACL response patterns.

# The Rajneeshees

The followers of Bhagwan Shree Rajneesh, a worldwide movement, established a community in eastern Oregon in 1981, after serious external political problems associated with the large central ashram in Poona, India, led Rajneesh to shut down the Poona operation and move to America (Carter, 1987). The group purchased a 64,000-acre ranch and took over a small town (Antelope) in the area. By 1985 there were 4 to 5 thousand people residing at the new site, which they named Rajneeshpuram, a development that aroused considerable controversy with local and state officials, leading to many legal battles with the state of Oregon and others (Latkin, 1992; Richardson, 1990). The Oregon group disbanded in 1985, after the arrest of some leaders, including the Bhagwan and his chief associate Ma Sheela, on criminal charges. The Bhagwan has since died, but the group continues to function in other countries as well as other, smaller sites in the United States.

Work by a group of psychologists from the University of Oregon and others made this one of the most thoroughly researched religious groups in history (Latkin, 1987, 1989, 1990, 1991, 1992, 1993; Latkin et al., 1987; Latkin et al., 1993, Latkin et al., in press; Sundberg et al., 1992; Sundberg et al., 1990; also see Carter, 1990; Palmer and Bird, 1992). The Oregon team administered a set of instruments to most participants there in October 1983 (635 of about 800 completed all instruments), as well as a follow-up survey of 150 of 200 randomly selected from the original 635 (only 100 randomly selected instruments of the 150 returned were analyzed for reporting in

Latkin et al., 1987). The instrumentation focused on demographic and personal background and attitudes, as well as psychological well-being information. Latkin (1987), in his dissertation, reported another set of responses of 232 participants to a number of personality inventories, some of which are also discussed in Latkin (1989, 1990). Sundberg et al. (1990) reported results of administering the California Psychological Inventory to 67 members; Sundberg et al. (1992) reported on administrations of the Thematic Apperception Test to Rajneesh members who had been high achievers prior to participating, as well as to a matched sample of nonparticipants in new religions. Follow-up work has been done, as well, on former Rajneeshpuram residents after that site disbanded (Latkin, 1993; Latkin et al., in press) that will be briefly discussed.[3]

Participants in this group differed somewhat from typical participants in the new religions reviewed earlier (Richardson, 1985b). Respondents to the Latkin et al. (in press) survey were 54% female, average age of 34 years, and 46% male, average age of 35. Seventy-four percent were married, and 65% said they were living with their spouse. Twenty-five percent had children, and 11% said they were living with them at Rajneeshpuram. Forty percent said they first heard of Rajneeshism from friends, 30% said they read books or listened to tapes of Bhagwan, and 10% said they visited a Rajneesh center to first learn about the Bhagwan. Their prior religious background was varied — 30% Protestant, 27% Catholic, 20% Jewish, 14% "none," 4% Hindu or Buddhist, and 4% "other," but only 40% characterized themselves as religious before joining.

Education level and orientation revealed by the Oregon team's research were particularly interesting, with 95% graduating from high school, and 64% with a college degree. A random sample of 100 showed that 24% had a master's degree, and 12% had a doctorate of some sort. The area of academic degree for those with a bachelor's, master's, or doctorate were: arts and humanities, 27%; social sciences, 33%; natural sciences and math, 10%; and professional, 10%. Self-reported political orientation was quite skewed, with only 2% saying they were conservative; the rest were radical (11%), very liberal (31%), somewhat liberal (20%), and "neither liberal nor conservative" (36%). When asked about income earned in a year prior to joining, only 16% said less than $10,000, and 19% said they had earned over $40,000. Forty-eight percent said they came from cities of over 100,000, with 35% from ones of over one-half million.

The typical sannyasin at Rajneeshpuram was, therefore, considerably different from the typical member of most of the other controversial new religions.[4] Sannyasins are older, much better educated, from a more financially successful background, and more politically liberal than participants in many of the groups that have been researched (Richardson et al., 1979; Wuthnow, 1976). A similar pattern of background characteristics was found in an earlier study of 300 sannyasins in the Poona community in 1980, which revealed that members were overwhelmingly from "occupations either of a creative kind, or in which their main role is service to others, particularly of a human development kind" (Wallis and Bruce, 1986, p. 201). Sociologist Lewis Carter's (1987) study of the development of the Oregon community also noted unique characteristics of members:

> Some writers ... make the mistake of assuming that Rajneesh recruitment follows the pattern of groups like the Hare Krishnas and Children of God. ... Rajneesh are almost uniformly older and at later states in their lives before turning to the movements, and rather than chance recruitment by strangers, ...Sannyasins indicate active pursuit of Rajneesh training after referral by friends. Some have been drawn by advertised therapies. Most have traveled widely and report earlier experiments in other religions and therapies. (p. 163)

These unique personal characteristics of sannyasins must be considered when interpreting data gathered by the Oregon researchers. Also, certain features of Rajneesh philosophy and organizational style — particularly their approach to sex roles — are relevant. As Latkin (1987, 1989) and Goldman (1988) noted, the Rajneesh group emphasized flexible gender roles and had a disproportionate number of women in managerial roles and in jobs — such as operating construction heavy equipment — usually reserved for men. This "androgynous" philosophy and practice could be expected to influence results of personality assessment, as Latkin's (1987) dissertation demonstrated. Also, the Rajneesh community practiced a very open and loving lifestyle for members, which Latkin (1987) called an "affect-oriented society" (p. 147).

The team of Oregon psychologists administered more standardized assessment instruments to Rajneesh members than has been given to participants of any of the new religions. Latkin et al. (1987) reported results of inventories on perceived stress (Cohen, Kamart, and Mermelstein, 1983), social support (Cohen and Hoberman, 1983), self-esteem (Rosenberg, 1965), and depression (Radloff, 1977). They also asked for self-assessed life satisfaction before and after becoming a sannyasin. The latter measure revealed that life satisfaction rating of members were extremely high, with 82% choosing the last level on a 9-point scale. The reports of life satisfaction prior to becoming a sannyasin showed only 5% in the last level, with most grouped in the middle of the 9-point scale. This is self-report data, taken from current members, which means results may be subject to some "biographical reconstruction" (Berger, 1967) and a selection bias, but nonetheless, the data show high levels of current satisfaction for those responding. The Cohen et al. (1983) Perceived Stress Scale was designed to tap unpredictability, uncontrollability, and overload experiences in the lives of those being studied. The Rajneesh mean was significantly lower at 15.22 ($SD$ = 7.64, $N$ = 79) than the mean of 23.34 ($SD$ = 7.62, $N$ = 543) for a normative sample, indicating much lower levels of perceived stress among sannyasins. Cohen and Hoberman's (1983) Interpersonal Support Evaluation List is made up of 40 true-false statements developed to measure perceived social resources. The Rajneesh sample had a mean of 37.91 ($SD$ = 1.51, $N$ = 78), compared to a normative sample mean of 36.5 ($SD$ = 7.4), indicating that the Rajneesh group perceived slightly higher levels of social support, with much less variation. The 20-item Center for Epidemiological Studies Depression Scale used by Radloff (1977) focuses on depression symptoms over the past week. Rajneesh participants had a mean of 5.86 ($SD$ = 5.55, $N$ = 86), indicating significantly less recent depression than several normative samples, for which Radloff reported means from 7.94 to 9.25 ($SDs$ from 7.53 to 8.58, $N$ = 4,996). Rosenberg's 10-item Self-Esteem Scale was developed to measure global feelings about the self (Rosenberg, 1965). The Rajneesh mean was 35.71 ($SD$ = 5.53, $N$ = 87), compared to means of 29.82 ($SD$ = 4.43, $N$ = 1,179) reported by Yancey, Rigsby, and MaCarthy (1972). The higher mean score indicated greater self-esteem for Rajneesh group members.

Latkin et al. (1987) suggested caution when interpreting their results because of (a) use of self-report data, (b) instruments having different meanings in different cultures, and (c) confounding of results because Rajneesh philosophy emphasizes the positive. The small $N$s on some scales also raise concerns about validity and reliability.

Latkin (1987) included results from several other inventories, directly chosen to allow testing of hypotheses about effects of the Rajneesh philosophy and practice concerning sex roles. A Self-Consciousness Scale developed by Feigenstein, Scheier, and Buss (1975) and revised by Kernis and Reis (1981) was administered, as was a slightly revised Coping Scale from Moos, Cronkite, Billings, and Finney (1982); the Cohen–Hoberman Inventory of Physical Symptoms (1983); the Job Diagnostic Index from Smith, Kendall, and Hulin (1969); a modified version of Wrightsman's Assumptions about Human Nature Scale (1974); and the Personal Attribute Questionnaire developed by Spence and Helmreich (1978) to measure gender-role orientation. Latkin also asked some separate questions about values, as well as administering the Rosenberg Self-Esteem Scale and the Depression Scale referred to earlier, along with obtaining considerable other data from demographic and personal background questionnaires. Latkin did in-depth interviews with 25 sannyasins as well. Note that Latkin gathered his data shortly after the Bhagwan and Ma Sheela left the Oregon commune, a disruptive factor that apparently impacted some results.[5]

Detailed results from Latkin's work cannot be given here, but some particularly germane conclusions are noted. Of interest are results of the Personal Attribute Questionnaire designed to show gender-role orientation. Both men and women scored higher on the Femininity Scale than on the Masculinity Scale, which means they valued positive, usually feminine attributes more than they valued positive, usually male attributes. Latkin examined the 16 specific items on which men and women differed and found some startling results on four items with significant differences (Latkin, 1987): "Males reported themselves to cry and have hurt feelings significantly more than women reported these attributes. On the other hand, women had higher scores on feelings of dominance" (p. 72). Men also ranked slightly, but significantly, higher on "feelings of superiority."

The Feigenstein Self-Consciousness Scale contains three subscales: (a) Private Self-Consciousness, focusing on internal thoughts and feelings; (b) Public Self-Consciousness, attending to perceptions of self as a social object; and (c) Social Anxiety, which deals with being ill at ease and uncomfortable in the presence of others. The Rajneesh sample scored significantly below normative means on the Public and Social Anxiety subscales and scored significantly above normative means on the Private Self-Consciousness scale. Thus, respondents seemed more introspective, but less concerned about other's opinions of themselves and less socially anxious than normative samples.

A discussion of the results from the Feigenstein Self-Consciousness Scale and the Rosenberg Self-Esteem Scale are presented in Latkin (1990). Scores for the Rajneeshees on the Self-Esteem Scale were nearly as high as the earlier use of the instrument reported in Latkin et al. (1987) — the mean was 33.4 ($SD = 3.9$, $N = 210$). These data, coupled with those just reported on the Self-Consciousness Scale, suggest that "The score on Private Self-Consciousness accords with the movement's belief that self-exploration is a legitimate and respectable avocation, but it contradicts the stereotypical notion that members of new religions or cults are easily persuaded" (Latkin, 1990, p. 91).

Results from one specific item of the Wrightsman Assumptions About Human Nature Scale, designed to indicate locus of control orientation, is also germane. That item is, "Our success in life is pretty much determined by forces outside our control." Ninety-three percent of the 226 sannyasins who responded disagreed with that statement, suggesting a strong internal locus of control orientation.

Scores on the Depression Scale were elevated considerably compared to the earlier administration reported in Latkin et al. (1987), with a mean of 12.96. Latkin attributed this to the fact that the Bhagwan and Ma Sheela had left the community and encountered considerable legal difficulties within the previous year, a very traumatic event for sannyasins. This interpretation is supported by responses to the Coping Scale, which asks respondents to list a stressful event that occurred during the past year and describe their reactions to it. The majority listed the Bhagwan's departure and related events.

Sundberg et al. (1990) presented results from administering the California Personality Inventory (CPI) to 67 Rajneeshees (34 women, 33 men). They found male and female scoring patterns to be quite similar, with especially high scores on the Independence and Flexibility scales of the CPI. That article also reported an analysis in terms of Gough's (1987) new structural system of interpreting CPI scores. This system categorizes individuals based on three variables: "Role (internalizing or detached vs. externalizing or involved), Temperament (norm favoring vs. norm doubting), and Realization (low-to-high levels of self-perceived realization, or competence)" (Sundberg et al., 1990, p. 10). Gough (1987) proposed four types of individuals — Alphas, Betas, Deltas, and Gammas — depending on their categorization on the three variables, and Sundberg et al. (1990, p. 11) claimed that 25% of respondents in the general population fall into each of the four categories. The Rajneesh group of 67 included only 2 who were not either Gammas (57%) or Deltas (40%), which means that only 2 were "norm favoring," and 75 were "norm doubting." Gammas are described as follows: "adventurous, clever, headstrong, progressive, and rebellious" (Sundberg et al., 1990, p. 11). Deltas are "more private and internally oriented and are described by the following terms: preoccupied, quiet, reserved, sensitive, and worrying" (pp. 11-12). Sundberg et al. (1990) stated, "Compared with most people on CPI norms, Rajneeshees showed considerable ability, social poise, and absence of rigidity, and at the same time, a strong dislike for conventional forms and rules" (p. 15). They speculated, however, that the demise of the group might have derived from the lack of balance in personality types, suggesting that any group, in order to survive, "requires some conventional norm-favoring participants" (p. 16).

Latkin's (1987) rich discussion of his results is well worth studying, as are other papers from this research, but enough results have been sampled to draw a few conclusions. First, the data reported in the 1987 study (gathered prior to the departure of the Bhagwan), although involving small Ns on some key scales, supports the position that sannyasins were living in a very positive atmosphere that contributed to a strong self-concept. Data from the later study (Latkin et al., 1987) also supports that general conclusion, with the caveat that loss of the leader was a traumatic event that apparently influenced responses on the Depression Scale dramatically. However, even in the face of the loss of the Bhagwan, impact of the philosophy of the group was evident in the results, especially concerning gender roles. Thus, this much-maligned group appeared to be succeeding to some extent in changing traditional approaches to gender in American society. That is no small feat and should be recognized by those who would only focus on the negative aspects of the Rajneesh experience in Oregon. The Sundberg et al. (1990) results also suggests that most members were strong, well-focused personalities, even if the group may have needed some other personality types in order to survive.

The Rajneesh group had built a strong, loving community, which members apparently found very satisfying. The sannyasins were able to act out their philosophy and express their emotions without fear of retribution, except by the greater society. The group may have simply attracted the type of person described in the inventories, of course, which would undercut the view that the community developed and promoted a unique, loving and supportive, less male-dominated philosophy. Given the length of time that most respondents had been sannyasins, it is apparent that even if the group only attracted such people, the organization and philosophy of the community fostered such individuals and allowed them to continue along that path of human development.

After the disbanding of Rajneeshpuram, Latkin's research continued (Latkin, 1993), with two mail surveys of former residents attempting to assess whether the experience of living in such an isolated and unique environment was detrimental to the long-term well-being of former residents, who were, on very short notice, forced to leave their encapsulating and supportive environment.[6] The second survey (n = 231) included the Depression Scale (Radloff, 1977) used in the earlier research, the

Somatization and Anxiety subscales of the Symptoms Check List (Derogatis, Lipman, and Covi, 1973), and 12 items from the MMPI Lie Scale (Dahlstrom, Welsh, and Dahlstrom, 1975), and other measures of social desirability (Paulhus, 1991) were used as well. The research revealed that former residents who responded still maintained ties and some degree of self-identification with the Rajneesh movement. There were significant positive correlations between the mental health scales and the Lie Scale, leading the researchers to control for score on the Lie Scale.[7] No detailed results will be given for space reasons, but Latkin (1993) concluded:

> Considering the severity of their change in life style and number of life events the Rajneeshees appear to be adjusted well. ... They had recently changed residences, occupations, hours of work, recreational and social activities, eating and sleeping habits, and financial status, but there was no evidence that these stressors had been deleterious to their mental health. (p. 105)

## Hare Krishna

The Hare Krishna group has been the focus of considerable psychological research in the past decade. One book reports results of a major personality assessment effort (Poling and Kenny, 1986); Arnold Weiss has done a dissertation out of which a number of articles have come (Weiss, 1987; Weiss and Comprey, 1987a, 1987b, 1987c; Weiss and Mendoza, 1990); and Michael Ross has produced four articles out of his research on an Australian Hare Krishna group (Ross, 1983a, 1983b, 1985). Some important aspects of these reports will be summarized.

*Ross's Australian research.* Ross (1983a) reported results from administering the MMPI, Goldberg's (1972) General Health Questionnaire, and the Eysenck Personality Inventory (1975) to the entire population of a Melbourne, Australia, Hare Krishna temple. The 42 members, who averaged 1.5 years in the movement, were found to be within the normal range on all tests. Ross (1983a) also presented the MMPI results to two outside assessors, who "found no associated elevation of related scales that would permit an assessment of psychopathology" (p. 418). Ross (1983a) concluded: "Clearly, the argument that Hare Krishna devotees are individuals who suffer from psychopathology, as some investigators have claimed, cannot be supported on the basis of the present evidence" (p. 418). He added that the longer one was a member, the more conventional the responses, the less anxious the respondents, and the less they felt socially alienated. Ross (1983a) said of the behavioral changes brought about by participation, such as cutting the quite high levels of drug use prior to joining: "This history of abstinence after joining the movement must rate as one of the more successful rehabilitation programs" (p. 418). He offered other strong conclusionary statements, based on his research:

> These devotees appeared extremely well adjusted. ... Most still visited
> their families and were visited by them; ... In short, the popular view of
> Hare Krishna devotees as brainwashed and maladjusted individuals
> who have been snatched from their families was shown to be fallacious.
> ... Deprogramming and other actions against these individuals and
> their right to practice a particular religion cannot be justified on the
> grounds that they have been "brainwashed." ... Those researchers who
> base conclusions on their perceptions of movements rather than on
> clinical and psychometric evaluation of members of each organization
> are in danger of exonerating the bad or condemning the normal.
> (1983a, pp. 419-420).

Ross (1985) reported a follow-up administration of the MMPI to 25 of the 42 members 4 years later. He said that the changes experienced, with one exception, were well within the normal range and were beneficial rather than harmful. The exception was increased anxiety of the 25 members.

*Poling and Kenny's Myers–Briggs application.* Poling and Kenny (1986) presented findings based on an application of the Jungian-based, Myers-Briggs 162-item personality assessment instrument (I. Myers, 1962) to 93 members from four different temples in the United States (Dallas; Philadelphia; Carrier, MI; and San Diego), which represented about 90% of the fully initiated members at those temples. They also administered the Rokeach (1960) Dogmatism Scale to 29 individuals at three temples.

Poling and Kenny were addressing two questions: Why do some young people join Hare Krishna, and Why do some persevere in their affiliation? To gain answers to these questions, Poling and Kenny engaged in an in-depth study of the Krishna, including (a) an analysis of Krishna beliefs and ritual behaviors, using a Jungian framework; (b) extensive fieldwork and participant observation at eight temples around the country, supplemented by biographical questionnaires, personality assessment, and in-depth interviews; and (c) administration of the aforementioned personality assessment instruments.

Phase 1 of the research led to the following conclusion (Poling and Kenny, 1986):

> (1) Krishna, ISKCON's [International Society of Krishna
> Consciousness) deity, may be viewed as a symbol of transformation
> stemming from man's collective and unconscious strivings toward
> transcendence; and (2) consciousness of Krishna is developed in
> ISKCON by redirecting sexual impulses and desires for sense
> gratification into devotional services involving sensory-emotive rituals.
> (p. i)

Phase 2 of the research led to the conclusion that "the devotees we observed displayed a high degree of homogeneity in terms of background, lifestyle, and personality traits" (p. i). They described the typical ISKCON preconvert as follows, based on their work and that of others:

> A socio-economically advantaged family background; an early socialization process characterized by discord as well as an identity crisis prior to membership in ISKCON; an orientation toward being a world-saver; a rejection of parental authority and value system coupled with the need for a strong, male authority substitute; extensive use of drugs prior to joining ISKCON; a tendency to view the material world as devoid of meaning and reality, a vegetarian diet and a tendency to seek a new self-identity in nontraditional, Asian religions. (1986, p. 1)

Phase 3 of the research used the Myers-Briggs inventory to categorize individuals into 1 of 16 different personality types. The 16 types are combinations of four basic attributes — thinking versus feeling, sensing versus intuiting, introversion versus extroversion, and judging versus perceiving. *Thinking* is primarily intellectual and ideational, with an emphasis on logic and rationality. *Feeling* is the emotive or evaluative function that brings a subjective element to judgments. *Sensing*, according to Poling and Kenny (1986), "promotes awareness of literal facts or sensory representations of tangible events and objects" (p. 44). *Intuition* involves perception through unconscious processes that are more irrational in character. *Introversion* refers to a focus on thoughts, feelings, perceptions, ideas, and fantasies, in contrast to *extraversion*, which directs awareness to tangible entities external to the observer. Introverts are more reflective and socially withdrawn, whereas extraverts tend to be outgoing and interested in others. *Judging* refers to a preference for an ordered and structured lifestyle, contrasted to *perceiving*, which indicates a preference for a more spontaneous, experientially oriented, and unstructured lifestyle, the last pair of attributes being added to Jung's theoretical scheme by I. Myers (1962).

Considerable homogeneity was found among the 93 Krishna devotees who took the Myers-Briggs inventory. Forty percent of those taking the test were classified as "ISTJ," which means they were introverted, sensory, thinking, and judging. Another 26% were classified as "ESTJ," which means they were extraverted, sensory, thinking, and judging.Thus 66% were classified as sensory, thinking, and judging. When looking at what percentages chose items classifying them on the separate attributes, the dominance of the STJ pattern stands out. Eighty-two percent were classified as sensory, 78% as thinking, and 90% as judging (55% chose introversion). This startling pattern was interpreted by Poling and Kenny (1986) to mean that considerable selection had taken place to have such a concentration of a unique personality type within the Krishna. They pointed out that only 1 out of 23 females in an earlier study (I. Myers and P. Myers, 1980) was of the ISTJ pattern that characterized 40% of the Krishna women tested. They also report administration of the inventory to samples of 29 Catholic high school women and 52 members of the Unitarian Church, which resulted in quite a different spread of personality types than those found with the Krishna sample.

Poling and Kenny (1986) said, "It is our contention that the high frequency of sensing types among our ISKCON subjects validates the presence of the sensate orientation initially identified through other sources of information including interviews, direct observation, and previous scholarship" (p. 63). They described the ISTJ personality as "painstaking, hardworking, systematic, and thorough," "often remarkably dependable," "stable, ... seldom enter[ing] into endeavors implusively," and "very hard to distract or discourage" (1986, p. 62). Their (1986) explanation of why sensates are attracted is provocative:

> We view ISKCON devotees as highly sensate-oriented pleasure seekers who perceive themselves as constantly in danger of falling victim to sense gratification as an end in itself. ... Our contention is that IKSCON devotees: (1) are preoccupied with the sensing process; and (2) are using thinking and judging to structure or control the sensate function. This explains the apparent paradox between the rejection of sense pleasure on the mundane level and its acceptance on the transcendent level. (p. 108)

Poling and Kenny (1986) noted that "ISKCON's categorical condemnation of the use of intoxicants of any kind (including caffeine) indicates a sensate preoccupation" (p. 118). They discussed the strict dietary rules as another indicator of controlling sensate pleasures. Most importantly, the redefinition and strict regulation of sexual behavior is viewed as a manifestation of a sensate preoccupation.

Thinking and judging help control the sensate impulses that plague ISKCON members. Major characteristics of the thinking function are "(1) the tendency to think in clear cut ways; (2) the tendency to accept dichotomies stressing true vs. false, one's own truth as absolute, coupled with the corresponding tendency to make errors with confidence; and (3) the tendency to value principles over persons" (Poling and Kenny, 1986, p. 127). This style can mean that devotees, when dealing with outsiders, are argumentative and confrontational. Judging has as major features:

> (1) tendency to conform to proper standards; (2) sustained effort in terms of projects; (3) a passion for a decisive, purposeful, planned life with a high degree of purposeful, self-regimentation and the acceptance of routine; and (4) a high degree of intolerance regarding the beliefs and lifestyles of others, coupled with dogmatic thinking. (1986, p. 135)

The last point about dogmatic thinking is also evidenced by scores on Rokeach's Dogmatism Scale, administered to 29 devotees at three temples (we are not told why there was a small *N*). ISKCON members had a mean score of 191 (*SD* = 22.3), which was about 2 standard deviations above the normative mean of 142 (*SD* = 27.9) for college students reported in Rokeach (1960).

Poling and Kenny (1986) noted "the remarkable correspondence between the predispositional factors of persons who join ISKCON and the structural factors of ISKCON itself" (p. 152). They referred to ISKCON as a "specialized institution in that its therapeutic techniques are designed solely for sensates" (1986, p. 154). This unique organization attracts and reinforces a new identity in devotees, who change from a materialistic sensate to a more spiritual one. Poling and Kenny (1986) characterized ISKCON interestingly:

> From 1967 to approximately 1975, ISKCON functioned as a voluntary detoxification unit for countercultural, drug-addicted youth with a "world-saver" mentality and a tendency to seek new identity in religion. ... Later, from 1975 to the present, ISKCON functioned ... as a rehabilitative program analogous to Alcoholics Anonymous. Individuals who had been successfully detoxed were now rehabilitated." (p. 152)

Poling and Kenny closed their book with a discussion of the so-called "brainwashing-deprogramming" controversy. They admitted that their work might be viewed as supportive of the brainwashing idea, because it identifies a strong set of predispositional factors that indicate susceptibility to certain types of religious influence. However, they pointed out that their study did not support the brainwashing notion in terms of the element of coercion, which they define as "physical incarceration and mind control" (1986, p. 163). They cited the ease with which devotees leave the movement, and the fact that there are large numbers of ex-devotees (more than there are members), and stated: "If ISKCON has employed brainwashing and mind-control techniques, these have been very successful" (1986, p. 164). They also noted that, although becoming a member was easier and more haphazard earlier in the movement's history, later a lengthy probationary period was instituted. Such a recruitment process does not resemble what most mean when they talk of so-called "brainwashing."

Poling and Kenny (1986) concluded that sensate personalities are attracted to the Krishna organization because of its unique features, and some of those who join remain for a time because of what the organization does for them. However, no one is coerced into joining or kept a prisoner after joining.

*Weiss's research.* Arnold Weiss's research on Krishna devotees included an assessment of the personality characteristics (Weiss and Comprey, 1987b), the personality factor structure of Krishna followers (Weiss and Comprey, 1987c), and a comparison of followers with psychiatric outpatients and "normals" (Weiss and

Comprey, 1987a), all using the Comprey Personality Scales (CPS; Comprey, 1970a, 1970b, 1980). Weiss (1987) also presented results of administering the RAND Corporation's Mental Health Inventory (MHI) developed by Ware (Ware, Johnston, Davies-Avery, and Brook, 1979; Veit and Ware, 1983), as well as results from relating an Acculturation Scale to the CPS and MHI data (Weiss and Mendoza, 1990).

All these comparisons were based on a sample of 186 devotees and 40 "sympathizers" (most of whom were in the process of becoming devotees), who represented about 5% of all Krishna followers in the United States at the time (Weiss, 1987, p. 33). The 132 men and 94 women who volunteered for testing averaged 30 years of age and 8.6 years in the Krishna movement. Marital status was 89 single, 101 married, 21 divorced, 10 separated, 3 cohabiting, and 2 widows. One hundred twenty-eight claimed no prior religious affiliation, 40 said they were Catholics, 20 were Protestant, 14 in other Christian religions, 11 Jewish, and 11 from various Eastern religions. They came from temples in San Diego, the District of Columbia, Pennsylvania, and Los Angeles, with the Los Angeles temple furnishing about 40% of Weiss's sample. One hundred sixteen of the devotees had some college education, 22 had bachelor's degrees, 10 had some graduate training, and 7 had graduate or professional degrees. One hundred eighty-eight were White, 13 were Black, 9 were Asian, 5 were Hispanic, with 11 unclassified. Thirty-three were from lower socioeconomic status origins, with 97 from the middle class, and 96 from the upper middle and upper classes (Weiss and Comprey, 1987c).

The 180-item CPS measures eight personality traits or constructs, including:

1. Trust versus Defensiveness (T). High scores indicate a belief in the basic honesty, trustworthiness, and good intentions of people.
2. Orderliness versus Lack of Compulsion (O). High scores are characteristic of careful, meticulous, orderly, and highly organized individuals.
3. Social Conformity versus Rebelliousness (C). Individuals with high scores accept society as it is, resent nonconformity in others, seek the approval of society, and respect the law.
4. Activity versus Lack of Energy (A). High-scoring individuals have a great deal of energy and endurance, work hard, and strive to excel.
5. Emotional Stability versus Neuroticism (S). High-scoring persons are free of depression, optimistic, relaxed, stable in mood, and confident.
6. Extraversion versus Introversion (E). High-scoring individuals meet people easily, seek new friends, feel comfortable with strangers, and do not suffer from stage fright.
7. Masculinity versus Femininity (M). High-scoring individuals tend to be rather tough-minded people who are not bothered by blood, crawling creatures, vulgarity, and who do not cry easily or show interest in love stories.

8. Empathy versus Egocentrism (P). High-scoring individuals describe themselves as helpful, generous, sympathetic people who are interested in devoting their lives to the service of others. (1987b, pp. 400-401)

Two additional scales — a Validity (V) scale and a Response Bias (R) scale — detect distorted responding and faking.

Results of the CPS administration to Krishna followers, when factor-analyzed to discern the personality structure of followers (Weiss and Comprey, 1987c), revealed that the CPS personality dimensions found appropriate for use with diverse groups also described the Krishna well, with one exception. That was the Social Conformity scale, on which Krishna scores displayed a score variance only one third that of norm groups of males and females. Failure of this factor to emerge was interpreted as deriving from the conformity requirements within the group, which in turn led to more homogeneity on this characteristic than with most other groups. Weiss and Comprey (1987c) concluded, however, that

> The most surprising outcome ... was not that the factor structure of personality underlying the CPS for Hare Krishna diverged from that for other groups but rather that it was so similar. ... What the present results show is that individuals in this Hare Krishna population subgroup, a minority United States culture possessing divergent habits, life style, and other characteristics, nevertheless can be described with respect to the same set of personality dimensions as that which previously has been found to be appropriate for use with what would be considered more typical individuals in the United States and other countries. (p. 327).

The assessment of personality characteristics (Weiss and Comprey, 1987b) revealed a number of significant differences, particularly for men, who differed on eight of the scales (R, T, O, C, S, E, M, and P). Krishna men were higher than the norm on O, C, S, E, and P, but below the norm on T and M. However, all scores were within the defined normal range (Comprey, 1980), except for the score on O, which was 1.44 standard deviations above the normal group mean. Thus, the male profile can be described as low on T and M and high on O, C, S, E, and P. Also, men were higher on R, compared to the norm group. Krishna women differed from the norm group only on T and O, being significantly below the norm for T and significantly above ($SD$ = 1.18), on O. Only scale O for women was out of the defined normal range, however.

The finding of a strong "compulsivity trait" among Krishna followers of both sexes (stronger with men) is called the "hallmark trait of the Hare Krishna personality" by Weiss and Comprey (1987b, p. 406). Nearly 23% of the sample (including 27% of the men) scored at the extreme range on the O scale. The compulsive personality is:

very meticulous, compulsive people who are highly organized, conscientious, punctual, neat and tidy. They are driven to complete tasks, feel compelled to correct errors, and often fall prey to obsessive behavior. Many individuals with moderately high scores on this scale are highly productive persons who capitalize on their obsessive-compulsive inclinations to accomplish amazing feats. ... Unfortunately, this behavior in adult life may have some negative side effects on their overall adjustment. (Comprey, 1980, p. 22)

Weiss and Comprey (1987b) spoke directly to whether this trait is a debilitating mental disorder, under the rubric of the *Diagnostic and Statistical Manual of Mental Disorders* (3rd ed., *DSM-III*; American Psychiatric Association, 1980). They noted that elevated scores on the O scale accompanied by high C scale scores has been suggested (Comprey, 1980, p. 65) as characteristic of the "compulsive personality disorder" of the *DSM-III*. However, they pointed out that Krishna followers are not out of the normal range on the C scale; although men are significantly higher than the norm on C, they do not have enough extreme scores to fit the profile of that disorder.

Weiss and Comprey (1987b) discussed the congruence between the structured Krishna lifestyle and the results of the CPS application. Their discussion mirrored that of Poling and Kenny (1986), whose classification of most Krishna followers as Judging and Thinking and as highly Dogmatic, parallels the Weiss and Comprey (1987b) finding of compulsivity as a dominant trait. The differences between Krishna men and women is indicative, Weiss and Comprey suggested, of more complex role requirements placed on Krishna men, who must practice their demanding religion, while also interfacing with the world to keep Krishna enterprises functioning.

In another article, Weiss (1987) presented an assessment of the mental health of the Krishna sample, using the RAND MHI, a measure of psychological distress and well-being. The 38-item self-report inventory contains correlated subscales measuring Mental Health, Psychological Distress, Psychological Well-Being, Anxiety, Depression, Loss of Behavioral/Emotional Control, General Positive Affect, Emotional Ties, and Life Satisfaction.

Weiss (1987) concluded that the Krishna samples (by sex) generally compared favorably with the normative samples on mental health. No significant differences were found between Krishna women and the normative sample on any of the nine subscales of the MHI. Krishna men were higher on three of the nine scales — Psychological Well-Being, General Positive Affect, and Loss of Behavioral/Emotional Control, the last of which was attributed to a "Type I error" (Weiss, 1987, pp. 29-30). Krishna men were found to score better than women on several of the subscales, a finding that was also noted with the normative samples, although Krishna women were less unhealthy, as measured by the MHI, than were normative women.

Weiss (1987) proposed a "positivity effect" for Krishna men, who showed the unusual pattern of being comparatively higher on Psychological Well-Being and

General Positive Affect, but without lower Psychological Distress scores:

> This male group responded as if happier, exhibiting more positive
> affect and behavior, and appearing to be more satisfied with their lives,
> and yet reporting anxiety, depression, and other unhappy feelings that
> were not different from those of normative men. ... Speculations are
> that this unusual effect may have arisen from a positiveness that Hare
> Krishna men derive from their religious experiences and life style or
> that it may represent an intentional "high" that they have fostered
> within themselves, perhaps unconsciously. (p. 32)

The conclusion drawn from this study is: "Psychological distress and well-being of Hare Krishna do not differ significantly from that of U.S. general population men and women, respectively, as measured on the MHI, with the exception of the 'positivity effect' for Hare Krishna males" (Weiss, 1987, p. 33). Weiss and Comprey (1987a) mentioned that "the estimated rate of mental disorder of this Krishna sample was not significantly different from that of American society as reported by the National Institute of Mental Health in 1984" (p. 722).

Weiss and Comprey (1987a) added to this picture of mental health normality, with a sophisticated treatment of CPS scores using a "stanine analysis" as part of comparing the Krishna sample with a well-studied psychiatric sample and a normative sample. Details are not given here; however, a summary gives the flavor of results:

> Outpatients exhibited multiple pathologic signs of reduced daily
> functioning, compulsive personality disorder, and general emotional
> maladjustment. Hare Krishnas, except for their hallmark personality
> characteristic, a strong compulsivity trait, scored within the normal
> psychological range. Reduced trust in society was exhibited in many
> members although the average trust was normal. (p. 721)

In his final article (Weiss and Mendoza, 1990), Weiss used the MHI and CPS to evaluate mental health and personality differences in acculturation among Krishna members. Design and validation of the Aculturation Index (AI), which is a measure of religiosity pertaining to the Krishna belief system and practices, is detailed in Weiss' dissertation (1985, pp. 73-93). The 53-item AI was designed to tap the degree of immersion into the Hare Krishna religion. Scores on the CPS and MHI subscales were treated separately as dependent variables in a multiple regression analysis. The Krishna samples (by sex) were trichotomized by choosing the extreme thirds on the AI for comparison purposes.

No association was found between scores on the AI and length of time in Hare Krishna (Weiss and Mendoza, 1990, p. 181). Some interesting relations were found when relating the CPS and MHI subscales to AI scores; an overall statement from Weiss and Mendoza (1990, p. 173) summarized their conclusions:

> Personality traits were mostly invariant with acculturation, and those traits on which the Hare Krishna differed from the norm group may be prerequisite to membership rather than being its consequences. Mental health was also largely invariable with acculturation, except that greater degree of acculturation was associated with greater subjective well-being.

In short, Weiss and Mendoza (1990) seemed to be saying that the Hare Krishna movement attracts a certain type of person and then encourages them to be more like that type of person, which causes those who remain to feel better about themselves. The authors also reported that men fare slightly better in this analysis than females, shown particularly by high AI men scoring significantly higher than low AI ones on all five positive attribute subscales of the MHI, indicating better mental health (p. 177).

These findings have implications, discussed by Weiss and Mendoza (1990), for the anticult position

> that greater cult involvement (as measured by higher acculturation) is associated with decreased mental health, as feared by some (Singer, 1979; Conway and Siegelman, 1982; Kilbourne and Richardson, 1986) and that less acculturation is more likely to be associated with normal mental health. (p. 180)

Weiss and Mendoza stated:

> Our results suggest the contrary. High AI groups for both genders reported significantly greater well-being than did their respective MHI norms, while not reporting significantly less distress than did the norms (a positivity effect). Also, low AI group scores on a few subscales were significantly lower than were the MHI norms.

## Summary Statement of Results of Present Review

There seems little reason to modify the overall conclusion cited earlier from the 1985 review (Richardson, 1985b, p. 221). Indeed, the statement can be made even stronger, based on the thorough and sophisticated research that has been done, particularly by the University of Oregon team, by Ross, and by Weiss and associates. The Rajneesh group had developed a lifestyle with more emotional openness and more gender equality than exists in normal life, and some quite well-educated and relatively high-status people, particularly a number of women, have chosen to be a part of that lifestyle. The Hare Krishna have developed a rigorous but apparently satisfying lifestyle for a few people, attracted by the very attributes that bring criticism from some detractors. Male Hare Krishna members seem to fare particularly well, despite (or perhaps because of) their "compulsivity." Shiloh group members, who had earlier displayed traits that might have been dysfunctional in normal society, have apparently overcome any possible problems and adapted quite well to their new noncommunal lifestyles. The same can be said for the Rajneeshees who participated in the follow-up research by Latkin after Rajneeshpuram disbanded.

Such results and conclusions are consistent with those of reviews by others, including Larson et al. (1992), which looked at the general relation of religion with psychological well-being in *The American Journal of Psychiatry* and the *Archives of General Psychiatry*, over a recent 10-year-period. Their research, which included some of the reports referred to herein, led to this conclusion (1992, p. 558):

> Consistent with several reviews, the present study found that when the religious variable is studied, it often has a positive association with measures of health, or mental health. Quite similar to the findings of the family medicine review, the dimensions of ceremony, social support, prayer, and relationships with God, although seldom assessed, were all found to have positive associations with mental health. (citations omitted)

Thus, it seems time to admit that participation in the new religions is similar to that of participation in other, more "normal" religious groups.[8] Such an admission would go far toward quelling the controversy about participation in such groups[9] and would seem preferable from the point of view of protecting religious freedom, as well as maintaining credibility for those professionals involved in research, therapy, and public policy development in the area of newer religious groups. It would also go far toward accepting more benign alternative explanations about why people choose to participate in such groups and the consequences of such participation.[10]

• • • • • • • • • • • • • • • • • • • • • • • • • •

# Notes

[1]     The term *cult* has many negative connotations and should be applied with great care by scholars,

whose use of the term fosters those negative connotations (Richardson, 1993a). I prefer the term *new religion* or *minority religion*, in an effort to avoid problems associated with the term cult.

2       Galanter recently updated his position on the relief effect (1978) in a provocative but well-received book (1989b), as well as editing a collection for the American Psychiatric Association on the topic of new religions and cults (1989a).

3       Latkin has also done some more sociological and social-psychological writing on the social control within the community and public reactions to the community that will not be discussed herein (Latkin, 1991, 1992). Also, the research the team has done an interesting subjective analysis of their research experience, focusing on problematic theoretical and methodological issues raised during the lengthy research project (Latkin, Littman, Sundberg, and Hagan, 1993). Palmer and Bird (1992) have also presented an insightful analysis of the way the Rajneesh philosophy integrated the tension between Esalen-style humanism and oriental-style veneration of the guru, the role played by therapy in the group, and some significant information about post-Rajneeshpuram activities and developments in the movement.

4       Certainly members of other newer religions have also aged and developed families: See Richardson (1994), for instance, which deals with later developments of the Children of God, now called The Family. However, the educational attainment and economic status of the Rajneeshees seem especially unique among the newer groups, as does their political orientation and the way they were recruited into the group.

5       One of the great virtues of the massive amount of research by Latkin, Sundberg, and others is that their data were gathered around the time of the demise of Rajneeshpuram. Thus, scholars are afforded a close look at the effects of that traumatic event on the individuals involved. The follow-up work is especially valuable (Latkin, 1993; Latkin, Sundberg, Littman, Katsikis, and Hagan, in press).

6       The survey was sent to 1,000 former residents, with half returned as undeliverable. Three hundred twenty people sent back the instrument, and 231 responded to a follow-up second instrument. The second survey containing mental health assessment instrumentation is focused on here.

7       Latkin (1993, p. 107) suggested that the social context and belief system may, in effect, cause social desirability responses to misrepresent effective levels of social desirability. He also acknowledged, however, that respondents may also be deliberately reporting inaccurately.

8       These results comport well with the studies that have taken place of children in some of the groups, such as The Family (formerly the Children of God). As a result of a number of accusations of child abuse by this group, a large proportion of their children worldwide (some 700) have been submitted to a number of different types of assessment, some using standardized instrumentation (Lilliston and Shepherd, 1994, for instance). Results show them comparing favorably with comparison age groups on educational accomplishments and other measures. See Richardson (1994) for a review of this situation and other studies of this group of children.

9       See Shupe and Bromley, 1980; Bromley and Richardson, 1983; Shapiro, 1983; Beckford, 1985; Barker, 1984; Kilbourne and Richardson, 1984, 1986b; Malony, 1987; Robbins, 1985; Robbins, Shepherd, and McBride, 1985; Anthony, 1990, Anthony, Robbins, and McCarthy, 1980; and Richardson, 1982, 1989, 1991, 1992a, 1992b, 1993a, 1993c, for discussions of the huge controversy that has developed concerning new religions in Western society.

10      The alternative explanation that engenders most support from the research done about participation is that of volition being exercised, both to join and to leave the groups, which most participants do shortly after involvement (Barker, 1984; Richardson, 1980, 1985a; Richardson, van der Lans, and Derks, 1986; Wright, 1983). People join for many reasons, including social experimentation, seeking meaning and community, a search for healing, or as an act of adolescent rebellion (Kilbourne and Richardson, 1985, 1986a, 1988; Levine, 1986; Richardson, 1985a). As noted in the articles reviewed herein, the effect of participation is usually ameliorative.

# References

American Psychiatric Association
    1980    *The diagnostic and statistical manual of mental disorders* (3rd ed.). Washington, DC: Author.

Anthony, D.
    1990    Religious movements litigation: Evaluating key testimony. In T. Robbins and D. Anthony (Eds.), *In gods we trust* (pp. 295-344). New Brunswick, NJ: Transaction.

Anthony, D., Robbins, T., and McCarthy, J.
    1980    Legitimating repression. *Society, 17,* 39-42.

Barker, E.
    1984    *The making of a Moonie: Choice or brainwashing?* Oxford: Blackwell.

Beckford, J.
    1985    *Cult controversies.* London: Tavistock.

Berger, P.
    1967    *The sacred canopy.* New York: Doubleday.

Bromley, D., and Richardson, J. (Eds.)
    1983    *The brainwashing / deprogramming controversy.* Toronto: Edwin Mellen.

Carter, L.
    1987    The "new renunciates" of the Bhagwan Shree Rajneesh: Observations and identification of problems of interpreting new religious movements. *Journal for the Scientific Study of Religion, 26,* 148-172.
    1990    *Charisma and control in Rajneeshpuram.* New York: Cambridge University Press.

Cohen, S., and Hoberman, H.
    1983    Positive events and social supports as buffers of life change stress. *Journal of Applied Social Psychology, 13,* 99-125.

Cohen, S., Kamart, T., and Mermelstein, R.
    1983    A global measure of perceived stress. *Journal of Health and Social Behavior, 24,* 385-396.

Comprey, A.
    1970a    *Comprey personality scales.* San Diego: Educational and Industrial Testing Service.
    1970b    *Manual for Comprey personality scales.* San Diego: Educational and Industrial Testing Service.
    1980    *Handbook for interpretations for the Comprey personality scales.* San Diego: Educational and Industrial Testing Service.

Conway, F., and Siegleman, J.
    1982    Information disease: Have cults created a new mental illness? *Science Digest, 90,* 88-92.

Dahlstrom, W., Welsh, G., and Dahlstrom, L.
    1975    *An MMPI handbook: Vol. 2. Research applications.* Minneapolis: University of Minnesota Press.

Derogatis, L., Lipman, R., and Covi, L.
    1973    The SCL-90: An outpatient psychiatric rating scale. *Psychopharmacological Bulletin, 1,* 13-28.

Eysenck, H.
1975     *Manual of the Eysenck personality questionnaire*. London: Hodder and Stoughton.

Feigenstein, A., Scheier, M., and Buss, A.
1975     Public and private self-consciousness: Assessment and theory. *Journal of Consulting and Clinical Psychology, 43*, 522-527.

Galanter, M.
1978     The "relief effect": A sociobiological model of neurotic distress and large group therapy. *American Journal of Psychiatry, 135*, 588-591.
1980     Psychological induction into the large-group: Findings from a modern religious sect. *American Journal of Psychiatry, 137*, 1574-1579.
1989a    *Cults and new religious movements*. Washington, DC: American Psychiatric Association.
1989b    *Cults, faith healing, and coercion*. New York: Oxford University Press.

Galanter, M., and Buckley, P.
1978     Evangelical religion and meditation: Psychotherapeutic effects. *Journal of Nervous and Mental Disease, 166*, 685-691.

Galanter, M., Rabkin, R., Rabkin, F., and Deutsch, A.
1979     The "Moonies": A psychological study of conversion and membership in a contemporary religious sect. *American Journal of Psychiatry, 136*, 165-169.

Goldberg, D.
1972     *The detection of psychiatric illness by questionnaire*. London: Oxford University Press.

Goldman, M.
1988     The women of Rajneeshpuram. *Center for the Study of Women Review, 2*, 18-21.

Gough, H.
1987     *CPI administrators guide*. Palo Alto, CA: Consulting Psychologists Press.

Kernis, M., and Reis, H.
1981     *Self-consciousness, self-awareness, and justice in reward allocation*. Unpublished manuscript.

Kilbourne, B., and Richardson, J.
1984     Psychotherapy and new religions in a pluralistic society. *American Psychologist, 39*, 237-251.
1985     Social experimentation: Self process or social role? *International Journal of Social Psychiatry, 31*, 13-22
1986a    The communalization of religious experience in contemporary religious groups. *Journal of Community Psychology, 14*, 206-212.
1986b    Cultphobia. *Thought, 61*, 258-266.
1988     A social psychological analysis of healing. *Journal of Integrative and Eclectic Psychotherapy, 7*, 20-34.

Kuner, W.
1983     New religions and mental health. In E. Barker (Ed.), *Of gods and men: New religious movements in the West* (pp. 255-263). Macon, GA: Mercer University Press.

Larson, D., Sherrill, K., Lyons, J., Craigie, F., Thielman, S., Greenwald, M., and Larson, S.
1992     Associations between dimensions of religious commitment and mental health reported in the *American Journal of Psychiatry* and *Archives of General Psychiatry:* 1978-1989. *American Journal of Psychiatry, 149*, 557-559.

Latkin, C.
1987     *Rajneeshpuram, Oregon — An exploration of gender and work roles, self-concept, and psychological well-being in an experimental community.* Unpublished doctoral dissertation, University of Oregon, Eugene.
1989     Gender roles in an experimental community. *Sex Roles, 21,* 629-652.
1990     Self-consciousness in members of a new religious movement: The Rajneeshees. *Journal of Social Psychology, 130,* 557-558.
1991     Vice and device: Social control and intergroup conflict. *Sociological Analysis, 52,* 363-378.
1992     Seeing red: A social-psychological analysis of the Rajneeshpuram conflict. *Sociological Analysis, 53,* 257-271.
1993     Coping after the fall: The mental health of former members of the Rajneeshpuram commune. *International Journal for the Psychology of Religion, 3,* 97-109.

Latkin, C., Hagan, R., Littman, R., and Sundberg, N.
1987     Who lives in utopia? A brief report on Rajneeshpuram research project. *Sociological Analysis, 48,* 73-81.

Latkin, C., Littman, R., Sundberg, N., and Hagan, R.
1993     Pitfalls and pratfalls in research on an experimental community: Lessons in integrating theory and practice from the Rajneeshpuram research project. *Journal of Community Psychology, 21,* 35-48.

Latkin, C., Sundberg, N., Littman, R., Katsikis, M., and Hagan, R.
In press    Feelings after the fall: Former Rajneeshpuram commune members' perceptions of and affiliation with the Rajneeshee movement. *Sociology of Religion.*

Levine, S.
1986     *Radical departures: Desperate detours to growing up.* San Diego, CA: Harcourt Brace.

Lilliston, L., and Shepherd, G.
1994     Psychological assessment of children in The Family. In J. Lewis and G. Metton (Eds.), *Sex, slander, and salvation* (pp. 47-56). Stanford, CA: Center for Academic Publications.

Malony, N.
1987     *Anticultism: The ethics of psychologists reactions to new religions.* Paper presented to annual meeting of the American Psychological Association, New York.

Moos, R., Cronkite, R., Billings, A., and Finney, J.
1982     *Health and daily living form manual.* Stanford, CA: University School of Medicine.

Myers, I.
1962     *The Myers-Briggs type indicator.* Palo Alto, CA: Consulting Psychologists Press.

Myers, I., and Myers, P.
1980     *Gifts differing.* Palo Alto, CA: Consulting Psychologists Press.

Nicholi, A.
1974     A new dimension of the youth culture. *American Journal of Psychiatry, 131,* 396-401.

Nordquist, T.
1978     *Ananda Cooperative Village: A study in the attitudes of a new age religious beliefs, values, and community.* Uppsala University: Religionshistorlska Institutionen Monograph Series.

Palmer, S., and Bird, F.
1992     Therapy, charisma and social control in the Rajneesh movement. *Sociological Analysis, 53*(S), S71-S85.

Paulhus, D.
    1991        Measurement and control of response bias. In J. Robinson, P. Shaver, and L. Wrightsman
                (Eds.), *Measurement of personality and social psychological attitudes* (Vol. 1, pp. 17-59).
                New York: Academic.

Poling, T., and Kenny, J.
    1986        *The Hare Krishna character type: A study in sensate personality.* Lewiston, NY: Edwin
                Mellen.

Radloff, L.
    1977        The CES-D scale: A self-report depression scale of research in the general population.
                *Applied Psychological Measurement, 1,* 385-401.

Richardson, J.
    1980        Conversion careers. *Society, 17,* 47-50.
    1982        Conversion, deprogramming, and brainwashing. *The Center Magazine, 15,* 18-24.
    1985a       The active vs. passive convert: Paradigm conflict in conversion/recruitment research.
                *Journal for the Scientific Study of Religion, 24,* 163-179.
    1985b       Psychological and psychiatric studies of new religions. In L. B. Brown (Ed.), *Advances in
                the psychology of religion* (pp. 209-223). New York: Pergamon.
    1989        The psychology of induction. In M. Galanter (Ed.), *Cults and new religious movements*
                (pp. 211-238). Washington, DC: American Psychiatric Association.
    1990        *New Oregon religions on trial.* Paper presented at annual meeting of the Pacific Sociological
                Association, Spokane, WA.
    1991        Cult/brainwashing cases and the freedom of religion. *Journal of Church and State, 33,* 55-
                74.
    1992a       Mental health of cult consumers: A legal and scientific controversy. In J. Schumaker (Ed.),
                *Religion and mental health* (pp. 233-244). New York: Oxford University Press.
    1992b       Public opinion and the tax evasion trial of Reverend Moon. *Behavioral Sciences and the
                Law, 10,* 53-63.
    1993a       Cult definitions: From sociological-technical to popular-negative. *Review of Religious
                Research, 34,* 348-356.
    1993b       Mergers, "marriages", coalitions, and denominationalization: The growth of Calvary Chapel.
                *Syzygy, 2,* 205-223.
    1993c       Religiosity as deviance: The negative religious bias in the use and misuse of the DMS-III.
                *Deviant Behavior, 14,* 1-21.
    1994        Update on "The Family:" Organizational change and development in a controversial new
                religious group. In J. Lewis and G. Melton (Eds.), *Sex, slander, and salvation.* Stanford,
                CA: Center for Academic Publications.

Richardson, J., Stewart, M., and Simmonds, R.
    1979        *Organized miracles.* New Brunswick, NJ: Transaction Books.

Richardson, J., van der Lans, J., and Derks, F.
    1986        Leaving and labeling: Voluntary and coerced disaffiliation from new religious movements.
                *Social Movements, Conflict, and Change, 8,* 385-393.

Robbins, T.
    1985        Government regulatory powers over religious movements: Deviant groups as test cases.
                *Journal for the Scientific Study of Religion, 24,* 237-251.

Robbins, T., Shepherd, W., and McBride, J. (Eds.)
    1985        *Cults, culture and the law.* Chico, CA: Scholars Press.

Rokeach, M.
  1960      The open and closed mind. New York: Basic Books.

Rosen, A., and Nordquist, T.
  1980      Ego developmental level and values in a yogic community. Journal of Personality and
            Social Psychology, 39, 1152-1160.

Rosenberg, M.
  1965      Social and adolescent self-image. Princeton, NJ: Princeton University Press.

Ross, M.
  1983a     Clinical profiles of Hare Krishna devotees. American Journal of Psychiatry, 140, 416-420.
  1983b     Mental health and membership in Hare Krishna: A case study. Australian Psychologist, 18,
            128-129.
  1985      Mental health in Hare Krishna devotees: A longitudinal study. American Journal of Social
            Psychiatry, 4, 65-67.

Shapiro, R.
  1983      Of robots, persons, and the protection of religious beliefs. Southern California Law
            Review, 56, 1277-1318.

Shupe, A., and Bromley, D.
  1980      The new vigilantes. Beverly Hills, CA: Sage.

Simmonds, R.
  1978      Conversion or addiction: Consequences of joining a Jesus Movement group. In J. Richardson
            (Ed.), Conversion careers (pp. 113-128). Beverly Hills, CA: Sage.

Simmonds, R., Richardson, J., and Harder, M.
  1976      A Jesus movement group: An adjective checklist assessment. Journal for the Scientific
            Study of Religion, 15, 323-337.

Singer, M.
  1979      Coming out of the cults. Psychology Today, 12, 72-82.

Smith, P., Kendall, L., and Hulin, C.
  1969      The measurement of satisfaction in work and retirement. Chicago: Rand McNally.

Spence, J., and Helmreich, R.
  1978      Masculinity and femininity: Their psychological dimensions, correlates, and antecedents.
            Austin: University of Texas Press.

Sundberg, N., Goldman, M., Rotter, N., and Smyth, D.
  1992      Personality and spirituality: Comparative TATs of high-achieving Rajneeshees. Journal of
            Personality Assessment, 59, 329-339.

Sundberg, N., Latkin, C., Littman, C., and Hagan, R.
  1990      Personality in a religious commune: CPIs in Rajneeshpuram. Journal of Personality
            Assessment, 55, 7-17.

Taslimi, C., Hood, R., and Watson, P.
  1991      Assessment of former members of Shiloh: The Adjective Checklist 17 years later. Journal
            for the Scientific Study of Religion, 30, 306-311.

Ungerleider, T., and Wellisch, D.
  1979      Coercive persuasion (brainwashing), religious cults and deprogramming. American Journal
            of Psychiatry, 136, 279-282.

Veit, C., and Ware, J.
    1983      The structure of psychological distress and well-being in the general population. *Journal of Consulting and Clinical Psychology, 51*, 730-742.

Wallis, R., and Bruce, S.
    1986      *Sociological theory, religion, and collective action.* Belfast: Queen's University.

Ware, J., Johnston, S., Davies-Avery, A., and Brook, R.
    1979      Mental health: Vol. 3. *Conceptualization and measurement of health for adults in the health insurance study.* Santa Monica, CA: RAND Corporation.

Weiss, A.
    1985      *Mental health and personality characteristics of Hare Krishna devotees and sympathizers as a function of acculturation into the Hare Krishna movement.* Doctoral dissertation, California School of Professional Psychology, Los Angeles. *Dissertation Abstracts International, 46*, 8b.
    1987      Psychological distress and well-being in Hare Krishna. *Psychological Reports, 61*, 23-35.

Weiss, A., and Comprey, A.
    1987a     Personality and mental health of Hare Krishna compared with psychiatric outpatients and "normals." *Personality and Individual Differences, 8*, 721-730.
    1987b     Personality characteristics of Hare Krishna. *Journal of Personality Assessment, 51*, 399-413.
    1987c     Personality factor structure among Hare Krishna. *Educational and Psychological Measurement, 47*, 317-328.

Weiss, A., and Mendoza, R.
    1990      Effects of acculturation into the Hare Krishna on mental health and personality. *Journal for the Scientific Study of Religion, 29*, 173-184.

Wrightsman, L.
    1974      *Assumptions about human nature: A social psychological approach.* Monterey, CA: Brooks/Cole.

Wuthnow, R.
    1976      *The consciousness reformation.* Berkeley, CA: University of California Press.

Wright, S.
    1983      Defection from new religious movements: A test of some theoretical propositions. In D. Bromley and J. Richardson (Eds.), *The brainwashing / deprogramming controversy* (pp. 106-121). Lewiston, NY: Edwin Mellen.

Yancey, W., Rigsby, L., and McCarthy, J.
    1972      Self esteem and social class. *American Journal of Sociology, 798*, 338-359.

# PART E
# THE SATANISM SCARE

## Introduction to the Readings

By the mid-1980s the controversy surrounding the better known "cults" that had

emerged into public awareness in the 1960s began to wane (e.g., Krishna Consciousness,

The Unification Church, The Children of God, Scientology). The membership of these

groups was stabilizing, and contrary to the dire warnings of the anti-cult movement, at

relatively small levels. From the hard-knocks taken in the press and the courts of law

these new religions had learned to tone-down their proselytizing and fund-raising

campaigns; in general they were seeking to appear more moderate in their practices.

To the public, and hence for the media, they were becoming "old news." Curiously, at

this juncture, the anti-cult movement began to switch its primary target of concern.

Satanism became the main subject of discussion at lectures, conferences, and press

meetings sponsored by anti-cult organizations (e.g., The American Family Foundation,

The Council on Mind Abuse). Charges of "brainwashing" and "mind-control" continued to be central to the warnings issued about this new danger to society. But the threat posed is now more obviously sinister and truly covert. Thousands of people, it is alleged, are engaged in the clandestine practise of the dark arts of magic, including the ritualistic abuse, even sacrifice of babies, children, and young women. In fact the self-appointed "experts" claim that every year tens of thousands of children are kidnapped or purposefully bred for abuse or sacrifice by an organized and international network of Satanists (e.g., Schwarz, 1988; Johnston, 1989; Langone and Blood, 1990). Our surprising ignorance of this horrible state of affairs is tribute, we are told, to the success of the Satanists in brainwashing their victims and participants.

Once again, however, the hard evidence to support these charges is missing. Generalizations have been made on the basis of the stories collected in clinical interviews by therapists, of varying abilities and qualifications, with supposed victims of Satanic ritual abuse. The claims of these therapists have sparked a larger and heated debate over the reliability or even reality of "repressed memories" and the causal links between the experiences remembered and "multiple personality disorders" (technically termed, since 1994, "dissociative identity disorders" by the American Psychiatric Association). Most claims of Satanic abuse refer to the abuse of children, based on accounts of such abuse provided many years later by adult "survivors." These survivors usually have entered psychological therapy for other reasons (e.g., Padzer and Smith, 1980; Mayer, 1991; Wright, 1994). By while in therapy, usually under the influence of hypnosis, they provide accounts of past abuses that are thought to be "repressed memories" of previously unacknowledged events. These memories have been systematically repressed, in part to simply avoid the pain associated with them, and in part as a result of sophisticated Satanist brainwashing or programming (e.g., Sakheim and Devine, 1992). The trauma of these experiences is thought to have caused the personalities of the survivors to fragment into many distinguishable alter egos. This creation of multiple personalities is also in part a psychological defense mechanism to cope with the pain of these memories, and a product of Satanist programming. The resultant tales of horror have been gathered, embellished, and widely disseminated by the anti-cult movement as proof of the need for renewed vigilance against this age-old nemesis of Christian culture. The books and lectures of the "moral entrepreneurs" crusading against this new Satanism are rife with detailed descriptions of the rites and deeds of diverse Satanist groups, though none claim to have ever witnessed a real Satanic ritual.

Many other psychologists and scholars are severely critical of the therapeutic methods used by the exponents of the Satanic ritual abuse diagnosis and they have called the veracity of the reported results into question (e.g., Mulhern, 1994; Spanos, Burgess and Burgess, 1994; Loftus and Ketcham, 1994; Wakefield and Underwager, 1994). Investigations by numerous police agencies, including a special department of the FBI, have yet to document a single case of Satanic ritual abuse or murder (Lanning, 1992). In fact no material evidence of any sort has ever been found of a crime committed by an organized Satanic group, nor of the existence of an international

Satanist conspiracy (Richardson, et al., 1991; Victor, 1993). Consequently, even some of the most staunch proponents of Satanic ritual abuse as a primary cause of multiple personality disorders have admitted that most of their patients may have confabulated their "memories" of ritual abuse (e.g., Ross, 1995: Preface). Nevertheless, the view persists that where there is so much supposed smoke, there must be some fire, and the fear of Satanism remains strong in some quarters.

As the first reading in this section by Randy Lippert carefully documents, however, the Satanism scare of today is probably a "socially constructed" social problem, comparable to the "Red Menace" (i.e., fear of communism) rampant in the United States during the 1950s. With the witting and unwitting aid of the media and various self-proclaimed "experts," rumour has carried the day. Such rumours are bolstered by the many social legends of Satanic conspiracies found throughout the history of the Christian West and enlivened by the vapid imagery of evil conjured up for popular consumption by hundreds of novels, movies, and television programs.

This is not to say that there are no Satanists. On the contrary, there are, though in very small numbers. The Satanists that exist, however, tend to fall overwhelmingly into two categories: they are either (i) self-styled and largely adolescent dabblers, or (ii) members of a few new and legally constituted Satanist groups. The best known example from the latter category is The Church of Satan, founded in San Francisco in 1966 by the flamboyant Anton LaVey (e.g., LaVey, 1969). While clearly sensationalistic, neither this group nor any of the similar groups spawned in its wake have ever run foul of the law. In fact, The Church of Satan has always been a rather disorganized group which probably never attracted more than a 1,000 members at the height of its popularity (Melton, 1992: 108-117). In the larger scheme of things, then, it is hard to say that such groups pose a serious threat to society. Nevertheless, the very existence of such blatantly deviant organizations is perplexing.

In the second reading, "Magical Therapy: An Anthropological Investigation of Contemporary Satanism," Edward Moody offers an early (1974) and still worthwhile explanation of why some people might join these legally constituted Satanist groups. Calling on several years of participant observation in such a group, and employing the "relative deprivation" perspective outlined in Part C of this reader, Moody provides a series of plausible social psychological insights into the motives of participants. He demonstrates, in some detail, the positive functions of such organizations for individuals with certain predispositions. In the process he also provides a good description of several of the rites and activities of a typical Satanist group (e.g., The Black Mass, Invocations of Lust). In the end, the Satanists he studied remain a rather unsavoury lot, but his analysis gives us good reason to recast their activities as more therapeutic than malevolent. These groups help socially dysfunctional individuals to adapt to mounting and stressful social pressures in their lives, and as such, he suggests, they warrant a somewhat more sympathetic and tolerant reception from the public. A similar line of analysis is followed in William Sims Bainbridge's *Satan's Power: Ethnography of a Deviant Psychotherapy Cult* (1978) and in many other attempts to explain the appeal of witchcraft groups in general (e.g., Kemp, 1993).

In the third reading, "Teenage Satanism as Oppositional Youth Culture," Kathleen Lowney gives us a close-up look at the processes shaping members of the first category of Satanists, "self-styled and largely adolescent dabblers." Here we have an ethnographic case study of how and why one group of rather marginalized kids in a typical American town turned to a loose amalgam of Satanic ideas and imagery to vent their frustration with their relative lack of social power. We hear how the teenagers themselves think of their activities as acts of cultural protest more than commitment to an alternative religion. These adolescents, Lowney concludes, are neither mentally disturbed nor breaking the law in any significant way. They are symbolically protesting against the hegemonic values of their local society, from which by choice and chance (e.g., their relative lack of athletic prowess) they are alienated. These are the relatively innocuous roots, as Lippert's analysis suggests (see Victor, 1993 as well), of most of the moral panics about Satanism experienced by North American communities in recent years (c.g., the city wide panic precipitated by reports of a teenage Satanic ritual suicide pack in Lethbridge, Alberta in 1989).

● ● ● ● ● ● ● ● ● ● ● ● ● ● ● ● ● ● ● ● ● ● ● ● ● ●

# References

Bainbridge, William Sims
    1978    *Satan's Power: Ethnography of a Deviant Psychotherapy Cult.* Berkeley, CA: University of California Press.

Johnston, Jerry
    1989    *The Edge of Evil: The Rise of Satanism in North America.* Dallas, TX: Word Pub.

Kemp, Anthony
    1993    *Witchcraft and Paganism Today.* London: Michael O'Mara Books.

Langone, M.D. and L.O. Blood
    1990    *Satanism and Occult-Related Violence: What You Should Know.* Weston, MA: American Family Foundation.

Lanning, K.
    1992    *Investigator's Guide to Allegations of Ritual Child Abuse.* Quantico, VI: Federal Bureau of Investigation.

LaVey, Anton
    1969    *The Satanic Bible.* New York: Avon Books.

Loftus, Elizabeth and Katherine Ketcham
    1994    *The Myth of Repressed Memories.* New York: St. Martin's Press.

Mayer, R.S.
    1991    *Satan's Children: Case Studies in Multiple Personality.* New York: G.P. Putnam's.

Melton, Gordon J.
    1992    *Encyclopedic Handbook of Cults in America*. Revised and Updated Edition. New York: Garland.

Mulhern, Sherrill
    1994    "Satanism, Ritual Abuse, and Multiple Personality Disorder: A Sociohistorical Perspective." *The International Journal of Clinical and Experimental Hypnosis* 42: 265-288.

Padzer, L. and Michelle Smith
    1980    *Michelle Remembers*. New York: Pocket Books.

Richardson, James T., Joel Best, and David G. Bromley, eds.
    1991    *The Satanism Scare*. New York: Aldine de Gruyter.

Ross, Colin A.
    1995    *Satanic Ritual Abuse: Principles of Treatment*. Toronto: University of Toronto Press.

Sakheim, D.K. and S.E. Devine
    1992    *Out of Darkness: Exploring Satanism and Ritual Abuse*. New York: Lexington Books.

Schwarz, Ted
    1988    *Satanism: Is Your Family Safe?* Grand Rapids, MI: Zondervan.

Spanos, Nicholas P., Cheryl A. Burgess, and Melissa F. Burgess
    1994    "Past-Life Identities, UFO Abductions, and Satanic Ritual Abuse: The Social Construction of Memories." *The International Journal of Clinical and Experimental Hypnosis* 42: 433-446.

Victor, Jeffrey S.
    1993    *Satanic Panic: The Creation of a Contemporary Legend*. Chicago: Open Court.

Wakefield, Hollida and Ralph Underwager
    1994    *Return of the Furies: An Investigation into Recovered Memory Therapy*. Chicago: Open Court.

Wright, Lawrence
    1994    *Remembering Satan*. New York: Alfred A. Knopf.

# THE CONSTRUCTION OF SATANISM AS A SOCIAL PROBLEM IN CANADA

## RANDY LIPPERT

*This paper examines the problem of Satanism using a social constructionist framework. Seventy-five Canadian news articles from 1980-1989 were examined and telephone interviews carried out to obtain a picture of how the problem is emerging, the groups involved, and the claims being made. An examination of the use of rhetoric in claims is undertaken. The role of the news media and American experts in promoting the problem is then explored. The theme of Satanism as a vehicle for other social problems, how claims about it constitute a symbolic crusade, and Satanism's natural history as a social problem in Canada are discussed.*

● ● ● ● ● ● ● ● ● ● ● ● ● ● ● ● ● ● ● ● ● ● ● ● ● ●

## Introduction

Satanism is an emerging social problem that is receiving attention from various organizations. The focus of this paper will be to examine the problem of Satanism in Canada using a social constructionist framework.[1] The emphasis of this paper is two-fold. First, I will identify the claims-makers and their claims about Satanism. I will use the framework outlined by Best (1987) to do this. Through this framework, the definitions of Satanism, the alleged extent of Satanism, and finally, the problems Satanism is supposedly associated with or is "causing" will be shown. Second, I will

Randy Lippert. "The Construction of Satanism as a Social Problem in Canada," *Canadian Journal of Sociology* 15, 1990: 417-439.

examine four basic themes to see how they apply to Satanism: the role of the Canadian news media, the role of experts from the United States, Satanism as a vehicle for other social problems, and the natural history of Satanism as a social problem.


## Methodology

A search of the Canadian periodical and newspaper indices, sociological, psychological, and educational computer data bases, and several criminological indices was made in order to obtain a picture of how Satanism is emerging and the individuals and groups involved.[2] Telephone interviews were carried out with these individuals and representatives of groups where possible to determine present views. The examination of the role of the media involved returning to the *Canadian Newspaper Index* and the *Canadian Periodical Index* to obtain a sample of articles. Every article pertaining to Satanism in a ten-year period (1980 to 1989 inclusive), under the headings of "Satanism," "demonology," "cults," and "mind control" was selected. Other possible headings such as "devil" and "devil worship" were consulted but no such headings were found to exist. The dates and the headings under which articles on Satanism appeared were recorded. Each of the seventy-five articles found was then examined for content.


## Claims-makers

Seven major categories of claims-makers were identified: police agencies and individual police officers; child welfare workers; the news media including talk show hosts; mental health professionals including social workers; participants and their families; cult monitoring organizations; and Christian religious leaders. Each type will be described separately.


### POLICE

From the first Canadian article about Satanism (27 May 1983) to articles appearing as recently as December, 1989, the police have been quoted making claims about Satanism. Articles between 1986 and 1988 reported statements about Satanism by individual members of the police. These statements arose from the investigation of crimes, but were not made on behalf of the organization to which individual police officers belonged. Rather, statements reflected officers' own views. Members of the RCMP, the Ontario Provincial Police, the Halton Regional Police (Ontario), and the

Calgary and Winnipeg City Police among others have been involved. Often these views were presented as if they came from experts in the field. Canadian police agencies began to officially recognize Satanism in 1989 when they began holding seminars on the subject. All of these seminars were conducted by individual members, known as experts, of police agencies in the US where police interest occurred much earlier, and where Satanism has apparently developed into a larger "problem." The police have played and continue to play a dominant role in the struggle for control of the definition of the problem of Satanism. The reason for their extensive involvement in claims-making will become clearer when the claims about Satanism are discussed later.

## CHILD WELFARE ORGANIZATIONS

Also making claims about Satanism are child welfare workers, and particularly those from the Children's Aid Society (CAS) in the province of Manitoba and in metropolitan Toronto.[3] Other groups of this type include the Institute For the Prevention of Child Abuse and, to a lesser extent, Childfind Alberta and the office of the Official Guardian of the Province of Ontario. Although these groups did not emerge until the latter part of 1986, they continue to play a dominant role in the construction of the problem of Satanism, with the exception of Childfind Alberta. A representative of this latter organization made a statement to the press early in 1987 concerning Satanism and its supposed link to missing children (*Montreal Gazette*, 1987a). Neither this alleged link nor the organization has been mentioned in the media since.

## THE NEWS MEDIA

Best (1989:260) refers to the news media as "secondary claims-makers." They can report others' claims in a neutral fashion, or "translate and transform them" (Best, 1989:260). Therefore, they act as both claims-maker and a forum for other claims-makers. Canadians receive much of their information about social problems from Canadian newspaper and magazine articles, but also from American television broadcasts. For example, when the Geraldo Rivera Show aired a two-hour special on Satanism in the winter of 1988, which apparently had the highest ratings of any two-hour syndicated program that has appeared on the National Broadcasting Company's network, a large number of Canadians were undoubtedly watching. Those watching Oprah Winfrey and Sally Jesse Raphael would have similarly seen coverage of Satanism (Pearson, 1989:21). In this way, it can be seen how an alleged problem in the US might become an alleged problem in Canada with little or no change in actual Canadian conditions. However, this migration of alleged problems might also be propagated by another source, as will be seen in the discussion of the role of American experts later on. Nevertheless, the news media are important in defining a new problem (Fishman, 1980; Tuchman, 1978; Gans, 1979). They play a role in shaping the public's perceptions (Johnson, 1989: 5) and, at the same time, show which interest groups are making claims. Because of the media's importance, a closer examination will be carried out later on.


## PROFESSIONALS

Professionals such as psychiatrists, psychologists, and social workers (those not dealing with children exclusively) have played a relatively minor role in claims-making in Canada compared to the three former groups.[4] From the latter part of 1986 until the second quarter of 1988, these professionals were quoted in the media as acknowledging the existence of Satanism as a problem, but the frequency of claims was far less than from the groups mentioned above. Most of these professionals were from the US and are quoted in Canadian media in a similar way to American police. In addition, the contrary view, that Satanism is not a problem, was claimed for the first time by one of these individuals from the US in an article in early 1987. A psychiatric paper on Satanism in adolescents (Bourget et al., 1988) was published in Canada in 1988, although interestingly enough the manuscript was sent in 1986. This seems to be the extent of the professionals' involvement.


## PARTICIPANTS

For the most part, participants in Satanism have not been involved in making claims about it.[5] The media reported on six adolescents in a small Ontario town who sought help from an Anglican priest to obtain counselling for demon possession. They associated this possession with practising Satanism in the second quarter of 1986 (*Globe and Mail*, 1986). Two teenage inmates at a young offender institution in Calgary, Alberta were interviewed by the media in early 1987. They claimed that they were practising members of Satanic cults in the Calgary area, but neither defined their involvement as problematic in any way (*Calgary Herald*, 1987a). The only other alleged participants making claims in the entire ten-year period this study covers have been school-aged children. This occurred in the much publicized Hamilton (1985-1987) (Marron, 1988; Kendrick, 1988) and Oshawa (1989), Ontario cases of ritual sexual abuse. These claims were made only indirectly through child welfare workers and foster parents and became defined as problematic by them.

The parents of participants were only slightly more involved. The mother of one participant was convicted of assault after allegedly trying to rescue her teenage daughter from a Satanic cult. The woman attacked a supposed cult member in Winkler, Manitoba in the second quarter of 1987 (*Winnipeg Free Press*, 1987a). Parents of a participant who committed suicide in Sackville, Nova Scotia in the same period blamed Satanism exclusively for their son's death, even though a media article indicated that he had been using illegal drugs prior to his death (*Maclean's*, 1987a). Parents of a participant who became a victim of an over-dose in Naniamo, B.C. in the same time period were quoted in one article as blaming their son's death on his lifestyle. An examination of their statements in the article, however, reveals that they did not claim the death was linked to Satanism as the media had implied (*Alberta Report*, 1987a). No other participants or their families were involved in claims-making in the ten-year period examined. This lack of claims-making has important implications that will be discussed later on.

## CULT MONITORING GROUPS

Two cult monitoring groups have been involved in claims-making in Canada. Representatives of the Montreal-based Project Cult, which is financed by the provincial government of Quebec, acknowledge the existence of Satanism in Canada. They have, however, consistently been quoted from 1987 through 1989, in five articles, as claiming that Satanism is not at all an extensive problem in Canada. In a telephone interview, a representative of the group related that Satanism may be a problem only for teenage "dabblers." He claimed that for those adolescents who have already been involved in crime, Satanism is an "attractive belief system" which can "cloak" and justify criminal behaviour before or after the fact (Kropveld, 1990). The executive director of the other group, the privately financed, Toronto-based Council on Mind Abuse (COMA), has since early 1989 adamantly claimed in three articles the exact opposite: that Satanism is a serious problem.[6] In a telephone interview with this representative, he affirmed this latter notion and related that he conducts "dozens of seminars on Satanism for professional groups, correctional workers, police, and child welfare workers" among others (Tucker, 1990).

## CHRISTIAN CHURCH LEADERS

The final type of claims-makers are Christian church leaders. Their involvement in claims-making has been steady from 1983 to 1989 with their claims appearing in at least one article for each year in which articles were found. No one church leader's claims appeared in more than one article. Their individual claims came from all over Canada and not from any particular denomination. From this, it appears as though the news media sought out local individual church leaders and asked them for comments.

In the aggregate they appear to be unified and of one group, but upon closer examination it becomes obvious that the media are responsible for this appearance. These individuals usually referred to Satanism as representing moral breakdown and/or the existence of evil. While all acknowledged the existence of Satanists and Satanism, most were far less adamant in their claims than the groups described above. There were two church leaders who were termed experts by the media, but they were only mentioned in one or two articles each. One is the American evangelist, Johnson, who now tours Canada and the US giving seminars on Satanism. The other is Clay, a chaplain at a western Canadian university (*Globe and Mail*, 1989a). Both are authors of books on cults (*Globe and Mail*, 1989a; *Calgary Herald*, 1989a) and both preach about the problem of Satanism.

## Claims

The framework used by Best (1987) is useful for analyzing the claims of claims-makers. He sees claims-making as a rhetorical activity and, therefore, as an effort to persuade audiences (Best, 1987:102). He breaks claims down into "categories of statements — grounds, warrants, and conclusions" (Best, 1987:102).

### GROUNDS

Grounds are further subdivided into "definitions, examples, and numeric estimates" (Best, 1987:104). No consistent definition of Satanism emerged from the claims about it. In only one article (*Toronto Star*, 1989a) was a definition given for ritual sexual abuse, a small part of the alleged problem. No other individual or group in any article in the ten-year period attempted to precisely define what was a problem or was not a problem. In three articles (*Toronto Star*, 1989a; *Calgary Herald*, 1989a; *Calgary Herald*, 1987b), however, a typology of four groups of Satanists was given and there was some basic agreement among these articles.[7] The first type, which there was limited agreement on, were termed "self-styled Satanists," and included "serial killers such as the Son of Sam" (*Toronto Star*, 1989a), but also "groups...who recruit teens through drugs and sex parties" (*Calgary Herald*, 1989a). According to an American police expert quoted in the 1987 *Herald* article, self-styled Satanists are "the ones most involved in criminal behaviour" and therefore "are a major threat." The second type of Satanists were teenage "dabblers," referred to earlier, who are apparently not fully committed to, but rather, sparingly use Satanic literature and paraphernalia. The third type were members of legitimate churches such as the American "Temple of Set" or the "Church of Satan." Lastly, there were the "hardcore [S]atanic cults who practice ritual human sacrifices" (*Calgary Herald*, 1989a) and "bastardize the beliefs" (*Toronto Star*, 1989a) of the legitimate Satanic churches.

## EXAMPLES

The examples of the practice of Satanism usually involved images of hooded figures carrying out horrific, bloody rituals in secluded graveyards. As with the missing children problem examined by Best (1987), this example is used by claims-makers because it "gives a sense of the problem's frightening, harmful dimensions" (Best, 1987:106).

## ESTIMATES OF EXTENT

The claims surrounding the extent of Satanism vary widely depending on the claims-maker. Estimates of the extent of Satanism can be further broken down into incident estimates, range claims, and growth estimates (Best, 1987:107), all of which will be shown below. The vague, imprecise way in which these estimates are worded adds to their persuasiveness. This will also be shown.

In the lone article that appeared in 1983 no attempts were made by claims-makers to estimate the extent of Satanism in the surrounding area or in Canada as a whole. In the second quarter of 1986 the Anglican priest, mentioned earlier, counselled six adolescents and claimed they were Satanists. Early in 1987 the first grand claims of both the extent of the problem and the number of Satanists — incident estimates — began to emerge. These claims were made mostly by both American and Canadian police cult experts, but also by participants, church leaders, and the media. One RCMP constable in Alberta claimed that "in Calgary alone there are supposedly 5000 practising Satanists" and that "they are prevalent throughout the province" (*Calgary Herald, 1987*b). An American expert talking about traditional Satanists stated: "My guess is probably under 100,000" (*Calgary Herald*, 1987b). No effort was made to clarify whether this was the number in Canada, the US, or both, or just how much "under 100,000" it was. The participant in the young offender institution in Calgary claimed that "he belongs to a 400 member Alberta-based cult"[8] (*Calgary Herald*, 1987a). The *Herald* claimed through an unnamed source that in this same institution "most of the 100...youngsters...have dabbled in the occult or are practising [S]atanic cultists" (*Calgary Herald*, 1987a). From this statement one could conclude that ninety-nine youngsters "dabbled" and only one was a cult member, since, again, no further clarification was forthcoming. In the second quarter of 1987 a church leader estimated that "30 members are in Winkler," a town of 5000 in Manitoba (*Winnipeg Free Press*,

1987). Late in 1987 the first Geraldo Rivera special on Satanism was aired. Rivera claimed that "over one million Satanists" were linked by a "highly organized, very secret network" (Pearson, 1989: 20). For Canadian viewers it was unclear how this number is distributed around the US and/or Canada, but if indeed one in three hundred people are Satanists in North America, little doubt is left that many are in Canada. In the second quarter of 1988 the press, through the emerging claims of child welfare workers, stated that "the [S]atanic twist...has cropped up in as many as 100 cases of alleged sexual abuse across this continent" (*Saturday Night*, 1988: 66). By using the word *continent*, the claims-maker avoided having to estimate just how many of those 100 cases were in Canada. Using rhetoric like this gives the impression that Satanism is an extensive problem in Canada.

Beginning in 1989 the claims about the extent of Satanism as a problem increased in both frequency and magnitude as the first child welfare worker and police seminars on the subject took place. At the same time, but to a much lesser extent, claims that Satanism is not an extensive problem (mostly from the Cult Project) increased; the media began to present the first indications of heading toward a more balanced view; and the first and only critical article concerning the claims about Satanism was published (Pearson, 1989). All claims about Satanism as an extensive problem came from the main claims-makers mentioned earlier. The following are typical of such claims.

In Winnipeg, Manitoba the press cited a city police officer who claimed: "Satanism is growing at an alarming rate in Winnipeg" and "Satanism is a billion dollar industry"[9] (*Winnipeg Free Press*, 1989). An American evangelist expert claimed: "Satanism is on the rise" (*Calgary Herald*, 1989a). The press in Calgary, Alberta, covering a police seminar, used the headline "Satanic Cults at Alarming Level, Says U.S. Educator." (*Calgary Herald*, 1989b). The use of the words *level* and *rise* in the claims above imply not only that these experts have an objective measure of Satanism (which, of course, they do not), but also that the previous measures have been compared and an increase found. In this same article an American expert was quoted: "It's happening all over North America. What we have to do is accept it as a problem" (*Calgary Herald*, 1989b). The press in Toronto claimed: "It's clearly becoming a problem" (*Toronto Star*, 1989b). The Ontario Association of Children's Aid Societies claimed that Satanism is the "child protection challenge of the 90's" (*Toronto Star*, 1989b). In the 1990s it may indeed become a challenge and it may be "accepted as a problem" in Canada, but this will ironically occur, in part, because of the use of rhetoric in growth, incidence estimates, and range claims such as those above, and not necessarily because more people have become involved in Satanism.

## WARRANTS

Best (1987: 108) defines warrants as "statements which justify drawing conclusions from the grounds" and tells us that they "are often implicit." Two warrants mentioned by Best (1987) in examining the missing children problem are also to be found in claims surrounding Satanism. They are "associated evils" and the "value of children" (Best, 1987: 109-10).

The list of associated evils in claims is substantial. These supposed problems allegedly linked to Satanism can be grouped into types. The first types are those problems that presumably lead participants to get involved in Satanism and then somehow lead to other types of alleged problems in a causal chain. The second types are claimed to be the result of Satanism. Only in Bourget et al.'s (1988) psychiatric study of adolescents is Satanism consistently referred to as if it were a symptom of other problems: it was not a result and not a cause. The following is a description of the types.

The first type included elements of popular culture: "heavy metal" rock music and the role-playing game "Dungeons and Dragons." These were claimed to lead adolescents into Satanism and in turn lead to such problems as drug abuse and suicide.[10] One or the other of these elements was mentioned in this way in seven articles from early in 1987 to the third quarter of 1989. One expert Christian couple in the Edmonton, Alberta area has, for two years, toured schools with a lecture and slide presentation on the "particularly sinister" effects of rock music (*Alberta Report*, 1988a).

The second type of associated evils were made up of the following: homicides, cruelty to animals or animal sacrifices, psychological problems, sexual abuse of children, vandalism, and miscellaneous crimes. Homicides were claimed to be the result of Satanism in thirty-four articles from the third quarter of 1986 until late in 1989. Cruelty to animals was claimed to be the result of Satanism in at seven articles during the same time period. Psychological problems such as misery, delusions, and brain-washing were claimed to be the result of Satanism in three articles from the second quarter of 1986 to early in 1988. Sexual abuse of children was claimed to be the result of Satanism in seven articles from the second quarter of 1986 to the second quarter of 1989. Vandalism, especially in graveyards, was claimed to be the result of Satanism in six articles from the first article in 1983 to early in 1989. Miscellaneous crimes, not including those above, were claimed to be the result of Satanism in twenty-four articles from the first article in 1983 to the last article in 1989. The crimes included theft, bestiality, assault, break and enter, kidnapping, cannibalism, white slave trading, necrophilia, possession of illegal drugs, suicide, shoplifting, child pornography, child prostitution, impersonating a peace officer, extortion, smuggling illegal drugs, sex with an underage person, arson, and teenage alcohol abuse. This list illustrates how police are involved in claims-making.

It was mentioned earlier that Satanists have been linked to the missing children problem by claims-makers in two articles early in Satanism's history as a problem. Also it was mentioned that one of the dominant groups of claims-makers was child welfare workers and other related groups dealing with children. Implicit in their claims is the notion that children are valuable. Another example of this comes from the RCMP constable from Alberta who claims: "Children are basically pure, they aren't corrupt." He follows this with: "To take a child and use it for a sacrifice is a horrendous thing" (*Calgary Herald*, 1987c). Because of this, the public is to assume that any problem facing children naturally requires action of some kind. Best (1987: 112) refers to this proposed action as "conclusions."

## CONCLUSIONS

Conclusions can be further broken down into goals of "awareness," "prevention," and "social control policies" (Best, 1987: 112-13). In examining the claims made about Satanism it becomes clear that the vast majority of conclusions emphasize awareness by publicizing the claims in the media. In later articles in 1989, however, an emphasis on prevention of Satanism by parents of adolescents emerges in three articles. Typical of the warning signs of involvement in Satanism suggested for parents by experts are "sudden withdrawal from family, [or] a shady crowd of new friends" (*Calgary Herald*, 1989c). These are almost identical to signs of any adolescent problem. Rob Tucker of COMA suggests to parents: "Watch your children. Watch the bedroom... Watch for knives. Watch for candles, goblets and robes. Check their artwork." (*Toronto Star*, 1989c).

These suggestions, along with the claims about popular culture mentioned earlier, seem to fall into the broader "anti-youth movement" which has a theme of "greater control over the young" suggested by Best (1987: 113) in his examination of the missing children problem. These suggestions also appear to stem from an even broader conservative ideology. Gusfield (1963) in his examination of the temperance movement and Zurcher et al. (1973) in their examination of an anti-pornography movement in the US found that such movements can be seen as "symbolic crusades" (Zurcher et al., 1973). They are ways "by which members of a status group could strive to preserve, defend, or enhance the dominance and prestige of their style of life against threats from individuals or groups whose life differed from theirs" (Zurcher et al., 1973). Campaigns to prevent Satanism and to create awareness of it may be symbolic crusades against what conservative claims-makers, such as Christian religious leaders or members of police forces, see as ever-increasing moral breakdown. These claims-makers seem to feel, as Zurcher et al.'s anti-pornography claims-makers did, that "traditional attitudes towards sexual behaviour, religion, work, education, authority,...and so on...[are] threatened" (Zurcher et al., 1973: 195). What symbol for moral breakdown could be more rhetorical for those adhering to such an ideology than

Satanism, which represents not merely digression from a conservative lifestyle, but a total and complete inversion of it. From a conservative point of view Satanism is the perfect symbol of evil and represents the worst possible state of today's moral order.

Conclusions for changes in social control policies will be discussed when the theme of Satanism as a vehicle for other problems and the natural history of the problem is examined later.

# Role of the Canadian news media

The examination of the claims-makers and their claims above showed that the news media is a dominant group in constructing the problem and that its claims involve the use of rhetoric. Therefore, a closer examination of the media follows.

In the search for news media articles covering the subject of Satanism in Canada, none were found between the first quarter of 1980 and the first quarter of 1983. Cursory glances in the indices from 1977-1980 indicated no articles either.[11] The years 1987 and 1989, however, saw the media reaching peaks in their coverage (see Figure 1).

Fishman (1980) suggests the following about why the news media's reports of Satanism would reach peaks or come in waves and then subside. He examined the news production process from within a television newsroom during a seven week crime wave in New York City. He sees a crime wave as a "theme in the news" and as a concept that editors need "to organize an otherwise confusing array of events into packages or groups of interrelated news items" (Fishman, 1980: 5-6). For themes to begin, or be sustained, new incidents to relate as instances of a theme are essential (Fishman, 1980: 8). However, reporters and editors depend a great deal on other news organizations for what their next news theme will be (Fishman, 1980: 7) and this can result in the following:

> As journalists notice each other reporting the same news theme, it becomes established within a community of media organizations. Journalists who are not yet reporting a theme learn to use it by watching their competition. And when journalists who first report a theme see others beginning to use it, they feel their original new judgement is confirmed. Within the space of a week a crime theme can become so hot, so entrenched in a community of news organizations that even journalists sceptical of the crime wave cannot ignore reporting each new incident [or perceived incident] that comes along. Crime waves have a life of their own. (Fishman, 1980: 8).

It can be seen from this how a news theme about Satanism that stems from one or two reported cases can become a theme for news media across the country,[12] or be imported from the US, and result in a wave of coverage. The wave may subside when new, more interesting themes are constructed somewhere in a news organization, growing until there is no longer space and time for coverage of Satanism. Waves may also subside when there are no longer incidents that, by any stretch of the imagination, fit the theme of Satanism.

---

**Figure 1 Articles about Satanism in Canadian popular magazines and seven major newspapers, 1983-1989**

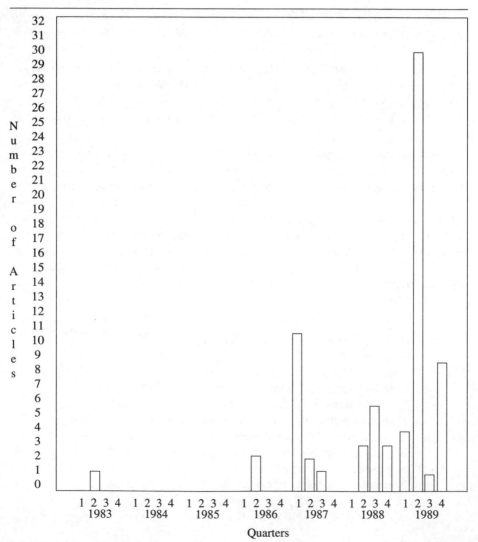

Best (1989) in his examination of statistical claims about the missing children problem suggests that statistics are rhetorical and are meant to persuade others that a problem is important (Best, 1989: 33). He suggests that there are three principles for claims-makers: *"big numbers are better than little numbers," "official numbers are better than unofficial numbers,"* and *"big official numbers are best of all"* (Best 1989: 32, his emphasis). The press in their treatment of Satanism follow these principles. For an example of this consider the case of the RCMP constable in Alberta mentioned earlier. This particular individual is mentioned in numerous articles as being an expert on the subject of Satanism. He is quoted as estimating "5000" Satanists in the Calgary area. In typical fashion the media and this expert do not differentiate among which of the four types of Satanists are being referred to. In only four of the seventy-five articles in the sample was this ever done. The criteria for defining someone as a Satanist is similarly left out. This number is "big" for a city of approximately 650,000 people. Only in one article is it mentioned that this is not the view of the RCMP as an organization, but rather a member of the RCMP who investigates Satanists on his own time. However, mentioning that a representative of a national police force had given the estimate makes it "official." This particular constable wrote a paper on Satanism for a university correspondence course. This paper was quoted from in a number of articles, and referred to by the media as a "report." Soon it took on a life of its own and in later articles was no longer accompanied by the qualifier that it was written for a university course.

Gusfield (1989) in referring to the role of the media in problem construction states: "The criminal, the prostitute, the drug addict and the other objects of problems may be seen as deplorable, as troubled, as dangerous, but they are endlessly dramatic and interesting" (Gusfield, 1989: 434). Such is the case with the Satanists — tales of the devil "provoke incredible fear" and interest in people (Kropveld, 1990). When Satanism is linked to crimes such as vicious child sexual abuse or murder, as it was in almost every article, it becomes even more so. Satanism sells magazines and newspapers. When the bodies in Matamoras, Mexico began to be discovered in March, 1989 Canadian newspapers had no less than twenty-nine articles on the subject. It didn't seem to matter that the "cult involved was an improvisation on an African religion that has nothing to do with Satan" (Pearson, 1989: 20). This lack of clarity in defining Satanism or Satanists aids the news media in producing more interesting stories, aids people in becoming "experts" on the subject and, as will be discussed later, makes it easier to attach Satanism to other problems, thus drawing more attention to them.

The media's coverage of a problem contributes to public acceptance of the definition. It is interesting, for instance, that the only psychiatric work in Canada on Satanism was submitted to the *Canadian Journal of Psychiatry* in March, 1986, but published two years later in April, *1988* after the media began extensive coverage of Satanism (see Figure 1). This suggests that Satanism was not enough of a problem, until the media defined it as such, to warrant publishing a paper on it. Similarly, COMA claims that it had no telephone calls from the public about "people believed to be dangerous Satanists" until the third quarter of 1987, after the first wave of media coverage. In the third quarter of 1988 they were receiving "10 calls per month" and in the same period in 1989 they were receiving "50 calls per month" (*Toronto Star*, 1989c). In addition, it should be pointed out that formal seminars on Satanism were held across Canada beginning in 1989, two years after media coverage began. It appears as media coverage increased, claims-making about Satanism and the existence of Satanists by members of the public[13] likewise increased.

This increase of reported cases of Satanism and media coverage of them, the dominant claims-makers might argue, is the inevitable result of and caused by an actual increase in the number of persons practising Satanism. However, it is also possible that through increased coverage, adolescents and others who would not otherwise have been aware of the existence and complexities of Satanic rituals, became interested in them either as a "dabbler" or constant practitioner. Another explanation for an apparent increase in the number of persons practising Satanism is that through increased coverage, greater public awareness of Satanism occurs and, as a result of extremely vague definitions provided in this coverage, more events are reported as Satanism.

## The American Experts

Various experts on Satanism have been mentioned above. One American police expert, Detective James Bradley, after giving a seminar on Satanism to sixty Canadian police officers, said: "your're going to see more of it in Canada" (*Globe and Mail*, 1989b). From this seminar, a Canadian deputy chief of police concluded: "It's obvious there was a much broader problem in the U.S. than we'd anticipated. Knowing how these things migrate, we think there may be more of a problem in Canada" (*Globe and Mail*, 1989b). I suggest that no one "knows" how actual conditions defined as problems move or spread. Canadian individuals are led to such dubious conclusions by, I suggest, "a marriage of convenience" whereby: 1) the lack of available experts in Canada leads the Canadian press to desperately search south of the border for them and 2) the entrepreneurial spirit of some individuals from the US is such that they cannot help but extend their expertise north of their border.

The following is another typical example of an American expert making claims about the nature of the problem in Canada. Retired Captain Dale Griffis from "thousands of kilometres away" (*Calgary Herald*, 1987b) somewhere in the US tells us: "In an area like Alberta, where you have a blighted economy, Satanism does well, because people are searching for answers" (*Calgary Herald*, 1987d). Whether Griffis ever visited Alberta, how he came to decide that it has a depressed economy, or how a depressed economy leads to Satanism is left unclear. What is made clear is that he is an expert and, therefore, such questions need not be raised.

American experts have been quoted in Canadian articles more often than Canadian experts have, which may help explain how Satanism can migrate to Canada from the US with or without the actual number of Satanists increasing. The effect of American television talk shows being beamed into Canada; vague estimates of the problem's geographical and numerical boundaries, and the use of American experts in the Canadian media and at Canadian seminars is that the American problem becomes indistinguishable from the Canadian one.

Significant evidence of the extent of Satanism, measured objectively, and proof that it does lead to crime and other problems seems to be of little importance for most of the dominant claims-makers in either country. How American claims-makers define it may be important for it becoming a problem in Canada.

Judging from the quotation in the Canadian media they are defining it as an extensive problem.[14] Quotations from experts add credibility to claims by the media. Labelling someone an expert similarly gives them credibility. Most experts quoted in the articles were members of police forces or evangelists. While the media do not publish the qualifications needed to be defined as an expert, Ken Lanning of the FBI offers the following: "you have [to] read two books on Satanism, which is more than anyone else read" (Pearson, 1989:21).

The benefits of being labelled an expert can be substantial. The religious couple in Alberta tour the school circuit and by 1988 they had completed fifty presentations; the American evangelist/author Johnson, who sold 20,000 copies of his book on Satanism, *The Edge of Evil*, and did ninety media interviews by 1989, tours the church circuit in Canada; the American police cult experts conduct seminars at Humber College in Ontario and at Mount Royal College in Alberta; and two reporters-turned-authors (Marron, 1988; Kendrick, 1988) published best-selling books on the Hamilton ritual sexual abuse case. One American police cult export charges $350 (US) per student at his seminars on Satanism around the US (Pearson, 1989: 22). All this from Satanism being defined as a problem and individuals being labelled as experts.[15]

An aid for conceptualizing the foregoing, and the relationship of what I consider the most important components in the social construction of a problem, is shown in Figure 2 below.

---

**Figure 2 An aid for conceptualizing the construction of a social problem.**

---

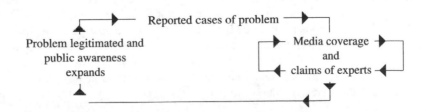

## Satanism as a Vehicle for Other Problems

Although conclusions were made of the "awareness" and "prevention types," in no articles in the ten-year period were claims-makers quoted as requesting new legislation or other government action to curb the alleged increase or reduce the numbers involved in Satanism in Canada. This, along with the fact that no articles ever dealt with Satanism without linking it to other problems, suggests that Satanism is a vehicle for other problems. Groups seem to use portions of the alleged Satanism problem to serve their interests. Both the temperance and anti-pornography movements mentioned earlier had extensive lists of "associated evils" attributed to them by claims-makers (Gusfield, 1963: 30-35; Zurcher et al., 1973: 189), which were almost identical to those found in the claims about Satanism. All of this suggests that there is a symbolic crusade transpiring. Perhaps it is not Satanism claims-makers are specifically concerned about, but rather a general anxiety about perceived threats to their conservative way of life.

While claims about Satanism are still not getting official government action, they do get public attention. News of a teenage suicide seems rather mundane (such stories are in the news media every day), but attach Satanism to it, especially to the cause of it, and a mundane claim becomes an interesting and important one. The minimum criteria for such a claim by the media and others is, for example, to find Anton Lavey's *Satanic Bible* at or near the scene, or perhaps for the teenager to have listened to "heavy metal" rock music, especially that of Ozzy Ozbourne,[16] prior to the tragedy. Such tangible "evidence" of the existence of Satanists lends persuasion to the claims of church leaders that Satan is everywhere. Similarly, the standard claims of the police about ever-increasing crime; of parents of drug abuse victims about the evils of drugs, and of child welfare organizations about child sexual abuse are enhanced when Satanism is suggested as the cause.

## The Natural History of Satanism

Social problems are said to follow a natural history (Spector and Kitsuse, 1987; Blumer, 1971). Satanism and the influence of the devil have been present in art, literature, and folklore for centuries. Only in 1983, however, did it enter the first stage of becoming a problem in Canada, because before "persons perceive it, address it, discuss it or do anything about it, the problem is not there" (Blumer, 1971:302). The five stages of a social problem proposed by Blumer (1971)[17] are emergence, legitimation, mobilization of action, formation of an official plan, and implementation of the plan. Satanism seems to have passed the emergence stage. Through the media, authors, religious leaders, psychiatrists, and other claims-makers the public has become aware of the problem and therefore it has emerged.

It seems that Satanism is currently at the end of the second stage, legitimation. The fact that seminars were held on it suggest that it was considered legitimate by those who attended. What was presented at the seminars is an important factor in whether it enters the next stage of mobilization. In a telephone interview with a representative of the Ottawa-Carleton (Ontario) CAS, it was related that members of the Ottawa CAS attended the September, 1989 seminar in Toronto, Ontario (Johnson, 1990). They in turn held a seminar in Ottawa for other members of CAS, and for Ottawa City Police, using what they had learned at the Toronto seminar. This suggests that what they had learned in Toronto, from Rob Tucker of COMA and others, was persuasively presented, and may have been considered legitimate by those attending. These seminars, however, were not open to the public. As Blumer (1971) points out: "do not think because a given social condition or arrangement is recognized as grave by some people in a society...that this means that the problem will break into the area of public consideration" (Blumer, 1971:303). Nevertheless, COMA receives fifty telephone calls a month on Satanism, which indicates that at least a proportion of the public considers it as a legitimate problem.

Another interesting fact came out of the examination of the *Canadian News Index* which suggests that Satanism has reached the legitimation stage. Early articles on Satanism were found under the heading of "mind control" or "cults," but beginning in 1987 Satanism was given its own heading, and only three articles from the 1987-1989 period examined were found under other headings. This change of headings suggests that Satanism is now considered a legitimate problem, separate from mind control and cults.

According to Blumer (1971:303), for Satanism to enter the mobilization of action stage the "advancing of proposals" is required. Such proposals, or "conclusions" for changes in social control policies, have not been called for by claims-makers and will not if Satanism is simply a vehicle for other problems and a symbol of threats as I have suggested. A precise definition of the problem would be required as well, not the vague sense of dissatisfaction which is being voiced now (Spector and Kitsuse, 1987: 144).

Spector and Kitsuse (1987) assert that "[o]ther things being equal, groups that have a larger membership, greater constituency, more money, and greater discipline and organization will be more effective in pressing their claims than those that lack these attributes" (Spector and Kitsuse, 1987: 43). The dominant claims-makers in Canada seem to have these characteristics in comparison to the Cult Project and this would suggest that the problem may enter Blumer's third stage, mobilization of action. One small part of the problem has already entered the third stage on a provincial level. The Ontario government's Official Guardian, whose office represents children in battles over custody, called, in the second quarter of 1989, for a special ritual abuse team to be set up. This team would be made up of lawyers and child welfare workers, among others, to investigate cases of Satanic sexual abuse (*Toronto Star*, 1989b). In a telephone interview with Wilson McTavish the Official Guardian, however, it was related that the team has yet to be set up (McTavish, 1990). Nevertheless, the ability of this group to precisely define their part of the problem leads to the mobilization of action, although only minimally.

On a national level, however, I suggest the problem will not enter the next stage, the mobilization of action, for the following reasons. The CAS is not a national organization: each province has similar groups but they differ and are not nationally linked. The Ontario CAS is funded by the Ontario government to protect children under provincial law. Their calls for action would likely be, therefore, directed to provincial and not federal governments. The RCMP, the closest thing to a national police force, does not seem to be making claims about Satanism, with the exception of interested members in Alberta. No other members or police forces as a whole appear to have enough power behind their claims, although their seminars were an "official" reaction to a certain extent.[18] Also, COMA is a small organization and likely does not have the power to play a large role in this effort. As was pointed out earlier, church leaders are not unified in their claims and the families of "victims" of Satanism, with probably only one exception, remain indifferent towards the issue. In addition, no formal "objective" study of Satanism has been carried out in Canada.[19] Therefore, no claims-makers have been able to add "objective" evidence produced by such studies to their rhetorical repertoire (Gusfield, 1981). Using these criteria, it seems that these groups are unlikely to succeed in propelling Satanism into the next stage on a national level. COMA, the Canadian news media, and psychiatrists, however, continue to show interest in it. As this is being written seminars continue, a second psychiatric study using a larger sample of adolescents than the previous one has recently been completed, as has a two-day, two-and-one-half-page special feature on Satanism in the *Ottawa Citizen* — a major newspaper circulated in a metropolitan area of 900,000.[20]

But the mobilization of action through social control agencies or legislation, given that Satanism is not simply a vehicle for other problems, using Blumer's framework raises other more basic questions for the move to this state and the next, the formation of an official plan. For instance, other than awareness campaigns what proposals could these groups possibly put forth to officials such as legislators?[21] Satanism, even among "dabblers," lies in the realm of religion. Would proposals for official action include a ban on the use of Satanist paraphernalia and literature? If this occurred other civil rights and religious groups would undoubtedly enter the debate, a situation governments would like to avoid. How could the federal or provincial governments be expected to draw the line between a Satanic bible and a Christian one, a right-side-up crucifix and an upside-down one? Perhaps only increases in informal controls, such as by "watching your children," are perceived as viable and this is why claims-makers have not been explicitly calling for increases in controls of the formal kind.

# Conclusion

The construction of Satanism as a social problem in Canada has been made possible by various claims-makers, particularly American experts and the Canadian news media. The efforts of these and other dominant claims-makers can be seen as a symbolic crusade against perceived threats to their conservative ideology and way of life. Through their use of rhetoric the problem has reached the legitimation stage in its natural history as a social problem.

An examination of Satanism suggests how influential news media and so-called experts, especially those from the US, are in constructing social problems in Canada. It also reveals how social problems can emerge, grow, and become legitimated quite apart from conditions of objective reality.

The dominant claims-makers offer a simple, inherently appealing answer to the complex questions that sociologists ask about the causes and nature of crime and deviance. The answer is evil in the form of Satanism. But after we rejoice at having found out that evil was responsible for such behaviour all along, where do we go from there? Explanations such as these[22] belong to past centuries, but even after decades of on-going scientific inquiry it appears that some cannot resist them.

● ● ● ● ● ● ● ● ● ● ● ● ● ● ● ● ● ● ● ● ● ● ● ● ●

# Notes

1    There is an on-going debate between two basic groups of scholars using this framework: the contextual constructionists and the strict constructionists (Best, 1989:xi-xiii). I acknowledge the value of the strict approach first outlined by Spector and Kitsuse (1987), and I realize that to a certain extent I too am making claims and, therefore, am playing a role in the construction of Satanism as a problem. However, I feel obligated to call into question and attempt to discredit, at times implicitly, some of the claims found in this paper.

2    There are obvious limitations in using the news media's view of the world as a measure of what claims-making activities are occurring, some of which I mention in the body of this paper. Another limitation should be taken into account when I attempt to quantify the types of claims being made about Satanism. The news media may be referring to the same cases but in different articles and therefore appear to be referring to different cases. Also, some will not come to the attention of the media. With these and other limitations in mind, for lack of a better available method and by complementing this one with interviews, I carried it out as described.

3    The claims-making of child welfare workers and police, which is examined in more detail later on, can be better understood when these individuals are seen as one of two types of "moral entrepreneurs" (Becker, 1963: 147). As "rule enforcers" — the first type — they will attempt to provide justification for their existence in claims, and therefore may "be more vehement than anyone else in their insistence that the problem they are supposed to deal with is still with us, in fact is more with us than ever before" (Becker, 1963: 156-57).

[4]     A possible exception to this is the first alleged case of Satanic ritual abuse in Canada which is described in a 1980 book entitled *Michelle Remembers*, written by a psychiatrist, Dr. Lawrence Pazder, and his patient, Michelle Smith. With statements like, "reports of Satanism in Victoria are not infrequent and...Satanism has apparently existed there for many years" (Pazder and Smith, 1980: xi-xii), it can be seen how this book may have laid the groundwork for claims-making that was to occur later in the 1980s.

[5]     It is conceivable, however, that participants may be making claims to counsellors such as psychiatrists and, because of rules regarding confidentiality, they have not come to the attention of the media and the public.

[6]     The claims-making of this representative might be better understood when he is seen as an example of the second type of "moral entrepreneur" — the "rule creator" (Becker, 1963: 147). Becker (1963: 147) describes this type as one who operates with an absolute ethic; what he sees is truly and totally evil with no qualification. While Satanism has not reached the stage whereby legislation is being drawn up, i.e., rules are being created, according to his claims this individual fits this description exactly. Therefore, he would likely be called upon for input, I suggest, in the event that it was decided by government that legislation be drafted to address the problem of Satanism, however unlikely this may be (as I suggest later on).

[7]     The definition for a Satanist is similar to that of an anti-state deviant in the Soviet Union during the purges (Connor, 1972: 407), of a witch in the sixteenth and seventeenth centuries (Currie, 1968: 15) and of a sexual psychopath in the US (Sutherland, 1950: 142), among others, in that it is extremely vague, or absent in claims-making altogether.

[8]     I was employed as a youth worker in a similar small, closed-custody facility under the same provincial government department 100 miles south of the one referred to for six months in 1989. If the adolescents at the Calgary institution were anything like those at the one in which I worked, and if admitting being involved in Satanism, even if they were not, was required in order for them to be interviewed, then I suggest the inmates would readily do so. The use of exaggeration, to say the least, was not uncommon among them either. None of the inmates I worked with ever mentioned involvement in Satanism or appeared to be involved. A lot of them enjoyed "heavy metal" music however, as I did at their age.

[9]     Conner (1972) examined the Soviet Purges (1936-1938) when millions of individuals, many of whom were completely innocent of any deviant acts, were labelled as deviants. He suggests that "[a]s a control institution, the NKVD [the soviet state police] had interests in maintaining itself and acquiring powers and resources — interest it could promote by detecting (or inventing) growing members of deviants" (Conner, 1972: 408). A similar situation seems to be occurring here, but on a much smaller scale, of course.

[10]    It is curious to me that "Dungeons and Dragons" is claimed to lead to such problems. While growing up my parents and parents of friends continuously rejoiced at our playing it because they claimed it kept us inside and "out of trouble"! Claims like those above are made by persons who clearly never played the game and, therefore, were never able to enjoy its emphasis on creativity and imagination, both of which, I suggest, are very positive attributes for impressionable adolescents.

[11]    During a period from 1978 to 1981 six articles on cattle mutilations on the Canadian prairies were identified under the headings of "Livestock and Livestock Industry" in the *Canadian Newspaper Index* and "Cattle" in the *Canadian Periodical Index*. I did not consider these articles to be about Satanism. While the possibility of a religious cult being responsible for these kills was mentioned in five of the six articles, it was done so in one sentence in the text of the article, not in the title, and only occasionally was the word *Satanic* used to describe the cult being referred to. In addition, in two of these five the premise was that a cult was not a viable explanation for these kills. Satanism, therefore, was by no means the main subject of these six articles or any other articles during this period.

12  Sutherland (1950: 144) in his examination of the diffusion of sexual psychopath laws made a similar statement regarding media coverage: "Any spectacular sex crime is picked up by the press associations and is distributed to practically all the newspapers in the nation; in addition, it is often described in news broadcasts" (Sutherland, 1950: 144). In this way the news media played a significant role in the spread of dangerous and futile sexual psychopath laws across many states in the US (Sutherland, 1950: 142).

13  I am not suggesting that news media accounts of what is occurring are mindlessly accepted by the public. There is likely a degree of scepticism among at least some viewers and readers. These sceptics were, however, mostly silent and not involved in claims-making during the ten-year period examined.

14  The problem being defined as extensive by persons in the US is reflected in, among other things, the publication of literature for social workers to assess and intervene with adolescents involved in Satanism (Wheeler et al., 1988) and for investigation of Satanic ritual crimes by police (Story, 1987). This is also seen in the production of police training videos about Satanism.

15  It would be arrogant not to point out that I too am capitalizing on Satanism being defined as a problem — it has provided me with subject matter to examine.

16  As an adolescent I was the proud holder of three Ozzy Ozbourne records and found some of his music, such as songs like "Believer," with lines like "You've got to believe in yourself or no one will believe in you," to be positive. All "heavy-metal" music is not negative and destructive as certain claims-makers would have the public believe. Gray (1989) examined in a historical context the periodic appearance of the popular music problem. He suggests that when claims-makers define music such as jazz, in the period in which it emerged, as a problem it "is an attempt to assert moral control over a world thought out of control" (Gray, 1989: 156). This suggestion is consistent with the notion of a symbolic crusade presented above and attaching Satanism to this recurring problem may be the latest attempt to gain attention from the public.

17  Although I acknowledge that the natural history of Spector and Kitsuse (1987: 142) "goes beyond" Blumer's, I chose the latter's because the problem of Satanism has not reached the point where official action is being taken and therefore it is adequate.

18  In Blumer's framework I think "official" has more to do with legislation. At this point in time police forces seem to be acting as advocacy groups and have not been given the mandate to act on the problem officially.

19  An "objective" study in the US was carried out by the Committee for the Scientific Examination of Religion, a Buffalo, New York-based religious research group. One of their findings was that while there are crimes that are committed in the devil's name, "Satanism is rarely the motivating factor for these crimes" (Toronto Star, 1989a).

20  This article (Ottawa Citizen, 1990a) marked the beginning of a dramatic increase in newspaper articles and Canadian television broadcasts about Satanism all across Canada. What followed this article can be described as a "moral panic" (Cohen, 1972). Unfortunately for purposes of analysis this newspaper article, the ones to follow it in the Ottawa Citizen (eight in just over three weeks) and in other major newspapers, and the broadcasts (approximately twelve in number) occurred outside of the sampling frame and the time period originally used. The Citizen, for example, is not indexed in either of the indices used to generate the original sample of articles. However, I did briefly examine each of the articles in the Citizen and the broadcasts available in the Ottawa area. I found that claims-making in them was typical as were the type of claims-makers and "experts" involved, the use of rhetoric, and media's fostering of cases of Satanism. This latter phenomenon occurred in an article on March 11 (Ottawa Citizen, 1990b). Between March 3 and 11 police made several arrests of individuals and laid charges connected with the sexual abuse of children in Prescott, Ontario, a town a few miles south of Ottawa. No evidence was presented then, or has come to light since, that indicates that Satanism was linked in any way to the charges. Despite this, the first line of the March 11 front page article reads: "A Satanic cult may have been involved in this town's growing child sexual abuse and homicide scandal"

(*Ottawa Citizen*, 1990b). The only quote from the Prescott police was: "We may very well run into something like that" (*Ottawa Citizen*, 1990b).

[21] Two American states have recently introduced legislation that would make animal sacrifices and the eating of human parts illegal. These would-be laws only address a small part of the alleged problem of Satanism, however.

[22] Tannenbaum (1938: 1-7) offers an extended discussion of the role of evil in explanations of crime and deviance.

# References

*Alberta Report*
 1987    "Sleuthing after subliminal Satanism." 15: 30-31.
 1988    "The 'witches' lethal brew." 14:30-31.

Beck, Howard S.
 1963    *Outsiders: Studies in the Sociology of Deviance*. London: Collier-Macmillan.

Best, Joel
 1987    "Rhetoric in claims-making: Constructing the missing children problem." *Social Problems* 34: 101-121.
 1989a   "Secondary claims-making: Claims about threats to children on the network news." *Perspectives on Social Problems* 1: 259-282.
 1989b   *Images of Issues: Typifying Contemporary Social Problems*. New York: Aldine De Gruyter.
 1989c   "Dark figures and child victims: Statistical claims about missing children." In Joel Best, ed., *Images of Issues: Typifying Contemporary Social Problems*. New York: Aldine De Gruyter.

Blumer, Herbert
 1971    "Social problems as collective behaviour." *Social Problems* 18(3): 298-306.

Bourget, Dominique, Andre Gagnon, and John Bradford
 1988    "Satanism in a psychiatric adolescent population." *Canadian Journal of Psychiatry* 33: 197-201.

*Calgary Herald*
 1987a   "Troubled teens turn to Satanism." March 29: A1.
 1987b   "Devil's disciples: Thousands 'worship' in Calgary." March 7: E1.
 1987c   "Satanism suspected in unsolved kidnap cases." March 7: A1.
 1987d   "Children described ritual murders, cannibalism." March 8: C7.
 1989a   "Satanism new fad: Evangelist." June 24: C7.
 1989b   "Satanic cults at alarming level, says U.S. educator." March 17: A19.

Cohen, Stanley
 1972    *Folk Devils and Moral Panics*. London: Granada.

Connor, Walter
 1972    "The manufacture of deviance: The case of the Soviet purge, 1936-1938." *American Sociological Review* 37: 403-413.

Currie, Elliot
 1968    "Crime without criminals: Witchcraft and its control in Renaissance Europe." *Law and Society Review* 3: 7-32.

Fishman, Mark
    1980      *Manufacturing the News.* Austin: University of Texas Press.

Gans, Herbert
    1979      *Deciding What's News.* New York: Pantheon Books.

*Globe and Mail*
    1986      "Priest counselling boys involved in Devil worship." May 12: A13.
    1989a     "Prairie towns bedeviled by rumors of Satanic rites." October 30: A16.
    1989b     "Satanic cults more active, expert warns." March 20: A1.

Gray, Herman
    1989      "Popular music as a social problem: A social history of claims against popular music." In
              Joel Best, ed., *Images of Issues: Typifying Contemporary Social Problems*, pp. 143-58.
              New York: Aldine De Gruyter.

Gusfield, Joseph
    1963      *Symbolic Crusade: Status Politics and the American Temperance Movement.* Urbana,
              Illinois: University of Illinois Press.
    1981      *The Culture of Public Problems: Drinking-Driving and the Symbolic Order.* Chicago:
              University of Chicago Press.
    1989      "Constructing the ownership of social problems: Fun and profit in the welfare state."
              *Social Problems* 36: 431-41.

Johnson, Connie
    1990      Ottawa-Carleton Children's Aid Society. Telephone Interview. February 1.

Johnson, John
    1989      "Horror stories and the construction of child abuse." In Joel Best, ed., *Images of Issues:
              Typifying Contemporary Social Problems*, pp. 5-19. New York: Aldine De Gruyter.

Kendrick, Martyn
    1988      *Anatomy of a Nightmare.* Toronto: Macmillan.

Kropveld, Michael
    1990      Cult Project. Telephone Interview. February 1.

*Maclean's*
    1987a     "Suicide and Satanism." March 30: 54.

Marron, Kevin
    1988      *Ritual Abuse.* Toronto: Seal Books.

McTavish, Wilson
    1990      Official Guardian of Ontario. Telephone Interview. February 13.

*Montreal Gazette*
    1987      "Satanists may be nabbing children: R.C.M.P. Officer." March 9: A8.

*Ottawa Citizen*
    1990a     "Satanism: Journey from the dark side." March 3: A1, B4, B5. Special feature.
    1990b     "Prescott police study possible link between sex crimes and cult." March 11: A1.

Pazder, Lawrence and Michelle Smith
    1980      *Michelle Remembers.* Toronto: Nelson.

Pearson, Patricia
    1989      "In search of the Satanists." *The Idler.* 25: 19-25.

*Saturday Night*
    1988        "Raising the Devil." 103: 66-70.

Spector, Malcolm and John Kitsuse
    1987        *Constructing Social Problems*. New York: Aldine de Gruyter.

Story, Donald
    1987        "Ritualistic crime: A new challenge to law enforcement." *Law and Order* 9: 81-83.

Sutherland, Edwin
    1950        "The diffusion of sexual psychopath laws." *American Journal of Sociology* 56: 142-48.

Tannenbaum, Frank
    1938        *Crime and the Community*. New York: Ginn and Company.

*Toronto Star*
    1989a       "New crimes linked to Devil worship." June 30: A12.
    1989b       "Satanism: The spectre of ritual child abuse." June 29: J1.
    1989c       "Alarming number of teenagers drawn to Satanism, expert says." October 1: A1.

Tuchman, Gaye
    1978        *Making News*. New York: Free Press.

Tucker, Robert
    1990        Council on Mind Abuse. Telephone Interview. February 1.

Wheeler, Barbara, Spence Wood, and Richard Hatch
    1988        "Assessment and Intervention with adolescents involved in Satanism." *Social Work* 33: 247-50.

*Winnipeg Free Press*
    1987        "Bible belt teens dabble with Satan." June 6: 1, 4.
    1989        "Satanism linked to increase in crime, child abuse." December 16: 1-2.

Zurcher, Louis, Jr., R. Fitzpatrick, Robert Cushing, and Charles Bowman
    1973        "The anti-pornography campaign: A symbolic crusade." In Robert Evans, ed., *Social Movements: A Reader and Source Book*, pp. 190-216. Chicago: Rand McNally.

# CHAPTER FOURTEEN

# MAGICAL THERAPY: AN ANTHROPOLOGICAL INVESTIGATION OF CONTEMPORARY SATANISM

## EDWARD J. MOODY

*There is a revival of Black Magic and Satanism in the West at the present time. Many well-educated individuals are practicing the Black Arts. In so doing they make themselves the target of the community's scorn and aggression. Why do they persist? They persist because their magic "works" by helping them to achieve the goals they desire. This paper attempts to indicate how magical rituals such as the Invocation of Lust and the Shibboleth Ritual help practicing Satanists, members of the Church of the Trapezoid, to accomplish their desires.*

● ● ● ● ● ● ● ● ● ● ● ● ● ● ● ● ● ● ● ● ● ● ● ● ● ● ●

The crashing music stops and in the sudden silence the air seems to throb and pulse. Then a candle flickers into life, and then another, and another. In their flickering light dark and shadowy figures can be seen, their shadows dancing grotesquely on the wall of the ritual chamber. From above, the Goat God gazes down upon the motionless tableau. Then a black-robed figure steps forward to the stone altar beneath the Baphomet and, as the gong is struck, lifts the gleaming sword high above the naked and motionless body of the young girl stretched supine upon the altar before him...

Africa? Medieval Europe? No! The time is the present and the setting is the First Church of the Trapezoid, the Church of Satan, San Francisco, California. The members of the congregation, many of them by day respected and ostensibly respectable

Edward J. Moody. "Magical Therapy: An Anthropological Investigation of Contemporary Satanism." In Irving I. Zaretsky and Mark P. Leone, eds., *Religious Movements in Contemporary America.* Princeton, NJ: Princeton University Press, pp. 355-382. Copyright Princeton University Press. Reprinted by permission of Princeton University Press.

citizens, are members of a group of witches and magicians practicing the Black Arts of witchcraft and magic. They are part of a contemporary rebirth of black and white magic in the modern and urban environment that is sweeping the Western world, a rebirth that is part of a growing interest in the occult and is seen in the growing number of cults or religions devoted to the "mystic arts."[1] Who are these people? Why do they risk exposure, ridicule even social sanction to practice the ancient art of Black Magic? Why do they become Satanists? It was in order to seek an answer to this and related questions that I joined the First Church of Satan. For two years I was an active member of the group, a participant-observer in the anthropological sense of the term, taking part in all aspects of the religion. Although the answer to my original question proved deceptively simple — people become black magicians because magic "works," it accomplishes many of the ends which the Satanists desire — an answer to the next obvious question, *how* magic "works," proved to be less obvious, and it is that topic which is the subject of this paper.

Anthropological, historical, and theological scholarship is filled with learned and semi-learned articles on the phenomenon of witchcraft. The mysterious power of magic has a fascination even for the staid and rational scholars of the West, and indeed it should have, for magic and evil are ubiquitous parts of the total "world view" of virtually every culture investigated to date.[2] Whether investigators acknowledge the existence of actual confessed witches (Crawford 1967) or not (Evans-Pritchard 1937), no study of any culture, including those of the West, would be complete without a description of beliefs about witches and witchcraft.

In 1967 I became aware of a new group of practicing witches and became fascinated by the possibility of investigating the Church of the Trapezoid and its members. Almost without exception anthropologists working in non-Western cultures have analyzed witchcraft as either behavior based on ignorance or lack of scientific knowledge (e.g. Parrinder 1963), as a social institution functioning to control deviant behavior (deviants could be accused of witchcraft and punished), or as an institutionalized outlet for the culture's forbidden aggressions. Virtually no one has viewed the institution from the point of view of the witches except to cite the culture's "folk" explanation for the abnormal and deviant behavior of the witches. Few modern writers apparently have actually encountered witches, a fact that has not prevented most of them from making ethnocentrically biased observations concerning the personality characteristics of the witch (see Caro Baroja 1964). Even those who have encountered self-confessed witches have been more interested in the social and psychological functions of the act of confession than in the functions of the practice of witchcraft itself. The modern view seems to be that there are no such things as witches except in the imagination of the members of a culture. The historical literature contains many references to witch crazes and even to confessions of witchcraft throughout European history, and though the validity of many of the statements is questionable due to the methods by which the statements were obtained — torture of various and sundry kinds — and the obvious biases of the investigators (Sprenger and Institoris 1948; Summers 1926; Robbins 1959), it is clear that Black Magic and

Satanism are not new phenomena, even in the West. The lack of scientific interest in the topic is therefore astounding.

Although it is not my intention to deal specifically with the sociology of witchcraft, an examination of witchcraft beliefs in various cultures reveals several common characteristics uniting those *accused* of witchcraft. Witchcraft is usually suspected of those who are envious, resentful or powerless. It is expected from people who are not full members of the community, whose position within the culture and society is not well defined and whose behavior is therefore somewhat unpredictable (these people are usually low on the scale of social status). Moreover, witchcraft in non-Western cultures does not operate at a distance but is expected in face-to-face relationships. The accusation of witchcraft may be made against mothers' brothers in a matrilineal society (Nadel 1952), co-wives or brothers in another type of social system (Lienhardt 1951), or even non-related individuals in a small community (Kluckhohn 1967), but all accusations come in relationships which are unavoidable but which tend to produce socially forbidden hostility (Lienhardt 1951). Accusations come in situations in which the relative status of the two persons is not rigidly defined, where expectations are not fixed, in the "cracks and crevices of the social system" as Mary Douglas puts it (1967). The accusation of witchcraft is an expression of fear: fear of the resentment and envy of those people who are in subordinate positions without legitimate means of either modifying their position or expressing the hostility which the accuser knows they must feel. The suspected witch is believed to be frustrated, powerless one — be she a wife from outside the husband's community or merely an asocial or marginal person like the traditional crone of Western witch beliefs, old, ugly, widowed or never married, and envious.

This characterization of persons accused of witchcraft in other cultures is a surprisingly accurate depiction of many if not all of the Satanists I encountered. They too turn to witchcraft out of envy and frustration. They desire successes denied them — money, fame, recognition, power — and with all legitimate avenues apparently blocked, with no apparent means by which legitimate effort will bring reward, they turn to Satanism and witchcraft. In some cases the resentment is that of a frustrated, hostile, but powerless figure who lacks legitimate means of striking back at supposed aggressors: the subordinate striking back at his boss by the only available means. The practice of witchcraft appears, in fact, to spring from the very sources which produce accusations of witchcraft: unfulfilled desire, frustration, envy, and need for "power."

It is easy to bring the accusation of witchcraft, to accuse others of hostility and anger, to accept the "boundless possibilities of sheer human malevolence...because we all know the depth of our own hearts" (Mair 1969: 13). Most of us know personally the anger of resentment and frustration, have said in our own hearts, "I wish he was dead," and have refused to accept our own inadequacy as a reason for the greater success of our rivals. It is easy to project this feeling into others and not unreasonable to expect them to have similar feelings.

The next obvious question is: Why do some turn to the Church of Satan, to Black Magic and the Occult? In answering this question, I will attempt to depict some of the characteristics of the individual who turns to magic. This depiction is a model, a type case, and certainly does not provide a list of characteristics which would allow one to predict just who becomes a Satanist and who does not. There are types of individuals who are more likely to become Satanists than others, but certainly the circumstances of various life crises — does the individual come into contact with some form of magic at a crucial time and so on — has an effect.

Upon becoming acquainted with the Satanists[3] I began searching for some traditional sociological pigeonhole into which I could put them. It wasn't easy to find. Famous and obscure, wealthy and poor, "successes" and "failures," upper to lower class, young and old, right-wing to left-wing political opinions — all were represented in the early Church membership, along with a baker's dozen or more assorted psychological "syndromes" ranging from transvestism to sadomasochism. A single factor seemed to typify all of them: all were deviant or abnormal in some aspect of their social behavior. Although they usually were behaviorally "normal" in most social contexts, in some areas each exhibited maladaptive or abnormal responses.[4]

By abnormal behavior I mean simply that they engaged in some behavior which was disturbing to other members, especially important members, of their society, behavior which deviated from established cultural norms. It is the position of the behavioral therapist that abnormal behavior is no different from "normal" behavior in its development or maintenance; it is simply socially incorrect (Ullman and Krasner 1969; 92-105). The abnormal person, behaviorally, is deficient in either his ability to perceive or receive social stimuli, or in the skills necessary to make the appropriate response. If he lacks these skills and responds in an "abnormal" or unpredictable fashion he is labeled abnormal by other members of society. Abnormal behavior is frequently no more than culturally unanticipated or unexpected behavior. The deviant's behavior is not so much disturbed as disturbing, for the person who does not play according to the rules casts doubt on the validity of the game and causes anxiety in the minds of others who do play according to the rules.

Other members of the social network frequently respond by excluding the deviant from social interaction and, by labeling him abnormal, creating at least a partial set of expectations for his behavior: the "crazy" role. In so doing they deny the "deviant" member of the system the accurate feedback necessary for him to evaluate his behavior. Thus deviants are placed in socially and often geographically marginal positions, defined interaction which will allow them to adapt their behavior via feedback, and forced to interact only with other marginal or abnormal individuals who reinforce abnormal responses. The deviant becomes locked into a vicious cycle with improper behavior leading to negative responses from others which increases anxiety or expectations of failure, which further inhibits behavior, which leads to more failure, which leads to more negative social response, and so on. The result can be generalization of an avoidance response, a desire to avoid negative responses from others as the result of aversive conditioning, which becomes extended to all social interactions. Such is the case among the pre-Satanists — individuals who will eventually become Satanists. Although a man may be successful in business, for example, the negative responses which he gets as a homosexual may influence his interactions generally. Failure due to inability to respond correctly in social situations results in a generalized feeling of inadequacy and negative self-evaluation, especially if he accepts the label of deviant placed upon him.

Lack of knowledge of the rules of the social game and the lack of success which springs from social ineptitude bring a general feeling of lack of power, of inability to achieve one's goals or to make the outcome favorable to oneself — simply put, inability to make the system respond.

The roots of abnormality among the pre-Satanists are not difficult to find. A great many of the Satanists whom I interviewed reported childhoods marred by strife: they spoke of broken homes, drunken parents, aggressive and hostile siblings, and so on. While it is not necessary to trace childhood causes — knowing that the pre-Satanist's behavior is abnormal is sufficient for analysis — this report indicates that the people who socialized the pre-Satanists were themselves frequently less than adequate social actors. It is not likely that socially inept agents could teach their children completely appropriate responses. It is, in fact, likely that the discriminations, generalizations, and responses taught were themselves abnormal and likely to bring negative or aversive consequences in social interaction, or, in some cases, were responses appropriate only in a specific social context and abnormal in other contexts.

Furthermore, social rules are constantly changing and, especially in our pluralistic culture, conflict between sets of rules is highly likely. The complex and diverse sets of rules, both overt and covert, which govern our behavior make it almost impossible to avoid some transgressions (see Wallenstein and Wylie 1947). Gluckman (1965) and others point out that the number of witchcraft accusations in a social group rises in times of culture change, such as when rural Africans move into an urban environment. It is at times such as these that the rules change and expectations are weak.

In summary, the various individuals who are members of the Satanic cult exhibit behaviors which are at variance with cultural norms. They suffer aversive consequences as result of this behavior: rejection, social failure, punishment, etc., and learn to perceive themselves as inadequate and powerless, unable to accomplish what they desire.

There are several ways in which they can alleviate the fear and anxiety that they feel in such a situation. Some "pre-Satanists" (the term I will use to designate Satanists before they join the Church) go to acknowledged socialization agents for help: to the Judeo-Christian religious practitioners, or to psychotherapists. Usually these attempts at behavior modification fail for one of several reasons. In both cases the pre-Satanist is asked by the practitioner to admit his inadequacy or abnormality, and although he may want help in learning the accepted social mores, the pre-Satanist usually balks at admitting that the source of his difficulty lies within himself. Moreover, in the case of the religious specialist, success is usually of a spiritual nature, while the Satanist is concerned with immediate results in the mundane world.

The pre-Satanists report that the psychotherapist usually spends a great deal of time attempting to get the individual to redefine his problems in terms with which the therapist can deal, terms familiar to the therapist but not meaningful to the pre-Satanist. The deviants' unwillingness to do this means that they do not do anything which the therapist perceives as warranting reinforcement, and their behavior soon becomes aversive to the frustrated therapist and his to them (Rickels and Anderson 1967).

And so the potential Satanist, anxious and socially inept, exhibiting behaviors and having feelings (so they say) which are forbidden and which cause them to doubt their own worth, are kept at the margins of society, denied feedback other than negative responses (Moody 1971). Poorly socialized, unaware of the "chains of causality" which bring results in social action, the pre-Satanists have no explanation for the successes of one person and the failures of others. The pre-Satanist too wants the rewards, the monetary successes and sexual conquests, that are the symbol of social adequacy in our culture. Unaware of the covert rules by which others operate, the type of implicit understanding which aids one in successful social interaction, the Satanist can see no good reason for the inordinate success of one man as opposed to another, just as they can, even more to the point, see no one good reason for their own failure.

And yet they have a sense of there being something moving and influencing both themselves and the world around them. It is difficult to accept a chaotic world. A world in which there are no expectations, in which all is unpredictable, is an anxiety-provoking world. And so they strain to structure the world and to make it systematic and consistent. They attempt to give a name to the unnamed forces which they feel moving and influencing them, the forces of sorcery, perhaps, or conscience; and they attempt to find an explanation for misfortune.

Frequently this attempt leads to magic. The step from our "rational" and "scientific" world to the world of magic is not a difficult one. Our Western world view is shot through with magical thinking. The Judeo-Christian notion of the world of Good has as its necessary complement the world of Evil; God is opposed to the Devil, the forces of white light and spirit are opposed by the legions of darkness and earthiness. It may be that this bipolar division of the categories of understanding is innate in man, but it is certainly true that the division is part of the Western tradition. To be a good Christian, one must believe, of necessity, in Evil and the Devil. Satan was, and is frequently used, as witchcraft is used in all societies, as an explanation for the otherwise inexplainable evils and misfortunes that befall man.

Given this world view, the pre-Satanist frequently takes his first step into the world of magic in an effort to make the world in which he lives predictable and therefore less anxiety-provoking. Astrology, card-reading, the tarot, crystal-gazing, and other forms of divination are an accepted part of even our sophisticated urban environment. It is possible to gain a sense of partial control over one's fate by reading daily horoscopes or divining the course of the cosmos. The concept of inexorable fate influencing man's future is appealing to many of the pre-Satanists. They are people troubled by a lack of self-esteem, by failure and doubt. And how much better it is for such a person to know that one's failure is not caused by personal shortcomings alone, but is also a function of great and mysterious powers, the power of evil, for example, before which *all* are relatively helpless. Fate or Satan serve as a reasonable explanation for the differential success.

For some individuals, this level of magical involvement is sufficient to reassure them and reduce their anxiety, and they may stop here and not move beyond. For others, the "seekers," in Catton's terminology (Catton 1968), astrology does not fill the bill. Although it may improve one's feeling that the world is predictable if one knows the rules of prediction, astrology does not guarantee success and may not improve one's success in social interaction appreciably. The pre-Satanist usually believes that further investigation is called for and more powerful means of control of one's fate necessary. Having been introduced to the notion of esoteric science through astrology, it is not a difficult step to the notion of a magic more amenable to individual control. Those who eventually become Satanists usually have begun with astrology but have come into contact with other types of magic in the magical subculture of the urban center (the "candle shops" and magic stores which sell occult supplies). Others have come to magic via the medium of magazines dealing with the occult. Astrology magazines frequently contain advertisements for occult groups which promise one the secrets of success, of magical control and power. The Rosicrucians come to mind, or the Keepers of the Golden Key. They promise the seeker the key to that success that he has always wanted but which has eluded him, the secrets of the ages which he has perhaps felt accounted for the success of others but which he himself has never learned.[5]

I am not sure why other occult groups fail the pre-Satanist. I believe that perhaps the lack of practical application, the lack of demonstrable effect of the teachings of many of these groups, the constant demands for money, serve to disillusion the pre-Satanists who have tried one or more of these organizations. In some cases he has actually attended meetings or lectures given by groups interested in such occult subjects as flying saucers, etc. (Catton 1968). In so doing, he moves into an occult subculture that operates in most major urban areas. The meeting place of the subculture vary from the lecture hall to the magic store where the implements for magical working may be purchased. Whatever the other results of this experience, the pre-Satanist has been brought into contact with people whose world view includes the possibility of forces and powers unknown to the ordinary man. It is usually in this context that the pre-Satanist first discovers the existence of Black Magic and, eventually, hears of Anton LaVey and the First Church of the Trapezoid.

Such an individual is the model convert. He is, in Toch's terms, "a disillusioned person, and disillusionment is a slow, surreptitious type of change... .It represents a cumulative record of the costs of adaptation. Whether it dies in its suppressed state or becomes publicized in awareness depends on the number and import of disillusioning experiences that are encountered...a person will tend to become disillusioned if he becomes actively involved in life situations for which he has been ill-prepared by socialization" (Toch 1965: 128). The pre-Satanist is such a person — marginal, unsuccessful, faced by experiences of which he has no knowledge and for which he has no precedent. He has been receiving negative responses from the social system and now wishes to begin "reduction of ties to a prior evaluative system and of aversive consequences for deviation from it" (Ullman and Krassner 1969: 206): Having consciously or implicitly identified the source of his problems as the evaluative system, an essentially Judeo-Christian system of his culture, the pre-Satanist wishes to reduce the anxiety caused him by behavior at variance with his culture and his beliefs. In reducing this cognitive dissonance (Festinger 1957), "if one's labeling of proper behavior and one's own behavior do not match, the procedure requiring the least effort is to alter one's concepts of proper behavior" (Ullman and Krassner 1969: 208). This is precisely what the Satanist does during his initial period of membership in the Church of the Trapezoid.

He is already at odds with the values of the larger society, and by changing that evaluation for the evaluation of a more highly esteemed but select group he can change his perception of himself and his world. And so he comes to witchcraft and, tautological though such an explanation may be, for the believer, Black Magic provides a solution. It solves the problem of the fragmented self, of guilt, of inadequacy, of anxiety, of lack of success, and it solves them "magically."

With few other options open to him, faced with the problems of fragmentation of self, social ineptitude, and a lack of any explanation for his failure and the success of others, the pre-Satanist turns from astrology and card-reading — "magic in sports clothes" as the High Priest Anton LaVey would say — to serious practice of magic. He has, from the behavioral point of view, two basic problems which he must solve: a high level of anxiety (the product of an unpredictable environment and the expectation of failure in social interaction); and some maladaptive behavioral characteristics which, based upon an incomplete or erroneous perception of the social situation coupled with an abnormal set of conditioned responses, lead to negative responses from those around him.

The would-be Satanist expresses his problem in terms of lack of power. His anxiety must be lowered, his maladaptive responses extinguished, and appropriate responses conditioned. This is all accomplished primarily through the ritual of the Satanic Church, and Black Magic rituals, I would like to devote the remainder of this paper to a discussion of the function and effect of various Satanic rituals on the Satanist himself.

The would-be Satanist asks, "Is there a secret to success?" Anton LaVey, High Priest and sorcerer, responds, "Of course, magic." The pre-Satanist asks, "Will you teach me?" LaVey replies, "If you are worthy." When after a series of tests and interviews the pre-Satanist is asked to become a member of the elite Inner Circle, his low opinion of himself is already slightly altered and, with social support of his new friends, his anxiety begins to diminish.

The Satanic novice, already disillusioned, has a concerted effort made to make him change the very basis of his value system. In addition to teaching the novice Satanist magic, his fellow witches and magicians teach him that he is "evil," but the definition of evil is changed. In some cases the new Satanist has harbored a nagging belief that he is evil — his deviant behavior is usually at odds with some aspect of the Judeo-Christian tradition in which most of us were raised — but his fears are at last out in the open. He is actively encouraged to speak of his evil (deviant) thoughts and deeds and lauded instead of reviled for them. It is a tenet of the Satanic theology that evil is relative to the time and place in which the deed is done — a sentiment which sounds very Boasian to an anthropologist — and only when one feels guilty about doing something is he really "doing wrong." The Satanists persuade their adherents that the Judeo-Christian value system was a trick perpetrated on our forefathers. It is the position of the Satanic church that the "white light magicians" (Christians) made sins of natural human impulses in order to be sure that people would transgress. They then, by making salvation dependent on belief in Christianity, "hooked" the population and made them dependent on the Christian church for freedom from fear. The Satanists, by contrast, persuade their new members to revel in their own humanity, to give free reign to their natural impulses and indulge their appetites without fear or guilt. Members are constantly reminded that man is the human *animal*, and members are encouraged to throw off the shackles of Christianity and rediscover the joy of living. "Evil" is redefined as human, free, unafraid, and joyful.

It is interesting to note in passing that the image which the Satanists adopt is virtually identical to the symbolic image of the witch in many cultures. The witch in all cultures is the symbolic antithesis of the well-socialized "good" member of society: free where the "normal" person is controlled, unreservedly sexual or aggressive where the good member of society obeys rules, animalistic where the ordinary member is spiritual. Witches are depicted as ugly, abnormal physically, and depraved; given to performing the most horrendous of acts, they are aggressive with absolutely no possible reason (witches kill innocent and helpless newborn infants and eat them). They are, in short, more animal-like and less social. It is an almost universal belief that witches can converse with animals, implying that they are closer to the animal world. In many parts of the world the witch is believed to have the power to actually turn himself into an animal, a clear indication of the animalistic aspect of the witch's nature. In the Western tradition, the Devil clearly stands midway between the completely animal (or physical) and the completely human (or spiritual). He has a mixture of animal and human parts: he is hermaphroditic with a man's torso but a woman's breasts, with human arms but animal legs. He is the very symbol of confusion between the animal and the spiritual. In some African tribes witches are believed actually to be reversed or inverted humans, going about on their hands upside down.

The Satanists accept most of this image, but change the associated semantic evaluation of "evil" from bad to, at the very least, natural. They deliberately set out to be the antithesis of Christianity, preaching indulgence rather than abstinence, strength rather than meekness, worldly rather than other-wordly orientation. They preach power rather than weakness and depict the image of the crucified Christ as "pallid incompetence nailed to a tree." The new member is likely to find himself praised and rewarded for the very thoughts and behaviors which brought him pain and scorn in the larger community. In Wallace's worlds, what has been initiated is a "ritual of salvation" in which the "desperate quest for an experience that knits together the raveled aspects of an identity into a new coherent synthesis" (Wallace 1966: 207) has temporarily ended, the individual's disorder partially molded into a more socially understandable if not generally acceptable pattern. This aspect of the Satanist's indoctrination obviously has characteristics of a religious "revitalization" movement in the truest sense, for it brings "organization into a rich but disorderly field by eliminating some of the materials (thus reducing the cultural repertoire to more manageable size) and combining what is left into a more orderly structure" (Wallace 1966: 211). For the new Satanist, the lack of predictability in social interaction has been reduced by removing certain elements and organizing the others into a more coherent and simpler whole. In a confused world of shifting values, often in an anomic urban world, such extraneous things as the "Golden Rule" and the "Seven Deadly Sins" have been eliminated and replaced with a pragmatic belief in man's basic animal nature. In the world of My Lai and Dallas, of massive retaliation and graft scandals, it is not difficult to argue that the Satanist's position is more realistic and that expectations based on their view of man as being self-aggrandizing and greedy are more likely to be accurate.

If the Satanist is brought to accept, even relish, his shortcomings, and believe in his own worth, if his guilt and anxiety are diminished, he is already on the way to more effective action, to a more successful social adaptation.

## The Black Mass and Other Blasphemies

For many individuals, as you might expect, the transition from Christian to Satanist is not as easily as I have pictured it. The ingrained and conditioned responses of a lifetime are not so easily altered. Many would-be Satanists, like that personification of evil the Hollywood vampire, still cower in guilt and fear before the charismatic power of the symbols of Christianity. Though they may want to be "evil," the conditioned fear or awe response ingrained by twenty tears of conditioning does not extinguish easily. Guilt may still inhibit their behavior, anxiety prevent them from giving up an old and fear-conditioned response and, facing in a new reality, developing a new behavioral adaptation.

It is for people such as these that the Black Mass is intended. Not only is it a symbolic expression of the opposition of the Satanists to the superstitions and rituals of Christianity, but it also has a more direct function. It is a blasphemy.

Behavioral therapists[6] tell us that there are several ways to modify an anxious or fearful response to a given stimulus. The anxiety response must be replaced by another response antithetical to fear or anxiety. The purpose of a blasphemy is to bring about a change in the Satanists' responses.[7] Any institution can be blasphemed, but the most frequent and popular target among the Satanists is Judeo-Christian symbols. The traditional Black Mass parodies the Christian Mass using urine for communion wine, a beet rubbed in vaginal fluid for the wafer and so on. The cross is hung upside down, and in some cults was and is used for other bizarre purposes of a sexual nature. A naked female was and is the altar, and in some instances the mass itself is ridiculed, the "Lord's Prayer" is recited backward, obscene phrases chanted in Latin, and so on.

Like the rat who is trained to expect food for bar-pressing when a light goes on, the Satanist has often been trained to feel guilty or awed in the presence of the Cross, or a priest, or even a nun. But like the rat when his response is no longer rewarded, the Satanists' guilt reaction often disappears when their fear response is no longer rewarded but in fact ridiculed by other Satanists (an aversive stimulus). The absence of lightning bolts from above or other aversive stimuli following a blasphemy weakens the conditioned response of fear. But as Ullman and Krassner put it, "the therapist who removes a particular behavior without helping to replace it with some more adjustive response to the situation in which the former behavior was emitted is doing only half his professional job" (1969:253).

In addition, a response antithetical to fear or anxiety must be and is conditioned to the old stimulus. The new response may vary. Some responses antithetical to anxiety are anger, disgust, or laughter. If one is made to consume the "bread and wine" mentioned previously (urine and vaginal fluid), the Christian ritual and its symbols will eventually become associated with or evoke a "disgust" response rather than "fear." In some rituals, aggression, another antithetical response, against the symbols is encouraged, breaking them, urinating on them, and yet another non-anxiety response is conditioned.

One of the most effective tactics is the use of laughter. Some blasphemies are grotesque burlesques or parodies of religious rituals and evoke laughter. Eventually the formerly anxiety-provoking stimuli bring disgust, anger, or laughter, but not fear.

As a result of religious rituals within the Inner Circle, the new Satanist is now going through a "personality" transformation, a modification of many formerly maladaptive anxiety-producing behaviors. He is becoming less anxious (the world is more predictable) and more sure of himself (he is learning to do magic). But this in itself would not be enough to insure continuing interest in the Church. LaVey has promised success and help via magic; and now he must and does make good his promise.

# An Example: The Invocation of Lust and Systematic Desensitization

An individual named Billy G., who became a member of the Satanic Church shortly after my initiation, is an almost classic illustration of the efficacy of "magic." The son of Fundamentalist Baptist missionaries, Billy G. had been raised in the Billy Graham tradition. He had been taught that most impulses which he had were "the Devil tempting him." By the time Billy G. was 18 and had moved away from what he termed the "up-tight" atmosphere of his home, he found that the Devil was after him a good deal of the time. He was being constantly beset by impulses which were, by his family's definition, "evil." Especially of his heterosexual interactions he was extremely anxious. He had been taught that any "lustful" thoughts about a female were wrong and sinful, and as a result he had great difficulty interacting with females. This problem had become so serious by the time he became a member of the Satanic Church that he could not stay in the presence of a young woman without showing symptoms of severe anxiety — sweating, alternate flushing or paling, and so on.

After joining the Satanic Church he began to relax a bit as his conception of what was "right" and "wrong" were altered, and along with them his perception of himself. Generally a little less anxious and guilty, Billy G. was still anxious about females and lacking in general social ability in heterosexual situations. He still had not been taught the "magical" power to attract and win females. To accomplish this he was instructed in both Greater and Lesser Magic, and I will use his case to illustrate a few additional facets of magical therapy.

It is worth noting that the explanations just given and those to be given do not reply on psychoanalytic theory, as do so many discussions of religion and magic. It is not necessary to postulate or even hypothesize about childhood traumas or deep-seated neuroses in order to explain the process of magical therapy. It may be true that many of the members of the Church have, by our culture's standards, neuroses — transvestism, for example, probably is a surface manifestation of "deeper" problems — but it is not necessary to deal with the problem on the deeper level in order to change the behavior. The associated problem is less one of psychopathology than sociopathology. The source of difficulty for the marginal or deviant man is not his inner thought so much as it is his external behavior based on those thoughts. Many of us have deviant thoughts from time to time, a situation which does not disturb our social relationships until those thoughts are expressed in action. It is my contention that changing behavior is all that is necessary for one to be adjudged "normal" by society. If society reacts favorably to one's behavior, then in most cases one's anxiety diminishes and one's rate of behavioral or social success increases. Change in behavior may require a change in values or meaning such as the reconditioning of responses to charismatic objects just described, but it is difficult and perhaps unnecessary to demonstrate changes in the "deeper" structure of the personality in order to show adaptation and even adjustment.

In Billy G.'s case his resocialization was begun the moment he stepped into the Inner Circle. Different behaviors and perceptions were reinforced; he was lauded for being natural and spontaneous. He was told that his sexual desires were commendable illustrations of a strong-willed person struggling against the trammels of a Christian dominated culture. He was soon better able to accept his desires as part of himself, not something ego-alien sent by the devil to torment him.

He was still faced with two additional problems, however: a high level of anxiety about heterosexual interaction and a lack of knowledge of approved social technique. Because of his socialization, he had been taught to fear women as sources of danger, especially if they were viewed as possible sexual partners. Subsequently his inept and fumbling attempts at any type of heterosexual contact, met by rejection, increased his anxiety. As is frequently the case in our society with its preoccupation with masculinity, his sexual inadequacies came to symbolize for Billy G. a more general social impotence and inadequacy, which caused him great anxiety. He was so anxious that his behavior was impaired, which raised his anxiety, and so on. He exhibited symptoms of an anxiety reaction in the presence of females and could not sustain an encounter with one.

The atmosphere of the Church, relaxed and amoral, began to effect a change in his attitude. Casual conversations about sex allowed him to voice his fears and attitudes without fear of ridicule or recrimination. But it was the general ritual itself which began to actually reduce his specific anxieties. Each ritual is performed before the "altar of flesh," the naked body of some young and usually attractive young witch (different witches play this role each week). For Billy G. the initial weeks he spent watching the ritual acted to systematically desensitize him to the anxiety-producing stimulus, the young woman's body.

Systematic desensitization (Haugen, Dixon, and Dickel 1958; Wolpe 1954, 1958) is the name of a general technique of behavioral therapy designed to take a previously anxiety-producing stimulus and condition a new response to it. In clinical practice, if a person is fearful of dogs he is asked to construct a hierarchy of ever more anxiety-producing situations involving dogs. He is then taught a response which is antithetical to anxiety, usually complete relaxation. When he is relaxed he is asked to imagine the least anxiety-provoking of the various scenarios involving dogs — looking at a dog through a telescope, for example. He repeats this procedure, relaxing each time the scene makes him tense or anxious, until he can imagine the scene without anxiety. He then proceeds to the next most anxiety-provoking image and repeats the process. If he tenses, he attempts to relax once again and goes back to the previously desensitized situation. This is kept up until he can imagine all the scenes involving dogs without fear. He is now desensitized. He has conditioned a new response, relaxation, to a previously fear-producing stimulus. The surprising fact is that his reaction to real dogs is usually discovered to have altered at the same time. The subject is able to generalize his new response to the extratherapeutic situation (Rackman 1966).

Billy G.'s initial period in the Church of the Trapezoid may be viewed as systematic desensitization. If we consider his problem as being strong fear or anxiety in response to women, his progress can be viewed as follows: initially he comes into contact with others who are friendly and accepting and who, by example, encourage him to voice his fears. They persuade him that he is not different or detestable. He begins to relax and modify his defensive posture. When at last he is invited to view the ritual it is a further symbol of acceptance and warmth, of belonging. In the darkness of the ritual chamber he is surrounded by friends, and he eventually relaxes. But when the candles are lighted he is face-to-face with the ultimate anxiety-producing stimulus, the body of an "evil" female. Although his initial reaction may be one of fear or anxiety, this soon begins to change (he is after all in an atmosphere conducive to relaxation). The witch on the altar makes no demands on him and does not move about; she just lies quietly. He sits in the darkness, his reactions masked, surrounded by friends — secure and safe from the negative consequences of his behavior. Eventually he relaxes. In the case of Billy G., I watched him, over a period of months, move forward through the rows of seats, coming closer and closer to the altar. Like the man envisioning ever more anxiety-provoking scenarios, he sometimes paused for several weeks before feeling confident enough to move forward again. Eventually he moved very close and even began assisting the young witch on and off the stone altar. Meanwhile he had begun talking to the female members of the Church, and eventually signs of anxiety diminished and then vanished. At this point he was instructed in both Greater and Lesser Magic concerning the Invocation of Lust and other phenomena associated with heterosexuality.

Greater and Lesser Magic are relatively easy to distinguish. Greater Magic is ritual magic in which the purposes of the ritual are usually specific, the structure of the ritual formalized (usually it takes place in a special ritual setting at a special time and so on), and the magical rationale for the success or failure of the ritual codified. Lesser Magic is a type of magic used to bring the results one wants in *daily* interactions with others in the *workaday* world. It is a specification, in magical terms, of rules of social interaction which resemble the work of Irving Goffman.

I stated previously that the Satanists were, prior to becoming members of the Church, poorly socialized individuals who were unaware of the subtle and often unwritten rules governing successful social interaction in various situations. It was for this reason that the successes and accomplishments of others around them often appeared "magical." The intermediary and implicit steps in the progress of a social interaction often were beyond their ken. For the pre-Satanist, social exchange frequently looked magical, progressing from stage A to result Z without apparently, as far as the Satanists were concerned passing from B to Y (if, indeed, they were aware of the existence of B or Y). Nowhere is this fact more obvious than in the necessity the Satanists feel for training their members in the subtle (and sometimes not so subtle) aspects of social interaction. As "Lesser Magic," the type of magical knowledge taught may range from how to flatter a girl to how to dress and groom oneself in order to be attractive to others. It is true in fact that a knowledge of these social mores does improve one's chances of success in the everyday world. Couching these rules in magical terminology merely underlines their importance and makes them more acceptable to the magician and the witch. If the desired goals — a date with a girl or more success in business — do follow lessons in Lesser and Greater Magic, the Satanist, not unreasonably, attributes his success to his new magical awareness. Ergo, the Satanist reasons, magic caused my success. To the other members of society it makes no difference what the motivation for socially appropriate behavior is; so long as the manifest behavior is culturally correct, the social response of others to the Satanist is positive.

In the case of Billy G., the Greater Magic he learned initially took the form of Love Magic. He was instructed in the art of preparing a love amulet and conjuring lust in his love object. Preparing a love amulet is a rather difficult and time-consuming thing to do. Exotic or rare ingredients must be gathered and ritually combined accordingly in a special setting. If one views this activity from the point of view of a behavioral therapist, it is easy to see why such activity would have the beneficial effects ascribed to it. Obviously the individual's confidence is being built up (or, if you prefer, his anxiety lessened). His fellow magicians swear to the efficacy of the amulet he is constructing and, since the magic of the group has already begun to work, making him feel better and more confident, he tends to believe them (perhaps because he wants to believe them). In addition, however, the process of desensitization is continuing. It is one thing to stand in a group of Satanists and converse with a young woman, quite another to consider sexual interaction with her. Frequently, as noted, sexual failure has come to symbolize the general inadequacy and lack of power one feels. The process of gathering the ingredients for the amulet and the actual preparation of the amulet, usually after long discussions with one's fellow magicians, allows one to consider sexual interaction, the obvious goal in creating the amulet, in non-anxiety provoking situations. Riding on a street car, sitting in one's room reading old magic texts, or talking with fellow Satanists in a casual setting is not anxiety-provoking. The Satanist, just as Billy G. did, gradually develops the ability to consider a formerly anxiety-provoking subject with some aplomb. This is a continuation of the process of desensitization.

But even this is not enough. Eventually, when the amulet is prepared, the act of seduction or heterosexual intercourse of some kind must be attempted. With his inappropriate behavior patterns, his strange or poorly developed social techniques, Billy G. would fail if he were turned loose at this point. He is not. First the theory of love magic is explained to him. He is taught that every individual gives off "vibrations" of one kind or another. To be successful as a lover you must transform yourself into a love magnet by focusing and concentrating these emanations. You must make yourself attractive to others, a "magnetic personality." To do this you must learn some more of the Lesser Magic. The Satanists, both male and female, are taught good grooming, social graces, how to indicate interest to another, and many other social techniques which many of us take for granted. They are taught to emphasize and capitalize on some characteristic of theirs that is appealing to others. Males and females both are taught how to give off an aura of mystery, or of power, or even of helplessness if that is the technique best suited to their particular personality. They are told that it is ridiculous for an individual who is short of stature and slight of build to attempt to use the powerful image. Rather they are taught that they must develop what they are to its fullest. A slight individual, and Billy G. was such a person, is told that he might be more successful if he adopted an "apple-cheeked, clean-cut, youthful image" that would appeal to the maternal instinct in women. This type of training not only increases the Satanist's knowledge of appropriate behavior, but gives him a relatively accurate picture of himself through the eyes of the "significant others" in his life. He develops a more realistic perception of himself and of his own capabilities, learning to magnify his strong points and de-emphasize his weaknesses.

He then begins to work his love magic in earnest. He utilizes his confidence-giving amulet, and with the aid, support, and encouragement of the rest of the congregation performs an Invocation of Lust at one of the weekly meetings. The form of weekly ritual is such that there is a basic or core ritual which can be modified for a variety of special purposes. Just as the Catholic Mass can serve as the basic vehicle for communion or baptism, the Satanic ritual can serve as the medium for an Invocation of Lust, or an Invocation of Destruction, or several other ritual purposes.

Without going into the details of the love magic — it involves the use of certain ritual objects, the preparation of certain types of candles, parchments, and so on — the ritual process in the conjuration of lust can be typified as encouraging the individual to give voice in a direct and graphic way to the desires that are moving him. For perhaps the first time, Billy G. was given support and encouraged to give vent to his secret wishes and dreams, but still in a safe ritual context (the progress of the action and the reaction of others is stereotyped and therefore predictable).

In order to avoid initial failure, the Satanist is told that there are others in the world who are powerful love magnets in their own right, and he is advised against choosing as his initial target a powerful person widely recognized as a sex figure. He would be unwise to choose Brigitte Bardot as his first choice, for example, for she might not only fail to respond to his yet undeveloped and comparatively feeble powers, but might also overwhelm his power with her own magnetic strength and leave him weaker than before (one does not attack an obviously magical and powerful figure such as Brigitte Bardot). Instead the Satanist is encouraged to build up his power gradually, to start with someone close at hand, someone within the group, for example. There were several girls in the group to whom Billy G. was attracted and he chose one of them as the subject of his first magical working.

Although he did not name her specifically in the ritual; it was not difficult to tell which female was the target of his magic. His success, once he began his magic, was virtually assured for several reasons. First, to be chosen was very flattering to the girl and indicated that her magic was working and making her powerful and attractive.

One of the main measures of the power of a witch is believed to be the power to enthrall, the ability to exercise the "command to look." Second, once the girl is aware that she is the desired person, to deny the efficacy of Billy G.'s magic would be to deny the efficacy of the system of magic from which she herself is gaining her own sense of adequacy and power. She usually surrenders, but not without a bit further resocialization. If Billy G. were to attempt just to drag her off to his apartment at this point, he would be rebuffed with the explanation that while his manipulative or Greater Magic was working, he needed to polish his Lesser Magic a little. The young witch in question usually helps him do this, explaining the Lesser Magic practices required to attract a girl and make her amenable to suggestion. She describes the proper technique for getting a date, what to do on a date, when to get more serious, and eventually even instructs him in seduction and love-making techniques, all as aspects of the Lesser Magic. Eventually, when he has performed all of the necessary behavioral steps, she allows herself to be seduced, a type of positive response or reward which is likely to condition Billy G.'s social behavior rather quickly, as any behavioral psychologist could tell you. His success is a validation of the magical power of the Church, its teachings, and of the amulet for Billy G. and he tends to listen with a great deal more attention and less skepticism to the next explanation of Lesser Magic techniques. If he now attempts another conquest — and Billy G., flushed with success, did — it is usually another witch whom he chooses as his subject, and he goes through the socialization process again at the hands of a different girl who has slightly different tastes and behavioral predilections. After several such encounters, he is ready to attempt a conquest outside of the same confines of the Satanic group. Confident, poised, and socialized in a number of different behavioral techniques, Billy G., like most Satanists, was successful. If he is not, he can now say with some assurance that it is not because he himself is unattractive but because he did not perform the magic correctly. This is a rather realistic assessment of the situation if "social graces" is substituted for "Lesser Magic." He discusses any failure with the other members of the group and solicits opinions about why the magic failed. He now has the source of feedback so necessary to the socialization process.

There is a "halo effect" in the process of interaction and behavioral modification. While he is learning seduction techniques, the Satanist is also learning a number of other generally valuable lessons about social expectations. His general level of adaptation to the demands of society becomes better. He grows more confident and socially adept and the general quality of his relationship with others improves. He has moved from anxiety and ineptitude to confidence and expertise, and in his eyes his success is attributed to magic. Perhaps by framing the resocialization process in terms of the subject's world view, even a magical world view, the socializing agents made the behavioral modifications easier for the individual to accept. They were certainly made more understandable.

# The Conjuration of Destruction: Assertive Responses and Therapy

Witches are believed to be aggressive and destructive. In part this is true. One of the common problems besetting many of the Satanists prior to their becoming members of the Church was, as previously mentioned, a pervasive sense of powerlessness, of victimization or manipulation by other individuals or uncontrollable forces. Frustrated and hostile because of this and because of his own inability to realize his desired goals or satisfy his needs, the Satanist is frequently a very aggressive individual who, because of the particular mores of our culture, feels very guilty about his forbidden and unacceptable hostilities. Often his perception of the aggressiveness and hostility of the natural and social environment around him is caused by his projection of his own unacceptable, hostile impulses into other individuals or even into inanimate objects.

Satanic theology encourages rather than discourages the Satanist's aggressiveness, but teaches him to be discriminating about the targets of his aggression. Only deserving victims are to be the targets of aggressive magic, only people against whom one has a right to feel hostile. This tendency is congruent with the image of the medieval witch. Rarely does one find an accusation of witchcraft against some marginal individual in medieval society without the victim being able to hypothesize some cause for the witch's anger: a request for a drink of water refused, a demand for help ignored, etc. The modern witch also directs his aggression against those individuals who have behaved badly toward him or her. Frequently these are people against whom the witch or magician would be powerless were it not for magic, people against whom there is no legitimate means of retaliation within the social code of the given culture and society (see McFarlane 1967). An individual's boss, a person's business acquaintance, anyone can be perceived as a deserving victim. Most curses that I witnessed were directed at some person against whom the curser had what he considered a legitimate grievance. A boss might have been unfair, or a business acquaintance cheated him in a way for which the boss was not legally liable. It is against these individuals that the Satanist is encouraged to react with magical aggression. "Be a lion in the path," the Satanic Bible urges, and "if a person smite you on your left cheek smash him on his right cheek" (LaVey 1969).

Such ritual aggression has a number of functions. First, and least obvious, it continues the process of resocialization. When an individual wants the group's help in cursing an enemy, he must persuade the group that his grievance is just. Although it is not common, I have on occasion heard a group of Satanists chastise another for bringing a problem to the group that he could and should have handled himself if he were indeed a powerful magician as he claimed. I have heard an individual's version of the situation challenged and, in the course of the discussion, alternative interpretations of the action of the transgressor put forth. This is a form of "taking the role of the other," and for the poorly socialized Satanist the additional perspectives of his fellows may suggest interpretations of the event that he himself had not considered but which now become part of his experience. Although virtually all of the Satanists have some "blind spots" in their social make-up when they come to the group, the blind spots of all the Satanists do not usually overlap and as a result there is always someone who has an alternative view or interpretation of the situation.

Second, in a situation in which the fledging Satanist may still feel anxious or inept, may feel used and manipulated, the use of ritual aggression provides a means of restructuring his response to the situation. You will recall that one of the effective techniques for eliminating the paralyzing anxiety response was to condition an antithetical response, a response which an individual could not maintain while simultaneously remaining anxious, to the same stimulus that previously had caused the anxiety reaction. We have discussed the use of relaxation, laughter, disgust, and a number of other hypothetically antithetical responses; anger is another effective alternative to anxiety (Wolpe 1958). If an individual has been conditioned to expect failure and negative responses from others because of that failure, he sometimes, and in the case of the Satanist frequently, develops a general anxiety about social interaction that is cued by almost any individual whom he perceives as being more adept or powerful than he. This anxiety can cripple and inhibit such a person's activity in many areas, sometimes becoming a generalized fear of social interaction. It is in this situation that the cursing or aggressive response is most effective. It has been demonstrated that if one can develop an assertive or aggressive response to a formerly anxiety-provoking symbol, the level of anxiety evoked by that symbol diminishes and eventually disappears. Small children may be taught by a behavioral therapist to yell threats at a noisy and frightening fire engine. "Get out of here you fire engine or I'll punch you in the nose," one three-year-old girl was taught to yell upon hearing fire sirens, and with that her anxiety reaction to the fire engine disappeared. For the Satanist, this aggressive response is turned on the people who are causing him difficulty and whom he cannot attack in any other way. "Rend his gagging tongue and close his throat...pierce his lungs with the stings of scorpions," reads the Invocation of Destruction in the Satanic Bible and some members write their own more personal curses.

Not only is the Satanist's anxiety reaction to the person in question diminished or eliminated by ritual cursing, but the aggressive response which might impair or destroy a necessary social relationship is kept within the confines of the ritual chamber and seldom allowed expression in direct face-to-face contact with the feared person. The Satanist, having learned to be assertive toward certain persons, can face them without fear.

The Satanist who has cursed a person then waits patiently for the inevitable destruction to descend on his victim. The curse is not usually designed to cause death — I observed only one death rune case during the two years that I was active in the Inner Circle — and eventually, when in the course of daily living the "victim" has some bad luck or misfortune, the Satanist chortles with satisfaction and murmurs, "Got him!"

The casting of a death rune is a more serious matter and is not taken lightly. Although the cause of the victim's death is purportedly magic, science explains voodoo death, as it is called (Cannon 1942; Wallace 1966: 178), in terms of the General Adaptation Syndrome in which anxiety is *created* instead of being eliminated and pressure is kept on the victim so that he cannot return to a state of physiological equilibrium. The physiological changes which accompany an anxiety reaction, endocrine changes in response to stress, eventually cause the victim to die of shock. In the one case I observed in which a death rune was cast, the victim, a former member of the group, was, after many warnings, cursed. Though he became quite ill with ulcers and left San Francisco, he was still alive when I last heard of him.

## Shibboleth

There is a special ritual called the Shibboleth ritual which is especially enlightening concerning the means by which resocialization takes place. In the Shibboleth ritual each Satanist comes to the meeting place dressed in the guise of the person or type of person whom he least understands or who causes him the most difficulty in life. During the course of the evening the Satanist is required to act like, think like, talk like, and in fact "be" that individual. At the end of the evening the hated individual is ritually killed and the Satanist is brought back to life in his own identity. During the course of the evening, however, he gets a great deal of feedback from others concerning his performance. In response to my performance of the "right-wing extremist" role, for example, I had the benefit of the opinion not just of run-of-the-mill Satanists, but was also criticized by some genuine right-wing extremists who were members of the group at that time. In this sense I was able to develop a much better knowledge of the expectations of the group of people whom I least understood and, in fact, subsequently interacted with the right-wing group much more successfully because of the experience. This is "taking the role of the other" in its purest form. Developing a knowledge of social expectations does enhance one's ability to interact in some form of an equivalence structure with previously misunderstood people. This is resocialization. In the context of the Satanic Church, the rationale for this ritual was that a better knowledge of others would enhance the Satanist's ability to manipulate them with Lesser Magic. Whatever the reason, the Satanists who took part in this ritual were more adept social actors because of it. Again they assumed magical reasons for their new success but, regardless of the reason, the results of this role-playing were the same: more successful adaptation (Wolpe 1954, 1958; Wolpe and Lazarus 1966; Kelly 1955).

# Ideological Rituals

There are a number of rituals which serve as ideological rituals. They serve to enunciate the position of the Satanists and teach the new Satanists, either directly or indirectly, the ethos and eidos of the subculture in which they now operate. These are rituals in which the animal nature of man, the similarity between his behavior and that of the animals, is demonstrated by delibrants dressed as men with animal heads who perform animalistically in the ritual, gradually shifting back and forth from human to animal.

The Black Mass can also be seen as an ideological ritual. The Satanists clearly recognize that the very name "Satanists" puts them in opposition to the accepted religions of the larger society and they express this position in the Black Mass in which the Christian practices and symbols are inverted and the ritual literally "turned upside down." The ritual becomes a ritual of the flesh rather than a ritual *de-emphasizing* the flesh and emphasizing the spirit, as is the case in Christianity.

# Magic Transformation

Finally, for the purpose of understanding the social effects of Satanic or magical therapy, there is the ritual of magical transformation. Most of us are familiar with the Bela Lugosi vampire who transforms himself into a bat and flies through the night to turn himself, when necessary, back into human form. The legends and myths from other cultures concerning witches are almost unanimous in their assertion that witches either associate with animals or can turn themselves into animals (Parrinder 1963:145-147). From the Satanic point of view this is a misunderstanding of the concept of magical transformation. The Satanists are well aware of the fate that befalls deviants and they are equally well aware, from bitter experience in many cases, that the fear of witches is not a thing of the past but still exists, bringing punishment and pain to the unwary witch. It is for this reason that they teach the members of the Church the art of magical transformation.

The member is taught that those fearful of his great power will attempt to destroy him if possible just as some of his predecessors were destroyed. He is taught that though he may be a powerful magician, he must use his magic not only to protect himself but to take advantage of the stupid and insensitive non-magicians of the world. It would be unwise, he is told, even though he knows he is a powerful magician or witch, to flaunt that fact in the faces of the fearful. Instead it is smarter and better magic to turn their fear and your power to your own advantage. For that reason, each day the magician magically transforms himself from Paimon the Powerful to Homer Smith, bank teller, and from 9 to 5 acts the part of Homer Smith. Inside he may be laughing at the inability of those around him to see through his disguise and reveling in the way he is using his magic to fool them and make them do his bidding. He takes delight in his raise at the bank, for he knows that it was his ability to practice the Lesser Magic of social manipulation that made it possible, and his magical transformation that enabled him to disguise his real purposes and his real identity. In the evening, safe in his room or secure in the ritual chamber, he can revert to his "true" self and become the powerful and vaunted magician that he knows he really is.

In the eyes of the larger society this former "deviant" may be thought to have undergone a pleasing and unexpected personality modification. Others, after all, do not know the motivations "behind" his changed behavior. They might become concerned if he expressed his motivations, but as he does not, for good magical reasons, the other members of his behavioral environment must and can base their judgment of him on his overt actions and his expressed motivations only.

The benefits of Satanism and Black Magic to the witch or magician are obvious: he need be less anxious or fearful, he is more able socially, and he is actually more successful in many spheres of activity due to his enhanced ability to interact with others. He now has, after all, a better knowledge of the expectations of the rest of the society, a better awareness of the rules of the cultural or social game. He has been taught to curb his maladaptive behavior and exhibit "proper" behavior in response to certain cues. If he attributes this new-found power and success to magic rather than to the insights of sociology, anthropology, or psychology, it is because such an interpretation is more in accordance with his world view and the categories of understanding which he uses to give structure and meaning to his world.

In fact, it is sometimes difficult to argue against his interpretation. If psychology explains personal interaction in terms of hypothesized "forces" at work, forces which are known and measured only though the perception of their effects, then how is that different, the Satanist asks, from magic? Satanists say, with some justification, "When magic becomes scientific fact we refer to it as medicine or astronomy" (LaVey 1969).

The benefits to society are equally numerous. Not only are all of the previous cultural functions of witchcraft still in effect — witches are still the focus of a community's aggression, still used to symbolize the anti-social and anti-cultural, still cited as an explanation of the evil and misfortune in the world — but there are, in the case of the contemporary Satanists at least, a number of other benefits as well.

The use of magical therapy helps to resocialize deviants and bring their behavior, for whatever reasons, closer to the cultural and social norms necessary to ensure the continued "smooth" running of the society. The Satanists are clearly better citizens after their magical therapy than before, if one is speaking in terms of social cohesion and equilibrium.

In addition, deviant behavior not modified is confined to a specific social context, a special time and place, and not allowed to spread into the wider social environment. The Satanists preach indulgence of all desires, but the indulgences they enjoy are confined to the Satanic context and are never forced on unwilling victims. The socially dysfunctional nature of some of the modes of gratification is kept from spreading and influencing the wider social environment.

## Summary

Why is witchcraft on the rise today? A resurgence of interest in Black Magic is today being reported not only in most of the Western world but in many other culture areas as well. I would like to speculate that perhaps the rise of witchcraft belief is an attempt by various people to regain a sense of control over their environment and their lives.

This seems to be a time when many of the gods of the Western world, like the old traditional gods of the urbanizing African, are being challenged. God is dead, but that means not just the Judeo-Christian god but also the gods of progress, science, and technology. We put our faith in "him," but now the god of progress is discovered to be a two-faced Janus about to extract a terrible price for our progress and comfort; the god of science has failed us and has not created the paradise we were led to expect, free from disease and ignorance and death. Instead he threatens us with destruction with either the apocalypse of atomic conflagration or a slow death by chemical pollution. The god of technology reveals his "true " face and our streams die, our lakes atrophy, and the very air is turned into a subtle poison. Like the Ashanti or the Bete, many people in the Western world today feel themselves "surrounded by undefinable dangers that their fathers never knew" (Paulme 1962). In such time the people look to new gods or try to refurbish the old ones. They need a method of making what is happening understandable, of coping with the contradictions in daily life and organizing them into a new meaning.

Now that external sources of truth, the experts and scientists, have failed us, many persons have begun to look within themselves for their source of wisdom and security. Some have begun to reassert the necessity of finding personal solutions. In a certain sense witchcraft is a product of these needs. If the world of the Satanist is a criterion, the Satanist is training himself to be assertive and powerful *as an individual.* Although he draws a sense of security from his association with powerful forces, he is finding inner sources of strength. He is casting off the need for powerful gods to protect and care for him, insisting that he is strong enough to care for himself. He commands the gods and does not beseech them. He is turning from an ethereal and other-worldly orientation to a somewhat more realistic assessment and concern with the mundane and real world.

Perhaps it is for this reason that marginal religions such as the Church of the Trapezoid should be encouraged. They appear in many cases to be revitalizations that spring, in response to a changing world, more directly from the needs of the individuals who comprise their membership.

Perhaps what is needed is greater tolerance for a multiplicity of alternative solutions from which various individuals may select the one most applicable to their particular needs. Perhaps we need more religions in which speaking in tongues is not a sign of abnormality, or in which "honest" aggression is accepted and recognized as a realistic response to some situations.

As the pace of change increases and the rules that have governed our social and cultural system seem more and more transitory, we will need other means of giving means to our environment, of bringing cosmos from chaos and making life predictable and understandable. The more flexible nature of marginal religions provides one answer. Whatever increases the individual's ability to adjust and adapt to the world in which he lives may be, perhaps must be, the criterion we ultimately use to evaluate new and initially marginal institutions in our society.

●●●●●●●●●●●●●●●●●●●●●●●●●●●

# Notes

[1]    It is not my intention to argue the question of whether or not the Satanic Church is indeed a religion as measured by some set of "universal" objective criteria. My definition of "religion" is a simple one which follows that developed by Wallace (1966: 107): "Religion is a set of rituals rationalized by myth, which mobilizes supernatural powers for the purpose of achieving or preventing transformations of state in man and nature."

A more complex problem is distinguishing the witches and the Satanists. The two terms are not mutually exclusive. Simply put, witches may have power even without making a pact with the Devil. Devil worship is a product of the Judeo-Christian tradition. Indeed, it is ironical that a good part of the Satanic practice used today may be the product of the overactive imagination of overzealous inquisitors rather than duplications of the "real" activities of the Devil worshipers of the time.

Most material on non-Western witchcraft has no mention of the Devil or Satan. Any mention of witchcraft in the West indicates that it was the learned opinion of the time that witches' power comes from a pact with Satan, "the Opposition." This is the structure of the institution today... .

[2]    The world view of every culture which I personally have investigated distinguishes between good and evil, the presence of evil frequently being given as the reason for or cause of misfortune.

[3]    Data was collected during a two-year period of participant observation. I would like to emphasize that the San Francisco Satanists are one group among many and that the forms of Satanism and witchcraft are many. I would also like to point out that the period of investigation was during the early stages of the Church of the Trapezoid's growth. A visit this year indicates changes in the composition of the membership and in the structure of the Church. Over the past three years, as the Church of Satan has become more institutionalized and less marginal, criteria for membership has been stiffened, and the process of advancement formalized.

[4]    "Normal" and "abnormal" are, in my opinion, relative terms. Not only are they culturally relative, but relative to social context. In some cases abnormal may mean that the individual exhibits "correct" responses, e.g. sexuality, in socially "incorrect" settings.

5    These groups — the Rosicrucians, the Keepers of the Golden Key, and others — promise literally that
     all the ills which plague the anxiety-ridden sociopath, sickness, failure, impotence, and so on, will be
     eliminated once the "Secrets of the Ages," the "esoteric knowledge of the ancient masters" is acquired.
     For the potential Satanist, convinced that there must be some key to his failure and other's success, this
     is an obvious answer.

6    There is some controversy over the efficacy of treating "symptoms" of the "deeper problem." Can one
     change more "basic" attitudes by modifying surface behavior is a question asked. The work of Bem
     (1967) and Bandura, Blanchard, and Ritter (1969) indicates that attitude change, regardless of the
     original cause of maladaptive responses, can and does *follow* modification of the maladaptive behavior
     rather than precede it.

7    As Wallace (1966: 106-107) points out, "all ritual is directed toward the problem of transformations of
     state in human beings or nature." Sometimes the purpose is to insure rapid transformation, sometimes
     to prevent it. The Satanists are more explicit about the ritual effects desired than any other religion I
     have encountered. In some cases they describe the effects in terms of magic, at other times their
     explanation is very sociological.

# References

Bandura, A., E.B. Blanchard, and B.J. Ritter
    1969    "The Relative Efficacy of Modelling Therapeutic Approaches for Producing Behavioral,
            Attitudinal, and Affective Changes." In L. Ullman and L. Krasner, eds., *Behavioral
            Approaches to Abnormal Psychology*. Englewood Cliffs, NJ: Prentice-Hall.

Bem, D.J.
    1967    "Self-Perception: The Dependent Variable of Human Performance." *Organizational
            Behavior and Human Performance* 2: 105-121

Cannon, Walter B.
    1942    "The 'Voodoo' Death." *American Anthropologist* 44: 164-181.

Caro Baroja, J.
    1964    *The World of Witches*. Chicago: University of Chicago Press.

Crawford, J.R.
    1967    *Witchcraft and Sorcery in Rhodesia*. London: Oxford University Press.

Douglas, Mary
    1967    "Witch Beliefs in Central Africa." *Africa* 37:72-80.

Evans-Pritchard, E.E.
    1937    *Witchcraft, Oracles and Magic Among the Azande*. Oxford: Clarendon Press.

Festinger, Leon
    1957    *A Theory of Cognitive Dissonance*. Evanston, IL: Row, Peterson.

Gluckman, Max
    1965    *Politics. Law, and Ritual in Tribal Societies*. Oxford: Blackwell.

Haugen, E., H.H. Dixon, and H.A. Dickel
    1958    *A Therapy for Anxiety Tension Reactions*. New York: Macmillan.

Kelly, M.W.
    1955    *The Psychology of Personal Constructs*. 2 vols. New York: W.W. Norton.

Kluckholm, Clyde
    1967      *Navaho Witchcraft*. Boston: Beacon Press.

La Vey, Anton S.
    1969      *The Satanic Bible*. New York: Avon Books.

Lienhardt, G.
    1951      "Some Notions of Witchcraft Among the Dinka." *Africa* 21: 303-318.

MacFarlan, M.G.
    1967      *Witchcraft Persecution in Essex, 1560-1690*. Unpublished Ph.D. dissertation.

Mair, Lucy
    1969      *Witchcraft*. New York: McGraw-Hill.

Moody, Edward J.
    1971      "Urban Witches." In J.P. Spradley and D.W. McCurdy, eds., *Conformity and Conflict: Readings in Cultural Anthropology*.

Nadel, S.F.
    1952      "Witchcraft in Four African Societies." *American Anthropologist* 54: 18-29.

Parrinder, Geoffrey
    1963      *Witchcraft: European and African*. London: Faber and Faber.

Paulme, Denise
    1962      Une Sociéte de la Cote d'Ivorie: Les Bété. Paris (Cited in Mair, 1969: 162-163).

Rackmann, S.
    1966      "Sexual Fetishism: An Experimental Dialogue." *Psychological Record* 12: 293-296.

Robbins, Russell H.
    1959      *The Encyclopedia of Witchcraft and Demonology*. New York: Crown Pub.

Sprenger, Jakob and Henricus Institoris
    1948      *Malleus malefarum*. London: Puskin Press.

Summers, Montague
    1926      *The History of Witchcraft and Demonology*. New York: University Books.

Toch, Hans
    1965      *The Social Psychology of Mass Movements*. Indianapolis, IN: Bobbs-Merrill.

Ullman, Leonard and L. Krasner
    1969      *Behavioral Approaches to Abnormal Psychology*. Englewood Cliffs, NJ: Prentice-Hall.

Wallenstein, J.S. and C.J. Wylie
    1947      "Our Law-Abiding Law Breakers." *Probation* 25: 107-112.

Wolpe, J.
    1954      "Reciprocal Inhibition as the Main Basis of Psychotherapeutic Effects." *AMA Archives of Neurology and Psychiatry* 72: 205-266.
    1958      *Psychotherapy by Reciprocal Inhibition*. Stanford, CA: Stanford University Press.

Wolpe, J. and A.A. Lazarus
    1966      *Behavior Therapy Techniques: A Guide to the Treatment of Neuroses*. New York: Pergamon.

# TEENAGE SATANISM AS OPPOSITIONAL YOUTH SUBCULTURE

## KATHLEEN S. LOWNEY

*This research offers an ethnographic portrait of a coven of teenage Satanists. It argues that the psychological, folklore, and constructionist perspectives on Satanists are lacking an important voice — the adolescent Satanists themselves. By listening to them, it becomes clear that Satanism allows them to challenge the dominant culture's norm's and values. Lacking the social power though, the Coven primarily used a symbolic critique, through the creation of a Satanic style.*

• • • • • • • • • • • • • • • • • • • • • • • • •

Satanism has been much discussed of late, primarily by the popular media and less so by the scholarly community. A very few analysts have seen it as a nonthreatening new religious movement, one among many that have attracted members since the 1960s. Many more people have seen Satanism as an unhealthy, perhaps even criminal enterprise that hurts all those who encounter it. In this view, Satanists are likely to be child abusers, murderers, and substance abusers, and are constantly looking for others to harm or to recruit. Children and adolescents are the most vulnerable to the seduction of the Devil's grasp; thus the activity must be stopped to prevent further innocents from being led astray down the path to Hell.

Those who see Satanism as dangerous have described it as "a belief system that uses occult magic and employs ritual practices that constitute a travesty of Christianity" (Moriarty and Story 1990, 187). For these individuals, religion "refers to Judeo-

Kathleen S. Lowney. "Teenage Satanism as Oppositional Youth Subculture." *Journal of Contemporary Ethnography* 23, 1995: 453-484. Copyright © 1995 Sage Publications Inc. Reprinted by permission of Sage Publications Inc.

Christian practices and belief system commonly associated with Western culture" (Moriarty and Story 1990, 187). Those who accept such a definition of Satanism are Christian evangelists (e.g., Larson 1989), ex-Satanists (e.g., Stratford [1987] 1991; Warnke 1972), and many in the psychiatric community (e.g., Moriarty and Story 1990; Wheeler, Wood, and Hatch 1988). They hold that Satanists are dangerous people — to others, especially innocent children, and even to themselves. They regard them as mentally disturbed individuals, often addicted to drugs or sadistic sexual practices. The psychiatric description that Satanists are "dysfunctional" or "sick" comes almost entirely from three sources: hospitalized teenagers diagnosed as Satanic practitioners (Belitz and Schacht 1992; Bourget, Gagnon, and Bradford 1988; Moriarty and Story 1990; Steck, Anderson, and Boylin 1992), prisoners whose crimes were said to have been inspired by Satanism, and ex-Satanists, many of whom subsequently converted to Christianity. Those who hold to this explanation proclaim that American moral values (religious faith, family unity, etc.) are breaking down, and that Satanism has flourished in such a morally bankrupt social environment.

This construction of Satanism has been prominently expressed in popular media, especially on television talk shows.[1] Talk show hosts rely on psychiatric experts to explain the danger to Satanists and to those they might victimize. According to this explanation, the cause of these "sick " or deviant behaviors is the Satanic faith that practitioners espouse. The most common prescription is counseling (be it exit counseling [religious in nature] or psychotherapy). Therapeutic intervention is seen as the sole means of releasing the person from the Devil's grip (e.g. Rudin 1990; Speltz 1990; and Tennant-Clark, Fritz, and Beauvais 1989).

The other primary explanation is a more social-scientific one. Satanism is understood to encompass a range of beliefs and practices: it can be simply mislabeled youthful playfulness, or it can be a social movement that is seemingly harmless though often flamboyant (Richardson, Best, and Bromley 1991a), or it may even be the rationale for criminal behavior (Crouch and Damphousse 1992; Taub and Nelson 1993).

In the earliest sociological literature, Satanism, or more precisely, certain organized Satanic groups that Taub and Nelson (1993) called the Satanic Establishment, were seen to have "achieved a measure of social legitimation" (p. 525) in the American religious plurality. These groups contain adult, not juvenile members: Alfred (1976) found that the vast majority of members in the Church of Satan were "middle class white people in their forties, thirties, and late twenties, including many professionals" (p. 194). Moody's (1974) study of the (Satanic) church of the Trapezoid, and Bainbridge's study (1978) of The Power, a Satanic cult, also characterized their members as adults. These establishment groups had a cohesive theology and praxis, and did not involve themselves in criminal conduct, nor did their values differ significantly from those of many other American organizations (Taub and Nelson 1993).

Recent sociological literature about Satanism has stressed a constructionist analysis of the moral panic created by claim-makers who advocated the psychiatric explanation (e.g., Forsyth and Olivier 1990; Lippert 1990; Richardson, Best, and Bromley 1991a) rather than an analysis of actual practitioners. So much of our knowledge about teenagers involved in what popular culture calls Satanism stems from the work of folklorists. Ellis (1982-1983, 1991b) has argued that teenagers act out local legends by visiting "haunted" sites, a practice called legend-tripping. He stated (1991b) that legend-tripping frequently includes acts of deviant behavior such as graffiti spray-painting, breaking and entering abandoned churches, and vandalizing graveyards. This is not "real" Satanism but ostentation, the physical re-enactment of local legends. The role-playing done on these legend-trips is "the significant thing to the adolescent, and the legend serves mainly as an excuse to escape adult supervision, commit antisocial acts, and experiment illicitly with drugs and sex. Both legend and trip are ways of saying 'screw you' to adult law and order" (Ellis 1982-1983, 64). Ellis has argued that, given the hysteria instigated by the moral panic, law enforcement officers, educators, mental health professionals, and parents have overreacted and inappropriately labeled legend-trippers as Satanists. Ellis comes close to arguing that there is little actual Satanic religious behavior among adolescents; what seems visible is more often simply misunderstood, mislabeled legend-trip activity.

The "disturbed" explanation given by the mental health professionals, the folklorists' legend-tripping explanation, and to a lesser extent the constructionist literature that explores the anti-Satanist claim-making agenda, assume that there is a dominant culture against which individual young adults are reacting with their "Satanic" behaviors. These explanations privilege this dominant culture, arguing that "healthy" teens would not feel alienated from peers, parents, community, and that these adolescents eventually will stop rebelling and join the "real," adult world. This theoretical privileging of one culture accomplishes two things: first, it keeps the analysis focused on "bad" or "sick" *individuals* rather than on the level of the social group, and second, it does not allow for an analysis of teenage Satanists as *social critics* of the dominant culture.[2]

The voices of adolescent Satanists are absent from the sociological literature. Gaines (1990) briefly discussed what she called "Satanteens," with little analysis of their beliefs. Crouch and Damphousse (1992) discussed "self styled" or "youth subculture" Satanists. They assume that all such Satanists "sometime engage in activities that are not only bizarre by conventional standards but also criminal" (p. 5). They offer no firsthand data to support this claim. Crouch and Damphousse agree with Taub and Nelson (1993) that youthful Satanists should be classified as members of the Satanic Underground, with its "reputed participation in antisocial or criminal behavior. Activities of these individuals or groups are less structured and lack the organizational dimensions of the Satanic Establishment" (p. 525).

Here again, theoretical dichotomies such as "Satanic Establishment" versus "Satanic Underground" are too simplistic. Critical questions must be asked about these descriptions of adolescent Satanism: "underground" to whom? "antisocial" according to whose moral perspective? "conventional" according to whose viewpoint? "less structured" according to whose standards? Terms such as these also imply a privileged position, in this case by the sociological analyst. These would not be the terms used by many youthful Satanists to describe their own activities.

Ethnographic accounts of modern-day adolescent Satanists are needed, including accounts of Satanists who are not hospitalized in a psychiatric facility, and accounts that give participants' explanation for their religious behaviors. In this article I analyze five years of fieldwork with the Coven, a Satanic adolescent subculture in a Southern community I shall call "Victory Village." What emerges from these data is far removed from the psychiatric interpretation. Although it is a "view from below" — the explanation constructed by the teenage Satanists themselves — it is *not* an examination of the Taub and Nelson's "Satanic Underground." The Coven did not participate in major criminal activities.

What the Coven did was to present a critique of the dominant culture of Victory Village. Thus the Coven is yet another example of how youth subcultures can challenge the hegemony of the dominant culture (e.g., Brake 1980; Cohen 1980; Fox 1987; Gaines 1990; Hebdige 1979[3]). Their subcultural opposition operated on several levels simultaneously: first, it was *collective* articulation of a cultural critique; second, it allowed them to establish and maintain a new self-concept; and third, it provided a symbolic challenge to the dominant culture's value system.

What the Coven did was to play with the social categories and boundaries of Victory Village. These were so accepted by many in the community that they had become almost imperceptible over time. The Coven made visible the dominant culture's valued statuses as it simultaneously rejected them. But its rejection of the dominant culture antagonized Victory Village.

To understand what the Coven got from its Satanic faith — even in the face of such rejection — requires listening to the story of Victory Village from these adolescents' perspective. I tell their story as they told it to me, first by explaining the dominant culture as they saw it and then by describing their critique of that culture. In particular, I focus on their development of a Satanic style as an expression of their opposition to Victory Village.

# Method

I have been on my college's Speaker's Bureau — a faculty list of those willing to speak to the community on topics related to their expertise — since I came to this institution in 1987. I was listed as an expert on "new religious movements/cults," because my doctoral dissertation focused on a well-know new religion. One day in

March of 1988, three calls came in to the Public Relations Department and were referred to me. The calls either asked me about, or informed me of, Satanic activities in neighboring high schools. The first and third calls were from Christian ministers who wanted me to speak to their youth groups about what was happening. The second call was from an employee of a nearby bookstore who knew of me, notifying me that during the last six weeks there had been over thirty-five special orders placed for *The Satanic Bible* (LaVey 1969). That very day I began interviewing members of the press, law enforcement, and school systems for their perspective on what was occurring. These interviews, plus background reading on Satanism (academic and popular), took up the bulk of my research time for the next two months. I also went to one of the youth groups, less as an expert than as a listener. From those Christian young adults I gathered not just names of possible Coven members, but also learned more about their behaviors and favorite hangouts.

For the next several months, I frequented locations where, according to the Christian youths, the Coven met. Primarily this meant going to the mall on Friday nights and observing until it closed. From the non-Satanist youth's descriptions of the Coven's style, I was able to identify possible members quite easily. Through background interviews with youth ministers and others, I learned of more names; sometimes members even were pointed out to me. Thus even before contact was made with the Coven, I was able to begin to sort out membership status and style matters. I sat and observed numerous interactions of the Coven while members played games, as well as their interactions with non-Satanic youth, the shopping public, food court workers, and mall security guards. Initially I observed from a distance; over time I would chat with some members and other young adults at the arcade. I was becoming a "social fixture" at the mall. These observations gave me some idea of the group's norms, structure, and argot prior to the interviewing phase.

Simultaneously, I began visiting other locations I heard the Coven discuss — in particular local bridges — but I went on Friday afternoons or Saturday mornings, when it was less likely that I would meet the group, because the Coven visited them after the mall closed on Friday nights. These visits gave me some sense of the less public activities of the Coven. I took photographs of these sites when I found evidence of Coven activities: Satanic graffiti, such as "Playing with black magic is fun" or Satanic pentagrams painted on trees to mark the way into a rural meeting site; non-Satanic graffiti but signed with Coven nicknames, such as one male who often went by the name of "Casper." He tended to paint "Casper loves." Not only could I trace his whereabouts with these messages, but I could also follow his romantic history as well.

I continued to talk with Christian youth groups; from them I realized that I needed to know more about high school culture. Therefore I continued to visit the mall and video arcade; I interviewed local merchants (bookstore, music store, alternative clothing stores, etc.) I also began to observe the areas of the high school parking lots when school was getting out.

After about one year, I became known as an "expert" in Satanism. This status opened some new research opportunities. I was given permission to attend an Occult Crime Workshop for Georgia law enforcement officers. I was the only non-law enforcement person present during the three day workshop. The workshop fit the model described by Hicks (1991a, 1991b, personal communication): a law enforcement officer presented a great deal of data — mostly clips from television talk shows. His analytical framework blended the psychiatric explanation — "Satanists were sickies" — with a heavy dose of conservative Christianity. He showed little understanding of religions (confusing Santeria with Voodoo, for instance) and labeled any new religious movement, such as the Unification Church, as Satanic. Claims about the growing number of Satanic or occult crimes were repeatedly made, with no evidence presented to support them. While there, I interviewed five police officers from various jurisdictions in Georgia, as well as local officers who also attended the workshop.

Throughout the course of the research, I was invited to attend or to lecture at the workshops on Satanism for social workers (local and state level), probation and parole officers (state level), and educators (local level). During these meetings I conducted interviews, primarily with those people who stayed afterward to discuss specific work-related incidents. I have interviewed local (Georgia) television reporters and print journalists, and I had several telephone interviews with a Florida television anchor who ran a week-long special on the evening news about teenage Satanism. Although certainly not systematic, it can be argued that the interviews with these professionals might well represent concerns about the "worst" cases of alleged Satanism among Georgia and Florida teenagers.

By mid-1989, some Coven members agreed to be interviewed. This took a long time to arrange due to ethical concerns about studying minors involved in Satanism without the informed consent of their parents or guardians.[4] More males than females agreed to one-on-one interviews, although there were several opportunities for informal group discussions (especially about makeup) with females during observations at the mall. Interviews were often unplanned. Twice members or former members showed up at my faculty office ready to talk.[5] I learned to keep a notebook, camera, and tape recorder with me. Interviews were most often unstructured. I let the member lead our discussion, and asked questions mostly for clarification. During later interviews, and only with certain subjects, I was more directive and brought up topics for discussion.

All the young adults interviewed were involved with the Coven, though membership status varied. I interviewed four very active members; two less active members; and two ex-members. From mid-1989 to 1991, I conducted over fifteen interviews; they ranged from just under one hour to several hours in length. Most often the interviews occurred in a setting chosen by the Coven member. This often meant that interviews were done outdoors, sometimes while sitting on the hood of a car, often with a car stereo playing in the background.

Interactions with the Coven, especially at first, were sometimes problematic.

They were not sure how to treat me and how much they could trust me. I was a teacher, yet not *their* teacher; I was an adult yet I had no real authority over them. Some of this awkwardness disappeared during the observational stage, especially after the Coven knew who I was and became used to me. We eventually negotiated a "friend role" (Fine 1987) that was comfortable for them and for me. I dressed casually during observations; I deliberately purchased compact discs at the music store for personal enjoyment when in the presence of the Coven; some members had much to say about my taste in music. These behaviors allowed interactions to occur that facilitated the friendship role. Perhaps the two most disconcerting issues that emerged during the research were religion and confidentiality. For eight years I have worn a Christian cross. It had become such a part of my presentation of self that I often forgot it was there. Coven members, once they felt comfortable around me, sometimes commented about it. Because I asked them about their jewelry and why they wore it, I responded in kind. Often this led into conversations about religion. I was expected to participate, not just observe, and I did, sometimes sharing moments in my life that were either religious highs or lows. These conversations were quite comfortable for me. Where religion became problematic was when adults who knew I was studying the Coven expected that my research goal was to talk members out of Satanism. In particular, some Christian adults felt strongly that I was letting them and/or the community down if I was not deconverting the teens. I was not always successful at explaining that deconversion was never my goal. Several times these adults asked me if I was a secret Satanist — Why else was I not trying to get the kids out of the Devil's grip?

Although religious issues were more problematic between myself and those outside the Coven, confidentiality was more difficult to negotiate with the Coven. As the research progressed, I learned that children of social acquaintances were involved. These teens were concerned that I would report their activities (especially Coven membership, sneaking out of the house, and underage drinking) to parents/guardians. As trust built up and they learned that I would not, this declined as an issue.

Only one other issue ever proved problematic — underage consumption of alcohol. For the most part, members never drank in my presence, or if they did, they were of legal age. Twice I was asked to provide alcohol for a gathering and both times I refused. This refusal had less to do with my concern than I would be stepping over an "ethical line in the sand" than that this could have led to my arrest for supplying alcohol to minors. Both times the request was withdrawn after my refusal, or turned into a joke that, "Oh yea, she doesn't drink ... she's allergic to alcohol ... she wouldn't know what the fuck to get anyway." The use of humor (by them or me) allowed the role of friend to be maintained.

During the years of data-gathering, over thirty-five young adults had at least some involvement with the Coven. Three were members throughout the entire study and to my knowledge considered themselves Satanists by the time I concluded my research, though they were no longer active in the Coven because they were in colleges away from home. All were White; almost all were from middle- or upper-middle-class families. A third of the membership was female; a female was the charismatic leader for over two years.

## The Dominant Culture

The acquisition of culture by any particular individual is a complex interactive process, mediated both by other individuals (parents, peers, siblings) and social institutions (religion, schools, mass media). A culture, however dominant it may be, "is not uniformly spread throughout a social system" (Fine and Kleinman 1979, 1); rather, culture is internalized to different degrees due to sociocultural variables such as social class, race, sex, and age. Victory Village's dominant culture, as it was internalized by its adolescents, can be summed up in one word — football. The high school team consistently ranked among the top twenty-five high school football teams in the nation. The team boasted a record that included two national championships and numerous state championships; in the last four years the team was featured on at least two national news programs.[6]

This football culture created multiple status hierarchies within the student body. From the Coven's perspective, these hierarchies amounted to an unmentioned but understood categorization of the entire student body. Richard, a non-Satanist high school junior, described the social structure of Victory Village High School this way:

Well, here's how it is .... There's the jocks and their ladies — they're on the top. Then their flunkies, cheerleaders, and the band. All *they* do is make the football jocks look good .... Then there's the geeks, oh, I mean the greeks. They're rich and White and let everyone know it .... Then the academics — yeah, that's most of us over there — study, work, go to [football] games if we want to, ya know, regular folks .... Then there's the others, you know, the artsy types — they're odd, but they have God-given talent, I guess ... .There's the freaks — druggies, or just the odd ones, they just don't fit in anywhere.

Although these groups tend toward intragroup activities, Fine and Kleinman (1979) has written that "it is erroneous to conceive of group members as interacting exclusively with each other. Small groups are connected with many other groups through a large number of interlocks, or social connections" (p. 8). So too, in Victory Village high schools, the organization of the schools forced a limited amount of mixing, primarily in classrooms, the parking lots, and lunchrooms. The groups also interacted outside of the high schools, in particular at the favorite adolescent leisure activity sites such as the shopping mall and theaters.

One of the ways groups differentiate themselves is through constructing unique styles. Style is

> the expressive elements used by an actor in his way of acting upon the
> world. This includes the way he organizes his experiences, his
> perceptions, and his cognitions at the psychological level, as well as
> his appearance, bearing, and life style .... Style indicates who one is,
> and where one is at — it indicates identity in a particular way (Brake
> 1974, 185).

Even dominant groups developed particular styles. The football players dressed conspicuously, in football jerseys, school colors, and sweats. They used a specialized argot to talk about their games, training procedures, and opponents. Cheerleaders also had a particular presentation of self — appropriate makeup, hairstyles, and weight — as well as a language of cheers and planning activities for the athletes. Band members had props such as uniforms and instruments, which readily identified them. Thus each group developed a unique style that both bonded members to each other and served to socially locate them.

Although these status hierarchies divided the student body, there was a unifying force in the high school, indeed in the community. Christian faith was normative in Victory Village. A woman, shopping in the local mall, expressed this "social fact" to two Coven females, when she yelled at them:

> Okay, you've made your point; you don't like my religion [the woman
> was wearing a Christian cross and had just come out of a Christian
> bookstore]. But this is a *Christian* community — we don't want you
> around either. So go, why don't you? Just leave, go somewhere, maybe
> Atlanta, some big city where there are more like you ... just go, before
> my daughter gets to high school next year.

Christianity permeated Victory Village. Prayers were said before football games. Weekly church attendance was customary among both adolescents and adults. Symbols of the faith were very visible; Christian crosses were commonplace as jewelry, especially among females. Most athletes and cheerleaders belonged to Christian organizations. Living the Christian lifestyle, as preached to adolescents, involved self-control of the body to be an excellent athlete, sexually chaste, and physically attractive. Thus membership in the larger body of the faithful to some degree mitigated the status divisions in Victory Village High School: adolescents saw each other frequently in church.

Nevertheless, some students were socially marginalized. Mark, an ex-member of the theater group and the most prolific of the Coven's graffiti artists, can serve as an example:

> I knew they didn't want me in class. They all sat together .... I let 'em

> ... What the hell did I care anyway? They never would have talked to
> me anyway. I made 'em uncomfortable — if they couldn't see me, they
> could go on the way they always were — praying a lot, yet being god
> damn mean to anyone below them .... I let 'em think they were better
> than me, .... 'cuz dammit, I knew the *truth*.

The "truth," for Mark, was Satanism. He described an incremental conversion
process, whereby social bonds developed both prior to and simultaneously with his
conversion to this Satanic group.[7]

> I never felt accepted at this school. Always felt different — sometimes
> that hurt, sometimes I was glad to be different. Who'd want to be like
> those motherfucking hypocritical Christians? ... Love your enemies —
> ya, let's see that attitude on the football field some Friday night! ...
> Then I noticed her one day, at lunch I think. She was an outsider too —
> could see that by her hair. But something was different .... She seemed
> proud of it. I began to find out about her; hang around her. She
> fascinated me, especially her appearance .... Everyday was something
> different ... She seemed exciting, daring others to challenge her .... So I
> got to know her, Zena. She was proud, proud of her uniqueness. I
> wanted that too — to feel better, no, *good* about myself. Don't remember
> just how it happened — maybe I was drunk when I finally did it — I
> finally asked her about it. And she showed me her *truth*. So I borrowed
> it [*The Satanic Bible*] for awhile ... If it worked for her, gave her all that
> fucking air of being above those shitty athletes and rich snobs ... well, I
> wanted it too.

Mark's story was typical. All of the Coven's membership shared this extremely
marginalized social location at the high school. Many had been members of the
"artistic" group — already a lower status group, but they did not want to continue
interacting with that group. Chris, a Coven member for three months, said, "I got tired
of all the rehearsals. I had better things to do with my time." So over a period of
months, the Coven was formed. It created a mechanism to *decrease* individual
marginality by inventing a new solidarity for its members, yet in so doing, its members
actually *increased* their social isolation by espousing a Satanic idioculture (Fine 1982)
and style that is the normative culture of Victory Village.

## The Coven's Critique of the Dominant Culture

Any group interacts with others over the course of time. These interactions serve critical functions in the construction of group beliefs, practices, and ideology. The marginalized status of some high school students in Victory Village, and their hostility to the in groups who had higher status in the school and community, led to the formation of the Coven. Over time, Satanic beliefs, practices, and rituals were constructed by members to serve two main purposes: first, to critique the dominant culture, and second, to create a new self-identity. As the Coven met these goals, it further marginalized its member from other students and the community. Coven members grew increasingly hostile to the outside world as they saw it, in particular due to the fact that the Coven felt Victory Village would never change. Coven members were not able to fit into the social structure of the high schools, no matter how hard they may have attempted to do so. At some point, they had decided to stop trying. Chris, one of the more visible male members, with his rock 'n roll t-shirts and his shoulder-length hair, said:

> Yeah, I know there's fucking no chance of changing this fucking town, [long pause] or even the damned school. But that doesn't mean I should just roll over and die — I am *here*, and so long as I can dress this way, think this way ... then they will have to deal with me, with us [the Coven]. It's fun to see them look scared, look the other way when I come down the hall .... Don't tell me I don't have power. So long as I'm in the Coven, so long as I believe, I have *lots* of power — least to rattle their chains. Not sure can ask for more.

This hostility became channeled into a streetwise analysis of the dominant culture; in other words, the Coven settled on the role of social critic. Its mere visual presence was challenging to some in the community, even *prior* to their understanding the group's religious convictions. To those who knew this, too, the Coven was seen as threatening to the community's social harmony. And the Coven perceived this. Mark, a long-time member and sometimes leader, said:

> I know lots of people in this fucking community wish we would disappear, or worse yet, be shipped off to [a local psychiatric hospital]. Too damned bad .... we're not going anywhere. I'm not sick ... least not the way *they* mean it. I'm fucking sick of always being put down 'cuz I don't play football. Well too damned bad. Why is chasing a fucking ball up and down a field such a fucking god-given talent in this community? If I did that, coach says I could be important. Well, hell *I am important*, dammit even though I fucking can't play football, *don't want to* play football. And if they don't see it, my friends [the Coven] do. We know we're important, see, if nothing else, we make *them* feel better about themselves .... They can pray for us [laughter]. Like I need their motherfucking prayers .... Their God is weak. He can't even make

[the county high school football] team win, even when they pray before a game ... and they think He will save the world, save them? Hell no .... God dammit, Satan is all power; so am I. I want nothing to do with *them*, the adults who run this shitty place, nor their fucking kids who prance around the field or cheer on 'their team.' No thanks, I will make my own way ... don't want to live like them, no way. Don't want to look like 'em, talk like 'em .... I don't want to be one of *them*, fucking never do I.

The Coven, like many subcultures, found its role, its cohesiveness in social criticism of the dominant culture from which it felt rejected. Lacking the social power to change that culture, Coven members chose to change themselves as a statement to Victory Village. Brake (1980, vii) has written that

subcultures arise as attempts to resolve collectively experienced problems arising from the contradictions in the social structure, and that they generate a form of collective identity from which an individual identity can be achieved outside that ascribed by class, education, and occupation. This is nearly always a temporary solution, and in no sense is a real material solution, but one which is solved at the cultural level.

And so the Coven members changed. Members created a Satanic subculture that diverged in both normative, cognitive, and behavioral aspects from the dominant culture of Victory Village. What the Coven created was a deliberate inversion of its perception of the dominant culture.

In particular, the Coven reversed what it perceived as the dominant culture's organization of space and time. The Coven chose to have its ritual sabbats[8] on Friday evenings, after the mall closed and at the same time as football games. "We try and get away from town, from the ass-kissing athletes playing their fucking games; that's where we do our thing." The Coven met in remote rural areas of the county. Their favorite ritual sites were bridges.[9] Although there were theological reasons for this,[10] there were other advantages. "We choose places that are one way in and one way out. That way we can see if anyone is coming and can stop the ritual. Our religion is for *us*, not just for anyone who wants to watch." In particular, the Coven kept a watchful eye out for law enforcement officers who might try to stop gatherings.[11]

By choosing remote rural sites for their rituals, the Coven acted out a central part of their oppositional subculture. Brake (1980, 35) has argued, "Physical space is not merely a simple territorial imperative, but symbolic of a whole life-style." Many of the bridges that the Coven used for ritual activity were in poor structural condition or actually closed to traffic. The Coven saw this as important. Mark best expressed this to me one night as he drew a map to one of the most remote Coven meeting sites.

> Our religion is about tearing down social lies and pointing out the truth, or as LaVey says, "Religion must be put to the question. No moral dogma must be taken for granted — no standard of measurement deified. There is nothing inherently sacred about moral codes. Like the wooden idols of long ago, they are the work of human hands, and what man has made, man can destroy!" We go to places that are in a state of decay — to show that the town is too!

During these nightime rituals, the Coven seemed to choose a state of nature over the dominant Christian culture. The faraway bridge sites allowed them to be in touch with nature. The Coven saw itself as a small group operating in darkness, ritually illuminated by sacred candles and a campfire, calling forth demons to do its bidding. "We like the dark while they sit in the fucking stadium, lit up like a Christmas tree." Simultaneous with the Coven's sabbats, other teens were sitting in the "sacred center" of the football stadium, lit by artificial lights, collectively acting out the social norms of civil Christianity — to win the athletic contest, to "win" the right high school member of the opposite sex's attention, to be a success at the "game of life," so that they could reside in Heaven forever.

These two ideologies also disagreed about temporality. Christianity has a linear sense of time — it holds that all events, in both history and personal biography, will culminate in the end time, the Second Coming of Jesus Christ. All phenomena led to this one salvific event. For Christians, therefore, all time has a *future* emphasis. Believers orient their actions toward this ultimate goal; to live with little or no sin is to look forward to the Second Coming with joy instead of dread. Football athletes, cheerleaders, and the band practice for next games or the next season. For the Coven, there was no ultimate goal toward which time was oriented. Rather, Satanists lived in and for the present.

> Life is the great indulgence — death, the great abstinence. Therefore, make the most of life — HERE AND NOW! There is no heaven of glory bright, and no hell where sinners roast. Here and now is our day of torment! Here and now is our day of joy! Here and now is our opportunity! Choose ye this day, this hour, for no redeemer liveth! (LaVey, 62).

Following LaVey, the Coven did not divide social reality into past, present, and future. There was only the present. Alice, a member for just several months, nevertheless was able to articulate this part of the Coven's worldview: "What I want now, is what I want. If my desires change, it is because there is a new now."

This disparity between their views of temporality only deepened the rift between the two worldviews. The Satanists could not comprehend living life toward a future heavenly goal that one might not even attain, while Christians considered the Satanists' emphasis on fulfilling one's desires in the present as hedonistic and self-indulgent, if not sinful.

Thus the two worldviews clashed; their theologies were antithetical. Christian deportment, success in relationships and on the football field — these were the dominant culture's values internalized by Victory Village's adolescents. But the Coven rejected these values, choosing instead to pray to Satan, living for the moment and for self. Although Coven membership fluctuated over the year, its theology remained relatively constant. The Coven was theologically eclectic, using *The Satanic Bible* (1969) and several other books, such as *The Necronomicon* (1980) as a basic framework. Here too, the Coven saw itself as opposing Christian reliance upon only one sacred text. Mark, a member for over sixteen months at the time of our interview, said, "We don't have to be tied to just one book, written ages ago. No words in red for us, we interpret the [Satanic] Bible as we see it. It speaks to me differently each fucking day. And I just live it out."

Thus personal experience was another theological source. Coven members brought to sabbat what was happening in their lives and the group ritually processed these life events. Several kinds of rituals were held; the most common involved members coming together at an isolated site, saying a few prayers to Satan, having a bonfire, drinking beer and wine coolers, criticizing Victory Village, and listening to rock music. Music offered both a way to ventilate emotions and to bond. "[M]usic is important because it articulates aspects of kids' lives, at a real or fantasy level" (Brake 1980, 157). As Mark said, "Like, I've had a shitty day. I'll go to sabbat, and be able to work through it all. Often I can't put it into words, but I'll play a song that says it all. Everyone understands then. I'm not too good with words, anyway."

The Coven's musical tastes shifted constantly. Their heavy metal favorites alternated between Megadeth, Motley Crue, Poison, Metallica, Guns and Roses, Ozzie Osbourne, and Anthrax; yet some members also like rap music and country songs.[12] More rarely "top 40" music could be heard from their portable stereo headsets. When questioned about this eclectic musical range, Chris, a guitar player himself, reported, "Yeah, I like metal music best ... guitars wailing. But mostly, it's what is being said. If it's bitching about the fucking world we've inherited, then I will probably like it ... but once and a while, I like a love song too." Coven members discussed both the structure of the music (guitar solos, etc.) and the lyrics. They seemed very aware of the lyrics, often interpreting them for me. In this, the Coven diverged from some of the findings in the literature about adolescents and heavy metal music (e.g., Prinksy and Rosenbaum 1987).

Music was also a critical component of what the Coven called its "sex rituals".[13] The Coven enjoyed discussing these rituals in a vage and secretive fashion in front of outsiders, particularly high school teachers, as a way of, as Alice put it, "shaking up the establishment." For instance, Zena, the charismatic leader, was known by the ritual name, The Sex Goddess. This Satanic name was often "dropped" before nonmembers (especially teachers) in an attempt to confound, embarrass, and worry the larger social world. And it worked. One local teacher called me after hearing such a conversation. "All they do is have sex. Sex and Satan. That's all they write about in class. I'm worried about them." Coven followers often laughed at the consternation their supposed sexual antics created. And yet despite their nomenclature, these rituals did not, to my knowledge, involve sexual intercourse. The sexual innuendos, however, clearly functioned as a source of power over nonmembers.

Most often these sex rituals involved the working of spells, often based on the sex chapter from *The Satanic Bible* (LaVey 1969), which focused on one member's sexual desire for someone else (either a member or a nonmember) and the spiritual mechanisms needed to accomplish that romantic goal. Spells tended to be highly personal in nature, composed by the individual but shared in the ritual context of sabbat. Members supported one another throughout the duration of the spell through prayer, conversation, listening to music as ritual activity, and confidence-building behaviors. Spells detailed the magical steps necessary to requite one's sexual desire for the other person. Mark shared a version of his spell for getting the girl of his dreams to go to a prom with him.

1. Pray to Satan about this every day. Ask for his guidance and support.
2. Change pattern of walking in the hallways in order to come into contact with the girl.
3. Begin to make eye contact with her.
4. Borrow/steal something of her [a pen].
5. Talk to her, initially about inconsequential things.
6. Talk to her about Satanism and how Satan is the most important person in his life, forever.
7. Use the personal object ritually to connect her to him forever. [This involved tying her pen to a pen of his. He carried them around for over two weeks.]
8. Eventually, ask her to the prom.

For each step in the spell, he had specific "Satanic prayers," which were to be repeated several times a day for the magic to become efficacious. These prayers consisted of poems that he had written, lyrics from love songs, passages from LaVey and other Satanic works about sex and love, and even a smattering of Emily Dickinson, whom he was studying in school. These prayers were the way he motivated himself to carry out these eight steps. The Coven provided a system of social and liturgical support for Mark; at least three sex rituals occurred during this two-week process. The sex rituals were collective encouragement — the prayers were heard by all; members supported Mark in his quest for a closer relationship with the female in question.

Through this ritual process, Mark structured his interactions with the female. He slowly progressed from being near her, to conversation, and he hoped, to a dating relationship. Slowly he gained enough confidence to approach this particular female (who was a fringe member of the group) and ask her out. By selecting a female who was at least somewhat familiar with Satanism, he further reduced his chances of romantic failure.

He reported that the ritual was a success, of a sort. The female did agree to go to the prom with him. However, he claimed to have had a miserable time. She "dressed up"; that is to say, she wore a prom dress, whereas Mark wore his typical attire, jeans and a heavy metal t-shirt. From that moment on, they seemed to have nothing in common. The date was "a motherfucking disaster." When asked to give a theological explanation for the apparent failure of his spell, Mark initially said that he had "just picked the wrong fucking broad to work it on." When he continued, "I guess she just wasn't really committed to my god. He [Satan] showed me that by getting us together, and then having her go *Christian* on me. Think she was a cheerleader or something." Neither Mark nor members in the Coven doubted their deity nor their belief system; the failure was due to inconsistent human followers. "I thought she was a true believer. But when I saw her all dressed up, I knew she wasn't. She wasn't as attractive to me then .... I had to keep asking myself *why* I had wanted to date her."

The Coven discussed this spell and its aftermath for some time, both in and out of Mark's presence. Eventually members constructed an explanation of what happened: Mark was being too "like them" (the Christians, the athletes) for even wanting to go to the prom, for wanting to date. This prom date entered into the group's folklore; five respondents told me some version of this story. In the social history of the Coven, this sex ritual concretized opposition to dyadic relationships, for they reflected all that was "bad" about the "others." From this point on, the Coven became an extended friendship network, but it did not condone dating relationships. To be dating was to be, in Alice's words, "a fucking cheerleader or at least acting like one." Thus the Coven's belief system was constructed so as to be flexible enough to allow members to view so-called "failures" as partial successes. These successes only further reinforced their Satanic, oppositional belief system.

This particular date/ritual was central to the Coven's subculture for yet another reason. It served as a "triggering event" (Fine 1982, 55) for the development of a normative style. Thereafter, the Coven standardized what was and was not acceptable clothing for its members. Whatever "the Christians," the athletes, or the cheerleaders wore was unacceptable.

## Satanic Style

The Coven recognized civil Christianity's control of the body for social purposes and explicitly rejected it. Coven members not only did not participate in the male athleticism and female presentation of self described above, they deliberately ridiculed it. Coven males laughed at the "jocks who spent time working out in a gym. This stress on athleticism robbed them, in the Coven's mind, of time for more enjoyable activities. Male members took pride in not looking athletic. Steven, tall, thin, with his hair flowing loosely about his shoulders, told me, "I don't want anyone to confuse me with *them*; I look different, I look like I want to look." For Coven males, this style entailed consistently wearing black clothing, often heavy metal t-shirts, and long hair, pulled back in a pony-tail. Ed, a clerk at the local mall who frequently interacted with Coven members, referred to the Coven's male members as "throw-backs to the sixties." During the first few months of existence, members wore black trenchcoats with the word Megadeth (the Coven's favorite heavy metal band at that time) on the back. This apparel was even more striking given that the trenchcoats were worn in weather well above seventy degrees.

Coven women, however, showed the most visible opposition to "the other way." For almost 14 months, two young women wore solid black clothing. For much of the same time, they wore black nail polish as well. However, this was not the most obvious stylistic shift. Zena, for well over a year, changed her appearance on an almost daily basis. She would dye her hair different shades; her favorites were fluorescent colors. Each day her newly colored hair would be sculpted into a unique design. Mark, who first learned of the Coven after speaking to Zena regarding her hair, explained: "To make such a drastic change everyday made the artificiality of the whole thing [appearance and presentation of self] so apparent to us. She was trying to ridicule their focus on self by overidentifying with it." However, Zena's most obvious flaunting of norms came when she settled on one particular hairstyle. She dyed her hair white, with a strip of black extending from ear to ear across the back of her head and another strip from forehead to neck. What she had created on her head was an upside down Christian cross. She quite consciously reversed symbols in an attempt to articulate her own theology. Over the next few months, this hairstyle became popular with other female members. Although not all the high school, let alone the community of Victory Village recognized the symbolism of the upside down cross, the difference in presentation of self alone, was enough to be labeled as deviant. Those who recognized her hairstyle as a symbolic expression of her belief system were quite shocked. While observing the Coven at the local shopping mall one evening, I overheard someone tell her that "God would never forgive her" for what she was proclaiming through her hairstyle.

Makeup also served to emphasize the Coven's defiance of the norms of Victory Village. Spurning makeup styles taught in fashion magazines, many female Coven members wore a very white foundation, black or dark purple eyeshadow, black blush, and either black or deep purple lipstick. Members reported that they enjoyed these colors. "The goal of makeup shouldn't be about attracting boys, but being true to oneself, being faithful to Him [Satan]." The females viewed their presentation of self as symbolic affiliation with and membership in the Truth that Satan represented. Thus

Alice, who wore not just purple blush, but for a brief time also wore a small hand-drawn Satanic pentagram near the outer corner of one eye, reported that, "I wear my makeup to say that I love Satan, just as *she* [one of the cheerleaders at the high school] wears her little gold cross to say that she is a Christian. Only hers is wrong; mine's right." Some female members admitted to "devouring [women's] magazines." They spent time learning what style (clothes, hair, makeup) was in fashion in order to reverse it. In this they were like some punk subcultures who have been studied (Fox 1987). Travers (1982) has argued that punkers "do know the ritual idiom that they violate, and in fact they know it in very fine detail because all their public life is lived in the narrow ground between normal appearances and illegal appearances (p. 281).

Many Coven members flaunted their opposition to Victory Village in yet another symbolic way. They wore jewelry that advertised their religious worldview. Some Coven females and one male would wear an upside-down Christian cross as an earring. This was an obvious inversion of Christian symbolism. However, other members chose to be more subtle, buying a set of tragedy and comedy mask stick pins. However, they would only wear the tragedy one. Even this more subtle component of their Satanic style drew comments. I witnessed two Coven females buying such pins. They first asked the clerk if the set could be broken up — they "only wanted to buy one of them." The clerk, nodding her head sympathetically, said, "I understand .... who would want to wear the depressing one, with the sad face, after all?" She seemed shocked when the members said, "We would, that's the fucking one we wanted to get." The purchase complete, the females opened their packages and threw the comedy pin away. The clerk stared after them, shaking her head and muttering about "they're trouble."

So the Coven flaunted their theological differences with the surrounding society through a new style. By changing their presentation of self, they literally embodied their change of social allegiance away from the community's standards toward those of their own making. Like punk styles before it, the Coven's style "ran counter to what the dominant culture would deem aesthetically pleasing" (Fox 1987, 349). However, style was not constructed *de novo*; the Coven appropriated style elements from Victory Village's dominant culture (Levine and Stumpf 1983). Makeup was not rejected, just makeup used as sexual enticement; religious symbolism was not repudiated, just Christian versions. The Coven practiced bricolage — the deliberate creation of, not just a Satanic style, but a Satanic self-concept from available cultural elements. Coven members believed they became powerful through their connection to the Devil.

> I can do anything when I am with my God. Doesn't matter what anybody says .... He gives me the power to do anything. I can be whatever I want to be ... no one can tell me what to do, when to do it. Let them fucking try ... He [the Devil] and I will show them who is the boss. I am.

By acquiring what they considered to be devilish power, Coven members achieved a significant goal — they reversed, in their perception, the high school's status hierarchies. They were no longer at the bottom among the "freaks," but were at the very top of the hierarchy — the Satanic chosen few. This new achieved status "worked" for them — they felt better about themselves.

Identity and self-concept are closely connected with one's social location. Both non-Satanist adolescents and the Coven used style as a way of proclaiming their social location. The difference is that one group, through its nonnormative stylistic content, proclaimed its opposition to the dominant cultural values. As their Satanic presentation of self became routinized and recognized by others for what it was, the Coven was sometimes challenged. A local video arcade was the scene of one confrontation. Five Coven members were in the arcade, surrounding a video game. Two non-Coven men (members of the junior varsity football team, according to the t-shirts they were wearing) approached the Coven and began ridiculing their Satanic appearance and faith. For a few moments, Coven members ignored the taunts. Then, after a short whispered conversation, one of the Coven men turned to the other students and said, "Leave us the fucking hell alone or else we'll fucking ...." His voice died out without completing the threat. While he was saying this, he was casually but deliberately running his finger through the upside down cross hairstyle of a female member who also was present. One of the challengers immediately took a step backward while fingering the Christian cross on his necklace. A few moments passed while each side stared intently at the other, then an employee approached the group and mumbled something akin to "We don't want trouble here." The football players left the arcade. Coven members enjoyed this exchange, often describing it and amplifying the encounter. According to members, the story typified how Satan and therefore the Coven were really the most powerful; after all, it was the *football players* who backed down after just a few moments of confrontation. Several weeks after the incident, Mark, who was present but was not the Coven spokesperson, said to me, "See, they didn't dear fight with us. Those motherfucking big guys were afraid of us .... and you ask what Satan has done for me lately?" Interactions such as this one simply reinforced the Coven's conclusion that it, and not the rest of Victory Village, was powerful and in control. In their minds, the status hierarchies had been completely reversed.

However, the stronger and more visible the Satanic style became, the stronger some in the community's concern became. Baron (1989) has noted that, "subcultures, and many of the activities that take place within them, represent 'symbolic violations of the social order' that provoke censure from the dominant culture" (p. 208). The Coven was not able to persuade Victory Village nor the high school to modify their value systems. Indeed, for some members of the community the Coven and its religious critique were considered so disturbing that they demanded social action. Victory Village mobilized to eliminate at least the outward signs of Satanism. There was talk of a high school dress code, which would prohibit visible signs of belonging to the Coven; law enforcement had, for all intents and purposes, closed off the Coven's favorite ritual site, Ghost Bridge, by patrolling it, and the local mall made it clear that, *as a group*, the Coven was not welcome inside — mall security forced them to leave for, according to a security officer, "other customers don't like them."

Despite this community hostility, their Satanic style empowered Coven members. Commitment to the style bonded the group to each other (Fox 1987) and to their new worldview. Thus the development of a Satanic style created a visible collective, though oppositional, identity for the Coven. Both the Coven and members of the community could see the visible accoutrements of Satanic commitment. Coven style norms were expressed through symbolic inversion (Lincoln 1989). It was only by changing themselves — their worldview, their bodies — that the coven could have any measure of success.

## Conclusion

Culture is transmitted to others through social interaction by parents, teachers, ministers, siblings, and peers. Christian values and norms permeated Victory Village. The statuses of churchgoer, athlete, and cheerleader were valued and rewarded. But the hegemony of this one culture invited a social critic, the Coven. However, the cultural combatants did not have equal social power.

That the Coven existed at all, in the face of so much opposition, at times seemed remarkable: "It is not the accomplishments of such projects [subculture's stated goals] per se that is of paramount importance; rather the very formation of such a group .... is itself a revolutionary action" (Lincoln 1989, 18). The Coven can illustrate the power of creating new social boundaries. Its continuation was predicted on the intense social bonding that developed within it, and on the ways in which the Satanic worldview gave meaning to members' lives. They transformed a marginal status into an achieved master status, central to their new, oppositional way of life. Lacking the material power to institute social change either in the high school's social structure or in the wider community, the Coven's critique could only operate at the symbolic level.

Analysis of the Coven shows that both the psychiatric and folklore explanations of adolescent Satanism are inadequate. These adolescents were not mentally disturbed, nor were they engaging in major criminal activity. What law-breaking they did — some underage alcohol consumption, minor vandalism of local bridges (spray-painting graffiti), and occasionally driving while intoxicated — are acts many non-Satanist teens also have committed. Nor were they experiencing "just" intergenerational rebellion against their parents. The Coven's critique went far deeper — it questioned the basic values of Victory Village — athleticism, Christianity, heterosexual dyads, and the nature of achievement, beauty, and power.

Yet the "form taken by this resistance [was] somehow *symbolic* or *magical*, in the sense of not being an actual successful solution to whatever is the problem" (Cohen

1980, ix-x). Clothing styles, haircuts, and prayer to Satan did not change the dominant culture of Victory Village. They were not meant to do so. The Coven chose these changes as its way of managing the alienation it found in the social structure of Victory Village and its educational facilities — managing it through confrontation. Oppositional subcultures thrive on conflict; they need it. It is only through confrontation with the dominant culture that their subcultures choices — moral, stylistic, sexual, aesthetic — can be constructed and routinized. Cultural belligerence was the central behavioral tactic of the Coven. It took pleasures in antagonizing Victory Village.

It is through their resistance to community norms that oppositional subcultures gain attention, albeit negative attention. Such opposition allows them to reduce their feelings of alienation or status frustration (Cohen 1955) by creating a new identity that is in contradistinction to their earlier, now rejected, socialization.

That a dominant culture reacts to an oppositional subculture's nonnormative behavior by labeling it as deviant or sick and in need of change — something the psychiatric explanation of Satanism has certainly done — may be sociologically understandable. Oppositional groups challenge the entire social system. Institutions of social control must then be utilized to maintain normative order. Thus it was not surprising, in recent years, to see American therapeutic and religious institutions as well as the mass media mobilized to prevent Satanism from spreading. Given the separation of church and state, these institutions can do little about what Taub and Nelson have called the Satanic Establishment. Such institutions were more able to mobilize themselves around claims about the deviant lifestyles of the alleged Satanic Underground, in particular as it might involve children and adolescents.

However, such claims about underground Satanic criminality, psychosis, substance abuse, and evil need to be investigated by sociologists. The central social actor in these claims — adolescents Satanists who are "out there" worshipping Satan — have been missing from both the popular and scholarly literature. By listening to their voices it can be shown that, at least for Victory Village's Coven, they were not about murder and mayhem, but social criticism. Their collective goal was not to abuse themselves nor others, but to confront a social system in which they no longer believed. Simplistic categorizations rarely capture the complexities of social life. The Coven was neither part of the Satanic Establishment nor the criminal Satanic Underground. It was an oppositional subculture that chose Satan as the symbol with which to critique its community. In its view, Satan gave members the ability to confront what they found distasteful in their community while giving them a new, important identity. Their theological and cultural inversion of Victory Village's norms was successful for them.

● ● ● ● ● ● ● ● ● ● ● ● ● ● ● ● ● ● ● ● ● ● ● ● ● ● ● ●

# Notes

1    Since 1980, there have been thirteen major talk shows about Satanism (Phil Donahue, Sally Jessy Raphael, Geraldo Rivera, and Oprah Winfrey). For an analysis of how Satanism was constructed on these talk shows, see Lowney (forthcoming).

2    Ellis argued that legend-tripping is mainly done in heterosexual dyadic pairs, not in larger social groupings. He alluded (1991b, 281) to clusters of adolescents who frequent trip sites. "A cluster that specializes in visits to 'haunted' spots may thus be termed an 'occult-oriented folk group,' since members often gather and share knowledge about other aspects of the supernatural and anomalous." But even he does not consider the possibility that adolescent Satanists are an organized social movement.

3    Certainly there are differences between the Coven and the subcultures discussed in these references, the primary one being social class: the Coven consisted almost entirely of middle- and upper-middle-class youths. Nevertheless, there are more similarities than differences.

4    My college's Human Subjects Committee and I communicated in writing about this research several times and met once. This research raised numerous ethical questions. I felt that I might be harming my potential research subjects if I contacted parents who were not aware of their children's activities and asked permission to interview their children about Satanism. Conversely, I felt uneasy contacting parents and obtaining informed consent to ask about "religion in general" when I knew I was interested in only Satanism. The committee for its part, struggled with statutes that did not adequately cover participant observation research. We reached a compromise position: it would be best if I did not interview teenager Satanists unless they had already told their parents about their involvement. I was permitted to obtain birthdate information from potential sources and often followed up with a contact when the person was no longer a minor. For this same reason, I have not collected data at Coven meetings, nor on the grounds of the high schools, because minors often were present. Some data were undoubtedly lost by operating under this compromise, however it provided the only opportunity for the research to continue.

5    Three other times underage members or ex-member showed up to talk with me. For ethical reasons I did not talk to these young adults.

6    For a detailed account of life in another "football town" that has many parallels with Victory Village, see Bissinger (1990). Gaines' (1990) analysis of Bergenfield, New Jersey also noted the linkage between football, social status, and religion.

7    His conversion seems to exemplify the Lofland-Stark model (1965) with two exceptions. Mark was uneasy saying that he was at a "turning point" in his life — he felt that he had always been different — and that high school was no worse, but also no better than previous times in his life. He also had a difficult time sorting out whether extracult attachments had been cut off *before* meeting the group or *after* cult bonds had been formed. On further reflection, Mark could not clearly state that he had *had* any bonds to anyone in the high school prior to joining this group.

8    Following LaVey (1969), the Coven used this term for its ritual meeting time.

9    Again, Ellis's analysis is correct, as far as it goes. Some of these bridges were local legend sites. However, Coven rituals were not connected to these legends.

10    LaVey (1969) has spoken of holding rituals between the four elements of air, water, fire, and earth. Clearly, a bridge meets that criterion.

11    Most law enforcement officers did not feel that the Coven "caused trouble." Their regulation of Coven activities was low-key and mostly focused on underage drinking and driving, spraypainting of graffiti, and bonfires not well doused. Local officers did not "handle" the Coven differently from other teens in the community. This approach was in stark contrast to other jurisdictions present at the Occult Crime

workshop I attended. In large measure the Victory Village law enforcement response was led by the sheriff and city police chief, who tried to prevent rumors from spreading.

12  The Coven might have been seen by some outsiders to be a heavy metal subculture. It was only in discussing the religious inversions that it became apparent how important the Satanic theology was in the subculture. It was the latter that set the Coven apart from heavy metal subcultures. See Gross (1990) for a profile of heavy metal subcultures.

13  For instance, this was the first Coven term I encountered during the research. They kept mentioning it, but it took almost a year before such a ritual was explained to me.

# References

Alfred, R.H.
1976    The church of Satan. In *The new religious consciousness*, edited by C.Y. Glock and R.N. Bellah, 180-202. Berkeley: University of California Press.

Bainbridge, W.S.
1978    *Satan's power: A deviant psychotherapy cult*. Berkeley: University of California Press.

Baron, S.W.
1989    Resistance and its consequences: The street culture of punks. *Youth & Society* 21:207-37.

Belitz, J. and A. Schacht
1992    Satanism as a response to abuse: The dynamics and treatment of Satanic Involvement in male youths. *Adolescence* 27:855-72.

Bissinger, H.G.
1990    *Friday night lights: A town, a team, and a dream*. Reading, MA: Addison-Wesley.

Bourget, D., A. Gagnon, and J.M.W. Bradford
1988    Satanism in a psychiatric adolescent population. *Canadian Journal of Psychiatry* 33:197-202.

Brake, M.
1974    The skinheads: An English working class subculture. *Youth & Society* 6:179-200.
1980    *The sociology of youth culture and youth subcultures*. London: Routledge & Kegan Paul.

Cohen, A.
1955    *Delinquent boys*. Glencoe, IL: Free Press.

Cohen, S.
1980    *Folk devils and moral panics: The creation of the mods and rockers*, 2d ed. New York: St. Martin.

Crouch, B.M. and K.R. Damphousse
1992    Newspapers and the antisatanism movement: A content analysis. *Sociological Spectrum* 12:1-20.

Ellis, B.
1982-3   Legend-tripping in Ohio: A behavioral survey. *Papers in Comparative Studies* 2:61-73.
1991a    Flying saucers from Hell: Alien abductions and Satanic cult abductions. *Magonia* 40:12-6.
1991b    Legend-trips and Satanism: Adolescents' ostensive traditions as cult' activity. In *The Satanism scare*, edited by J.T. Richardson, J. Best, and D.G. Bromley, 279-95. New York: Aldine de Gruyter.

Fine, G.A.
    1982        The Manson family: The folklore traditions of a small group. *Journal of the Folklore Institute* 19:47-60.
    1987        *With the boys: Little league baseball and preadolescent culture.* Chicago: University of Chicago Press.

Fine, G.A., and S. Kleinman
    1979        Rethinking subculture: An interactional analysis. *American Journal of Sociology* 85:1-20.

Forsyth, C.J., and M.D. Olivier
    1990        The theoretical framing of a social problem: Some conceptual notes on Satanic cults. *Deviant Behavior* 11:281-92.

Fox, K.J.
    1987        Real punks and pretenders: The social organization of a counterculture. *Journal of Contemporary Ethnography* 16:344-70.

Gaines, D.
    1990        *Teenage wasteland: Suburbia's dead end kids.* New York: Harper-Collins.

Gross, R.L.
    1990        Heavy metal music: A new subculture in American society. *Journal of Popular Culture* 24:119-30.

Hebdige, D.
    1979        *Subculture: The meaning of style.* London: Methuen & Company.

Hicks, R.
    1991a       In pursuit of Satan: The police and the occult. Buffalo, NY: Prometheus.
    1991b       The police model of Satanic crime. In *The Satanism scare*, edited by J.T. Richardson, J. Best, and D.G. Bromley, 175-89. New York: Aldine de Gruyter.

Larson, B.
    1989        *Satanism, the seduction of America's youth.* Nashville: Thomas Nelson.

LaVey, A.S.
    1969        *The Satanic bible.* New York: Avon.

Levine, H.G., and S.H. Stumpf
    1983        Statements of fear through cultural symbols: Punk rock as reflective subculture. *Youth & Society* 14:417-35.

Lincoln, B.
    1989        *Discourse and the construction of society: Comparative studies of myth, ritual, and classification.* New York: Oxford.

Lippert, R.
    1990        The construction of Satanism as a social problem in Canada. *Canadian Journal of Sociology* 15:417-39.

Lofland, J., and R. Stark
    1965        Becoming a world saver: A theory of conversion to a deviant perspective. *American Sociological Review* 30:863-974.

Lowney, K.
    Forthcoming        Speak of the devil: Talk shows and the social construction of Satanism. In *Perspectives on Social Problems*, volume 6, edited by J. A. Holstein and G. Miller. Greenwich, CT:JAI.

Moody, E.J.
    1974        Magical therapy: An anthropological investigation of contemporary Satanism. In *Religious movements in contemporary America*, edited by I.I. Zarctsky and M.P. Leone, 355-82. Princeton, NJ: Princeton University Press.

Moriarty, A.R., and D.W. Story
    1990        Psychological dynamics of adolescent Satanism. *Journal of Mental Health Counseling* 12:186-98.

*The Necronomicon*
    1980        Edited with an Introduction by Simon. New York: Avon.

Prinsky, L.E., and J.L. Rosenbaum
    1987        Leer-ics or lyrics: Teenage impressions of rock 'n' roll. *Youth & Society* 18:384-97.

Richardson, J.T, J. Best, and D.G. Bromley, eds.
    1991a       *The Satanism scare*. New York: Aldine de Gruyter.

Richardson, J.T., J Best, and D.G. Bromley
    1991b       Satanism as a social problem. In *The Satanism scare*, edited by J.T. Richardson, J. Best, and D.G. Bromley, 3-17. New York: Aldine de Gruyter.

Rudin, Marcia
    1990        Cults and Satanism: Threats to teens. *NAASP Bulletin* 74:46-52.

Speitz, A.M.
    1990        Treating adolescent Satanism in art therapy. *The Arts in Psychotherapy* 17:147-55.

Stratford, L.
    [1987] 1991           *Satan's underground: The extraordinary story of one woman's escape*. Gretna, LA: Pelican.

Sleck, G.M., S.A. Anderson, and W.M. Boylin
    1992        Satanism among adolescents: Empirical and clinical considerations. *Adolescents* 27:904-14.

Taub, D., and L.D. Nelson
    1993        Satanism in contemporary America: Establishment or underground. *Sociological Quarterly* 34:523-41.

Tennant-Clark, C.M., J.J. Fritz, and F. Beauvais
    1989        Occult participation: Its impact on adolescent development. *Adolescence* 24:757-72.

Travers, A.
    1982        Ritual power in interaction. *Symbolic Interaction* 5:277-86.

Victor, J.
    1989        A rumor-panic about a dangerous Satanic cult in western New York. *New York Folklore* 15:23-49.
    1991        The dynamics of rumor-panics about Satanic cults. In *The Satanism scare*, edited by J.T. Richardson, J. Best, and D.G. Bromley, 221-36. New York: Aldine de Gruyter.

Warnke, Mike
    1972        *The Satan seller*. Plainfield, NJ: Logos International.

Wheeler, B.R., S. Wood, R.J. Hatch
    1988        Assessment and intervention with adolescents involved in Satanism. *Social Work* 33:547-50.

# VIOLENCE AND NEW RELIGIOUS MOVEMENTS

## Introduction to the Readings

For many people talk of NRMs calls to mind rather graphic and disturbing images of the Branch Davidian compound burning in Waco, Texas, or of hundreds of bloated bodies turned face down in the mud, the victims of mass suicide, in Jonestown, Guyana. But these events of 1993 and 1978 are exceptional, given the large number of marginal religious groups in existence the world over. In recent years, of course, there have been other spectacular instances of "cult-related" violence: the murder suicides of members of the Solar Temple in Quebec, Switzerland, and France (in October, 1994 and December, 1995), and the Aum Shinrikyo subway poisonings in Tokyo (May, 1995). Most of the violence associated with "cults," however, is of a more mundane variety, both in kind and frequency. Groups like the Black Muslims, Synanon, Hare Krishna, Scientology, The House of Judah, The Children of God, and various fringe

Mormon and Christian fundamentalist groups have made their way into the news as a result of accusations and incidents of assault, murder, resistance to civil authorities, issuing death threats, harassing opponents or defectors, stock-piling arms, and abusing or molesting children. Relative, however, to the levels of crime present in our societies and the increased frequency with which some of these charges have also been levelled at more conventional religions (e.g., the many charges of child molestation levelled against members of the Catholic Church), these incidents are unexceptional. When a Methodist breaks the law, it must be remembered, his or her religious affiliation is rarely considered newsworthy. Such is not the case for members of marginal religions, who almost always have their "cult" affiliations identified or even emphasized, regardless the relevance of such affiliations to the crimes supposedly committed. Media reports of cult-related violence tend to be sensationalistic, mixing exaggeration with guess work. Further, all accusations of such behaviour become grist for the propaganda mills of the anti-cult movement (Melton, 1992).

This said, we are still left with the daunting and important task of trying to better comprehend how and why incidents like the Jonestown and Waco massacres occur. We now know much more about the factual record of these events as the instant analysis of journalists has given way to more scholarly research (e.g., Chidester, 1988; Wright, 1995). In the case of the Branch Davidians, the research should give us cause for concern about the capacity of American law enforcement officials to cope with incidences of religiously related violence. In the first reading in this section, Thomas Robbins and Dick Anthony, two of the most prolific students of NRMs, point out a crucial difference between the tragedies of Jonestown and Waco: in Waco, unlike Jonestown, exogenous factors, namely the mistaken assumptions, decisions, and actions of the agents of the Bureau of Alcohol, Tobacco, and Firearms (BATF) and of the Federal Bureau of Investigation (FBI), were instrumental in precipitating the loss of 80 lives, including many innocent children (see the other essays in Wright, 1995). In the case of Jonestown, and one assumes a group like the Solar Temple, endogenous variables, features of the religious life of the groups themselves, largely account for the resulting violence. Of course, similar endogenous factors played some role in Waco as well and, as Robbins and Anthony warn, each case of violence must be examined in terms of a unique conjunction of several endogenous and exogenous variables.

Seeking to derive some generalizable insights from our experiences, Robbins and Anthony discuss the role of three interrelated endogenous factors that appear to be common to most contemporary incidences of religiously inspired mass violence: (1) group commitment to an apocalyptic belief system, (2) a heavy investment in charismatic styles of leadership, and (3) processes of social encapsulation leading to heightened boundary tensions with the surrounding society. The presence of all three of these elements can make for a volatile mix, readily susceptible to combustion in the presence of some perceived or real external threat. The value of these insights are independently demonstrated, with reference to the mass-suicide of 917 followers of the Peoples Temple at Jonestown, in the other two readings in this section, John Hall's "The

Apocalypse at Jonestown" and Edgar Mills' "Cult Extremism: The Reduction of Normative Dissonance." These accounts provide a rich descriptive context for scrutinizing how a particular NRM was led into violence, and they add nuances to the links hypothesized by Robbins and Anthony.

Hall provides an excellent and balanced overview of the history of Jim Jones, the leader of the Peoples Temple, and Jonestown, his socialist/religious experiment in the jungles of South America. It is must be realized, Hall argues, that in belief and practice there is little to differentiate the Peoples Temple from other kinds of "other-worldly sects," both those revered (like the Puritans that help found America), and those reviled yet tolerated (like the Jehovah's Witnesses). Viewed objectively, many of the core features of Jonestown, so abhorred after the fact, are part of the "stock-in-trade" of deeply committed religious groups throughout the ages (e g , the absolute theocratic authority of Jim Jones, the use of mortification and other techniques of social control, the demanding regimen of everyday life, and even the persecution complex of Jim Jones and his followers). To understand the bizarre turn of events at Jonestown, Hall argues, we must further understand the idiosyncratic impact of the ideologies of racial integration and protocommunism promoted by Jim Jones, along with certain of his personal fears and strategic failings. Until near the end, Hall's analysis suggests, there need not have been a final "white night" of true death in Jonestown.

Mills' essay demonstrates, once again, how common forms of social psychological theorizing can be used to improve our grasp of even extraordinary religious events like the tragedy at Jonestown. Paradoxically, he argues, much that NRMs must do to maintain their corporate integrity in a hostile environment inevitably increases the likelihood of violence within these groups, and thus between them and the very civil authorities they wish to avoid. The interpretive key, he suggests, is the "reduction of normative dissonance." The generation of ever greater consensus and conformity in NRMs, a mark of their "religious" success, ironically serves to destabilize these groups by interfering with the natural contrast of opinions that tempers the decisions and actions of all groups. It induces, that is, what social psychologists have called a "shift to risk" — a willingness for the group to act more immoderately than any of its members would as individuals. In the wrong circumstances this process can prove lethal. Such certainly proved to be the case at Waco, where it would appear that the BATF and the FBI, as much as the Branch Davidians, succumbed to this same deleterious process.

● ● ● ● ● ● ● ● ● ● ● ● ● ● ● ● ● ● ● ● ● ● ● ● ● ●

# References

Chidester, David
    1988      *Salvation and Suicide: An Interpretation of Jim Jones, the Peoples Temple, and Jonestown.*
              Bloomington, IN: Indiana University Press.

Melton, J. Gordon
    1992      "Violence and the Cults." Pp. 361-393 in J.G. Melton, *Encyclopedic Handbook of Cults in*
              *America.* Revised and Updated Edition. New York: Garland.

Wright, Stuart A., ed.
    1995      *Armageddon in Waco: Critical Perspectives on the Branch Davidian Conflict.* Chicago:
              University of Chicago Press.

# CHAPTER SIXTEEN

# SECTS AND VIOLENCE: FACTORS ENHANCING THE VOLATILITY OF MARGINAL RELIGIOUS MOVEMENTS

## THOMAS ROBBINS and DICK ANTHONY

In the aftermath of the fiery deaths of the Branch Davidians in Texas, the issue of violence in marginal religious ("cults") has been highlighted in popular consciousness.[1] While spectacular mass violence such as exploded in Jonestown, Guyana, and more recently in Waco, Texas, is very rare, smaller-scale instances of deadly violence have been associated with a variety of groups in recent decades. The Manson Family, Synanon, Hare Krishna, the Lundgren group, the House of Judah, several polygamous "fringe Mormon" groups, the Bhagawan movement of Sri Rajneesh, the Order of the Solar Temple, and the followers of Lindberg "Black Jesus" Sanders are just some of the other religious groups which have experienced violent episodes and whose leaders have been accused of wrongdoing in this connection. This chapter explores the factors that operate to enhance the volatility of relatively new or marginal religious groups.

Why are marginal or noninstitutionalized religious movements more volatile or potentially violent than institutionalized churches (assuming the validity of the premise)? What factors determine how much physical danger a group may pose to its members or others? There are indeed so many factors that may be identified as bearing upon these issues that the initial aim of this paper is simply to group, list, and briefly explore these factors.

We may initially list the factors pertinent to our inquiry under two headings: *exogenous* and *endogenous* factors. The former include factors related to the hostility, stigmatization, and persecution that "religious outsiders" often receive at the hands of

Thomas Robbins and Dick Anthony, "Sects and Violence: Factors Enhancing the Volatility of Marginal Religious Movements," in Stuart Wright, ed., *Armageddon in Waco*. Chicago: University of Chicago Press, 1995, pp. 236-259. Copyright © 1995 the University of Chicago Press. Reprinted by permission of the University of Chicago Press.

forces in the social environment in which they operate. The latter category denotes properties of a movement: its leadership, beliefs, rituals, and organization. Exogenous and endogenous variables are interrelated (Richardson 1985); indeed, the separation and mutual autonomy of these factors may ultimately seem illusory.[2] Nevertheless, in this paper we will focus primarily on the endogenous conditions and processes within religious movements which appear to enhance volatility and the potential for violence. We note, however, the importance of exogenous factors, which Melton (1985) emphasizes: "Given the high level of tension with society under which some nonconventional groups have been forced to operate, it is not surprising that the violent tendencies of some cult leaders have emerged" (p. 57). Violence generally erupts "only after a period of heightened conflict" in which "both sides" have contributed to escalation (p. 58).

It is worth noting, however, that the relative weight or significance of the contribution of exogenous and endogenous factors may vary from one situated event to another. Thus to elicit a fatal violent response from Jim Jones's Peoples Temple required only that a congressman and a press entourage visit Jonestown and attempt to return to the United States with a handful of defectors. In contrast, to set off the immolations in Waco (assuming that the Davidians were responsible for setting the fire), what had to transpire was not only the initial military-style raid on the "cult compound" by the Bureau of Alcohol, Tobacco, and Firearms (BATF) but also the subsequent breaking down of the walls of the compound by armored vehicles and the insertion of CS gas. It may therefore be a viable thesis that the role or weight of exogenous factors was smaller at Jonestown compared to Waco. Or to put it another way, the Branch Davidian community at Waco was less internally volatile or violence-prone than the Peoples Temple settlement in Guyana.

Unfortunately, evaluation of the relative salience of exogenous and endogenous contributions to particular explosive events are highly controversial and sometimes elicit accusations of "blaming the victim." Resolving these issues is beyond the scope of the present survey, which will try to identify and group the most salient characteristics of movements which often operate to enhance volatility and the likelihood of violence. It should be noted that no factor discussed below produces violence automatically or autonomously. The eruption of violence generally reflects the interaction of several endogenous conditions with exogenous variables.

Pertinent endogenous factors may be tentatively grouped under three headings: (1) factors related to the consequences of *apocalyptic* beliefs and fervent millennial expectations; (2) factors related to the nature and characteristic volatility of *charismatic* leadership, and (3) residual factors that are more loosely interrelated but that might be viewed as relating to the significance of some social movements as communal-ideological *systems* with "boundaries" and systemic problems that may be given different priorities by different groups and leaders, who may attempt to resolve them in different ways. These headings do not denote single variables, but ensembles of variables. As with the distinction between endogenous and exogenous factors, the autonomy or separate identity of these groups of variables is ultimately illusory. "Charismatic," "apocalyptic," and "communal-systemic" factors are often closely interrelated; moreover, the same condition or pattern may sometimes be classified under more than one heading.

This survey is written from a sociological perspective. Factors related to the alleged phenomenon of "mind control," to the degree to which they have any validity, may entail some of the conditions and patterns that will be discussed under the headings delineated above. On the other hand, a partly autonomous and pertinent realm of factors may entail the predispositions and personality patterns of persons who are attracted to movements or ideologies of a certain kind, that is, militant, authoritarian, apocalyptic, or charismatically led (Anthony and Robbins 1994; Jones 1989), although we cannot devote much space here to a discussion of individual psychodynamics. We will deal first with the impact of apocalyptic beliefs.

## Apocalypticism

Apocalyptic belief systems and millennial visions of the imminent "last days" or "end times" appear to characterize almost all violent religious sects. Such notions certainly characterized the Branch Davidians at Waco led by David Koresh. Originally a Seventh Day Adventist, Vernon Howell (David Koresh) was initially captivated by the grim apocalyptic message of the church-sponsored revivalist "Revelation Seminars" featuring "dramatic, even frightening images in a multimedia portrayal of Armageddon" (McGee and Clairborne 1993, 10) conducted by evangelist Jim Gilley. In the Branch Davidians, Howell found a special attention and emphasis given to the culmination of the end time, mystically represented in the seven seals, which could be opened only by a new prophet (see Tabor, this volume).

Jim Jones, prophet-leader of the ill-fated Peoples Temple, also developed a complex apocalyptic vision that was drawn from several sources. "With elements of socialism, messianism, and biblical prophecy, Jones crafted a worldview that made an impending apocalypse plausible." Jones "used biblical imagery to persuade his followers that they were on a divine pilgrimage through a wasteland to paradise" (Jones 1989, 212).

Distinctly apocalyptic and millennial worldviews have characterized a number of religious groups that have experienced violent altercations with outsiders, including the early Mormons (Boyer 1992, 1993), early Anabaptists and radical Reformation Protestants (Boyer 1992, 1993; Cohn 1961; Palmer 1994), and groups involved in pre-Jonestown episodes of mass/collective suicide such as the Old Believers in early modern Russia who immolated themselves (Cherniavsky 1970; Crummey 1970; Robbins 1986) or the violent Circumcellion fringe of the Donatist "Church of Martyrs" in late antiquity in North Africa (Frend 1950; Knox 1950; Robbins 1989).[3]

What is it about apocalyptic beliefs that may encourage volatility and enhance the likelihood of violence? The perceived imminence of the last days may be expected to relativize conventional norms and rules. Received arrangements are seen to be doomed! Apocalyptic visions thus have inherent antinomian implications. More specifically, apocalyptic movements often anticipate that an environing climate of violence will pervade the last days and that, in particular, persecutory violence will be directed against "The Saints" or "The Elect," that is, against the spiritual vanguard that the movement represents. The latter must therefore prepare themselves to defend their enclave, to survive to inherit the world. A defensive survivalist orientation may crystallize.

This was certainly the view of David Koresh, who frequently quoted the second Psalm, "The Kings of the Earth set themselves, and the rulers take counsel against the Lord and against His Anointed" (quoted in Boyer 1993, 30). Koresh clearly anticipated a government assault, and the actual military-style raid that the BATF perpetrated against the Waco Davidian settlement in late February 1993 "seemed to those inside to validate at least part of Koresh's prophecy. The Branch Davidians and their leader began preparing for the end" (McGee and Clairborne 1993, 11). After the shoot-out began, Koresh may well have wished to find a peaceful resolution to the confrontation. He was probably inhibited from surrendering to the BATF not only because his power would then be destroyed but also because his apocalyptic vision would be compromised if the confrontation ended "not with a bang but with a whimper."

Anticipation of ruthless persecution tends to be encouraged by beliefs that assign to the apocalyptic group a special sanctity and a special key role in the unfolding of end times or in the birth of a new order. Such beliefs, however, do not necessarily follow from a commitment to an apocalyptic scenario (Sharot 1982).

Perhaps what renders apocalyptic spirituality potentially explosive is that it is often linked to something broader and deeper to which we may apply Ronald Knox's terms "enthusiasm" or "ultra-supernaturalism" (Knox 1950). The enthusiast "expects more evident results from the grace of God than we others." Faith must fully transform devotees, who are therefore set apart from ordinary folks and live on a higher plane. The enthusiast prophet "insists that members of his society (movement), saved members of a perishing world, should live a life of angelic purity, of apostolic simplicity" (Knox 1950, 2); although in practice what has historically resulted from this orientation is "strange oscillations of rigorism and antinomianism," as emancipation from conventional rules validates the speciality of the Elect.

Enthusiasm, according to Knox, implies "a different Theology of Grace" whereby the "traditional doctrine" that "grace perfects nature" is supplanted by the idea that "grace has destroyed nature and replaced it. The saved man has come out into a new order of being, with a new set of faculties appropriate to his state; David must not wear the panoply of Saul" (Knox 1950, 2). Enthusiasts need not be violent — indeed religious enthusiasm can motivate pacifism, as in early Quakerism; however, an antinomian volatility can sometimes proceed from the phenomenological condition of

God's Elect, who, "although they must perforce live cheek by jowl with the sons of perdition, *claim another citizenship and own another allegiance*" (Knox 1950, 2, our emphasis). When true religious enthusiasts submit themselves to public law and authority, which they may often readily do, it is "always under protest."

> Worldly governments, being of purely human institution, have no real mandate to exercise authority, and sinful folk have no real rights, although out of courtesy their fancied rights must be respected. Always the enthusiast hankers after a theocracy in which the anomalies of the present situation will be done away, and the righteous bear rule openly. Disappointed of this hope, a group of sectaries will sometimes go out into the wilderness and set up a little theocracy of their own, like Cato's senate at Utica. The American continent has more than once been the scene of such an adventure, in these days, it is the last refuge of the enthusiast (Knox 1950, 3).[4]

Clearly, apocalypticism or apocalyptic enthusiasm is not inexorably violent. Indeed, apocalypticism is somewhat like religion writ large; it reflects and hypostatizes the moral duality of religion, which can bind persons together and uplift them but can also provoke paranoid anxieties and fierce antipathy toward the dehumanization of the ungodly. Apocalyptic images of the future may often impart a particular volatile quality to a group. However, throughout history such volatile apocalypticism has often been elicited or intensified by the exogenous factor of *persecution*. Consider, for example, the violent Anabaptist chiliasm of the early sixteenth century which culminated in the seizure of Munster (or "New Jerusalem") by apocalyptic visionaries who eventually came to be led by Jon Bockelson, "a monomaniacal young tailor who, like David Koresh, anointed himself Messiah, imposed his absolute rule with the aid of loyal lieutenants and demanded free access to his female followers" (Boyer 1993, 30). Bockelson's followers "saw Munster as the birthplace of Christ's new world order as foretold in the final chapter of the Book of Revelation" (Boyer 1993, 30). Yet, as Norman Cohn (1961, 274) notes, "most Anabaptists were peaceful folk who in practice were quite willing, except in matters of conscience and belief, to respect the authority of the state." Yet, "even the most peaceful Anabaptists were ferociously persecuted and many thousands were killed." Anabaptist hostility to the state was thereby reinforced. Anabaptists "interpreted their sufferings in apocalyptic terms as the great onslaught of Satan and Antichrist against the Saints, as those 'messianic woes' that were to usher in the Millennium" (Cohn 1961, 275). In this context Anabaptists became obsessed by an expected "Day of Reckoning" when the mighty would be overthrown by the faithful and Christ would return to establish the millennium and place the sword of retribution in the hands of the rebaptized and purified saints. Thus, alongside the persisting "tradition of peaceful and austere dissent" there emerged a new expression of "an equally ancient tradition of militant chiliasm" (Cohn 1961, 275).[5]

The exogenous factor of persecution is only one limiting condition on any explanation of religious violence and sectarian volatility in terms of apocalyptic worldviews. Consideration must also be given to the fact that apocalyptic beliefs are increasingly common, and only a tiny minority of groups and movements expressing such ideologies appear to have violent proclivities or to pose a threat to civil peace. David Koresh may have engaged in deviant practices, "But his alienation and core doctrines are shared by millions of Americans, perhaps even a majority.....the general contours of Koresh's beliefs were neither unique nor particularly unusual" (Boyer 1993, 30). Churches that embrace prophetic, millennial doctrines are presently experiencing rapid growth in the United States, where such currents have always run powerfully (Boyer 1992, 1993).

Are some varieties of apocalypticism more associated with violence and volatility than other varieties? We have already discussed "enthusiasm," as delineated by Ronald Knox (1950), however, it is clear that most apocalyptic religious enthusiasts are fairly peaceful. Some writers have identified "exemplary dualism" as an apocalyptic mystique that is particularly volatile (Anthony and Robbins 1978; Jones 1989). "Exemplary dualism" denotes an apocalyptic orientation in which contemporary sociopolitical or socioreligious forces are viewed as exemplifying absolute contrast categories in terms not only of moral virtue but also of eschatology and the millennial destiny of humankind. An example of such a worldview is the old Protestant millennial identification of the papacy with Antichrist and the "Whore of Babylon." Exemplary dualism detranscendentalizes apocalypticism. It confers ultimacy or contemporary religiopolitical conflicts that are seen to have cosmic significance. The present authors originally developed this concept in an analysis of the ideology of the Unification Church (Anthony and Robbins 1978) and it has been subsequently applied to Jim Jones and the Peoples Temple by Jones (1989), a seminar student of Anthony. In Jim Jones's worldview:

> Themes of destruction, redemption, flight and salvation taken from the book of Isaiah were used to justify a prophecy of the destruction of the fattened nations and escape of the righteous into a new nation... the United States, its institutions and even its standards of beauty were portrayed as the "beast" — totally irredeemable — to be overcome by the "redeeming remnant." Well-versed in both doctrinal and operational aspects of the conflict of opposing forces of absolute good and evil, members of the Peoples Temple were prepared for sacrifice, struggle and an apocalyptic "final showdown" (Jones 1989, 212).

Exemplary dualism is volatile because it confers deep eschatological significance on the social and political conflicts of the day, thereby raising the stakes of victory or defeat in immediate worldly struggles. Thus communism, radical feminism, the papacy, and exotic cults have all been identified by some Protestant millenarians with the biblical Beast or the "Whore of Babylon." Yet there are surely many more groups with an exemplary-dualist worldview that there are violent or highly volatile movements. Indeed, the arguably exemplary-dualist Unification Church, though labeled a "destructive cult" by anticult crusaders, has not been shown to be violent or volatile.

As John Hall (1989, 1990) observes, the Peoples Temple community at Jonestown represented the type of the "other-worldly apocalyptic sect." Such groups, "typically founded by charismatic leaders, establish a radical separation between themselves and the established social world, which they regard as hopelessly evil" (Hall 1989, 78). Yet as Hall (1990) notes in an analysis of the Jonestown tragedy, there have been many more world-rejecting apocalyptic sects than there have been violent (and particularly suicidal) movements. According to Hall, most apocalyptic sects conceptually situate themselves "on the other side of the apocalypse" in the sense that they define themselves as inexorably "saved" — the corrupt world will be destroyed but they will survive by God's grace — and thus they are safe and cannot be hurt by the hostility of outsiders; they need not anticipate or prepare for violent conflict. A different kind of apocalyptic sect, however, a "warring sect," prosecutes a holy war "to vanquish the infidels from dominion over a world where they exercise their evil ways" (Hall 1989, 78). Jim Jones's problem was that under his leadership the Peoples Temple was unable to opt clearly for either pattern. The relocation to Guyana (from California) was a retreatist tactic and an attempt to insulate the group from outside pressure. But this strategy was undercut by Jones's emphasis (somewhat similar to that of David Koresh) on the inescapability of conflict with an overpowering and relentless enemy. Although probably functional in terms of sustaining internal solidarity and control, Jones's paranoid themes undercut the insulated sanctuary conception that many world-rejecting sects construct and which enable them to condemn the surrounding society as hopelessly corrupt while making a partial de facto accommodation with the society. "Jones vacillated between an ethic of confrontation and an ethic of sanctuary" (Hall 1987, 298). Mass suicide, conceived as a vehicle for what Robert Lifton has called "revolutionary immortality," finally united "the divergent public threads of meaningful existence at Jonestown — those of political revolution and religious salvation" (Hall 1987, 300).

In an analysis of the Bishop Hill community, whose volatile charismatic leader, Eric Jansen, was murdered in 1850, Hall notes that his ideal typical conceptions of two different kinds of apocalyptic movements are often conflated in practice, "especially when believers who want to 'flee' this world find themselves embroiled in conflict with their own detractors" (Hall 1989, 78). Thus, as Hall emphasizes, the key to apocalyptic violence and suicide ultimately lies in the dynamics of tension between an apocalyptic community and an external political order. An apocalyptic sect may demonize the external order. The escalation of external pressure "thus forces a choice between the sacred and evil," which becomes "a question of honor, and it is the seedbed of martyrdom" (Hall 1987, 296).

It is possible to speculate as to what variety of apocalyptic or millenarian orientation is most conducive to volatility and violence.[6] It would appear, however, that millenarian-apocalyptic worldviews are most likely to be associated with volatility and violence when they are embodied in charismatic "messianic" leaders who identify the millennial destiny of humankind with their own personal vicissitudes and demonize any opposition to their aspirations and personal aggrandizement. "Koresh, of course, identified *himself* as the Lord's anointed and saw the standoff at Waco as the literal fulfillment of an intensifying campaign by demonic earthly rulers to destroy the righteous remnant" (Boyer 1993, 30, emphasis in original). To the volatility and destructive potential associated with fervent apocalyptic-millenarian expectations is added the volatility and instability associated with charismatic, messianic leadership. It is to the latter issue that we now turn.

## Charismatic Leadership

Charismatic authority is a factor (or embodies a number of conditions) that may affect the volatility and violent potential of religious movements. The importance of this factor probably exceeds that of apocalypticism. Charismatic authority is really a hallmark, almost by definition, of noninstitutionalized movements that therefore partake of whatever instability or volatility is associated with charismatic leadership. Apocalyptic beliefs, on the other hand, characterize many relatively institutionalized churches with stable bureaucratic structures with little destructive potential. Apocalyptic, even millenian, beliefs are not unique to marginal or noninstitutionalized churches or movements, the Seventh-Day Adventist Church and various fundamentalist churches are examples of stable organizations that adhere to apocalyptic (e.g., premillennial) expectations.

Nevertheless, despite the existence of institutionalized churches with doctrinal commitments to apocalyptic visions, there may be a sense in which charismatic leaders and apocalyptic scenarios fit together. Prophecies presuppose prophets, and apocalyptic beliefs are often associated with "world-rejecting" sects whose stance of total rejection of, or opposition to, the broader environing society requires the legitimization of a revered charismatic prophet with a compelling vision (Wallis 1984: Wallis and Bruce 1986a). Institutionalized or institutionalizing apocalyptic movements that are becoming more accommodating to conventional society appear to be prone to defections by volatile followers who become attracted to new and frequently schismatic prophets proclaiming new messages entailing new and nonaccommodative extrapolations of the original millenarian vision. Nonaccommodative apocalyptic sects often experience continual schisms entailing conflicts between competing leaders with differing extrapolations of an original vision. "Offbeat sects are composed of people who are fearful about the future, who hope that by placing their faith in some charismatic leader they will eradicate the past and protect their lives against unknown and unseen dangers" (Fogary 1993, 486).

Ultimately the volatility of movements with charismatic leaderships is related to the intrinsic volatility or *precariousness* of charismatic authority (Wallis 1984; Wallis and Bruce 1986a), which lacks institutional supports. As Wallis (1993, 176) notes, "Charismatic leadership is a fundamentally precarious status." This is largely because the charismatic leaders' claim to authority "rests purely on subjective factors. The 'gift of grace' may evaporate in the eyes of the claimant or his followers in the face of failure." In this connection Johnson (1979) has published a perceptive analysis of how steps that Jim Jones took in response to threats to his charismatic authority created new situations with elements that potentially undercut his authority, which in turn required new responses such that Jones and his community became locked into a spiraling process of increasing authoritarianism, anxiety, and volatility.

The responses that charismatic leaders make to perceived threats to their authority will often tend to embellish this authority and extrapolate it in an increasingly authoritarian and absolutist direction. "Jim Jones required frequent tests of faith and commitment from his core followers: signing false confessions, suffering public humiliation, drinking unidentified fluids and then restraining expressions of fear or hysteria on being told they were being poisoned" (Wallis 1984, 117). Ofshe (1980) describes various dramatic and traumatic devices (e.g., male vasectomies, abortions, recoupling of sexual dyads) whereby Chuck Dederich and the leadership of Synanon was able "to force out members who were a potential threat to the stability of the power structure" or had less intense commitment (p. 125; see also Wallis 1984, 117). In this way the followers of a charismatic leader may be directly or indirectly prepared for future violence as the leader consolidates a disciplined cadre of devotees who have shed their inhibitions against taking extreme actions in behalf of the prophet's vision.

The evolution of charismatic leadership too often operates to embellish or intensify a basic definitional quality of charismatic leadership: the absence of accountability and of inhibitions on the impulsivity and freedom of the leader. This inhibition of restraint is the other side of the precariousness of charismatic authority, that is, both institutional *restraints* and institutional *supports* are lacking. Both characteristics increase group volatility. Lacking both immediate restraints and long-term supports, a charismatic leader will be tempted to use his authority to try to simplify the environment within the group by eliminating sources of dissension, normative diversity, and alternative leadership. This will attenuate the cross-pressures that operate to inhibit followers from accepting extreme demands made on them by an eccentric leader (Mills 1982).

These institutional (or anti-institutional) processes interact with certain social-psychological patterns to enhance volatility. What Lifton (1979) calls the "deification of idiosyncrasy" refers to the tendency for the devotees of charismatic leaders to interpret in deep and legitimating terms actions on the part of a leader which might otherwise appear irresponsible, selfish, or destructive. Continual repetition of this dynamic may in effect condition the followers to accept with enthusiasm increasingly bizarre behavior on the part of the leader. It can also encourage such behavior on the part of the charismatic leader, who becomes freer to innovate and act in an eccentric manner without eliciting disapprobation. The leader may also feel increasingly impelled to act forcefully to meet the expectations of the devotees.[7]

A key element of the precariousness of charisma is the uncertainty of succession, which cannot be routinized and institutionalized without threatening the subjective basis of charisma. The result is continual factionalism within movements pervaded by charismatic authority and a looming threat of a crisis of succession when the erstwhile leader departs. As analyzed by Rocheford (1985), the failure of the Hare Krishna sect to institutionalize the charisma of the deceased founding prophet, Sri Prahupada, interfaced with financial difficulties to enhance factionalism and dissidence in the movement in the early 1980s. Escalating internal conflict led to the murder of a dissident in 1986 (Huber and Gruson 1987).

An additional threat to the authority of a charismatic leader derives from tendencies toward institutionalization, which may be prompted by the administrative staff, and which have the effect of isolating the leader, restraining his freedom of action, and sometimes leading to his actual deposition (Wallis 1984, 109-18; Johnson 1992). To resist such tendencies charismatic leaders may engage in continual crisis-mongering, whereby a movement is kept in such turmoil that stable institutional structures and routines cannot be consolidated (Bird 1993; Hiller 1975; Wallis and Bruce 1986a). "Routinization may be resisted by perpetual environmental change and the shifting of goals" (Hiller 1975, 334). Sudden policy shifts and a rapid succession of commitment rituals such as the vasectomies at Synanon are relevant here, as are grand upheavals such as the Maoist "Great Proletarian Cultural Revolution" in China (Hiller 1975) in the late 1960s, by means of which Mao Tse-tung undermined the institutionalized Communist party bureaucracy, but which ultimately degenerated into factional violence. Finally, a particularly precarious mode of crisis-mongering entails attempts to continually escalate tension between the movement and forces in the socio-organizational environment such that the external threat is continually thematized. The risk of this tactic may be illustrated by the lynching of the controversial Mormon prophet Joseph Smith, whose paramilitarist tendencies contributed significantly to the hostility his movement evoked in Missouri and Illinois.[8]

The nature and evolution of charisma can thus "provide opportunities for charismatic leaders to indulge the darker desires of their subconscious. Through effective resistance to the threat of institutionalization charismatic leaders may be able to render followers exclusively dependent upon them, eliminating constraints or inhibitions on their whims, leading to the possible emergence of unconventional sexual practices and violence" (Wallis and Bruce 1986a, 117).[9] The absence of institutional restraints on charismatic leaders combines with the lack of structural supports, to render charismatic leadership precarious and enhance volatility.

The late Roy Wallis was an outstanding contributor to the analysis of charismatic leadership in religious movements and its relation to apocalyptic worldviews and to violence (Wallis 1982, 1984, 1993; Wallis and Bruce 1986a, 1986b). Wallis developed a tripartite typology of religious movements in terms of world-rejecting, world-accepting and world-accommodating orientations (Wallis 1984). Millenarian and apocalyptic beliefs are said to be intrinsic to world-rejecting movements, which see "themselves as islands of sanity or righteousness in a hostile and degenerate world" (Wallis and Bruce 1986a, 122).[10] Yet, "so great a break with prevailing society can only be justified by the authority of someone perceived to be truly extraordinary. Thus such extremes of world-rejection are normally founded or fostered by a charismatic leader" (Wallis and Bruce 1986a, 122, emphasis in original), who may often resist institutionalization tendencies (which threaten to challenge his authority as well as mitigate the group's apocalyptic vision and world-rejecting stance) by continually shifting policies and practices within the movement and keeping the latter in turmoil. In the process the leader systematically "eliminates the sources of inhibition upon his translation of every new whim or inspiration into practice" (1986a, 123). The leader's power may thus become increasingly absolute. In increasing group volatility and the potential for violence, the defense of precarious charisma interfaces with the provocative quality of world-rejection. "Movements which sharply reject the world around them tend to provoke a reciprocal hostility which in turn creates anxiety, fear and paranoia and thus heightens the potential for violence as well as sex to be aspects of the leader's id which come to the fore" (Wallis and Bruce 1986a, 126).

It would appear logical that the tendencies described above will be more intense and strongly developed the more the leader exercises direct, personal control over a local, spatially concentrated community of believers (as opposed to a spatially dispersed or decentralized movement). Peoples Temple communities in San Francisco and Los Angeles did not suicidally self-destruct and initially denied reports that their vanguard community in Guyana, which was under Jim Jones's personal direction, had done so.[11] It also follows that the degree of institutionalization in a charismatically led movement may inhibit violence and volatility. In a comparison of the ill-fated Peoples Temple with the Unification Church, Galanter (1989, 121-25) notes that the latter, which experienced extreme conflict with forces in its environment in the early 1980s, was partly bureaucratized and spatially decentralized such that the individual devotee's relationship to the charismatic leader, "Father" Moon, was mediated by a "middle-management" strata that imparted to the movement some insulation against possible impulsive reactions on the part of the exalted leader. Smaller communities of believers may thus be most susceptible to any violent and antinomian proclivities of the charismatic leader (Bird 1993). Thus, in the period from 1969 to 1985 violent explosions took place in connection with movements led by Charles Manson, Lindberg "Black Jesus" Sanders[12] and Jim Jones. In contrast, "the larger charismatic groups of the 1970s, on the other hand, were relatively free from violence... they were usually run by a reasonably well-organized bureaucratic structure that served to mute the impact of their leaders' idiosyncrasies." They were also less isolated. "In addition, they had considerable visibility so that local and state authorities were fairly aggressive in scrutinizing potential areas of illegal activity and intervening when signs of violent behavior appeared" (Galanter 1989, 192).

Finally it is worth noting that charismatic authority tends to be volatile not only in consequence of its intrinsic precariousness but also in terms of its lack of legitimacy in American culture. As Bryan Wilson (1975, 1987) and others have noted, charismatic authority is viewed in the modern North American and European setting as legitimate exclusively in the "unserious" realms of entertainment and sports. In the areas of religion, charismatic leaders are likely to be met with challenge and skepticism from the media.

## Movement as Systems

Before concluding this paper we want to briefly explore some residual factors that are somewhat related to both apocalypticism and charisma. According to Marc Galanter (1989) a cult or charismatic group operates as a social system. It has a primary task of basic transformation function, which entails transforming input from the environment into a form that meets system needs, that is, converting and socializing recruits. A monitoring function monitors, regulates, and coordinates the action of component parts of the system. A feedback function enables the system to obtain information on how effectively it is carrying out its primary task. Negative feedback is vital to long-term self-regulation of the system but also poses a short-term threat to the system by undermining participants' morale and sometimes challenging group beliefs. The suppression of negative feedback is a constant temptation, which, however, may ultimately impair the system. Finally, charismatic social systems have a dimension of boundary control, protecting the systems from external threats.

Most outbreaks of violence associated with religious movements entail escalating boundary tension. This possibility is accentuated when communal systems turn in upon themselves such that recruitment is de-emphasized and the system's "energies now come to focus primarily on close monitoring of its members" (Galanter 1989, 121). This occurred at Jonestown and coincided with intensified demands for commitment to the leader's increasingly bizarre beliefs. The theme of apocalyptic doom became increasingly prominent among those beliefs and "soon became intertwined with the group's monitoring function" (Galanter 1989, 122). Negative feedback was suppressed, which, together with the attenuation of outreach, increasingly isolated the group from the outside community. In this context the imperative of preventing penetration of the system boundary was heightened. "The arrival of Congressman Ryan portended the imminent disruption of the group's control over its boundary, and thereby precipitated the final events as Jonestown" (Galanter 1989, 124). The integrity of the system was threatened in several ways: the threatened exodus of some defectors with Ryan "posed a challenge to the group's monitoring of the membership"; the intrusion of the U.S. state via Ryan "meant that the suppression of negative feedback could no longer be absolute." "Once it became apparent that his cult's boundary could no longer be secured, Jones chose to preserve its identity in spirit if not in living membership" (Galanter 1989, 124).

Galanter also applies his model to an analysis of the destructive confrontation of the Philadelphia police with MOVE, which culminated in authorities dropping a bomb on the house containing the group and inadvertently destroying a whole neighborhood. In the years preceding the final showdown with authorities, the anarchic ecology movement stopped actively recruiting "and its energies were channeled into monitoring its members" (Galanter 1989, 126). The group "increasingly cut back on the feedback it would accept from the surrounding community, shielding its members from opposing views" (p.126). The group boarded up the house it occupied, electronically blasted obscenities at the neighborhood and refused to listen to the complaints of neighbors, which eventually elicited the intervention of the police, who tragically overreacted. Galanter concludes:

> MOVE and the Peoples Temple can show how a hostile confrontation can ensue at the boundary between a charismatic group and the surrounding community. Protective functions on both sides of the group's boundary may become intensified, leading to mutual provocation and paranoia. If neither party takes steps to defuse the situation, grave consequences can result. This vulnerability to escalating destructiveness across the boundary of charismatic groups should not go unnoticed in dealing with terrorists and nations that have turned to religious fundamentalism with a vengeance. (Galanter 1989, 128).

An analysis of the tragedy of Waco in terms of Galanter's social system/boundary tension model cannot be undertaken here, but could be a fruitful enterprise.

Two other factors or realms of factors should be mentioned. Crusaders against cults have put forward analyses in terms of mind control (brainwashing, coercive persuasion, thought reform). Our objections to these orientations need not be repeated here (see Anthony and Robbins 1994). The best formulation along these anticult lines is by Anderson (1985), who discusses dimensions of deception and "psychological coercion" in "cultic systems." Groups that score high on the multidimensional variables of deception and coercion may not necessarily be dangerous or volatile, but the great power they exercise over the members renders them potentially destructive.

Finally it is worth considering whether certain kinds of movements — apocalyptic, militant, authoritarian — attract certain kinds of persons whose aggressiveness or submissiveness may accentuate the volatility of the group and the prerogatives of a wild leader. Recently the authors (Anthony and Robbins 1994) have re-evaluated the well-known work of Robert Lifton (1961), which is often considered to be an analysis formulated in terms of brainwashing. However, insomuch as Lifton is concerned with (voluntary or coerced) conversion to a totalist perspective and not simply forced behavioral compliance, he sees adoption of a totalist worldview as a product of the interaction of the content of a totalist ideological milieu and personality patterns that predispose certain persons to ideological absolutism (Anthony and Robbins 1994). "Ideological totalism" entails "the coming together of immoderate ideology with equally immoderate individual (totalist) character traits — an extremist meeting ground between people and ideas" (Lifton 1961, 419).

Lifton was strongly influenced by Erik Erikson's work on the constellation of psychological characteristics of people who convert to totalistic social movements, which Erikson had originally referred to as "totalism." Lifton's analysis of those few of his subjects who actually changed their attitudes significantly in a pro-Maoist direction when exposed to Maoist indoctrination is largely in terms of Erikson's totalism concept, which included notions of polarized identities and "negative external conscience" that Erikson had employed to analyze the psychological appeal of both fascism and communism (Anthony and Robbins 1994). To oversimplify radically, the prototalist personality escapes from an oppressively self-critical "negative identity" through immersion in an absolutist ideological totalism. His or her polarized identity is reconstructed in an absolutist manner such that the devotee identifies with the group, the cause, or the leader as the embodiment of the highest standard of heroic virtue and the foundation of the devotee's new idealized or grandiose self-image. Weaknesses and negative qualities, which the convert may once have condemned in himself, are projected onto "them," that is, the designated ideological scapegoats in an exemplary dualist world-view: Jews, counterrevolutionaries, occultists, or others (Anthony and Robbins 1978, 1994).[13] Persons with such identities are available for militant and even violent action against "them," or will readily approve of such actions taken by the leader and his close associates. A concentration of such totalistic types in the movement will reduce the inhibitions against extreme measures.[14]

To sum up, the endogenous potential for violence is likely to be enhanced when communal groups are energized by a fervent millenarian vision, and when the membership has totalist psychological characteristics, and when the group is under the direct personal control of a charismatic leader with an exalted messianic self-conception and a determination to resist any encroachments on his authority or constraints upon his freedom of action. A proselytizing outreach to the broader society may inhibit volatility and promote a stabilizing reality-testing. Conversely, an absence of open communication and interaction with outsiders may disinhibit violence and heighten volatility. Of course much will depend upon the specific content of the apocalyptic worldview, particularly if there is an expectation of persecution and violence against the group, and if the group views itself as the exclusive vanguard of a new order or saved remnant. Volatility may also be encouraged if political elements mitigate the otherworldly character of the apocalyptic scenario, if demonic qualities are attributed to sociopolitical or socioreligious forces or to opponents of the group, and if the unsaved or those bereft of grace are viewed as having sharply diminished claims to consideration. Much will also depend upon the particular personality of the leader, although his or her character might be expected to deteriorate somewhat over time to the degree that his authority is direct, absolute, and legitimated in grandiose millenarian terms.[15] The personality characteristics of members in these groups can also be important. Totalistic members who identify the grandiose elements of their polarized self-concepts with the personality of the leader, and who project their negative identities upon scapegoated contrast groups, tend to increase the volatility of the group. Finally the role of exogenous or environmental factors will always be crucial: many Branch Davidians might still be alive today if the BATF had initially exercised more restraint in dealing with a group which, notwithstanding its weapons stockpile, had no history of nonintramural violence.

# Postscript

Dangerous confrontations and "cult-related violence" are likely to continue in the future. As the year 2000 approaches, apocalyptic excitation may be expected to intensify. Returning from a conference at which an earlier draft of this paper was presented, the senior author, while making a connection at O'Hare Airport, read the following on the first page of the "Evening Update" to the late edition of the *Chicago Tribune* (November 2, 1993):

> FIVE HUNDRED IN SUICIDE SECT ARE DETAINED:
> Ukrainian police have detained some 500 young followers of a religious sect in Kiev in a bid to prevent any possible suicides. The detentions were necessary, police said, because the sect, The White Brotherhood, which claims the world will come to an end Nov. 24, had called on its followers to take their own lives. The followers were in Kiev for a meeting of the sect led by former communist official, Marina Krivonogova-Zvigun, who now calls herself Maria Devi Christos. The sect members were detained for violations of passport and residency regulations. Many of them have rendered their identification papers illegible and defaced their photographs. Following orders from sect leaders, the detainees are refusing to tell police their names, ages and residence.

● ● ● ● ● ● ● ● ● ● ● ● ● ● ● ● ● ● ● ● ● ● ● ● ● ● ●

# Notes

[1]  In this report we will focus primarily on *confrontational* violence involving conflict between factions within movements or more particularly, tension between a group and individuals, other groups, and authorities in the group's environment. Other modes of "cult-related" violence, such as child abuse through corporal punishment or the withholding of modern medical treatment, have specialized concomitants (e.g., "faith healing" doctrines or biblical literalism applied to corporal punishment). We will neglect these specialized subtypes of cult-related violence and probe instead the factors pertinent to violent *confrontations,* particularly violent actions which are seemingly perpetrated by a religious movement or its leadership.

[2]  This is particularly the case when a violent episode culminates a spiraling process of mutual antagonism and recrimination between a religious group and the broader community. The concept of "deviance amplification," which was developed by British sociologists to analyze the spiraling process of mutual escalation of conflict between deviants and authorities, was applied to conflicts involving the Church of Scientology by Wallis (1977) and has been critically evaluated as a tool for understanding sectarian tensions by Hammond and Beckford (1983). Deviance amplification entails feedback processes between societal labeling and increased endogenous deviance. It can be applied in terms of both the short-term unfolding of violent confrontation (Palmer 1994) and the long-term escalation of conflict ultimately leading to violence (Robbins 1986).

[3]  The Russian "Old Believers," who experienced mass suicides through immolation at the end of the seventeenth century, thought that purification by fire would open the seventh seal (Robbins 1986, 1989).

[4]  Knox discusses the doctrine, which was articulated by John Wycliffe but which can be identified in later groups such as the Hussites, Anabaptists, and early Quakers, that *dominion is founded on grace* (Knox 1950, 88, 108-9, 123-24, 133, 147-49, 585). The exercise of rule as well as rights to property and other values is legitimately vouchsafed only to the saints. Knox argues that the early Quaker principle of nonresistance, which condemns the bearing of arms, was grounded in the Anabaptist view of dominion. The doctrine of the latter "was not that nobody has a right to take the sword, but that no worldly person has a right to take the sword. Dominion is founded on grace; if you are not in a state of grace, you have, strictly speaking, no rights and therefore no authority either to govern or to make war — least of all on the saints" (Knox 1950, 148). But "dominion" can refer to a number of things including the right to rule, to property, to possess women, or to properly conduct sexual liaisons, and even to continue to live. Thus the sinister underside of the doctrine that dominion proceeds from grace is that "the worldling has no rights" (Knox 1950, 585). The principle thus converges with Robert Lifton's formulation of "the dispensing of existence" as a key element of "ideological totalism" whereby "those who have not seen the light, have not embraced the truth, are in some way in the shadows — bound up with evil, tainted — and do not have a right to exist as full equals" (Lifton 1985, 64; see also Lifton 1961, 433-34). Finally, some recent examples of the principle that dominion presupposes grace might be found in the idea, imputed to the Unification Church, that all property rightfully belongs to Father Moon and must be emancipated from the realm of sin (Bromley 1985), or the reported revelation to David Koresh that all marriages and couplings except his were adulterous.

[5]  Robbins (1986, 1989) attempts to disentangle the interrelationship of apocalyptic fanaticism and fierce persecution in the deviance amplification process which produced immolative mass suicides in settlements of Old Believers in Russia at the end of the seventeenth century.

[6]  Sharot (1982, 13-14) defines millenarianism as an orientation which "seeks the destruction of the natural and social orders as a prelude to a perfect society and state of being." He reproduces a typology of millenarian variations initially formulated by Talmon (1962, 125-48, 1966, 159-200). On a partly a priori basis we can speculate that volatility is enhanced when a millenarian movement sees itself as surviving to enjoy (or rule) the millennium and, moreover, having a part in bringing about the

millennium, and when there is an expectation that the advent of the millennium will be preceded by an apocalypse of upheavals, calamities, and wars. Wessinger (1994) identifies "pre-millennial" movements, which purvey the expectation that "collective terrestrial salvation will be accomplished in a catastrophic manner," as particularly prone to volatile authoritarian leadership. Wessinger has generalized the concept of pre-millennialism beyond the specific Protestant fundamentalist tradition of dispensational pre-millennialism, which envisions a Great Tribulation under the auspices of Antichrist preceding the second coming of the messiah. The dominant "pre-tribulationist" variation expects true Christians to be "raptured" and spared the Tribulation. In contrast, "post-tribulationist" perspectives expect Christians to have to survive the rigors of the Tribulation. Post-tribulationist groups, which include Aryan supremacist groups associated with the Christian identity movement, may be particularly susceptible to becoming involved in violent confrontations because their emphasis on emerging chaos and persecution "sometimes leads them toward a 'survivalist' lifestyle — retreat into defendable, self-sufficient rural settlements where they can, they believe, wait out the coming upheavals" (Barkun 1994, 47).

7    According to FBI advisor, psychiatrist Murray Miron, "The adulation of this confined group (the Waco Davidian community) works on this charismatic leader (Koresh) so that he in turn spirals into greater and greater paranoia... He's playing a role that his followers have cast him in" (quoted in *Time*, May 3, 1993, 35).

8    Moore (1986) argues that Joseph Smith pursued a risky strategy of advertising Mormon deviance and eliciting hostility and persecution in order to build commitment and solidarity within the Mormon movement.

9    An important analysis of sex, violence, and religion in religious movements has been published by Wallis and Bruce (1986a). The analysis is based on four groups: the Manson Family, Synanon, the Peoples Temple (Jonestown) and the Children of God, all of which have been associated with deviant sexual patterns and implicated (except the Children of God) in violent events (see also Wallis 1982a). The authors conclude that deviant sexual practices and violence are often concomitant in religious movements because they are indirectly interrelated as consequences of the lack of institutional restraint on charismatic leaders. In attempting to prevent the emergence of rationalized structures and routines which would challenge inherently precarious charismatic authority, "the leader eliminates the sources of inhibition upon his translation of every new whim or inspiration into practice" (Wallis and Bruce 1986a, 123). According to Wallis, charisma is an essentially descriptive concept that can, however, be employed as an *explanatory* factor in the analysis of the development of deviant patterns in groups and in analyzing the actions of leaders (Wallis 1993).

10   Wallis (1993) refers to Wallis and Bruce (1986a) as "Wallis 1986a," although the article appears as a chapter in a volume by Wallis and Bruce (1986c).

11   In the late seventeenth century Russian Old Believers, who were divided between extremists and antisuicidal moderates, were organized in terms of separate quasi-monastic communities (Crummey 1970). The dynamics of charismatic leadership within each community was probably a factor in determining which settlements experienced suicidal events. As the extremists were consumed by their own lethal frenzy, the moderates ultimately came to dominate the movement (Robbins 1986, 1989).

12   A small (six-person) quasi-Christian group met a cataclysmic end in Memphis in 1983. Led by Lindberg Sanders, self-proclaimed "Black Jesus," "the group had come to believe that an imminent lunar eclipse would lead to an Armageddon, and they acted on this deluded shared belief" (Galanter 1989, 192). They took a local police official hostage and barricaded themselves in a small house, ultimately murdering the hostage and perishing to the last man in a shoot-out with police. Sanders had nearly been committed to a mental hospital a few days prior to the shoot-out (Galanter 1989).

13   Erikson's theory of totalism both influenced and was influenced by the better known work *The Authoritarian Personality* (Adorno et al. 1950), which still inspires research in which "authoritarian traits are correlated with religious fundamentalism and other variables (Altemeyer 1988).

[14]   The leaders of totalistic apocalyptic movements may be disproportionately recruited from persons exhibiting such traits.

[15]   These characteristics are likely indicators not only of intrinsic volatility and violent proclivities on the part of movements but also of those properties which make certain religious movements appear particularly objectionable in the view of observers and which are thus most likely to elicit hostile reactions.


# References

Adorno, Theodore, Else Frenkel-Brunswick, Daniel Levinson, and R. Nevett Sanford
    1950    *The Authoritarian Personality.* New York: Norton.

Altemeyer, Bob
    1988    *Enemies of Freedom.* New York: Jossey-Bass.

Anderson, Susan
    1985    "Identifying Coercion and Deception in Social Systems." In *Scientific Research on New Religions,* edited by Brock Kilbourne, pp. 12-23. Proceedings of the Annual Meetings of the Pacific Division of the American Association and the Advancement of Science meeting jointly with the Rocky Mountain Division. San Francisco: AAAS.

Anthony, Dick, and Thomas Robbins
    1978    "The Effect of Detente on the Growth of New Religions: Reverend Moon and the Unification Church." In *Understanding the New Religions,* edited by Jacob Needleman and George Baker, pp. 80-100. New York: Seabury.
    1994    "Brainwashing and Totalitarian Influence." In *Encyclopedia of Human Behavior,* edited by V. S. Ramchandran. San Diego: Academic Press.

Barkun, Michael
    1994    "Reflections after Waco: Millennialists and the State." In *From the Ashes: Making Sense of Waco,* edited by James Lewis, pp. 41-50. Lanham, MD: Rowman and Littlefield.

Bird, Frederick
    1993    "Charisma and Leadership in New Religious Movements." In *Handbook of Cults and Sects in America,* vol. 3A, *Religion and the Social Order,* edited by David Bromley and Jeffrey Hadden, pp. 75-92. Greenwich, CT: JAI Press.

Boyer, Paul
    1992    *When Time Shall Be No More: Prophecy Belief in Modern America.* Cambridge: Belknap/ Harvard University.
    1993    "A Brief History of the End of Time." *New Republic* (May 17): 30-33.

Bromley, David
    1985    "Financing the Millennium: The Economic Structure of the Unificationist Movement." *Journal for the Scientific Study of Religion* 24 (3): 253-75.

Cherniavsky, Michael
    1970    "The Old Believers and the New Religion." In *The Structure of Russian History,* edited by M. Cherniavsky, pp. 140-88. New York: Random House.

Cohn, Norman
    1961    *Pursuit of the Millennium.* New York: Oxford.

Crummey, Richard
    1970    *The Old Believers and the World of Antichrist.* Madison: University of Wisconsin.

Frend, W. C.
    1950    *The Donatist Church.* London: Oxford.

Fogarty, Robert
    1993    "Sects and Violence: 'Cults,' Guns, and the Kingdom." *Nation* (April 12): 485-87.

Galanter, Marc
    1989    *Cults: Faith, Healing, and Coercion.* New York: Oxford.

Hall, John
    1987    *Gone From the Promised Land.* New Brunswick, NJ: Transaction.
    1989    "Jonestown and Bishop Hill." In *New Religious Movements, Mass Suicide, and the Peoples Temple,* edited by Rebecca Moore and Fielding McGehee III, pp. 77-92. Lewiston, NY: Edwin Mellen.
    1990    "The Apocalypse at Jonestown." In *In Gods We Trust,* edited by Thomas Robbins and Dick Anthony, pp. 269-94. New Brunswick, NJ: Transaction.

Hammond, Annette, and James Beckford
    1983    "Religious Sects and the Concept of Deviance." *British Journal of Sociology* 34 (2): 208-9.

Hiller, Harry
    1975    "A Reconceptualization of the Dynamics of Social Movement Development." *Pacific Sociological Review* 17 (3): 342-59.

Huber, John and Lindsay Gruson
    1987    "Dial OM for Murder." *Rolling Stone* 497: 53-59.

Johnson, Benton
    1992    "Of Founders and Followers." *Sociological Analysis* 53 (S): S1-S15.

Johnson, Doyle Paul
    1979    "Dilemmas of Charismatic Leadership: The Case of the Peoples Temple." *Sociological Analysis* 40 (4): 315-23.

Jones, Constance
    1989    "Exemplary Dualism and Authoritarianism at Jonestown." In *New Religious Movements, Mass Suicide, and the Peoples Temple,* edited by Rebecca Moore and Fielding McGehee, pp. 209-30. Lewiston, NY: Edwin Mellen.

Knox, Ronald
    1950    *Enthusiasm.* London: Oxford. Reprinted London: Collins Press.

Levi, Kenneth, ed.
    1982    *Violence and Religious Commitment: Implications of Jim Jones' Peoples Temple Movement.* University Park, PA: Penn State.

Lewis, James
    1994    *From the Ashes: Making Sense of Waco.* Lanham, MD: Rowman and Littlefield.

Lifton, Robert
    1961    *Chinese Thought Reform and the Psychology of Totalism.* New York: Norton.
    1968    *Revolutionary Immortality.* New York: Norton.
    1979    "The Appeal of the Death Trip." *New York Times,* January 7.
    1985    "Cult Processes, Religious Totalism, and Civil Liberties." In *Cults, Culture, and the Law,* edited by Thomas Robbins, William Shepherd, and James McBride. Chico, CA: Scholars Press.

McGee, Jim, and William Clairborne
    1993        "The Waco Messiah." *Washington Post, National Weekly Edition.* May 17-23, 10-11.

Melton, J. Gordon
    1985        "Violence and the Cults." *Nebraska Humanist* 8 (2): 51-61.
    1992        *Encyclopedic Handbook of Cults in America.* Rev. ed. New York: Garland Press.

Mills, Edgar
    1982        "Cult Extremism: The Reduction of Normative Dissonance." In *Violence and Religious Commitment,* edited by Kenneth Levi, pp. 75-102. University Park: Penn State University Press.

Moore, R. Laurence
    1986        *Religious Outsiders.* New York: Oxford University Press.

Ofshe, Richard
    1980        "The Social Development of the Synanon Cult." *Sociological Analysis* 41 (2): 109-27.

Palmer, Susan
    1994        "Excavating Waco." In *From the Ashes: Making Sense of Waco,* edited by James Lewis, pp. 99-111. Lanham, MD: Rowman and Littlefield.

Richardson, James
    1985        "The 'Deformation' of New Religions." In *Cults, Culture, and Charisma,* edited by Thomas Robbins, William Shepherd, and James McBride, pp. 163-75. Chico, CA: Scholars Press.

Robbins, Thomas
    1986        "Religious Mass Suicide before Jonestown." *Sociological Analysis* 41 (1): 1-20.
    1989        "The Historical Antecedents of Jonestown." In *New Religious Movements, Mass Suicide, and the Peoples Temple,* edited by Rebecca Moore and Fielding McGehee, pp. 51-77. Lewiston, NY: Edwin Mellen.

Rocheford, E. Burke
    1985        *Hare Krishna in America.* New Brunswick, NJ: Rutgers University Press.

Sharot, Stephen
    1982        *Messianism, Mysticism, and Magic.* Chapel Hill: University of North Carolina.

Talmon, Yonina
    1962        "Pursuit of the Millennium: The Relationship between Religious and Social Change." *Archives Européens de Sociologie* 3: 125-48.
    1966        "Millenarian Movements." *Archives Européens de Sociologie* 7: 159-200.

Wallis, Roy
    1977        *The Road to Total Freedom: A Sociological Analysis of Scientology.* New York: Columbia.
    1982        "Charisma, Commitment, and Control in a New Religious Movement." In *Millennialism and Charisma,* edited by Roy Wallis, pp. 73-140. Belfast: Queens University.
    1984        *The Elementary Forms of the New Religious Life.* London: Routledge and Kegan Paul.
    1993        "Charisma and Explanation." In *Secularism, Rationalism, and Sectarianism,* edited by Eileen Barker, James Beckford, and Karel Dobbelaere, pp. 167-79. Oxford: Clarendon Press.

Wallis, Roy, and Steven Bruce
    1986a       "Sex, Violence, and Religion." In *Sociological Theory, Religion, and Collective Actions,* edited by Roy Wallis and Steven Bruce, pp. 115-27. Belfast: Queens University.
    1986b       *Sociological Theory, Religion, and Collective Actions.* Belfast: Queens University.

Wessinger, Catherine
   1994     "Varieties of Millenarianism and the Issue of Authority." In *From the Ashes: Making Sense of Waco*, edited by James Lewis, pp. 55-73. Lanham, MD: Rowman and Littlefield.

Wilson, Bryan
   1975     *The Noble Savage: The Primitive Origins of Charisma.* Berkeley: University of California.
   1987     "Factors in the Failure of the New Religious Movements." In *The Future of New Religious Movements*, edited by David Bromley and Phillip Hammond, pp. 30-35. Macon GA: Mercer University.

# CHAPTER SEVENTEEN

# THE APOCALYPSE AT
# JONESTOWN

## JOHN R. HALL

The events of November 1978 at Jonestown, Guyana have been well documented, indeed probably better documented than most incident in the realm of the bizarre. Beyond the wealth of "facts" that have been drawn from interviews with survivors of all stripes, there remain piles of as yet unsifted documents and tapes. If they can ever be examined, these will perhaps add something in the way of detail, but it is unlikely they will change very much the broad lines of our understanding of Jonestown. The major dimensions of the events and the outlines of various intrigues are already before us. But so far we have been caught in a flood of instant analysis. Some of this has been insightful, but much of the accompanying moral outrage has clouded our ability to comprehend the events themselves. We need a more considered look at what sort of social phenomenon Jonestown was, and why, and how the Reverend Jim Jones and his staff led the 900 people at Jonestown to die in mass murder and suicide. On the face of it, the action is unparalleled and incredible.

The news media have sought to account for Jonestown largely by looking for parallels in history. Yet we have not been terribly enlightened by the examples they have found, usually because they have searched for cases that bear the outer trappings of the event but have fundamentally different causes. Thus, at Masada, in 73 A.D. the Jews who committed suicide under siege by Roman soldiers knew their fate was death, and they chose to die by their own hands rather than at those of the Romans. In World War II Japanese kamikaze pilots acted with the knowledge that direct, tangible, strategic results would stem from their altruistic suicides, if they were properly

John R. Hall. "The Apocalypse at Jonestown," in Thomas Robbins and Dick Anthony, eds., *In Gods We Trust — New Patterns of Religious Pluralism in America.* Second, Revised and Expanded Edition. New Brunswick, NJ: Transaction Pub., 1990, pp. 269-293. Reprinted by permission of Transaction Publishers. Copyright © 1990 by Transaction Publishers; all rights reserved.

executed. And in Hitler's concentration camps, though there was occasional cooperation by Jews in their own executions, the Nazi executioners had no intentions of dying themselves.

Besides pointing to parallels that don't quite fit, the news media have portrayed Jim Jones as irrational — a madman who had perverse tendencies from early in his youth. They have labeled the Peoples Temple a "cult," perhaps in the hope that a label will suffice when an explanation is unavailable. And they have quite correctly plumbed the key issue of how Jones and his staff were able to bring the mass murder/suicide to completion, drawing largely on the explanations of psychiatrists who have suggested the concept of "brainwashing" as the answer.

But Jones was crazy like a fox! Though he may have been "possessed" or "crazed," both the organizational effectiveness of the Peoples Temple for more than fifteen years and the actual carrying out of the mass murder/suicide show that Jones and his immediate staff knew what they were doing.

Moreover, the Peoples Temple only became a cult when the media discovered the tragedy at Jonestown. As an Indiana woman whose teenager died there commented: "I can't understand why they call the Peoples Temple a cult. To the people, it was their church...."[1]

It is questionable whether the term cult has any sociological utility, for as Harold Fallding has observed, it is a pejorative term most often used by members of one religion to describe a heretical or competing religion, of which they disapprove (1974, p. 27).[2] Of course, even if the use of the term "cult" in the press has been sloppy and inappropriate, some comparisons — for example, to the Unification church, the Krishna Society, and the Children of God — have been quite apt. But these comparisons have triggered a sort of guilt by association. In this view, Jonestown is not such an aberrant case among numerous exotic and bizarre religious cults. The only thing stopping some people from "cleaning up" the cult situation is the constitutional guarantee of freedom of religion.[3]

Finally, the brainwashing concept is an important but nevertheless incomplete basis for understanding the mass murder/suicide. There can be no way to determine how many people at Jonestown freely chose to drink the cyanide-laced Flav-r-ade distributed after word was received of the murders of U.S. Representative Leo Ryan and four other visitors at the airstrip. Clearly, over 200 children and an undetermined number of adults were murdered. Thought control and blind obedience to authority — brainwashing — surely account for some additional number of suicides. But the obvious cannot be ignored — that a substantial number of people, brainwashed or not, committed suicide. Since brainwashing occurs in other social organizations besides the Peoples Temple, it can only be a necessary but not a sufficient cause of the mass murder/suicide. The coercive persuasion involved in a totalistic construction of reality may explain in part *how* large numbers of people came to accept the course proposed by their leader, but it leaves unanswered the question of *why* the true believers among the inhabitants of Jonestown came to consider "revolutionary suicide" a plausible course of action.

In all the instant analysis of Jones' perversity, the threats posed by cults, and the victimization of people by brainwashing, there has been little attempt to account for Jonestown sociologically or as a religious phenomenon. The various facets of Jonestown remain as incongruous pieces of seemingly separate puzzles, and we need a close examination of the case itself in order to try to comprehend it.

In the following discussion, based on ideal-type analysis and *verstehende* sociology (Weber, 1977, pp. 4-22), I will suggest that the Peoples Temple Agricultural Project at Jonestown was an apocalyptic sect. Most apocalyptic sects gravitate toward one of three ideal typical possibilities — preapocalyptic Adventism, preapocalyptic war, or postapocalyptic other-worldly grace. Insofar as the Adventist group takes on a communal form, it comes to approximate the postapocalyptic tableau of other-worldly grace. Jonestown, I argue, was caught on the saddle of the apocalypse: it had its origins in the vaguely apocalyptic revivalist evangelism of the Peoples Temple in the United States, but the Guyanese communal settlement itself was an attempt to transcend the apocalypse by establishing a "heaven-on-earth." For various reasons this attempt was frustrated. The Jonestown group was drawn back into a preapocalyptic war with the forces of the established order, and thus "revolutionary suicide" came to be seen as a way of surmounting the frustration, of moving beyond the apocalypse to heaven, albeit not on earth.

In order to explore this idea, let us first consider the origins of Jonestown and the ways in which it subsequently came to approximate the ideal typical other-worldly sect. Then we can consider certain tensions within the Jonestown group with respect to its other-worldly existence in order to understand why similar groups did not (and are not likely to) encounter the same fate.

## Jonestown as an Other-Worldly Sect

An other-worldly sect, as I have described it in *The Ways Out* (1978), is a utopian communal group that subscribes to a comprehensive set of beliefs based on an apocalyptic interpretation of current history. The world of society-at-large is seen as totally evil, in its last days, at the end of history as we know it. It is to be replaced by a community of the elect — those who live according to the revelation of God's will. The convert who embraces such as sect must, therefore, abandon any previous understanding of life's meaning and embrace the new world view, which itself is capable of subsuming and explaining the individual's previous life, the actions of the sect's opponents, and the demands that are placed on the convert by the leadership of the sect. The other-worldly sect typically establishes its existence on the "other" side of the apocalypse by withdrawing from "this" world into a timeless heaven-on-earth.

In this millennial kingdom, those closest to God come to rule. Though democratic consenuality or the collegiality of elders may come into play, more typically a preeminent prophet or messiah, who is legitimated by charisma or tradition, calls the shots in a theocratic organization of God's chosen people.

The Peoples Temple had its roots in amorphous revivalistic evangelical religion, but in the transition to the Jonestown Agricultural Mission it came to resemble an other-worldly sect. The Temple grew out of the interracial congregation Jim Jones had founded in Indiana in 1953. By 1964 the Peoples Temple Full Gospel Church was federated with the Disciples of Christ (Kilduff and Javers, 1978, p. 20). Later, in 1966, Jones moved with 100 of his most devout followers to Redwood Valley, California. From there they expanded in the 1970s to San Francisco and Los Angeles, which were more promising locales for liberal, interracial evangelism. In these years before the move to Guyana, Jones largely engaged himself in the manifold craft of revivalism. He learned from others he observed — Father Divine in Philadelphia and David Martinus de Miranda in Brazil — and Jones himself became a purveyor of faked miracles and faith healings (*Newsweek*, December 4, 1978, pp. 55-56). By the time of the California years, the Peoples Temple was prospering financially from its somewhat shady tent meeting-style activities and from a variety of other money-making schemes. It was also gaining political clout through the deployment of its members for the benefit of various politicians and causes.

These early developments make one wonder why Jones did not establish a successful but relatively benign sect like the Jehovah's Witnesses, or, alternatively, why he did not move from a religious base directly into the realm of politics, as did the Reverend Adam Clayton Powell when he left his Harlem congregation to go to the U.S. House of Representatives. The answer seems twofold.

In the first place, Jim Jones appears to have had limitations both as an evangelist and as a politician. He simply did not succeed in fooling key California religious observers with his faked miracles. And for all his political support in California politics, Jones was not always able to draw on his good political "credit" when he needed it. A certain mark of political effectiveness is the ability to sustain power in the face of scandal. By this standard, Jones was not totally successful in either Indiana or California. There always seemed to be investigators and reporters on the trails of his various questionable financial and evangelical dealings (Kilduff and Javers, 1978, pp. 23-25, 35-38).

Quite aside from the limits of Jones' effectiveness, the very nature of his prophecy directed his religious movement along a different path from either worldly politics or sectarian Adventism. Keyed to the New Testament Book of Revelations, Adventist groups receive prophecy about the apocalyptic downfall of the present evil world order and the second coming of Christ to preside over a millennial period of divine grace on earth. For all such groups, the Advent itself makes irrelevant social action to reform the institutions of this world. Adventist groups differ from one another in their exact eschatology of the last days, but the groups that have survived, e.g., the Seventh

Day Adventists and Jehovah's Witnesses, have juggled their doctrines that fix an exact date for Christ's appearance. They have thus moved away from any intense chiliastic expectation of an imminent appearance to engage in more mundane conversionist activities that are intended to pave the way for the Millennium (Clark, 1949, pp. 34-50; Lewy, 1974, p. 265).

Reverend Jones himself seems to have shared the pessimism of the Adventist sects about reforming social institutions in this world — for him, the capitalist world of the United States. It is true that he supported various progressive causes, but he did not put much stake in their success. Jones' prophecy was far more radical than those of contemporary Adventist groups: he focused on imminent apocalyptic disaster rather than on Christ's millennial salvation, and his eschatology therefore had to resolve a choice between preapocalyptic struggle with "the beast" or collective flight to establish a postapocalyptic kingdom of the elect. Up until the end, the Peoples Temple was directed toward the latter possibility.

Even in the Indiana years Jones had embraced an apocalyptic view. The move from Indiana to California was justified in part by his claim that Redwood Valley would survive nuclear holocaust (Krause, Stern, and Harwood, 1978, p. 29). In the California years the apocalyptic vision shifted to CIA persecution and Nazi-like extermination of blacks. In California also, the Peoples Temple gradually became communalistic in certain respects. It established a community of goods, pooled resources of elderly followers to provide communal housing for them, and drew on state funds to act as foster parents by establishing group homes for displaced youths.

In its apocalyptic and communal aspects, the Peoples Temple more and more came to exist as an ark of survival, Jonestown — the Agricultural Project in Guyana — was built, beginning in 1974, by an advance crew that by early 1977 still amounted to less than 60 people, most of them under 30. The mass exodus of the People's Temple to Jonestown really began in 1977 when the Peoples Temple was coming under increasing scrutiny in California.

In the move to Guyana, the group began to concertedly exhibit many dynamics of an other-worldly sect, although it differed in ways that were central to its fate. Until the end, Jonestown was similar in striking ways to contemporary sects like the Children of God and the Krishna Society (ISKCON, Inc.). Indeed, the Temple bears a more than casual, and somewhat uncomfortable, resemblance to the various Protestant sects that emigrated to the wilderness of North America beginning in the seventeenth century. The Puritans, Moravians, Rappites, Shakers, Lutherans, and many others like them sought to escape religious persecution in Europe by setting up theocracies where they could live out their own visions of the earthly millennial community. So it was with Jonestown. In this light, neither disciplinary practices, the daily round of life, nor the community of goods at Jonestown seem so unusual.

The disciplinary practices of the Peoples Temple — as bizarre and grotesque as they may sound — are not uncommon aspects of other-worldly sects. These practices have been played up in the press in an attempt to demonstrate the perverse nature of the group, in order to "explain" the terrible climax to their life. But, as Erving Goffman has shown in *Asylums* (1961), sexual intimidation and general psychological terror occur in all kinds of institutions, including mental hospitals, prisons, armies, and even nunneries. Indeed, Congressman Leo Ryan, just prior to his fateful visit to Jonestown, accepted the need for social control: "...you can't put 1,200 people in the middle of a jungle without some damn tight discipline" (quoted in Krause, Stern, and Harwood, 1978, p.21). Practices at Jonestown may well seem restrained in comparison to practices of, say seventeenth-century American Puritans who, among other things, were willing to execute "witches" on the testimony of respected churchgoers or even children. Meg Greenfield observed in *Newsweek*, reflecting on Jonestown, that "the jungle is only a few yards away" (December 4, 1978, p. 132). It seems important to recall that some revered origins of the United States lie in a remarkably similar "jungle."

Communal groups of all types, not just other-worldly sects, face problems of social control and commitment. Rosabeth Kanter (1972) has convincingly shown that successful communal groups in the nineteenth-century United States often drew on mechanisms of mutual criticism, mortification, modification of conventional dyadic sexual mores, and other devices in order to decrease the individual's ties to the outside or to personal relationships within the group and thus to increase the individual's commitment to the collectivity as a whole.

Such commitment mechanisms are employed most often in religious communal groups, especially those with charismatic leaders (Hall, 1978, pp. 225-26). Other-worldly communal groups, where a special attempt is being made to forge a wholly new interpretation of reality, where the demand for commitment is especially pronounced, in a word, where it is sectarian — these groups have tremendously high stakes in maintaining commitment. Such groups are likely to seek out the procedures that are the most effective in guaranteeing commitment. After all, defection from "the way" inevitably casts doubt on its sanctity, no matter how it is rationalized among the faithful. Thus, it is against such groups that the charges of brainwashing, chicanery, and mistreatment of members are leveled most often. Whatever their basis in fact, these are the likely charges of families and friends who see their loved ones abandon them in favor of committing material resources and persona to the religious hope of a new life. Much like other-worldly sects, families suffer a loss of legitimacy in the defection of one of their own.

The abyss that comes to exist between other-worldly sects and the world of society-at-large left behind simply cannot be bridged. There is no encompassing rational connection between the two realities, and therefore the interchange between the other-worldly sect and people beyond its boundaries becomes a struggle either between "infidels" and the "faithful" from the point of view of the sect, or between rationality and fanaticism from the point of view of outsiders. Every sectarian action has its benevolent interpretation and legitimation within the sect, and a converse interpretation is given from the outside. Thus, from inside the sect, various practices of "confession," "mutual criticism," or "catharsis sessions" seem necessary to prevent deviant world views from taking hold within the group.

In the Peoples Temple, such practices included occasional enforced isolation and drug regimens for "rehabilitation" that were like contemporary psychiatric treatment. From the outside, all this tends to be regarded as brainwashing, but insiders will turn the accusation outward, claiming that it is those in the society-at-large who are brainwashed. Though there really can be no resolution to this conflict of interpretations, the widespread incidence of similar patterns of "coercive persuasion" outside Jonestown suggests that its practice there was not so unusual, at least within the context of other-worldly sects, or total institutions in general for that matter.

What is unusual is the direction that coercive persuasion or brainwashing took. Jones worked to instill devotion in unusual ways — ways that fostered the acceptability of "revolutionary suicide" among his followers. During "white nights" of emergency mobilization, he conducted rituals of proclaimed mass suicide, giving "poison" to all members, and saying they would die within the hour. According to one defector — Deborah Blakey — Jones "explained that the poison was not real and we had just been through a loyalty test. He warned us that the time was not far off when it would be necessary for us to die by our own hands" (cited in Krause, Stern, and Harwood, 1978, p. 193). This event initially left Blakey "indifferent to whether she "lived or died." A true believer in the Peoples Temple was more emphatic. Disappointed by the string of false collective suicides, he said in a note to Jones that he hoped for "the real thing" so that they could all pass beyond the suffering of this world.[4]

Some people yielded to Jim Jones only because their will to resist was beaten down; others — including many "seniors," the elderly members of the Peoples Temple — felt they owed everything to Jim Jones, and they provided him with a strong core of unequivocal support. Jones apparently allowed open dissension at "town meetings" because, with the support of the seniors, he knew he could prevail. Thus, no matter what they wanted personally, people learned to leave their fates in the hands of Jim Jones and to accept what he demanded. The specific uses of coercive persuasion at Jonestown help to explain how (but not why) the mass murder/suicide was implemented. But it is the special use, not the general nature, of brainwashing that distinguishes Jonestown from most other-worldly sects.

Aside from brainwashing, a second major kind of accusation about Jonestown, put forward most forcefully by Deborah Blakey, concerns the work discipline and diet there. Blakey swore in an affidavit that the work load was excessive and that the food served to the average residents of Jonestown was inadequate. She abhorred the contradiction between the conditions she reported and the privileged diet of Reverend Jones and his inner circle. Moreover, because she had dealt with the group's finances, she knew that money could have been directed to providing a more adequate diet for everyone.

Blakey's moral sensibilities notwithstanding, the disparity between the diet of the elite and that of the average Jonestowner should come as no surprise: it parallels Erving Goffman's (1961, p. 48ff.) description of widespread hierarchies of privilege in total institutions. Her concern about the average diet is more to the point. But here, other accounts differ from Blakey's report. Maria Katsairs, a consort of Reverend Jones, wrote her father a letter extolling the virtues of the Agricultural Project's "cutlass" beans that were used as a meat substitute (Kilduff and Javers, 1978, p. 109). And Paula Adams, who survived the Jonestown holocaust because she resided at the Peoples Temple house in Georgetown, expressed ambivalence about the Jonestown community in an interview after the tragedy. But she also remarked: "My daughter ate very well. She got eggs and milk everyday. How many black children in the ghetto eat that well?"[5]

The accounts of surviving members of Jones' personal staff and inner circle, like Katsaris and Adams, are suspect, of course, in exactly the opposite way to those of people like the "Concerned Relatives." But the inside accounts are corroborated by at least one outsider, *Washington Post* reporter Charles Krause. On his arrival at Jonestown in the company of U.S. Representative Leo Ryan, Krause noted that "contrary to what the Concerned Relatives had told us, nobody seemed to be starving. Indeed, everyone seemed quite healthy" (Krause, Stern, and Harwood, 1978, p. 41).

It is difficult to assess these conflicting views. Beginning early in the summer of 1977, Jones set in motion the mass exodus of some 800 Peoples Temple members from California. Though Jonestown could adequately house only about 500 people at that time, the population climbed quickly beyond that mark. At the same time the population mushroomed beyond the agricultural potential of the settlement. The exodus also caused Jonestown to become top heavy with less productive seniors and children. Anything close to agricultural self-sufficiency thus became a more elusive and long-range goal.

As time wore on during the group's last year of existence, Jones himself came more and more fixated on the prospect of a mass emigration from Guyana, and in this light, any sort of long-range agricultural-development strategy seemed increasingly irrational. According to the *New York Times*, the former Jonestown farm manager, Jim Bogue, suggested that the agricultural program would have succeeded in the long run if it had been adhered to.[6] But with the emerging plans for emigration, it was not followed and thus became merely a charade for the benefit of the Guyanese government.

This analysis would seem to have implications for the *internal* conflicts about goals at Jonestown. Jim Jones' only natural son, Stephan Jones, and several other young men in the Peoples Temple came to believe in Jonestown as a socialist agrarian community, not as an other-worldly sect headed up by Jim Jones. Reflecting about his father after the mass murder/suicide, Stephan Jones commented: "I don't mind discrediting him, but I'm still a socialist, and Jim Jones will be used to discredit socialism. People will use him to discredit what we built, Jonestown was not Jim Jones, although he believed it was."[7]

The seniors, who provided social security checks, gardened, and produced handicraft articles for sale in Georgetown in lieu of heavy physical labor, and the fate of agricultural productivity both reinforce the assessment that Jim Jones' vision of the Peoples Temple approximates the other-worldly sect as an ideal type. In such sects, as a rule, proponents seek to survive *not* on the basis of productive labor, as in more "worldly utopian" communal groups, but on the basis of patronage, petty financial schemes, and the building of a "community of goods" through prosyletizaiton (Hall, 1978, p. 207). This was the case with Jonestown. The community of goods that Jones built up is valued at more than $12 million. As a basis for satisfying collective wants, any agricultural production at Jonestown would have paled in comparison to this amassed wealth.

But even if the agricultural project itself became a charade, it is no easy task to create a plausible charade in the midst of relatively infertile soil reclaimed from dense jungle. This would have required the long hours of work that Peoples Temple defectors described. Such a charade could serve as yet another effective means of social control. In the first place, it gave a purposeful role to those who envisioned Jonestown as an experimental socialist agrarian community. Beyond this, it monopolized the waking hours of most of the populace in exhausting work, and it gave them a minimal — though probably adequate — diet on which to subsist. It is easy to imagine that many city people, or those with bourgeois sensibilities in general, would not find this their cup of tea in any case But the demanding daily regimen, however abhorrent to the uninitiated, is widespread in other-worldly sects.

Various programs of fasting and work asceticism have long been regarded as signs of piety and routes to religious enlightenment or ecstasy. In the contemporary American Krishna groups, an alternation of nonsugar and high-sugar phases of the diet seems to create an almost addictive attachment to the food that is communally dispersed (Hall, 1978, p. 76; cf. Goffman, 1961, pp. 49-50). And we need look no later in history than to Saint Benedict's order to find a situation in which the personal time of participants was eliminated for all practical purposes, with procedures of mortification for offenders laid out by Saint Benedict in his *Rule* (1975; cf. Zerubavel, 1977). The concerns of Blakey and others about diet, work, and discipline may have some basis, but probably they have been exaggerated. In any case, they do not distinguish Jonestown from other-worldly sects in general.

One final public concern with the People's Temple deserves mention because it parallels so closely previous sectarian practices. The Reverend Jim Jones is accused of swindling people out of their livelihoods and life circumstances by tricking them into signing over their money and possessions to the Peoples Temple or to its inner circle of members. Of course Jones considered this a "community of goods," and he correctly pointed to a long tradition of such want satisfaction among other-worldly sects. In an interview just prior to the tragedy, Jones cited Jesus' call to hold all things in common.[8] There are good grounds to think that Reverend Jones carried this philosophy into the realm of a con game. Still it should be noted that in the suicidal end, Jones did not benefit from the wealth in the way a large number of other self-declared prophets and messiahs have.[9]

Like its disciplinary practices and its round of daily life, the community of goods in the Peoples Temple at Jonestown emphasizes its similarities to other-worldly sects — both the contemporary ones labeled cults by their detractors and historical examples that are often revered in retrospect by contemporary religious culture. The elaboration of these affinities is in no way intended to suggest that we can or should vindicate the duplicity, the bizarre sexual and psychological intimidation, and the hardships of daily life at Jonestown. But it must be recognized that the settlement was much less unusual that some of us might like to think. The practices that detractors find abhorrent in the life of the Peoples Temple at Jonestown prior to the final "white night" of murder and suicide are the core nature of other-worldly sects. Therefore, it should come as no surprise that practices like those at Jonestown are widespread, both in historical and contemporary other-worldly sects. Granted that the character of such sects — the theocratic basis of authority, the devices of mortification and social control, and the demanding regimen of everyday life — predisposes people in such groups to respond to the whims of their leaders, no matter what fanatic and zealous directions they may take. But given the widespread occurrence of other-worldly sects, the other-worldly features of Jonestown are insufficient in themselves to explain the bizarre fate of its participants. If we are to understand the unique turn of events at Jonestown, we must look to certain distinctive features of the Peoples Temple — traits that make it unusual among other-worldly sects — and we must try to comprehend the subjective means of these features for some of Jonestown's participants.

## Persecution at Jonestown

If the Peoples Temple was distinctive among other-worldly sects, it is for two reasons. First, the group was more thoroughly integrated racially than any other such group today. Second, the People's Temple was distinctively protocommunist in ideology. Both of these conditions, together with certain personal fears of Jim Jones (mixed perhaps with organic disorders and assorted drugs), converged in his active mind to give a special twist to the apocalyptic quest of his flock. Let us consider these matters in turn.

In Peoples Temple, Jim Jones had consistently sought to transcend racism in peace rather than in struggle. The origins of this approach, like most of Jones' early life, are by now shrouded in myth. But it is clear that Jones was committed to racial harmony in his Indiana ministry. In the 1950s his formation of an interracial congregation met with much resistance in Indianapolis, and this persecution was one impetus for the exodus to California (Kilduff and Javers, 1978, pp. 16-17, 19-20, 25).[10] There is room for debate on how far Jones' operation actually went toward achieving racial equality, or to what degree it simply perpetuated racism, albeit in a racially harmonious microcosm (Kilduff and Javers, 1978, pp. 86-7; Krause, Stern, and Harwood, 1978, p.

41). But Peoples Temple fostered greater racial equality and harmony than that of the larger society, and in this respect it has few parallels in present-day communal groups.[11] It also achieved more racial harmony than is evidenced in mainstream religious congregations. The significance of this cannot be assayed easily, but one view of it has been captured in a letter from a 20-year-old Jonestown girl. She wrote to her mother in Evansville, Indiana that she could "walk down the street now without the fear of having little old white ladies call me nigger."[12]

Coupled with the commitment to racial integration and again in contrast to most other-worldly sects, the Peoples Temple moved strongly toward ideological communism. Most other-worldly sects practice religiously inspired communism — the "clerical" or "Christian" socialism that Marx and Engels railed theories of Marx, Lenin, and Stalin. By contrast, it has become clear that, whatever the contradictions other socialists point to between Jones' messianism and socialism (Moberg, 1978), the Reverend Jim Jones and his staff considered themselves socialists. In his column, "Perspectives from Guyana," Jones (1978, p. 208) maintained that "neither my colleagues nor I are any longer caught up in the opiate of religion...." (reprinted in Krause, Stern, and Harwood, 1978, p. 208). Though the practices of the group prior to the mass murder/suicide were not based on any doctrinaire Marxism, at least some of the recruits to the group were young radical intellectuals, and one of the group's members, Richard Tropp, gave evening classes on radical political theory.[13] In short, radical socialist currents were unmistakably present in the group.

It is perhaps more questionable whether the Peoples Temple was religious in any conventional sense of the term. Of course, all utopian communal groups are religious in that they draw true believers together who seek to live out a heretical or heterodox interpretation of the meaningfulness of social existence. In this sense, the Peoples Temple was a religious group, just as Frederick Engels (1964a; 1964b) once observed that socialist sects of the nineteenth century were similar in character to primitive Christian and Reformation sects. Jim Jones clearly was more self-consciously religious than were the leaders of the socialist sects. Though he preached atheism and did not believe in a God that answers prayer, he did embrace reincarnation. A surviving resident of Jonestown remembers him saying that "our religion is this — your highest service to God is service to your fellow man." On the other hand, it seems that the outward manifestations of conventional religious activity — revivals, sermons, faith healings — were, at least in Jim Jones' view, calculated devices to draw people into an organization that was something quite different. It is a telling point in this regard that Jones ceased the practice of faith healings and cut off other religious activities once he moved to Jonestown. Jones' wife, Marceline, once noted that Jim Jones considered himself a Marxist who "used religion to try to get some people out of the opiate of religion."[14] In a remarkable off-the-cuff interview with Richard and Harriet Tropp — the two Jonestown residents who were writing a book about the Peoples Temple — Jones reflected on the early years of his ministry, claiming: "What a hell of a battle that [integration] was — I thought 'I'll never make a revolution, I can't even get those fuckers to integrate, much less get them to any communist philosophy.'"[15]

In the same interview, Jones intimated that he had been a member of the U.S. Communist party in the early 1950s. Of course, with Jones' Nixonesque concern for his place in history, it is possible that his hindsight, even in talking with sympathetic biographers, did not convey his original motives. In the interview with the Tropps, Jones also hinted that the entire development of the Peoples Temple, down to the Jonestown Agricultural Project, derived from his communist beliefs. This interview and Marceline Jones' comment give strong evidence of Jim Jones' early communist orientation. Whenever this orientation began, the move to Jonestown was predicated on it.

The socialist government of Guyana was generally committed to supporting socialists seeking refuse from capitalist societies, and they apparently thought that Jones' flexible brand of Marxism fit well within the country's political matrix. By 1973 when negotiations with Guyana about an agricultural project were initiated, Jones and his aides were professing identification with the world historical communist movement.

The convergence of racial integration and crude communism gave a distinctly political character to what in many other respects was an other-worldly religious sect. The injection of radical politics gave a heightened sense of persecution to the Jonestown Agricultural Project. Jim Jones himself seems both to have fed this heightened sense of persecution to his followers and to have been devoured by it himself. He manipulated fears among his followers by controlling information and spreading false rumors about news events in the United States (Moberg, 1978, p. 14). With actual knowledge of certain adversaries and fed by his own premonitions, Jones spread these premonitions among his followers, thereby heightening their dedication. In the process, Jones disenchanted a few members who became Judas Iscariots and who in time brought the forces of legitimated external authority to "persecute" Jones and his true believers in their jungle theocracy.

The persecution complex is a stock-in-trade of other-worldly sects. It is naturally engendered by a radical separation from the world of society-at-large. An apocalyptic mission develops in such a way that persecution from the world left behind is taken as a sign of the sanctity of the group's chosen path of salvation. Though radical and political persecution are not usually among the themes of other-worldly persecution, they do not totally break with the other-worldly way of interpreting experience. But the heightened sense of persecution at Jonestown did reduce the disconnection from society-at-large that is the signature of other-worldly sects.

Most blacks in the United States have already experienced persecution; and if Jim Jones gave his black followers some relief from a ghetto existence (which many seem to have felt he did), he also made a point of reminding those in his group that persecution still awaited them back in the ghettos and rural areas of the United States. In the California years, for example, the Peoples Temple would stage mock lynchings of blacks by the Ku Klux Klan as a form of political theater (Krause, Stern, and Harwood, 1978, p. 56). And, according to Deborah Blakey, Jones "convinced black

Temple members that if they did not follow him to Guyana, they would be put into concentration camps and killed" (quoted in Krause, Stern, and Harwood, 1978, p. 188).

Similarly, white socialist intellectuals could easily become paranoid about their activities. As any participant in the New Left movement of the 1960s and early 1970s knows, paranoia was a sort of badge of honor to some people. Jones exacerbated this by telling whites that the CIA listed them as enemies of the state.

Jones probably impressed persecution upon his followers to increase their allegiance to him. But Jones himself was caught up in a web of persecution and betrayal. The falling-out between Jones and Grace and Tim Stoen seems of primary importance here. In conjunction with the imminent appearance of negative news articles, the fight over custody of John Victor Stoen (Grace's son whom both Jones and Tim Stoen claimed to have fathered) triggered Jones' 1977 decision to remove himself from the San Francisco Temple to Guyana (Krause, Stern, and Harwood, 1978, p. 57).[16]

We may never know what happened between the Stoens and Jones. According to Teri Buford, a former Jonestown insider, Tim Stoen left the Peoples Temple shortly after it became known that in the 1960s he had gone on a Rotary-sponsored speaking tour denouncing communism.[17] Both sides have accused the other of being the progenitors of violence in the Peoples Temple.[18] To reporters who accompanied Representative Ryan, Jones charged that the Stoen couple had been government agents and provocateurs who had advocated bombing, burning, and terrorism.[19] This possibility could have been regarded as quite plausible by Jones and his staff because they possessed documents about similar alleged FBI moves against the Weather Underground and the Church of Scientology.[20] The struggle between Jones and the Stoens thus could easily have personified to Jones the quintessence of a conspiracy against him and his work. It certainly intensified negative media attention on the Temple.

For all his attempts to curry favor with the press, Jones failed in the crucial instance: the San Francisco investigative reporters gave much coverage to the horror stories about the Peoples Temple and Jones' custody battle. Jones may well have been correct in his suspicion that he was not being treated fairly in the press. After the mass murder/suicide, the managing editor of the *San Francisco Examiner* proudly asserted in a January 15, 1979 letter to the *Wall Street Journal* that his paper had not been "morally neutral" in its coverage of the Peoples Temple.[21]

The published horror stories were based on the allegations by defectors — the Stoens and Deborah Blakey being foremost among them. We do not know how true, widespread, exaggerated, or isolated the incidents reported were. Certainly they were generalized in the press to the point of creating an image of Jones as a total ogre. The defectors also initiated legal proceedings against the Temple, and the news articles began to stir the interest of government authorities in the operation. These developments were not lost on Jim Jones. In fact, the custody battle with the Stoens seems to have precipitated Jones' mass suicide threat to the Guyanese government. Not coincidentally, according to Jim Jones' only natural son, Stephan, the first "white night" drills for mass suicide were held at this point. Stephan Jones connects these events with the appearance of several negative news articles.[22]

With these sorts of events in mind, it is not hard to see how it happened that Jim Jones felt betrayed by the Stoens and the other defectors, and persecuted by those who appeared to side with them — the press and the government foremost among them. In September 1978 Jones went so far as to retain the well-known conspiracy theorist and lawyer, Mark Lane, to investigate the possibility of a plot against the Peoples Temple. In the days immediately following, Mark Lane — perhaps self-servingly — reported in a memorandum to Jones that "even a cursory examination" of the available evidence "reveals that there has been a coordinated campaign to destroy the Peoples Temple and to impugn the reputation of its leader." Those involved were said to include the U.S. Customs Bureau, the Federal Communications Commission, the Central Intelligence Agency, the Federal Bureau of Investigation, and the Internal Revenue Service.[23] Lane's assertions probably had little basis in fact. Although several of these agencies had looked into certain Temple activities independently, none of them had taken any direct action against the Temple, even though they may have had some cause for so doing. The actual state of affairs notwithstanding, with Lane's assertions Jones had substantiation of his sense of persecution from a widely touted conspiracy theorist.

The sense of persecution that gradually developed in the Peoples Temple from its beginning and increased markedly at Jonestown must have come to a head with the visit of U.S. Representative Leo Ryan. The U.S. State Department has revealed that Jones had agreed to a visit by Ryan, but that he withdrew permission when it became known that a contingent of Concerned Relatives as well as certain members of the press would accompany Ryan to Guyana.[24] Among the Concerned Relatives who came with Ryan was the Stoen couple; in fact, Tim Stoen, was known as a leader of the Concerned Relatives group.[25] Reporters with Ryan included two from the *San Francisco Chronicle*, a paper that had already pursued investigative reporting on the Peoples Temple, as well as Gordon Lindsay, an independent newsman who had written a negative story on the Peoples Temple for publication in the *National Enquirer* (This article was never published) (Krause, Stern, and Harwood, 1978, p. 40). This entourage could hardly have been regarded as objective or unbiased by Jones and his closer supporters. Instead, it identified Ryan with the forces of persecution, personified by the Stoens and the investigative press, and it set the stage for the mass murder/suicide that had already been threatened in conjunction with the custody fight.

The ways in which the People's Temple came to differ from more typical other-worldly sects are more a matter of degree than of kind, but the differences profoundly altered the character of the scene at Jonestown. Though the avowed radicalism, the interracial living, and the defector-media-government "conspiracy" are structurally distinct from one another, Jim Jones incorporated them into a tableau of conspiracy that was intended to increase his followers' attachment to him but ironically brought his legitimacy as a messiah into question, undermined the other-worldly possibilities of the Peoples Temple Agricultural Project, and placed the group on the stage of history in a distinctive relationship to the apocalypse.

# Jonestown and the Apocalypse

Other-worldly sects by their very nature are permeated with apocalyptic ideas. The sense of a decaying social order is personally experienced by the religious seeker in a life held to be untenable, meaningless, or both. This interpretation of life is collectively affirmed and transcened in other-worldly sects that purport to offer heaven-on-earth beyond the apocalypse. Such sects promise the grace of a theocracy in which followers can sometimes really escape the "living hell" of society-at-large. Many of the Reverend Jones' followers seem to have joined the Peoples Temple with this in mind. But the predominance of blacks, the radical ideology of the Temple, the persistent struggle against the defectors, and the "conspiracy" that formed around them in the minds of the faithful gave the true believers' sense of persecution a more immediate and pressing aura, rather than an other-worldly one.

Jones used these elements to heighten his followers' sense of persecution from the outside, but this device itself may have drawn into question the ability of the supposed charismatic leader to provide an other-worldly sanctuary. By the middle of October 1978, a month before Representative Ryan's trip in November, Jones' position of preeminent leadership was beginning to be questioned not only by disappointed religious followers, but also by previously devoted seniors, who were growing tired of the endless meetings and the increasingly untenable character of everyday life, and by key proponents of collective life, who felt Jones was responsible for their growing inability to deal successfully with Jonestown's material operations.

Once these dissatisfied individuals circumvented Jones' intelligence network of informers and began to establish solidarity with one another, the conspiracy can be said truly to have taken hold within Jonestown itself. If the times were apocalyptic, Reverend Jones was like the revolutionary millenarians described by Norman Cohn (1970) and Gunther Lewy (1974). Rather than successfully proclaiming the postapocalyptic sanctuary, Jones was reduced to declaiming the web of "evil" powers in which he was ensnared and to searching with chiliastic expectation for the imminent cataclysm that would announce the beginning of the kingdom of righteousness.

Usually other-worldly sects have a sense of the eternal about them — having escaped this world, they adopt the temporal trappings of heaven, which amounts to a timeless bliss of immortality (Hall, 1978, pp. 72-79). But Jim Jones had not really established a postapocalyptic heavenly plateau. Even if he had promised this to his followers, it was only just being built in the form of the Agricultural Project. And it was not even clear that Jonestown itself was the promised land. Jones did not entirely trust the Guyanese government, and he was considering seeking final asylum in Cuba or the Soviet Union. Whereas other-worldly sects typically assert that heaven is at hand, Jones could only hold it out as a future goal — one that became more and more elusive as the forces of persecution tracked him to Guyana. Thus, Jones and his followers were still within the throes of the Apocalypse as they conceived it — the forces of good fighting against the evil and conspiratorial world that could not tolerate a living example of a racially integrated American socialist utopia.

In the struggle against evil, Jones and his true believers took on the character of what I have termed a "warring sect," fighting a decisive Manichean struggle with the forces of evil (Hall, 1978, pp. 206-207). Such a struggle seems almost inevitable when political rather than religious themes of apocalypse are stressed. And it is clear that Jones and his staff acted at times within this militant frame of reference. For example, they maintained armed guards around the settlement, held "white night" emergency drills, and even staged mock CIA attacks on Jonestown. By so doing, they undermined the plausibility of an other-worldly existence. The struggle of a warring sect takes place in historical time, where one action builds on another and decisive outcomes of previous events shape future possibilities. The contradiction between this earthly struggle and the heaven-on-earth Jones would have liked to proclaim (e.g., in "Perspectives from Guyana") gave Jonestown many of its strange juxtapositions — of heaven and hell, of suffering and bliss, of love and coercion. Perhaps even Jones himself, for all his megalomaniacal ability to transcend the contradictions that others saw in him, and that caused him to be labeled an "opportunist," could not endure the struggle for is own immortality. If he were indeed a messianic incarnation of God, as he sometimes claimed, presumably Jones could have either won the struggle of the warring sect against its evil persecutors or delivered his people to the bliss of another world.

In effect, Jones had brought his flock to the point of straddling the two sides of the apocalypse. Had he established his colony beyond the unsympathetic purview of defectors, Concerned Relatives, investigative reporters, and government agencies, the other-worldly tableau perhaps could have been sustained with less repressive methods of social control. As it was, Jones and the colony experienced the three interconnected limitations of group totalism that Robert Jay Lifton (1968, p. 129) described with respect to the Chinese Communist Revolution — diminishing conversions, inner antagonism of disillusioned participants to the suffocation of individuality, and increasing penetration of the "idea-tight milieu control" by outside forces.[26] As Lifton noted, revolutionaries are engaged in a quest for immortality. Other-worldly sectarians short-circuit this quest in a way by the fiat of *asserting* their immortality — positing the timeless heavenly plateau that exists *beyond* history as the basis of their everyday life. But under the persistent eyes of external critics and because Jones himself exploited such "persecution" to increase his social control, he could not sustain the illusion of other-worldly immortality.

On the other hand, the Peoples Temple could not achieve the sort of political victory that would have been the goal of a warring scct. Since revolutionary war involves a struggle with an established political order in unfolding historical time, revolutionaries can only attain immortality in the widescape victory of the revolution over the "forces of reaction." Ironically, as Lifton pointed out, even the initial political and military victory of the revolutionary forces does not end the search for immortality. Even in victory, revolution can be sustained only through diffusion of its principles and goals. But, as Max Weber (1977, p. 1,121) observed, in the long run it seems impossible to maintain the charismatic enthusiasm of revolution; more pragmatic concerns come to the fore, and as the ultimate ends of revolution are faced against everyday life and its demands, the question for immortality fades, and the immortality of the revolutionary moment is replaced by the myth of a grand revolutionary past.

The Peoples Temple could not begin to achieve revolutionary immortality in historical time because it could not even pretend to achieve any victory against its enemies. If it had come to a pitched battle, the Jonestown defenders — like the Symbionese Liberation Army against the Los Angeles Police Department S.W.A.T. Team — would have been wiped out.

But the Peoples Temple could create a kind of immortality that is not really a possibility for political revolutionaries. They could abandon apocalyptic hell by the act of mass suicide. This would shut out the opponents of the Temple. They could not be the undoing of what was already undone, and there could be no recriminations against the dead. It could also achieve the other-worldly salvation Jones had promised his more religious followers. Mass suicide bridged the divergent public threads of meaningful existence at Jonestown — those of political revolution and religious salvation. It was an awesome vehicle for a powerful statement of collective solidarity by the true believers among the people of Jonestown — that they would rather die together than have their lives together subjected to gradual decimation and dishonor at the hands of authorities regarded as illegitimate.

Most warring sects reach a grisly end. Occasionally they achieve martyrdom, but if they lack a constituency, their extermination is used by the state as proof of its monopoly on the legitimate use of force. Revolutionary suicide is a victory by comparison. The event can be drawn upon for moral didactics, but this cannot erase the stigma that Jonestown implicitly places on the world that its members left behind. Nor can the state punish the dead who are guilty, among other things, of murdering a United States Congressman, three newsmen, a Concerned Relative, and those many Jonestown residents who did not willingly commit suicide.[27]

Though they paid the total price of death for their ultimate commitment and though they achieved little except perhaps sustenance of their own collective sense of honor, those who won this hollow victory still cannot have it taken away from them. In the absence of retribution the state search for the guilty who have remained alive and the widespread outcry against cults take on the character of scapegoating.[28] Those most responsible are beyond the reach of the law. Unable to escape the hell of their own lives by creating an other-worldly existence on earth, they instead sought their immortality in death, and left it to others to ponder the apocalypse that they unveiled.

● ● ● ● ● ● ● ● ● ● ● ● ● ● ● ● ● ● ● ● ● ● ● ● ● ● ●

In addition to the references cited in this article, it is based on personal interviews by the author conducted in Georgetown, Guyana, and in California during the summer of 1979.

# Notes

1  *Louisville Courier-Journal*, 23 December 1978, p. B1.

2  Fallding does not want to "plunge into relativism," so he tries to retrieve the term "cultism" for sociological use by defining it as ascribing sacred status to anything in the profane, actualized world. But this just displaced the problem of "false religion" onto the definition of "profane," which itself can only be defined within a religious perspective!

3  Even the constitutional guarantee is under fire. Prior to the Jonestown events, the U.S. Justice Department (texts in Krause, Stern, and Harwood, 1978, pp.171-85) had carefully examined the legal issues involved in investigating religious sects, and determined against such action. But since Jonestown, there have been suggestions, for example by William Randolph Hearst, in the *San Francisco Examiner* (10 December 1978, p. 28), and a law professor, Richard Delgado, in the *New York Times* (27 December 1978, p. A23), that totalitarianism in the name of religion should not qualify for constitutional protection. Also, the *Washington Post* (16 December 1978, p. 3) reports that mainline churches have been reexamining their stands on freedom of religion in light of the Jonestown events.

4  *San Francisco Examiner*, 6 December 1978, p. 10.

5  *San Francisco Examiner*, 10 December 1978, p. 9.

6  *New York Times*, 24 December 1978, pp. 1, 20.

7  *San Francisco Examiner*, 10 December 1978, p. 9.

8  *San Francisco Examiner*, 3 December 1978, p. 16.

9  The list of these religious swindlers, if it is kept by God's angels someplace, must be a long one indeed! Some would want to suggest that even in the end, Jim Jones plotted to make off with the loot. One theory holds that he planned to escape with his personal nurse at the conclusion of the cyanide poisonings. But this theory seems far-fetched to the *New York Times* (25 December 1978, p. 15) reporter who attended the Guyanese coroner's inquest where it was proposed. It did not account either for the bequeathing of Temple assets to the Communist party of the Soviet Union or for the suicidal "lost hope" that Jones expressed in the taped portion of the mass murder/suicide episode.

10  *Time*, December 4, 1978, p. 22.

11  Only one contemporary, explicitly interracial communal group immediately comes to mind — Koinonia Farm in Georgia, a Christian group founded in the 1940s.

12  *Louisville Courier-Journal*, 23 December 1978, p. B1.

13  *San Francisco Examiner*, 8 December 1978, p. 1.

14  *New York Times*, 26 November 1978, p. 20.

15  *San Francisco Examiner*, 8 December 1978, p. 16

16  Kilduff and Javers (1978, pp. 77-78) cite the imminent appearance of negative news articles as a cause of Jones' departure.

17  *New York Times*, 1 January 1979, p. 35.

18  *San Francisco Examiner*, 6 December 1978, p. 1; *Louisville Courier-Journal*, 22 December 1978, p. 5.

[19]    *San Francisco Examiner*, 3 December 1978, p. 14.

[20]    *New York Times*, 6 December 1979, p. 16; *Columbia (Mo.) Tribune*, 6 January 1979, p. 6.

[21]    "Letter to the Editor, " *Wall Street Journal*, 5 January 1979, p. 21.

[22]    *San Francisco Examiner*, 17 December 1978, p. 5.

[23]    *New York Times*, 4 February 1979, pp. 1, 42.

[24]    *San Francisco Examiner*, 16 December 1978, p. 1.

[25]    *New York Times*, 1 January 1979, p. 35.

[26]    The Peoples Temple perhaps had already begun to undergo the third of Lifton's limitations — the "law of diminishing conversions" — before the move from San Francisco to Guyana.

[27]    On the trip into Jonestown with Ryan, Peoples Temple lawyer Mark Lane told reporter Charles Krause (1978, p. 37) that perhaps ten percent of Jonestown residents would leave if given a chance but "90 per cent... will fight to the death to remain." The U.S. State Department originally suppressed the tape recording of the mass murder/suicide, but I have listened to a pirated copy of it, and the event clearly involved a freewheeling discussion of alternatives, with vocal support as well as pointed resistance voiced for the proposed "taking of the potion." (*New York Times*, 10 December 1978, p. A28; 25 December 1978, p. A16).

[28]    *Washington Post*, 16 December 1978, p. 3; *New York Times*, 27 December 1978, p. A23.

# References

Benedictus, Saint
    1975       *The Rule of Saint Benedict*. New York: Doubleday Image (Originally c. 525?).

Clark, Elmer T.
    1949       *The Small Sects in America*. 1st. rev. ed. New York: Abindon-Cokesbury Press.

Cohen, Norman
    1970       *Pursuit of the Millennium*. 2nd ed. New York: Oxford University Press.

Engels, Frederick
    1964a      "The Peasant War in Germany." In Reinhold Niebuhr, ed., *Karl Marx and Frederick Engels on Religion*. New York: Shocken (originally 1850).
    1964b      "The Book of Revelation." In Reinhold Niebuhr, ed., *Karl Marx and Frederick Engels on Religion*. New York: Shocken (originally 1883).

Fallding, Harold
    1974       *The Sociology of Religion*. Toronto: McGraw-Hill.

Goffman, Erving
    1961       *Asylums: Essays on the Social Situations of Mental Patients and Other Inmates*. Garden City, NY: Doubleday Anchor.

Greenfield, Meg
    1978       "Heart of Darkness." *Newsweek*, 4 December, 132.

Hall, John R.
    1978       *The Ways Out: Utopian Communal Groups in an Age of Babylon*. Boston: Routledge and Kegan Paul.

Jones, Jim
    1978       "Perspectives from Guyana." *Peoples Forum* (January). [Reprinted in Krause, Stern, and
               Harwood, 1978: 205-210.]

Kanter, Rosabeth
    1972       *Commitment and Community: Communes and Utopias in Sociological Perspective.*
               Cambridge, MA: Harvard University Press.

Kilduff, Marshal and Ron Javers
    1978       *The Suicide Cult: The Inside Story of the Peoples Temple Sect and the Massacre In
               Guyana.* New York: Bantam.

Krause, Charles, Lawrence M. Stern, and Richard Harwood
    1978       *Guyana Massacre: The Eye Witness Account.* New York: Berkeley Books.

Lewy, Gunther
    1974       *Religion and Revolution.* New York: Oxford University Press.

Lifton, Robert Jay
    1968       *Revolutionary Immortality: Mao Tse-Tung and the Chinese Cultural Revolution.* New
               York: Vintage.

Marx, Karl and Frederick Engels
    1959       "Manifesto of the Communist Party." In Lewis S. Fewer, ed., *Marx and Engels: Basic
               Writings on Politics and Philosophy.* Garden City, NY: Doubleday Anchor (originally
               1848).

Moberg, David
    1978       "Prison Camp of the Mind." *In These Times* (13 December): 11-14.

Weber, Max
    1977       *Economy and Society.* Edited by G. Roth and Claus Wittich. Berkeley, CA: University of
               California Press (originally 1922).

Zerubavel, Eviatar
    1978       "The Benedictine Ethic and the Spirit of Scheduling." Paper read at the meetings of the
               International Society for the Comparative Study of Civilizations, Milwaukee, Wisconsin.

CHAPTER EIGHTEEN

# CULT EXTREMISM: THE REDUCTION OF NORMATIVE DISSONANCE

### EDGAR W. MILLS, JR.

*Although holy wars, ritual sacrifice, and self-flagellation are well-known uses of violence by religious groups, the appearance of any violence in a religious context remains shocking to contemporary Americans. It is clear, however, that physical violence may indeed become a property of a religious group and be a highly probable experience for the majority of its members. In discussing this matter, let us at the beginning eliminate from consideration both isolated instances of individual violence and the situations created by a leader's sudden shift to violent behavior, since these, though often having social sources, constitute individual deviance rather than group violence. Instead, we will concentrate upon the conditions under which a group may develop so that to be a member is to have a high probability of engaging in violent behavior, even though both the individual's early socialization and the group's ethical norms and values eschew violence.*

*In particular, I will discuss how normative dissonance serves as a source of order and a constraint upon extreme behavior in groups, in addition to giving individuals a significant degree of moral autonomy. The reduction of normative dissonance, which interferes with the full working out of goal-directed rationality in groups, removes this constraint and reduces individual autonomy.*

*Beginning with a summary of recent findings on the Jonestown incident of November 1978, I will examine several converging discussions of normative dissonance that illuminate the more general phenomenon as it affects groups and organizations. At the end I will return with a further application to People's Temple.*

●●●●●●●●●●●●●●●●●●●●●●●●●●●

Edgar W. Mills, Jr. "Cult Extremism: The Reduction of Normative Dissonance," in Ken Levi, ed., *Violence and Religious Commitment*. University Park: Pennsylvania State University Press, pp. 75-87. Copyright 1982 by The Pennsylvania State University. Reproduced by permission of the publisher.

# Violence at Jonestown

A plausible account of sources of the suicide/murder debacle of People's Temple may be developed from the news reports and analyses of late 1978 as well as from more recent discussions by social scientists and other investigators.

People's Temple certainly was more than anything else an extension of the beliefs, plans, and needs of its charismatic leader, Jim Jones. Conflicting tendencies in the organization, present almost from its inception, interacted with changes in Jones's own mind and leadership style and were exacerbated by events in the surrounding society to produce the desperate situation of early November 1978 in Guyana. The processes involved may be grouped under six headings.

*Recruitment of Vulnerable People* Jones's members came largely from three groups: blacks, the elderly, and alienated or confused young whites. Each group has experienced in the larger society some degree of discrimination and deprivation, and many responded to Jones's emphases upon social structural change and amelioration of need. People with depravation backgrounds, even when attracted by an activist program, are probably more susceptible than most people to conspiracy interpretations and to the trapped feelings that led to Jones's retreatist strategies. Further, as Coser (1975) and others have shown, the encouragement of intellectual flexibility needed to exercise independent judgment

> is directly associated with status position. Those who occupy high-status positions are expected to use their judgment, to weigh alternatives, and to be guided in their actions by moral principles, cognitive assessment, and commitments to goals. Those who occupy low [status] positions have much less leeway and fewer options...; for them specific activities are more frequently prescribed in detail, and their relation to a goal is not always clear. (p. 252)

Coser cites evidence regarding both speech and behavior patterns to show that not only low status but traditional, less complex social structures are associated with low autonomy and high behavioral conformity. Thus the elderly and minority recruits generally came from segments of the population most vulnerable both to Jones's conspiratorial theories and to his absolutist control policies.

*Isolation* Increasing control over the exchange of information with the outside world, coupled with suppression of internal dissent, created prolonged intellectual isolation of People's Temple members. Melton (1979:15) regards this isolation as necessary for "the internal logic of a paranoid world view...to work itself to a conclusion." At the same time, especially after the move to Guyana, lack of contact with any outside sources that might have reinforced variant views or action tendencies left members entirely dependent upon the leadership group for value and norm confirmation. In this setting the elaborate resocialization processes undertaken by Jones (both with his central leadership group of 100 and with the larger membership) could proceed with little fear of contradiction and the cultural standards internalized during childhood socialization could be easily eroded.

*Undermining Trust Relationships* The series of moves, from Indiana to California to Guyana, along with increasing residential isolation, cut members off from extended family contact and from friendships formed prior to joining. The disruption of such external ties paralleled the fracturing of family relationships within People's Temple. Proscription of normal sexual contact between spouses, mutual observation and reporting of deviance to leaders, redirecting the sexual activity of women to Jones, separation of children from family environment, and other techniques undermined the normal family bonds that would have provided a base of independence from People's Temple and its leader.

*Heightening of Frustration* In addition to promoting the disruption of relationships and isolation from the outside world, Jones's policies gradually increased the frustration level within the group. Intense demands for service to the organization, all-night meetings, physical exhaustion, overcrowding of living quarters, the contrast between members' privation and Jones's privilege, anxiety about loved ones, fear of arbitrary power — all combined to heighten frustration, which in turn made aggressive behavior more likely.

*Suppression of Alternatives* Safety valves such as internal criticism, democratic procedures, and even voluntary departure from the group were increasingly forbidden. The powerful emphasis upon loyalty was, by the Guyana period, couched in absolutist terms which neither brooked significant deviation nor gave opportunity to influence events. With the heightening of frustration, the blocking of normal relationships, and the suppression of both voice and exit alternatives, the potential for violence grew steadily.

*Legitimation of Violence* Both precept and example made violent means more and more acceptable within People's Temple. Jones's feelings of persecution led to greater reliance on weapons and security measures. The resocialization and disciplinary techniques within the group became quite harsh. Moreover, both real and imagined harassment from without lent plausibility to Jones's interpretation of narrowing options and the closing noose of fascist hostility. Finally, the concept of revolution was given fresh power by the co-optation of a central Christian symbol (taking the cup together) to express a violent rejection of the persecuting world. Revolutionary suicide became acceptable not only through conceptual integration but also through repeated rehearsals that took away its shock value and added legitimacy to the act.

The probability of violence directed either outward or inward is maximized by these six groups of processes. When we are confronted with the Jonestown murder/ suicides it is relatively convincing to adduce these as reason for the tragedy. Yet we have not thereby understood the breakdown of normative order within the group which could lead ostensibly religious, humane, normal people to mass destruction.

Sometimes it helps to stand an issue on its head. Let us, instead of asking "Why violence in Jonestown?" ask the opposite question: "Why not violence in every group" In view of the aggressive tendencies in every human being and the probability that one person's aggressiveness will excite another's, why does violence *not* break out in every group? What is it that restrains violence in most situations and whose absence or breakdown allows violent behavior to emerge in the rare instance? An account of the sources of normative order is essential to understanding how it fails under conditions such as those described above. The remainder of this chapter discusses a major source of normative order in groups and illustrates how its breakdown can create conditions in which the probability of violent action is very high.

## Legitimated Inconsistency

Let us begin with another effort to turn a familiar view around. Kanter declares that in utopian communities "the problem of securing total and complete commitment is central" (1972:65). Beginning with this premise, she offers an impressive conceptual framework from which are derived six mechanisms for building commitment. Our question, however, is whether more commitment is always better. Granted that too little commitment in a group leads to its failure, is there such a thing as too much commitment? I suggest that in most groups the commitment mechanisms are damped and inhibited by the interplay of complex and partially inconsistent norms and values of the group and of its environment. Loss of this damping process leads to a kind of supercommitment in which autonomy, both in moral judgment and role behavior, is replaced by unquestioning obedience, even to participation in violence.

We exist morally within a value space whose boundaries are set by the varied and partly inconsistent values and norms of our reference orientations, including our own standards internalized through earlier socialization. Our moral decisions are made in relation to these boundaries so as to keep us always within this space legitimized by norms and values to which we give some loyalty. This is not a simple equilibrating or homeostatic process consisting of tension reduction and return to a quiet state. Rather it corresponds more to the dynamic life space described in Kurt Lewin's field theory of behavior (1936). As he points out, psychological forces are properties of the environment rather than of the person and moral forces belong to the valuative and normative environment to which each of us refers his or her own inner standards.

The most important fact about this value space is the inconsistency of the various positions that form its boundaries. That is, we accord to several normative sources some degree of legitimacy, and by balancing their credibility, using one set of values or norms to counter another, we create a measure of moral autonomy for ourselves. Individuals thus can make independent decisions without forfeiting group approval or incurring severe guilt because full agreement does not exist within our value space. Its absence is not due simply to interpersonal disagreement about values and norms but also to our own intrapersonal conflicts between normative expectations. The phenomenon of conflicting norms as a fixed characteristic of social systems has been noted by many writers, though not always as a source of autonomy in decision making. One of the most famous of these writers is Robert S. Lynd, who regarded "contradictions among assumptions" as sources of "extreme complexity, contradictoriness and insecurity" for Americans (1940:59, 105). Lynd cites as conflicting assumptions of American life the following, among others:

> 5. Everyone should try to be successful. *But*: The kind of person you are is more important than how successful you are.
> 15. Children are a blessing. *But*: You should not have more children than you can afford.
> 16. No man deserves to have what he has not worked for. It demoralizes him to do so. *But*: You cannot let people starve. (1940:60-62)

He further cites psychoanalyst Karen Horney on the same point: "These contradictions embedded in our culture are precisely the conflicts which the neurotic struggles to reconcile" (1940:102, cited from Horney 1937:289).

Although Horney thus views contrasting assumptions as harmful to individuals, Lynd comes close to pointing out the practical usefulness of such contrasting pairs:

> One [assumption] may be thrown into the scale as decisive in a given situation at one moment, and the other contrasting assumption may be invoked in the same or a different situation a few moments later. It is precisely in this matter of trying to live by contrasting rules of the game that one of the most characteristic aspects of our American culture is to be seen. (1940: 59)

Both Lynd and Horney were so focused upon a rational model of decision making and upon self-consistency as essential to mental health that they did not see the utility of legitimated inconsistency for retaining personal autonomy.

A more perceptive analysis of contrasting norms and values is found in Robert K. Merton's treatment of "sociological ambivalence." One of the earliest and best examples is his discussion of the physician's role as

> a dynamic alternation of norms and counternorms...[which] call for potentially contradictory attitudes and behaviors....This alternation of subroles *evolves* as a social device for helping people in designated statuses to cope with the contingencies they face in trying to fulfill their functions....*Only through such structures of norms and counternorms...can the various functions of a role be effectively discharged.* (1976: 58)

Here contrasting norms (of which Merton lists 21 pairs; see 1976: 67-69) are not the stuff of neurosis nor of insecurity but rather are means for preserving role effectiveness under widely varying conditions of practice. We might generalize that a measure of autonomy in the physician's role thus is rooted in legitimated normative inconsistency, and it makes possible resistance to extreme pressures by invoking contrary norms without loss of role or status.

Contrasting norms and values, however, are not only mechanisms by which role consistency and autonomy may be retained in spite of rationally contradictory behavior. They also are definers of the situation, and in particular they are dampers of commitment. If, for example, a group member holds as a supreme value the good of the group, or perhaps the divine perfection of the leader, the member's family may suffer severely unless the increasingly extreme demands from the group trigger in the member a countervalue of family welfare. This countervalue causes the member to limit his or her commitment to group or leader and to balance their demands against those of the family. By the same token, of course, commitment to the family's welfare is damped by the value placed upon the group's needs. What is important in the example is not the role conflict engendered but the opportunity, indeed the necessity, to choose between commitments that are mutually limiting yet both legitimate for group members. One retains role and status by honoring different loyalties under differing conditions.

To eliminate one side of this contrasting value set is both to decrease the ground for role autonomy and fundamentally to alter the member's commitment by removing the damper. For the group to destroy family ties and refuse legitimacy to the needs of spouse and children (or to provide for those needs in an entirely separate way) effectively releases commitment to group needs from one significant limiting countervalue. As group demands become more extreme there is less basis for refusing them. Thus (to the degree that a member accepts the redefined value structure), as commitment to group needs grows more complete and less damped by countercommitments, role autonomy declines. The consequences for the group include both the loss of a source of criticism and correction (the member with multiple loyalties) and the greater possibility of unquestioning obedience to demands for extreme behavior such as violence to self or others.

An important consequence is that agents of violence or other antisocial behavior need not actually approve their own actions to engage in them. It is sufficient that their inhibiting or damping norms or values be reduced in effectiveness. That is, the ordinary morality of individuals is sustained by their contrasting loyalties to inconsistent standards, with the consequent necessity to keep correcting their behavior whenever allegiance to one norm threatens severe violation of another (thus we refer to "healthy skepticism"). The loss of this damping effect thus releases behavior from its principal inner restraint and allows group influence to carry the individual far beyond what he or she would ordinarily approve.

The observed tendency of leaders to surround themselves with lieutenants who support the leader uncritically likewise greatly reduces the operation of contrasting value sets and leaves the leader vulnerable to extremes of behavior, which can then have dire consequences for the group.

Explanations using legitimated inconsistency are common in the social sciences. Roger Brown (1965:704-706) summarizes social psychological research on the "shift to risk" phenomenon, in which individuals become more likely to take risks after participating in group discussions of the issues. He finds that the findings cannot be explained by a theory based on a single value but rather:

> We value both risk and caution, according to the circumstances. At present we can only say that a story-problem involving risk may engage either the value on caution or the value on risk. The group decision will be more extreme than the individual decision, in the direction of the value engaged, whichever that direction may be. (705)

Broad, culturally based values thus act in opposite directions and may be engaged at different times. I am suggesting that such values receive social support external to the individual through his or her reference orientations, and that the elimination of discrediting of a varied reference set causes the individual to lack an effective range of counterbalancing values that can serve as dampers upon potentially extreme behavior.

In sociological theory, the introduction of pattern variables by Parsons and Shils (1951: 76ff.) was an attempt to systematize the choices in human behavior. Heading their discussion "Dilemmas of orientation and the pattern variables," Parsons and Shils sketched a "system of choices" resembling the value space described above and defined by five continua whose poles constitute the pattern variables. Like Brown, they failed to state clearly the function of these variables in maintaining the individual autonomy but the "dilemma" character of the choices suggests both their role in self-determination within the larger sociocultural system and the damping effect that each pole has upon tendencies toward its opposite.

Yet a third example suggests legitimated inconsistency as useful in managing normatively ambiguous problems. Some recent research on attitudes toward abortion (Barnartt and Harris 1980; Arney and Trescher 1976) suggests that attitudes fall empirically into two subsets that differ in the type of reason given for an abortion. The hard or physical concerns involve circumstances (mother's health endangered, probable deformed child, pregnancy due to rape) in which a woman is forced to become a mother under unfair conditions that are not her fault. The soft or social subset of attitudes consists of elective options (do not want more children, feel they cannot afford more, parents not married) in which the possibility of abortion arises not from coercive circumstances but from a rational decision not to complete what seems to have been voluntarily begun. I believe these two subsets invoke different cultural values that constitute a contrasting pair (in Merton's sense): the hard or coercive reasons refer to the value placed on freedom of action and a mother's right to decide without being forced, and the soft or elective reasons engage the value placed on personal responsibility to see through a task one has begun, regardless of preference. Abortion is thus approved or disapproved depending on which of the two values is primarily heeded. Both values are held by most Americans, with each serving to damp extreme tendencies either toward liberalism or toward unfair coercion. Both are valued, as Brown says, but "according to the circumstances."

## Rationality and the Generation of Slack

Just as normative dissonance allows individuals to create autonomy for themselves by means of legitimated inconsistent behavior, so at the social-system level the presence of contrasting norms and values assures a ferment of differences that both encourages innovation and interferes with system efficiency. In moderation this dynamic protects against supercommitment and undamped tendencies to extreme behavior.

Alvin Gouldner, discussing reciprocity and autonomy in functional theory (1959), points out the need of individuals (as parts) to maintain a degree of functional autonomy from the larger system. Further, he says,

> a need of systems, which possess parts having degrees of functional autonomy, is to inhibit their own tendencies to subordinate and fully specialize these parts. In short, they must inhibit their own tendencies toward "wholeness" or complete integration if they are to be stable. The system model…is not one in which the system is viewed as a "plunger" playing an all-or-none game, but as a minimax player seeking to strike a federalizing balance between totalitarian and anarchist limits. (159-160)

Later, Gouldner says:

> It is of the essence of social roles that they never demand total role involvement by the actors but only segmental and partial involvements. [The significance of] the part's involvement in multiple systems [is]...not only that such a functionally autonomous part will be refractory to system steering but that it will tend to oscillate and initiate changes. (162)

What Gouldner describes in social-system terms can be restated in the language of cultural norms and value. Multiple reference orientations ally a group member with socially legitimated values and norms that are somewhat at odds with each other, making the individual refractory to behavioral steering by a single loyalty and inducing him or her to "oscillate and initiate changes." As a result, stable groups (religious and otherwise), even those with strong orthodoxies, tend to allow degrees of lukewarmness and to develop a tolerance for what Everett Hughes called "the rhythms and cycles of birth, growth, and decline and death" (1958:21). The balance that groups thus strike between Gouldner's "totalitarian and anarchist limits" arises from members' own multiple loyalties.

It is but one step more to recognize that these indeterminacies by which individual moral autonomy and group stability are sustained are inimical to any hard-headed rationality that seeks to bring all of life under a single principle rigorously and unswervingly applied. Therefore, the value space within which an individual exercises freedom of choice, which is protected by his or her multiple reference loyalties, is constantly in danger of being reduced by leaders who aspire to total rationality, to complete devotion to a cause. Reduction of value space (and thus of moral autonomy) to a unidimensional line, in which obedience rather than decision making is called for, deprives the group of the alternative criteria by which potentially extreme forms of behavior are inhibited. Thus the larger system becomes vulnerable to mobilization of its obedient parts into violent action undamped by contrasting norms. As Kanter says, "All human groups may need to strike balances, for social life is full of such tradeoffs" (1972:234).

The tension between throughgoing rationality and the moral autonomy of individuals is also illuminated by economist Albert Hirschman's *Exit, Voice, and Loyalty* (1970). Noting the classical economic model of perfect competition, he evokes "the image of a relentlessly taut economy" in which "society as a whole produces a comfortable...surplus, but every individual firm considered in isolation is barely getting by, so that a single false step will be its undoing. As a result, everyone is constantly made to perform at the top of his form..." Classical economic theory thus idealizes the taut economy and regards slack as fault or failure.

Yet, as Hirschman shows in some detail, slack is constantly generated both in economic and in organizational terms. Performance (judged on rational, goal-oriented grounds) is continually being undermined in a kind of social entropy. "Firms and other organizations are conceived to be permanently and randomly subject to decline and decay, that is, to a gradual loss of rationality, efficiency, and surplus-producing energy, no matter how well the institutional framework within which they function is designed" (1970:15). Hirschman's comments evoke echoes of Hughes, Gouldner, and others who find that the goal-oriented organization is difficult to maintain at full rigor and gradually evolves into a more complex system. The white heat of total commitment is replaced by softer demands that recognize both the legitimacy of individual needs and also the importance of the "cycles and turning points" of the calendar as regulators of fluctuating commitment. Like these sociologists, Hirschman finds that "slack fulfills some important, if unintended or latent, functions." It acts "like a reserve that can be called upon," offering a degree both of stability and of emergency resources to an organization which, if always taut, would be much more volatile and vulnerable to environmental changes.

Normative dissonance likewise may be seen as slack by goal-oriented leaders, since it legitimates inconsistent behavior by members. Yet it both protects the organization from extreme volatility and produces for it a level of collective wisdom not available to fully taut groups with supercommitted members.

## Conclusion: The Slide toward Violence

The idea of normative dissonance has led us in several directions. At the level of the individual, the presence of contrasting sets of norms and values creates a degree of autonomy and develops skill in weighing alternatives, charting one's own course among them, and managing inner dissonance arising from multiple reference orientations. Members of groups may thus legitimately behave inconsistently, invoking differing standards at various times. Retaining some degree of commitment to contrasting norms provides a natural damper upon tendencies to extreme behavior and thus protects the individual from demands for supercommitment in any direction.

At the group level, the presence of multiple loyalties in a broad value space among members may, depending upon the leader's ideology, be perceived either as slack interfering with pursuit of group goals or as breadth and depth that members contribute to the group's wisdom in decision making. In either case the strict rationality of goal-oriented behavior is modified by slack that diverts energy and subverts efforts to rationalize commitment. Since this kind of slack is constantly being generated in an open group, drastic measures must be taken by leaders if they are to achieve a taut organization with supercommitted members. Such measures characterize totalitarian societies, though-reform or brainwashing programs, extreme militant cults or movements, and many tightly run mission-oriented organizations. The summary of reasons for the Jonestown tragedy earlier in this paper reflects just such measures:

physical and social isolation, control of information flow, undermining trust relationships, suppression of alternatives. Without them, the moral field of the group, with its natural normative dissonance, would have made impossible the legitimation and use of violence by the majority of members. These measures served to destroy the damper effect upon which member autonomy rests and so to prepare the group to slide toward violence.

I want to emphasize that the violence itself came from Jim Jones and the leadership cadre, through their use of the mounting frustration they generated among followers. The relative absence of normative dissonance within a group does not in itself produce violence — many examples exist of wholehearted and unquestioning devotion to a cause or leader that does not issue in violence. Rather, the absence of this natural damping process robs the group and its members of their principal protection against demands for supercommitment, for unquestioning obedience. Further, this happens more easily among religious cults than sects, since the latter are rooted in longstanding traditions which themselves contain normative dissonance and serve to define norms and values that effectively damp tendencies to extreme behavior. Among cults, however, the absence of a nurturing tradition within their environing society leaves their members more susceptible to the demand for total obedience to leader commands. (See Stark and Bainbridge 1979 for a useful discussion of sects and cults.)

A final comment may help to place this discussion within the larger context of theories of social behavior. I am clearly presenting yet another member of the family of dissonance or incongruence theories. Cognitive dissonance and balance theories among sociologists are familiar members of this family. The dynamic for behavior in most such discussions (and thus their explanatory power) is based on the individual's effort to *reduce* dissonance and to re-equilibrate his or her inner life to a normal or tolerable level. They are essentially homeostatic theories of behavior motivated by the attempt to reduce dissonance. While they are surely sound in part, I am proposing that individuals also learn to *value* dissonance and to cultivate it as a source of autonomy in the face of demands for conformity or commitment to group goals. Thus normative dissonance, like the role complexity of which Coser has written in similar vein (1975), offers opportunity for self-directed change and management of group loyalty precisely by sustaining the dissonance rather than reducing it. People who are unwilling or unable to tolerate such dissonance, or who are caught up in groups that destroy the social supports for multiple reference orientations, are likely to become collaborators in the reduction of their own moral freedom to reluctant obedience. While the slide toward violence is not thereby made inevitable, the way is opened for an entire group to act in ways that each individual in it would have abhorred.

● ● ● ● ● ● ● ● ● ● ● ● ● ● ● ● ● ● ● ● ● ● ● ● ● ●

# References

Brown, Roger
    1965    *Social Psychology.* New York: The Free Press.

Coser, Rose Laub
    1975    "Complexity of Roles as a Seedbed of Individual Autonomy." In Lewis A. Coser, ed., *The Idea of Social Structure.* New York: Harcourt, Brace, Jovanovich.

Gouldner, Alvin
    1959    "Reciprocity and Autonomy in Functional Theory." In Llewellyn Gross, ed. *Symposium on Sociological Theory.* New York: Harper and Row.

Hirschmann, Albert
    1970    *Exit, Voice, and Loyalty.* Cambridge: Harvard University Press.

Horney, Karen
    1937    *The Neurotic Personality of Our Time.* New York: Norton, 1937.

Hughes, Everett C.
    1958    *Men and Their Work.* New York: The Free Press.

Kanter, Rosabeth
    1972    *Commitment and Community.* Cambridge, Mass.: Harvard University Press.

Lynd, Robert S.
    1940    *Knowledge for What?* Princeton, N.J.: Princeton University Press.

Merton, Robert K.
    1976    *Sociological Ambivalence and Other Essays.* New York: The Free Press.

Parsons, Talcott and Edward A. Shils, eds.
    1951    *Toward a General Theory of Action.* Cambridge: Harvard University Press.

# THE CULTURAL SIGNIFICANCE OF NEW RELIGIOUS MOVEMENTS

## Introduction to the Readings

Some sociologists of religion see the rise of so many NRMs in the late twentieth century as indicative of the continued need for some vibrant spiritual dimension to life, even in the midst of the triumph of science, technology, and consumerism (e.g., Mol, 1976; Stark and Bainbridge, 1985; Finke and Stark, 1992). Other sociologists of religion (e.g., Berger, 1967; Fenn, 1978; Wilson, 1988), convinced that our societies are becoming increasingly secular, interpret the rise of NRMs as the desperate last gasps of religion. Determining which view is more accurate is extremely difficult, because the data at hand lends itself to either interpretation (see e.g. Tschannen, 1991; Warner, 1993). Though never clearly articulated before, a survey of the scattered literature on the possible cultural significance of NRMs suggests general agreement, for example, on three interrelated points: the rise of NRMs reflects (1) a strong movement towards the extension and even institutionalization of religious and cultural pluralism; (2) an extension of religious individualism and voluntarism; and (3), an extension of the demand for a more experiential basis for belief. This simply means that more people today expect to be able to freely choose more aspects of their religious beliefs and practices, from a wider array of possibilities (both from within and without their own cultural heritage). Moreover, the choices are being guided increasingly by an interest in specific new experiences or the felt experience of an improvement in one's well being. In other words, on both counts, tradition and custom are giving way as the prime determinants of people's religious orientations (see Bibby, 1987; Roof and McKinney, 1987).

Seen in one light, these developments (if true) suggest that religion as it has commonly existed for thousands of years is dying. The three patterns of change reflect the increased "privatization" of religion. It is losing its public significance as a source of generalized meaning and order and becoming an aspect of people's leisure time. Seen in another light, these developments do not point so much to the demise of religion, as its natural transformation and adaptation to new social circumstances. The new religions effecting this adaptation may well succeed in making things religious far more relevant, once again, to the daily lives of individuals in our postmodern societies. Of course choosing between these two interpretive options hinges on what we think about several other issues basic to the study of religious phenomena, like the very definition of religion, our assessment of the psychological and sociological functions of religion, and whether we think humans are in some sense intrinsically religious. These long-standing concerns carry us well beyond the confines of this limited collection of readings. They are indirectly addressed, however, in each of the three readings chosen for this final section.

The first reading, Susan Palmer's "Women's 'Cocoon Work' in New Religious Movements: Sexual Experimentation and Feminine Rites of Passage," was chosen for several reasons. First, as Palmer (1994), Jacobs (1984), Aidala (1985), Davidman (1990) and many others have demonstrated, the sexes tend to experience NRMs differently. The reasons why women join, remain members of, or quit NRMs tend to be distinct from why men do. This is an important variable not adequately considered in the rest of the readings in this book nor in the social scientific literature on NRMs in general (see Davidman and Jacobs, 1993). Second, like Robbins and Bromley (1992), Palmer argues that NRMs seem to be operating as forums for significant social experimentation. In other words, in their practices as well as their very existence NRMs are actively facilitating the emergence of patterns of heightened pluralism and voluntarism in our societies. Third, Palmer documents how NRMs are particularly involved in diverse collective experiments with alternative forms of sex and gender identities and relations. Typologically she distinguishes at least three distinct approaches to sex and gender relations in different NRMs: sex complementarity groups (e.g., The Unification Church), sex polarity groups (e.g., The International Society of Krishna Consciousness), and sex unity groups (e.g., Scientology). In each kind of group we find women seeking different kinds of solutions to their disaffection with either the ambiguity, harshness, or insufficiency of the changes brought about in their lives by the counter-culture, feminism, and the new economic realities of the dual income family. As James Hunter stipulates in the second section of this reader, the de-institutionalization of the private sphere of life has de-stabilized accepted patterns of courtship, sexuality, marriage, reproduction, and child-rearing in our society. Such intimate activities are at the core of the quest for meaning in our lives and most NRMs are dedicated to the reform, organization, legitimation, and regulation of these very activities. As such they can provide "safe havens" or "cocoons" within which individuals can practice alternative life-styles, for a time or, in a few instances, permanently.

The second reading, Phillip Lucas' "The New Age Movement and the Pentecostal/ Charismatic Revival: Distinct Yet Parallel Phases of a Fourth Great Awakening?", uniquely demonstrates how even new religious movements of seemingly antithetical natures share a number of common traits, traits which may be indicative of a broader transformation of the religious environment of North America. Simultaneously this reading points to a crucial measure of continuity between the present and the past by suggesting a connection between the religious fervour of recent years and the Great Awakenings that have periodically marked the religious history of North America. Different historians delineate the number and the dates of the movements of religious revival, called Great Awakenings, that have swept over the United States and (to an lesser extent) Canada in different ways. But to probe the significance of the rise of NRMs Lucas somewhat rhetorically asks us to compare the religious changes we are witnessing with three earlier periods of significant cultural change: The First Great Awakening (1730-1760), The Second Great Awakening (1800-1830), and The Third Great Awakening (1890-1920) (McLoughlin, 1978). Seen in this light, the thematic continuity he detects between the New Age and the Pentecostal/Charismatic movements, with their starkly contrasting "theologies," may be more important than any differences. In his analysis of these common themes we encounter the movement towards greater religious pluralism, voluntarism, and the demand for religious experience. This essay also introduces students, of course, to two other important and highly diverse aspects of the study of NRMs not directly addressed in previous readings, namely the nature of the two movements being compared.

In the third and final reading, Phillip Hammond, a veteran observer of the contemporary religious scene in America, directly inquires about the significance of NRMs. The three themes of pluralism, voluntarism, and to a lesser extent the demand for experience emerge from his analysis as well. But here, unlike the first two readings, these developments are interpreted as unintentionally advancing the secularization of American society. Highlighting the impact of the rise of NRMs on the link between the family and religion on the one hand, and the state and religion on the other hand, Hammond paints a bleaker picture of the future of religion. His analysis provides an important illustration of the wisdom of the traditional sociological inclination to heed the unanticipated consequences of peoples' actions. Actions taken by both sides in the cult controversy, the NRMs and the anti-cult movement, with the intention of protecting and improving the religious life and rights of Americans, actually may have hastened the systematic marginalization of religious organizations, new and old.

● ● ● ● ● ● ● ● ● ● ● ● ● ● ● ● ● ● ● ● ● ● ● ● ● ●

# References

Aidala, Angela
  1985      "Social Change, Gender Roles, and New Religious Movements." *Sociological Analysis* 46 (3): 287-314.

Berger, Peter L.
  1967      *The Scared Canopy: Elements of a Sociological Theory of Religion.* Garden City, NY: Doubleday.

Bibby, Reginald
  1987      *Fragmented Gods: The Poverty and Potential of Religion in Canada.* Toronto: Irwin.

Davidman, Lynn
  1990      "Women's Search for Family and Roots: A Jewish Religious Solution to a Modern Dilemma." Pp. 385-407 in T. Robbins and D. Anthony, eds., *In Gods We Trust.* 2nd edition. New Brunswick, NJ: Transaction Pub.

Davidman, Lynn and Janet Jacobs
  1993      "Feminist Perspectives on New Religious Movements." Pp. 173-190 in D.G. Bromley and J.K. Hadden, eds., *Religion and The Social Order, Volume 3, The Handbook on Cults and Sects in America, Part B.* Greenwich, CT: JAI Press.

Fenn, Richard K.
  1978      *Toward a Theory of Secularization.* Ellington, CT: Society for the Scientific Study of Religion.

Finke, Roger and Rodney Stark
  1992      *The Churching of America, 1776-1990.* New Brunswick, NJ: Rutgers University Press.

Jacobs, Janet L.
  1985      "The Economy of Love in Religious Commitment." *Journal for the Scientific Study of Religion* 23 (2): 155-171.

McLoughlin, William G.
  1978      *Revivals, Awakenings, and Reform: An Essay on Religion and Social Change in America, 1607-1977.* Chicago: University of Chicago Press.

Mol, Hans
  1976      *Identity and the Sacred: A Sketch for a New Social Scientific Theory of Religion.* New York: The Free Press.

Palmer, Susan Jean
  1994      *Moon Sisters, Krishna Mothers, Rajneesh Lovers: Women's Roles in New Religions.* Syracuse, NY: Syracuse University Press.

Robbins, Thomas and David Bromley
   1992      "Social Experimentation and the Significance of American New Religions: A Focused
              Review Essay." Pp. 1-28 in M. Lynn and D. Moberg, eds., *Research in the Social Scientific
              Study of Religion*, Vol. 4. Greenwich, CT: JAI Press.

Roof, Wade Clark and William McKinney
   1988      *American Mainline Religion: Its Changing Shape and Future.* New Brunswick, NJ: Rutgers
              University Press.

Stark, Rodney and William Sims Bainbridge
   1985      *The Future of Religion - Secularization, Revival and Cult Formation.* Berkeley, CA:
              University of California Press.

Tschannen, Oliver
   1991      "The Secularization Paradigm: A Systematization." *Journal for the Scientific Study of
              Religion* 30 (4): 395-415.

Warner, Stephen R.
   1993      "Work in Progress Toward a New Paradigm for the Sociological Study of Religion in the
              United States." *American Journal of Sociology* 98 (5): 1044-1093.

Wilson, Bryan R.
   1988      "'Secularization': Religion in the Modern World." Pp. 953-966 in Stewart Sutherland et
              al., eds., *The World's Religions*. London: Routledge.

# WOMEN'S 'COCOON WORK' IN NEW RELIGIOUS MOVEMENTS: SEXUAL EXPERIMENTATION AND FEMININE RITES OF PASSAGE

## SUSAN J. PALMER

On the basis of research into alternative women's roles in eight new religious movements, this study addresses conflicting views concerning the relationship between gender role ambiguities and women's participation in the sexual innovations developing in NRMs, summed up as the "empowerment" versus the "neopatriarchy" school of thought. A close study of the literature and histories of these groups suggests that they are more varied, flexible, and experimental in their patterns of sexuality than previous studies would indicate; and that, for the majority of members, involvement is a transitory phenomenon, providing them with opportunities for participating in laboratories of sexual experimentation. Adopting a "gendered" approach to the issue of "cult conversion," this study argues that contemporary women find protective, supportive microsocieties in NRMs, which enable them to try out a spectrum of clearly defined roles that prepare them to choose a more personally gratifying adult mode when they eventually defect. By temporarily inhabiting the stylized feminine roles in NRMs and submitting to their leaders' erotic/ascetic ordeals, members appear to undergo a self-imposed psychological metamorphosis, or "cocoon work," which in many ways resembles the ritual process found in feminine rites of passage in traditional societies.

In contrast to the depth of interest shown by historians and anthropologists in women's participation in utopias (Foster 1981; Kern 1981; Moore 1977), ecstatic cults (Cohn 1970; Lewis 1971), and Christian heresies (Pagels 1988; Ruether 1983), the issue of women's experiences in contemporary nonconventional religions has not been adequately addressed. Fieldwork in the area of NRM sex roles is limited (Wagner

Susan J. Palmer. "Women's 'Cocoon Work' in New Religious Movements: Sexual Experimentation and Feminine Rites of Passage." *Journal for the Scientific Study of Religion* 32, 1993: 343-355.

1982; Wallis 1982; Richardson, Stewart, and Simmonds 1979; Wessinger, forthcoming), and only a few "gendered" approaches to "cult conversion" processes (Grace 1985; Rochford 1985; Barker 1984) have been written. Thus, the appeal for women of communities practicing spiritually based forms of celibacy, polygamy, eugenics, or "free love" remains enigmatic.

Robbins (1988) identifies a rift between those scholars who stress the *empowerment* of women in unconventional spiritual groups (Babb 1986; Bednarowski 1980; Haywood 1983; Neitz 1988) and an opposing "camp" (Aidala 1985; Davidman 1991; Rose 1987) who portray NRMs as a *backlash* against the feminist movement and a retreat into conservative family patterns within enclaves of patriarchy. Jacob's study of women's defection from NRMs (1984), for example, presents NRMs as magnifying the patriarchal patterns of authority found in mainstream religions. Since social control in charismatic communities is greater, Jacobs (1984:158) argues, "the overall effect is a system in which men are dominant, women are submissive and the exercise of male power leads to almost total subordination of the female devotees." Interestingly, scholars of nineteenth-century "new religions" tend to find their women "empowered," whereas studies of contemporary NRMs (with the notable exception of Wicca) often stress the theme of feminine degradation, a view reflected in literature of the anticult movement (Ritchie 1991) and in the press — as summed up by *The Guardian* (1991:33): "The degrading treatment of women in many religious cults today reads like a chapter from the dark ages. Yet 200 years ago, women were leaders of a number of sects, asserting feminine equality (and even superiority) within them. What went wrong?"

Perhaps the most objective and comprehensive analysis of the relationship between current gender ambiguities and youth's conversion to NRMs appears in Aidala's seminal study (1985). Aidala argues that communal NRMs are responding to the erosion of norms regulating gender roles occurring in the larger society. She demonstrates that members of religious communes (as opposed to secular ones) exhibit a low tolerance for the shifting interpretations of masculinity and femininity. She proposes an "elective affinity" between the clear-cut sex roles found in charismatic groups and the need perceived in contemporary youth to resolve gender-related ambiguities. She finds that, unlike the individualistic experimentation occurring in secular communes, where the rules governing sexual behavior are ill-defined, religiously based gender roles are rigid and absolute. While Aidala (1985:297) notes among her groups "a great diversity in sexual and gender role ideology," she emphasizes their universal patriarchal character. In her view, joining religious communes represents a *flight* from feminism, modernity, and the moral ambiguity that characterizes our pluralistic society. The static, rigid quality of new religious sex roles, therefore, she interprets as a *rejection of or reaction against* the more fluid and experimental approaches prevailing in the secular sphere.

In this study I propose a "gendered" specification and modification of Aidala's central argument: that communal NRMs provide ideological resolutions to moral ambiguity and gender confusion. First, evidence shows that new religious sex roles are considerably more diverse than Aidala acknowledges, challenging previous classifications as "patriarchal" or "feminist." Second, they are more *fluid* in their patterns of gender and authority than Aidala's more static portrait suggests — and, if observed over a period of time, exhibit flexibility and a commitment to experimentation. Third, given the high attrition rates found in NRMs, and striking affinities between the "liminal period" (Turner, 1968) and new religious sexual experiments, I argue that the "cult experience," for most female participants, can best be understood as fulfilling a similar function to the feminine rites of passage found in traditional societies.

This study will demonstrate the wide variety of feminine roles available in NRMs, and will analyze the various routes to resolving gender ambiguity outlined in these movements. Eight groups were selected for study, as examples of NRMs in which women's roles were radically alternative, highly developed, and mutually contrasting:

The International Society of Krishna Consciousness (ISKCON)
The Unification Church (UC)
The Rajneesh Movement (currently known as Osho Friends International)
The Institute for the Harmonious Development of the Human Being (IDHHB)
The Raelian Movement International
The Northeast Kingdom Community Church (NEKC)
The Ansaaru Allah Community (AAC)
The Institute of Applied Metaphysics (IAM)

Information on their gender roles was gathered from a variety of sources, including NRM literature, videocassettes of leaders' discourses, field research, and over 150 interviews with members and ex-members.

## The Diversity of New Religious Women's Roles

Aidala (1985:297) insists that "in none of the religious communes did ideological formulation or practice pose a direct challenge to the traditional allocation of greater social and economic power to men. Many groups actively promoted traditional inequalities. Those that did not denied the reality of inequalities which allowed traditional patterns to continue." Many of the groups studied here challenge this statement. The Raelian Movement, for example, deliberately encourages homosexual and bisexual expression (Palmer 1992). Rajneesh and Brahmakumari leaders are overwhelmingly female (Babb 1986; Barker 1991; Gordon 1986). Leaders' speeches conveying notions of radical or conservative romantic feminism (Ruether 1983), denouncing men as world spoilers and exalting women as world saviors, appear in such NRM literature as *A New Vision of Woman's Liberation* (Rajneesh 1987), *Adi Dev the First Man* (Chander 1981), and *Sensual Meditation* (Vorilhon 1986).

The most striking feature of women's roles in new religious movements, besides their diversity, is their clarity and simplicity. This clarity seems to be achieved by emphasizing *one* role and de-emphasizing or rejecting others. Krishna-conscious women, for example, are defined as "mothers" by title and by occupation, even if unmarried or childless (Knott 1987; Rochford 1985). The sexually expressive Rajneeshee is a "lover" in relation to Bhagwan Shree Rajneesh (metaphorically speaking) and to the male disciples; but she was not permitted to give birth or raise her existing children during the communal phase, and the role of "wife" is still considered demeaning (Belfrage 1981; Milne 1986). Women in the Raelian Movement are defined as sensually aware, bisexual "playmates" and tend to reject marriage in favor of "free love," and avoid procreating in anticipation of being cloned by extraterrestrials (Vorilhon 1986; Palmer 1992).

Even many NRMs that appear to foster "traditional" roles deviate widely from the mainstream (and from each other) in their interpretations of woman's domestic role. Exemplary "wives" in the Institute of Applied Metaphysics are postmenopausal, childless "handmaidens" and work partners to their considerably younger "lords" (Morris 1986). "Wives" in the Ansaaru Allah Community are heavily veiled and come in sets of four, since the Nubian household should (ideally) feature a Domestic Wife, a Cultured Wife, an Educated Wife, and a Companion Wife (As Sayyid 1988). In their role of "breeder," AAC women are exhorted to usher in the 144,000 pure Nubian children to "rapture" their parents when the satanic reign of the "paleman" ends in the cataclysm of 2000 (As Sayyid 1987). In spite of this literary emphasis on the ideal Muslim family, real-life Ansaars live in same-sex dormitories, separated from their children, and are permitted to cohabit with their spouses once every three months in the "Green Room," in accordance with their founder's racialist eugenics theory (Philips 1988). Unificationist women have opted for a wider range of roles — but only one role at a time. They begin their careers in the movement as celibate "sisters," and then become "daughters" of Reverend Moon when he blesses them in marriage to one of their "brothers." These marriages remain unconsummated for three or more years, during which time the "wives" strive to mature into "The Ideal Woman" (Grace 1985).

Thus, a survey of a corner of the "spiritual supermarket" suggests that a contemporary North American woman who is seeking alternative spiritual, sexual, and social experiences is presented with a remarkable range of possibilities. She can be a celibate "sister," a devoted "wife," a domineering "lover," a veiled "Nubian Bride," an immortal "Yin-Tang Unit," a "breeder" of the perfect race, an ageless, celibate "daughter" with magical powers, a "quadrasexual playmate," or an asexual shaman.

New religious models of gender also vary widely. Aidala (1985:294) found three basic approaches to understanding gender relations: "biblically based understandings of patriarchy, bio-mystical complementarity and subjectivist denials of gender differences."

These three approaches apply to the eight groups explored here and correspond to Allen's typology (1987:21) of sex polarity/sex complementarity/sex unity, describing three philosophical notions of sex identity developed within Christendom. Some elaboration is required in order to increase the relevance of this model to eclectic and "oriental import" NRMs, as follows[1].

*Sex Complementarity* groups endow each sex with unique spiritual qualities, and emphasize marriage as the union of spiritual opposites in order to form a whole androgyne. Gender and marriage continue in the afterlife, marriage to the dead is possible, and weddings and procreation assist in ushering in the Millennium. A dual or androgynous godhead overshadows these communities. The Unification Church, Northeast Kingdom, and Institute of Applied Metaphysics conform to this view.

*Sex Polarity* groups regard the sexes as spiritually different, and as useless or obstructive to the other's salvation. The notion of sex pollution is importantly present and the sexes are segregated so as to avoid weakening each other's spiritual resolve. Levels of salvation might be quite different for men and women since they are unequal. ISKCON and the Ansaars espouse this view, whereas the Rajneeshee and the Brahmakumaris might be described as "reverse sex polarity" groups, where women are vaunted as spiritually more powerful than men.

*Sex Unity* groups view the body and its gender as a superficial layer of false identity obscuring the immortal, asexual spirit. Groups espousing this view might adopt "unisex" clothing and cultivate androgynous social *personae*, or they might "play act" traditional sex roles while maintaining a psychological detachment from these roles. In shamanistic or gnostic groups there is often the notion that by transcending the limits of social/sexual identity, the adept can release the powerful spiritual potentialities. The IDHHB, Scientology, and the Raelians espouse this view.

While these models are not necessarily unique to NRMs, and feminist theorists like Mary Daly, Dana Densmore, and Valerie Solanas have articulated versions of androgyny and sex polarity that are no less radically alternative (Castro 1984), new religions appear to offer more scope for collective and individual experimentation in praxis. Women in secular society, whether they define themselves as lesbian feminists or as Real Women, must confront conflicting notions of gender in moving from the private through the different sectors of the public sphere. The secretary, for example, will expect sex unity in her paycheck, will "act out" sex polarity in the synagogue or the YMCA locker room — but might yearn for sex complementarity in the course of her Friday night dinner date. Elaborate "facework" is required in our pluralistic society as women move from one arena to the next (Goffman 1959; Westley 1983). Within intentional communities, however, *one* model of gender prevails. Dress codes, rituals, work roles, and authority patterns tend to reflect a single, clear-cut model of male-female relations.

Creation myths educate new religious women in the mysteries of sexuality and offer theodicies to explain the ongoing war between the sexes that is waging outside their utopias. These myths convey clear-cut models of gender — as, for example, when the 3,500-year-old warrior Ramtha (channelled by J.Z. Knight) relates the myth of how one god, Duvall-Debra, split into male and female and how the two became enemies "through jealousy, possessiveness and ... superiority" (*Ramtha Intensive:*

*Soulmates,* 1987). The notion of sex unity is dramatized in the *Creation Story Verbatim* (Gold 1973) when "god" recalls how he sent a spaceship to save human specimens when Atlantis was flooded, and how the ship's captain "goofed" by rescuing two males, so that one of them had to undergo a sex-change operation, and then even god couldn't tell which was which.

New feminine archetypes hold out keys to understanding — or at least testing — who woman is and what her potential might be. These narratives establish the guidelines for courtship rituals, marital relations, and sexual ethics in spiritual communities. Informants described the therapeutic and empowering effects of inhabiting these roles. One ex-Ansaar observed, "I felt superior wearing the veil, because it was not easy .... I had to put away western ideas of beauty and fashion and become a Muslim .... It made me feel godly. It made me feel like Eve when I learned that Eve dressed this way after the world got populated .... Also, Sarah, Abraham's wife — and all other righteous women in the Bible." Unificationist women are encouraged to relate their own sad experiences of the "abuse of love" with Eve's tragic seduction at the hands of Satan. Participants in the 1983 "Conference on Eve," held at Barrytown, New York even described encountering Eve and conversing with her during their "travels in the spirit world."[2] Within these carefully supervised playing fields, women can explore the potential and limitations of new religious models of gender in their daily life.

# The Experimental Quality of NRM Patterns of Gender

A striking feature of new religions, when observed over a period of time, is their flexibility in trying out different patterns of authority and gender. This experimentation occurs on two levels: the collective and the individual.

## COLLECTIVE EXPERIMENTS

A close study of NRMs' short histories reveals a tendency to "flip-flop" in policies for awarding leadership posts determined by gender. Two outstanding examples of this pattern are the Institute of Applies Metaphysics (IAM) and the Rajneesh movement. In the early days of IAM (1963-1975) women were leaders, but after the "Yin-Yang units" were formed, husband and wife were defined as equal halves of a whole person, and took part in ritual and work life as a team. Women's authority began to plummet in 1983 after the founder Winifred Barton was deposed by her husband (Morris 1986). A similar mood of experimentation can be found throughout the history of the Rajneesh Movement. During the 1981-1985 communal phase in Rajneeshpuram, women were conspicuous in leadership positions. After the "Sheela scandal" in 1985, however, the group became disillusioned with the utopian notion that women were less aggressive than men, and the international communes began to appoint male leaders. This experiment was abandoned after the group settled back in Poona, and women took over the reins again.

Even "patriarchal" groups fostering nostalgic recreations of perfect families from a mythic golden age are wont to improvise. The ascephalous Northeast Kingdom Community will occasionally modify its conservative gender roles, as when the women in Island Pond put aside their head coverings during working days, in response to a collective revelation received by the elders in Boston in April, 1991.[3] The AAC leader, As Sayyid as Imaam Isa, after instructing women since 1969 to wear a face veil, accept polygamy, and devote their energies to housework, suddenly announced in the January 1992 *Nubian Village Bulletin* his change of title to "The Lamb, Liberator of Women," and advised women to discard the veil, wear "pantoons," and embrace monogamy. Today women are permitted (in theory) to "peddle" crafts on public streets, drive cars, and preach in the mosque.

Exercises permitting members to "play-act" the opposite sex are found in several therapeutically oriented NRMs. The Raelians hold a transvestite banquet dance on the final night of the Sensual Meditation Camp, and, as one member put it, "We show the opposite sex what we don't like about the way they treat us!" The Rajneesh hold a "Sexual Fantasies" party at the end of their "Tantra" therapy groups in Poona, and one participant described how one man dressed as a prostitute, another dressed as Lolita, and one woman came as a male "flasher." The IDHHB practice "gender-erasing" in the "Daysnap" exercise, which requires participants to vocally assume the personalities of "Helpful Herbie," "Gross-out Gertrude," "Doubtful Danny," or "Condescending Connie" (Palmer 1976). Est trainees "make asses of themselves" in a role-playing exercise described by Rhinehart (1976:150-151):

> In two of the most difficult roles, women are asked to play the role of a
> loud, stupid, blustering drunk, and men are asked to play a "cute" ten-
> year old girl reciting a silly flirtatious poem about herself: the women
> being asked to be aggressively masculine, the men pertly feminine.

## INDIVIDUAL EXPERIMENTATION

The experimentation in gender and sexual mores found in NRMs can also be observed taking place on the individual level. As Robbins and Bromley (1992:3) pointed out, new members who "adopt the convert role and collaborate in the process of self-reconstruction often conceive of themselves as engaged in experimentation." Several informants for this study described conversion careers in which they had moved through a series of spiritual movements, assuming serial feminine identities and experimenting with various forms of celibacy, polygamy, and/or pantagamy.

The interview data and sex ratio surveys challenge prevailing notions that "cultwomen" are the passive victims of the ineluctable forces of charisma, "brainwashing," or "patriarchal authority," who will submit to whatever sexual excesses emanate from the leader's dark libido. Our informants made it clear they chose *which* experiment to participate in, and for specific personal reasons. The interviews suggest that women are drawn to groups that offer them the roles they feel comfortable inhabiting, an escape route from the too-demanding roles in the modern family, or an initiation into a longed-for role that eluded them in secular life. A comparison of sex ratios indicates that some movements hold a stronger appeal for one sex than for the other. Men outnumber women two to one in the Unificationist Church (Barker 1984; Grace 1985), whereas women outnumber men by a considerable margin in the Brahmakumaris (Babb 1986), and by a slight margin in the Rajneesh Movement (Braun 1984; Gordon 1986; Milne 1986). Groups that espouse the "reverse sex polarity" view and promote feminine leadership appear to attract more women than men.

Contributing to the argument that women select NRMs that serve their particular needs is evidence that different age sets are represented in different movements, as are specific classes of women. The great majority of women attending Spiritualist seances are in late middle age or elderly (Haywood 1983), whereas the mean age of women in the Rajneesh Movement is between 31 and 35 (Braun, 1984; Carter 1987). ISKCON, however, appeals to girls in their late teens and early twenties (Judah 1974). Studies of the Rajneesh have consistently shown that the disciples tend to be highly educated professionals from the middle to upper-middle class (Wallis 1982). Women in the ACC are recruited from the middle to lower-middle classes and are exclusively black (Philips 1988). Single mothers appear to find the Northeast Kingdom Community attractive, whereas many of the Rajneesh and Raelian women interviewed had postponed or rejected childbearing in favor of a career, and had lived out of wedlock with a number of men before joining the movement.

New religious sexual experiments might be seen as a *series*, dedicated to solving specific sets of social problems confronted by contemporary women. NRM literature offers theodicies that account for the failure of marriage in the secular realm, and advertise spiritual solutions to problems of intimacy that resonate with different audiences. A Krishna devotee, for example, described her parents' brutality throughout her childhood, and claimed that the male authority in ISKCON offered women a benign "protection," because it was based on a "spiritual line of discipline succession." A *chela* of Elizabeth Clare Prophet described how she had suffered during divorce, and how "Guru Ma made me understand that my former marriage was only a *karmic* relationship — something we had to work out from our previous lives." Having recently married a celibate "soulmate" in the Church Universal and Triumphant, she happily anticipated her eventual reunion with her "twin flame" into an androgynous, enlightened being. A Rajneesh "lover" recounted her pain in losing her two-year-old daughter to leukemia, and her relief in joining the Rajneesh commune, where motherhood was not an option, and where she could "surrender to Bhagwan" and assuage her grief through short-term, pluralistic love affairs with the "beautiful, soft swamis."

# The "Cult Experience" and Contemporary Rites of Passage

Aidala's study does not address the issue of defection. While my findings corroborate her observations concerning the appeal of the ideological certainty of new religious gender roles to youth, it appears significant that between 80 and 90% of members participate in these alternative patterns of sexuality for one, two, or even three years — and then leave. Sociologists consistently have maintained that NRMs exhibit high rates of voluntary defection and that the average length of membership is less than two years (Barker 1984; Judah 1974; Ofshe 1976; Skonovd 1983; Wright 1988). Bird and Reimer (1982) found that in the Unification Church at least 80% of members defected within two years. In ISKCON less than 600 disciples out of the original 10,000 initiated under Swami Prabhupada have remained in the movement.[4] The Rajneesh Foundation International claimed 250,000 members in 1985, but Belfrage (1981) described a common pattern of defection by Poona visitors, following their impulsive decision to "take sannyas" (initiation). Of the Ansaar's leader, Philips (1988:37) noted, "every two or three years he has a major turnover of followers."

"The temporality of membership should alter dramatically the way in which unconventional religious movements are perceived," noted Wright (1988:163). The high attrition rate suggests that joining spiritual families rarely turns out to be a satisfactory solution to the ambiguity surrounding gender issues, but rather that NRMs in general (and their sexual innovations in particular) provide laboratories for individual and collective social experimentation. This interpretation, however, cannot be applied to lifelong participants who commit themselves to furthering the group's collective goals. When Unificationist couples remain together to raise their "perfect children," and aging Brahmakumari leaders maintain their vows of celibacy as they instruct future generations in the *gyan*, these members have evidently rejected the experimental mode to forge a new culture.

The theory that NRMs provide experiences analogous to those found in traditional rites of passage has been convincingly argued by a number of scholars. As Melton and Moore (1982:46) wrote, "the phenomenon of the 'cult experience' ... must be seen within the context of states of transition — particularly the transition from adolescence to young adulthood." Turner (1968) pointed to the hippie movement, and Levine (1984) to "radical groups" as fulfilling a function similar to traditional rites of passage.

Prince (1974) pursued a similar line of argument, but adopted the metaphor of "cocoon work," suggesting a process of psychological healing and maturation.

These authors point to a *lacuna* in our society, which has set individuals adrift as the role of public ritual has declined in the wake of secularization. "Instead of having one's change in situation acknowledged clearly and publicly with social support and with knowledgeable ritual elders to usher one through the limbo of the transition," Melton and Moore (1982:50) noted, "in modern culture one is all too often left to one's own devices, having to seek out social support and 'ritual elders' wherever they may be found." Rites of passage are an urgent imperative in our pluralistic society, they insist, if only because the coming of age in America involves confronting so many complex and depressingly insoluble problems. One of the major dilemmas, they agree, is that of choosing one's sexual orientation and code of sexual ethics. Prince (1974:271) asked, "What is it to be a man, or a woman, a father, or a mother? Educated side by side and equipped for identical roles in the same universities, how can male and female find differences and sexual identity?" He described the pessimism of contemporary youth at the prospect of adopting their parents' way of life, which they seem to feel is "a blueprint for disaster."

Aidala (1985:289) accounts for this attitude as follows: "As horizons expand beyond the family unit, traditional gender roles into which they have been socialized ... fail to resonate with emerging social-cultural realities." It seems fair to assert that woman's coming of age today is even more problematic than man's, requiring not only the initiation into women's mysteries, but also into the public realm of professional life — until recently an almost exclusively male domain. Toffler (1974) spoke of "overchoice," and Glendon (1985) deplored women's "role overload" in the "New Family." For women facing pluralistic and open sets of possibilities, their gender identities must be "accomplished" (McGuire 1992) and sexual relationships "negotiated" (Rose 1987).

It might be argued that new religious founders play a role comparable to traditional societies' "ritual elders" in youth's search for authority — for some authentic voice to outline the true shape of their sexuality which reflects the divine cosmos. The certainty of charismatic *gurus* on matters of sexual morality contrasts sharply with the rather "wishy-washy" stances of mere priestly authorities (Bibby 1987:164), rendering them attractive to disoriented youth. While Turner (1968) and Foster (1981) insisted that the distinctive features of the liminal period of individual rites of passage can also be seen in larger, more complex social transitions, it is, however, important to distinguish between the two contexts. In contrast, to the approved shamans or priestly authorities, the well-established social statuses, and the predictable ceremonies of long traditions, Foster (1981:9) observed,

> the prophet-founders of millennial movements face a more difficult task. They must begin to create a new way of life and status relationships at the very same time that they are trying to initiate individuals into

those not yet established roles. In short, the desired end point is often unclear.

None of these theorists has addressed the issue of whether these ritual processes are different for men than they are for women — an oversight that apparently also exists in anthropological literature, where "discussions of female initiation ceremonies are fewer by far [than of male] and often their function is clear: a severe suppression of female sexuality and symbolic expression of female inferiority" (Myerkoff 1982:123). An exception is found in Lincoln (1991:101), who argued that Van Gennep's *rite de passage* model is based on a study of male initiations, and proposes a trope of insect metamorphosis as more descriptive of women's initiations. Lincoln (1981) suggested that female rites of passage follow a tripartite structure of enclosure, magnification, and emergence, and that these dramas celebrate woman's new reproductive function and invest sacred power in her body, thus ensuring the future of her society. Women's roles in NRMs, which are usually far more stylized and confining than the roles of men (Aidala 1985:311), might be analyzed within this framework. For the collective, woman's body is often a symbol of the commune, the maternal womb from whence the "New Man" will emerge. The Lamb eloquently expresses this notion:

> We are the caterpillar that crawled around on the ground alongside the snake in America ... . We metamorphosed step by step into a perfect being. We wore all kinds of African attire ... like bones in our ears ... The destination of the caterpillar was he would be painted by the hand of the Artist of the Universe ... . So we walked around cloaked in our cocoon (the veil, Jallasbiyah) awaiting the great day when we would unfold the cocoon and come forth in our beauty as a nation. (*Nubian Village Bulletin*, 1992, Ed.1:15)

On the individual level, women experience the "enclosure" of a stiff, cocoon-like group identity, and give birth to a new feminine identity — which is frequently better suited to living in the larger society. Studying the process of Ansaar apostates, one might argue that they retreat behind the veil so as to undergo a period of racial deconditioning and psychological metamorphosis, until they are ready to expand beyond the boundaries of the sect; and they emerge perhaps better equipped to cope with the problems of being an African-American woman in a white society.

## SEXUAL INNOVATIONS AND LIMINALITY

Some of the more singular features of NRM sex roles — their ideological rigidity, their surrealism or postmodernist qualities — can be better understood within the framework of Turner's thoughts on liminality. Turner (1968) outlined Van Gennep's three stages, and expands upon the second. The initial "separation" stage involves a symbolic death of the novice to his or her former sociocultural state, and the third stage of "reaggregation" involves rejoining the community. The second "liminal" period is found to be the most central to the ritual process. Described as a "social limbo" of ritual time and space, the liminal period has three major components: the communication of *sacra*, the encouragement of *ludic recombination*, and the fostering of *communitas*.

The communication of *sacra* can be observed in the instruction female novices receive in new religious narratives, creation myths, and iconography of female saints or deities. Besides these exhibitions, there are ritual actions, stylized postures and greetings, and community dances that reflect sacred models of sex identity.

Some of the more outrageous sexual innovations found in these groups begin to "make sense" if considered *ludic recombination*. NRM courting rituals — the Rajneesh "Tantric" exercises, the Raelian transvestite balls, the IDHHB "Objective Sex" workshops, the "Moonie" matchings and mass marriages — might strike the outsider as extreme versions — even parodies — of "mainstream" American courting rituals, and many of them imply harsh critiques of the poorly organized and minimally supervised "dating game" practiced in secular society. These playful recombinations of American cultural traits resemble the "unusual, even bizarre and monstrous configurations ... masks, images, contraptions, costumes" found in traditional rites of passage.

The clear-cut, spiritually based gender roles outlined in new religious literature invite participation in *communitas*, the "direct, spontaneous and egalitarian mode of social relationship, as against hierarchical relationships among occupants of structural status-roles" (Turner and Turner 1982:202). A recurring theme in interviews was woman's hope of rebuilding better relationships with men, based on the mutual recognition of each other's essential spiritual status — which outweighed the sexual element. One Krishna-conscious "widow" noted, "When I talk to my godbrothers and godsisters, there's a special understanding. We all know we are spirit-souls and have lived on this earth in many different bodies for hundreds of thousands of years. We know our godbrothers respect us and would never treat us as instruments of sense gratification." A Rajneesh "supermom" explained the "heart connection" she felt with the male sannyasins in a commune, which enabled her to navigate the emotional pitfalls of a "free love" lifestyle:

> The swamis here are more available than most men. You can confront
> them, pour your guts out and they don't just walk away. That's because
> they're coming from the heart space, they have a commitment to the
> spiritual search, so they are more vulnerable — and not afraid to show
> their emotional side.

What these women appear to be describing is the experience of *communitas*, a generic bond outside the limits of social structure; a transient condition that liberates them from conformity to general norms, and opens a space for experimentation.

I would argue that the deceptively conservative roles of "wife" or "mother" present opportunities for a process of self-reconstruction that is no less radical than that observed in "feminist" groups; that some of these "traditional" roles, on closer examination, appear no less deviant than those found in "free love" NRMs; and that their stiff, stylized quality suggests that the women who inhabit them are not embracing a permanent life-style, but rather trying on a modern version of the ritual mask. "Wives" in the Ansaars, ISKCON, Unification Church, and CUT might dress up and play the role with gusto, but in most cases are not actually permitted to live with, sleep with, clean up after, or cook for their "husbands."

Whether the group espouses sex unity, complementarity, or polarity, a common thread running through their rhetoric is the notion of the androgyne. Women and men, whether they practice monogamy, celibacy, or "free love," set aside their individuality and strive to build a collective identity, to experience "communion" (Kanter 1972) with the opposite sex, and to merge into an undifferentiated whole. Rejecting hierarchical relationships and social status, initiates embrace the symbolism of totality, the resexuality of childhood innocence or the perfection of androgyny. New religions function as protective microsocieties where women can recapture a sense of innocence, and slowly recapitulate the stages of their sexual/social development in a new cultural setting. These "traditional" women, therefore, also seek "empowerment," albeit of another kind. As Gross observed (1987), societies that segregate the sexes through gender-based work roles and dress codes seem to be particularly successful in conjuring up an aura of mystery, charm, and taboo around the opposite sex. For this reason, the phenomenon of modern women choosing to inhabit the stylized roles in NRMs might be better understood *not* as a rejection of pluralism and contemporary experimentation (Aidala 1985), nor as a lifelong choice to opt for traditional family values in the face of gender uncertainty in the larger society (Davidman 1991), but rather as the ancient and familiar search for the powerful religious and social epiphanies available within the ritual passage.

# Conclusion

This study has endeavored to prove that one of the significant cultural contributions of NRMs is their provision of a modern equivalent to the feminine rites of passage found in traditional societies, which allow women to engage in an intensive process of self-reconstruction. While utopian sexual innovations have usually been interpreted as collective rites of passage (Foster 1981), or as "commitment mechanisms" (Kanter 1972) designed to bind members to the whole community to become the hierophants or parents of the next generation, there is evidence to show that the majority of members eventually reject the authority of their ad hoc "ritual elders" and instead use these rites of passage for individual ends. The significance of our apostates' erotic/ascetic ordeals, whether in retrospect they found them to be repressive or empowering, resides in their ritual aspects. Thus, while NRMs are obviously not indistinguishable from traditional rites of passage, but rather might be seen as near substitutes, the experiences of their women — while perhaps not authentically "liminal" — at least are "liminoid."

The data suggest that the innovations in sex roles and sexual mores presently developing in NRMs, far from representing a conservative reaction against "mainstream" experimentation and feminism, might more accurately be characterized as offering even *more* extreme, intensified, and diverse versions of the ongoing experimentation already occurring outside these utopias. The highly organized and strictly supervised group experiments occurring in NRMs appeal to prospective members as safe havens in which they might engage in more radical forms of experimentation than are possible in the secular sphere. Our informants appeared to be reacting not so much to gender ambiguity per se (Aidala 1985:287), but rather to the disorganized and haphazard ways in which "sexual experiments" were being conducted in the larger society.

While inhabiting these new, postmodernist Eves, Sitas, and Fatimahs, if only for a few months or years, these women apostates had found an arena for the symbolic and ritual expression of their own half-formulated and conflicting notions of sexuality, and its place in the divine cosmos. For the researcher, investigating these alternative and sacred patterns of sexuality tends to confirm Durkheim's theory on religion's representational and interpretive function (Durkheim 1912). By replicating, resolving, and even parodying the pluralistic approaches towards sexuality prevailing in our transitional age, new religious Eves and Adams hold up fragments of a mirror, inviting society to see itself and to become self-conscious.

●●●●●●●●●●●●●●●●●●●●●●●●●

## Notes

1      These categories also overlap with Rosemary Ruether's typology (1983:199) of eschatological, liberal, and romantic.

2      "Conference on Eve" materials from Unificationist women's conference at Barrytown seminary, April 3, 1983.

3      This innovation was explained during a visit to the Island Pond Community in April 1991.

4      This estimate was communicated by a former temple president in Canada, who had been initiated by Prabhupada in 1968.

# References

Aidala, Angela
1985      Social change, gender roles, and new religious movements. *Sociological Analysis* 465:287-314.

Allen, Prudence, RSM.
1987      Two medieval views on woman's identity: Hildegard of Bingen and Thomas Aquinas. *Studies in Religion* 16:21-36.

As Sayyid as Imaam Isa as Haadi al Mahdi
1988      *Hadrat Faatimah, the daughter of the Prophet Muhammad (PBUH)*. Brooklyn: The Tents of Kedar.

As Sayyid as Imaam Isa as Haadi al Mahdi
1987      *The paleman*. Brooklyn: The Tents of Kedar.

Babb, Lawrence
1986      The Brahmakumaris: History as movie. In *Redemptive encounters: Three modern styles in the Hindu tradition*, edited by Lawrence Babb, 110-155. Berkeley: University of California Press.

Barker, Eileen
1984      *The making of a Moonie: Choice or brainwashing?* New York: Basil Blackwell.
1991      *New religious movements: A practical introduction*. London: HMSO.

Bednarowski, Mary Farrell
1980      Outside the mainstream: women's religion and women religious leaders in nineteenth century America. *Journal of the American Academy of Religion* 48:207-231.

Belfrage, Sally
1981      *Flowers of emptiness*. New York: Dial Press.

Bibby, Reginald W.
1987      *Fragmented gods: The poverty and potential of religion in Canada*. Richmond Hill: Irwin.

Bird, Frederick and William Reimer
1982      Participation rates in new religious movements and para-religious movements. *Journal for the Scientific Study of Religion* 21:1-14.

Braun, Kirk
1984      *Rajneeshpuram: The unwelcome society*. West Linn, OR: Scouts Creek Press.

Carter, Lewis
1987      The new renunciates of Bhagwan Shree Rajneesh. *Journal for the Scientific Study of Religion* 26:148-172.

Castro, Ginetta
1984      *Radioscope du feminism americain*. Paris:Presses de la Fondation Nationale des Sciences Politiques.

Changer, Jagdish
1981      *Adi Dev, the First Man*. Prajapita Brahma Kumaris World Spiritual University. Singapore, Malaysia: Kim Hup Lee Printing.

Cohn, Norman
1972      *The pursuit of the millennium*. New York: Oxford University Press.

Davidman, Lyn
1991    *Tradition in a rootless world: Women turn to Orthodox Judaism.* Berkeley: University of California Press.

Durkheim, Emile
1964    *The elementary forms of religious life.* (1912) New York: Free Press.

Foster, Lawrence
1981    *Religion and sexuality: Three American communal experiments of the nineteenth century.* New: Grove Press.

Glendon, Mary Ann
1985    *The new family and the new property.* Toronto: Butterworth.

Goffman, Erving
1959    *The presentation of self in everyday life.* Garden City, NY: Doubleday Anchor.

Gold, E.J.
1973    *The Creation Story Verbatim: The Autobiography of God.* No. 64 of 200 copies bound by Djinn and Eddin, Crestline, California: IDHHB Publishing.

Gordon, James
1986    *The golden guru.* Lexington: Stephen Greene Press.

Grace, James H.
1985    *Sex and marriage in the Unification Church.* Lewiston, NY: Edwin Mellen Press.

Gross, Rita
1987    Tribal religions: Aboriginal Australia. In *Women in world religions,* edited by Arvind Sharma, 37-58. Albany: State University of New York Press.

Haywood, Carol L.
1983    The authority and empowerment of women among spiritualist groups. *Journal for the Scientific Study of Religion.* 22:156-165.

Jacobs, Janet
1984    The economy of love in religious commitment: The ceconversion of women from non-traditional movements. *Journal for the Scientific Study of Religion.* 13:155-71.

Judah, Stillson J.
1974    *Hare Krishna and the counterculture.* New York: Haworth.

Kanter, Rosabeth Moss
1972    *Commitment and community: Communes and utopias in a sociological perspective.* Cambridge, MA: Harvard University Press.

Kern, Louis
1961    *An ordered love.* Chapel Hill: University of North Carolina Press.

Knott, Kim
1987    Men or women or devotees? In *Women in world's religions, past and present,* edited by Ursula King. 112-116. New York: Paragon House.

Levine, Saul
1984    *Radical departures: Desperate detours to growing up.* Toronto: Harcourt Brace Jovanovich.

Lewis, I.M.
1971    *Ecstatic religion: An anthropological study of spirit possession and shamanism.* Harmondsworth, England: Penguin.

Lincoln, Bruce
1991    *Emerging from the chrysalis: Rituals of women's initiation.* New York: Oxford University Press.

McGuire, Meredith
    1992    Gendered spirituality and quasi-religious ritual. Paper presented at the Society for the
            Scientific Study of Religion in Washington, D.C.

Melton, Gordon and Robert L. Moore
    1982    The cult experience: Responding to the new religious pluralism. New York: Pilgrim Press.

Milne, Hugh
    1986    Bhagwan the god that failed. London: Caliban Books.

Moore, Lawrence R.
    1977    In search of white crows: Spiritualism, parapsychology and American Culture. New York:
            Oxford University Press.

Morris, Madeline
    1986    IAM: A group portrait. Unpublished senior essay, Yale University.

Myerkoff, Barbara
    1982    Rites of passage: Process and paradox. In Celebration: Studies in festivity and ritual, edited
            by Victor Turner, 109-135. Washington: Smithsonian Institute Press.

Neitz, Mary Jo
    1988    Sacramental sex in modern witchcraft. Paper presented at the Midwest Sociological Society,
            Minneapolis.

Nubian Village Bulletin
    1992    Shahru Yamahua 21, A.T. Brooklyn: The Tents of Kedar.

Ofshe, Richard
    1976    Synanon: The people's business. In The new religious consciousness, edited by Charles
            Glock and Robert Bellah, 116-137. Berkeley: University of California Press.

Pagels, Elaine
    1988    Adam, Eve and the serpent. New York: Random House.

Palmer, Susan J.
    1976    Shakti! The spiritual science of DNA. Unpublished Masters thesis. Concordia University,
            Montreal.
    1992    Playmates in the Raelian movement: Power and pantagamy in a UFO cult. SYZYGY:
            Journal of Alternative Religion and Culture(1):227-245.

Philipe, Abu Ameenah bilal
    1988    The Ansar cult in America: Riyadh, Saudi Arabia: Tawheed.

Prince, Raymond
    1974    Cocoon work: Contemporary youth's concern with the mystical. In Religious movements
            in contemporary America, edited by Irving Zaretsky and Mark P. Leone, 255-274. Princeton:
            Princeton University Press.

Rajneesh, Bhagwan Shree
    1987    A new vision of women's liberation. Poona, India: Rebel Press.

Ramtha Intensive: Soulmates
    1987    Eastsound, WA: Sovereignty Inc.

Reuther, Rosemary Radford
    1983    Sexism and god talk. Boston: Beacon Press.

Rhinehart, Luke
    1976    The book of est. New York: Holt, Rhinehart and Winston.

Richardson, James T., Mary W, Stewart, and Robert Simmonds
1979     *Organized miracles: A study of a contemporary youth communal, fundamentalist organization.* New Brunswick, NJ: Transaction.

Ritchie, Jean
1991     *The secret world of cults.* London: Angus and Robertson.

Robbins, Tom
1988     *Cults, converts and charisma.* London: Sage.

Robbins, Tom and David Bromley
1992     Social experimentation and the significance of American new religions: A focused review essay. In *Research in the Social Scientific Study of Religion*, Vol. 4, edited by Monty Lynn and David Moberg. Greenwich, CT: JAI Press.

Rochford, Burke Jr.
1985     *The Hare Krishna in America.* New Brunswick, NJ: Rutgers University Press.

Rose, Susan
1987     Women warriors: The negotiation of gender in a charismatic community. *Sociological Analysis* 48:245-258.

Skonovd, L. Norman
1983     Leaving the cultic milieu. In *The brainwashing deprogramming controversy: Sociological, psychological, legal and historical perspectives,* edited by David Bromley and James Richardson, 91-106. Lewiston, NY: Edwin Mellen Press.

Toffler, Alvin
1974     *Future shock.* New York: Bantam Books.

Turner, Victor
1968     *The ritual process.* Chicago: Aldine.

Turner, Victor and Edith Turner.
1982     Religious celebrations. In *Celebrations: Studies in festivity and ritual,* edited by Victor Turner 201-219. Washington, DC: Smithsonian Institute Press.

Vorilhon, Claude (Rael)
1986     *Sensual meditation.* Tokyo: AOM Corporation.

Wagner, Jon ed.
1982     *Sex roles in contemporary communes.* Bloomington: Indiana University Press.

Wallis, Roy
1982     *Millenialism and charisma.* Belfast: Queen's University Press.

Wessinger, Catherine, ed.
forthcoming     *Women outside the mainstream: Female leaders in marginal religions in 19th and 20th century America.* Urbana: University of Illinois Press.

Westley, Frances
1983     *The complex forms of religious life: A Durkheimian view of new religious movements.* Chico, CA: Scholars Press.

*Women and abuse in cults.*
1991     The Guardian 9 May:33.

Wright, Stuart
1988     Leaving new religions: Issues, theories and research. In *Falling from the faith: Causes and consequences of religious apostasy,* edited by David G. Bromley, 143-165. Sage, CA: Newbury Park.

# THE NEW AGE MOVEMENT AND THE PENTECOSTAL/CHARISMATIC REVIVAL: DISTINCT YET PARALLEL PHASES OF A FOURTH GREAT AWAKENING?

PHILLIP C. LUCAS

## Introduction

In her address delivered to the centennial celebration of the American Society of Church History (1988), historian of American religions Catherine Albanese sought to identify the broad outlines of an emerging, ethnically (that is, characteristic of America as a *nation*) American religion. In the concluding portion of that address, she briefly highlighted a series of rather startling convergences between the New Age movement and Christian fundamentalism. The convergences she identified included each movement's focus on personal transformation, healing, direct spiritual experience, the reality of continuing revelation, a peculiarly American species of religious materialism, and a democratized spirituality that "fell forward" into visions of the millennium.[1]

I became interested in probing these convergences within a phenomenological framework and observing how they were manifested in each movement's characteristic rituals, cosmology, institutions, spiritual practices, attitude towards contemporary society, and doctrines. Did significant convergences or parallels really exist between such seemingly different religious movements? If so, what light did this shed on the religious character of the American soil from which they sprang?

At the same time, in obedience to what Ninian Smart has called the "contextual imperative,"[2] I wanted to examine the parallels and convergences between the two groups in the context of the socio-historical period within which they both rose to prominence, the 1960s and 1970s. Were there particular societal conditions during this

Phillip C. Lucas. "The New Age Movement and the Pentecostal/Charasmatic Revival: Distinct Yet Parallel Phases of a Fourth Great Awakening?" in James R. Lewis and J. Gordon Melton, eds., *Perspectives on the New Age*. Albany, NY: State University of New York Press, 1992, pp. 189-211. Reprinted from *Persepectives on the New Age* by R. Lewis and G. Melton (eds.) by permission of the State University of New York Press.

period of which the New Age movement and the fundamental resurgence were two manifestations? Were these movements two alternative strategies created to address a shared experience of socio-political crisis? Additionally, were these two movements possible harbingers of an emerging national religious synthesis?

As I began examining the primary sources, conducting oral interviews, engaging in participant observation of worship services, and analyzing recent sociological survey data bearing on each group's belief systems, it became clear that the groups clustered under the fundamentalist umbrella evinced significant differences in lifestyle, worldview, attitude toward ecstatic experience, and liturgical practices. I discovered that the two groups under this umbrella that most clearly converged with the New Age movement in the way Albanese had suggested were the Pentecostals and the charismatics. As a consequence, I decided to narrow the focus of my examination to the parallels, convergences, and *contrasts* between these two movements and the New Age movement.

The most promising socio-historical perspective I found from which to view both the contrasts and the convergences between New Agers and Pentecostals/charismatics was that advanced by William McLoughlin in his influential essay *Revivals, Awakenings, and Reform*. McLoughlin's thesis is that American culture periodically renews itself by what he terms "great awakenings." These are periods of between thirty and forty years when a fundamental reorientation takes place in our belief or value system, ethical norms, and institutional structures. When the period has ended, those values, norms, and institutions have become better adapted to actual social and environmental conditions.[3] According to McLoughlin, the period 1960–1990 saw the beginning of America's Fourth Great Awakening.

In a schema developed through Anthony F. C. Wallace's 1956 essay "Revitalization Movements," McLoughlin argued that during the early stages of a great awakening, the major institutions of society, i.e. churches, schools, police, courts, jails, and government, begin to malfunction and lose their legitimacy in the eyes of a growing number of individuals. As society moves into a period of cultural distortion (when the routine "mazeways" become blocked and out of touch with contemporary needs), a revivalist, traditionalist movement characteristically arises that blames the societal crisis on a collective failure to adhere to the traditional beliefs, mores, and values of the culture.[4] This movement awaits God's apocalyptic retribution on society and advocates a way of life that is essentially a return to the "basics," to the purity and vitality of an idealized time of beginnings. Throughout this essay, I will probe whether the Pentecostal/charismatic movement can best be understood as one part of the Fourth Great Awakening's revivalist, traditionalist phase (which, to be sure, includes the larger fundamentalist resurgence).

In the middle stages of a great awakening, prophetic movements arise which advance new sets of religious and social norms for individual and group behavior. The leaders of these widely dispersed movements then begin to attract the more flexible (usually the younger) members of the society, who are willing to experiment with new economic, political, and familial arrangements (sometimes in a communal context), as well as new sexual mores.[5] The ideological reorientation that McLoughlin believes is occurring during the Fourth Great Awakening includes "a new sense of the mystical unity of all mankind and of the vital power of harmony between man and nature," an image of God that is life supporting, nurturing, and more immanent than transcendent, and an ethic of cooperation, service, and mutual care.[6] This essay will also consider evidence which indicates that the New Age movement, in significant ways, articulates these ideological reorientations and thus represents the progressive, future-oriented, experimental phase of our current great awakening.

McLoughlin's "multi-phase" framework, if it proves solid, will help to explain the contrasts between the two movements. But what about the convergences and parallels? I will attempt to understand these as rooted in the fact that both movements draw on a shared American heritage of beliefs, experiences, myths, and traditions. One of the most important of these is the old revivalistic belief that "God has yet further light to shed upon his revelations."[7] The others include, in McLoughlin's list, individualism, pietism, perfectionism, and millenarianism.[8]

I will also attempt to show that each of these movements offers solutions to a common problem: the crisis that American society has faced as a result of the profound socio-cultural disorientation of the 1960s and 1970s. The two movements can then be viewed as in some ways distinct, and in other ways generic, moments in a greater pattern of societal revitalization. Both will be seen to share in the larger awakening's desire to transform both the individual and society. In addition, their underlying structures of thought will be seen to manifest in parallel ways two characteristic themes that McLoughlin identifies as areas of emphasis during a great awakening.

One of these themes is the emphasis on the immanence of the divine as opposed to its transcendence. During awakenings God is felt to be present again in the world — in visions, in sacred utterances and revelations, in charismatic spiritual leaders and in the natural environment.[9]

The second theme is that of a great battle between the powers of evil and the powers of good that ends in the cleansing of all darkness and disharmony from the world and in the appearance of a transformed humanity.[10] This theme ties into part of America's cultural mythos: the belief that we are a chosen people, a new Israel ordained by God to lead the world (through virtuous living) into a glorious era of peace, prosperity, brotherhood, and equality.[11]

# Defining "New Age Movement," "Charismatic," and Pentecostal"

Before I begin my analysis, it is necessary to delineate what I mean by the New

Age movement, as well as by such terms as *Pentecostal* and *charismatic*.

My reading of the primary material and of studies by scholars such as Catherine Albanese, Gordon Melton, Robert Ellwood, and Mary Bednarowski has led me to identify the New Age movement as an American social and religious phenomenon that has four major distinguishing characteristics. First, there is the belief that the earth and its people are on the verge of a radical spiritual transformation. This transformation will occur at the level of human consciousness and will entail a dawning awareness of the oneness of the human family and the intimate relationship that exists between the human species and the entire fabric of the natural world. Second, there is the eclectic embrace of a wide array of healing therapies as well as spiritual beliefs and practices. These include, among others, yoga, various forms of meditation, crystal healing, macrobiotics, reincarnation, the western esoteric tadition, tantra, and trance channeling. Third, the New Age involves the adoption of an ethic of self-empowerment, which focuses on the realization of individual goals and aspirations as the prerequisite for efficacious societal transformation. Fourth, there is the desire to reconcile religious and scientific worldviews in a higher synthesis that enhances the human condition both spiritually and materially.[12]

The New Age movement has its roots in the many alternative religions that have emerged and spread in this country since the mid-1800s, especially Swedenborgianism, Spiritualism, New Thought, and those movements that have attempted to harmonize Western and Eastern religious traditions, such as transcendentalism and Theosophy.[13] The movement is hard to pin down in quantitative terms, because it has no central organization whose membership can be counted and because there is no definitive way of delimiting its boundaries.[14] Its breadth can be observed, however, in the various directories, journals, and "networking" publications it produces. Even a rough count of New Agers is complicated by the facts that a wide variety of beliefs and practices are commonly situated under the New Age "umbrella" and that there are many persons who identify themselves with particular denominations and who nevertheless subscribe to many of these beliefs and practices. For example, in a new and yet unpublished sociological survey conducted by Wade Clark Roof and Phillip Hammond, 27 percent of Roman Catholic, Greek Orthodox, Episcopalian, and Lutheran respondents indicated a belief in astrology, and 31 percent of these same respondents indicated a belief in reincarnation.[15] However, even if the movement cannot be measured accurately in quantitative terms, it is clear that it has made a significant impact on American society over the last twenty years and is steadily growing in influence and in media exposure.

A word need now be said concerning this paper's use of the two related terms, *Pentecostal* and *charismatic*. By Pentecostal, I refer to those American denominations — including the Assemblies of God, the United Pentecostal Church, International, the Church of God (Cleveland, Tennessee), the Church of God in Christ, the International Church of the Foursquare Gospel, and the Pentecostal Holiness Church — that were formed at the beginning of the twentieth century as a result of doctrinal and liturgical controversies within the Holiness movement.[16]

These controversies eventually resulted in the emergence of churches that placed primary emphasis on the doctrine of charismatic gifts following a "baptism of the Holy Spirit," and on spontaneity of emotional expression during worship. After slow expansion through their first forty-five years, these churches began growing rapidly during the 1960s. The Assemblies of God alone have experienced a growth rate of about 400 percent between 1965, when it numbered five hundred thousand members, and 1985, when it numbered two million.[17]

By the term *charismatic* I refer to the movement that began in the late 1950s and early 1960s when members of non-Pentecostal denominations began experiencing a Pentecostal-type "baptism of the Holy Spirit." Those experiencing the baptism for the most part did not join classical Pentecostal churches but rather sought to renew their own denominations from within. This renewal gained national publicity in the 1960s and spread to such mainstream denominations as Roman Catholicism, Lutheranism, Episcopalianism, and Methodism.[18]

The Pentecostal and the charismatic movements have mushroomed into the largest Christian movement of the twentieth century. A Gallup Poll taken in 1979 showed that 19 percent or 29 million adult Americans identified themselves as "Pentecostal" or "charismatic" Christians.[19] As documented in David Barrett's 1988 report on the movement, there are now over 176,000,000 Pentecostals and 123,000,000 Protestant and Catholic charismatics worldwide. In North America alone, Barrett documents 22,550,000 Pentecostalists and 43,212,000 charismatics.[20]

## Invisible Realms of Sacred Power and Experience: A Parallel Rediscovery

The first of the parallels I wish to consider concerns what may be termed each movement's attempt at *rediscovery of invisible realms of sacred power* and each movement's emphasis on *ecstatic, emotional experience* of this power. In the Pentecostal/charismatic movement this experience occurs generally in its participant-oriented worship, with religious emotions being freely expressed through upraised hands, dancing, and spontaneous shouts of praise. This behavior is in sharp contrast to the more restrained worship of mainstream churches.

In contrast to the skepticism regarding the supernatural that has prevailed in mainline religious culture since the upheavals of the 1960s, Pentecostals and charismatics believe that the Holy Spirit intervenes directly in their daily lives, performing tangible miracles. These manifestations of divine grace begin with the foundational "baptism of the Holy Spirit," which Pentecostals believe endues them with the same spiritual gifts as were given to the early Christian community. When a person experiences one of more of these gifts, s/he understands s/he has received the "second blessing" and has visible evidence that the Holy Spirit is now intimately at work in his or her life, these supernatural gifts include the ability to prophesy, to speak in foreign tongues, to interpret these tongues, to sing in the Spirit, to utter words of wisdom, to discern spirit entities, and to exorcise demons.

The late humanistic psychologist and father of the human potential movement Abraham Maslow spoke of the spiritual vacuum created in the believer's life when subjective religious experience is forgotten or devalued in a tradition and replaced by a dry, external set of behaviors, dogmas, and forms, devoid of feeling and intensity.[21] More than one commentator has attributed the popularity of the Pentecostal/charismatic movement to its ability to transcend dry formalism and to mediate continuing encounters with divine power for its adherents.[22]

The New Age movement, too, is strongly oriented to experiential encounters with sacred power. Many of those who participate in this movement were part of the counterculture generation of the sixties, who left the mainstream churches in droves because of what they perceived as rigid moralism, verbalism, and general inability to mediate ecstatic spiritual experience. They turned to the mystical, experience-centered new religious movements where transformative contact with sacred power was offered though such spiritual practices as yoga, meditation, chanting, and sacred dance.

Many New Agers accept the existence of a universal energy that differs from more common forms of energy like heat and light. This universal power is believed to undergird and permeate all existence. It goes by many names, including *prana, mana, odic force, orgone energy,* and *ch'i.*[23] The Pentecostal/charismatic movement's concept of the Holy Spirit is in some ways analogous to this. It is the divine force moving behind the miraculous events of healing, prophesy, glossolalia, and exorcism. It is the point where God's sacred power enters the human realm and manifests itself tangibly to human agents.

The main difference between these concepts lies in how they are conceived in cosmological and theological terms. As befits the traditionalist character of the Pentecostal/charismatic movement, this sacred power is conceived of within a strict, biblical paradigm. It is the Holy Spirit, the Spirit of Truth sent by Christ to comfort and enlighten all true Christians. The experience of the Holy Spirit is conceived of as a supernatural event, an intervention of divine grace in human affairs. Just as the Holy Spirit has "spoken through the prophets" in Old Testament times to reawaken Israel to the responsibilities of its convenant with Yahweh, so now, also, Pentecostals and charismatics believe, God is pouring out the Holy Spirit on his elect to reawaken them to their divine calling in Christ. Pentecostals/charismatics accept the traditional Christian dualisms of spirit and matter, heaven and earth, natural and supernatural. Their experience of the Holy Spirit is thus a divinely given pretaste of the heavenly realm where they will spend eternity after physical death.

For New Agers the sacred power they experience is conceived of, according to Albanese, as a *natural* energy that permeates, not only the physical body, but the entire created cosmos. It is believed to follow natural laws, like electricity, and to be wholly impersonal. The energy is, in fact, matter vibrating at a higher rate of vibration than the matter we see in physical forms. It is part of a subtle realm of vibration that permeates the natural world and, in a sense, sustains all natural forms with their essential life force. It is not God's supernatural intervention that makes an experience of this power available, but rather (as befits the pragmatic, science-affirming, and experimental character of the New Age movement) specific spiritual practices and methods that put a person in harmony with it and thus allow the person to act as its conductor and receptacle. This energy can be exchanged freely in interpersonal relationships through sexuality (i.e., in tantric practices) and can be channeled in various healing therapies.[24]

The literature of both movements articulates these ideas with a striking language of spiritual forces and empowerments. Take this example from Sun Bear, a Native American and poplar New Age teacher: "The invisible powers that are the spirit-keepers come to us, and when we lock ourselves into their energy we conduct it; we are working together, like electricity when it flows through certain kinds of crystals."[25] Or consider this typical example of the language used by Pentecostalists and charismatics to describe this sacred power: "[Pentecostalism] has reminded us that the Holy Spirit makes worship come alive, that the Holy Spirit is not the power stored in unused batteries, but a live current running though our every action."[26] Albanese has posited that an undernoticed feature of America's religious heritage is a metaphysical, mystical strain that knits together self, God, and nature in a way that is directly experienced and provides empowerment in material life.[27] This strain, which has its roots in Native American religions, transcendentalism, early American folk traditions, and the metaphysical healing movements of the nineteenth century, resonates strongly in both the Pentecostal/charismatic and the New Age movement's emphasis on personal encounters with sacred power. The Pentecostal/charismatic emphasis on deeply emotional, ecstatic encounters with the divine also finds paradigmatic antecedents in the recurrent outbreaks of evangelical revivalism that have swept America ever since the First Great Awakening between 1730 and 1760.

Keeping this in mind, one can examine instructively several parallel ways through which the New Age and Pentecostal/charismatic movements believe that they experience sacred power and contact noncorporeal intelligence. One of the most prominent of these ways for many New Agers is through the phenomenon popularly known as "channeling." A channeler is believed to be a human vehicle through whom beings from other dimensions of existence can address persons in this world. To enter the special trance state, the channeler's mind is disengaged from involvement with the sensory/time world. This state of disengaged attention purportedly allows disembodied entities to use the channel's physical faculties to lecture, counsel, and teach a human audience.[28] The channeling phenomenon has grown more and more popular with New Agers over the past decade. It is estimated that over one thousand active channelers now practice in the Los Angeles area alone.[29]

Many of the New Age groups have claimed to be channels of revelatory material from advanced spiritual beings. For example, the popular New Age teacher Ram Dass

(Richard Alpert) uses guidance he receives from the entity of the astral plane he calls "Emmanuel," who is channeled through East Coast housewife Pat Rodegast.[30] New Age philosopher and teacher David Spangler claims that he was the channel through which a being identifying itself as "Limitless Love and Truth" dictated the essence of Spangler's New Age bestseller *Revelation: The Birth of the New Age.*

The Pentecostal/charismatic movement's parallels to channeling are the phenomena termed "speaking in tongues" and "prophecy." Charismatic writer Don Basham, describes speaking in tongues as "a form of prayer in which the Christian yields himself to the Holy Spirit and receives from the Spirit a supernatural language with which to praise God." [31] The "tongues" phenomenon is usually unintelligible to listeners, and so a second person is often required who, also inspired by the Holy Spirit, is able to "interpret" the tongues message for the community of believers.

Margaret Poloma, who has researched both the charismatic movement in Catholicism and the Assemblies of God, defines prophecy as "a gift of the Holy Spirit through which a person speaks in the name of God by giving an exhortation, reporting a vision, providing a revelation, or interpreting a glossolalic utterance."[32] This can take place in various contexts, including speaking out at meetings in English with a message for the group, interpreting a vision one has received in private prayer, or interpreting a dream.[33] Like the information "channeled" to New Agers, the primary content of this "gift of the spirit" can be described as messages of encouragement, consolation, correction, and future direction.

Some commentators have remarked that these spiritual guidances or ecstatic utterances have similarities to those evidenced by shamans in traditional folk religions.[34] What is clear is that, both for New Agers and Pentecostals/charismatics, these events are experienced as a dramatic breakthrough of sacred power into the ordinary world, as an intensely personal, often ecstatic interaction with this power, and as compelling evidence of the proximity of other realms of being.

Another parallel has to do with each movement's avowed experiential contact with spirit beings, whether they are called angels, demons, spirit guides, spirit helpers, nature spirits, or angelic presences. The reality of demons and angels has long been a fundamental element of Pentecostal cosmology. The activity of the demonic host was believed to be increasing significantly in modern times because of the imminence of the Second Coming. To combat this activity, the authority to exorcise or cast out demons had been given to "spirit-baptized" believers.[35] Pentecostal revivalists such as Oral Roberts and Gordon Lindsay were noted for their power to cast out evil spirits.[36] Sensational stories of exorcism, replete with physical violence, foaming at the mouth, and uncontrolled cursing, abound in Pentecostal groups.[37]

Charismatics, too, believe in a personal devil and discern its influence in the smallest detail of their lives. They take regular steps to protect themselves from demonic attacks and perform rituals that use divine power to disperse perceived demonic presences. In numerous books, tapes, and pamphlets, Satan and his minions are portrayed as responsible for all the world's pain, disease, and suffering. Charismatics envision the spiritual realm as inhabited by angels as well as demons, though angels receive far less attention. Some charismatic groups invoke the angels to protect their homes and families from harm.[38] A member of an independent charismatic which I interviewed saw angels as being intimately involved in human lives:

> There are other angels that work in allegiance with God — they're called ministers. . . . There are a lot of instances in the Old and New Testaments where they directly contacted people, spoke to them, came face to face with them or spoke in dreams, visions, things like that. I believe that that's still going on.[39]

Many New Age groups also emphasize the reality of other-than-human persons, though these entities are rarely envisioned within the traditional biblical framework that the Pentecostals and charismatics use. Those groups that have incorporated Native American or shamanic beliefs and practices invoke the aid of spirit helpers and guardians, who help a person cope with and master hidden spirit forces. These helpers, related to the animal and plant kingdom, are also used in healing practices. Some of these practices closely parallel Pentecostal demon exorcism in that a harmful spirit being is removed from a person whose state of health or state of mind has purportedly been adversely affected by the spirit's presence.[40] The Holy Order of Mysterion, Agape, Nous, and Sophia (MANS), a New Age group founded in the late 1960s in San Francisco, invoked angelic beings in its secret Temple Services and has given each member a special medallion to help ward off negative spirit influences. Findhorn-related groups in America teach "attunements" to nature spirits and *devas*, or spirit beings who rule various plant kingdoms. These attunements, according to Findhorn community members, aid the production of garden vegetables and other crops.[41]

The significant parallel between these beliefs is that each assumes a functional, dynamic relationship between spirit beings (however conceived) and humans. These beings are experienced as *real* and as part of a subtle, sacred dimension that constantly interacts with mundane reality. These beliefs represent, in fact, a cosmological vision similar to that of traditional peoples, who perceive the cosmos as populated with a multitude of malevolent and benevolent noncorporeal entities, who act as causative agents in processes such as disease, plant growth, and human psychological breakdown.

For the traditionalist Pentecostals and charismatics, these spirit beings are conceived as players within a biblically based cosmological battle between the demonic and angelic hosts. Though the exact visions differ from group to group within the Pentecostal/charismatic movement, all contain the belief that Satan is a fallen archangel who, with his armies of demons, conducts spiritual warfare against God and the angelic hosts for the souls of humans. This battle has reached its final stages, and, though God's final victory is assured, the souls of humans are still in the balance. Writers within the Pentecostal/charismatic movement such as Dave Hunt warn that communication with any discarnate entity other than Jesus and the angels is a kind of necromancy that can lead to demonic possession. New Age practices such as channeling and seeking guidance from inner spirit helpers are roundly condemned by these writers.[42]

The cosmological assumptions underpinning the New Age movement's understanding of spirit beings are quite different. As befits its scientific, futuristic character, the New Age movement views the universe as an ever-expanding and evolving reality where persons learn to realize and manifest their innate potentials, however these are conceived. Jesus is one of many discarnate teachers who may be contacted for guidance and healing. Harmful spirit beings do exist, but protective practices, derived from Native American traditions and from the Western occult tradition, are used to combat their influence. New Agers do not believe that spirit beings are arrayed in some vast cosmic struggle for human souls but rather view them as mankind's generally benevolent helpers and guides.

By calling the ecstatic utterances of their adherents "prophecies of the Holy Spirit," Pentecostals and charismatics can enjoy the community-affirming experience of spontaneous guidances and revelations from the realm of the sacred while remaining within their traditional biblical worldview. But however the phenomena are conceptualized by their respective adherents, glossalia, prophesying, and channeling are parallel methods of intense, immediate encounter with sacred power and of the reception of "further light" and revelation on both personal and cosmological issues from sacred beings.

## A Parallel Commitment to Sacred Community

Both the New Age movement and the Pentecostal/charismatic movement place a high value on the reintegration of the alienated individual into some form of sacred community. The problem of disintegrating social cohesion and community became particularly acute during the 1960s and 1970s due to such factors as the increased mobility of the work force, the breakup of neighborhoods (through urban decay, riots, and suburbanization), the weakening of the nuclear family, and the increasing depersonalization of life wrought by anonymous bureaucracies and large scale institutions.

In the New Age movement, the attempt to form new structures of social cohesion has taken several forms. The first of these is the creation of intentional communities, where like-minded individuals pool resources and share an urban home or a farm. Richard Fairfield's *Communes USA* (1972) documents the extensive communal experiments that grew out of the 1960s counterculture. The best known of these, the Lama Foundation in New Mexico, the Farm in Tennessee, the Ananda Cooperative Community in California, and the Chinook Community on Whidby Island, Washington State, were among the first to identify with the New Age vision. A host of New Age

groups have sponsored communal living arrangements during their institutional histories
The creation of intentional communities ties in with the desire of many New Agers to
build a planetary society. The communities are believed to provide models for the
larger society of how individuals can learn to cooperate, share resources, and discover
a deeper sense of human solidarity.

Similarly, both white and black Pentecostals, during their first fifty years of
institutionalized existence, tended to be tight-knit religious communities on the fringes
of society. Though these groups have advanced in socio-economic terms, they still
promote an intense experience of communal identity and belonging.[43] During the
charismatic renewal of the 1960s and 1970s, some middle-class converts began
establishing communal living arrangements, sharing households and incomes like the
early apostolic community described in the Book of Acts.

The New Age movement's one-world vision is paralleled in the Pentecostal/
charismatic movement's transcendence of conventional denominational, national, and
ethnic boundaries. American Pentecostalism has gone expansionist. Pentecostal-style
worshippers are now found within all 150 traditional non-Pentecostal ecclesiastical
confessions and families, in 8,000 ethnolinguistic cultures, and in myriads of state-
sponsored churches worldwide.[44] Commentators speak of a "grass roots ecumenism"
within the Pentecostal and charismatic communities and of the sharing of a common
religious language. Though many differences remain between specific groups within
the movement as a whole (as in the case of the New Age movement), the emphasis in
recent times has been on unity in the Holy Spirit rather than on theological
argumentation.

From all this it is clear that both movements seek to create an intense experience
of community and to promote actively a worldwide spiritual sister-brotherhood that
transcends entrenched racial, national, ethnic, and class boundaries. The worldwide
reach and vision of these two movements reflect one of the peculiar traits of the
American religious character — its belief that America has been especially chosen by
God to lead the rest of the world to some form of spiritual and political enlightenment.
This national megalomania is clearly apparent in the highly successful missionizing
efforts of the Pentecostal/charismatic movement and in the New Age's planetary
vision and alliances with various international religious, environmental, and healing
movements.

At the same time, these movements can be seen as reflecting in the sphere of
religious communities the realities of late twentieth-century internationalism in the
economic and political spheres. With the shrinking of the planet as a result of mass
communication, air travel, and unprecedented cultural exchange, these movements
can be seen as a part of a larger readjustment of American religion to current
geopolitical realities and trends.

## Parallels in the Healing and Transformation of Self

Another significant convergence between New Agers and Pentecostal/charismatics is each group's focus on personal healing and transformation. Albanese posits that the healing self and planet constitutes the central agenda of the New Age movement.[45] Such healing is a form of personal transformation, and for a large segment of New Agers, personal transformation is at the core of a person's spiritual journey. This focus on the self traces its roots back to the humanistic psychology movement, which was launched in 1961 by Masow. He and those he influenced sought a middle way between the extremes of Freudian psychoanalysis and Skinnerian behaviorism. The movement sought to switch emphasis from the study of pathological behavior to the study of healthy individuals who had learned to "actualize" their full potential. The establishment in 1962 of the Esalen Institute at Big Sur, California, provided a laboratory where human potential theorists could test ideas and techniques on persons seeking to break through what was perceived as modern society's harsh psychological and social conditioning. Theorists found parallels between the emotional opening-up processes of Western cathartic psychotherapies, Maslow's peak experiences, and the altered states of consciousness experienced by practitioners of Eastern techniques of meditation.[46] Thus was born a synthesis of Western psychology (especially the transpersonal variety) and Eastern religion that became normative for the New Age movement.[47] Many New Age groups use techniques derived from humanistic psychology to bring about radical alterations of perspective and personality in their adherents.

The Pentecostal/charismatic movement also focuses a great deal of attention on the personal healing and transformation of its adherents. The "second blessing" or "baptism of the Holy Spirit" is viewed as the major transformative event in a person's life. One of the charismata is the gift of spiritual healing, which is usually administered through a laying on of hands. (This hands motif is paralleled in the numerous therapies of "healing hands" used in the New Age movement.)

Following the "baptism of the Holy Spirit" in the charismatic movement, great emphasis is placed on personal growth and the realization of one's potential. By the late 1970s, New Age group dynamics, popular psychology, New Thought teachings, and meditation techniques had permeated both modernist and traditionalist segments of the charismatic movement. Charismatic leaders like Josephine Ford were recommending the development of democratic, Esalen-type group structures and processes for their prayer groups.[48] Interpersonal honesty and non-verbal forms of communication such as handholding, embracing, and massage were encouraged.[49] Ruth Carter Stapleton, a nationally known charismatic, founded her "Holovita" retreat center outside Dallas in 1978, where she offered an eclectic mix of spiritual therapies including direct visualizations and meditation.[50] (Visualization techniques are, of course, a common staple of New Age self-help therapy.)[51]

Popular New Thought themes such as positive thinking and achieving personal prosperity had gained such adherence in the Pentecostal/charismatic movement by the mid-1980s that conservative Christian leaders were lamenting: "The people are so engaged in making money, subconsciously mammon has become their god until this has clouded, in many places, the real fervor, fire, and New Testament zeal that comes with Pentecostal experience."[52] In 1987, a special six-part series of the John Ankerberg television show highlighted the degree to which such New Age practices as visualization, seeking advice from an inner guide, rebirthing, and listening to relaxation tapes have permeated the Pentecostal/charismatic movement.[53]

Ankerberg and other charismatic leaders often condemn the New Age movement's "anti-Christlike" exaltation and empowerment of the self. But it must be acknowledged that, however much it may be packaged in revivalistic Christian idioms, Pentecostals and charismatics make direct appeals to the suffering individual self and promise *personal* healing, happiness, and prosperity. The fact that this is done within a traditionally salvationist perspective does not change its actual effect on, and appeal to, the personal self of its adherents As Robert Fuller's *Alternative Medicine and American Religious Life* makes clear, there is a long tradition in America of interest in self-culture and nonmedical healing methods. During the Second Great Awakening of the early nineteenth century, an attempt was made to collapse the distance between the stern Calvinist God and humankind. One manifestation of this attempt was a greatly increased interest in direct encounters with the invisible healing power, whether through the instrumentality of revivalist laying on of hands, or through alternative healing systems like homeopathy, mesmerism, and Grahamism. This phenomenon appears to be repeating itself during our current Awakening, whether through the charismatic movement's healing "gifts" or through the New Age's plentiful offerings of alternative healing methods such as crystal healing, polarity therapy, and acupuncture.[54] Clearly, it is in each of these movement's ability to offer an efficacious alternative means to heal and empower body, mind, and soul that we must look for their continued popularity and growth.

## Parallel Visions of a New World

Another set of convergences has to do with the elaborate eschatologies that dominate the worldviews of both movements. The scenarios differ in detail but agree on the imminence of a worldwide societal breakdown and the establishment of a spiritually transfigured world community. New Agers generally (Ruth Montgomery and Ramtha are prominent exceptions) envision a "soft" apocalypse wherein much that is of value from our present civilization can be salvaged while the new world community is being built. The Pentecostal/charismatic vision of massive destruction, like the apocalyptic vision in the New Testament that is its prototype, is far less sanguine about the prospects of the modern world. It expects a more radical and sudden breakdown of this civilization and less human energy in bringing the new world about.

Pentecostals have, from their inception as a movement, taught a dispensational premillennialism that entailed the idea of an imminent secret extraction (or "rapture") of the saints to a place of safety, immediately followed by a period of tribulation, the Second Coming of Christ, and a thousand-year messianic reign on earth. Some commentators, following the lead of Robert Mapes Anderson, have argued that this eschatological motif, which permeated the movement's earliest literature and resurfaced in the Latter Rain Revival of the 1940s, is the integrating nucleus of the Pentecostalist message.[55] For these scholars classical Pentecostalism constituted a wholesale rejection and condemnation of the present world order and a longing for its actual destruction so that the millenial reign of the saints could begin.[56] Among modern Pentecostalists and charismatics, these apocalyptic views are quite prominent, and much speculation exists concerning how current events fit into biblical prophecies of the end of times. Books like Hal Lindsey's *Late Great Planet Earth* and Doug Clark's *Final Shockwaves to Armageddon* are hugely popular within this movement.[57]

As Robert Bellah has observed about the new religions of the 1960s and early 1970s, many of which were later identified with the New Age movement:

> [they] share a very negative image of established society as sunk in materialism and heading for disaster. Many of them have intense millenial expectations, viewing the present society as in the last stage of degradation before the dawning of a new era. . . . All of these groups . . . have withdrawn fundamentally from contemporary American society, see it as corrupt and illegitimate, and place their hope in a radically different vision.[58]

Mirroring the Second Coming hopes of Pentecostals, New Agers with theosophical backgrounds speak of the appearance in the last days of a new avatar of the status of Jesus and Buddha. Students of the Arcane School actively advocate this position and have circulated worldwide copies of a prayer invoking the avatar's appearance.[59] A number of "channeled" messages speak of various catastrophic "earth changes" that will accompany the coming period of planetary illumination.

The latest examples of New Age millennialism occurred in 16 August 1987, when thousands of New Agers gathered at "power centers" around the world to herald the "harmonic convergence." According to New Age spokesperson Jose Arguelles, this event not only signaled

> the return to Quetzalcoatl but the elimination of Armageddon as well. To some it may even be as another Pentecost and second coming of

Christ. Amidst spectacle, celebration, and urgency, the old mental house will dissolve, activating the return of long-dormant archetypal memories and impressions. Synchronized with the descent of the new mental house, these "return" memories and impressions, corresponding to actual collective archetypal structures, will saturate the field and create the impulse toward the new order and lifestyle.[60]

Donald Dayton has observed that, historically, movements that provide their adherents with an intense experience of divine power also seem to develop a fascination with prophetic and apocalyptic themes and long for a corresponding transformation of the world order.[61] This observation is surely borne out in the two movements we have been studying, who have responded to the societal traumas of the 1960s with varying degrees of world rejection and millennialist visions.

# Parallel Anti-Institutionalism and Democratization of Spiritual Authority

The last parallel has to do with each movement's anti-institutional attitudes and tendencies toward democratization. Pentecostals have from their beginnings been criticized for the undignified nature of their worship services, during which the "Holy Spirit" was allowed to move through any believer without institutional control. Early Pentecostal leaders found ready adherence among rural working-class people who viewed the formal liturgies and extensive bureaucracies of larger denominational churches with a mixture of suspicion and fear.[62]

The charismatic revival of the 1960s and 1970s has adopted a modified version of these attitudes and tends to be decentralized in its authority structures. Leadership is often based on personal charisma rather than formal bureaucratic training within an institutional hierarchy. This movement's most characteristic form is the small prayer group and the "covenant community," which has minimal structure so that it can remain open to the spirit and provide intimate support for its members.[63]

The New Age movement is well known for its anti-institutional and decentralized character. The majority of New Agers embrace a loose form of organization called "networking," in which informal contacts among New Age groups are maintained by newsletters, shared phone lists, and word of mouth. Decision making in many groups is through consensus, a process wherein a sense of shared responsibility is promoted. The locus of authority for most New Agers tends to reside within the individual. The disciple or seeker decides which teachings or groups meet his needs based upon interior spiritual guidance.

The Pentecostal/charismatic movement's locus of authority also tends to be the individual, who receives the gifts of the Spirit from within and who seeks a "spirit-informed" interpretation of Scripture. These spiritual gifts are not the special province of a priesthood or bureaucratic hierarchy, but are rather seen to be freely distributed by God to all believers. While it is true that some groups have authoritarian *interior* structures, they nevertheless tend to reject the authority claims of normative societal institutions such as the public school and legal systems. Ultimately, as Catherine Albanese argues, the strategy of many New Agers and charismatics toward mainline churches and institutions seems to be to disappear in their midst and to transform them from within. The creation of large separate institutions could only impede this strategy.[64]

The striking underlying similarities between these movements should not make us lose sight of the very real differences between them. The history of the Pentecostal movement reaches back into the general context of nineteenth-century American Protestantism, with its pre-versus-post-millennialist and fundamentalist-versus-modernist controversies and its questions concerning the proper degree of spontancity that should be allowed in worship services. The development of twentieth-century Pentecostalism, including the charismatic renewal, has all taken place within the larger socio-historical development of American Protestantism. Its political and moral views, theology, and liturgy thoroughly reflect this fact. Being linked in many ways with the conservative, fundamentalist wing of American Protestantism, Pentecostals and charismatics generally espouse social and political stands that reflect conservative values. These include a pro-life stance on abortion, opposition to homosexuality and the legalization of marijuana, a traditional view of the role of women in society, and support for prayer in public schools.[65]

Though it has important historical roots in the alternative religious movements of the nineteenth century, the contemporary New Age movement is largely a phenomenon of the late twentieth century, The movement's socio-political views and values, including its emphasis on individual freedom and self-empowerment, its willingness to innovate and experiment, and its acceptance of planetary, as opposed to an ethnocentric or national, perspective, all resonate with identifiable thematic currents in modern society. New Agers' stands on social issues generally fall at the opposite end of the spectrum from those of Pentecostals and charismatics. Despite the elements of Judeo-Christian tradition in America that can be found within it, the New Age movement is essentially universalist and eclectic (as opposed to exclusivist) in its appropriation of religious traditions and practices.

## Summary and Conclusion

It is now possible to posit answers to some of the questions that initiated this inquiry. There do indeed exist significant convergences and parallels between the Pentecostal/charismatic and New Age movements. First, both movements represent attempts to bring an experience of sacred power into the daily lives of ordinary people.

The actual means of accomplishing this and the theological models for comprehending these experiences may differ, but the underlying theme remains the same. As McLoughlin has observed, in an awakening the divine's manifestations are no longer limited to the institutional churches and their functionaries. Instead, these manifestations occur in intense, personal encounters with all levels of humanity, even the lowliest. The spiritual and physical worlds intermingle and the boundaries between the two become permeable.[66] The emphasis in both movements on personal experiences with sacred power, whether through channeling, speaking in tongues, prophesying, meditation, laying on of hands, or exorcism, can be understood as aspects of this characteristic manifestation of a great awakening. This democratization of numinous experience can be seen as part of the necessary wresting way from conventional authorities of their hegemony over societal norms, so that the currents of revitalization being pioneered by alternative religious movements can gain some legitimacy in the larger culture.

Second, both movements place a high value on the reintegration of the individual into an intimate, stable, and meaningful sacred community. In each movement this community ultimately extends beyond conventional ethnic, class, national, regional, and denominational boundaries to embrace the human race as a whole. Third, both of these movements place a strong emphasis on the healing and inner transformation of the wounded, fragmented modern individual through various nonmedical means. Finally, each movement sees itself as part of a planetary spiritual transformation that it is helping to bring about, a transformation wherein the locus of authority will be the individual rather than an institution.

Do these convergences tell us something important about the unique religious character of America and its future? That is, are these continuities with the country's religious heritage and yet something that points beyond that heritage to some future synthesis that is as yet in the making?

This essay has demonstrated that each of these movements has its common American features. Each ties into a core part of our longstanding cultural mythos: that we are a chosen people ordained by the divine to embody a glorious new society where peace, community, material prosperity, and equality reign. Though America itself may be the proving ground for this new vision, it is ultimately a vision that Americans feel compelled to share and implement among the rest of humanity. This worldwide vision has a great deal to do with the heterogeneity of the nation's populace. Many of the world's countries have concrete ties of family and tradition to the United States. Each in a sense has a stake in the American experiment. The ability of both the New Age and the Pentecostal/charismatic movements to transcend conventional boundaries and reach out to humanity at large is a reflection of this reality.

The individualistic, egalitarian, and democratizing roots of America's early history are also reflected in both movements' democratization of revelation and mystical experience and in their anti-institutional attitudes. The longstanding revivalistic belief that "God has yet further light to shed upon his revelations" is reflected in each of these movements' privileging of inner voices, visions, and ecstatic utterances over tradition and dogma. Finally, America's pragmatic concern with this worldly success and material prosperity is strongly reflected in each movement's acceptance of prayer, positive thinking, or visualization as methods for enhancing the individual's spiritual and material conditions.

If indeed a national religious synthesis or consensus is in the making, it will certainly include at least these abovementioned core elements of America's religious heritage. The New Age's attempt to reconcile scientific and religious worldviews in a higher synthesis that enhances the human condition in the here and now is also likely to be part of any emergent religious ethos. Science (and its concrete fruits) has come to dominate modern American society to such an extent that any religious worldview that did not integrate it in some way would be unable to gain a foothold in the majority's thinking. The pragmatic, thisworldly orientation of the American character could never accept a worldview that took people too far afield from the immediate and the concrete. I would also expect that the New Age's individualistic eclecticism and preference for decentralized forms of internal structuring would be characteristic of any emergent consensus on American soil.

William McLoughlin's interpretation of the present era as a Fourth Great Awakening has proved useful for identifying the socio-historical factors that may have served as catalysts for the rapid emergence of these movements as well as for understanding them as distinctive yet parallel strategies for dealing with a collective experience of societal crisis. McLoughlin's model of a great awakening, which I discussed briefly at the beginning of this essay, posits a five stage process. In the first stage, growing numbers of individuals within a society begin to lose their bearings and to show signs of psychological or physical illness. This slowly begins to break the institutional bonds of society, especially at the level of families. In the second stage, people begin to shift the blame for their problems away from themselves and onto societal institutions such as churches, schools, courts, and government. Political rebellion, demonstrations, and schisms in churches lead to civil and ecclesiastical disorder. At this stage, there characteristically arise nativist or traditionalist movements that attempt to call people back to traditional beliefs, values, and behavioral norms.[67] In the third stage of an awakening, prophetic movements arise whose adherents articulate a new understanding of the nature and will of God and new social norms for individual and collective behavior. Because of the voluntaristic, pluralistic religious and political structure of our society, these movements have a widely dispersed leadership and outreach in the American context.[68] In the fourth stage, these prophetic movements begin to attract persons willing to experiment with the new "mazeways" or life styles they advocate.[69] In the final phase of an awakening, the prophetic movements win over the undecided majority who, though they themselves have not experienced conversion, are sufficiently impressed by the doctrines and behavior of the prophetic movements that they accept their values and practices. Thus is born the new consensus that remains dominant until the next period of cultural strain and distortion.[70] McLoughlin maintains that the most rigid and reactionary traditionalists are seldom able to make the transition to the new consensus, and soon become a small, dissident minority, clinging to old ways.[71]

Following McLoughlin's schema, I would assert that the Pentecostal resurgence of the 1960s and 1970s represents one dimension of the traditionalist, revivalist stage of our current Great Awakening. This movement, like the fundamentalist movement of which it is a part,[72] preaches a return to biblical values and a traditional life style. Theologically and morally, it is suspicious of innovation and experimentation. This assertion deviates slightly from McLoughlin's interpretation of Pentecostalism, which sees it as part of the third stage of our current Awakening. McLoughlin bases this judgment on the pietistic, ecstatic dimensions of Pentecostalism, which he views as the Awakening's response to a loss of faith in old religious doctrines and rituals.[73] While I am in agreement with McLoughlin that such a loss of faith in fact occurred during the 1960s and 1970s, I would argue that the Pentecostalist movement is in essence a strategy for dealing with this loss that hearkens backwards to earlier traditions, attitudes, and life styles. It is therefore out of tune with larger societal trends and is not articulating new mazeways that the majority of Americans will adopt over the next generation.

I would also argue that the New Age movement is one of the movements spawned during our present Awakening that is experimental and future-oriented in its effort to create mazeways that are better adapted to current societal conditions. McLoughlin's assertion that the counterculture movement of the 1960s and 1970s, with its radical politics, communes, interest in Eastern religions, and ecological sensitivity, is a part of the Fourth Great Awakening's third and fourth stages basically concurs with this interpretation. As I have shown, the New Age movement is strongly rooted in the counterculture movement of the 1960s and 1970s.

This leaves the charismatics, who, for the sake of simplicity, I have considered as essentially the same as the Pentecostals throughout the body of this essay. In actuality, charismatics are distinct in several ways. Though they embrace a traditionally Christian theology and worldview, they tend to be far more open to modern social currents and experimentation in matters of life style, spiritual practice, worship, and self-therapy than classical Pentecostals. McLoughlin places the charismatic movement in the third and fourth stages of our current Awakening.[74] This I agree with, for it is clear that the movement has had a powerful effect on the mazeways of the mainstream churches. Ultimately, charismatics may represent a kind of mediating movement, drawing from the strengths of both traditionalists and futurists, formulating their own unique synthesis, and then attempting to revitalize the weakened religious mainstream.

If these observations are accurate, it may be necessary to revise McLoughlin's model somewhat. For, rather than fading into insignificance, as he suggests happens with traditionalist movements after the revivalist phase of an awakening, it is clear from the statistical data quoted earlier that the Pentecostals are still growing rapidly and show no signs of slowing down in the near future. The number of charismatics as well as those with no religious affiliation (who, as Albanese suggests, may be most likely to identify with the New Age movement) is also steadily increasing. As a consequence, it may be more accurate to say that the stages in our present awakening are not occurring within predictable chronological intervals, but in fact are occurring simultaneously.

It is still a matter of debate whether *any* of these three movements has created new social and religious norms that will become the dominant mazeways in twenty-first-century America. However, the growing national concern with environmental issues and the increasing globalization of our culture on the religious, political, and economic fronts would appear to bode well for a larger acceptance of such New Age themes as "the global village," planetary spiritual community, and the healing of self and the planetary ecosystem.

Ultimately, it is too soon to tell whether these movements were indeed part of a larger "Great Awakening" in late twentieth-century American society. Such judgment can only be made from the perspective of historical hindsight. Nevertheless, each of these movements has clearly had an impact on American society across traditional boundaries of race, creed, class, and nationality and may turn out to have been key harbingers and catalysts of fundamental societal transformation.

• • • • • • • • • • • • • • • • • • • • • • • •

# Endnotes

[1]   Catherine L. Albanese, "Religion and the American Experience: A Century After," *Church History* 57:337-51.

[2]   Ninian Smart, *Religion and the Western Mind* (London: Macmillan Press Ltd, 1987), 14.

[3]   William G. McLoughlin, *Revivals, Awakenings, and Reform: An Essay on Religion and Social Change in America, 1607-1977* (Chicago: University of Chicago Press, 1978), 10

[4]   Ibid., 14

[5]   Ibid., 22.

[6]   Ibid., 214-15.

[7]   Ibid., 18.

[8]   Ibid., xiv.

[9]   Ibid., 19-20.

[10]  Ibid.

[11]  Ibid., 21.

[12]  For an excellent analysis of the theological fundamentals of New Age religion, see Mary Farrell Bednarowski's *New Religions and the Theological Imagination in America* (Bloomington: Indiana University Press, 1989).

[13]  J. Gordon Melton, *Encyclopedic Handbook of Cults in America* (New York: Garland Publishing, 1986), 108-09.

[14]  Ibid., 116.

[15]  Sociological survey entitled *Values and Belief Study*, conducted September 1988. Project headed by Wade Clark Roof and Phillip Hammond.

[16]  Grant Wacker, "America's Pentecostals: Who They Are," *Christianity Today*, 16 Oct. 1987, 20.

[17]  Terry Muck, "Spiritual Lifts," *Christianity Today*, 16 Oct. 1987, 14-15.

[18]   Wacker, "American Pentecostals," 20.

[19]   Ibid., 16.

[20]   David B. Barrett, "The 20th Century Pentecostal/Charismatic Renewal in the Holy Spirit, With Its Goal of World Evangelization," in Stanley Burgess and Gary McGee, eds., *Dictionary of Pentecostals and Charismatic Movements* (Grand Rapids: Zondervan Publishing House, 1988), 1-9.

[21]   Abraham H. Maslow, *Religions, Values, and Peak Experiences* (New York: Viking Press, 1970), viii.

[22]   For instance: Seraphim Rose, *Orthodoxy and the Religion of the Future* (Platina: Saint Herman of Alaska Brotherhood, 1983), 149; Richard Quebedeaux, *The New Charismatics II* (San Francisco: Harper and Row, 1983), 217-18; Carol Flake *Redemptorama: Culture, Politics, and the New Evangelicalism* (Garden City: Anchor Press, 1984), 221-22.

[23]   Melton, *Handbook of Cults*, 113-14.

[24]   Catherine L. Albanese, *Nature Religion in America: From the Algonkian Indians to the New Age* (Chicago: University of Chicago Press, 1990), 281-82.

[25]   Sun Bear, *The Path of Power, as told to Wabun and to Barry Weinstock* (Spokane: Bear Tribe Publishing, 1983), 245-46.

[26]   Muck, "Spiritual Lifts," 15.

[27]   Albanese, "Religion and the American Experience," 339, 345.

[28]   Brooks Alexander, "Theology from the Twilight Zone," *Christianity Today*, 18 Sept. 1987, 22.

[29]   Alexander, "Theology from the Twilight Zone," 23.

[30]   Ibid., 24.

[31]   Don Balsam, *A Handbook On Holy Spirit Baptism* (Monroeville: Whitaker Books, 1973), 80.

[32]   Margaret M. Poloma, *The Charismatic Movement: Is There a New Pentecost?* (Boston: Twayne Publishers, 1982), 246.

[33]   Mary Jo Neitz, *Charisma and Community: A Study of Religious Commitment within the Charismatic Renewal* (New Brunswick: Transaction Books, 1987), 42.

[34]   Rose, *Orthodoxy*, 170.

[35]   Robert Mapes Anderson, *Vision of the Disinherited: The Making of American Pentecostalism* (New York: Oxford University Press, 1979), 199-202.

[36]   For an expanded treatment of Pentacostalist spirit exorcism, see David E. Harrell, *All Things are Possible* (Bloomington: Indiana University Press, 1975),

[37]   Neitz, *Charisma and Community*, 32.

[38]   Ibid.

[39]   Donna Bilow, Interview with author, Goleta, California, 9 August 1989.

[40]   Michael Harner, *The Way of the Shaman* (New York: Bantam Books, 1982), 145-61.

[41]   See Paul Hawkin, *The Magic of Findhorn* (New York: Harper and Row, 1975).

[42]   David Hunt, *The Seduction of Christianity: Spiritual Discernment in the Last Days* (Eugene: Harvest House Publishers, 1985), 172-88. See also Constance E. Cumbey, *The Hidden Dangers of the Rainbow* (Shreveport: Huntington House, 1983).

[43]   Flake, *Redemptorama*, 221.

[44]   Barrett, *Pentecostal/Charismatic Renewal*, 1.

[45]   Albanese, "Religion and American Experience," 348.

[46]   As Gordon Melton has shown, the Theosophical movement has been instrumental in introducing Eastern mysticism and meditation to the American public since the late nineteenth century. See *The Encyclopedia of American Religions*, 3d ed. (Detroit: Gale Research Inc, 1989), 129-32.

47    Win McCormack, "The Rajneesh Files: 1981-1986," *Oregon Magazine, Collector's Edition* (Portland: New Oregon Publishers, Inc., 1985), 85-86.

48    Quebedeaux, *The New Charismatics II*, 229.

49    Neitz, *Charisma and Community*, 238.

50    Poloma, *The Charismatic Movement*, 95; Quebedeaux, *The New Charismatics II*, 230.

51    See, for instance, Hunt, *Seduction of Christianity*, 137-48; Shakti Gawain, *Creative Visualization* (New York: Bantam New Age Books, 1978); "Under Fire: Two Christian Leaders Respond to Accusations of New Age Mysticism," *Christianity Today*, 18 Sept. 1987, 17-21.

52    Wacker, "American Pentecostals," 21.

53    Transcript of the John Ankerberg Show, "The New Age and the Church," undated.

54    Robert C. Fuller, *Alternative Medicine and American Religious Life* (New York: Oxford University Press, 1989).

55    Donald W. Dayton, *Theological Roots of Pentecostalism* (Metuchen: The Scarecrow Press, Inc., 1987), 143.

56    Anderson, *Vision of the Disinherited*, 201-2.

57    Hal Lindsey, *The Late Great Planet Earth* (Grand Rapid, Michigan: Zondervan, 1970) and Doug Clark, *Final Shockwaves to Armageddon* (Vail: Doug Clark Ministries, 1982).

58    Robert Bellah, "New Religious Consciousness and the Crisis in Modernity," in Charles Glock and Robert Bellah, eds., *The New Religious Consciousness* (Berkeley: University of California Press, 1976), 343-44.

59    Melton, *Handbook of Cults*, 115.

60    Jose Arguelles, *The Mayan Factor: Path Beyond Technology* (Sante Fe: Bear and Company, 1987), 169-70.

61    Dayton, *Theological Roots*, 144.

62    Erling Jorstad, *The Holy Spirit in Today's Church: A Handbook of the New Pentecostalism* (Nashville: Abingdon Press, 1973), 13.

63    Killian McDonnell, "Catholic Charismatics: A Critique," *Commonweal*, 5 May 1972, 210-11.

64    Albanese, "Religion and American Experience," 348.

65    For statistical support of these statements, see Chapter 6 of Wade Clark Roof's and William McKinney's *American Mainline Religion* (New Brunswick: Rutgers University Press, 1987), 186-228.

66    McLoughlin, *Revivals, Awakenings, and Reform*, 20.

67    Ibid., 12-14.

68    Ibid., 16-17.

69    Ibid., 19-20.

70    Ibid., 22.

71    Ibid., 16.

72    As mentioned in my introduction, I view the Pentecostalist movement as a subset of the fundamentalist revival of the 1960s, 1970s, and 1980s. In terms of theology, biblicism, moral and political attitudes, use of telecommunications, and regional strength, enough similarities exist to justify this view.

73    McLoughlin, *Revivals, Awakenings, and Reform*, 191-92.

74    Ibid., 192-93.

# CULTURAL CONSEQUENCES OF CULTS

## PHILLIP E. HAMMOND

## Introduction

The prospectus sent to participants in the conference on the future of new religious movements included the statement that we were "to anticipate what the future holds for these groups and, by extension, *for American society as a whole.*" Those underlined words are the subject of this essay, the only essay in the volume that blithely ignores the new religious movements themselves, so to speak, and instead speculates generally about America in the twenty-first century in light of the fact that NRMs came on the scene during the final third of the twentieth. How might the culture and institutions of this country — and not just *this* country, but, by extrapolation, any country that has experienced the influx of NRMs during the 1960s and 1970s — be influenced? One consequence, of course, has already been discussed: the emergence of an anticult movement, which may leave residues of its own. What might be other consequences?

My concern here will be focused on socio-cultural reverberations somewhat removed from the NRMs themselves. Because of the distance between cause and effects, therefore, the links may be less observable — requiring an analysis such as this even to make visible their potential — but, at the same time, these links may be decidedly more vulnerable to manifold other influences. What appears in the mid-1980s to be a plausible and likely fallout of NRMs into the broader culture may, because of the multitude of these intervening factors, develop along paths quite at odds with the projections here.

Phillip Hammond. "Cultural Consequences of Cults," in David G. Bromley and Phillip Hammond, eds., *The Future of New Religious Movements*. Macon, GA: Mercer University Press, 1987, pp. 261-273.

Nonetheless, if for no other reason than the "spirit of the game" invites it, some speculation into the direct influences of NRMs on the broader society seems appropriate in a book such as this. It should be clear that I am estimating neither what the future holds for today's NRMs — the proper task of virtually all the rest of this volume's essays — nor the likelihood of the NRM's own goal achievement, a somewhat different issue. Rather, I am trying to assess what, if any, unintended cultural consequences will follow from the fact that during the 1960s, 1970s, and into the 1980s, the industrial nations of the world experienced a range of new religious movements in their midst. As J. Milton Yinger tells us regarding "deviant religious groups" generally, their importance rests "on the nature of their cultural challenges, not their memberships." (Yinger, 1982:233) We might expect, therefore, that it is precisely in the arena of unintended outcomes where impact will, in the long run, be more lastingly felt. Such, in any event, is what this essay is about.

## The American Past and Its Trajectory

Benton Johnson, writing in 1981 about the NRMs, notes that, generally speaking, they have no "adequate theory of society," and thus — even though they may have revised some people's religious consciousness — they are unlikely to produce the social changes they themselves seek (Johnson, 1981:62). As he recognizes, however, to assert that NRMs will fall short of *their* societal aims is not at all to say that they will have no societal *impact*. Assessment of impact is, to be sure, the privilege of the historian looking backward. But, if American history is any guide, one can venture some guesses in our day, informed by the unintended consequences of prior periods when new religious impulses were felt and expressed.

Thus, during the First Great Awakening (c. 1730-60), the ostensible theological thrust was evangelical, but the unintended consequence was the further (and irrevocable) disestablishment of Puritan Protestantism. During the Second Great Awakening (c. 1800-1830), the theological impulse was again evangelical, but the broader outcome was a pattern of religious voluntarism that has persisted to this day. Similarly, in the decades following the Civil War, the theology took a radical turn in the direction of liberalism, but the more lasting impact could be said to be the institutionalization of religious pluralism. If one were to summarize two centuries of religious change, then, one might say that whatever their theological intentions, the periods of religious ferment led to ever greater levels of individual choice.

And what of the present period? Accepting McLoughlin's analysis (1978) that the current scene is, indeed, a period of religious ferment — a period in which the ostensible thrust is toward "eastern," "mystical," or at least unconventional theologies — we might note that the long-range consequences of this thrust may well be quite otherwise. Just as the previous awakenings have capitalized on an ever-increasing individualism — whatever their doctrinal definition of the situation — so, too, do the NRMs of the current day not only flow from this individualism but also help institutionalize it at yet another notch higher. Their impact on the culture at large, then, may lie not so much with the substance of their novel theologies as with the increased demands they make on the ethic of individualism.

## A General Cultural Outcome

A first observation to be made, therefore, stems from Rodney Stark's point in the first chapter of this book regarding the regulation of the "religious economy": just as new religious movements have greater chance of emerging and thriving in a relatively unregulated religious economy, so does the appearance of NRMs serve to further deregulate that economy. At the individual level, this increase in individual religious choice means simply that even greater choice — in whether and how to be religious — is likely to ensue. At the *cultural* level, however, it may mean more. It may, by offering novel religious choices, be offering broader value choices as well. Thus Glock and Wuthnow, after comparing the "conventionally" religious and the "nonreligious" with the "alternatively" religious in their Bay Area survey, note:

> By and large, to be alternatively religious represents a sharper and more pervasive break with the conventional than does being nonreligious. The differences between the conventionally and alternatively religious on canons of personal morality are in every instance greater than between the conventionally religious and the nonreligious. The same applies to political outlook and political attitudes... .Unlike the nonreligious, the alternatively religious break with the conventionally religious in other realms of life. Thus, the alternatively religious in all comparisons are the least likely of the three orientations to attach great importance to the "creature comfort" items....Openness to alternative life-styles is also more characteristic....These results...are not an artifact of group age....Among both youth and matures, the alternatively religious are more sharply and pervasively in conflict with the conventionally religious on all of the issues examined....(1979:62-63)

One might say, using the parlance coming out of the 1960s, that NRMs have provided an avenue for a counterculture to take root and be expressed. The consequence in the next century will be a yet more variegated culture.

More precision than this is desirable, however, because, over and beyond the sheer addition of religious options, might there be a multiplier effect with reverberations felt elsewhere in society as well? I think at least two such reverberations can be identified and predicted with fair accuracy. They are; (1) the further weakening of the link between religion and family, and (2) the further erosion of "established" religion. In neither instance can these outcomes be said to be intended by any NRM, yet both will be more characteristic of our society in the next century, in part because of the NRMs in this one. No doubt there will be many other cultural consequences as well, but these two seem almost certain.

## The Link Between Religion and Family

In one of the most seminal essays in all of sociology of religion, Talcott Pasons wrote that

> it is to be taken for granted that the overwhelming majority will accept the religious affiliations of their parents — of course with varying degrees of commitment. Unless the whole society is drastically disorganized there will not be notable instability in its religious organization. But there will be an important element of flexibility and opportunity for new adjustments within an orderly system which the older church organizations...did not allow for (1963:65)

The "element of flexibility" Parsons had in mind is the ease with which persons can switch denominations without family heresy. For the Lutheran-raised son or daughter, a change to the Methodists is not a rejection of parental religion, for example, but merely an exercise in culturally circumscribed choice. Similarly, Catholics raised in an ethnic parish can remain Catholic even while leaving their ethnic parochial background, and Jews have at least Orthodox, Conservative, and Reform options without dropping out of their familial faith. However wrenching individual cases may be, the religious culture of America, Parsons asserted, made room for adjustments in the religion-family link; one did not have to reject the latter in order to make a change in the former.

All of this flexibility rested on a fairly low rate of defection from all religion, however. That is to say, the assumption that one denomination is about the equivalent of any other presumes only a few in each generation will exercise the option of rejecting religion altogether. Otherwise, an important cultural feature of Americans — visible at least since de Tocqueville's visit in 1831 — would be seriously challenged. "Each sect worships God in its own fashion," de Tocqueville observed, "but all preach the same morality." (1969:290) President Eisenhower was merely echoing the same sentiment in 1952 when he declared our government to be "founded in a deeply felt religious faith — and I don't care what it is." (Quoted in Herberg, 1960:84)

New religious movements in the sixties, seventies, and eighties *have* challenged this cultural assumption, however. Surely it is no coincidence that the strongest expressions of anticult feeling come not from established churches but from families who, in seeing their children join a religious group outside of the mainstream, regard those children as somehow "lost." Cults, in other words, call into question the link between religion and family.

And well they might. While the number of cult members is still so small as not to show up in samples of the normal population, we can nonetheless see that the cultural assumption of only negligible defection from all religion is seriously in doubt. The next two tables provide the evidence.

Table 1 makes clear that defection among Catholics and Jews has risen from the generations born before 1931 to the generations born since. Approximately one in ten in the older group departed their religious legacy whereas nearly two in ten, and then one in four, in subsequent groups have done so. Protestants, however, show no such trend. Is this because they are religiously more loyal? Probably not, inasmuch as their "defection" rate, while not increasing through time as do those of Catholics and Jews, is consistently much higher. The explanation would seem to be in the far greater options available to Protestants to change from parental denomination while still remaining Protestant. If, therefore, we look not at all kinds of defection from parental religion but just at the proportion of such defections that constitute departure from all religions, we find that Protestants are not that different from Catholics and Jews.

---

**Table 1   The proportion, by year of birth, of Catholics and Jews and Protestants (age 18+) who do not share the religious affiliations of their parents***

| Parental Religion | Year of Birth | | |
| --- | --- | --- | --- |
| | 1931 or earlier | 1932-1946 | 1947 and since |
| Catholic | 13(1122) | 17(764) | 22(827) |
| Jewish | 10(135) | 16(56) | 25(57) |
| Protestant | 35(2361) | 37(1239) | 33(1090) |

---

*These data (and those of table 2) are derived from the combined 1973-1980 General Social Surveys of the National Opinion Research Center of the University of Chicago. They were made available through the Inter-University Consortium on Political and Social Research of the University of Michigan, and their analysis is the work of Samuel Mueller of the Department of Sociology, University of Akron. Professor Mueller's aid is gratefully acknowledged. It must be noted that the right-hand-most column contains those who, by their youth, have not yet lived through their "high-risk" defecting period (and thus deflate the true percentage) plus those who, because of their young adulthood, have not yet returned to the fold (and thus inflate the true percentage). The trend is nonetheless clear for Catholics and Jews in table 1 and for all in table 2.

Catholics and Jews lead the way, of course; their choices remain restricted once departure from parental religion occurs. Nonetheless, the figures of Table 2 are remarkable across the board because *in every denomination defection into no religion is on the increase among those departing from parental religion.* Moreover, these defections double and then triple across the three age cohorts. The strong if flexible link Parsons could assume in 1963 is now obviously weakened to a great degree.

Where do new religious movements fit in? They would appear to be both product and producer of this weakened link. First of all, only with the link weakened were NRMs able to recruit members and become a visible force. Second, their very success not doubt contributes to the further weakening of the family-religion link. It is important to recognize that this last assertion is cultural, not individual, however. No doubt the enthusiastic early generations of NRM members will take great care to raise *their* children in the parental religion. But the wider consequence — of demonstrating that, indeed, children can depart markedly from parents' affiliations — is surely to weaken even further the tie between family and religion.

One might raise the question, therefore, following Parsons's trenchant analysis early in the 1960s, whether or not we have experienced a "notable instability in...religious organization." In other words, have new religious movements contributed to the disruption of a long-standing cultural pattern in the United States linking the family with religion? Robbins and Anthony, who have followed closely this particular aspect of NRMs, would suggest the answer is yes.

Cults operate as surrogate extended families and, moreover, provide novel therapeutic and spiritual mystiques which confer meaning on

---

**Table 2   The proportion, by year of birth, of those who, having defected from parental religion, have departed religious affiliation altogether**

---

|  | Year of Birth | | |
| --- | --- | --- | --- |
| Parental Denomination | 1931 or Earlier | 1932-1946 | 1947 and Since |
| Catholic | 23(13) | 47(17) | 55(22) |
| Jewish | 33(15) | 69(16) | 64(25) |
| Methodist | 8(39) | 13(31) | 29(24) |
| Lutheran | 9(22) | 21(28) | 40(30) |
| Presbyterian | 7(41) | 15(54) | 28(46) |
| Episcopal | 21(34) | 38(42) | 48(40) |
| White Baptist | 9(33) | 13(31) | 29(24) |
| Black Baptist | 18(18) | 29(21) | 39(18) |

> social processes...no longer...easily legitimated by...traditional
> ideologies. In so doing, however, they exploit the weaknesses of
> existing institutions (churches, nuclear families, psychiatry) and perhaps
> pose a threat to these institutions. (1979:88-89)

One cultural consequence of the emergence of new religious movements in the 1960s, 1970s, and 1980s, therefore, will probably be a dramatic further loosening of the link between religion and family.

# Erosion of Established Religion

A second cultural consequence of current new religious movements will likely be the erosion, through legal decision making, of the power of those religions with long-standing roots in the American culture — the so-called mainline denominations, including Catholicism and Judaism. More accurately, perhaps, what will happen is the *further* erosion of such religion, because what is occurring is, in reality, but another step in the same direction established religion has already been forced to go on previous occasions. Thus, in a quite literal sense, when the framers and ratifiers agreed on the No Establishment Clause of the First Amendment, they assured a decline in the power and prestige of whichever denomination *would* have been chosen had establishment been allowed. Similarly, the passing of all vestiges of state establishment — completed finally in Massachusetts in 1833 — left all denominations on a voluntary footing, a decline in power if not in prestige.

The kind of legal erosion being brought on by contemporary NRMs is more subtle than in these earlier instances, however. A closer parallel with the present is the case of Mormon polygamy, wherein the court, confronted by the unprecedented claim to plural marriage (Reynolds v. United States, 98 US 145 [1879]), responded not only by declaring the practice unconstitutional but also by making explicit the fact that governments, not churches, determine which behaviors are acceptable. Churches retained their power to *preach* doctrines of choice, then, but it was not clear they had lost the power necessarily to *act* on them. In a similar fashion, I would argue, the great number of legal challenges brought by new religious movements in our own day — even though, by and large, the courts have upheld the right of NRMs to be different — will have the consequence of further eroding religious power.

The context for this argument is the well-known tension between the Free Exercise Clause and the No Establishment Clause of the First Amendment. Put baldly, the argument is that every extension of what is permitted as free exercise of religion by *individuals* leads to a diminution in the rights of religious collectivities because it calls into question their prior privileged position. The more widespread a benefit becomes, in other words, the less value that benefit will have to those who were earlier its sole beneficiaries. This argument is complicated, however, and no doubt controversial as well, so we must proceed slowly.

The idea is hardly new that legal decisions may lead unintentionally to consequences quite at odds with those decisions' stated purposes. Thus, for example, court cases enabling Native Americans to extend their tribal sovereignty give rise to that sovereignty's possible arbitrary use, which gives rise to the need to protect individual rights, which then undermines tribal sovereignty (Medcalf, 1978). The decision is made that children attending schools in poor districts are entitled to the same enriched education received by students in wealthy districts, but local communities therefore no longer control admissions, curriculums, or standards of excellence. This notion — that individual rights are won at the expense of those collectivities intermediary between persons and central governments — is well known.

In the church-state scene, however, there is an additional element inasmuch as the individuals whose rights get recognized in ground-breaking cases are oftentimes representatives of the religious collectivities whose power *as collectivities* is being compromised. As James A. Beckford says, "Religious groups...voluntarily take their testimony into courtrooms and are thereby seduced into rationalizing their deepest convictions in return for legal credibility." (1983:10 MS.)

This phenomenon is easier to see *ex post facto*, of course. Thus, in upholding the right to proselytize in hostile neighborhoods, the court made explicit the right of government to control proselytizing. (Cantwell v. Connecticut, 310 U.S. 296 [1940]) Or in granting conscientious objector status to persons not "religiously" motivated, the court took on the *de facto* task of defining religion (United States v. Seeger, 380 U.S. 163 [1965]); Welsh v. United States, 398 U.S. 333 [1970]), a task it had hitherto assiduously claimed to avoid (United States v. Ballard, 322 U.S. 78 [1944]). Viewing with alarm these threats to "established" religious communities that often result unintentionally from the further broadening of individual rights, some "conservationists" have called for a purposive strengthening through legal recognition of so-called "mediating structures." Inevitably, however, such an argument runs into the problem I have identified here.

> In general, we are more relaxed about "no establishment" than is the
> present approach of the courts, and more adamant about "free exercise."
> We would wish the courts to take more seriously the institutional
> integrity of religion, rather than its current tendency of privatizing
> religion by focusing on individual beliefs and motivations. (Kerrine
> and Neuhaus, 1979:14)

Such is the wish, perhaps, but it is not at all clear how one can be "more adamant" about individual free exercise and at the same time insist on continued (or renewed) recognition of religion's "institutional integrity" — not, at least, if religion retains a single meaning. If the courts will grant the right of conscientious objection to someone who does not believe in God, what special right can be claimed by someone who does? Or by one belonging to a group based on such a belief?

New religious movements, I am asserting, have intensified this process by requesting — and, for the most part, being granted — extensions of religious rights. Thus, on issues not only of evangelizing but also of soliciting funds, tax exemption, and political involvement by religious groups, NRMs have stretched existing boundaries, with the consequence that government feels the need (or is asked) to intervene in matters that once were entirely internal to churches. (See Kelley, ed., *Government Intervention in Religious Affairs*, 1982, for discussions of these matters.) Ironically, it is a No Establishment case involving Transcendental Meditation that allows us to see how this erosion process works.

The circumstances of this case were peculiar, to say the least. Followers of Maharishi Mahesh Yogi were teaching meditation techniques in five public schools in New Jersey. Upon examination by the Federal courts, the practice was declared "religious" and thus in violation of the No Establishment Clause. All three judges agreed that TM is religious because its "substantive characteristics" resemble those of other systems found to constitute religion in prior cases. For one of these concurring judges, however, this "look-alike" test was not enough.

> I am convinced that this appeal presents a novel and important question that may not be disposed of simply on the basis of past precedent. Rather...the result reached today is largely based upon a newer, more expansive reading of "religion" that has been developed in the last two decades in the context of free exercise...cases but not, until today, applied by an appellate court to invalidate a government program under the establishment clause. (Malnak v. Yogi, 592 F. 2d 197 [1979])

Judge Adams then proceeded to write a fairly lengthy opinion that at the end, offers a legal definition of religion, precisely an outcome established religious traditions would avoid and will no doubt resist. Along the way, however, the judge considers the "mediating structures" position of two understandings of religion — a "broad" one with respect to Free Exercise issues so that individual conscience is given greatest rein and a "narrow" one with respect to No Establishment issues, thus protecting the favored status of religious collectivities clearly recognized as such. The result, he says, would be a 'three-tiered system of ideas": (1) those that are unquestionably religious and thus free from government interference but also barred from government support, (2) those that are unquestionably nonreligious and thus subject to government regulation and eligible for support, and (3) those that are religious only under the dual definition, thus free from government regulation but eligible for government support. The hypothetical outcome is that the third category would get favorable treatment, which leads to clearly unconstitutional preferences.

The point is, something like this situation already occurs, leading the government to outlaw more and more of what is religious on No Establishment grounds *because* it has been recognized as religious on Free Exercise grounds. Thus, says Beckford, many governments used to

> justify a variety of arrangements for giving *bona fide* (i.e., generally recognized) religious groups a number of official privileges. Indeed, the privileges used to make very good sense from the States' point of view at a time when religious groups served as the foremost defenders of general culture and as agents of socialization (1983:7MS)

Insofar as the substance of "general culture" is *challenged*, however, then the "official privileges" are also challenged.

In the realm of education alone, first publicly funded but church-operated schools, then clerical teachers, then a religious curriculum, then sponsored devotionals, have been outlawed from public schools because the *de facto* Protestant nature of such things was challenged by Catholics, Jews, and non-believers whose Free Exercise rights had permeated the culture. (See my discussion [1984] of a 1920s Georgia Supreme Court "Bible-reading" issue for a clear illustration of how a case decided on Establishment grounds arose from such Free Exercise considerations.)

After the fact, the process is not mysterious; the particularism assumed to be universal is shown to be a particularism by the act of recognizing yet other particularisms. New religious movements since the 1960s, I am suggesting, are hastening this process by revealing in yet new ways how "Judeo-Christian" has been our conception of religion. As non-Judeo-Christian variations gain legal status, therefore, the effect will be further erosion of heretofore established religion.

There is an even larger irony on this point, exposed by those fundamentalists who would reimpose school prayer, declare this nation to be "Christan" or otherwise restore religious particularism — of just what stripe they, of course, dare not say. The irony comes from the failure of these people to recognize their lineage in the left-wing, arminian, egalitarian, nonconforming, and sectarian branch of Protestantism that was at least half of the impulse for the First Amendment in the first place. What Robert Bellah (1982) calls "romantic cultural particularism" joined forces with secular individualism two centuries ago to create the church-and-state situation we have today. Considering the path of development since 1789, NRMs are hardly unusual, then, but instead represent further occasions by which established religion is eroded.

# Conclusion

If the above two predictions can be made with some confidence, one might generalize further. New religious movements in the last third of the twentieth century will lead to yet another increase in institutionalized individualism, just as previous episodes of religious ferment did. And if this is so, are we not led to conclude even more generally that, just as NRMs could take root and grow only in an already secularized soil, so does the success of those NRMs — however limited — indicate even further secularization? After all, we have just argued that individuals will experience even greater freedom from families, and churches will experience even greater loss of influence. Is it not reasonable to conclude, therefore, that religion will decline yet another step?

A coauthor here, Bryan Wilson, has been the most eloquent spokesman for this point of view (Wilson, 1975; 1976; 1979), and probably the majority of sociologists of religion agree. Yet the appearance of NRMs on the contemporary scene has led some observers to the opposite conclusion — that the "sacred" may be "returning" (for example, Bell, 1977. See also Anthony, Robbins, and Schwartz, 1983, for a summary of the debate.) Surely both sides cannot be correct.

Or can they? Perhaps the arguments advanced in the foregoing pages suggest a resolution of this apparent dilemma. Imagine that the "sacred" is always and everywhere being encountered. That is to say, with Durkheim, social life lived entirely on the profane level is impossible, which means that the "unquestioned" is forever intruding in human affairs. But whether this sacred is regarded as "religion" depends upon the accretion of a number of other characteristics, foremost among them being the degree to which the sacred impinges upon lives and the degree to which it is expressed in supernatural terms.

Looking backward, moreover, we can see yet other accretions: (1) the supernatural expression of the sacred has often been elaborated into systematic theology, (2) which, in the West, has been largely Christian, (3) embodied primarily in the church, (4) the "purest American" branch of which is Protestant evangelical. As long as religion, with these accretions, remained highly institutionalized — as long as Protestant evangelicalism retained a near-monopoly, to use Rodney Stark's formulation — then as new encounters with the sacred occurred, they were likely to be perceived in the culturally prescribed manner, and one person's God resembled the next person's God, one church acted much as all other churches, and so forth.

Given this view, secularization might thus be conceived as the systematic dismantling — or "unpeeling" — of those accretions. Thus in America, Protestant evangelicalism lost hegemony; the church had to compete with other Christian bodies; Christianity became one religion in the marketplace; and informal expressions of the sacred came to exist alongside systematic theology, much of which could in fact be rendered in "natural" terms, which finally may have lost all relevance in some people's lives. This development did not mean the disappearance of the sacred but rather the loss of its accretions and thus its recognizability as religion.

In the resulting "secular" setting, new encounters with the sacred take place, but — insofar as they draw upon cultural traditions some distance from Western Christian traditions — they appear to some as not religious at all and to others as a "return" of the sacred. The new religious movements of the 1960s and 1970s seem to have met with such mixed reactions, as indeed they would if they were simultaneously two things: (1) authentic efforts to express the sacrd, and (2) believable *because* of the dismantling of previous accretions of the sacred.

The NRMs can never duplicate the course taken by, say, Christian sects in America, therefore. Even more doubtful is their likelihood of achieving cultural hegemony. But the new religious movements of the final third of the twentieth century must be seen nonetheless as intrusions of the sacred into cultural life, even if they are, at the same time, both products of the secularization preceding their appearance and facilitators of yet more to come. Even if the NRMs manage to hang on as religious alternatives, in other words, they carry the cultural implication not that sacralization is taking place but quite the opposite.

● ● ● ● ● ● ● ● ● ● ● ● ● ● ● ● ● ● ● ● ● ● ● ● ●

# References

Anthony, Dick, T. Robbins, and P. Schwartz
    1983        "Contemporary Religious Movements and the Secularization Premise." *Concilum* vol. 161
                (January): 1-8

Beckford, James A.
    1983        "The State and Control of New Religious Movements." *Acts of the 17th International
                Congress for the Sociology of Religion.* Paris.

Bell, Daniel
    1977        "The Return of the Sacred?" *British Journal of Sociology* 28: 4-14.

Bellah, Robert N.
    1982        "Cultural Pluralism and Religious Particularism." In *Freedom of Religion in America,*
                edited by Henry B. Clark, III, 33-52. Los Angeles: Center for Study of the American
                Experience, University of Southern California.

Glock, Charles Y., and Robert Wuthnow
    1979        "Departures from Conventional Religion." In *The Religious Dimension,* edited by Robert
                Wuthnow, 47-68. New York: Academic Press.

Hammond, Phillip E.
    1984        "The Courts and Secular Humanism: How to Misinterpret Chruch/State Issues." *Society*
                vol. 21, no. 4 (May-June): 11-16.

Herberg, Will
    1960        *Protestant, Catholic, Jew*. Garden City NY: Doubleday Anchor.

Johnson, Benton
    1981        "A Sociological Perspective on the New Religions." In *In Gods We Trust*, edited by
                Thomas Robbins and Dick Anthony, 51-66. New Brunswick NJ: Transaction Books.

Kelley, Dean M., ed.
    1982        *Government Intervention in Religious Affairs*. New York: The Pilgrim Press. Is a good
                description of the range of issue wherein government is asked (or feels the need) to
                intervene in religious activity brought on by NRM's "free exercise": methods of solicitation,
                tax exemption, political involvements of religious bodies, evangelizing.

Kerrine, Theodore M., and Richard John Neuhaus
    1979        "Mediating Structure: A Paradigm for Democratic Pluralism," In *The Annals of the
                American Academy of Political and Social Science* 446 (November): 10-18.

McLoughlin, William G.
    1978        *Revivals, Awakening, and Reform*. Chicago: University of Chicago Press.

Medcalf, Linda
    1978        *Law and Identity: Lawyers, Native Americans, and Legal Practice*. Beverly Hills CA: Sage
                Publications

Parsons, Talcott
    1963        "Christianity and Modern Industrial Society." In *Sociology Theory, Values, and Sociological
                Change*, 33-70. Edited by E.A. Tiryakian, New York: The Free Press.

Robbins, Thomas, and Dick Anthony
    1979        "Cults, Brainwashing, and Counter-Subversion" in Dean M. Kelley, ed., *The Annals of the
                American Academy of Political and Social Science* 446 (November): 78-90.

de Tocqueville, Alexis
    1969        *Democracy in America*. Edited by George Lawrence. Garden City NY: Doubleday Anchor.

Wilson, Bryan
    1975        "The Secularization Debate," *Encounter* 45:77-83.
    1976        *Contemporary Transformations of Religion*. Oxford: Oxford University Press.
    1979        "The Return of the Sacred," *Journal for the Scientific Study of Religion* 18:268-80.

Yinger, Y.M.
    1982        *Countercultures: The Promise and the Peril of a World Turned Upside Down*. New York:
                Free Press. Re "deviant religious groups": "Their importance rests on the nature of their
                cultural challenge, not their membership" (233).

**APPENDIX**

# CULTS AND THE INTERNET

# NRMS, THE ACM, AND THE WWW: A GUIDE FOR BEGINNERS

TIM COTTEE, NICKY YATEMAN and LORNE DAWSON

## Introduction

The internet or World Wide Web (WWW) is a resource for information on new religious movements (NRMs) and the anti-cult movement (ACM) that is growing rapidly and constantly changing. Access to the WWW provides a very quick and diversified way of learning about the basic beliefs and activities of a great many new religions and their secular and religious opponents. Both sides of the "cult controversy" have displayed a remarkable willingness and capacity to harness this new mode of communication, for legitimate educational and more suspect propagandistic and commercial purposes (e.g., the sale of books, taped lectures, and videos). This paper is designed simply to provide an initial insight into the variety of information available and how to access it. Once a basic competency in using the internet has been obtained, finding information about NRMs is relatively easy. Sifting through the kinds of information available, however, can be quite time consuming. It is important to keep in mind that almost anyone can establish a "web page" on the internet — a site where their ideas can be expressed — so considerable discretion must be exercised. What you read may or may not be accurate or even true. The web pages established by religions themselves, individual members, members of the ACM, or other interested organizations (like academic societies) are almost inevitably bias. This does not mean that the WWW is an unreliable educational resource. It simply means that the reader must make more of an effort than is common with other conventional sources of information (like library books, or even magazines) to discern the explicit and implicit agendas at work. In most cases, as the following guide clearly indicates, the opinions of web page authors are fairly obvious.

It is also important to point out that the internet allows for rapid and constant change in the sources and types of information available. Please keep this in mind when using the information provided in this guide. Sites we cite may no longer exist, they may have moved or transformed themselves in some way. This is only a snap shot of some of the kinds of sites active at the time that this paper was prepared (the fall of 1995). We are only providing a sampling of useful sites that are illustrative of the WWW as a resource for studying NRMs and the cult controversy as a whole.

You can never be certain what you will find in searching the internet. The quantity, quality, and complexity of web pages is quite variable. Often you will discover hundreds of web sites and the prospect of looking at them all can be disheartening. But do not be discouraged. Keep the following two points in mind: (i) the most useful information will be found at the beginning of your search list, and (ii), many web pages will appear multiple times on your search list. This means that you will come to a point in your search when some of the sites listed have only a tangential, if any, connection with your original search topic. Usually you can confidently stop reviewing your search list when this begins to happen. Also you should pay attention to the address listed in the abstract of each web page. For example, if you are searching for web pages on Theosophy, you may notice that one web page has the address Http://zeta.cs.adfa.oz.au/spirit/theosophy and another the address Http://zeta.cs.adfa.oz.au/spirit/theosophy/**overview.html**. The only difference between the two addresses is the extension added to the second one. This simply means that it will take you to a further development of the first page, and you could reach both pages by going to the first site. You can save yourself a lot of time if you are able to recognize the pages that are extensions of other pages, or even the pages that you have already visited that are listed somewhat differently. The "search engines" used to direct your research (explained and discussed below) are not infallible and you will come across listings for the same site multiple times.

Each site on the WWW usually has several or many words or phrases in bold print (or another colour) that are "active." By clicking on these words, or "links," with your mouse you move to other menus with more detailed information about the subject in question. These menus may in turn have more active links to more menus with even more specific or different kinds of information.

## Searching The World Wide Web

The World Wide Web (WWW) is like a large library. Like any library it has catalogues and indexes that can be used to locate the book(s) you are interested in. On the internet these devices are called "search engines" and they are essential to finding anything on the WWW, as this "library" is growing at an estimated 20% every month and the sheer volume of information available is mind-boggling.

There are numerous free and effective search engines available on the net. We have a preference for three of them: Yahoo, Infoseek Net Search, and Lycos Inc. We have tried almost all of the free WWW search tools and found that by using these relatively easy devices together you can find almost anything on any topic. Certainly the topic of "cults" as it is carried on the WWW can be examined exhaustively.

## Yahoo

Address: http://www.yahoo.com/

Yahoo is not so much a WWW search engine as a directory. Even though it is updated regularly, it sometimes lags behind the true search tools in listing newer information or "locations" on the net. Yahoo is arranged in a series of hierarchical menus going from the general to the more specific. For instance, to find the listings for "cults," you click on "Society and Culture," then on "Religion," then on "Cults." The true strength of any WWW search tool is how many "hits," or different locations, the tool finds for a given topic. At the time of writing, Yahoo had 19 different hits for "cult," and 1543 for "religion." Yahoo has the further advantage of being easy to use for inexperienced "web surfers."

## Infoseek Net Search

Address: http://www2.infoseek.com/

Infoseek is a true search engine. You enter in a query or set of search terms such as "cult," "krishna consciousness," or "magic modern Canada," and it searches an immense database to find locations that contain your search term. A limitation is that the free version of *Infoseek* will only give you the first 100 hits it finds. Of course you can register with them and pay to get more hits, but that is not usually necessary. As of this writing, entering a query for "cult" gives 100 hits, as does the query "religion."

## Lycos, Inc.

Address: http://lycos-tmp1.psc.edu/

Lycos is also a true search engine. It works in an almost identical manner to Infoseek. Your enter a query and it searches a database for locations that contain your term. Why use it then in addition to Infoseek? There are four reasons. First, in a general sense, given the amazing growth rate of the WWW, no search tool can keep up. Therefore by using multiple search engines you can find some locations on one "engine" that were not available on others. Second, there is no limit to the number of hits that Lycos will give you. Third, Lycos will also search for your term in languages other than English. Fourth, Lycos orders its hits by scoring them. A 1.0 score contains an exact match to your query, a 0.0 means there is no match. Lycos only gives hits with a score of 0.10 or better. These features give Lycos a great deal of strength in searching. As of writing, entering a query for "cult" gives 2007 hits with scores of 0.10 or better. Entering "religion" gives only 158 hits.


# A Sampling of Relevant Sites on the Net

Here we provide a limited annotated bibliography of typical sites dealing with NRMs available on the WWW (as of the fall of 1995). Three groupings are presented: (1) general information sites about NRMs or links to data on many different organizations; (2) web pages operated by explicitly anti-cult organizations; and (3) pages set in place by various sources dealing with aspects of specific NRMs. No attempt is made in this limited context to explain the nature of the groups whose web pages are sampled. To that end one might consult such sources as Timothy Miller, ed., *America's Alternative Religions* (Albany, NY: State University of New York Press, 1995), J. Gordon Melton, *The Encyclopedic Handbook of Cults in America*, Revised Edition (New York: Garland Pub., 1992), or Robert S. Ellwood and Harry B. Partin, *Religious and Spiritual Groups in Modern America*, Second Edition (Englewood Cliffs, NJ: Prentice-Hall, 1988).


## SOME GENERAL INFORMATION SITES

http://www.algonet.se/~teodor/cult/welcome.htm

This site provides a good general start for searches about NRMs on the net. There many links to various organizations. But as the general reading on the definition and characteristics of "cults" demonstrates, the author of this page tends to adopt a negative view of NRMs.


http:/ex-cult.org/

This page has many links to other pages. It provides a kind of directory of almost all aspects of the anti-cult movement: the different primary organizations (e.g., The Cult Awareness Network, The American Family Foundation), their publications, addresses, contacts and activities. The page is very extensive and clearly designed to advance the anti-cult cause.


http:/www.kosene.com/people/ocrt/cults.htm

This pages provides multi-part definitions of terms like "cult," "sect," and "denomination" as forwarded by members of the mass media, sociologists, Christians and so on. The page gives links to ways of evaluating the potential danger posed by any religious group, without denouncing any specific NRMs.

## SOME OF THE ANTI-CULT ORGANIZATION SITES

http://www.tacoma.net/~refocus/

This page is operated by a support group called reFocus (Recovering Former Cultists Support Network). It is not particularly informative, consisting at the moment of addresses for recovery centres and support groups, as well as contacts with former members of NRMs willing to help anyone leave a cult.

http://virtumall.com/mindcontrol/

This is the home page of Steven Hassan, a former member of the Unification Church and author of *Combatting Cult Mind Control* (Rochester, VT: Park Street Press, 1988). The page is designed to establish and legitimate Mr. Hassan's claim to "expertise" on the topic of cults and to promote his book, tapes, and other anti-cult materials. Amongst other things, one can access his discussion of the features of a "destructive cult," and advice about how to respond to such cults.

http://www.xnet.com/~can/index.htm

This is the home page of the Cult Awareness Network, probably the best known anti-cult organization currently in existence. The page primarily offers ways to contact the organization and obtain more information and assistance. Books on cults and information packets on many specific NRMs are advertised for sale, along with subscriptions to the group's newsletter. Sample articles are also provided.

## SOME SITES DEALING WITH SPECIFIC NRMS (IN ALPHABETICAL ORDER)

### Eckankar

http://www.Eckankar.org/

"Eckankar teaches simple spiritual exercises to experience the light and sound of God. As we practice the spiritual exercises, we learn to recognize the presence of the Holy Spirit in our lives. We learn that each of us is Soul, a spark of God sent to this world to gain spiritual experience."

This page is maintained by the Eckankar organization. Amongst other things it outlines some of the basic beliefs and practices, introduces Sri Harold Klemp, the

Living Eck Master, advertises the literature available from the group, offers information on membership and upcoming Eckankar seminars. There is even a link to a on-line spiritual exercise through which you can begin to learn how to soul travel. It is a useful site for gaining a initial sense of the interests and style of this NRM.

http://inlink.com/~rife/eck_main.html

This site provides a complete on-line book entitled *The Making of A Spiritual Movement* by David C. Lane. The book claims to "expose" the Eckankar religion and originally arose out of a term paper written on Eckankar. The page is definitely anti-Eckankar. Many links to other sites are provided, mostly others set up by David Lane.

## Gnosticism

http://www.webcom.com/gnosis/welcome.html

"The Gnostic sacraments are ritual punctuations, magnifications of the essential mysteries within" (*Socielas Gnostica Norvegia*).

This page is maintained by a practitioner of gnosticism, and consequently all of the links provided are positive. Some of these links are not of much use for scholarly research, but others, like the links to primary sources and documents, are of value.

## Krishna Consciousness

http://www.webcom/~ARA/index.html

"Krishna Consciousness is not something imposed on the mind. On the contrary, it's already inside each of us, waiting to come out, like fire in a match."

This page outlines the beliefs of the International Society for Krishna Consciousness. There is a biography of the group's founder A.C. Bhaktivedanta Swami Pradhupada, and information on their literature and centres throughout the world.

http://www.peg.apc.org/~shelter/

This page is maintained by a "pure devotee" of A.C. Bhaktivedanta, who is following the primary directive of the Krishna Consciousness movement to spread the writings of Bhaktivedanta and other gurus of this movement, going back to Chaitanya Mahaprabhu in 16th century India. Interestingly, while promoting the creed and practice, this site seems rather critical of the Krishna Consciousness organization as it has developed over the past two decades.

## Neo-Paganism

http://www.cc.1.org/~es8/FAQS/paganism.txt

"Neo-Pagans hold a reverence for the earth and all its creatures, generally see all life as interconnected, and tend to strive to attune one's self to the manifestations of this belief ..." (alt.pagan).

The material on this page is drawn from the newsgroup alt.pagan. There is a listing of "Most Frequently Asked Questions" (FAQS) about modern pagan practice (e.g., "Are you guys Satanists?"), with responses. The page is informative, though obviously designed to provide the movement with some positive publicity.

http://www.lysator.liu.se/religion/neopagan/mdex.html

This page provides a fairly comprehensive survey of various kinds of groups generally placed under the heading "pagan," as well as links to material on the rituals and tools of neo-paganism, primary source texts, and many other things like a guide to stores that cater to the needs of neo-pagans. The page is administered by a non-pagan and hence relatively free of any bias and provides a good introduction to the neo-pagan worldview and community.

## Nichiren Shoshu

http://www.primenet.com/~martman/ns.html

"The True Law enables people to understand the eternal nature of their lives and dispels their ignorance of causality ... the True Buddha is Nichiren Daishonin, and he did directly declare the True Law."

This page is maintained by members of the Templetaisekiji and it offers a fairly comprehensive introduction to the basic beliefs and practices of Nichiren Shoshu Buddhists, as well as many texts and parables drawn from the Lotus Sutra, the Gosho, and the life of Nichiren Daishonin.

## Rajneeshism

http://earth.path.net/osho/

"This moment is the door to the divine. My whole effort here is to pull all my people away from the past and from the future, and just make them available to the intense beauty of the present" (Osho).

This page is dedicated to Osho — the name adopted by the controversial Indian guru Bhagwan Shree Rajneesh in his last years, after being expelled from the United States following the collapse of his large utopian community in Oregon in the late 1980s. It gives a synopsis of Osho's beliefs, work, writings, and life. There are links to books written by Osho (who was very prolific), as well as his meditations, his centres around the world, and other related sites on the Internet.

## Rosicrucianism

http://www.cts.com/~rosfshp/wdex.html

"... salvation is simply but succinctly defined as the result of knowledge of one's true self, and adjusting life to spiritual principles."

This site offers nearly complete information on the beliefs and practices of the Rosicrucians. Short articles are available on their philosophy and there are links to many full online texts.

## Scientology

http://www.theta.com/goodman/index.htm

"Scientology is an applied religious philosophy and technology resolving problems of the spirit, life and thought."

This the Church of Scientology's semi-official home page. The author is Leisa Goodman, the Media Relations Director for the mother church of Scientology in Los Angeles, California. The page offers extensive links to church publications on a diverse array of topics (booklets and magazine articles) and hence provides an introduction to many of their basic beliefs and practices. Rather uniquely it also offers a scholarly appraisal of the "religiousness" of Scientology of about 10 pages, written by Lonnie D. Kliever, a professor of Religious Studies at Southern Methodist University. Scientology is often accused of being more a psychotherapy or even business than a religion. This defense of the religious status of the group makes for interesting reading.

http://copper.ucs.indiana.edu/~sgoehrin/scientology/home.html

The author of this page warns readers from the start that he is "not friendly" towards the Church of Scientology. The same author first started the *alt.religion.scientology* newsgroup to discuss the negative aspects of Scientology. Many links are provided to the pages of other critics of the church and many more are slated to be added.

## Spiritualism

http://www.iris.brown.edu/iris/RIE/alternative/spiritualism.html

This page provides a brief synopsis of the Spiritualist Movement. It is written by David Cody, a Ph.D. graduate from Brown University. It is primarily factual, and basically unbiased. In addition to beliefs and practices it mentions famous believers in Spiritualism. The description is limited to the Spiritualist Movement of the nineteenth century.

## Theosophy

http://zcta.cs.adfa.oz.au/spirit/theosophy/overview.html

"There is no religion higher than the truth."

This is a page of extensive links to every significant site dealing with Theosophy on the net. There are many essays and links to Introductory pages, as well as to the writings of Theosophy's mysterious and charismatic founder, Helena Blavatsky.

## Transcendental Meditation

http://www.best.com/~mmy/

"This home page is a gathering place, a 'cafe-newstand,' for friends around the world who share a common interest in Transcendental Meditation as taught by Maharishi Mahesh Yogi."

This page provides an introduction to Transcendental Meditation (TM) and is part of the process of legitimating and promoting TM. There are two primary links provided: "Authoritative Information and Sources" and "Casual Collections of Information and Resources," as well as links to "Most Frequently Asked Questions" about TM and to Maharishi University (in Fairfield, Iowa).

http://minet.org/

Here there are many links to anti-Transcendental Meditation sites and some neutral sites, including links to articles pertaining to the study of the TM movement, such as those contained in the on-line magazine at the site we next list.

http://www.crl.com:80/~jmknapp/trancenet/

Trancenet is set up in a magazine format and claims to present independent research on the TM technique. At the time of this review, however, every article took a negative view of the claims and influences of TM. Due to the magazine format, though, this orientation may be subject to change.

## UFO Cults

http://www.harvornet.com/ufos/ufopage.html

This site brings together not only information regarding those persons who believe in saviours from the stars, but also speculative and scientific information on the existence of extraterrestrial life forms. This is the most complete page of its kind on the WWW, and is constantly growing.

**The Unification Church**

http://www.cais.com/unification/

"True love transcends all limitations. It is the reality underlying human life in all its manifestations. Therefore true love is the key to world peace and harmony." Rev. Sun Myung Moon

This page is put on the web by Damian Anderson, a member of The Unification Church since 1977. It is very extensive, with links presenting the life, teachings and public works of Rev. Sun Myung Moon, the founder and charismatic leader of the movement. The information is available in eight languages and other languages are planned.

## Concluding Comments

As is evident from the few web pages reviewed above, almost every page has been created to serve some vested interest. Pages where the author has no personal stake in the content are rare. But this does not mean that the internet is an illegitimate resource for scholarly research. There are numerous primary source documents on the net and the web is the easiest way to contact new religious groups, some of their members, members of various anti-cult organizations, or many scholars interested in NRMs. These are the kind of first-hand sources of information that the average person would otherwise find difficult, time consuming, and maybe even expensive to pursue. The ready access provided by the WWW to people and their beliefs and activities, scattered throughout the world, represents a new and exciting opportunity. But surfing the WWW suggests that its full potential for disseminating substantial and significant scholarly work on NRMs has yet to be realized. At present, propaganda of one form or another rules the web. We suspect, however, that this may soon begin to be corrected, if only through advertising books like this one (*Cults in Context*) on the net. More neutral sites, maintained by truly reputable sources, are needed.

● ● ● ● ● ● ● ● ● ● ● ● ● ● ● ● ● ● ● ● ● ● ● ● ●